EBURY PRESS

1 3 5 7 9 10 8 6 4 2

Ebury Press, an imprint of Ebury Publishing
20 Vauxhall Bridge Road
London SW1V 2SA

Ebury Press is part of the Penguin Random House group of companies
whose addresses can be found at global.penguinrandomhouse.com

Penguin
Random House
UK

First published by Ebury Press in 2019
This edition published in 2020

www.penguin.co.uk

A CIP catalogue record for this book is available from
the British Library

ISBN 9781529104943

Typeset in 10.51/15.85 pt Sabon LT Std
by Integra Software Services Pvt. Ltd, Pondicherry

Printed and bound in Great Britain by Clays Ltd, Elcograf S.p.A.

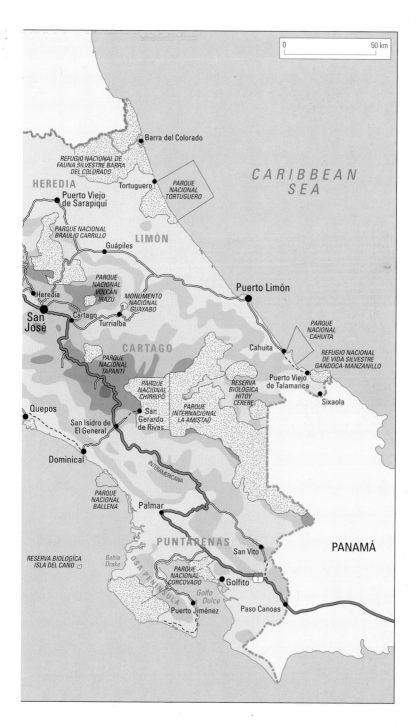

Introduction to

Costa Rica

Hemmed in between the Pacific and Atlantic oceans near the narrowest point of the Central American isthmus, the tiny republic of Costa Rica is often pictured as an oasis of political stability in the midst of a turbulent region. This democratic and prosperous nation is also one of the most biodiverse areas on the planet, an ecological treasure house whose varied habitats – ranging from rainforests and beaches to volcanoes and mangrove swamps – support a fascinating variety of wildlife, much of it now protected by an enlightened national conservation system which is widely regarded as a model of its kind.

Though this idyllic image might not do justice to the full complexities of contemporary Costa Rican society, it's true that the country's long democratic tradition and complete absence of military forces (the army was abolished in 1948) stand in sharp contrast to the brutal internal conflicts which have ravaged its neighbours, while the country has also largely escaped the natural disasters which have afflicted so many other Central American states. This reputation for peacefulness has been an important factor in the spectacular growth of Costa Rica's tourist industry – up to a million visitors are expected to visit the country during the year 2002, mainly from North America. Most of all, though, it's the country's outstanding natural beauty which has made it one of the world's prime eco-tourism destinations, with visitors coming to walk trails beneath the vaulting canopy trees of million-year-old rainforests; to climb the volcanoes that punctuate the country's mountainous spine; or to explore the high-altitude cloudforest, home to the jaguar, the lumbering tapir and the resplendent quetzal.

Admittedly, tourism has made Costa Rica less of an "authentic" experience than some travellers would like: it's hard to go anywhere in the country without bumping into white-water rafters or surfers, and more and more previously remote spots are being bought up by foreign entrepreneurs. Still, few Costa Ricans have anything bad to say about their country's popularity with visitors – perhaps simply because they know which side their bread's buttered. But as more hotels open, malls go up, and foreigners flock to the country, there's no doubt the country is experiencing a significant social change, while the darker side of foreign involvement in the country – sex tourism, real-estate scams and conflicts between foreign property-owners and poorer locals – are all on the increase.

Costa Rica's long democratic tradition and complete absence of military forces stand in sharp contrast to the brutal internal conflicts which have ravaged its neighbours

Despite such problems, revenue from tourism is one of the reasons Costa Ricans – or *Ticos*, as they are generally known – now enjoy the highest rate of literacy, health care, education and life expectancy in the isthmus. That said, Costa Rica is certainly not the middle-class country that it's often portrayed to be – a significant percentage of people still live below the poverty line – and while it is modernizing fast, its character continues to be rooted in distinct local cultures, from the Afro-Caribbean province of Limón, with its Creole cuisine, games and patois, to the traditional *ladino* values embodied by the *sabanero* (cowboy) of Guanacaste. Above all, the country still has the highest rural population density in Latin America, and society continues to revolve around the twin axes of countryside and family: wherever you go, you're sure to be left with mental snapshots of rural life, whether it be horsemen trotting by on dirt roads, coffee-plantation day-labourers setting off to work in the

dawn mists of the Highlands, or avocado-pickers cycling home at sunset.

Where to go

Though everyone passes through it, hardly anyone falls in love with **San José**, Costa Rica's underrated capital. Often dismissed as an ugly urban sprawl, the city enjoys a dramatic setting amid jagged mountain peaks, plus some excellent cafés and restaurants, leafy parks, a lively university district and a good arts scene. The surrounding **Valle Central** is the country's agricultural heartland, and also home to several of its finest volcanos, including the huge crater of Volcán Poás and the largely dormant Volcán Irazú, a strange lunar landscape high above the regional capital of Cartago.

Though nowhere in the country is further than nine hours' drive from San José, the far north and the far south are less visited than other regions. The broad alluvial plains of the **Zona Norte** are often overlooked, despite featuring active Volcán Arenal, which spouts and spews within sight of the friendly tourist hangout of Fortuna, affording arresting night-time scenes of blood-red lava illuminating the sky. Off-the-beaten-path travellers and serious hikers will be happiest in the rugged **Zona Sur**, home to Mount Chirripó, the highest point in the country. Further south, on the outstretched feeler of the Osa Peninsula,

Fact file

● The Republic of Costa Rica lies on the Central American isthmus between the Atlantic and Pacific oceans, consisting of a mountainous backbone – rising to 3819m at the summit of Mount Chirripó, its highest point – flanked by low-lying coastal strips. Though set in one of the most geologically active regions on Earth, Costa Rica has suffered less from earthquakes and volcanic eruptions than its northern neighbours – the worst incident in modern times was the earthquake which struck near Cartago in April 1910, killing 1750 people.

● The country's population is largely of Spanish extraction, though there's a substantial community of English-speaking Costa Ricans of African origin along the Caribbean coast, along with a few thousand indigenous peoples. Costa Rica is a young country: out of its population of slightly over 3 million, more than a third are aged under 15; men currently enjoy a life expectancy of 72, women of 77.

● Costa Rica's main exports are coffee and bananas, though in recent years income from these products has been overtaken by that from tourism. The country's recent prosperity has also been partly funded by massive borrowing – per capita, Costa Rica's levels of debt are among the highest in the world. Despite widespread poverty, the free and compulsory primary education system means that the country boasts a literacy rate of 90 percent, the best in Central America.

Biodiversity under protection

Despite its small size, Costa Rica possesses no less than five percent of the world's total biodiversity, in part due to its position as a transition zone between North and South America, and also thanks to its complex system of interlocking micro-climates, created by differences in topography and altitude. This biological abundance is now safeguarded by one of the world's most enlightened and dedicated conservation programmes – about 25 percent of Costa Rica's land is protected, most of it through the country's extensive system of national parks.

Costa Rica's national parks vary from the tropical jungle lowlands of Corcovado to the grassy volcanic uplands of Rincón de la Vieja, an impressive and varied range of terrain which has helped the country become Central America's prime ecotourism destination. Outside the park system, however, land is assailed by deforestation – ironically, there are now no more significant patches of forest left anywhere in the country except in protected areas.

Parque Nacional Corcovado protects the last significant area of tropical wet forest on the Pacific coast of the isthmus and is probably the best destination in the country for walkers – and also one of the few places where you have a fighting chance of seeing some of the wildlife for which Costa Rica is famed.

In the northwest, the cattle-ranching province of **Guanacaste** is often called "the home of Costa Rican folklore", and *sabanero* (cowboy) culture dominates here, with exuberant ragtag rodeos and large cattle haciendas. **Limón** province, on the Caribbean coast, is the polar opposite to traditional ladino Guanacaste, home to the descendants of the Afro-Caribbeans who came to Costa Rica at the end of the nineteenth century to work on the San José–Limón railroad – their language (Creole English), Protestantism and the West Indian traditions remain relatively intact to this day.

Close to the **Pacific coast**, Monteverde has become the country's number-one tourist attraction, pulling in the visitors who flock here to walk trails through some of the last remaining cloudforest in the Americas. Further down the coast is the popular beach of Manuel Antonio, with its picture-postcard ocean setting, plus the equally pretty but far less touristed beaches of Sámara and Nosara on the Nicoya Peninsula.

The country with no army

"We are a country with more teachers than soldiers . . . and a country that turns military headquarters into schools." So President Ricardo Jiménez Oreamuno rousingly described Costa Rica in 1922, and his oft-repeated quote still neatly sums up the country's status as an island of relative peace in a turbulent region. The reason for Costa Rica's continued stability whilst so many of its neighbours descended into dictatorship and civil war during recent decades are manifold, and include the comparative lack of ethnic tensions, a long-standing tradition of social equality and democracy, and also the fact, almost unheard of in the modern world, that Costa Rica has no army.

The decision to abolish the country's armed forces was taken by President Figueres in 1948. Figueres's motives were not entirely utopian, representing a pragmatic bid to save valuable resources and to limit the political instability that had been the scourge of so many Latin American countries. Even so, despite the subsequent success of Costa Rica's bold experiment, things are not entirely rosy. Today, to compensate for the absence of a national military body, the police forces are powerful, highly specialized and, in some cases, heavily armed.

When to go

Although Costa Rica lies between 8° and 11° north of the equator, temperatures, governed by the vastly varying altitudes, are by no means universally high, and can plummet to below freezing at higher altitudes. Local microclimates predominate and make weather unpredictable, though to an extent you can depend upon the two-season rule. From roughly May to mid-November you will have afternoon rains and sunny mornings. The rains are heaviest in September and October and, although they can be fierce, will impede you from travelling only in the more remote areas of the country – the Nicoya Peninsula especially – where dirt roads become impassible to all but the sturdiest 4WDs. In the dry season most areas are just that: dry all day, with occasional blustery northern winds blowing in during January or February and cooling things off. Otherwise you can depend on sunshine and warm temperatures.

In recent years Costa Rica has been booked solid during the peak season, the North American winter months, when bargains are few and far between. The crowds peter out after Easter, but return again to an extent in June and July. During peak times you have to plan well in advance, faxing the hotels of your choice, usually prepaying or at least putting down a deposit by credit card, and arriving armed with faxed confirmations and a set itinerary. Travellers who prefer to play it by ear are much better off coming during the low or rainy season (euphemistically called the "green season"), when many hotels offer discounts. The months of November, April (after Easter) and May are the best times to visit, when the rains have either just started or just died off, and the country is refreshed, green, and relatively untouristed. *been there !*

Toucans and tapirs

Costa Rica's position as a land bridge between the temperate north and the tropical south has given it a beguiling diversity of animal life, including tropical creatures such as the jaguar, temperate-zone animals like the deer, and some unusual, seemingly hybrid combinations such as the coati and the tapir. It's also home to no fewer than 850 species of bird – more than the US and Canada combined – along with a quarter of the world's known butterflies and thousands of moths, bees and wasps.

While it has an extraordinary wealth of bird and animal life, Costa Rica isn't a zoo. Most animals are very shy – and in some cases, centuries of hunting has driven them to take refuge in the most impenetrable terrain. That said, the average visitor to one of the national parks or reserves has a fair chance of spotting one or two unfamiliar creatures, most likely the bright-beaked toucan, the common paca (a large, harmless rodent which forages on the forest floor) or the coati (which looks like a cross between a racoon and an anteater), along with a few smaller bird species. You will, however, have to be extremely lucky to get a glimpse of one of the country's larger mammals, such as the jaguar, ocelot or tapir.

Temperature and rainfall

	Caribbean coast		San José and the Highlands		Pacific coast	
	Max	Min	Max	Min	Max	Min
January °C	27	19	24	14	31	22
Average rainfall (mm)	137		15		25	
February °C	28	21	26	14	32	22
Average rainfall (mm)	61		5		10	
March °C	29	22	26	15	32	22
Average rainfall (mm)	38		20		18	
April °C	30	23	24	17	31	23
Average rainfall (mm)	56		46		74	
May °C	31	24	27	17	30	23
Average rainfall (mm)	109		229		203	
June °C	31	24	26	17	31	23
Average rainfall (mm)	196		241		213	
July °C	31	24	25	17	31	23
Average rainfall (mm)	163		211		180	
August °C	31	24	26	16	30	23
Average rainfall (mm)	170		241		201	
September °C	31	23	26	16	29	23
Average rainfall (mm)	244		305		208	
October °C	30	22	25	16	29	23
Average rainfall (mm)	305		300		257	
November °C	28	20	25	16	29	23
Average rainfall (mm)	226		145		259	
December °C	27	20	24	14	31	23
Average rainfall (mm)	185		41		122	

28

things not to miss

It's not possible to see everything that Costa Rica has to offer in one trip – and we don't suggest you try. What follows is a selective and subjective taste of the country's highlights: great places to stay, outstanding national parks, spectacular wildlife, and even good things to eat and drink – arranged in five colour-coded categories to help you find the very best things to see, do and experience. All entries have a page reference to take you straight into the guide, where you can find out more.

01 **Arenal Volcano** Page **208** ● One of the Western hemisphere's most active volcanoes, Arenal's upper slopes are periodically doused in flows of red-hot lava.

02 Coffee Page **41** Sample a cup of Costa Rica's most famous export, and the foundation of the country's prosperity.

03 Monkeys Page **412** • Costa Rica is home to four species of monkey, including the white-faced capuchin monkey (pictured above).

04 Irazú Volcano Page **145** • The blasted lunar landscape at the summit of Irazú is one of Costa Rica's most stirring natural sights, with fantastic views on a clear day all the way to the Caribbean.

05 **Fruit** Page 38 • Costa Rica's tropical fruit ranges from the ubiquitous banana to the exotic mamones chinos (a kind of lychee), anona (which tastes like custard) and marañón, whose seed is the cashew nut.

06 **Corcovado National Park** Page 377 • The towering coastal rainforest of Corcovado National Park is one of Costa Rica's finest destinations for walking and wildlife-spotting.

I've been there !

07 **Museo de Jade** Page 91 • Visit the world's largest collection of pre-Columbian jade artefacts at the Museo de Jade in San José.

Thai
is
Not a
leatherback
!! ???!!

08 **Leatherback turtles** Page **286** • Hundreds of magnificent leatherback turtles come ashore near Tamarindo to lay their eggs every year.

09 **Carnival, Puerto Limón** Page **165** • Young bloods and grandparents alike take to the streets during Costa Rica's raciest carnival.

10 **Manuel Antonio National Park** Page **344** • The perennially popular Manuel Antonio National Park boasts four beaches, mangroves, tropical forest and stunning coastal scenery.

11 Tortuguero Canal Page **187** • Ride the boat ride north from Puerto Limón along the Tortuguero Canal, past luxuriant tropical vegetation and colourful wooden houses on stilts.

12 Nosara Page **281** • Nosara's unspoilt beaches are excellent for beachcombing and wildlife-spotting.

13 Teatro Nacional, San José
Page **90** • Central America's grandest theatre, built in imitation of the Paris Opéra with money raised by a tax on coffee.

14 **Poás Volcano** Page **126** • Poás is among the world's most easily accessible active volcanoes, with a history of eruptions that goes back eleven million years.

16 **Rara Avis** Page **218** • Kingfishers, toucans, vultures and oropéndolas (whose curious nests are pictured below) are among the birds found at the Rara Avis rainforest reserve, one of Costa Rica's premier ecotourism destinations.

Seen em !

Seen em

15 **Birdwatching** Page **59** • Costa Rica is home to some of the most colourful birds in the Americas, including hummingbirds, scarlet macaws, toucans and the resplendent quetzal.

xix

17 Sámara Page **278** • Relaxing Playa Sámara enjoys some of the most spectacular sunsets on the Pacific coast.

18 White-water rafting Page **55** • White-water rafting is one of Costa Rica's most popular outdoor activities, with a range of rivers to suit all abilities.

done it! wow!

19 Santa Elena Cloudforest Reserve

Page **307** • One of Costa Rica's spectacular cloudforest reserves, Santa Elena has excellent trails through misty and mysterious vegetation.

20 Baird's tapir Page **411** • Halfway between an elephant and a cow, Baird's tapir is one of Costa Rica's most remarkable – and elusive – inhabitants.

21 Calle Real, Liberia

Page **247** • Now restored to its original nineteenth-century glory, Liberia's Calle Real is the country's finest surviving colonial street.

22 **Cowboys** Page **235** • Guanacaste is home to Costa Rica's cowboys, or *sabaneros* – iconic figures whose ranching skills and bull-fighting prowess have become part of national legend.

23 **Xandari Plantation Hotel** Page **124** • Spend a night at the beautiful Xandari Plantation Hotel, set in a coffee plantation amidst the scenic heights of the Valle Central.

24 **Santa Rosa National Park** Page **253** • The beautiful Santa Rosa National-al Park is home to a rare stretch of dry tropical forest.

25 **Arco Iris Eco-lodge** Page **297** • Relax amidst the attractively landscaped grounds of the Arco Iris Eco-lodge in peaceful Santa Elena.

26 **Rincón de la Vieja National Park** Page **249** • Clouds of sulphurous smoke and steaming mudpots dot the dessicated slopes of Rincón de la Vieja Volcano, one of the country's most thermally active areas. *been there done that!*

27 El Sano Banano

Page **323** • Swing in a hammock at the characterful El Sano Banano lodge, just outside the popular beach village of Montezuma.

28 Playa Cocles Page **180** • One of the most appealing beaches on the entire Caribbean coast, with pristine tropical scenery, a hassle-free atmosphere and excellent accommodation.

contents

using the Rough Guide

We've tried to make this Rough Guide a good read and easy to use. The book is divided into five main sections, and you should be able to find whatever you want in one of them.

front section

The front colour section offers a quick tour of Costa Rica. The **introduction** aims to give you a feel for the place, with suggestions on where to go. We also tell you what the weather is like and include a basic country fact file. Next, our authors round up their favourite aspects of Costa Rica in the **things not to miss** section – whether it's great food, amazing sights or a special hotel. Right after this comes the Rough Guide's full **contents** list.

basics

You've decided to go and the Basics section covers all the **pre-departure** nitty-gritty to help you plan your trip. This is where to find out which airlines fly to your destination, what paperwork you'll need, what to do about money and insurance, about internet access, food, security, public transport, car rental – in fact just about every piece of **general practical information** you might need.

guide

This is the heart of the Rough Guide, divided into user-friendly chapters, each of which covers a specific region. Every chapter starts with a list of **highlights** and an **introduction** that helps you to decide where to go, depending on your time and budget.

Likewise, introductions to the various towns and smaller regions within each chapter should help you plan your itinerary. We start most town accounts with information on arrival and accommodation, followed by a tour of the sights, and finally reviews of places to eat and drink, and details of nightlife. Longer accounts also have a directory of practical listings. Each chapter concludes with **public transport** details for that region.

contexts

Read Contexts to get a deeper understanding of what makes Costa Rica tick. We include a brief history, articles about **conservation** and **environmental issues**, a detailed further reading section that reviews dozens of **books** relating to the country, and a **language** section which gives useful guidance for speaking Spanish, Tico-style, and a glossary of words and terms that are peculiar to the country.

index + small print

Apart from a **full index**, which includes maps as well as places, this section covers publishing information, credits and acknowledgements, and also has our contact details in case you want to send in updates and corrections to the book – or suggestions as to how we might improve it.

contexts 389–444

index + small print 447–455

map symbols

symbols

maps are listed in the full index using coloured text

Interamericana		★	Bus stop
Road		✈	Airport
Pedestrianized road		✉	Post office
Railway		ⓘ	Information centre
Trail/path		⬧	Place of interest
International boundary		⁝	Ruin
Chapter boundary		⬥	Museum
Waterway		ⓢ	Bank
Ferry route		⚑	Garden
Rocks		⬛	Fuel station
Peak		⌂	Lodge
Mirador			Building
Cave		╄	Church
Waterfall			Beach
Accommodation		⊞	Cemetery
Restaurant			National Park
Campsite			Park

basics

basics

Getting there from North America

The easiest way to get to Costa Rica from the US and Canada is to fly; there are daily non-stop flights to San José from Miami, Dallas and Houston, and direct flights from a number of other cities. Fares are very competitive, and airlines match each other almost to the dollar. There are also numerous air, hotel and car packages available, as well as a variety of escorted tours focusing on nature expeditions, wildlife, ecology or just relaxing on the beach. Alternatively, you can travel overland from the US through Mexico and Central America, though this amounts practically to a major expedition in its own right, rather than a way of simply getting to the country.

Shopping for air tickets

Barring special offers, the cheapest of the airlines' published fares is usually an **Apex** ticket, although this will carry certain restrictions: you have to book – and pay – at least 21 days before departure, spend at least seven days abroad (maximum stay three months), and you may be penalized if you change your schedule. Some airlines also issue **Special Apex** tickets to under-24s, often extending the maximum stay to a year. Others offer **youth** or **student fares** to under-25s; a passport or driving licence are sufficient proof of age, though these tickets are subject to availability and can have eccentric booking conditions. It's worth remembering that most cheap return fares involve spending at least one Saturday night away and that many will only give a percentage refund if you need to cancel or alter your journey. Check the restrictions carefully before buying a ticket.

You can normally cut costs further by going through a specialist flight agent – either a **consolidator**, who buys up blocks of tickets from the airlines and sells them at a discount, or a **discount agent**, who in addition to dealing with discounted flights may also offer special student and youth fares and a range of other travel-related services such as insurance, car rentals, tours and the like. Bear in mind, though, that penalties for changing your plans can be stiff. Remember, too, that these companies make their money by dealing in bulk – don't expect them to answer lots of questions.

Some agents specialize in charter flights, which may be cheaper than anything available on a scheduled flight, but again departure dates are fixed and withdrawal penalties are high (check the refund policy). If you travel a lot, discount **travel clubs** are another option – the annual membership fee may be worth it for benefits such as cut-price air tickets and car rental. Don't, however, automatically assume that tickets bought through a travel specialist will be cheapest – once you get a quote, check with the airlines and you may turn up an even better deal. Be advised, also, that the pool of travel companies is swimming with sharks. Exercise caution and never deal with a company that demands cash up front or refuses to accept payment by credit card.

Regardless of where you buy your ticket, the fare will depend on when you fly. Prices are steepest during the Christmas period, from mid-December through the first week in January. Most airlines offer little variety in prices throughout the rest of the year, though Continental's fares increase in the summer from mid-June to mid-August, which it considers high season. Flying at the weekend will bump up fares by about $50; all the prices ranges quoted below are for midweek, low-season travel, unless otherwise stated.

Airlines in North America

American Airlines ☎1-800/433-7300, ⓦ www.aa.com. Non-stop flights from Miami and Dallas to San José.

Continental Airlines ☏1-800/231-0856, ⊛www.continental.com. Non-stop flights from Houston and Newark.

Iberia ☏1-800/772-4642, ⊛www.iberia.com. Non-stop flights from Miami to San José.

Lacsa ☏1-800/225-2272. Non-stop flights from Miami and Dallas to San José. Also direct flights from New York, LA, New Orleans and Toronto.

Mexicana ☏1-800/531-7921, ⊛www.mexicana.com. Flights from LA, San Francisco, San José (California), Denver, San Antonio, Chicago, Newark and Miami; all involve a plane change in Mexico City, and a stop in Guatemala City.

Flight agents

Air Brokers International, 323 Geary St, San Francisco, CA 94102 (☏1-800/883-3273). Consolidator.

Council Travel, 205 E 42nd St, New York, NY 10017 (☏1-800/743-1823), plus branches nationwide. Discount travel agent, with student discounts.

Educational Travel Center, 438 N Frances St, Madison, WI 53703 (☏1-800/747-5551). Student/youth discounts.

Leisure Tyme Travel ☏1-800/322-TYME. Discount air fares.

STA Travel, 48 E 11th St, New York, NY 10013 (☏1-800/777-0112). Discounts for students under 25.

Travel CUTS, 187 College St, Toronto, ON M5T 1P7 (☏416/979-2406), plus branches nationwide. Student travel organization.

Flights from the US

It takes just under three hours to fly from Miami to San José, and around three to four hours from Houston and Dallas. Flight times from New York and Los Angeles are usually around eight hours, including plane changes.

You can fly **non-stop** to San José from Miami, Dallas or Houston with American, Continental, Iberia or Lacsa (see above for details). Of these, Lacsa (the Costa Rican carrier) usually offers the cheapest fares **from Miami** and **Dallas** (from around $400–500), while **from Houston**, Continental's flight starting at around $330 is the best value. American and Continental both fly from many US cities to Dallas, Miami or Houston to connect with the flight to Costa Rica.

The best fares **from New York** are on Continental via Houston and Lacsa via San Salvador ($500–600), while American Airlines has a direct flight for about $750. Continental also offers the cheapest fare **from Chicago** ($600), via Houston. From **the West coast**, the cheapest flights ($500–700) are on Lacsa (from Los Angeles via Mexico City), and on Mexicana (from San Francisco via Mexico City and Guatemala City).

Flights from Canada

There are no non-stop flights to San José from Canada. The cheapest fare **from Toronto** is on Lacsa's thrice-weekly service via Havana (CDN$808; 6hr 45min), while American Airlines' daily flight costs only a little more (CDN$836; 8hr), but involves a plane change in Miami. **From Montréal**, American is the best bet, with daily flights, also requiring a plane change in Miami (CDN$846; 8hr 45min). The quickest and cheapest flight **from Vancouver** is on American with a change of planes in Dallas (CDN$898; 10hr).

Packages and organized tours

There's a huge variety of **package tours** to Costa Rica from North America: check the travel sections of the Sunday papers for the latest offers. Typical of the trips offered by airlines is American Airlines' three-day package, including flights, transfers and a hotel in downtown San José for $442, or a five-day package staying at the beach for $736.

North American specialist tour operators

Above the Clouds Trekking, PO Box 398, Worcester, MA 01602-0398 (☏1-800/233-4499, ⊛www.abovethecloudstreks.com). Ten-day trips including challenging treks, rafting through rainforests and guided ecological tours.

Adventures Abroad, 2148-20800 Westminster Hwy, Richmond, BC V6V 2W3 (☏1-800/665-3998, ⊛www.adventuresabroad.com). Excellent tours for small groups, with a strong cultural focus.

American Airlines Fly Away Vacations (☏1-800/321-2121). Hotel, sightseeing and car-rental packages, as well as several eco-adventure tours.

Backroads, 1516 5th St, Berkeley, CA 94710-

1740 (☎1-800/462-2848, ⓦwww.backroads.com). Walking, biking and hiking vacations.

Eco-Adventures Special Interest Tours and Travel, 960 N San Antonio Road, Suite 201, Los Altos, CA 94022 (☎1-800/227-3026). Nature and wildlife tours ranging from one to three weeks, including rafting, camping and bird-watching.

Elderhostel, 75 Federal St, Boston, MA 02110 (☎617/426-8056, ⓦwww.elderhostel.org). Extensive network of educational and activity programmes, including twelve-day nature-study trips and two-week educational trips studying environment and history. Participants must be over 55 (companions may be younger).

Euro-Global Travel, 5670 Wilshire Blvd, LA, CA 90036 (☎1-800/235-5222, ⓦwww.costaricavacations.net). Flight, hotel and car packages, and guided nature tours.

GAP Adventures, 264 Dupont St, Toronto, ON M5R (☎1-800/465-5600 or 416/922-8899, ⓦwww.gap.ca/world/index). Two-week trekking and public-transport trips along the coast, visiting rain- and cloudforests and national parks.

Green Tortoise Adventure Travel, 494 Broadway, San Francisco, CA 94133 (☎415/956-7500 or 1-800/TORTOISE, ⓦwww.greentortoise.com). Inexpensive tours (Nov–April) to off-the-beaten-track destinations throughout Costa Rica and Central America aboard converted buses with sleeping space.

Imagine Travel Alternatives, PO Box 13219, Burton, WA 98103 (☎1-800/777-3975, ⓦwww.primechoice.com/imagine). Makes travel arrangements for independent travellers and runs some escorted small-group tours.

International Expeditions Inc, 1 Environs Park, Helena, AL 35080 (☎1-800/633-4734,

ⓦwww.ietravel.com). Group or independent all-inclusive natural-history tours.

Nature Expeditions International, 474 Willamette St, PO Box 11496, Eugene, OR 97440 (☎1-800/869-0639, ⓦwww.natureexp.com). Small-group expeditions led by specialists in anthropology, biology and natural history.

Questers Worldwide Nature Tours, 257 Park Ave South, New York, NY 10010 (☎1-800/468-8668, ⓦwww.questers.com). Upmarket nature tours.

REI Adventures, PO Box 1938, Sumner, WA 98390-0800 (☎1-800/622-2236, ⓦwww.rei.com/travel). Biking, hiking, rafting tours and adventure travel.

Overland to Costa Rica

Costa Rica's international bus company, Ticabus, runs a good **overland bus** service between Guatemala, Honduras, El Salvador, Nicaragua and Costa Rica, and on south into Panamá.

Ticabus leaves **Guatemala City** daily for San José at 12pm. It's a two-and-a-half-day trip, entailing nights (at your own expense) in San Salvador and Managua. From **Tegucigalpa** in Honduras, Ticabus leaves daily at 7.30am for San José, arriving 48 hours later (with an overnight stop in **Managua**, again at your own expense). From Managua you can also get a Nicaraguan SIRCA bus (daily at 6am) or, more comfortably, a Ticabus (daily at 6am & 7am); in both cases the journey takes eleven hours. Additionally, a deluxe service run by Transnica leaves Managua daily at 7am, taking only eight hours.

Getting there from the UK and Ireland

There are no direct flights from the UK to Costa Rica. Getting there by plane involves a change of aircraft (and sometimes airline) in the US, usually in Miami or Houston, while some cheaper routings also involve a change of plane in Europe. The quickest flights can get you to Costa Rica in as little as 13 hours, including changes.

Flying to Costa Rica from the UK can be surprisingly good value. European airlines' **fares** to Costa Rica vary according to whether it's **low season** (generally mid-Jan to June & Sept–Nov) or **high season** (July, Aug & Dec to mid-Jan). There should be no problem fixing flexible return dates or tickets valid for a long period, and there's always some deal available for **students** or young people, though don't expect big reductions. Note that flights to Costa Rica fill up early at most times of the year, and it's best to book as far ahead as you can.

Unless you're lucky enough to unearth a bargain last-minute offer, the best deals are found by booking well in advance. The cheapest tickets (sometimes referred to as Apex tickets) invariably mean committing yourself to flight dates and times, with heavy penalties if you change your plans. In general, the further ahead you book and the shorter your stay abroad, the cheaper the ticket. Be aware though that you'll almost always save money by booking through a specialist **flight agent** (see p.13) rather than going directly to the airline. You may also find good deals in the classified ads of newspapers, particularly on Sundays (in London, try *Time Out*, the *Evening Standard* and free magazines like *TNT*), and on the Internet – try Ⓦ www.cheapflights.co.uk, Ⓦ www.deckchair.co.uk, Ⓦ www.ebookers.com or Ⓦ www.last-minute.com.

The quickest and easiest way of getting to San José is **via the US** – a routing which involves only one stopover. Continental have flights via Houston, while American Airlines fly via Miami and United via Chicago or New York (expect flight times to be a bit longer on

the last routing). Of the three, Continental generally have the lowest fares (around £525 in low-season, £645 in high) and offer an excellent service, with swift connections in Houston.

The cheapest low-season fare from the UK is with Martinair via Amsterdam and Miami (4 weekly) for about £440, while Iberia fly via Madrid and Miami daily for about £470 – however, both these routes are time-consuming and inconvenient, with two stopovers and a total flying time of at least 18 hours.

Alternatively, you could fly to either the US or Europe with any relevant airline and once there switch to a different airline for your onward flight to San José. British Airways, for example, have flights to Miami which connect to the American Airlines departure for San José; the whole trip costs a reasonable £500 in low season. Obviously there are all kinds of options, although you might find yourself with a long wait between flights.

Airlines in Britain

American Airlines ☏ 0845/778 9789, Ⓦ www.aa.com
British Airways ☏ 0845/722 2111, Ⓦ www.britishairways.com
Continental ☏ 0800/776464, Ⓦ www.continental.com
KLM (for Martinair) ☏ 0870/507 4074, Ⓦ www.klm.com
Iberia ☏ 020/7830 0011, Ⓦ www.iberia.com
United Airlines ☏ 0845/844 4777, Ⓦ www.ual.com.

Flight agents in Britain

Bridge the World, 47 Chalk Farm Road, London NW1 8AN (☎020/7916 0990, ⓦwww.bridgetheworld.com). Specializing in round-the-world tickets, with good deals aimed at the backpacker market.

Flightbookers, 177–178 Tottenham Court Rd, London W1P 0LX (☎020/7757 2000, ⓦwww.ebookers.com). Low fares on an extensive range of scheduled flights.

Journey Latin America, 12–13 Heathfield Terrace, London W4 4JE (☎020/8747 8315, ℻8742 1312, ⓦwww.journeylatinamerica.co.uk). Latin American specialists, adept at arranging unusual itineraries at competitive fares. They also offer tours (see below).

North South Travel, Moulsham Mill Centre, Parkway, Chelmsford, Essex CM2 7PX (☎ & ℻01245/608291, ⓦwww.northsouthtravel.co.uk). Friendly, competitive travel agency, offering discounted fares worldwide – profits are used to support projects in the world, especially the promotion of sustainable tourism.

STA Travel (London call centre ☎020/7361 6144, northern call centre ☎0161/830 4713, ⓦwww.statravel.co.uk). Branches at: 86 Old Brompton Rd, London SW7; 117 Euston Rd, London NW1 2SX; 38 Store St, London WC1E 7BZ); 25 Queen's Rd, Bristol BS8 1QE (☎0117/929 4399); 38 Sidney St, Cambridge CB2 3HX (☎01223/366966); 75 Deansgate, Manchester M3 2BW (☎0161/834 0668); 88 Vicar Lane, Leeds LS1 7JH (☎0113/244 9212); 36 George St, Oxford OX1 (☎01865/792800). Worldwide specialists in low-cost flights, with particularly good deals for students and under-26s.

Trailfinders (ⓦwww.trailfinders.co.uk). Branches at 42–50 Earl's Court Rd, London W8 6FT (☎020/7938 3366); 194 Kensington High St, London W8 (☎020/7938 3939); 58 Deansgate, Manchester M3 2FF (☎0161/839 6969); 254–284 Sauchiehall St, Glasgow G2 3EH (☎0141/353 2224); 22–24 The Priory, Queensway, Birmingham B4 6BS (☎0121/236 1234); 48 Corn St, Bristol BS1 1HQ (☎0117/929 9000). One of the best-informed and most efficient agents for independent travellers.

Packages and organized tours

A number of operators offer **specialist tours** to Costa Rica – rainforest hiking, bird-watching and natural history tours are particularly popular. All the tour operators listed below

offer one or all of these activities, as well as booking flights. **Walkers** should contact their local ramblers' association, who may have information on tours to Costa Rica.

Specialist tour operators in Britain

Exodus, 9 Weir Rd, London SW12 0LT (☎020/8675 5550, brochure requests ☎020/8673 0859, ⓦwww.exodus.co.uk). Experienced adventure-tour operators offering a range of Central American itineraries, including several two-week tours of Costa Rica (from £1080).

Explore Worldwide, 1 Frederick St, Aldershot GU11 1LQ (☎01252/760000, brochure requests 01252/760100, ⓦwww.explore.co.uk). Competitively priced range of hotel-based tours (14–21 days) in Central America.

Journey Latin America, 12–13 Heathfield Terrace, London W4 4JE (☎020/8747 8315, ℻8742 1312, ⓦwww.journeylatinamerica.co.uk). Specialist in flights, packages and adventurous, tailor-made trips to Latin America, including two 11-day Costa Rica tours (from £1620).

Reef and Rainforest Tours, Prospect House, Jubilee Rd, Totnes, Devon TQ9 5TN (☎01803/866965, ℻865916, ⓦwww.reefrainforest.co.uk). Ecotours and "research programmes" on which you can work with scientists, collecting data, photographing animals and the like. The Costa Rican programme includes a humpback whale research project off the Osa Peninsula, plus birding, natural history and adventure tours.

South American Experience, 47 Causton St, London SW1P 4AT (☎020/7976 5511, ℻7976 6908, ⓦwww.southamericanexperience.co.uk). Tailor-made itineraries of Latin America – the 19-day tour to Costa Rica takes in San José, Manuel Antonio, Tortuguero, Volcán Poás and Monteverde. Good-value flights too, including tickets with multiple stopovers.

Sunvil Holidays, Sunvil House, Upper Square, Old Isleworth, Middlesex TW7 7BJ (☎020/8568 4499, brochure requests ☎020/8757 4747, ⓦwww.sunvil.co.uk). Flexible fly-drive itineraries, with accommodation in a number of areas including Sámara and Nosara.

Travelbag Adventures, 15 Turk St, Alton, Hants GU34 1AG (☎01420/541007, ℻541022, ⓦwww.travelbag-adventures.co.uk). Hotel-based tours for small groups throughout Central America.

Trips Worldwide, 9 Byron Place, Clifton, Bristol BS8 1JT (☎0117/987 2626, ℻987 2627, ⓦwww.tripsworldwide.co.uk). Tailor-made tours to

Central America, and particularly strong on Costa Rica, with prices to suit all budgets.

Flights from Ireland

There are no direct flights from Ireland to Costa Rica. Your best option is to fly **via the US**, where you can connect with flights to San José (see p.10). Delta has the widest range of flights from Dublin (and several from Shannon) to New York and Atlanta, from where you can get an onward flight to San José, though you'll probably have to change planes at least once more (see p.10). On Aer Lingus from Dublin and Shannon, you can get same-day connections to San José, via New York (JFK) and Mexico City. Fares from Dublin and Belfast start at around IR£550.

Airlines in Ireland

Aer Lingus (🌐 www.aerlingus.com) Dublin ☎ 01/705 3333
British Airways (🌐 www.britishairways.com)

Belfast ☎ 0345/222111; Dublin ☎ 0141/222 2345
British Midland (🌐 www.britishmidland.co.uk) Belfast ☎ 0345/554554; Dublin ☎ 01/283 8833
Delta (🌐 www.delta.com) Belfast ☎ 028/9048 0526; Dublin ☎ 1800/414767

Flight and tour agents in Ireland

Maxwell's Travel, D'Olier Chambers, 1 Hawkins St, Dublin 2 (☎ 01/677 9479, 📠 679 3948). Very experienced Latin American specialist, and the Irish agent for many of the tour operators listed on p.13.
Trailfinders, 45 Dawson St, Dublin 2 (☎ 01/677 7888, 🌐 www.trailfinders.co.uk). Irish branch of this expert flight agent and independent travel agent.
USIT, 19 Aston Quay, O'Connell Bridge, Dublin 2 (☎ 01/602 1777, 🌐 www.usit.campus.co.uk); Fountain Centre, College St, Belfast BT1 6ET (☎ 028/9032 4073). All-Ireland student travel agents, with 17 offices in Ireland throughout the Republic and the North (mainly on campuses).

Getting there from Australia and New Zealand

There are no direct flights from Australia or New Zealand to Costa Rica – the quickest and easiest option is to fly via the US. Qantas, Air New Zealand, United Airlines and American Airlines all sell through-tickets to San José (the first two in conjunction with Continental and TACA). Alternatively, you could get a flight to LA or Mexico City, and then either an add-on fare to San José – the year-round flat fare costs A$780/NZ$860 from LA and A$350/NZ$390 from Mexico City – or travel overland. Yet another option, if you're not in a hurry, is to fly via Asia.

The **low season** for travel to Costa Rica is from mid-January to the end of February, and October to the end of November; **high season** is mid-May to August and December to mid-January; the rest of the year is **shoulder seasons**. Seat availability on most international flights out of Australia and New Zealand is often limited, so it's best to book several weeks ahead. Note that tickets purchased from **discount travel agents** (see p.15) often undercut airlines' published fares – they'll also have the latest information on special offers. Flight Centres and STA Travel generally offer the lowest fares; it's also worth checking 🌐 www.travel.com.au, 🌐 www.travelforless. co.nz and 🌐 www.sydneytravel.com for discounted fares. If you intend to see something of

Mexico or other Central American countries en route to Costa Rica, you may want to check out the various **airpasses** on offer (see p.32 for details).

Very few **round-the-world** tickets include Costa Rica, although it's possible to visit it as a side trip (at extra cost) with the more flexible packages, such as the Star Alliance 1 ticket, from Ansett and Air New Zealand, and the One World Explorer from Qantas. An increasing number of Australian and New Zealand operators offer **specialist tours** to Costa Rica; activity and natural history tours are particularly popular, and there are a number of good surfing packages. See the list of specialist tour operators on p.16 for more details.

Fares

From Australia, the cheapest fares **to San José** are via LA on Air New Zealand–TACA, or with Qantas/Air New Zealand and Continental via LA and Houston (both from around A$2300/A$2900 low/high season). American Airlines' fares to San José via LA are higher (A$2699/$3059 low/high season). If you only want a ticket **to LA**, the cheapest fares are on United Airlines, Qantas and Air New Zealand (A$1179/2499 in low/high season). Air New Zealand can get you **to Mexico City** for A$2429–2959; Qantas and United Airlines' fares are more expensive at A$2669–3199. Fares are higher travelling **via Asia**, but include an overnight stop in the carrier's home city, with the best deals on All Nippon Airways (ANA) via Osaka, and Korean Airlines via Seoul (A$1429–1899). The best-value flights to Mexico City are with JAL (A$1529–$1999), with an overnight stop in Tokyo. Fares from all eastern Australian cities are generally the same; fares from Perth and Darwin are about A$200 more.

From New Zealand, as from Australia, the best through-tickets **to San José** are via LA on Air New Zealand–TACA, or with Qantas/ Air New Zealand and Continental via LA and Houston (both from around NZ$2600/$3200 low/high season). American Airlines' fares to San José via LA are higher (NZ$2899/3299 low/high season). If you just want a flight **to LA**, the cheapest are on Qantas (NZ$1599–2699), Air New Zealand and United Airlines (NZ$1899–2699), and American Airlines (NZ$1999–2899). All these airlines also fly **to Mexico City**

(NZ$2599–3099). **Via Asia** the best deals to LA are on Korean Air via Seoul (NZ$2099–2599), and to LA and Mexico City on JAL via Tokyo or Osaka (NZ$1899–$2599). All the above fares are from Auckland; expect to pay an extra NZ$150 for Christchurch and Wellington departures.

Airlines in Australia and New Zealand

Air New Zealand (ⓦwww.airnz.com) Australia ☎13 2476, New Zealand ☎0800/737 000 or 09/357 3000. Daily flights from Sydney, Brisbane, Melbourne and Adelaide to LA, either direct or via one of Honolulu, Tonga, Fiji or Papeete; with onward connections to San José on TACA International or via Houston on Continental Airlines.

All Nippon Airways (ⓦwww.ana.co.jp) Australia ☎1800/257 015 or 02/9367 6711 (no NZ office). Several flights weekly from Brisbane and Sydney to Los Angeles, with an overnight stop in Osaka included in the fare.

American Airlines American Airlines (ⓦwww.aa.com) Australia ☎1300/650 747, New Zealand ☎0800/887 997.

Continental Airlines (ⓦwww.flycontinental.com) Australia ☎02/9321 9242, New Zealand ☎ 09/308 3350. Onward connections from LA via Houston to San José.

Japan Airlines (ⓦwww.japanair.com) Australia ☎02/9272 1111, New Zealand ☎09/379 9906. Several flights weekly from Sydney, Brisbane, Cairns and Auckland to LA and Mexico City, with an overnight stopover in either Tokyo or Osaka included in the fare.

Korean Airlines (ⓦwww.koreanair.com) Australia ☎02/9262 6000, New Zealand ☎09/307 3687. Several flights weekly from Sydney, Brisbane and Auckland to LA, with an overnight stop in Seoul included in the fare.

Qantas (ⓦwww.qantas.com.au) Australia ☎13 1313, New Zealand ☎09/357 8900 or 0800/808 767. Daily flights to LA from major Australian and New Zealand cities, with onward connections to San José on Continental via Houston or direct on TACA International.

United Airlines (ⓦwww.ual.com) Australia ☎13 1777, New Zealand ☎09/379 3800. Daily direct flights to LA from Sydney, Melbourne and Auckland, with onward connections to San José.

Discount travel agents in Australia and New Zealand

Anywhere Travel, 345 Anzac Parade, Kingsford,

Sydney (☏ 02/9663 0411,

℮ anywhere@ozemail.com.au). Discount flight agent offering discounted flights, as well as accommodation, tours and car rental.

Budget Travel, 16 Fort St, Auckland, plus branches around the city (☏ 09/366 0061 or 0800/808 040). Long-established agent offering budget air fares and accommodation packages.

Destinations Unlimited, 220 Queen St, Auckland (☏ 09/373 4033). Discount fares plus a good selection of tours and holiday packages.

Flight Centre (ⓦ www.flightcentre.com.au) Australia: 82 Elizabeth St, Sydney (☏ 02/9235 3522), plus branches nationwide (for the location of your nearest branch call ☏ 13 1600); New Zealand: 350 Queen St, Auckland (☏ 09/358 4310), plus branches nationwide. Competitive discounts on air fares and a wide range of package holidays and adventure tours.

Northern Gateway, 22 Cavenagh St, Darwin (☏ 08/8941 1394, ℮ oztravel@norgate.com.au). Low-cost flights from Australia's top end.

STA Travel (ⓦ www.statravel.com.au) Australia: 855 George St, Sydney; 256 Flinders St, Melbourne; plus branches nationwide (for the location of your nearest branch call ☏ 13 1776; for telesales call ☏ 1300/360 960);. New Zealand: 10 High St, Auckland (☏ 09/309 0458, telesales ☏ 09/366 6673), plus branches nationwide. Discounted fares for students and under-26s, plus visas, student cards and travel insurance.

Student Uni Travel, 92 Pitt St, Sydney (☏ 02/9232 8444, ℮ sydney@backpackers.net), plus branches nationwide. Student/youth discounts and travel advice.

Thomas Cook (ⓦ www.thomascook.com.au) Australia: 175 Pitt St, Sydney (☏ 02/9231 2877); 257 Collins St, Melbourne (03/9282 0222); plus branches nationwide (for the location of your nearest branch call ☏ 13 1771; for telesales call ☏ 1800/801 002); New Zealand: 191 Queen St, Auckland (☏ 09/379 3920, ⓦ www.thomascook.co.nz). Low-cost flights, plus tours, accommodation and travellers' cheques.

Trailfinders (ⓦ www.trailfinders.com.au), 8 Spring St, Sydney (☏ 02/9247 7666); 91 Elizabeth St, Brisbane (☏ 07/3229 0887); Hides Corner, Shield St, Cairns (☏ 07/4041 1199). Independent travel specialist.

USIT Beyond, cnr Shortland St & Jean Batten Place, Auckland (☏ 09/379 4224 or 0800/788 336, ⓦ www.usitbeyond.co.nz), plus branches nationwide. Student/youth travel specialists.

Specialist tour operators in Australia and New Zealand

Adventure Associates, 197 Oxford St, Bondi Junction (☏ 02/9389 7466 or 1800/222 141, ⓦ www.adventureassociates.com). Escorted small-group tours from San José, including a seven-day bus, boat and hiking tour through the rainforests of Corcovado National Park and the Isla del Caño. They also arrange independent trekking, mountain-biking, white-water rafting, canal trips and sports-fishing, plus city stopovers and cruises in and around Costa Rica.

Adventure Specialists, 69 Liverpool St, Sydney (☏ 02/9261 2927 or 1800/634465). Adventure trips (8–22 days) from San José, including white-water rafting, rainforest hikes, national park visits and horse-riding.

The Adventure Travel Company, 164 Parnell Rd, Parnell, Auckland (☏ 09/379 9755, ℮ advakl@hot.co.nz). Wide selection of adventure tours throughout Central America.

Adventure World, 73 Walker St, Sydney (☏ 02/9956 7766 or 1300/363 055, ⓦ www.adventureworld.com.au), plus branches in Melbourne, Brisbane, Adelaide and Perth; 101 Great South Rd, Remuera, Auckland (☏ 09/524 5118). Five-day tour around San José and a seventeen-day rainforest and national parks tour, including Volcán Poás and Tortuguero.

Birding Worldwide, Level 3, 818 Whitehorse Road, Box Hill, VIC 3128 (☏ 03/9899 9303, ⓦ www.birdingworldwide.com.au). Three-week bird-watching tour offering the chance to discover some of Costa Rica's 850 species of birds.

Contours, 1/84 William St, Melbourne. (☏ 03/9670 6900 or 1800/331 378, ℮ contourstravel@bigpond.com). Specialists in stopovers in San José and tours to the Caribbean and Central America.

Exodus, c/o Peregrine Adventures, 258 Lonsdale St, Melbourne (☏ 03/9662 2700 & 1300/655 433; ⓦ www.peregrine.net.au), plus branches in Brisbane, Sydney, Adelaide and Perth. Eight-week overland tours trucking between Mexico City and Panamá City; fourteen-day coast-to-coast off-road cycling adventures through Costa Rica's jungles; plus wildlife-spotting and rainforest boat tours.

Wiltrans/Maupintour, 189 Kent St, Sydney (☏ 02/9255 0899, ⓦ www.mauintour.com). All-inclusive seven-day guided tours from San José (Oct–July) including rafting, rainforest hikes through Carara Reserve and a descent of Volcán Irazú by bike.

Red tape and visas

Citizens of the US, Canada, the UK and most Western European countries can obtain a ninety-day entry stamp for Costa Rica without needing a visa. Citizens of Australia, New Zealand and Ireland do not need a visa, either, but are only issued a thirty-day entrance stamp. Whatever your nationality, you must in theory show your passport, a valid onward air or bus ticket, a visa for your next country (if applicable) and proof of "sufficient funds" (around $400 per month), but if you arrive by air the last is rarely asked for. Most other nationalities need a visa; always check first with a Costa Rican consulate concerning current regulations. For most nationalities, a thirty-day visa will cost about $25.

Your **entrance stamp** is very important: no matter where you arrive, make sure you get it. You have to carry your passport (or a photocopy) with you at all times in Costa Rica. If you are asked for it and cannot produce it, you may well be detained and fined.

The easiest way to **extend your entry permit** is to leave Costa Rica for 72 hours – to Panamá or Nicaragua, say – and then re-enter, fulfilling the same requirements as on your original trip. You should, although it is at the discretion of the immigration officer, be given another ninety- or thirty-day stamp. If you prefer not to leave the country, you can apply for a permit or visa extension at the **Departamento de Migración** in San José (see p.108) – (e) dmigracion@ns.migracion. go.cr) – a time-consuming and often costly business. You'll need to bring all relevant documents – passport and three photographs, onward air or bus ticket – as well as proof of funds (credit cards and/or travellers' cheques). If you do not have a ticket out of Costa Rica you may have to buy one in order to get your extension. Bus tickets are more easily refunded than air tickets; some airlines refuse to cash in onward tickets unless you can produce or buy another one out of the country. Note that you will pay approximately ten percent tax on all air tickets bought in Costa Rica.

If, for whatever reason, you overstay your ninety- or thirty-day limit, you must get an **exit visa** in order to be allowed to leave the country. This involves going to the Departamento de Migración in San José with your passport and onward ticket. The

visa, normally granted within one to three days, gives you thirty days in which to leave the country and costs $38; you will also have to pay overstayers' fees of $1.50 per month. These fees have been subject to abrupt change (always upwards) recently, so make sure you ask exactly how much you will be required to pay and ensure that you have sufficient funds – either in colones or dollars – to fork out when you leave. Any reputable tour operator (see p.33) should be able to help you through the red tape, although this will cost a further $15–20. For more information on visa requirements, check the Costa Rican Ministry of Foreign Affairs Web site at (w) www.rree.go.cr.

Costa Rica has no such thing as a **Working Holiday Visa**. If you plan to stay for a long period, you need a Resident's Permit, which is extremely difficult to get hold of – you'll need to appoint a Costa Rican resident (friend, family or a lawyer) to act on your behalf, fill in stacks of paperwork, and then wait as long as six months for your application to be processed. Be warned that the Costa Rican government is currently cracking down heavily on illegal residents; without a permit you risk being deported and not allowed to re-enter the country for ten years. If you're **studying**, or on a **volunteer programme** (see p.63), the organization or school may sort out visas for you; check in advance.

Costa Rica's stringent regulations governing **the stay of children** were put in place to counteract the number of people bringing children into the country from the US to defy

Costa Rican embassies

Australia 11/30 Clarence St, Sydney
(⊕02/9261 1177)
Canada 135 York St, Suite 208, Ottawa,
Ontario, K1N 5T4 (⊕613/562-2855)
Ireland no representation; contact the UK
embassy
New Zealand no representation; contact the
Australian embassy
UK 14 Lancaster Gate, London W2 3LH
(⊕020/7562 2855)
US 2114 S St NW, Washington, DC 20008
(⊕202/234-2945, ⊚www.
costa-embassy.org)

custody arrangements or trials. Officially, if one parent, rather than both, is travelling with their child, that child is not permitted to remain in Costa Rica for more than thirty days unless the travelling parent asks permission, in person, supported by the other parent's request in writing, from the Costa Rican Child Protection Agency, the Patronato Nacional de la Infancia, C 19, Av 6, San José (in the Tribunales de la Justicia complex). That said, the Costa Rican authorities take a very dim view of this method, preferring that both parents are with the child when permission to stay is requested. It becomes even more tricky if a child is coming to Costa Rica without his or her parents: in this case you have to contact the Costa Rican embassy or consulate in your home country to get a notarized permit.

Insurance

A typical travel insurance policy usually provides cover for the loss of baggage, tickets and – up to a certain limit – cash or cheques, as well as cancellation or curtailment of your journey. Most of them exclude so-called "dangerous" sports unless an extra premium is paid. Read the small print and benefits tables of prospective policies carefully; coverage can vary wildly for roughly similar premiums. Many policies can be chopped and changed to exclude coverage you don't need.

If you do take medical coverage, ascertain whether benefits will be paid as treatment proceeds or only after return home, and whether there is a 24-hour medical emergency number. When securing baggage cover, make sure that the per-article limit – typically under £500/US$730 – will cover your most valuable possession. If you need to make a claim, you should keep receipts for medicines and medical treatment, and in the event you have anything stolen, you must obtain an official statement from the police. Bank and credit cards often have certain levels of medical or other insurance included and you may automatically get travel insurance if you use a major credit card to pay for your trip.

In the **UK and Ireland**, travel agents and tour operators are likely to require some sort of insurance when you book a package holiday, though according to UK law they can't make you buy their own (other than a £1 premium for "schedule airline failure"). If you have a good all-risks home insurance policy it *may* cover your possessions against loss or theft even when overseas. Many private medical schemes such as BUPA or PPP also offer coverage plans for abroad, including baggage loss, cancellation or curtailment and cash replacement as well as sickness or accident.

Rough Guide travel insurance

Rough Guides now offers its own travel insurance, customized for our readers by a leading UK broker and backed by a Lloyds underwriter. It's available for anyone, of any nationality, travelling anywhere in the world.

There are two main Rough Guide insurance plans: Essential, for basic, no-frills cover; and Premier – with more generous and extensive benefits. Alternatively, you can take out annual multi-trip insurance, which covers you for any number of trips throughout the year (with a maximum of 60 days for any one trip). Unlike many policies, the Rough Guides schemes are calculated by the day, so if you're travelling for 27 days rather than a month, that's all you pay for. If you intend to be away for the whole year, the Adventurer policy will cover you for 365 days. Each plan can be supplemented with a "Hazardous Activities Premium" if you plan to indulge in sports considered dangerous, such as skiing, scuba-diving or trekking. Rough Guides also does good deals for older travellers, and will insure you up to any age, at prices comparable to SAGA's.

For a policy quote, call the Rough Guide Insurance Line on UK freefone ⊤ 0800/015 0906, US freefone ⊤ 1-866/220-5588, or, if you're calling from elsewhere, ⊤ +44 1243/621046. Alternatively, get an online quote at ⓦ www.roughguides.com/insurance.

Americans and Canadians should also check that they're not already covered. Canadian provincial health plans usually provide partial cover for medical mishaps overseas. Holders of official student/ teacher/youth cards are entitled to meagre accident coverage and hospital in-patient benefits. Students will often find that their student health coverage extends during the vacations and for one term beyond the date of last enrolment. Homeowners' or renters' insurance often covers theft or loss of documents, money and valuables while overseas, though conditions and maximum amounts vary from company to company.

Health

Health-wise, travelling in Costa Rica is generally very safe. Food tends to be well and hygienically prepared, so bugs and upsets are normally limited to the usual "travellers' tummy". Water supplies in most places are clean and bacteria-free, and outbreaks of infectious diseases such as cholera are rare.

In general, as in the rest of Latin America, it tends to be local people, often poor or without proper sanitation or quick access to health care, who contract infectious diseases. If you do fall ill or have an accident, medical treatment in Costa Rica is very good but very expensive: extensive health insurance is a must (see "Insurance", opposite).

Inoculations

No compulsory **inoculations** are required before you enter Costa Rica. You may, however, want to make sure that your polio, typhoid, and hepatitis A and B jabs are up-to-date, though none of the diseases is a major risk. **Rabies**, a potentially fatal illness, should be taken very seriously. There is a vaccine, comprising a course of three injections that has to be started at least a month before departure and which is effective for two years – though it's expensive and serves only to shorten the course of treatment you need. If you're not vaccinated, stay away from dogs, monkeys and any other potentially biting or scratching animals. If you do get scratched or bitten, wash the wound at once, with alcohol if possible, and seek medical help immediately.

Medical resources for travellers

Australia and New Zealand

Travellers' Medical and Vaccination Centres (ⓦ www.tmvc.com.au), 7/428 George St, Sydney (ⓣ 02/9221 7133); 2/393 Little Bourke St, Melbourne (ⓣ 03/9602 5788); 27–29 Gilbert Place, Adelaide (ⓣ 08/8212 7522); 5/247 Adelaide St, Brisbane (ⓣ 07/3221 9066); 5 Mill St, Perth (ⓣ 08/9321 1977); 270 Sandy Bay Rd, Sandy Bay, Hobart (ⓣ 03/6223 7577); 5/8–10 Hobart Place, Canberra (ⓣ 02/6257 7156); 5 Westralia St, Darwin (ⓣ 08/8981 2907); 1/170 Queen St, Auckland (ⓣ 09/373 3531); 147 Armagh St, Christchurch (ⓣ 03/379 4000); Shop 15, Grand Arcade, 14–16 Willis St, Wellington (ⓣ 04/473 0991).

North America

Center for Disease Control, 1600 Clifton Rd NE, Atlanta, GA 30333 (ⓣ 404/639-3311, ⓦ www.cdc.gov/travel/travel.html). Publishes outbreak warnings, suggested inoculations, precautions and other background information for travellers, and has a very useful Web site.
International Association for Medical Assistance to Travellers (IAMAT), 417 Center St, Lewiston, NY 14092 (ⓣ 716/754-4883, ⓦ www.sentex.net/~iamat); 40 Regal Rd, Guelph, ON N1K 1B5 (ⓣ 519/836-0102). Non-profit organization supported by donations, which can provide a list of English-speaking doctors in Costa Rica, climate charts and leaflets on various diseases and inoculations.
International SOS Assistance, PO Box 11568, Philadelphia, PA 19116 (ⓣ 1-800/523-8930 in the US, ⓣ 1-800/363-0263 in Canada, ⓦ www.internationalsos.com). Members receive pre-trip medical info and the use of overseas emergency services designed to complement travel insurance coverage.
Travel Medicine, 351 Pleasant St, Suite 312, Northampton, MA 01060 (ⓣ 1-800/872-8633). Sells first-aid kits, mosquito netting, water filters and other health-related travel products.

UK

British Airways Travel Clinic (28 clinics nationwide; call ⓣ 01276/685040 or visit ⓦ www.britishairways.com for your nearest branch). Vaccinations, tailored advice from their online database and a complete range of travel healthcare products. No appointment is necessary at the branch at 156 Regent Street, London W1 (Mon–Fri 9.30am–5.15pm, Sat 10.00am–4.00pm; ⓣ 020/7439 9584).
Hospital for Tropical Diseases Travel Clinic, 2nd Floor, Mortimer Market Centre, off Capper Street, London WC1E 6AU (Mon–Fri 9am–5pm by appointment only; the consultation fee of £15 is waived if you have your injections here; ⓣ 020/7388 9600). A recorded Health Line (ⓣ 09061/337733; 50p/min) gives information on illness, hygiene and immunizations.
MASTA (Medical Advisory Service for Travellers Abroad). Operates a prerecorded 24hr Travellers' Health Line (ⓣ 0906/822 4100; 60p per min), giving written information tailored to your journey by return of post.
Trailfinders, 194 Kensington High Street, London W8 7RG (Mon–Fri 9am–5pm, Thurs until 6pm, Sat 9.30am–4pm; ⓣ 020/7938 3999). Immunization clinic; no appointment needed.
Yahoo! Health, ⓦ www.health.yahoo.com. Information about specific diseases and conditions, drugs and herbal remedies, plus advice from health experts.

Sun trouble

Sunstroke, dehydration and diarrhoea are the likeliest sources of illness in Costa Rica, and capable of making you very sick indeed. Costa Rica is just 8°–11° north of the Equator, which means a blazing-hot sun directly overhead. To guard against **sunburn** take at least factor-15 sunscreen and a good hat, and wear both even on slightly overcast days, especially in coastal areas. Even in places at higher altitudes where it does not feel excessively hot, such as San José and the surrounding Valle Central, you should protect yourself. **Dehydration** is another possible problem, so keep your fluid level up, and take rehydration salts (Gastrolyte is readily available). **Diarrhoea** can be brought on by too much sun and heat sickness. It's a good idea to bring an over-the-counter remedy like Lomotil from home – it should only be taken for short periods, however, as extensive use leads to

A traveller's first-aid kit

Among the items you might want to carry with you, especially if you're planning to go hiking, are:
❏ Antiseptic cream
❏ Plasters/band aids
❏ Imodium (Lomotil) for emergency diarrhoea treatment
❏ Paracetamol/aspirin
❏ Rehydration sachets
❏ Calamine lotion
❏ Hypodermic needles and sterilized skin wipes
❏ Iodine soap for washing cuts (guards against humidity-encouraged infections)
❏ Insect repellent
❏ Sulphur powder (fights the sand fleas/chiggers that are ubiquitous in Costa Rica's beach areas)

constipation, which is equally uncomfortable and inconvenient while travelling.

Water

The only areas of Costa Rica where it is best not to drink the tap water (or ice cubes, or drinks made with tap water) are the port cities of **Limón** and **Puntarenas**. Bottled water is available in these towns; drink from these and stick with known brands, even if they are more expensive. Though you'll be safe drinking tap water elsewhere in the country, it is possible to pick up **giardia**, a bacterium that causes stomach upset and diarrhoea, by drinking out of streams and rivers – campers should pick up their water supplies from the national park waterspouts, where it's been treated for drinking.

If you can't do this for some reason, the time-honoured method of **boiling** will effectively sterilize water, although it will not remove unpleasant tastes. A minimum boiling time of five minutes (longer at higher altitudes) is sufficient to kill micro-organisms. Boiling water is not always convenient, however, as it is time-consuming and requires supplies of fuel or a travel kettle and power source. **Chemical sterilization** can be carried out using either chlorine or iodine tablets or a tincture of iodine liquid. When using tablets it is essential to follow the manufacturer's dosage and contact time. Tincture of iodine is better; add a couple of drops to one litre of water and leave to stand for twenty minutes. **Pregnant women** or people with **thyroid problems** should consult their doctor before using iodine sterilizing tablets or iodine-based purifiers. Inexpensive iodine removal filters are recommended if treated water is being used continuously for more than a month or if it is being given to babies.

Malaria and dengue fever

Although some sources of information – including perhaps your GP – will tell you that you don't need to worry about **malaria** in Costa Rica, it is a risk, although admittedly very small. Around 800 cases of malaria are reported annually, about half of these being tourists. If you want to make absolutely sure of not contracting the illness, and intend to travel extensively anywhere on the **Caribbean coast**, especially in Puerto Limón and south towards Cahuita and Puerto Viejo, you should take a course of prophylactics (usually chloroquine rather than mefloquine), available from your doctor or clinic.

Though a minimal health risk to travellers, some incidences of **dengue fever**, another mosquito-borne illness, have been reported in the past few years: local papers often carry scare stories about outbreaks in San José's suburbs and the area immediately south of Puerto Limón. Symptoms are very like malaria, but with extreme aches and pains in the bones and joints, along with fever and dizziness. The only cure for dengue fever is rest and painkillers, and the only way to avoid it is to make sure you don't get bitten by mosquitos, since there's currently no vaccine available for it. On rare occasions, the illness may develop potentially fatal complications, though this usually only affects people who have caught the disease more than once.

Snakes

Snakes abound in Costa Rica, but the risk of being **bitten** is incredibly small – there has been no instance of a tourist receiving a fatal bite in recent years. Most of the victims of Costa Rica's more venomous snakes are field labourers who do not have time or the resources to get to a hospital. Just in case, however, travellers hiking off the beaten track may want to take specific antivenins plus sterile hypodermic needles. If you're worried, you can buy **antivenin** at the University of Costa Rica's snake farm in Coronado, outside San José (see p.141), where herpetologists (people who study snakes) are glad to talk to visitors about precautions.

If you have no antivenin and are unlucky enough to get bitten, the usual advice is to catch or kill the specimen for identification (since administering the wrong antivenin can cause death), though in practice it's usually impossible to do this – indeed it's probably best not to try, especially if faced with one of the larger vipers.

In general, prevention is better than cure. Before undertaking any activity where you're likely to come across a snake, stop off at the San José Serpentario (see p.92) and take a good look at some of Costa Rica's more poisonous specimens, so that you can theoretically identify – and avoid – them in the wild. As a rule of thumb, you should approach rainforest cover and grassy uplands – the kind of terrain you find in Guanacaste and the Nicoya Peninsula – with caution. Always watch where you put your feet and, if you need to hold something to keep your balance, make sure the "vine" you're grabbing isn't, in fact, a surprised snake. Be particularly wary at dawn or dusk – before 5.30am or after 6pm. Many snakes start moving as early as 4.30pm, particularly in dense cloudforest cover. In addition, be careful in "sunspots" – places in dense rainforest cover where the sun penetrates through to the ground or to a tree – snakes like to hang out there, absorbing the warmth. Above all, though, don't be too alarmed. Thousands of tourists troop through Costa Rica's rainforests and grasslands each year without encountering a single snake.

HIV and AIDS

HIV and **AIDS** (in Spanish, SIDA) is present in the country, but isn't prevalent (travelling around you'll see government-sponsored educational directives, such as billboards aimed at persuading heterosexual couples to "be faithful to your wife and save both your lives"). That said, the same commonsense rules apply here as all over the world: sex without a **condom**, especially in some of the popular beach towns, is a serious health risk. Condoms sold in Costa Rica are not of the quality you find at home; best bring them with you. Though hospitals and clinics in Costa Rica use sterilized equipment, you may want to bring sealed hypodermic syringes anyway.

Information and maps

The glossy promotional bumf handed out by Costa Rican embassies and consulates is pretty to look at but largely useless for independent travellers. Costa Rica has no tourist office in North America, the UK or Australasia. US and Canadian residents can call a toll-free tourist information hotline (☎1-800/343-6332), which is answered by English-speaking ICT (see p.76) staff in San José. Alternatively, check out the tourist board's Web site at ⓦwww.tourism -costarica.com.

Information

The best source of information about Costa Rica is the **Instituto Costarricense de Turismo** (ICT), Apartado 777, San José 1000, Costa Rica (☎506/223-1733, ℗223-5452) – you can write to them from abroad for information, although it may take a while to receive a reply, and you'll probably just get the same glossy pamphlets and brochures that are handed out at embassies.

You're better off going in person to the ICT office (see p.76), located in the unprepossessing bunker underneath the Plaza de la Cultura in central San José, where the friendly bilingual staff will do their best to answer any queries you may have. On request, they'll also offer you a free map of the city and a very useful comprehensive bus timetable with recent additions and changes corrected on the spot. The office also has a full (though not necessarily up-to-date) list of practically all the hotels in the country, with prices, addresses and telephone numbers, a list of museums and their opening hours, and details of many San José restaurants and nightclubs. The small ICT booth at the **Santamaría International Airport** doesn't offer free timetables but may have the hotel lists. Otherwise, there are no tourist offices offering independent (unbiased) information outside the capital. As a rule you have to rely on locally run initiatives, often set up by a small business association or the chamber of commerce, or hotels and tourist agencies.

A number of Costa Rican **tour operators**, based in San José, can offer information and guidance when planning a trip around the country, though these may not be as objective as they could be; see p.33 for details.

Maps

The maps dished out by Costa Rican embassies and the ICT are basic and somewhat out-of-date; it's best to arm yourself with general maps before you go. The best **road map**, a colourful spread giving a good rendition of all the major routes and national parks, is the *Costa Rica Road Map* (1:650,000; Berndtson & Berndtson), available from good map stores or by mail from Hauptstr. 1a, D-82256 Fürstenfeldbruck, Germany (℗49-8141/16280). Another excellent map, clearly marked with contour details, gas stations, national parks and roads, is *Costa Rica* (1:500,000) available from World Wide Books and Maps (see p.24). Road and park markings are less distinct on Nelles Verlag's large *Central America*, focusing on Costa Rica (1:900,000), but it's handy if you are travelling throughout the isthmus. Buy it at specialist travel or map stores or write direct to Nelles Verlag, Schleissheimer Str. 371b, D-80935 München, Germany.

In Costa Rica it's a good idea to go to one of San José's two big downtown bookstores, Librería Universal or Librería Lehmann (see p.107) and look through their stock of **maps**, which are contoured and show major topographical features like river crossings and high-tide marks. You buy them in sections; each costs about $2. You could also try going to the government maps bureau, the **Instituto Geográfico Nacional**, in San José at Av 20, C 5/7, which sells more lavishly detailed colour maps of specific areas of the country.

Considering it's such a popular hiking destination, there are surprisingly few good maps of Costa Rica's **national parks**. Those given out at ranger stations are very general; your best bet is to get hold of the book *Parques Nacionales de Costa Rica/National Parks of Costa Rica* (separate editions in Spanish and English), published by the National Parks Service and usually available in San José bookshops such as Librería Universal or Librería Lehmann (see above). Although rather cramped, not too detailed and of little practical use for walking the trails, these maps (of all the parks currently in existence) do at least show contours and give a general idea of the terrain, the animals you might see and the annual rainfall.

If you are going to be doing a lot of **driving**, pick up *The Essential Road Guide for Costa Rica* by Bill Baker ($9.95), widely available in San José bookstores, which features well-marked maps, tips and quite a bit of tourist information.

Map outlets

Australia and New Zealand

Mapland, 372 Little Bourke St, Melbourne (℡ 03/9670 4383).
The Map Shop, 6 Peel St, Adelaide (℡ 08/8231 2033).
Mapworld, 173 Gloucester Street, Christchurch (℡ 03/374 5399, ⓦ www.mapworld.co.nz).
Perth Map Centre, 1/884 Hay St, Perth (℡ 08/9322 5733).
Specialty Maps, 46 Albert St, Auckland (℡ 09/307 2217).
Travel Bookshop, Shop 3, 175 Liverpool St, Sydney (℡ 02/9261 8200).
Walkers Bookshop, 96 Lake Street, Cairns (℡ 07/4051 2410).
Worldwide Maps and Guides, 187 George St, Brisbane (℡ 07/3221 4330).

UK

Daunt Books, 83 Marylebone High St, London W1M 3DE (℡ 020/7224 2295); 193 Haverstock Hill, London NW3 4QL (℡ 020/7794 4006).
John Smith and Sons, 26 Colquhoun Ave, Glasgow G52 4PJ (℡ 0141/221 7472, ⓦ www.johnsmith.co.uk).

National Map Centre, 22–24 Caxton St, London SW1H 0QU (℡ 020/7222 2466, ⓦ www.mapsnmc.co.uk).
Stanfords (ⓦ www.stanfords.co.uk), 12–14 Long Acre, London WC2E 9LP (℡ 020/7836 1321); c/o British Airways, 156 Regent St, London W1R 5TA (℡ 020/7434 4744); 29 Corn St, Bristol BS1 1HT (℡ 0117/929 9966).
Waterstone's, Deansgate, Manchester M3 2BW (℡ 0161/837 3000, ℻ 0161/835 1534, ⓦ www.waterstonesbooks.co.uk).

US and Canada

The Complete Traveler Bookstore, 199 Madison Ave, New York, NY 10016 (℡ 212/685-9007).
Open Air Books and Maps, 25 Toronto St, Toronto, ON M5R 2C1 (℡ 416/363-0719).
Rand McNally, 444 N Michigan Ave, Chicago, IL 60611 (℡ 312/321-1751); 150 E 52nd St, New York, NY 10022 (℡ 212/758-7488); 595 Market St, San Francisco, CA 94105 (℡ 415/777-3131); 1201 Connecticut Ave NW, Washington, DC 20003 (℡ 202/223-6751). For other locations, or for maps by mail order, call ℡ 1-800/333-0136 (ext 2111).
Traveler's Bookstore, 22 W 52nd St, New York, NY 10019 (℡ 212/664-0995).
Ulysses Travel Bookshop, 4176 St-Denis, Montréal, PQ (℡ 514/843-9447).
World Wide Books and Maps, 736 Granville St, Vancouver, BC V6Z 1E4 (℡ 604/687-3320).

Internet and email access

Two recommended sites from which to being an **Internet** search for information on Costa Rica are ⓦ www.centralamerica.com and ⓦ www.incostarica.net, both of which have links to thousands of Costa Rica Web sites, including most official sites and countless others set up by Costa Rica aficionados in the US. Other sites with relevant links include ⓦ www.latinguia.com and ⓦ www.terra.co.cr. Weekly news on the country in English can be found at ⓦ www.ticotimes.co.cr, and Costa Rica's leading daily newspaper is online at ⓦ www.nacion.co.cr .

For issues specific to tourism, ⓦ www.costaricadestino.com (run in conjunction with a weekly Costa Rican TV programme of the same name on Channel 7) features tourist sites and attractions as well as undiscovered places in the country. If you have a special interest in eco-tourism check the Web site of Tourism Concern (🌐 www.tourismconcern.org.uk) or try the Association of Progressive Communication (🌐 www.apc.org), which also deals with global development and human-rights issues. GreenNet (🌐 www.gn.apc.org), an offshoot of the APC, promotes environmentally and culturally responsible tourism.

Many Costa Rican **hotels** and **businesses** now have email. If you don't know their email address, it's worth trying the establishment's name followed by @racsa.co.cr – a common termination for email addresses in Costa Rica. Beware **real-estate advertisements** on the Internet. Costa Rica is property scam heaven, and there are lots of shady deals around; if you have any intention of buying property in the country, wait until you arrive.

Costs, money and banks

Costa Rica is the most expensive country in Central America. Just about everything – from ice-cream cones and groceries to hotel rooms, meals and car rental – costs more than you might expect. Some prices, especially for upper-range accommodation, are comparable with those in the US, which never fails to astonish American travellers and those coming from the cheaper neighbouring countries. That said, prices have dropped from their peak of a few years ago, when Costa Rica developed a reputation as being overpriced, and you can, with a little foresight, travel reasonably cheaply throughout the country.

The US **dollar** has long been the second currency of Costa Rica, and we quote dollar prices throughout the Guide. However, outside the tourist areas nobody really refers to dollars. The vast majority of Costa Ricans get paid in **colones**, and buy and sell in colones, and you would do well to get the hang of the currency as soon as possible.

Currency

Though the US dollar is often used in Costa Rica, the official currency is the **colón** (plural *colones*) – named after Colón (Columbus) himself. It is divided into 1, 2, 5, 10 and 20 colón **coins**, which are silver, and the newer gold coins, which come in 1, 5, 10 and 25 denominations. The silver and gold coins are completely interchangeable, with the exception of in public payphones, which do not yet accept the gold coins. **Notes** are available in 50, 100, 500, 1000 and 5000 colones. You'll often hear colones colloquially referred to as "pesos", and the 1000-colón note is sometimes called the *rojo* (red). The colón floats freely against the US dollar – at the time of writing the exchange rate was around 320 colones to \$1, but inflationary pressures and devaluation mean that it will inevitably change considerably over the lifetime of this edition.

Obtaining colones outside Costa Rica is possible, but only by ordering them from your bank well in advance of your departure; otherwise, wait until you arrive and change some at the airport or border post. If you miss banking hours, dollar bills in small denominations will do fine.

Costs

Costa Rica has always been more pricey than its Central American neighbours, due to the relatively high (18–25 percent) **taxes** levied in restaurants and hotels.

Even on a rock-bottom hotel and lunch-

25

counter or takeout meal **budget**, you're looking at spending $25 a day for lodging, three meals and the odd bus ticket. Campers and hardy cyclists have been known to do it on $15 a day, but this entails sleeping either in your tent or in some pretty dire places. You will be far more comfortable if you count on spending at least $20 a day for accommodation and $12 for meals.

The good news is that some things are still inexpensive. **Bus** travel is geared toward Costa Ricans, not foreigners, so stays cheap – about 25¢ to $1 for local buses, around $4 or $5 for long-distance (3hr or more) trips, and rarely rising above $10. Eating, too, needn't be that pricey if you eat your main meal of the day at one of Costa Rica's good-value **sodas** (see "Eating and Drinking", p.38), while fruit, beer, theatre seats and trips to the movies will all seem very reasonable to visitors from most other countries. For notes on **tipping** in Costa Rica, see the Directory on p.67.

Moneychanging and banks

Outside San José there are effectively no official **bureaux de change** in Costa Rica – the Juan Santamaría airport does have one, but service is very slow and rather surly. In general, official and legitimate moneychanging entails going to a bank, a (usually upper-range) hotel or, in outlying areas of the country, to whoever will do it – a tour agency, the friend of the owner of your hotel who has a Chinese restaurant . . .

When heading for the more remote areas, try to carry sufficient colones with you, especially in small denominations – you may have trouble changing a 5000 bill in the middle of the Nicoya Peninsula, for example. Going around with stacks of mouldy-smelling colones may not seem safe, but you should be all right if you keep them in a money belt, and it will save hours of time waiting in line. That said, however, if you are doing a lot of travelling, it's comforting to know that many of even the smallest end-of-the-world towns have a branch of at least one bank.

Efficient and air-conditioned **private banks**, the majority of which are in down-town San José, will relieve you of your dollars and give you colones in good time and good humour, requiring only your passport and about five minutes to process the

transaction. Private banks in San José include Banco Mercantil, Banco Metropolitano, Banco Popular, Banco de San José, BANEX and Banco del Comercio (for addresses, see San José's "Listings" on p.107). Outside San José the most common branches are Banco Popular, BanCrecen and Scotiabank. Private banks in Costa Rica can legally charge what they like for com-mission; the norm is about $3 per transac-tion.

Banking hours vary slightly from branch to branch but tend to be Monday to Friday 8.30am to 3.30pm for state banks and slightly longer for private ones, with very few banks opening on Saturdays. Most Costa Rican banks now have **ATMs,** though despite the fact that they carry VISA and Plus signs, foreign-issued cards at present only work in the ATMs of private banks such as Banco Popular, not in those of state banks such as Banco de Costa Rica and Banco Nacional.

If you're stuck in San José without cash in an emergency, you could approach the guys who hang out on the pedestrian mall at the western end of Avenida Central whispering "dólares" and "cambio". However, this should be used only as a last resort when you're absolutely stuck for colones, as it's technically illegal and you could find yourself scammed.

Banks may not accept bent, smudged or torn dollars, although street traders usually will. It's also worth noting that, due to a recent influx of **counterfeit $100 bills**, some shops and even banks, are unwilling to accept them. If you bring any into the coun-try, make sure that they are in mint condition.

Credit cards

Credit cards can come in very handy as a back-up source of funds, and they can even save on exchange-rate commissions; just be sure someone back home is taking care of the bills if you're away for more than a month. You'll find them especially useful in Costa Rica for making deposits for hotels via fax or phone and for renting a car. In outly-ing areas, however, like the Talamanca coast, Quepos and Manuel Antonio and Golfito, some businesses may levy a six per-cent charge for credit card transactions; you may be better off taking plenty of cash.

In general, **Visa** and **Mastercard** are widely accepted, although retailers tend to accept only one or the other, so it's handy to have both. **Amex** is somewhat less useful, though you certainly won't have any problem using it in the higher-class hotels or to pay for air tickets and rental cars. Some retailers and hotels only accept the local Costa Rican credit card, called "Su Tarjeta" (ST).

Both state and private banks in Costa Rica can give you **cash advances** on your credit card (in either colones or dollars, provided they have enough dollars on hand) with relative ease, though not all will accept Mastercard (try Scotiabank or Banco de San José). Bring your passport as identification.

Travellers' cheques

Undeniably the safest way to keep your money, **travellers' cheques** should be brought in US dollars only – Costa Rican bank tellers will only stare blankly at other currencies. North American brands of travellers' cheques, including Amex, Citibank and Visa are most familiar to Costa Rican banks; they'll change Barclays' US-dollar cheques too, although they might look askance for a minute before deciding they're legit. Don't expect to use travellers' cheques as cash in Costa Rica except in mid- or top-range hotels and guest houses that regularly cater to foreigners.

The usual **fee** for travellers' cheque sales is one or two percent, and it pays to get a selection of denominations. Make sure you keep the purchase agreement and a record of cheque serial numbers safe and separate from the cheques themselves. In the event that cheques are lost or stolen, the issuing company will expect you to report the loss forthwith to their office in San José: most companies claim to replace lost or stolen cheques within 24 hours.

Another way of carrying funds is **Visa Travel Money** (Ⓦ www.visa.com), a disposable debit card pre-paid with dedicated travel funds which you can access from` over 627,000 Visa ATMs in 120 countries. In the UK, many Thomas Cook outlets sell the card.

Wiring money

Having **money wired** from home is never convenient or cheap, and should be considered a last resort only. In Costa Rica you can have money wired to Western Union, in San José at C 9, Av 2/4 (Ⓣ 204-4000 or toll-free 800/777-7777, Ⓦ www.westernunion.co.cr), or the Costa Rican company, Servicios Internacionales Unigiros SA in San José at Av 1, C 1/3 (Ⓣ 255-1033). Both companies' fees depend on the destination and the amount being transferred. The funds should be available for collection at the office within minutes of being sent. You can also have money wired directly from a bank in your home country to a bank in Costa Rica; a cumbersome process, because it involves two separate institutions. The person wiring the funds to you will need to know the telex number of the bank the funds are being wired to.

Youth and student discounts

Full-time students are eligible for the **International Student ID Card** (ISIC), which may entitle the bearer to some discounts at museums in Costa Rica. For US and Canadian card holders, there's also a health benefit, providing up to $3000 in emergency medical coverage and $100 a day for sixty days in hospital, plus a 24-hour hotline to call in the event of a medical, legal or financial emergency. The card, which costs $16 for US students, CDN$15 for Canadians, £5 in the UK and A$10 for Australians, is available from Council Travel, STA and Travel CUTS (see p.10 & p.13 for addresses). More useful is **local student ID**, which may offer discounts at museums and theatres – they're available to visitors on language courses and other education programmes (see p.64).

Getting around

Costa Rica's public bus system is excellent, cheap and quite frequent, even in remote areas. Getting anywhere by bus with a lot of baggage can be a problem, however, and between trips you should try to find somewhere secure to leave your luggage (your San José hotel, for example). Taxis regularly do long- as well as short-distance trips and are a fairly inexpensive alternative to the bus, at least if you're travelling in a group.

Car rental is more common here than in the rest of Central America, but is expensive, and as Costa Rica has one of the highest accident rates in the world, driving can be a little hair-raising. **Domestic airlines** are reasonably economical, especially since Costa Rica's difficult terrain makes driving distances longer than they look on the map. A number of **tour operators** in San José (see p.33) organize individual itineraries and packages with transport included, well worth checking out before making any decisions about heading out on your own.

By bus

Travelling by **bus** is by far the cheapest way to get around Costa Rica. The most expensive journey in the country (from Puerto Jiménez on the Osa Peninsula to San José) costs $7, while fares in the mid- to long-distance range vary from $2.50 to $5. **Tickets** on most mid- to long-distance and popular routes are issued with a date and a seat number; you are expected to sit in the seat indicated. Make sure the date is correct; even if the mistake is not yours, you cannot normally change your ticket or get a refund. Neither can you buy **return** bus tickets on Costa Rican buses, which can be quite inconvenient if you're heading to very popular destinations like Monteverde, Jacó and Manuel Antonio at busy times – you'll need to jump off the bus as soon as you arrive and buy your return ticket immediately to assure yourself of a seat.

The majority of the country's buses are in fairly good shape, although they're usually

Finding your way around Costa Rican towns

In Costa Rica there is only one vision of urban planning: the grid system. However, there are a number of peculiarities that it is essential to come to grips with if you want to find your way around with ease. The following rules apply to all cities except Limón.

Typically, you'll see addresses written as follows: Bar Esmeralda, Av 2, C 5/7 (abbreviated from Avenida 2, Calles 5/7). This means that Bar Esmeralda is on Avenida 2, between Calles 5 and 7. Bar Lotto, C 5, Av 2, on the other hand, is on the corner of Calle 5 and Avenida 2. Apartado (Aptdo) means "postbox", and bis means, technically, "encore": if you see "Av 6 bis" in an address it refers to another Avenida 6, right next to the original one.

Many directions, in both written and verbal form, are given in terms of metres rather than blocks. In general, one block is equivalent to 100m. Thus "de la Escuela Presidente Vargas, 125 metros al sur, cincuenta metros al oeste", translates as "from the Presidente Vargas School, 125 metres south [one block and a quarter] and 50 west [half a block]". More confusingly, verbal directions are also commonly given in relation to landmarks which everyone – except the visitor – knows and recognizes, and which, frustratingly, may not even exist any longer. This is something to get the hang of fast: taxi drivers will often look completely bewildered if given street directions, but as soon you come up with a landmark, the proverbial light bulb goes on.

not air-conditioned and there's very little room for luggage. Most comfortable are the **Ticabuses** – old US Greyhounds with good seats, adequate baggage space, air-conditioning and very courteous drivers – that run from San José to Panamá or to Managua.

San José is the hub for virtually all bus services in the country; indeed, it's often impossible to travel from one place to another without backtracking to the capital. Different companies have semi-monopolies on various regions; for a rundown of destinations and routes, including international services, see pp.109–112.

Some popular buses, like the service to Golfito, ought to be **booked in advance**, though you may be lucky enough to get on without a reservation. Services to popular tourist areas in high season – especially Monteverde – get booked up very fast, so again you should buy your ticket several days in advance. For updated information on bus timetables check ⓦwww.yellowweb.co.cr/crbuses.html; for more details of bus companies and terminals, see p.109.

Most buses in Costa Rica now have buzzers or bells to signal to the driver that you want to get off, though you may still find a few people using the old system of whistling, or shouting "¡*parada!*" ("stop!"). The atmosphere in Costa Rican buses is generally friendly, and if the driver starts to drive away while you're halfway out of the back door trying to get off, your fellow passengers will erupt in spontaneous help.

Though there are no **toilets** on the buses, drivers make (admittedly infrequent) stops on longer runs. Often a lunch or dinner stop will be made at a roadside restaurant or gas station; failing that, there is always a bevy of hardy food and drinks sellers who leap onto the bus proffering their wares.

If you don't fancy the local buses, a private bus service geared for tourists, **Interbus**, offers air-conditioned services to many of the country's tourist spots, travelling from San José to the Fortuna/Arenal area, the beaches of Guanacaste, Puerto Limón, Cahuita and Puerto Viejo. Fares are between $20 and $60 one-way, which often works out at about 1000 per cent more expensive than the local service – the upside is that there's no crowding, and the service is direct and doesn't stop to pick up passengers on the road, as public buses do. Interbus operates from mid- or upmarket hotels in the areas it serves, which is where you should ask about schedules. For a full rundown of services, contact Interbus (☎283-5573, ℉283-7655, ⓦwww.costaricapass.com). The similar but cheaper **Gray Line** (☎220-2126, ℉220-2393, ⓦwww.fantasy.co.cr) runs direct services between several San José hotels and many tourist spots. Fares are about $20 one-way.

Driving

Although there's little traffic outside the Valle Central, the common perception of **driving** in Costa Rica – imagined as an endless dodging around cows and potholes, whilst big trucks nudge your rear bumper in an effort to get you to go faster around that next blind bend – may deter you from driving in the country. It's perfectly possible to drive and survive, however, and with your own vehicle you'll get to see the country much better than from the windows of a bus or plane. Citizens of the US, Canada and the UK need only a **valid driver's licence** or an international driver's licence to operate a vehicle in Costa Rica. Residents of other countries should check with their nearest Costa Rican consulate. In **Australia**, international drivers' licences can be obtained from state motoring organization offices in major towns and cities, or contact the Australian Automobile Association, 212 Northbourne Ave, Canberra ACT 2601 (☎02/6247 7311, ⓦwww.aaa.asn.au). In **New Zealand**, contact the New Zealand Automobile Association at 17/99 Albert St, Auckland (☎09/377 4660, ⓦwww.aa.co.nz) or your local AA office.

In recent years a system of fines (*multas*) for infractions like **speeding** has been introduced in Costa Rica. The limit on the highways is either 75km/hr or 90km/hr; marked on the road surface or on signs. If you're caught speeding you could find yourself paying anything up to $65. Do not, under any circumstances, try to bribe a traffic cop, as this could land you in far more serious trouble. If a motorist – especially a trucker – in the oncoming direction flashes his headlights at you, you can be almost certain that traffic cops with speed-trapping radar are up ahead.

Gas is reasonably priced, and positively cheap by European standards: about $15 a tank on a medium-sized car or about $30 for

Car safety in Costa Rica

The road traffic accident rate in Costa Rica is phenomenal – and rising. Most tourists see at least one accident on the roads during their time in the country, and though Costa Ricans blame bad road conditions, the real cause is more often poor driving – you're advised to drive extremely defensively. Sections of washed out, unmarked or unlit road add to the hazards, as do mechanically unsound buses and big trans-isthmus trucks.

Another hazard of driving in Costa Rica involves car crime. A recent scam involves thieves entering car rental companies' parking lots and making slow punctures in the tyres of hire cars. Unsuspecting drivers then take these cars out onto the road until the puncture eventually forces them to pull over, at which point the thieves (who have been following) stop to offer help before robbing the visitor of all their belongings and the car, leaving them stranded by the roadside. The lesson is be sure to check your tyres carefully, especially if renting from an airport office. However, in the lifetime of this book the scam of the month will probably have moved on.

The Instituto de Turismo offers tourists the following advice:
❏ If your vehicle is bumped from behind, do not stop on the roadway or shoulder. Drive to the nearest public area and call for the police.
❏ Keep your doors locked and windows shut, especially in San José.
❏ If someone suspicious approaches your vehicle at a red light or stop sign, blow your horn.
❏ Do not pull over for flashing headlights. An emergency or police vehicle has red or blue flashing headlights.
❏ If you become lost, find a public place, like a service station, to consult your map or ask for directions.
❏ If someone tells you something is wrong with your vehicle do not stop immediately. Drive to the nearest service station or other well-lit public area.
❏ Keep valuables in the trunk or out of sight, and your car locked at all times.
❏ Do not pick up hitchhikers.
❏ Do not leave the keys in your vehicle or the motor running when you stop to use the telephone or the ATM.
❏ If you suspect you are being followed, go to the nearest well-lit public area and call the police.
❏ In case of emergency call 911.

a big 4WD. If you're unlucky enough to have an **accident** in Costa Rica, don't attempt to move the car until the traffic police arrive: call the National Insurance Institute (℡800/800-8000), who will send an inspector to check the vehicles involved to assess who caused the accident – vital if you're using a hire car.

If you intend to drive in the rainy season (May–Nov), especially on the Nicoya Peninsula, or to Santa Elena and Monteverde, or anywhere at all off the beaten track, you'll need to rent a **four-wheel drive** (4WD). Make sure someone explains the four-by-four function before you set out, and note that some car-rental companies will refuse to rent you a regular car if you intend to go to Monteverde from May through to November, due to the poor condition of the roads.

Car rental

Car rental in Costa Rica is expensive. Expect to pay about $350 per week (including insurance) for a regular vehicle, and up to $500 for a large 4WD. Rental days are calculated on a 24-hour basis: thus, if you pick up your car on a Tuesday at 3pm for a week, you have to return it before that time the following Tuesday. The minimum age for rental is usually 25, and you'll need a credit card, either Mastercard or Visa, which has sufficient credit for the entire cost of the rental. Although the majority of companies are based in San José, you can often arrange to pick up your car in another part of Costa Rica and drop it off at the airport when you leave. It's also worth knowing that most tour operators in Costa Rica can arrange car hire much more cheaply than if you organize it yourself through one of the overseas operators listed below.

Car rental companies in Costa Rica tend to be located in San José, at the international airport, and at the new airport in Liberia; you can also rent cars in various towns around the country – of the Costa Rican rental agencies, Elegante and Europcar/Prego have the largest network of regional offices. Renting outside San José often works out a bit more expensive than from the capital, but it can save you the drive on the tricky Interamericana highway from the capital to your destination. Prices can vary considerably from agency to agency (Europcar/Prego and Adobe are both recommended). During peak season (especially Christmas, but any time from December to March) it's essential to have a car reserved before you arrive.

Car rental companies in San José

In all the following, where two numbers are given, the first is the company's downtown office, the second, the airport office.
ADA, Av 18, C 11/13 (☏233-7733; ☏441-1260)
Adobe, C 7, Av 8/10 (☏221-5425)
Avis, C 42, Av Las Americas (☏293-2222)
Budget, Paseo Colón, C 30 (☏223-3284)
Elegante, C 10, Av 13/15, Barrio México (☏221-0066; ☏ 233-8605)
Europcar/Prego, C 36/38 (☏257-1158, ⓦwww.pregorentacar.com)
Hertz, C 38, Paseo Colón (☏221-1818)
Hola, in front of the *Best Western Irazú* on the airport highway (☏231-5666, ⓦwww.hola.net)
National, C 36, Av 7 (☏233-4044)
Thrifty, C 3, Av 13 (☏257-3434)
Tico, Paseo Colón, C 24/26 (☏222-8920; ☏443-2078)

Car rental companies abroad

Australia

Avis ☏13 6333, ⓦwww.avis.com
Budget ☏1300/362 848, ⓦwww.budget.com
Dollar ☏02/9223 1444 or 1800/358 008, ⓦwww.dollarcar.com.au
Hertz ☏1800/550 067, ⓦwww.hertz.com

New Zealand

Avis ☏09/526 5231 or 0800/655 111, ⓦwww.avis.com
Budget ☏0800/652 227 or 09/375 2270, ⓦwww.budget.com
Hertz ☏09/309 0989 or 0800/655 955, ⓦwww.hertz.com

North America

Avis ☏1-800/331-1084, ⓦwww.avis.com
Budget ☏1-800/800-6000, ⓦwww.budget.com
Dollar ☏1-800/421-6868, ⓦwww.dollar.com
Hertz ☏1-800/654-3001 in the US, ☏1-800/263-0600 in Canada, ⓦwww.hertz.com
National ☏1-800/CAR RENT, ⓦwww.nationalcar.com

UK

Avis ☏8706/060100, ⓦwww.avis.co.uk
Budget ☏0800/181181, ⓦwww.budget.com
Europcar ☏0345/222528, ⓦwww.europcar.co.uk
Hertz ☏0870/844 8844, ⓦwww.hertz.co.uk
Holiday Autos ☏0870/400 0011, ⓦwww.holidayautos.com
Thrifty ☏01494/442110, ⓦwww.thrifty.co.uk

Car rental essentials

You have to exercise caution when renting a car in Costa Rica, where it is not uncommon for rental companies to claim for "damage" they insist you inflicted on the vehicle. It is by far the best policy to rent a car through a Costa Rican travel agent. If you are travelling on a package, your agent will sort this out. Otherwise, go into an ICT-accredited travel agent in San José (see p.23) and ask them to arrange rental for you. This should be no more expensive than renting on your own and will help guard against false claims of damage and other accusations; rental companies will be less willing to make trouble with an agent who regularly sends them clients than with individual customers who they may not see again.

Make sure to check the car carefully before you sign off the damage sheet. Check the oil, brake fluid, gas (to make sure it's full) and that there is a spare tyre with good air pressure and a jack. For example, look up the Spanish for "scratches" (*rayas*) and other relevant terminology first, so you can at least scrutinize the rental company's assessment. Keep a copy of this document on you.

Take the maximum insurance (around $20/day) possible – because of the country's high accident rate, you need to be covered for damage to the vehicle, yourself, any third party and public property.

The DJ pilot

Pilot Peter Wohlleben offers one of the best experiences in Costa Rica in his fleet of modern single- and twin-engine planes. Not only will he fly you anywhere in the country (providing there's an airstrip), he'll also programme his vast collection of CDs to provide a musical accompaniment to the amazing sights below.

Especially recommended are the early-morning volcano trips ($119 per person; 90min). Banking at a 45° angle above Poás, Barva and Irazú – and sometimes Arenal, although planes can't get too close because of the activity – gives you the best volcano views in the country, enhanced by the well-chosen accompanying tunes. Other tours include the popular trip over Poás (to Beethoven's Fifth Symphony), landing at Tortuguero for breakfast and a boat ride ($179 per person for half a day). For reservations and further details of customized tours and charters contact Pitts Aviation (☏ 296-3600, ⓦ www.pitts-aviation.com).

By air

Costa Rica's two **domestic air carriers** offer reasonably economical scheduled services between San José and many beach destinations and provincial towns. Sansa is the state-owned domestic airline; Travelair is its commercial competitor. Both fly small twin-propeller aircraft, and service more or less the same destinations.

Of the two, **Travelair** (☏ 220-3054, ⓕ 220-0413, ⓦ www.travelair-costarica.com), which flies from Tobias Bolano airport in Pavas, 7km west of San José, is more reliable and has more frequent services on some runs. **Sansa** (☏ 221-9414, ⓕ 255-2176, ⓦ www.flysansa.com) flies from Juan Santamaría airport, 17km northwest of San José, and is cheaper but less dependable than Travelair. On both airlines, make your reservations as far as possible in advance, and even then be advised that a booking means almost nothing until the seat is actually paid for. Reconfirm your flight in advance of the day of departure and again on the day, if possible, as schedules can change at short notice.

If you're planning to cover a lot of ground in a limited amount of time, Sansa's **Costa Rica Air Pass** ($280/$320 for 1/2 weeks; $140 for each additional week) allows you unrestricted use of all their services. If you're travelling throughout Central America, a **TACA regional airpass** (ⓦ www.tacaregional.com) allows unlimited travel on the domestic airlines of Guatemala, Honduras, Nicaragua and Panama, as well as Costa Rica.

While flying around the country in the small aircraft operated by domestic airlines and air-charter companies is both convenient and exhilarating, the **accident rate** for light aircraft in Costa Rica is worryingly high: in 2000 there were seventeen light-plane crashes – 82 percent of them have since been attributed either to pilot error or adverse weather conditions. The national aviation authority is trying to combat the high accident rate with new safety measures which will come into place in the lifetime of this guide.

Air-charter companies

Aerobell, Tobias Bolano airport, Pavas (☏ 290-0000, ⓕ 296-04600). Very professional operation with friendly and efficient staff. Charter flights all over the country in twin-engine planes ($275 an hour to charter a 5-seater plane).

Alfa Romeo Aero Taxi, Puerto Jimenez, opposite the cemetery (☏ & ⓕ 735-5112). Zona Sur air charter company specializing in local short-hop trips.

Helicopteros Turisticos Tropical, Tobias Bolano airport, Pavas (☏ 220-3940, ⓦ www.heli-tour.com). Helicopters for charter and sightseeing tours.

Pitts Aviation, ☏ 296-3600, ⓕ 296-1429, ⓦ www.pitts-aviation.com.

TACSA, Tobias Bolano airport, Pavas (☏ 232-1317, ⓕ 232-1469). International and national flights from $250 to $550 per hour.

For a rundown of Sansa and Travelair **schedules**, along with their addresses and phone numbers, see "Moving on from San José" on p.112.

While fares will be at least double that of Sansa and Travelair, **air taxis** (journeys can cost anywhere from $125 to $550 per planeload) can prove a reasonably cheap way to get to the beaches and more remote areas if several people split the expense. Most charter planes operate from Tobias Bolaños airport in Pavas.

By bicycle

Costa Rica's terrain provides easy **cycling** compared with neighbouring countries and, as there's a good range of places to stay and eat, you don't need to carry the extra weight of a tent, sleeping bag and stove. Always carry warm clothes and a cycling jacket, however, wherever you are. As for **equipment**, rear panniers and a small handlebar bag (for maps and camera) should be enough. Bring a puncture repair kit, even if your tyres are supposedly unbustable. You'll need a bike with a triple front gear – this gives you 15 to 21 gears, and you will really need the low ones. Make sure, too, that you carry and drink lots of water – five to eight litres a day in the lowlands.

There is very little **traffic** outside the Valle Central, and despite their tactics with other cars – and pedestrians – Costa Rican drivers are probably the most courteous to cyclists in Central America. That said, however, bus and truck drivers do tend to forget about you as soon as they pass, sometimes cutting you up or forcing you off the road. **Roads** are generally good for cyclists, who can dodge the potholes and wandering cattle more easily than drivers, although bear in mind that if you cycle up to Monteverde, one of the most popular routes in the country, you're in for a slow trip: besides being steep there's not much traction on these loose gravel roads. Although road signs will tell you that cycling on the Interamericana (Pan-American Highway, or Hwy-1) is not permitted, you will quickly see that people do anyway.

San José's best **cycle shop** is Bicimania, at the corner of Paseo Colón and C 26. They have all the parts you might need, can fix your bike, and may even be able to give you a bicycle carton for the plane.

Tour operators

The Costa Rican tourist boom of the last ten years has led to a proliferation of **tour operators**. Market research shows that about fifty percent of travellers to Costa Rica arrive with only their return flight and the first few nights of accommodation booked; they then set about planning tours in situ in San José.

Wandering around the city, you face a barrage of tour agencies and advertisements: if you want to shop around it could take some time to sort yourself out. The following is not a comprehensive list of tour operators in Costa Rica, but all those that we've listed are experienced and recommendable, offering a good range of services and tours. They're all licensed (and regulated) by the ICT.

There are scores of others – be especially wary of fly-by-night operators, of which there are plenty. You often see, for instance, posters advertising cheap "packages" to Tortuguero or to Monteverde, both for about $80–100 – less than half the price of a regular package. These cut-price tours are not packages at all, and never worth the price: in some cases you will be responsible for your own transport, accommodation will be the most basic, and no tours, orientation or guidance will be given – something you can easily arrange on your own, for the same price or less.

Tour operators in Costa Rica

Camino Travel, C 1, Av 0/1 (ⓣ 257-0107, ⓕ 257-0243, ⓔ caminotr@racsa.co.cr). Young, enthusiastic staff with high standards and a mainly European clientele. Experienced in both upmarket and independent travel, selling individual tours and booking good-quality accommodation from their range of country-wide contacts. Can also help with bus and transport information and car rental. Convenient downtown office.

Costa Rica Expeditions, C Central, Av 3 (ⓣ 257-0766, ⓕ 257-1665, ⓦ www.costaricaexpeditions.com). Longest-established and most experienced of the major tour operators, with superior accommodation in Tortuguero, Monteverde and Corcovado, a superlative staff of guides and tremendous resources. You can drop into the busy downtown office and talk to a consultant about individual tours.

Costa Rican Trails, Av 15, C 23/25 (ⓣ 221-3011, ⓕ 257-4655, ⓦ www.costaricantrails.com). Small, friendly and very professional agency who will visit you in your hotel room to discuss their range of tailor-made and flexi-drive holidays in all price ranges. They're also experts in adventure sports, including rafting and motorbike tours.

Ecole Travel, C 7, Av 0/1 (ⓣ 223-2240, ⓕ 223-4128, ⓦ www.travelcostarica.net). Small agency, popular with backpackers, offering well-priced tours to Tortuguero and hiking trips to Chirripó (4 days) and the Osa Peninsula (3 days). They also run boats from Moín docks near Puerto Limón to Tortuguero.

Expediciones Tropicales, Av 11/13, C 3 bis
(☎257-4171, ☏257-4124,
🖳www.costaricainfo.com). Well-regarded agency
with knowledgeable guides which runs the popular
"Four-in-One" day-tour of Volcán Poás and nearby
sights ($79; 11hr), as well as a host of other trips
from San José at competitive prices.
Horizontes Nature Tours, C 28, Av 1/3 (☎222-
2022, 🖳www.horizontes.com). Highly regarded
agency concentrating on rainforest walking and
hiking, volcanos and bird-watching, all with an
emphasis on natural and cultural history. Specialists
in mountain biking and horse-riding as well.
OTEC, C 3, Av 1/3 (☎256-0633, ☏257-7671,
📧gotec@racsa.co.cr). Large agency specializing in
adventure tours including fishing, trekking, surfing
and mountain biking, plus hotel reservations and car
rentals. One of the few – if not the only – agency
which claims to offer student discounts.
Serendipity Adventures, Turrialba (☎556-2592,
☏556-2593, 🖳www.serendipityadventures.com).
Superior travel agency specializing in individual
custom-made tours for self-formed groups with a

sense of adventure. Serendipity make a point of
searching out undiscovered parts of Costa Rica, and
are also experts in canyoning and rappelling, as well
as being the only company in Costa Rica to offer hot-
air balloon trips. Tours are not cheap, however,
starting at $2000 per person for eight days.
Simbiosis Tours, Apt 6939-1000 San José,
(☎259-3605, ☏259-9430,
📧cooprena@racsa.co.cr). Tour company offering
package tours to one of six co-operatives in Costa
Rica. The co-operatives are composed of low-income
rural families living a modest lifestyle and sharing a
common goal of exploring new and sustainable land
uses. Projects managed by the co-ops and featured
in various packages include lodges, restaurants,
private reserves, nature trails, horse-riding and
organic farms.
SpECOps (☎232-4028, 🖳www.specops.com).
Adventure education group, comprising US Special
Forces veterans and expert Costa Rican guides
which specializes in white-knuckle thrills, jungle
survival courses and adventure film and photography.

Accommodation

Most towns in Costa Rica have a good range of places to stay, and even the smallest settlements will usually have some basic lodgings. The best budget accommodation tends to be found in the less touristy areas, and caters more for locals than foreigners. Accommodation in the middle and upper price ranges can be overpriced, though facilities and services are generally of a very good standard – you may need $45–70 a night (especially in San José, and in the high season) to find somewhere comfortable.

The larger places to stay in Costa Rica are usually called **hotels**. **Posadas**, **hostals**, **hospedajes** and **pensiones** are smaller, though *posadas* can sometimes turn out to be quite swanky, especially in rural areas. **Casas** tend to be private guesthouses, while **albergues** are the equivalent of lodges. **Cabinas** are common in Costa Rica: they're usually either a string of motel-style rooms in an annexe away from the main building or, more often, separate self-contained units.

Usually – although not always – they tend toward the basic, and are most often frequented by budget travellers. More upmarket versions may be called "villas" or "chalets". Anything called a **motel** – as in most of Latin America – is not likely to be used for sleeping.

Few hotels except those at the upper end of the price range have double beds, and it's more common to find two or three single beds. **Single travellers** will generally be

Accommodation price codes

All the accommodation in this book has graded using the following price codes. The prices quoted are for the **least expensive double room in high season**, and do not include the 18.46 percent national tax which is automatically added onto hotel bills.

❶ less than $10	**❷** $10–20
❸ $20–30	**❹** $30–50
❺ $50–75	**❻** $75–100
❼ $100–150	**❽** over $150

charged the single rate even if they're occupying a double room, though this may not be the case in popular beach towns and at peak seasons.

Incidentally, wherever you are staying, don't expect to get much reading done in the evenings. Light bulbs are very wan, even in good hotels, and avid after-dark readers may want to bring their own reading lamp (plus adaptor). Also bear in mind that in Costa Rican hotels the term **hot water** can be misleading. Showers are often equipped with squat plastic nozzles: these are water heaters. Inside is an electric element which heats the water coming through to a warm, rather than hot, temperature. Some of the nozzles have a button that actually turns on the element. Under no circumstances should you touch this button or get anywhere near the nozzle when wet – these contraptions may not be quite as bad as their tongue-in-cheek name of "suicide showers" suggests, but there's still a distinct possibility you could get a nasty shock. The trick to getting fairly hot water is not to turn on the pressure too high. Keep a little coming through to heat the water more efficiently.

Reservations

Costa Rica's hotels tend to be chock-full in high season (Nov–April), especially at Christmas, New Year and Easter, so **reserve well ahead**, particularly for youth hostels and good-value hotels in popular spots. Many hotels, even the budget ones, have faxes, and email is also becoming increasingly common, so the easiest and surest way to reserve in advance is with a credit card by fax or email. Once on the ground in Costa Rica, phone or ⓕ again to reconfirm your reservation. Some establishments will ask you to reserve and pay in advance – the more popular hotels and lodges require you to do this as far as thirty days ahead,

although they will accommodate you any time if they have space.

For many travellers, this level of preplanning is impractical. If you prefer to be a little more spontaneous, you should travel in the low season, from roughly after Easter to mid-November, when you can safely leave making reservations until you arrive in the country. During these months it's even possible to show up at hotels on spec – there will probably be space, and possibly even a low-season discount of as much as fifty percent. Another budget option is to arrange to **stay with a Tico family**; see p.81 for details.

Pensiones and hotels

When travelling, most Costa Ricans and nationals of other Central American countries stick to the bottom end of the market and patronize traditional *pensiones* (a fast-dying breed in Costa Rica, especially in San José) or established Costa Rican-owned hotels. If you do likewise you may well get a better price than at the tourist or foreign-owned hotels, although this is not a hard and fast rule. Though standards are generally high, at the **lower end** of the scale, you should expect to get what you pay for – usually clean but dim, spartan rooms with cold-water showers. If you think you might have a choice or like to shop around, it's perfectly acceptable to ask to see the room first.

The majority of accommodation catering to foreigners is in the **middle range**, and as such is reasonably priced – although still more expensive than similar accommodation in other Central American countries. Hotels at the lower end of this price range will often be very good value, however, giving you private bath with hot water, perhaps towels, and maybe even air conditioning (which, it has to be said, is not really necessary in

Abanico	Ceiling fan
Ventilador	Desk fan
Aire-acondicionado	Air conditioned
Baño colectivo/ compartido	Shared bath
Agua caliente	Hot water
Agua fría	Cold water
Cama matrimonial	Double bed
Sencillo	Single bed
Impuestos	Taxes
Hora de salida	Check-out time (usually 2pm)

most places; a ceiling fan generally does fine). At the upper end of this price range a few extras, like TV or breakfast, may be thrown in.

Resorts and lodges

There are many **resorts** scattered throughout Costa Rica, ranging from swanky hotels in popular areas like Manuel Antonio to **rainforest lodges** in areas of outstanding natural beauty, with superior service and excellent food and tours. Although often very expensive – and firmly out of reach of budget travellers – they're generally well worth the price .

B&Bs

Until recently many hotels offered breakfast in their room rates as a matter of course, but this is becoming less common and, if breakfast is offered at all, it will probably cost extra. However, a new breed of **B&Bs** has sprung up in recent years, often owned by expats and similar to their North American or UK counterparts: rooms in homes or converted homes with a "family atmosphere". For more information, write to the Costa Rica Bed and Breakfast Group, c/o Debbi McMurray-Long, PO Box 025216-1638, Miami, FL 33102-5216, US.

Camping

Though **camping** is fairly widespread in Costa Rica, gone are the days when you could pitch your tent on just about any beach or field. With more and more people coming to the country, local residents in small beachside communities, especially, are getting very upset with campers leaving rubbish on the beach. You'll have a far better relationship with locals if you ask politely whether it's OK to camp; if you're directed to a nearby campsite, this isn't because the locals don't like the look of you, but because they're trying to keep their environment clean.

In the beach towns especially you will usually find at least one well-equipped **private campsite**, with good facilities including lavatories, drinking water and cooking grilles; staff may also offer to guard your clothes and tent while you're at the beach. You may also find **hotels**, usually at the lower end of the price scale, whose owners will let you pitch your tent in the grounds and use the showers and washrooms for a fee – ask around. Though not all **national parks** have campsites, the ones that do usually offer high standards and at least basic facilities, with lavatories, water, and often cooking grilles – all for around $2 per person per day. In some national parks you can bunk down at the **ranger station** if you call well in advance; for more details, see p.51.

There are three general rules of camping in Costa Rica: first, never leave your tent or anything of value inside it unattended, or it may not be there when you get back. Second, never leave your tent open except to get in and out, unless you fancy sharing

❏ Groundsheet
❏ Backpack
❏ Lightweight (summer) sleeping bag, except for climbing Chirripó, where you may need a three-season bag
❏ Rain gear
❏ Mosquito net
❏ Maps
❏ Torch
❏ Knife
❏ Matches, in a waterproof box
❏ Firelighter
❏ Compass
❏ Insect repellent
❏ Water bottles
❏ Toilet paper
❏ Sunglasses
❏ Sunblock
❏ Plastic bags (for wet clothes/refuse)

your sleeping quarters with snakes, insects, coati or toads. Finally, take your refuse with you when you leave.

Youth hostels

Costa Rica has a small network of twelve good and reasonably priced **youth hostels**, many of them in prime locations. They usually cost around $12–20 per night, and can be conveniently booked from Toruma hostel in San José (see p.84). As with all accommodation in Costa Rica, bookings should ideally be made three months in advance if you're coming in high season – reserve by ⓕ or phone directly with the hostel or through Toruma.

All twelve hostels can be reached by public transport and follow conservation regulations based on the sustainable development principle. Most of them have a range of double, triple and family rooms, and bed linen, towels and soap are included in the price.

Youth hostel associations

Australia and New Zealand

Australian Youth Hostels Association (ⓦ www.yha.com.au), 422 Kent St, Sydney (ⓣ 02/9261 1111); 205 King St, Melbourne (ⓣ 03/9670 9611); 38 Sturt St, Adelaide (ⓣ 08/8231 5583); 154 Roma St, Brisbane (ⓣ 07/3236 1680); 236 William St, Perth (ⓣ 08/9227 5122); 69 Mitchell St, Darwin (ⓣ 08/8981 2560); 28 Criterion St, Hobart (ⓣ 03/6234 9617). Annual membership A$52 for first year, A$32 per subsequent year.

Youth Hostels Association of New Zealand (ⓦ www.yha.co.nz), 173 Gloucester St, Christchurch (ⓣ 03/379 9970). Annual membership NZ$40 (NZ$60 for two years, NZ$80 for three).

Costa Rica

Red Costarricense de Albergues Juveniles (RECAJ), Paseo de los Estudiantes, Av Central, C 29/31, San José (ⓣ & ⓕ 224-4085).

North America

Hostelling International/American Youth Hostels (ⓦ www.hiayh.org), 733 15th St NW, Suite 840, Washington, DC 20005 (ⓣ 202/783-6161). Annual membership $25 (under-18s free; over-54s $15; families $35).
Hostelling International/Canadian Hostelling Association, Room 400, 205 Catherine St, Ottawa, ON K2P 1C3 (ⓣ 1-800/663-5777 or 613/237-7884). Annual membership $26.75 (under-18s free when accompanied by parents).

UK and Ireland

Youth Hostel Association (ⓦ www.yha.org.uk), Trevelyan House, 8 St Stephen's Hill, St Albans, Herts AL1 2DY (ⓣ 0870/870 8808). London membership desk and booking office: 14 Southampton St, London WC2 7HY (ⓣ 020/7836 8541). Annual membership £12 (under-18s £6).
An Oige, 61 Mountjoy St, Dublin 7 (ⓣ 01/830 4555, ⓦ www.irelandyha.org). Annual membership IR£10.
Youth Hostel Association of Northern Ireland, 22 Donegal Rd, Belfast BT12 5JN (ⓣ 028/9031 5435, ⓦ www.hini.org.uk). Annual membership £8.
Scottish Youth Hostel Association, 7 Glebe Crescent, Stirling FK8 2JA (ⓣ 0870/155 3255, ⓦ www.syha.org.uk). Annual membership £6.

Eating and drinking

The best way to describe most Costa Rican food is to apply that evasive adjective "unpretentious". Ticos call their cuisine *comida típica* ("native" or "local" food). Simple it may be, but tasty nonetheless, especially when it comes to the interesting regional variations found along the Caribbean coast, with its Creole-influenced cooking, and in Guanacaste, where there are vestiges of the ancient indigenous peoples' love of maize. For more on the cuisine of these areas, see the relevant chapters in the Guide.

Típico dishes you'll find all over Costa Rica usually include rice and some kind of meat or fish, often served as part of a special plate with coleslaw salad, in which case it's called a **casado** (literally, "married person"). Often described as the national dish of Costa Rica, the ubiquitous **gallo pinto** ("painted rooster") is a breakfast combination of traditionally red and white beans with rice, sometimes served with *huevos revueltos* (scrambled eggs). The heavy concentration on starch and protein reveals the rural origins of Costa Rican food: *gallo pinto* is food for people who are going out to work it off.

Of the dishes found on menus all over the country, particularly recommended are **ceviche** (raw fish "cooked" in lime juice with coriander and peppers), **pargo** (red snapper), **corvina** (sea bass), and any of the ice creams and **desserts**, though these can be too sickly-sweet for many tastes. The fresh **fruit** is especially good, either eaten by itself or drunk in *refrescos* (see p.41). Papayas, pineapple and bananas are all cheap and plentiful, along with some less familiar fruits like *mamones chinos* (a kind of lychee), *anona* (which tastes like custard) and *marañón*, whose seed is the cashew nut.

Eating out

Eating out in Costa Rica will cost more than you might think, and has become even more expensive over the past few years. Main dishes can easily run between $7 and $9, and then there's those sneaky **extra charges**: the service charge (10 percent)

and the sales tax (15 percent), which bring the meal to a total of 25 percent more than the menu price. Add this all up, and dinner for two can easily come to $20 or even $25 just for a single course and a couple of beers. **Tipping** (for more on which, see p.67) is not necessary, however.

The cheapest places to dine in Costa Rica, and where most workers eat lunch, their main meal, are the ubiquitous **sodas**, halfway between the North American diner and the British greasy café. Sodas offer filling set *platos del día* (daily specials) and *casados*, combinations of rice, beans, salad and meat or fish, for about $3. Most do not add sales tax (although restaurants masquerading as sodas, like *El Parque* in San José, do). You usually have to go to the cash register to get your bill. Sodas also often have takeout windows where you can pick up snacks such as the delicious little fingers of bread and sugar called *churros*. Many sodas are vegetarian, and in general **vegetarians** do quite well in Costa Rica. Most menus will have a vegetable option, and asking for dishes to be served without meat is perfectly acceptable.

Because Costa Ricans start the day early, they are less likely to hang about late in restaurants in the evening, and establishments are usually empty or **closed** by 10 or 10.30pm. **Non-smoking sections** are uncommon, except in the most expensive establishments; if you're looking for a smoke-free environment, try the vegetarian sodas.

Fruits

Anona	Custard fruit; sweet, thick, ripe taste: one of the best fruits in the country
Carambola	Starfruit
Cas	Pale flesh fruit with sweet-sour taste,
Chinos	Usually used for *refrescos*
Fresas	Strawberries
Granadilla	Passion fruit; small yellow fruits, sharp and sweet
Guanábana	Soursop; very large green mottled fruit, with sweet white flesh tasting like a cross between a mango and a pear; mostly found on the Caribbean coast
Guayaba	Guava; very sweet fruit, usually used for making spreads and jams
Limónes	Lemons
Mamones chinos	Spiny-covered red or yellow fruits that look diabolical but reveal gently flavoured lychee-type fruit inside; somewhat like peeled green grapes, but sweeter and more fragrant. Usually sold in small bags of a dozen on street corners or buses
Maracuyá	Yellow fruit with bitter taste, often used in *refrescos*; delicious when sweetened
Mora	Blackberries
Naranja	Orange
Papaya	Papaya/pawpaw; large round or oblong fruit with sweet orange flesh. Best eaten with fresh lime juice, and very good for stomach bugs
Pejibaye	A Costa Rican speciality, you'll find this small green-orange fruit almost nowhere else. Like its relative, the coconut, it grows in bunches on palm trees: the texture is unusual, as is the nutty flavour
Piña	Pineapple
Sandía	Watermelon
Tamarindo	A large pod of seeds, covered in a sticky, light-brown flesh; the unique taste – at once tart and sweet – is best first sampled in a *refresco*
Zapotes	Large sweet orange fruit, with a dark-brown outer casing

Vegetables

Aguacates	Avocados
Chayote	Resembling a light-green avocado, this vegetable is tender and delicate when cooked, and excellent in stews and with meat and rice dishes
Fruta de pan	Breadfruit; eaten more as a starch substitute than a fruit
Hongos	Mushrooms
Palmito	Heart-of-palm; the inner core of palm trees, usually eaten on salads, with a somewhat bitter taste and fibrous texture
Plátanos	Plantains; eaten sweet
Zanahorias	Carrots

Dishes

Arreglados	Meat and mayonnaise sandwiches on greasy bread buns
Arroz…	Rice…
…con pollo	…with chicken
…con carne	…with meat
…con pescado	…with fish
…con mariscos	…with seafood
…con camarones	…with shrimps/prawns
Bocas	Small snacks, usually eaten as an accompaniment to a beer
Casado	Plate of meat or fish, rice and salad, sometimes served with fried plantains
Ceviche	Raw fish, usually corvina, "cooked" in lime juice, onions, chillies and coriander

Chicarrones	Pork rinds
Chilasquilas	Tortillas and beef with spices and battered eggs
Empanadas	Meat or vegetable patties
Frijoles molidos	Mashed black beans with onions, chilli peppers, coriander and thyme
Gallo pinto	"Painted rooster"; breakfast dish of rice and beans
Gallos	Small sandwiches
Pan de maíz	Corn bread; white rather than yellow
Picadillo	Potatoes cooked with beef and beans
Sopa negra	Black-bean soup with egg and vegetables
Tacos	Tortilla filled with beef or chicken, cabbage, tomatoes and mild chillies
Tamal	One of the best local specialities, usually consisting of maize flour, chicken or pork, olives, chillies and raisins all wrapped in a plantain leaf
Tortilla	Thin, small and bland bread, served as an accompaniment to meals and, especially in Guanacaste, breakfast

Meat

Bistec	Steak
Cerdo	Pork
Jamón	Ham
Lomito	Cut of beef *(filet mignon)*

Fish and Seafood

Atún	Tuna
Corvina	Sea bass
Langosta	Lobster
Mariscos	Seafood/shellfish
Pargo	Red snapper
Trucha	Trout

Ingredients and condiments

Aceite	Oil
Aceitunas	Olives
Ajo ("al ajillo")	Garlic (in garlic sauce)
Cebolla	Onion
Cilantro	Coriander
Frijoles	Beans
Huevos	Eggs
Leche	Milk
Queso	Cheese
Salsa	Sauce

Desserts

Cajeta	Dessert made of milk, sugar, vanilla and sometimes coconut
Helados	Ice cream
Milanes	Delicate chocolate fingers
Queque	Cake
Queque seco	Pound cake
Tamal asado	Cake made of cornflour, cream, eggs, sugar and butter
Tres leches	Boiled milk and syrup-drenched cake

REGIONAL DISHES
Caribbean

Pan bon	Sweet glazed bread with fruit and cheese
Patacones	Plantain chips, often served with *frijoles molidos* (see above)
Rice and beans	Rice and beans cooked in coconut milk
Rundown	Meat and vegetables stewed in coconut milk

Guanacaste

Chorreados	Corn pancakes
Horchata	Hot drink made with corn or rice and flavoured with cinnamon
Natilla	Sour cream
Olla de carne	Rich, hearty meat stew
Pinolillo	Milky corn drink
Rosquillas	Corn doughnut
Tanelas	Scone-like corn snack

Drinking

Mellow-tasting Costa Rican **coffee** is some of the best in the world, and it's usual to end a meal with a small cup. The best blends are export, which you can buy in stores and are served at some cafés. If you order it with milk (*café con leche*), it's traditionally served as a pitcher of coffee with a separate pitcher of heated milk, so you can mix it to your liking. Also good are **refrescos**, cool drinks made with milk (*leche*) or water (*agua*), fruit and ice, all whipped up in a blender. You can buy them at stalls or in cartons, though the latter tend to be sugary. You'll find **herb teas** throughout the country; those served in the Caribbean province of Limón are especially good. In Guanacaste you can get the distinctive **corn-based drinks** *horchata* and *pinolillo*, made with milk and sugar and with a grainy consistency.

In addition to the many imported American **beers**, Costa Rica has a few local brands, which are not bad at all. Most popular is Imperial (light draught, American-style), followed by Bavaria (sweeter, more substantial and slightly nutty). Of the local low-alcohol beers, Bavaria Light is a good option; Tropical is a bit more watery.

Wine, once a rare commodity, has become far more common in mid- and top-range restaurants, where you'll often find good Chilean varieties on offer. **Spirits** tend to be associated with serious drinking, usually by men in bars, and are rarely consumed by local women in public. There is an indigenous hard-liquor drink, **guaro**, of which Cacique is the most popular brand. It's a bit rough, but good with lime sodas such as Squirt or Lift. For an after-dinner drink, try Café Rica, a creamy liqueur made with the local coffee.

Bars

Costa Rica has a variety of **places to drink**, from shady macho domains to pretty beachside bars, with some particularly cosmopolitan establishments in San José. The capital is also the place to find the country's last remaining **boca bars**, atmospheric places which serve *bocas* (tasty little snacks like tapas) with drinks; though historically these were free, nowadays even in the most traditional places you'll probably have to pay for them (for more on San José's boca bars, see p.104). In even the smallest town with any foreign population – either expat or tourist – you'll notice a sharp split between the places frequented by locals and those that cater to foreigners. Gringo grottos abound, especially in the beach towns, with at least one bar aspiring to some kind of cosmopolitanism. These places tend to have a wide bar stock, at least compared to the limited *guaro*-and-beer menu of the local bars. In many places, especially port cities like Limón, Puntarenas and Golfito, there is the usual contingent of rough, rowdy bars where testosterone-fuelled machos go to drink gallons and fight; it's usually pretty obvious which ones they are – they advertise their seediness with a giant Imperial placard parked right in front of the door so you can't see what's going on inside.

Most bars typically **open** in the morning, any time between 8.30 and 11am, and **close** at around 11pm or midnight. **Sunday** night is usually dead: many bars don't open at all and others close early, around 10pm.

Coffee in Costa Rica

There are two types of coffee available in Costa Rica: export quality (*grano d'oro*), typically packaged by either Café Britt or Café Rey and served in good hotels and restaurants; and the lower-grade blend, usually sold for the home market. Costa Rica's export-grade coffee is known the world over for it mellowness and smoothness. The stuff produced for the domestic market, however, is another matter entirely. Some of it is even pre-sweetened, so if you ask for it with sugar (*con azúcar*), you'll get a saccharine shock. Among the best coffees you'll find in Costa Rica are La Carpintera, a smooth, rich, hard bean grown on Cerro de la Carpintera in the Valle Central, and Zurquí, the oldest cultivated bean in the country, grown for 150 years on the flanks of Volcán Barva. Strong, but with a silky, gentle taste, Café el Gran Vito, grown by Italian immigrants near San Vito in the extreme south of the country, is an unusual grade of export bean, harder to find than those grown in the Valle de el General and the Valle Central.

Though Friday and Saturday nights are, as usual, the busiest, the **best nights** to go are often those during the week, when you can enjoy live music, happy hours and other specials. The drinking age in Costa Rica is 18, and many bars will only admit those with a *cédula* (ID). A photocopy of your passport page is acceptable.

Mail and telecommunications

Costa Rica's recently privatized postal system (⊛www.correos.go.cr) is reasonably efficient, though you may have problems sending and receiving letters from remote areas. The Costa Rican state electronics company, the ICE (Instituto Costarricense de Electricidad) provides international telephone, fax and internet services via RACSA, the telecommunications subsidiary.

Mail

Even the smallest Costa Rican town has a **correo** (post office), but the most reliable place to mail overseas is from San José's lime-green Correo Central (main post office; see p.108). Airmail letters to Canada and the US cost 20¢ and take about ten days to arrive; letters to Europe cost about 25¢ and take two weeks or more; while letters to Australasia cost 30¢ and take three or four weeks.

Most post offices have a **lista de correos** (Poste Restante, General Delivery) – an efficient and safe way to receive letter mail, especially at the main office in San José. They will hold letters for up to four weeks at a charge of 15¢ a letter (though in smalller post offices you may not be charged at all). Bring a photocopy of your passport when picking up mail, and make sure that correspondents address letters to you under your name exactly as it appears on your passport.

One thing you can't fail to notice is the paucity of **mailboxes** in Costa Rica. In the capital, unless your hotel has regular mail pickup, the only resort is to hike down to the Correo Central. In outlying or isolated areas of the country you will have to rely on hotels or local businesses' private mailboxes. In most cases, especially in Limón province, where mail is very slow, it's probably quicker to wait until you return to San José and mail correspondence from there. **Opening hours** for nearly all Costa Rica's *correos* are Monday to Friday 7.30am to 5.30pm or 6pm, and Saturdays 7.30am to noon.

Although letters are handled fairly efficiently, **packages** are another thing altogether – the parcels service both coming and going gets snarled in paperwork and labyrinthine customs regulations, besides being very expensive and very slow. If you must send parcels, take them unsealed to the *correo* for inspection.

Email

Most towns of any size in Costa Rica now have at least one **Internet café**, while places popular with tourists will usually have many more; charges are low, usually $0.75–$1 for 30 minutes. In addition, all Costa Rican post offices – even the most rural – now offer Internet access with prepaid cards which you can buy in the post office (300 colones for 30min, 500 for 1hr).

Telecommunications

Calls **within Costa Rica** are very cheap and **calling long-distance** can work out very

Useful phone numbers

International information ☎ 124

International operator (for collect calls)
☎ 116 or 09

Calling-card access codes
AT&T ☎ 0800/011-4114
BT ☎ 0800/044-1044
Canada Direct ☎ 0800/015-1161
MCI ☎ 0800/012-2222
Sprint ☎ 0800/013-0123

For all other countries, look in the White
Pages (the Costa Rican phone book).

reasonably if you ring directly through a pub-
lic telephone network, and avoid calling from
your hotel or other private business. The
cheapest rates run from 10pm to 7am night-
ly: calls during this period cost $1 per
minute to the UK and Australasia; $0.65 per
minute to the US and Canada.

The **country code** for the whole of Costa
Rica is ☎ 506. There are no area codes, and
all phone numbers now have seven digits.
You can **call collect** to virtually any foreign
country from any phone or payphone in
Costa Rica; simply dial ☎ 09 or ☎ 116 to get
an English-speaking operator, then tell them
the country code, area code and number;
note, however, that this method costs twice
as much as dialling direct. Holders of AT&T,

MCI, Sprint, Canada Direct or BT calling-card
holders can make calls from payphones in
Costa Rica. Simply dial the relevant access
code (see below); charges will automatically
be billed to your calling-card account.

If you have to pay for a call on the spot, the
most convenient way to use a private line in
a hotel (though this can be expensive; check
before you go ahead), at a local *pulpería* (gen-
eral store; usually more reasonably priced) or
from the San José Radiográfica office (see
p.108), where you can also make overseas
calls, send and receive faxes, and use direc-
tories. It's not a good idea to use colones in a
payphone to make **international calls**; you're
better off using a **telephone card** (available
from newsstands, *pulperías* and supermar-
kets – see below).

Coin-operated **payphones** accept 5-, 10-
and 20-colón coins, though it's often difficult
to find one in working order, while many
have been replaced with "Chip" **card-
phones**. If you're making an international
call or want to avoid the bother of finding a
payphone that works, **chip 199 cards** work
well, though you'll need to find a special
Chip phone to use them. The **197 cards** can
be used in all public phones, but are best
avoided, with engaged lines and faulty serv-
ices common. Both cards come in denomi-
nations of 500, 1000 or 3000 colones for
national calls, and $10 or $20 for internation-
al calls; stock up in major towns and cities if
you intend to use them on a regular basis –
rural areas often run out of them.

The media

Though the Costa Rican media generally pumps out relatively anodyne and conservative coverage of local and regional issues – shadowing the antics of the president and the political elite with dogged tenacity – it is possible to find good investigative journalism, particularly in the daily *La Nación*. There are also a number of interesting local radio stations, though TV coverage leaves something to be desired.

Newspapers

In San José, all **domestic newspapers** are sold on the street by vendors. Elsewhere you can find them in newsagents and *pulperías* (general stores). All are tabloid format, with colourful, eye-catching layout and presentation.

Though the Costa Rican press is free, it does indulge in a certain follow-the-leader journalism. Leader of the pack is the daily **La Nación**, voice of the (right-of-centre) establishment and owned by the country's biggest media consortium; other highbrow dailies and television channels more or less parrot its line. Historically, *La Nación* has featured some good investigative reporting, as in the recent Banco Anglo corruption scandal and Costa Rica's continuing drug-trafficking problems. It also comes with a useful daily pull-out arts section, **Viva**, with listings of what's on in San José – the classifieds are handy for almost anything, including long-term accommodation.

Scarcely less serious is **La República**, even if they do have a tendency to slap a football photo on the front page, no matter what's happening in the world. **Al Día** is the populist "body count" paper, which will give you a feel for the kind of newspaper read by most Costa Ricans. Alternative voices include **La Prensa Libre**, the very good left-leaning evening paper, and the thoughtful weekly **Esta Semana**, which offers longer, in-depth articles and opinion pieces. **Mesoamerica**, based in San José, gives a solid weekly review and impartial analysis of politics, economics and society in Central America. You can consult it in libraries or take out a subscription by writing to ICAS, Aptdo 1524-2050, San Pedro, Costa Rica.

The weekly **Semanario Universidad**, the voice of the University of Costa Rica, certainly goes out on more of a limb than the big dailies, with particularly good coverage of the arts and the current political scene. You can find it on or around campus in San José's university district of San Pedro, and also in libraries.

Costa Rica's version of *Newsweek*, **Rumbo**, is a rather dull weekly, featuring thinly researched articles on sociological themes such as jealousy and infidelity alongside features on current politics in the region. Owned by the same group as *La Nación*, it also produces a dreadful women's magazine called **Perfil**.

Local **English-language papers** include the venerable and serious **Tico Times**, intended specifically for tourists, with articles on activities and holidays, and the freesheets *Costa Rica Explorer*, *Vista Costa Rica* and the glossy magazine *Friends in Costa Rica* (check out the ITC and other tourist outlets for copies). These can be a good source of information for travellers: the adverts regularly feature hotel and restaurant discounts. As for the **foreign press**, you can pick up recent copies of the *New York Times*, *International Herald Tribune*, *USA Today*, *Miami Herald*, *Newsweek*, *Time* and sometimes the *Financial Times* in the souvenir shop beside the *Gran Hotel Costa Rica* in downtown San José and La Casa de Revistas on the southwest corner of Parque Morazan. Of the San José bookstores (see p.107), Librerías Lehmann and Universal keep good stocks of mainstream and non-mainstream foreign magazines; the Mark Twain Library at the Centro Cultural Costarricense-Norteamericano (see p.95) also receives English-language publications.

For publications in other languages, go to the relevant cultural centre.

Radio

There are lots of **commercial radio stations** in Costa Rica, all pumping out techno and house, along with a bit of salsa, annoying commercials, and the odd bout of government-sponsored pseudo-propaganda promoting the general wonder that is Costa Rica. Some of the more interesting **local radio stations** have only a limited airtime, such as Radio Emperador (104.7FM) and Radio Costa Rica (930AM). Radio Alajuela (98.3FM/1280AM) features Costa Rican singers, along with some talk spots, from 8.30pm to midnight. Radio America Latina (780AM) has a fascinating advice show (10.30–11pm) – how to live your life better, be happy, find God – while Radio Monumental (93.5FM/670AM), broadcast from the Burger King Palace in central San José, is a politically themed talk show. Another fascinating programme is El Club del Taxista Costarricense – the "Costa Rican taxi driver's club" – broadcast by Radio Columbia (98.7FM/760AM) from 9.30 to 11pm. This social and political talk show, now in its 22nd year, was initially directed only at taxi drivers, but its populist appeal has led to it being adopted by the general population.

Television

Most Costa Rican households have a **television**, beaming out a range of wonderfully awful Mexican or Venezuelan *telenovelas* (soap operas) and some not-bad domestic news programmes. On the downside, Costa Rica is also the graveyard for 1970s American TV, the place where *The Dukes of Hazzard* and other such delights, dubbed into Spanish, come back to haunt you.

Channel 7 is the main national station, particularly strong in local and regional news. Other than its news show, Telenoticias, Costa Rica has few home-grown products, and Channel 7's programming comprises a mix of bought-in shows from Spanish-speaking countries plus a few from the US. **Channel 6** is the main competitor, very similar in content; **Channel 19** has mostly programmes and movies from the US dubbed into Spanish. The Mexican cable channels are good for news, and even have reports from Europe. Many places also subscribe to **CNN** and other cable channels, like HBO, Cinemax and Sony Entertainment, which show wall-to-wall reruns of hit comedy shows and films.

Crime and personal safety

As you might expect in a country which in 1999 received one million tourists, nearly all of them vastly better off than the average Costa Rican, opportunistic theft and petty scams are on the increase. Generally, though, Costa Rica is still considered a very safe country, and what crime there is tends to be opportunistic, rather than violent. The main thing travellers have to worry about is pickpocketing.

In **downtown San José** you need to be wary at all times. Street crime, especially chain- and watch-snatching and pickpocketing, is on the rise, perpetrated by delinquent gangs of kids called *chapulines* (literally "grasshoppers") who are too young to prosecute under Costa Rican law. Wear a money belt, and never carry anything of value – money, tickets or passport – in an outside pocket.

It has also been known for **luggage** to be stolen while you are distracted or while it is being kept supposedly secure in a left-luggage facility. Never hand your baggage to strangers, except airport porters who have official identification. If storing your luggage in a hotel or guesthouse while you are travelling around the country, make sure it is locked, has your name prominently written on it, and that you have left instructions for it not to be removed by anyone but yourself, under any circumstances.

Car theft – both of cars and things inside them – also occurs. You should not leave anything of value in a parked car – even locked in the trunk – anywhere in Costa Rica, day or night. In addition, never park your car on the street in San José, the Valle Central towns, Puntarenas or Limón; use the *parqueos* (guarded parking lots). Heavily touristed national park parking places are also vulnerable.

The bottom line is that if you take the common-sense **precautions** outlined above, you should get by unscathed. In addition, keep photocopies of your passport, air ticket, travellers' cheques and insurance policy in a safe place, separate from

Emergency telephone numbers

The three-digit numbers do not require coins

All emergencies	☏911
Police	☏117
Red Cross ambulance	☏128
Fire	☏118
Traffic police	☏222-9330 or 222-9245

the originals. Note, too, that you're required by law to **carry ID** at all times – for foreigners this means carrying your passport, though in practice a photocopy of the pages containing your personal information and the one with your Costa Rican entry stamp will suffice, since the police understand tourists' reluctance to go about with their passports all the time.

Reporting a crime

In recent years, the **police** (*guardia*) presence in San José has increased dramatically. If you have anything stolen you will need to report the incident to the nearest police post: do this right away. In San José, the most convenient method is to head for the Organismo de Investigación Judicial (OIJ; ☏221-5337 or 222-1365) in the Tribunales de la Justicia, or "La Corte" (the Supreme Court), in San José at Av 6/8, C 15/19. You're less likely to get robbed in rural areas; if you do, go to the nearest *guardia rural*, who will give you a report (you'll do better if you speak Spanish, or are with someone who does).

Any **tourist-related crime**, such as overcharging, can be addressed to the ICT in San José (see p.76) – they have a good reputation for following up letters and reports of incidents. For a list of **embassies** in San José, see p.107.

Women travellers

Educated urban women play an active role in Costa Rica's public life and in the workforce, while woman in more traditional positions are generally accorded the respect due to their role as mothers and heads of families. Despite this, however, any woman under the age of thirty can invariably expect to be the object of a certain amount of machismo.

Although the fact that in some parts of the country the idea of a woman travelling on her own is culturally foreign, in general, people are friendly and helpful: solo women travellers get the *pobrecita* (poor little thing) vote, because they're *solita* (all alone), without family or man. Nonetheless, Costa Rican men may throw out unsolicited comments (*piropos*) at women in the street: "*mí amor*", "*guapa*", "*machita*" ("blondie"), and so on. If they don't feel like articulating a whole word, they may stare or hiss – there's a saying used by local women: "Costa Rica's full of snakes, and they're all men."

Blonde, fair-skinned women are in for a quite a bit of this, whereas if you look remotely Latin you'll get less attention. This is not to say you'll be exempt from these so-called compliments, and even in groups, women are targets. Walk with a man, however, and the whole street theatre disappears as if by magic. The accepted wisdom is to pass right by and pretend nothing's happening. If you're staying in Costa Rica for any time, though, you may want to learn a few responses in Spanish; this won't gain you any respect – men will look at you and make *loca* (crazy) whirligig finger gestures at their temples – but it may make you feel better.

None of this is necessarily an expression of sexual interest: it has more to do with a man displaying his masculinity to his buddies than any desire to get to know you. Sexual assault figures in Costa Rica are low, you don't get felt up or groped, and you rarely hear *piropos* outside the towns. But for some women, unhappily, this machismo can be endlessly tiring, and may even mar their stay in the country.

In recent years there has been a spate of incidents allegedly involving Rophynol, the so-called **date-rape drug** (legal and available over the counter in Costa Rica), whereby women have been invited for a drink by a man, or sent a drink from a man in a bar, which turns out to be spiked with the drug (often by the bartender, who's in on the game). In the worst cases, the women have woken up hours later having no recollection of the missing time, and have been convinced they were raped. This is not to encourage paranoia, but the obvious thing to do is not accept opened drinks from men and be careful about accepting invitations to go to bars with unknown men. If you do, order a beer and ask to open the bottle yourself.

Geography, climate and the seasons

For such a small country (51,000 square kilometres or 19,700 square miles), Costa Rica is home to an enormous diversity of terrain, climates and geographical zones, formed from the stark contrasts between mountainous areas, agricultural valleys, and the hot, tropical lowlands.

Seasons

In much of Costa Rica the weather adheres to the **two-season pattern** of many tropical countries, alternating between **dry** (Dec–April) and **wet** (May–Nov) seasons. March and April are usually the hottest months, while cool winds from the North American winter-weather systems can make some days in December, January and February a bit cool. Note that although Costa Rica is in the northern hemisphere – it lies 8–11° above the equator – the dry season is referred to locally as *verano* (summer) and the wet as *invierno* (winter), which can cause some confusion for North American and European visitors.

There is currently a move in Costa Rica to refer, somewhat euphemistically, to the wet season as the **"green season"** – no doubt because "wet" scares off potential visitors with visions of monsoon-like deluges. In fact it's not all that wet, except in the Valle Central, where downpours, typically in the afternoon, can be fierce, especially in September and October, though even here you'll enjoy plenty of sunshine early in the day. Ticos say that the hotter it is in the morning – and it can get quite fiercely hot in San José – the harder it will rain in the afternoon.

Access to some national parks, especially Corcovado, is very limited in the rainy season – the Osa Peninsula on which Corcovado is located receives 2500–5000mm of rain a year, most of it between May and November. Driving is tougher in the wet season too, and you'll need a sturdy 4WD to get you around the Nicoya Peninsula or up to Monteverde. These caveats aside, the wet season should not deter you from travelling in Costa Rica: it rains most of the year on the Atlantic side anyway, and Guanacaste and the Pacific coast do not have such a pronounced rainy season. Simply focus your activities in the period between about 7am and noon, bring an umbrella, be prepared to get drenched from time to time, and get used to your clothes smelling a little mouldy. If you are in Costa Rica during July and August and notice there's been no rain for days, you may have caught the *veranillo* (little summer), a fortnight or so of dry weather that usually occurs at this time.

Dry-season days are characterized by more or less cloudless skies and cooler temperatures, especially in the highlands. The air is a pleasant temperature at higher altitudes and generally dry, with rare, unseasonal showers. The dry season is most pronounced in Guanacaste, the Nicoya Peninsula and the Valle Central.

Climates and microclimates

Although officially termed "subtropical", a mosaic of **microclimates** – comprising a total of at least twelve bona fide climate zones – makes it impossible to describe Costa Rica's climate accurately in one shot. **Altitude** is the prime factor in determining temperature and vegetation, and changes can be extreme and localized. Temperatures can range from 35°C on either of the coasts to below freezing atop Mount Chirripó, Costa Rica's highest point.

Four **mountain ranges** traverse the country – running roughly from northwest to southeast the low Cordillera de Guanacaste, the Cordillera de Tilarán and the Cordilleras Central and Talamanca – forming between their spines five distinct areas: the highlands of the Valle Central, the tropical lowlands of the Pacific and Caribbean coasts, the tropical plains of the Zona Norte, and the hot, dry lowlands of Guanacaste.

The fertile **Valle Central**, the geographical fulcrum of the country, is an intermountain plateau lying between the Cordilleras Central and Talamanca. Here you'll experience the classic highland climate found in other Central American countries – the place where coffee grows, elites settle, and economic and industrial wealth gathers. The climate is rosily described as "perpetual summer", a year-round 22–25°C, while higher altitudes around the Valle bask in a "perpetual spring", though it can actually be quite chilly in some of the mountain towns.

The eastern slopes of the Cordillera Central down to the **Caribbean coast** is relatively flat, hot and humid; ideal for growing fruit, especially bananas. Puerto Limón, Tortuguero and Barra de Colorado are hot and humid year-round, receiving an enormous amount of rain. South of Puerto Limón there is a "little summer", or small and unpredictable dry season, in September and October, just when the Valle Central is getting drenched. The **Pacific Coast** (including the Zona Sur) is also hot and humid year-round, but experiences its dry season later than the Caribbean coast, from December to March. The **Zona Norte** can get oppressively hot and humid, with temperatures around 26–30°C. **Guanacaste** can also be very hot, but the effect here is mitigated by the area's relative dryness.

National parks and reserves

Costa Rica protects 25 percent of its total territory under the aegis of a carefully structured system of national parks, wildlife refuges and biological reserves – in all there are currently some 75 designated protected areas. Established gradually over the past thirty years, their role in protecting the country's rich fauna and flora against the expansion of resource-extracting activities and human settlement is generally lauded.

Many people think that Costa Rica's national parks are a kind of tropical version of those in North America, while some visitors imagine them as huge outdoor zoos. On the contrary, it's important to understand from the start that you're not guaranteed to see any of the larger mammals that live in the parks: although you'll most likely see some of the more common or less shy animals, you would be very lucky indeed to spot a jaguar, ocelot or tapir. Above all, it's important to understand that the national parks were not created specifically with tourism in mind and to realize that it's not

the rangers' exclusive function to cater to tourists, although the government does recognize the invaluable cash brought in by the industry.

In total, the parks and reserves protect approximately four percent of the world's total **wildlife species** and **life zones**, among them rainforests, cloudforests, *páramo* (high-altitude moorlands), swamps, lagoons, marshes and mangroves, and the last remaining patches of tropical dry forest in the isthmus. Also protected are areas of historical significance, including a very few pre-Columbian settlements, and places

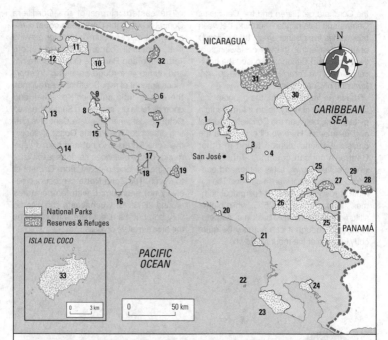

National Parks, Biological Reserves, Wildlife Refuges & Principal Private Reserves

1. Parque Nacional Volcán Poás
2. Parque Nacional Braulio Carrillo
3. Parque Nacional Volcán Irazú
4. Monumento Nacional Guayabo
5. Parque Nacional Tapantí
6. Parque Nacional Volcán Arenal
7. Reserva Biológica Bosque Nuboso
    Monteverde & Reserva Santa Elena
8. Parque Nacional Palo Verde
9. Reserva Biológica Lomas Barbudal
10. Parque Nacional Rincón de la Vieja
11. Parque Nacional Guanacaste
12. Parque Nacional Santa Rosa
13. Parque Nacional Marino las Baulas
14. Refugio Nacional de Fauna Silvestre
    Ostional
15. Parque Nacional Barra Honda
16. Reserva Natural Absoluta Cabo Blanco
17. Reserva Biológica de Guayabo y Negritos
18. Refugio Nacional de Fauna
    Silvestre Curú
19. Reserva Biológica Carara
20. Parque Nacional Manuel Antonio
21. Parque Nacional Marino las
    Ballenas
22. Reserva Biológica Isla del Caño
23. Parque Nacional Corcovado
24. Refugio Nacional de Fauna
    Silvestre Golfito
25. Parque Internacional la Amistad
    (Costa Rica & Panamá)
26. Parque Nacional Chirripó
27. Reserva Biológica Hitoy-Cerere
28. Refugio Nacional de Vida Silvestre
    Gandoca-Manzanillo
29. Parque Nacional Cahuita
30. Parque Nacional Tortuguero
31. Refugio Nacional de Fauna
    Silvestre Barra del Colorado
32. Refugio Nacional de Vida Silvestre
    Caño Negro
33. Parque Nacional Isla del Coco

considered to be of immense scenic beauty – valleys, waterfalls, dry lowlands and beaches. Costa Rica has also taken measures to protect beaches where marine turtles lay their eggs, as well as a number of active volcanos.

For a **history** of the park system in Costa Rica, see Contexts.

Definitions

A **national park** (*parque nacional*) is typically a large chunk of relatively untouched wilderness – usually more than 2500 acres – dedicated to preserving features of outstanding ecological or scenic interest. These are the

Park terminology

puesto	post (ranger post)
sendero	trail
area de acampar	camping area
agua potable	drinking water
peligro	danger
area restringado	restricted area
entrada/salida	entrance/exit

most touristy of the protected areas, typically offering walking, hiking or snorkelling opportunities, while a couple even have historical exhibits. Though habitation, construction of hotels and hunting of animals is prohibited in all national parks, "buffer zones" are increasingly being designated around them, where people are permitted to engage in a limited amount of agriculture and hunting. In most cases, park boundaries are surveyed but not demarcated – rangers and locals know what land is within the park and what is not – so don't expect fences or signs to tell you where you are.

Although it also protetcts valuable ecosystems and conserves areas for scientific research, a **biological reserve** (*reserva biológica*) generally has less of scenic or recreational interest than a national park, and hunting and fishing are usually prohibited. A **national wildlife refuge** (*refugio nacional de vida silvestre* or *refugio nacional de fauna silvestre*) is designated to protect the habitat of wildlife species. It will not be at all obviously demarcated, with few, if any, services, rangers or trails, and is generally little visited by tourists.

There are also a number of **privately owned reserves** in Costa Rica, chief among them community-initiated projects such as the now famous reserves at Monteverde and nearby Santa Elena. While the money you pay to enter these reserves does not go directly to the government, they are almost never money-grabbing places; the vast majority are conscientiously managed and have links with national and international conservation organizations. For more on how national parks and protected areas link up in Costa Rica's conservation strategy, see Contexts.

Visiting Costa Rica's parks

All national parks have entrance **puestos**, or ranger stations, often little more than a small

hut where you pay your fee and pick up a general map. Typically the main ranger stations – from where the internal administration of the park is carried out, and where the rangers sleep, eat and hang out – are some way from the entrance puesto. At some parks you will only deal with the entrance puesto, while at others it's a good idea to drop by the main administration centre, where you can talk to rangers (if your Spanish is good) about local terrain and conditions, enquire about drinking water, and use the bathroom. In some parks, such as Corcovado, you can sleep in or camp near the main stations. Usually these provide basic but adequate accommodation, be it on a campsite or a bunk, and a friendly atmosphere.

Outside the most visited parks – Volcán Poás, Volcán Irazú, Santa Rosa and Manuel Antonio – **opening hours** are erratic. Many places are open daily, from around 8am to 3.45pm, though there are exceptions, while other parks may open a little earlier in the morning. Unless you're planning on camping or staying overnight, there's almost no point in arriving at a national park in the afternoon. In all cases, especially the volcanos, you should aim to arrive as early in the morning as possible to make the most of the day and, in particular, the weather (especially in the wet season). You'll usually find a ranger somewhere, even if he or she is not at the puesto. If you hang around for a while and call "¡Upe!" (what people say when entering houses and farms in the countryside), someone will appear.

The only central office where you can make reservations and get detailed, up-to-date **information** or buy **permits**, where required, is the Fundación de Parques Nacionales (FPN; Av 15, C 23/25, San José, ☎257-2239, ⓦwww.minae.go.cr/accvc), who will contact those parks for which you need reservations, chiefly Santa Rosa, Corcovado and Chirripó (see the individual accounts in the Guide for more details). Other parks can be visited on spec.

All parks now charge an **entrance fee** of $6 per day. If you want to camp overnight in any park, you'll have to pay for both days – $12 in total.

Park organization

In order to decentralize the national park system and to shift some of the administrative

National parks

National park	Location	Topography	Wildlife	Activities
LA AMISTAD	border with Panamá	rainforest	mammals, birds	hiking
VOLCÁN ARENAL	136km NW of San José	volcanic	birds, mammals	volcano-watching, hiking
BALLENA	192km SW of San José	marine	coral, mammals, fish	diving, snorkelling
BARRA HONDA	330km E of San José	subterranean caves	bats, reptiles, birds	caving (via Liberia)
LAS BAULAS	301km NW of San José	beach, marine	turtles	turtle-watching
BRAULIO CARRILLO	20km N of San José	cloudforest, rainforest	birds, reptiles, mammals	hiking, birding
CAHUITA	195km SE of San José	marine, beaches	coral, reptiles, mammals	swimming, walking, snorkelling
CHIRRIPÓ	151km S of San José	mountain peaks, páramo	mammals, birds (incl. quetzal)	hiking, climbing
CORCOVADO	380km SW of San José	rainforest	mammals, amphibians, reptiles	hiking
GUANACASTE	250km NW of San José	rainforest, tropical dry forest	butterflies, moths, birds, mammals	hiking
GUAYABO NAT. MONUMENT	84km SE of San José	rainforest	mammals, birds	archeology, history, walking
VOLCÁN IRAZÚ	54km SE of San José	volcanic	birds	volcano-watching
ISLA DEL COCO	500km offshore	volcanic, rainforest	marine life	diving
MANUEL ANTONIO	132km SW of San José	rainforest, mangroves, beaches	mammals, marine life, reptiles	hiking, swimming
PALO VERDE	240km NW of San José	limestone hills, savannah	birds, mammals	bird-watching, hiking
VOLCÁN POÁS	56km N of San José	volcanic, dwarf cloudforest	mammals, birds	volcano-watching
RINCÓN DE LA VIEJA	253km NW of San José	rainforest, savannah	birds	hiking, volcano-watching
SANTA ROSA	261km NW of San José	tropical dry forest	mammals, turtles	hiking, history, turtle-watching
TAPANTÍ	40km SW of San José	primary montane forests	mammals, birds	hiking
TORTUGUERO	254km NE of San José	rainforest, beach	turtles, mammals, birds	turtle-watching (via road/water)

and day-to-day responsibitilities to the areas in which the parks are located, Costa Rica was formally divided in 1994–95 into **eight conservation areas**. It's useful to become familiar with these as, in the future, all parks and reserves will be discussed more and more in relation to the area to which they correspond.

In the middle of the country, the **CENTRAL VOLCANIC MOUNTAIN RANGE** contains the most accessible national parks, near San José and easily visited on a day-trip. Closest to the capital is **Braulio Carrillo National Park**, protecting tropical wet forest and cloudforest and containing its own volcano, Volcán Barva. The little-known **Juan Castro Blanco National Park** sits above **Volcán Poás National Park**, one of the most visited in the country; **Irazú National Park**, centred on another volcano, lies to the southeast. Nearby is the archeological site of **Guayabo National Monument**, a pre-Columbian settlement on the slopes of the Cordillera Central.

The tiny **ARENAL** conservation area, in the west of the Zona Norte, comprises the relatively new **Volcán Arenal National Park**, established to protect the lava trails and the flora and fauna on the slopes of Volcán Arenal. You can still watch the night-time eruptions, when lava streams down the sides of the mountain, for free, provided the top isn't obscured by cloud.

LA AMISTAD conservation area, located largely in the extreme south of the country and continuing east to encompass parts of the Caribbean province of Limón, includes giant **La Amistad International Park** – a joint venture betwen Costa Rica and Panamá that protects large areas of mammalian habitat and huge tracts of virtually impenetrable montane forests. Popular with hikers and backpackers, **Chirripó National Park** is named for Mt Chirripó, at 3820m the highest point in Costa Rica. The wet and dense **Tapantí National Park** lies close to the Valle Central, while in the east, Limón province holds little-visited **Hitoy-Cerere Biological Reserve**, tiny **Cahuita National Park**, established to conserve some of the last remaining coral reef in Costa Rica, and, in the southeast, **Gandoca-Manzanillo Wildlife Refuge**, an area of protected mangroves and low-lying swamps.

In the northeast corner of the country the **TORTUGUERO PLAINS** conservation area covers an enormous expanse 1330 square kilometres and comprises **Tortuguero National Park**, established to protect the nesting grounds of several species of marine turtle, and the wet lowland tropical forest of **Barra del Colorado Wildlife Refuge**. Largely impenetrable except by water, this area protects an enormous range of mammal and marine life, as well as some 400 different species of birds.

GUANACASTE conservation area, in the northwest of the country, includes **Guanacaste**, **Rincón de la Vieja** and **Santa Rosa National Parks**. It covers a wide variety of altitudes, from sea level to nearly 2000m at the top of Rincón de la Vieja volcano. Of most interest here are the surviving pockets of tropical dry forest and the good hiking trail up Rincon de la Vieja.

Straddling the Nicoya Peninsula and southern Guanacaste, **TEMPISQUE** covers **Palo Verde National Park**, **Las Baulas National Marine Park**, **Barra Honda National Park**, **Isla de Guayabo**, **Negrito**, **Pájaros Island Biological Reserves** and **Lomas Barbudal Biological Reserve**. This is a tremendously varied, if little visited, collection of protected areas, varying from subterranean caves in Barra Honda and turtles in Las Baulas to seasonal wetlands in Palo Verde – well worth the effort of getting off the beaten track.

The **OSA** conservation area in the extreme southwest of Costa Rica protects some of the most diverse tropical forest in the Americas. Comprising **Corcovado National Park** on the Osa Peninsula, the **Golfito Wildlife Refuge** and the **Piedras Blancas National Park** on the mainland, it also encompasses the **Marine National Park Ballena** and **Caño Island Biological Reserve**, both excellent snorkelling and scuba-diving destinations.

There's also a satellite category of parks that do not fit neatly into geographical or biological areas: **Manuel Antonio National Park** on the Pacific coast, protecting an area of astounding scenic beauty, including beaches and jungle trails; the Pacific lowland **Carara Biological Reserve**, a haven for crocodiles and other reptiles and amphibians; the unique and very localized habitat of **Cabo Blanco Absolute Nature Reserve** on the tip of the Nicoya Peninsula; and the remote **Isla del Coco National Park**,

Guardaparques

A **guardaparque** is a park ranger, working long hours and long shifts – often twenty days on and eight days off – for basic pay. You will sometimes see *guardaparques* in the more remote areas of the country setting out on foot to patrol the park against **poaching**. Poaching of birds and animals – including famous and endangered species such as the quetzal and the jaguar – for sale to zoos or individuals is common, as is the hunting of animals for meat by locals within protected areas. *Guardaparques* also often go on patrol at night, alone and armed only with a torch.

Many are locals, and extremely knowledgeable about their patch of terrain, while others are university students of biology, botany or ecology who may have studied abroad and who are working for the parks service as part of their education. The service also relies on a cadre of dedicated international **volunteers** to help out at the more remote ranger stations. If you fancy giving up some time, see p.63 for more details; you have to be pretty brave to do this, as you are expected to do everything that a ranger does.

In general, visitors to Costa Rica's National parks will find *guardaparques* friendly and very informative. Though only part of their job is to provide tourist information – don't expect them to provide you with a *Jungle Book* repertoire of adventures – sometimes they will, if gently encouraged, tell you about their encounters with fearsome bushmasters or placid tapirs. Independent travellers and hikers might want to ask about the possibility of joining them on patrol during the day (you'll probably have to speak some Spanish). This can be a great experience, and in some cases – especially if you're travelling alone – it's the only safe way to see certain parks, since some, like Corcovado, are not really safe to walk around solo.

500km off the Costa Rican coast in the Pacific Ocean, which safeguards marine life and many endemic land-living species of reptiles and birds.

Outdoor activities

Costa Rica is famous for year-round adventure tourism and outdoor activities, and in recent years has seen a proliferation of well-organized day-trips, packages and guided outings (see p.33 for details of tour operators) – in many ways the country is now much better set up for tour groups than for individual travellers who want to rough it on their own. For further information on sporting activities in Costa Rica pick up the twice-monthly *Costa Rica Outdoors* magazine or visit Ⓦwww.costaricaoutdoors.com – they specialize in fishing, but cover other sports too.

Hiking and walking

Almost everyone who comes to Costa Rica does some sort of **hiking** or **walking**, whether it be through the rainforest, on grassy uplands or drylands, or ambling along beaches or trails in parks with less demanding terrain.

From lowland tropical forest to the heights of Mount Chirripó, there are opportunities for walking in all kinds of terrain, often for considerable distances. Make sure to **bring** sturdy shoes or hiking boots and a hat, sunblock, umbrella and lightweight rain gear. It helps to have binoculars, too, even if you don't consider yourself an avid birder or animal-spotter; it's amazing what they pick up that the naked eye misses. In certain areas, like Corcovado – where you'll be doing more walking than you've ever done before, unless you're in the Marines – most people also bring a tent. In the high *páramo* of Chirripó, you'll need to bring at least a sleeping bag.

There are a number of things you have to be careful of when hiking in Costa Rica. The chief danger is **dehydration**: always carry lots of water with you, preferably bottled, or a canteen. In 1992 two hikers died in Barra Honda National Park when they ventured along unfamiliar trails in the midday heat without sufficient water and became lost. Bring a hat and sunscreen to protect yourself against sunstroke, and use both, even if it's cloudy.

Each year many hikers **get lost**, although they're nearly almost always found before it's too late. If you're venturing into a remote and unfamiliar area, bring a map and compass and make sure you know how to use both. To lessen anxiety if you do get lost, make sure you have matches, a torch and, if you are at a fairly high altitude, warm clothing. It gets cold at night above 1500m, and it would be ironic to end up with hypothermia in the tropics.

White-water rafting

After hiking and walking, **white-water rafting** is probably the single most popular activity in Costa Rica. Some of the best rapids and rivers to be found south of Colorado are here, and a mini-industry of rafting outfitters, most of them in San José, has grown up. Elsewhere in the country your hotel or lodge might provide a guided rafting trip as an inclusive or extra tour.

White-water rafting entails getting in a rubber dinghy with about eight other people – including a guide – and paddling, at first very leisurely, down one of the rivers listed below, working together with the guide to negotiate exhilarating rapids of varying difficulty. Overall it's very safe, and the ample life jackets and helmets help. **Wildlife** you are likely to see from the boat includes crocodiles, caimans, lizards, parrots, toucans, herons, kingfishers, iguanas and butterflies. Most trips last a day, though some companies run overnight or weekend excursions. They **cost** between $70 and $90 for a day, including transport, equipment and lunch. Dress to get wet, with sunscreen, a bathing suit, shorts and surfer sandals or gym shoes.

Rafters classify their rivers from Class I (easiest) to Class IV (pretty hard – don't venture onto one of these until you know what you're doing). The **most difficult** rivers in Costa Rica are the Class III–IV Ríos Reventazón and Pacuaré (both reached from the Valle Central via Turrialba) and some sections of the Río Naranjo around Manuel Antonio National Park. **Moderately easy** Río Sarapiquí (Zona Norte) is a Class II river with some Class III rapids. The gentlest of all is Corobicí in Guanacaste, a Class I flat water.

White-water-rafting outfitters

Aguas Bravas, Aptdo 1500-2100 (℡ 292-2072, ℻ 229-4837, ⓦ www.aguas-bravas.co.cr). Small company operating mostly on the Sarapiquí river and specializing in summer camps for kids aged 10–17 and family-orientated rafting excursions. They also offer kayaking tours and trips in non-motorized dinghies.

Aventuras Naturales, Aptdo 10736-1000, San José (℡ 225-3939, ℻ 253-6934, ⓦ www.adventurecostarica.com). Wide choice of tours and levels including day-trips on the Ríos Reventazón, Sarapiquí and Corobicí, two-day trips on the Río Pacuaré (with an overnight stay at the *Pacuaré Jungle Lodge*) and three- or four-day expeditions on the Río General near Chirripó.

Costa Rica Whitewater, C Central, Av 3, San José (℡ 257-0766, ℻ 257-1665, ⓦ www.costaricaexpeditions.com). Part of the long-established Costa Rica Expeditions (see p.33), this company has been rafting for over twenty years, with a good selection of day-trips and longer excursions, most of them fairly difficult.

Costa Sol Rafting, Aptdo 8-4390-1000, San José (℡ 293 2150, ℻ 293-2155, ⓦ www.costasolrafting.com). Day-trips on the more difficult rivers, some overnighters, and ocean kayaking.

Ríos Tropicales, Aptdo 472-1200, San José (℡ 233-6455, ℻ 255-4354, ⓦ www.riostropicales.com). One of the larger outfitters, with challenging trips on the Reventazón, Pacuaré and Corobicí rivers – a good choice for experienced rafters.

Kayaking

More than twenty rivers in Costa Rica provide good **kayaking**, especially the Sarapiquí, Reventazón, Pacuaré, General and Corobicí. The small towns of Turrialba, in the Valle Central, and Puerto Viejo de Sarapiquí, in the Zona Norte, are good bases for customized kayaking tours, with a number of specialist operators or lodges that rent boats, equipment and guides. Costa Sol Rafting (see opposite) run "kayaking clinics": crash courses lasting from half a day or more where you can learn how to handle a kayak.

Sea kayaking has become increasingly popular in recent years. This is an activity for experienced kayakers only, and should never be attempted without a guide. The number of rivers, rapids and streams pouring from the mountains into the oceans on both coasts can make currents treacherous, and any kind of boating, especially kayaking, is potentially dangerous without proper supervision.

Swimming

Costa Rica has many lovely **beaches**, most of them on the Pacific coast. You do have to be careful swimming at many of them, however, as more than 200 **drownings** occur each year – about four or five a week. Most are unnecessary, resulting from **rip tides**, strong currents that go from the beach out to sea in a kind of funnel. Rip tides are created by an excess of water coming into the beach and seeking a release for its extra energy. When the water finds an existing depression on the ocean floor, or creates one from its own force, it forms a kind of swift-moving current, much like a river, over this depression. Rip tides are always found on beaches with relatively **heavy surf**, and

Rip tides in Costa Rica

Some of the most popular and frequented beaches in Costa Rica are, ironically, also the worst for **rip tides**:

Playa Doña Ana (Central Pacific)
Playa Jacó (Central Pacific)
Manuel Antonio's Playa Espadilla
  (Central Pacific)
Playa Tamarindo (Guanacaste)
Playa Avellana (Guanacaste)
Playa Junquillal (Guanacaste)
Playa Bonita (Limón)
Punta Uva (Limón)
Cahuita, the first 400m of beach (Limón)

can also form near river estuaries. Some are permanent, while some "migrate" up and down a beach.

People who die in rip tides do so because they **panic** – it is undeniably unnerving when you find yourself being carried at what seems an alarming rate, 6 or 10km an hour, out to the wide blue ocean. They also try to swim against the current, which is a useless enterprise. The combination of panic and an intense burst of energy exhausts people fast, causing them to take in water. Tragically, many people who die as a result of rip currents do so in water that is no more than waist-high. The important thing to know about rip tides is that, while they may drag you out to sea a bit, they won't take you far beyond the breakers, where they lose their energy and dissipate. They also won't drag you under – that's an **undertow** – and there are far fewer of those on Costa Rica's beaches. The best advice if you get caught in rip currents is to relax as much as possible, float, call for help from the beach, and wait until the current dies down. Then swim back towards the beach at a 45° angle; not straight in. By swimming back at an angle you'll avoid getting caught in the current again.

The other thing you have to be careful of is fairly heavy **swells**. Waves that might not look that big from the beach can have a mighty pull when you get near their break point. Many people are hurt coming out of the sea, backs to the waves, which then clobber them from behind. Best come out of the sea sideways, so that there is minimum body resistance to the water.

In addition to the above precautions, never swim alone, don't swim at beaches where turtles nest (this means, more often than not, sharks), never swim near river estuaries (pollution and rip tides), and always ask locals about the general character of the beach before you swim.

Diving and snorkelling

Though **diving** is less of a big deal in Costa Rica than in Belize or Honduras's Bay Islands, there are a few worthwhile dive sites, the best of them along the extreme northwest of the **Pacific coast**, such as Santa Elena Bay's Murciélago and Catalina Islands.

You can also theoretically **snorkel** all along

the Pacific coast – Playa Flamingo in northern Guanacaste has clear waters but not a lot to see, while Playa Panamá and Bahía Ballena also have good snorkelling. For people who want to see an abundance of underwater life, the small **reef** near Manzanillo on the Caribbean coast is the best; the nearby reef at Cahuita has suffered in recent years from erosion and is now dying.

Diving outfitters in Costa Rica

Aquamor Adventures, Manzanillo ☏ 391-3417, ✉ aquamor@racsa.co.cr. Excellent dive operation situated within the Gandoca-Manzanillo Marine Refuge, with night dives, certification courses and tours. Employs local captains and works in alliance with the Talamanca Dolphin Foundation.

Bill Beard's Diving Safaris, Playa Hermosa ☏ & ℻ 672-0012, ✉ diving@racsa.co.cr. Experienced operator in the northern Guanacaste region. PADI certification courses.

Costa Rica Adventure Divers, Bahía Drake ☏ 385-9541, ⓦ www.costaricadiving.com. Boat dives, dive courses and snorkelling around Bahía Drake and the pristine reef of nearby Isla de Caño.

Ocotal Beach Resort and Marina, Playa Ocotal ☏ 222-4259, ℻ 223-8483, ✉ ocotal@centralamerica.com. PADI certification courses and five- and seven-day dive trips to offshore islands.

Rich Coast Diving, Playa del Coco ☏ 670-0176, ✉ dive@richcoastdiving.com. Snorkelling and scuba-diving trips.

Surfing

Surfing is very good on both of Costa Rica's coasts, although there are certain beaches that are suitable during only parts of the year. You can surf all year round on the **Pacific**: running north to south the most popular beaches are Boca de Barranca, Naranjo, Tamarindo, Jacó, Hermosa, Quepos, Dominical and, in the extreme south near the Panamá border, Pavones. On the **Caribbean** coast the best beaches are at Puerto Viejo and Punta Uva further down the coast.

The **north Pacific Coast and Nicoya Peninsula** is probably the prime surfing area in the country, with a wide variety of breaks and lefts and rights of varying power and velocity. Within Santa Rosa National Park, **Playa Naranjo** gives one of the best breaks in the country (Dec–March) and has the added attraction of good camping facilities, though you'll need your own 4WD to reach them. **Playa Potrero Grande**, only accessible by boat from Playa del Coco, offers a very fast right point break.

Moving down to the long western back of the Nicoya Peninsula, **Playa Tamarindo** has three sites for surfing, though parts of the beach are plagued by rocks. While they don't offer a really demanding or wild ride, Tamarindo's waves are very popular due to the large number of hotels and restaurants in the town nearby. **Playa Langosta**, just south of Tamarindo, offers right and left point breaks, a little more demanding than Tamarindo. **Playa Avellanas** has a good beach break, locally called the *Guanacasteco*, with very hollow rights and lefts, while **Playa Nosara** offers a fairly gentle beach break, with rights and lefts. Remote and difficult to reach, **Playas Coyote**, **Manzanillo** and **Mal País** have consistent lefts and rights and several points.

Near Puntarenas on the **Central Pacific Coast**, **Boca Barranca** is an estuary with a very long left, while **Puerto Caldera** has a good left. **Playa Jacó** is not always dependable for good beach breaks, and the surf is not too big. Further south, **Playa Hermosa** is better, with a very strong beach break. The adjacent **Playas Esterillos Este**, **Oeste** and **Bejuco** offer similarly good beach breaks.

On the south Pacific coast, **Playita Manuel Antonio** is good when the wind is up, with beach breaks and left and right waves. Southwards, **Dominical** offers great surfing, with strong lefts and rights and beautiful surroundings. Down at the very south of the country, past Golfito, **Playa Pavones** boasts one of the longest left points in the world, very fast and with a good formation.

The best surfing beaches on the **Caribbean coast** lie towards the south, from Cahuita to Manzanillo villages. **Black-Sand Beach** at Cahuita has an excellent beach break, with the added bonus of year-round waves. **Puerto Viejo** is home to "La Salsa Brava", one of the few legitimate "big waves" in Costa Rica, a very thick, tubular wave formed by deep water rocketing towards a shallow reef. Further south **Manzanillo** has a very fast beach break in lovely surroundings and with good camping.

Further north towards Puerto Limón are a couple of beaches that, while not in the class of Puerto Viejo, can offer experienced surfers a few good waves. **Playa Bonita**, a few kilometres north of Limón, is known for its powerful and dangerous left; only people who really know what they are doing should try this. Similarly, the left-breaking waves at **Isla Uvita**, just off the coast from Puerto Limón, are considered tricky.

If you're interested in **learning to surf**, Alvaro Solano (☏643-2830 or 643-1308), Costa Rica's national surfing champion, gives lessons at Playa Jacó on the Central Pacific coast.

Fishing and sports-fishing

Costa Rica has hit the big time in the lucrative **sports-fishing** game. Both coasts are blessed with the kind of big fish serious anglers love – marlin, swordfish, tarpon and snook among them. The most obvious characteristic of sports-fishing is its tremendous **expense**: some three- or four-day packages run upwards of $3000. **Quepos** and **Golfito** have long been good places to do a little fishing, while some areas, like **Barra del Colorado** in the northeast and **Playa Flamingo** in Guanacaste, have turned into monothematic destinations, where a rather expensive brand of sports-fishing is really all that's on offer. Although good fishing is possible all year round, **January** and **February** are the most popular months.

Sports-fishing is just that: sport. The vast majority of fish are returned to the sea alive. Marty Bernard's No Frills Sports-fishing Tours (☏228-4812, ✉nofrills@racsa. co.cr) is famous in Costa Rica for teaching total amateurs how to snag huge tarpon and guapote (rainbow bass) in a day; it offers a "no fish, no pay" deal and all-inclusive day tours for $500, which, odd though it may seem, is a good price. See the accounts of Barra del Colorado in Limón province (p.184), Los Chiles in the Zona Norte (p.335), Quepos in the Central Pacific (p.369) and Golfito in the Zona Sur (p.000) for local sports-fishing opportunities. The *Tico Times* has a fishing columnist, Jerry Ruhlow, who regularly reports on the current best fishing spots.

Casual anglers can find cheaper and more

low-key fishing opportunities in the country's many trout-rich **freshwater rivers,** or in **Laguna de Arenal,** where rainbow bass fishing is especially good.

Bird-watching

One oft-repeated statistic you'll hear about Costa Rica is that the country boasts more than 850 species of birds (including migratory ones), a higher number than all of North America. Consequently, the **birding** is impressive, and it's likely that at the very least you'll spot hummingbirds, scarlet macaws, toucans, kingfishers and a variety of trogons. The resplendent quetzal, found in the higher elevations of Monteverde, Braulio Carrillo National Park, and the Talamanca mountain range, is elusive, but can still be spotted (the tiny hamlet of San Gerardo de Dota, close to the Cerro de la Muerte and signposted from the stretch of Interamericana which runs between Cartago and San Isidro de El General, is by far the best place to see quetzals).

Serious birders have a few **tour operators** to choose from, all of them in San José. Of those listed on p.33, Horizontes and Costa Rica Expeditions are the best bets. The *Albergue de Montana Talari* in Rivas (see p.359) runs weekly tours through the south of Costa Rica guided by professional ornithologists ($660 per person all-inclusive). In addition, Mi Quaber Travel and Tours in San José (☏258-3341, ℉255-4493, ⓦwww.crdirec.com/qabek) runs popular one-day quetzal-spotting trips to Cerro de la Muerte.

Cycling and mountain biking

Only certain places in Costa Rica lend themselves well to **mountain biking**. In general the best areas for extensive biking are Corcovado National Park, Montezuma village to Cabo Blanco Absolute Nature Reserve on the Nicoya Peninsula, and Santa Rosa National Park in Guanacaste. The Fortuna and Volcán Arenal area is also increasingly popular: you can bike to see the volcano (although not up it) and around the pretty Laguna de Arenal.

There are plenty of bike **rental shops** throughout the country; you may also be able to rent one from local tour agencies. Prices are generally around $5 an hour, $25

or so for the day. See "Getting Around" for more on independent cycling around Costa Rica.

Biking tours in Costa Rica

Bi.Costa Rica ☏258-0303, ℉258-0606, ⓦwww.yellowweb.co.cr/bicostarica.html. Expert bike tour operators who organize custom-made tours throughout the country for experienced cyclists only. Hotel stop-overs are well chosen and itineraries both challenging and imaginative.
Ríos Tropicales ☏233-6455, ℉255-4354, ⓦwww.riostropicales.com. This white-water rafting specialist also arranges bike-rides up and around Poás and Irazú volcanos and a ten-day coast-to-coast tour on demand.

Horse-riding

Almost everywhere you go in Costa Rica, with the exception of waterlogged northern Limón province, you should be able to hook up with a **horseback tour**. Guanacaste is probably the best area in the country for riding, where a cluster of excellent haciendas (working cattle ranches) also cater to tourists, offering bed, breakfast and horse hire. They're covered in detail in our chapter on Guanacaste.

Riding **on the beach** on the Nicoya Peninsula, especially at Montezuma in the south and Sámara on the west coast, is also very popular. Horses are rented by the hour. However, there has been a history of mistreatment of horses in these places, including their being overworked and not allowed sufficient water in the midday heat. Don't expect the animals here to be in as good shape as sleek thoroughbreds back home, but if you see any extreme cases of mistreatment complain to the local tourist information centre or local residents.

Horse-riding tours

Buenavista Lodge, 31km northeast of Liberia. Horse-riding tours in the Rincón de la Vieja area.
Finca Los Caballos, Montezuma, Nicoya. Riding tours for guests only, with horses for all levels and trips along beaches, to waterfalls and through rainforest.
Hacienda Barú, between Quepos and Dominical on the Caribbean coast (see pp.362 & 363). Rides and horseback tours into the rainforest and around the hacienda's private reserve.

Laguna Horseback Riding, Zarcero, 52km northwest of Alajuela. Horse-riding with a small local operator in scenic mountainous region.
Mr Big J, Cahuita. Friendly tour company organizing rides through Cahuita National Park, the

jungle and along the lovely Black-Sand Beach.
Volcán Turrialba Lodge, near Turrialba. Five-hour rides ($25 per person) up to the volcano and through remote and spectacular cloudforest.

Public holidays and festivals

Though you shouldn't expect the kind of colour and verve that you'll find in fiestas in Mexico or Guatemala, Costa Rica has its fair share of holidays and festivals, or *feriados*, when all banks, post offices, museums and government offices close. In particular, don't try to travel anywhere during Semana Santa, Holy (Easter) Week: the whole country shuts down from Holy Thursday until after Easter Monday, and buses don't run. Likewise, the week from Christmas to New Year invariably causes traffic nightmares, overcrowded beach towns and a suspension of services.

Provincial holidays, like Independence Day in Guanacaste (July 25) and the Limón Carnival (the week preceding October 12) affect local services only, but nonetheless the shutdown is drastic: don't bet on cashing travellers' cheques or mailing letters if you're in these areas at party time.

January 1 New Year's Day. Celebrated with a big dance in San José's Parque Central.
March 19 St Joseph's Day (El dia de San José). Patron saint of San José and its province.
Ash Wednesday Countrywide processions; in Guanacaste they're marked by horse, cow and bull parades, with bullfights (in which the bull is not harmed) in Liberia.
Holy Week Semana Santa. Dates vary annually but businesses will often close for the entire week preceding Easter weekend.
April 11 Juan Santamaría Day. Public holiday to commemorate the national hero who fought at the Battle of Rivas against the American adventurer William Walker in 1856.

May 1 Dia de los trabajadores (Labor Day).
June 20 St Peter's and St Paul's Day.
July 25 Independence of Guanacaste Day (Guanacaste province only). To mark the annexation of Guanacaste from Nicaragua in 1824.
August 2 Virgin of Los Angeles Day. Patron saint of Costa Rica.
August 15 Assumption Day and Mother's Day.
September 15 Independence Day, with big patriotic parades celebrating Costa Rica's independence from Spain in 1821.
October 12 El dia de la Raza (Columbus Day; Limón province only). Centred on the carnival, which takes place in the week prior to October 12.
November 2 All Soul's Day.
Christmas Week The week before Christmas is celebrated in San José with fireworks, bullfights and funfairs.
December 25 Christmas Day. Family-oriented celebrations with trips to the beach and much consumption of apples and grapes.

Shopping

Compared with many Latin American countries, Costa Rica does not have an impressive crafts or artisan tradition. However, there are some reasonable souvenirs to buy, such as carved wooden salad bowls, plates and trays. Wherever you go you'll see hand-painted wooden replica ox-carts, originating from Sarchí, in the Valle Central (see p.129) – perennial favourites, especially when made into drinks trolleys.

Reproductions of the pre-Columbian pendants and earrings displayed in San José's Museo Nacional, the Museo de Oro and the Museo de Jade are sold both on the street and in shops. Much of the stuff is not real gold, however, but gold-plated, which chips and peels: check before you buy.

Costa Rican **coffee** is one of the best gifts to take home. Make sure you buy export brands Cafe Britt or Cafe Rey and not the lower-grade sweetened coffee sold locally. It is often cheaper to buy bags in the supermarket rather than in souvenir shops, and cheaper still to buy beans at San José's Mercado Central. If you want your coffee beans roasted to your own taste, go to the *Café Gourmet* in San José for excellent beans and grinds. For more on coffee, see p.41.

In the absence of a real home-grown crafts or textile tradition, generic **Indonesian** dresses and clothing – batiked and colourful printed cloth – are widely sold in the beach communities of Montezuma, Cahuita, Tamarindo and Quepos (near Manuel Antonio). In some cases this craze for all things Indonesian extends to slippers, silver and bamboo jewellery, and so on; prices aren't bad.

If you have qualms about buying goods made from **tropical hardwoods**, ask the salesperson what kind of wood the object is made from, and avoid mahogany, laurel and purple heart. Other goods to avoid are coral, anything made from tortoise shells, and furs such as ocelot or jaguar.

Consumer goods manufactured anywhere other than Costa Rica have a 100 percent tax levied on their importation, so it's worth bringing the items listed in the box below from home.

Things to bring from home

- ❏ Batteries
- ❏ Film
- ❏ Binoculars
- ❏ Watches (plastic, digital is best)
- ❏ Alarm clock
- ❏ Cassette tapes
- ❏ Insect repellent
- ❏ Tampons
- ❏ Spare spectacles prescription
- ❏ Contact lens supplies
- ❏ Condoms
- ❏ Non-soap facial cleansers and shower gels
- ❏ Combination lock
- ❏ Towel
- ❏ Contraceptive pills
- ❏ Electrical adaptor (two-prong, US-style)
- ❏ Umbrella (make sure it's sturdy and compact, especially if coming in the rainy season; those sold in Costa Rica tend to be flimsy)

Gay and lesbian Costa Rica

Costa Rica has good reputation among gay and lesbian travellers, and continues to be a generally hassle-free destination for gay and lesbian tourists. Costa Rica has a large gay community by Central American standards, and to a smaller extent a sizeable lesbian one too, though it's pretty much confined to San José; there's also a large community of transvestite/transsexual prostitutes (*travestís*) in the capital.

Although there have been some incidents of police harassing gays in bars, in general you will be met with respect, and there's no need to assume that everyone is a raving hetero-Catholic poised to bash gays. Part of this tolerance is due to the subtle tradition in Costa Rican life and politics summed up in the Spanish expression "*quedar bien*", which translates roughly as "don't rock the boat" or "leave well alone". People don't ask you about your sexual orientation or make assumptions, but they don't necessarily expect you to talk about it unprompted, either.

There are few formal **contacts** in Costa Rica for gay and lesbian travellers, and it is difficult to find an entrée into gay life (especially for women) without knowing local gays and lesbians. Check the *Gay and Lesbian Guide to Costa Rica* on the net (@www .members.aol.com/gayrica/guide.html) or pick up *Gayness*, the monthly newspaper for Costa Rica's gay community, from downtown newsstands in San José. The two easiest points of contact for foreigners are **Déjà Vu**, a mainly gay disco in San José (see p.104), and the University of Costa Rica – you can check with the Vida Estudantíl office on the fourth floor of Building A for gay-oriented events. See "Drinking and Nightlife" in our San José chapter for details of other bars.

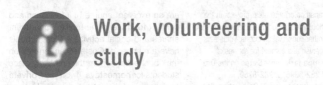

Work, volunteering and study

Costa Rica's all-round appeal makes it a good place to learn Spanish, and language-study tours and volunteer work projects (many of which are tax-deductible for travellers from the US) are extremely popular.

Volunteer work and research projects

There's a considerable choice of **volunteer work** and **research projects** in Costa Rica – some include food and lodging, and many can be organized from the US (see p.64). As an example, University Research Expeditions sends teams each year on two-week expeditions to replant lost trees and measure soil and plant characteristics. The team shares a rented house in a rural area of southern Costa Rica.

A good resource **in the US** for language study and volunteer work programmes is *Transitions Abroad*, a bimonthly magazine focusing on living and working overseas available from Dept TRA, Box 3000, Denville, NJ 07834 (🌐www.transabroad.com). Prospective **British** volunteers should contact the Costa Rican Embassy in London (see p.18). In **Australia**, details of current student exchanges and study programmes are available either from the Costa Rican consul (see p.18) or from the AFS, PO Box 5, Strawberry Hills, Sydney (☎02/9281 0066, 🌐www.afsaus.org.au). In **New Zealand**, contact the AFS, PO Box 11046, Wellington (☎04/384 8066 or 0800/600 300, 🌐www.afs.org/partners/nzlhome).

Volunteer programmes in Costa Rica

Amigos de las Aves, 32-4001 Río Segundo de Alajuela (☎441-2658). Works to establish breeding pairs of scarlet and great green macaws. Volunteers are welcome to help care for the birds; no food or lodging offered.

ANAI, Aptdo 170–2070, Sabanilla (☎224-6090 or 3570, 🖷253-7524, 📧anaicr@correo.co.cr). Based in southern Talamanca, ANAI trains people to farm

organically and manage forests sustainably. There are also volunteer programmes to help protect the Gandoca-Manzanillo Refuge and the turtles that come to the Caribbean coast each year (May–July), and working on ANAI's experimental farm (officially for a minimum of six months, but three-month stays can be arranged). Lodging and food included.

ASVO (Association of Volunteers for Service in Protected Areas), contact the director of International Voluntary Programmes (☎223-4533 ext. 135-182). Government-run scheme enabling volunteers to work in the national parks, helping guard protected areas, write reports and give environmental classes. Minimum two months.

DINADECO (Office of National Community Development; ☎235-0896, 🖷253-1745, 📧l.fallas@gobnert.go.cr). Costa Rican government institution which promotes citizen participation, family development, human-rights awareness and sexual equality. Foreigners are invited by the institution's International Cooperation Programme to get involved with individual development in small towns.

Earthwatch in the US: 3 Clock Tower Place, Suite 100, Maynard, MA 01754 (☎ 1-800/776-0188, 📧info@earthwatch.org). In the UK: 57 Woodstock Road, Oxford OX2 6HJ (☎ 01865/318838, 🖷01865/311383, 🌐www.earthwatch.org). Leatherback turtle study in Tamarindo, helping with a turtle hatchery and relocating threatened nests. From $1695.

Global Volunteers, 375 E Little Canada Rd, St Paul, MN 55117, US (☎ 800/487-1074, 🖷 51/482-0915, 🌐www.globalvolunteers.org). Volunteer program helping to maintain trails in the Santa Elena Cloud Forest Reserve ($1600).

Humanitarian Foundation (☎282-9862, 📧gnystrom@racsa.co.cr). Volunteers are placed in various programmes helping orphans, battered women, indigenous people and street children. $200 initial fee plus $225 per month for room and board.

Monteverde Institute, Aptdo 69–5655, Monteverde (☎645-5053, 🖷645-5219,

ⓔ mvipac@racsa.co.cr). Volunteer projects in the Monteverde cloudforest including teaching, fieldwork on trails and other conservation efforts. Volunteers must know Spanish and commit for six weeks.

Proyecto Campanario, near Sierpe on the Osa Peninsula (☎ 282-5898, ⓕ 282-8750, ⓔ volunteer@campanario.com). Research station and ecotourist project which sometimes offers free or discounted lodging and meals in exchange for work on and around the reserve. Must be able to swim.

Volunteer programmes in the US

Caribbean Conservation Corp, PO Box 2866, Gainesville, FL 32602 (☎ 1-800/678-7853, in Costa Rica ☎ 225-7516, ⓦ www.ccturtle.org). Volunteer research work on marine turtles at Tortuguero.

Global Service Corps, 300 Broadway, Suite 28, San Francisco, CA 94133-3312 (☎ 415/788-3666 ext 128, ⓦ www.globalservicecorps.org). Service programmes in Costa Rica.

University Research Expeditions, University of California, Berkeley, CA 94720-7050 (☎ 510/642-6586, ⓦ www.berkeley.edu). Environmental and animal behaviour studies.

Volunteers for Peace, 43 Tiffany Rd, Belmont, VT 05730 (☎ 802/259-2759, ⓦ www.vfp.org). Volunteer projects in Costa Rica and other Central American countries.

Study programmes and learning Spanish

As with most things, you will pay more in Costa Rica for a course in Spanish than in Guatemala or Mexico. There are so many schools in **San José** that choosing one can be a problem. Though you can arrange a place through organizations based in the US (see below), the best way to choose is to visit a few, perhaps sit in on a class or two, and judge the school according to your own personality and needs. This is not always possible, though, especially in high season (Dec–April), when many classes will have been booked in advance. At other times the drop-in method should be no problem at the majority of the schools we've listed.

Some of the **language schools** mentioned opposite are Tico-run; some are branches of international (usually North American) education networks. Instructors are almost invariably Costa Ricans who speak some English. School noticeboards are an excellent source of information and contact for travel opportunities, apartment shares and social activities. Most schools have a number of Costa Rican families on their books with whom they regularly place students for **homestays**. If you want **private tuition**, any of the schools listed below can recommend a tutor. Private rates run from $10 to $30 (£7–20) an hour.

US contacts for study programmes in Costa Rica

Bernan Associates, 4611-F Assembly Dr, Lanham, MD 20706 (☎ 1-800/274-4888). Distributes UNESCO's encyclopedic *Study Abroad*.

Council on International Educational Exchange (CIEE), 205 E 42nd St, New York, NY 10017 (☎ 1-888-COUNCIL, ⓦ www.ciee.org). The non-profit parent organization of Council Travel, CIEE runs summer, semester and academic-year programmes in Costa Rica.

Studyabroad.com (ⓦ www.studyabroad.com). A useful website on studying abroad, with listings and links to programmes worldwide.

World Learning, Kipling Road, PO Box 676, Brattleboro, VT 05302 (☎ 802/257-7751, ⓦ www.worldlearning.org). Runs a "School for International Training" which organizes accredited college semesters abroad, comprising language and cultural studies, and other academic work. It also has a summer programme for high-school students called "Experiment in International Living".

Language schools in Costa Rica

Academia Latinoamericana de Español, Aptdo 1280-2050, San Pedro, San José (☎ 224-9917, ⓕ 225-8125, ⓔ espalesa@racsa.co.cr). Friendly school close to the Toruma Youth Hostel in San José. Small groups (4–6) and intensive courses (20hr weekly; $155), with morning or afternoon schedules; homestay programmes cost a further $135 per week. There's a 15 percent discount to Hostelling International cardholders; all materials included.

Central American Institute for International Affairs (ICAI), Aptdo 10302, Otoya 1000, San José (☎ 233-8571, ⓕ 221-5238). Spanish tuition, cultural events and field trips, with an emphasis on learning through conversation. Good resources include a reference library, international directories and a travel office that can arrange weekend excursions. Two- or four-week programmes (4hr daily), with a minimum of six students per class.

Centro Cultural Costarricense-Norteamericano, Spanish Programme, c/o Aptdo 1489-1000, San José (T 225-9433, F 224-1480, W www.cccncr.com). Primarily a centre for cross-cultural exchange, but also offers Spanish lessons. The unrivalled facilities include a theatre, a gallery and the Mark Twain Library, which has an excellent stock of English and Spanish publications.

Centro Linguistico Conversa, C 38, Av 3/5, San José (T 221-7649, F 233-2418, E conversa@racsa.co.cr). Well-established institute that also teaches English to Ticos. Classes have a minimum of six students (5hr 30min daily), with thorough teaching that puts the emphasis on grammar. The four-week programme includes accommodation either with a Tico family, in a separate lodge with private bath and bedrooms, or at the centre's five-acre farm, 10km outside San José.

Costa Rica Spanish Institute (COSI), PO Box 1366-2050, San Pedro (T 253-9272, F 253-2117, W www.cosi.co.cr). Small classes in San Pedro, as well as a "beach programme" in Playa Ballena near Dominical. Homestays are arranged, as are private lessons and cultural activities.

Costa Rican Academy of Language, Av 0, C 25/27 (T 233-8938 or 233-8914, F 233-8670, E crlang@racsa.co.cr). Small, friendly and Costa Rican-owned school, with a multinational clientele (including many Germans and Swiss) and a conversational approach to learning, based on current affairs. There are also Latin dance classes every afternoon, and trips to discos to practise the steps.

ICADS (T 234-1381, F 234-1337, W www.icadscr.com). Month-long Spanish immersion programmes including lectures and activities emphasizing environmental issues, women's studies, economic development and human rights, with optional afternoon internships in grassroots organizations.

Instituto Britanico, Aptdo 8184, San José, 1000 (T 225-0256, F 253-1894, E instbrit@racsa.co.cr). Courses for all levels of proficiency, including tailor-made courses focusing on specific vocabulary (like business Spanish) and one-week courses in basic "survival" Spanish. You can also study in Liberia, Guanacaste.

Instituto Profesional de Espanol para Extranjeros, Aptdo 562-2050, San Pedro, San José (T 283-7731, F 225-7860, W www.ipee.com). Small school priding itself on its cosy atmosphere, total-immersion methodology and small groups (maximum six people). All ages and levels of Spanish are catered for, and courses run year round, from one week to six months or more. Facilities include free email access, and field trips, excursions and homestays are also arranged.

Montaña Linda Language School, Orosí (T & F 533-2153, W www.montanalinda.com). Popular school in a gorgeous location southeast of San José run by a friendly and knowledgeable couple. Tuition is either one-to-one or in tiny classes up to a maximum of three people, with the choice of concentrating on grammar or conversation. Accommodation is provided in a nearby hostel ($99 for five nights, including four 3hr classes and two meals daily; $120 for five classes; $225 for ten), and a wide range of tours and sightseeing activities are available. Recommended.

Universal de Idiomas, Aptdo 751-2150, Av 2, C 9, San José (T 223-9662, F 223 9917, W www.universal-edu.com). Well-established school with three-day crash courses and month-long programmes (3–4hr tuition daily). Homestays, tours, and dancing and cooking lessons can also be arranged.

Universidad Veritas, Aptdo 1380-1000, Zapote, San Pedro (T 283-4747, F 225-2907, E iee@veritas.ac.cr). Intensive month-long ($500) and 12-week ($1380) courses catering to all levels of Spanish, with 20 hours' tuition weekly, plus courses in other subjects including Costa Rican history, culture and literature. Homestays, student residences and tours available.

Directory

BUSINESS HOURS Hours fluctuate from establishment to establishment, but generally banks open Monday to Friday 8.30am to 3.30pm; government offices, Monday to Friday 8am to 5pm; and stores, Monday to Friday 9am to 6pm or 7pm. In rural areas shops often close for lunch. Stores and post offices open on Saturday mornings, as do a very few banks. Practically everything closes on Sundays.

DANCING Costa Ricans love to dance, and it's common to see children who have barely learned to stand up grooving and bopping, much encouraged by their parents. Consequently, there are many good discos, mainly in San José. Your popularity at discos or house parties will have something to do with how well you can dance; if you're really keen you might want to take salsa and merengue lessons before you come. Fitting in at a disco is easier for women, who simply wait to be asked to dance; not only are men expected to go out and hunt down female dance partners, but also to lead, which means you have to know what you're doing. For a list of dance schools in San José, see p.102.

DEPARTURE TAX Currently $17 if leaving by air, but check with your travel agent or airline in Costa Rica before you depart. The tax is not included in the price of your air ticket. You must leave sufficient funds in dollars or colones to pay it, and will be expected to show the stamp that confirms payment to the *migración* officer when you leave. If you're leaving overland you may have to buy a departure stamp ($2–3).

ELECTRICITY The electrical current in Costa Rica is 110 volts – the same as Canada and the US – although plugs are two-pronged, without the round grounding prong.

GAMBLING Casinos have sprung up in many – usually upmarket – hotels, and are increasingly to be found even in smaller beach or provincial hotels, generally ruining the landscape and lowering the tone with their red carpets, fake wood, orange lighting and besuited dealers. Slot machines, card games and roulette wheels are among the games on offer in these palaces of kitsch.

LANGUAGE The language of Costa Rica is Spanish. Although tourists who stay in top-end hotels will find that "everyone speaks English" (a common myth perpetrated about Costa Rica), your time here will be far more meaningful if you arm yourself with at least a 100-word Spanish vocabulary. Communicating with *guardaparques* and people at bus stops, asking directions and ordering *bocas* – not to mention finding salsa partners – is facilitated by speaking the language. For more on Costa Rican Spanish, see Contexts, p.493.

LAUNDRY There are very few laundrettes in Costa Rica, and they're practically all in San José (see p.108 for a list). Furthermore, laundrettes are rarely self-service – someone does it for you – and charge by the kilo. Most hotels will have some kind of laundry service, although charges are often outrageously high.

PHOTOGRAPHY Film is extremely expensive in Costa Rica, so bring lots from home. Although the incredibly bright equatorial light means that 100ASA will do for most situations, remember that rainforest cover can be very dark, and if you want to take photographs at dusk you'll need 200 or even 400ASA. San José is the only place in the country where you can process film; for a list of outlets, see p.108.

PROSTITUTION Prostitution is legal in Costa Rica. While there is streetwalking (largely confined to the streets of San José, especially those in the red-light district immediately west and south of the Parque Central), many prostitutes work out of bars. Bars in San José's "Gringo Gulch" (more or less on C 7, Av Central/5) tend to cater to and attract more foreign customers than the bars in the red-light district, which are frequented by Ticos. Steetwalkers around C 12 look like women but are not. *Travestís* are transsexual or transvestite prostitutes; they don't take kindly to being approached by jokers. In recent years Costa Rica has gained a reputation as a destination for sex tourism, and more specifically for child-sex tourism. The government is trying to combat this with a public information campaign and strict prison sentences for anyone caught having sex with a minor.

TIME Costa Rica is in North America's Central Standard time zone (the same as Winnipeg, New Orleans and Mexico City) and 6hr behind GMT.

TIPPING Unless service has been exceptional, you do not need to leave a tip in restaurants, where a ten percent service charge is automatically levied. Taxi drivers are not usually tipped, either. When it comes to nature guides, however, the rules become blurred. Many people – especially North Americans, who are more accustomed to tipping – routinely tip guides $3–10 per day. If you are utterly delighted with a guide it seems fair to offer a tip, although be warned that some guides may be made uncomfortable by your offer – as far as many of them are concerned, it's their job.

TOILETS The only place you'll find so-called "public" conveniences – they're really reserved for customers – is in fast-food outlets in San José, gas stations and roadside restaurants. When travelling in the outlying areas of the country you may want to take a roll of toilet paper with you. Note that except in the poshest hotels – which have their own sewage system/septic tank – you should not put toilet paper down the toilet. Sewage systems are not built to deal with paper, and you'll only cause a blockage. There's always a receptacle provided for toilet paper.

guide

guide

San José

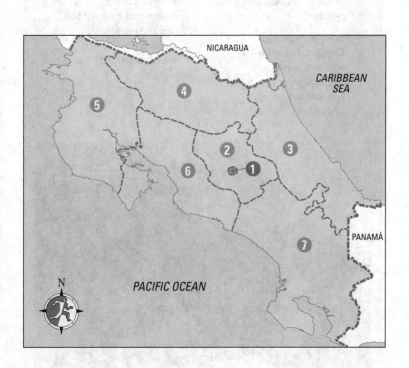

NICARAGUA

CARIBBEAN
SEA

④

⑤

②

③

⑥ ①

PANAMÁ

⑦

N

PACIFIC OCEAN

CHAPTER 1 # Highlights

✳ **Teatro Nacional** p.90 San José's most elegant building, and a little piece of Europe in the heart of the tropics.

✳ **Museo de Jade** p.91 A compelling exhibition of jade artefacts created by Costa Rica's indigenous peoples.

✳ **Parillada Argentina** p.100 Excellent Argentine-run café with superb empanadas to take away and massive, meaty lunches.

✳ **La Villa** p.103 Atmospheric San Pedro bar frequented by students and intellectual-types, and serving tasty bocas.

✳ **La Plaza** p.104 Archetypical Latin American disco, designed like a giant bull ring and packed with dancing couples and superb tuxedoed waiters.

San José

Sprawling smack in the middle of the fertile Valle Central, **SAN JOSÉ**, the only city of any size and administrative importance in Costa Rica, has a spectacular setting, ringed by the jagged silhouettes of soaring mountains – some of them volcanos – on all sides. At night, from high up on one of those mountains, the valley floor twinkles like a million Chinese lanterns, while on a sunny morning the sight of the blue-black peaks pink-shearing the sky is undeniably beautiful.

That's where the compliments end, however. Costa Ricans who live outside the capital are notoriously hard on the place, calling it, with a mixture of familiarity and contempt, "**Chepe**" – the diminutive of the name José – and writing it off as a maelstrom of stress junkies, rampant crime and other urban horrors. Poor Chepe is much maligned by just about everyone: you're hard pressed to find one among the 800,000 odd *Josefinos* willing to say much good about their city's pothole-scarred streets and car-dealership architecture, not to mention the choking black diesel fumes, kamikaze drivers and chaotically unplanned expansion. Travellers, meanwhile, talk about the city as they do about bank line-ups or immigration offices: it's a pain, but it's unavoidable. That said, however, while most visitors simply see the city in passing before heading out to Costa Rica's "real" attractions, for anyone with a little more time it is worth getting to know Chepe a bit better – many people even end up perversely fond of the place, modern malls, fast-food outlets, neon billboards and all.

San José has a sprinkling of excellent **museums** – some doubly memorable

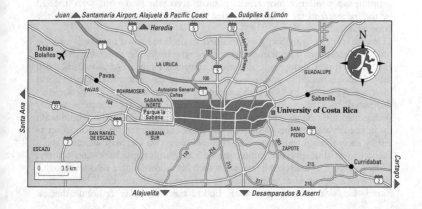

for their bizarre locations – a couple of elegant buildings and landscaped parks. Cafés and a few art galleries dot the streets and, occasionally, wandering around the leafy *barrios* of **Amón** and **Otoya**, with their colonial-era wooden houses, you could imagine yourself walking through the streets of an old European town. In the gridlocked **centre** things are more hectic, with vendors of fruit, lottery tickets and cigarettes jostling one another on street corners, and seemingly thousands of shoestores tumbling out onto sidewalks. Though you can sometimes sense an underlying order behind the chaos, walking around town means, more often than not, keeping your eyes glued to the ground to avoid stepping in deep open drains or in one of the boxes of multi-coloured clucking chicks sold by street-corner hopefuls. **Street crime** is on the rise, and pedestrians adopt the defensive posture (bags clutched securely, knapsacks worn on the front, determined facial expression) that you see in so many other big cities. All in all, walking in San José is a stressful experience, which is a shame, because exploring on foot is really the best way to get around.

Today, one in four Costa Ricans lives within the San José metropolitan area, and the capital is beginning to suffer from pressure on land due to the population density in the Valle Central and to rural migration. Most *Josefinos* live in the **suburbs**, now awash with the mega-supermarkets and American-style malls that have colonized San José in the last few years, though some districts, like comfortable **Escazú** and hip **San Pedro** (home to the campus of the University of Costa Rica), still merit a visit in their own right.

Some history

San José was established in 1737 at the insistence of the Catholic church in order to give a focal point to the scattered populace living in the area. For the next forty years, **Villa Nueva de la Boca del Monte**, as it was cumbersomely called, remained a muddy village of a few squalid adobe houses, until coffee was first planted in the Valle Central in 1821 (see p.121), triggering the settlement's expansion.

The single most crucial event in determining the city's future importance, however, was Central America's **declaration of independence** from the Spanish crown in 1821. Following the declaration, Mexico's self-proclaimed "emperor", General Agustín de Iturbide, ordered Costa Rica's immediate annexation, a demand which caused a rift between the citizens of Heredia and Cartago, who supported the move, and those of Alajuela and San José, who saw it for what it was: a panicky imperialist attempt to stifle Latin America's burgeoning independence movements. A short **civil war** broke out, won in 1823 by the *independentistas*, who moved the capital from Cartago to San José in the same year.

Despite its new status, San José remained a one-horse town until well into the nineteenth century. The framed sepia photographs in the venerable *Balcón de Europa* restaurant show wide dirt roads traversed by horse-drawn carts, with simple adobe buildings and a few spindly telegraph wires. Like the fictional town of Macondo in García Marquez's *One Hundred Years of Solitude*, this provincial backwater attracted piano-teaching European flotsam – usually young men looking to make their careers in the hinterland – who would wash up in the drawing rooms of the country's nascent bourgeoisie. Accounts written by early foreign tourists to San José, including two German scientists and a French journalist, give the impression of a tiny, stultifying backwater society: "The president of the republic has to sit with his followers on a wooden bench," they wrote, aghast, after attending a church service. In the city's houses they found dark-skinned young women, bound tight in white crinoline dresses, patiently conjugating French verbs, reflecting the degree to which Costa Rica's earliest cultural affiliations and aspirations lay with France. Even the mansions of former *finqueros* (coffee barons) in San José's Barrio Amón – especially the Alianza Francesa – resemble mansions in New Orleans or Port-au-Prince, with their delicate French ironwork, Moorish-influenced latticework, long, cool corridors of deep-blooded wood and brightly painted exteriors.

By the 1850s, fuelled largely by the tobacco boom, the city had acquired the trappings of bourgeois prosperity, with leafy parks, a few paved avenues and some fine examples of European-style architecture. Grand urban houses were built to accommodate the new class of burgeoning burghers, coffee middlemen and industrialists; these Europhile aspirations culminated in 1894 with the construction of the splendid **Teatro Nacional** – for which every molecule of material, as well as the finest craftsmen, were transported from Europe.

During the twentieth century, San José came to dominate nearly all aspects of the Costa Rican life. Not only the seat of government, since the 1970s it has become the Central American headquarters for many foreign non-governmental organizations, raising its international profile considerably. Multinationals, industry and agribusiness also started to base their national and regional offices here, creating what at times can seem to be a largely middle-class city, populated by an army of neatly suited, briefcase-toting office and embassy workers.

Arrival

Arrival in San José is straightforward, even if you don't speak Spanish, since all the machinery to get you into town is well oiled and there's less opportunistic theft than at most other Central and South American arrival points.

By air

Most international **flights** arrive at the modern new terminal at Juan Santamaría International Airport (℡ 441-0744), 17km northwest of San José and 3km southeast of Alajuela. The **ICT office** here (daily 8am–4pm; ℡ 442-1820 or 442-8542) can supply maps and give advice on accommodation. There's also a **correo** (Mon–Fri 8am–5pm), next to the departure tax window, and a **bank**, downstairs on the departure level (Mon–Fri 6.30am–6pm; Sat & Sun 7am–1pm); colones are not necessary for taxis, but you'll need them for the bus.

The best way to get into San José is by **taxi**, which takes about twenty minutes in light traffic and costs $12–14, depending what part of the city you are headed to. Official airport taxis are orange and line up outside the terminal. You'll have no problems getting a cab, as the drivers will stampede for your business when you're practically still in customs. Take a deep breath and make sure to agree the fare before you get in the cab. Some taxi drivers take travellers who haven't made accommodation bookings to hotels where they get commission – these might be more expensive than you were bargaining for, so be firm about where you want to go. Taxi drivers accept dollars as well as colones.

The Alajuela–San José **bus** (every 3min between 5am & 10pm; every 15min at other times) stops right outside the airport's undercover car park. Though it's much cheaper than a taxi, this is an intercity service and not really geared up for travellers, since there are no proper luggage racks inside and the buses are nearly always full – you can just about get away with it if you're carrying only a light backpack or small bag. Drivers will indicate which buses are on their way to San José (a 30min journey) and which to Alajuela. The fare is about 200 colones (about $0.75 – payable in local currency); pay the driver. The bus drops passengers in town at Av 2, C 12/14, where there are plenty of taxis around.

By bus

International buses from Nicaragua, Honduras, Guatemala and Panamá pull into the Ticabus station, Av 4, C 9/11 (ⓣ221-8954), next to the yellow Soledad church. Since buses can arrive at odd hours, you may want to take refuge at one of the 24-hour eating spots nearby on Av 2 before looking for a room. One of the cheapest is the *Casa del Sandwich* on the corner of C 9, and there's a taxi rank around the corner on Av 2 between C 5 and 9. Coming from Managua on Sirca, you'll arrive at the terminal at C 7, Av 6/8: taxis can be flagged down on C 7.

The closest thing San José has to a **domestic bus station** is **La Coca-Cola**, named after an old bottling plant that used to stand on the site five blocks west of the Mercado Central at Av 1/3, C 16/18 (the main entrance is on C 16). Buses arrive here from the north and west (including Monteverde), most of the beaches of the Nicoya Peninsula, Liberia and Puntarenas. The name La Coca-Cola not only applies to the station proper – which is quite small and the arrival point for only a few buses – but also the surrounding area, where many more buses pull in. Like many bus stations, La Coca-Cola is well on its way to being an unredeemed hellhole – noisy, hemmed in by small, confusing streets crammed with busy market traders, and invariably prowled by pickpockets. Lugging your bags and searching for your bus stop around here makes it very hard not to look like a confused gringo, thus increasing the chances that you'll become the target of opportunistic theft: best to arrive and leave in a taxi. Be especially careful of your belongings around the **Tilarán terminal** (C14, Av 9/11), which is also used by buses to Monteverde: people waiting here for the 6.30am bus to Monteverde seem to be particularly at risk of attempted theft.

For details on getting out of the city from La Coca-Cola, see "Moving on from San José" on p.109.

Information

San José's **ICT office** (Mon–Fri 9am–5pm; ⓣ223-1733, ⓕ223-5452, ⓦwww.tourism-costarica.com) is underneath the Plaza de la Cultura, C 5, Av 0/2. It has free maps, leaflets and binders in which you can check out photos of hotels before you book, and – most crucially – free leaflets detailing the national bus schedule. They also hand out the free monthly *Culture Calendar*, which details concerts and festivals throughout the country.

In addition, the Sistema Nacional de Areas de Conservación (National System of Conservation Areas), or SINAC, runs a free phone line giving information in English and Spanish about Costa Rica's **national parks** – call ⓣ192 Monday to Friday 8am to 5.30pm. They can provide information on individual parks, particularly about transport and camping facilities. Basic information about opening hours, entrance tariffs and an explanation of the national parks system can be found at ⓦwww.minae.go.cr/areas/sinac.htm. In San José you can get information, buy entrance tickets and make reservations for park shelters at the **Fundación de Parques Nacionales** office, Av 15, C 23/25, Barrio Escalante (℡ 257-2239, ℱ 222-4732, ℮ *azucena@ns.minae.go.cr*).

City transport

Once you've got used to the deep gutters and broken pavements, San José is easily negotiated **on foot**, and several blocks in the city centre around the Plaza de la Cultura have been completely pedestrianized. There is little need to take **buses** within the city centre, though the suburban buses are useful, particularly if you are heading out to Parque la Sabana, a thirty-minute walk west along Paseo Colón; to Escazú, twenty minutes' ride to the west; or to the University of Costa Rica and San Pedro, ten minutes' ride to the east.

Buses stop running after around 10–11pm and **taxis** become the best way to get around. These days street crime is noticeably on the rise, and most *Josefinos* advise against walking alone after dark, woman especially. Be especially wary, even during the day, in the streets around the Coca-Cola bus terminal and the Parque Central, Av 2 and the Plaza de la Cultura. A few places have a bad reputation day and night, including Barrio México in the northwest of the city and the red-light districts of C 12, Av 8/10, and Av 4/6, C 4/12, just southwest of the centre. The **dangers** are mainly mugging, purse-snatching or jewellery-snatching rather than serious assault, and many people walk around without encountering any problems at all. However, taxis are cheap enough that it is probably not worth taking the risk.

Buses

Fast, cheap and frequent buses connect the centre of the city with virtually all of San José's neighbourhoods and suburbs, and generally run from 5am until 10–11pm. **Bus stops** in the city centre area seem to change every year. Currently, most buses to San Pedro, Tres Ríos and other points east leave from the stretch of Avenida Central between C 5 and C 15. You can pick up buses for Paseo Colón and Parque Sabana (labelled "Sabana-Cementerio") at the bus shelters on Av 2, C 5/7. In an enlightened move, city authorities are hoping to

San José's street system and addresses

San José, along with all Costa Rican towns of any size, is planned on a grid system, intersected by an Avenida Central (later called Paseo Colón) which runs east–west, and a Calle Central, which runs north–south. From Av Central, parallel *avenidas* run to the north (odd numbers) and to the south (even numbers). From Calle Central, even-numbered calles run to the west and odd numbers to the east. Avenidas 8 and 9, therefore, are actually quite far apart. Similarly, Calles 23 and 24 are at opposite ends of the city. When you see bis (literally "encore" – again) in an address it denotes a separate street, usually a dead end (tell your taxi driver it's a *calle sin salida*), next to the *avenida* or *calle* to which it refers. Av 8 bis, for example, is between Av 8 and 10. "0" in addresses is shorthand for "Central": thus Av 0, C 11 is the same as Av Central, C 11.

Most times, locals – and especially taxi drivers – won't have a clue what you're talking about if you try to use street numbers to find an address. When possible, give directions in relation to local landmarks, buildings, businesses, parks or institutions. In addition, people use metres to signify distance: in local parlance 100 metres equals one city block.

Useful bus routes

The following is a rundown of the main inner-city routes, all of which stop along Av Central or Av 2 in the centre of town. If in doubt, ask "*¿dónde está la parada para...?*" ("Where is the stop for...?").

Sabana–Cementerio buses travel west along Paseo Colón to Parque Sabana, and are ideal for going to any of the shops, theatres and restaurants clustered around Paseo Colón, the Museo de Arte Costarricense or Parque Sabana.

Sabana–Estadio services run basically the same route, with a tour around Parque Sabana. Good for the neighbourhoods of Sabana norte and Sabana sur.

Sabanilla–Bethania buses run east through Los Yoses and beyond to the suburb of Sabanilla.

San Pedro (also **La U**) or **Tres Ríos** buses will also take you east through Los Yoses and on to the University of Costa Rica and the hip neighbourhood of San Pedro. Other buses serving San Pedro are: Vargas Araya, Santa Marta, Granadilla, Curridabat and Cedros.

move the bus stops out of the centre proper in order to cut traffic and pollution (most city buses belch an impressively black stream of diesel from their exhaust pipes).

All buses have their routes clearly marked on their windshields, and usually the **fare** too. These are payable either to the driver or his helper when you board and are usually 60 colones (25¢), though the faster, more comfortable *busetas de lujo* (luxury buses) to the suburbs, cost upwards of 80 colones (40¢). The traditional method of stopping the bus to get off is for men to whistle and women to call out *¡Parada!* (stop), but bus drivers have recently taken to putting up testy signs saying "los monos gritan, los pajaros silvan, por favor toca el timbre" ("monkeys yell, birds whistle, please use the bell").

Taxis

Taxis are cheap and plentiful, even at odd hours of the night and early morning. Licensed vehicles are red with a yellow triangle on the side, and have "SJP" ("San José Publico") licence plates. A ride anywhere within the city will cost $1–1.5, and about double that to get out to the suburbs. The starter fare – about $0.50 – is shown on the red digital read-out, and you should always make sure that the meter is on before you start (ask the driver to *toca la maría, por favor*). Some drivers may claim that the meter doesn't work – if this is the case, it's best either to agree a fare before you start out or find another taxi whose meter is working. Many drivers are honest – don't immediately assume everyone's trying to cheat you. After midnight, taxis from the El Pueblo centre charge forty percent extra. These are institutionalized higher fares, and you shouldn't attempt to negotiate. Tipping is not expected.

By car and bike

There's no need to **rent a car** specifically for getting around San José – indeed, most Ticos advise foreigners against driving in the city, at least until they're familiar with the aggressive local style of driving. In addition, most of the city's streets are one-way, though sometimes unmarked as such, and cars left on the street anywhere near the city centre are almost guaranteed to be broken into or stolen. Secure **parqueos** (guarded parking lots) dot the city; if you do rent a car, use them. Check their opening times, however, as although some are 24-hour, most close at 8 or 8.30pm. If you have to leave your car on the street, most areas have a man whose job is to guard the cars – look for the fellow with the truncheon and expect to pay around 300 colones. If driving in the centre of the city, keep your windows rolled up and your doors locked so no one can reach in. For a list of car **rental companies**, see p.31.

It's generally not a good idea to **cycle** in San José. Diesel fumes, potholes and un-cycle-conscious drivers don't make for pleasant cycling. although riding in the suburbs or Parque la Sabana is easier and less hazardous to your health.

Accommodation

After a period of rapid growth – and high prices – in the hotel business during the tourism boom of the early 1990s, San José is at last getting more quality hotel rooms, with fairer prices in all categories, although characterful, friendly and good-value budget-to-moderate options are still elusive. Rock-bottom hotels tend, with a few exceptions, to be depressing cells that make the city seem infinitely more ugly than it is. The other recent major accommodation event in San José has been the arrival of international **hotel chains**, many of whose names – *Radisson*, *Holiday Inn* and *Best Western* – will be familiar to North Americans and Europeans. While some are comfortable and have an excellent service, they don't offer much in the way of local colour. It's also worth noting that while these hotels employ Costa Ricans, most of their profits are repatriated to the company's home country, and at least one of these chains – *Barceló* – has been repeatedly accused of infringing the country's environmental laws.

Accommodation price codes

All the accommodation in this book has graded using the following price codes. The prices quoted are for the least expensive double room in high season, and do not include the 18.46 percent national tax which is automatically added onto hotel bills. For more details on accommodation in Costa Rica, see p.35.

❶ less than $10	❷ $10–20
❸ $20–30	❹ $30–50
❺ $50–75	❻ $75–100
❼ $100–150	❽ over $150

If you are coming in **high season** (Dec–May), and especially over busy periods like Christmas and Easter, be prepared to reserve (and, in some cases, even pay) in advance – places that require money in advance may give you a bank account number in Costa Rica for you to wire money to. Room **rates** vary dramatically between high and low seasons – the prices we quote are for a double room in peak season, and you can expect to get substantial discounts at less busy times.

Many of San José's rock-bottom hotels have cold-water showers only. Unless you're very tough, you'll want some form of **heated water**, as San Jose can get chilly, especially from December to March. At the budget end of the spectrum, so-called "hot" water is actually often no more than a tepid trickle, produced by one of the eccentric electric contraptions you'll find fitted over showers throughout the country (see Basics, p.35) – it's still better than cold water, however.

Central San José

Though staying in one of the budget hotels in the **city centre** is convenient, the downside is noise and pollution – Avenida 2 and parts of Avenidas 1, 3 and

Staying with a Costa Rican family

There's no better way to learn about life off the tourist trail and to practise your Costa Rican Spanish than staying with a Tico family. Usually enjoyable, sometimes transformative, this can be a fantastic experience, and at the very least is sure to provide some genuine contact with Costa Ricans.

One of the better established "B&B with a family" organizations in San José is Turcasa (℡ 258-3881, ℻ 258-3865, Ⓦ www.microempresa.co.cr/sertico), which offers three categories of accommodation, from A to C, ranging from $12 to $18 a night. A is the "*Lujosa*" (luxury) option, which usually gets you private bath, TV and phone; B means that you will share a bathroom with other guests, while C gets you a bathroom shared with your host family. Most of the homes are in San Pedro, Montes de Oca and Guadaloupe (east of the city). Tell Turcasa if you have any special needs, and they will do their best to find a family that suits you (and whom you suit). Restrictions are few, and vary according to the household. Stays can last anything from week to a month, and many travellers use the family home as a base while touring the country. You'll have your own key, but in most cases it would be frowned upon if you brought someone home for the night. The one rule that always applies is that guests and hosts communicate in Spanish.

Another recommended organization is Bell's Home Hospitality (℡ 225-4752, ℻ 224-5884, Ⓦ www.ilisa.com/bells), run by a long-time resident of Costa Rica, Vernon Bell, and his wife Marcela, who arrange for individuals, couples and families to stay in private rooms in a family home, with private or shared bath. Breakfast is included in the price, with evening meals and airport transfers available for a small additional cost. The Bells also run tours, mostly day-trips, to places like Volcán Poás, Sarchí and even one-day island cruises.

Other points of contact for homestays as well as longer-term apartment rentals and houseshares include adverts in the *Tico Times* – although homestays and flats listed here tend to be expensive – and the (Spanish) classifieds in *La Nación*. Language schools may be able to put you in contact with a family even if you are not a student at the school in question, while the bulletin boards at the University of Costa Rica work well for students who want to live with a family or share with other students. In the last case, however, you are more likely to be sharing with fellow foreigners – it's very hard to find an apartment or house-share with Tico students, as most of them live at home while going to university.

★ **BUS STOPS**

Alajuela, Volcan Poás & International Airport	**M**
Cahuita, Puerto Viejo de Talamanca & Sixaola	**A**
Cartago	**O**
Golfito	**E**
Guápiles	**A**
Liberia & Playa del Coco	**F & K**
Limón	**A**
Los Chiles & Zarcero	**C**
Nicoya, Sámara & Tamarindo	**G**
Peñas Blancas & La Cruz	**H**
Playa Hermosa & Playa Panamá	**I**
Puerto Jiménez	**B**
Puntarenas	**N**
Río Frío & Puerto Viejo de Sarapiquí	**A**
Santa Cruz & North Guanacaste Beaches	**L**
San Isidro de El General	**J**
Tilarán & Monteverde	**D**

5 can be noisy, but this is not a hard-and-fast rule, as the city authorities seem to like to change bus routes (the source of most street noise) every few years. The very cheapest rooms are in the insalubrious area immediately around La Coca-Cola, and while there are a couple of clean and well-run budget places here, the area is generally best avoided unless you've got an early bus to catch or are an aficionado of seedy hotels.

Not too far from downtown, in quieter areas such as **Paseo Colón**, **Los Yoses** and **Barrios Amón** and **Otoya**, is a group of more expensive hotels, many of them in old colonial homes.

Budget

B&B Costa Rica, Av 2, C 29, 50m south of *Kentucky Fried Chicken* (☎ 253-4166, ⨍ 225-8527, ⓔ iespcr@racsa.co.cr). Small, super-value hotel a bit out of the centre but on bus routes to San Pedro, run by a friendly family who also organize a Spanish school (ⓦ www.professionalspanish.com). Prices include breakfast and tax; single rooms ($15) are particularly good value. ❸

Bellavista, Av 0, C 19/21 (☎ 223-0095). Friendly place, with lively murals depicting scenes from *Caribeña* life and prices which offer rare good value this close to the centre. Rooms are a bit dark and musty, and walls are thin, but all have private bath with hot water, and ceiling fans do what they can to provide a semblance of fresh air. It's close to the Limón bus stop, and rooms at the front get bad noise from buses. ❸

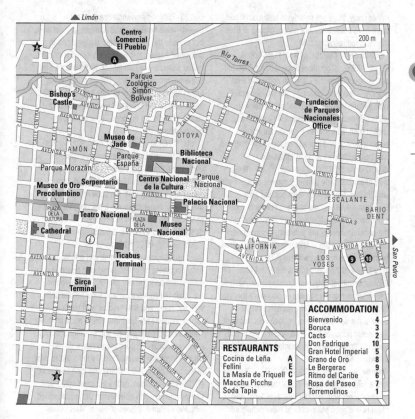

Map labels: Limón, Centro Comercial El Pueblo, Río Torres, Parque Zoológico Simón Bolívar, Bishop's Castle, AVENIDA 13, AVENIDA 11, AVENIDA 9, AVENIDA 5, AMÓN, Museo de Jade, Parque España, OTOYA, AV 11 BIS, AVENIDA 15, AVENIDA 13, AVENIDA 11, AVENIDA 9, AVENIDA 7, Fundacion de Parques Nacionales Office, Biblioteca Nacional, Parque Morazán, Museo de Oro Precolumbino, Serpentario, Centro Nacional de la Cultura, Parque Nacional, AVENIDA 3, ESCALANTE, AVENIDA 5, BARIO DENT, PLAZA DE LA CULTURA, Teatro Nacional, Palacio Nacional, AVENIDA CENTRAL, PLAZA DE LA DEMOCRACIA, Museo Nacional, AVENIDA 1, AVENIDA 3, Cathedral, LA CALIFORNIA, AVENIDA 2, LOS YOSES, AVENIDA CENTRAL, San Pedro, 9, 10, Ticabus Terminal, AVENIDA 6, AVENIDA 8, Sirca Terminal, AV 10 BIS, AVENIDA 10, AVENIDA 12, AVENIDA 14, AVENIDA 16, CALLE CENTRAL

0 — 200 m

ACCOMMODATION

Bienvenido	4
Boruca	3
Cacts	2
Don Fadrique	10
Gran Hotel Imperial	5
Grano de Oro	8
Le Bergerac	9
Ritmo del Caribe	6
Rosa del Paseo	7
Torremolinos	1

RESTAURANTS

Cocina de Leña	A
Fellini	E
La Masía de Triquell	C
Macchu Picchu	B
Soda Tapia	D

Bienvenido, C 10, Av 1/3 (☏ 233-2161, ☏ 221-1872). One of the best downtown budget options, this family-run establishment has small clean rooms with private bath, and friendly staff who are particularly helpful with bus timetables and can arrange tours, but do not push to sell them to you. Near La Coca-Cola, it's great if you want to catch an early bus, though the area is a bit dodgy. Credit cards accepted – unusual in this category. ❷

Boruca, C 14, Av 1/3 (☏ 223-0016, ☏ 232-0107). Central, basic and rather charmless hotel in the Coca-Cola district with small, musty and dark rooms – it's very cheap and clean, though, and has a secure atmosphere and friendly family management. ❶

Casa Leo, Av 6 bis, C 13/15 (☏ 222-9725). A good alternative if the *Casa Ridgway* (see below) is full, this small guesthouse has dorms ($9 per person in a mixed-sex dorm) and basic private rooms (❸) with shared bath and kitchen – all spotlessly

clean and good value. The house can be hard to find; look for it next to the train tracks and tell your taxi driver it's a *calle sin salida*.

Casa Ridgway, C 15, Av 6/8 (☏ 233-6168 or 221-8299, ☏ 224-8910). Near the Ticabus stop, this homely Quaker guesthouse is San José's best budget option and a great place to meet other travellers. Accommodation includes clean single-sex dorms ($10 per person), plus private singles ($12) and triples ($20) with communal bathrooms (there are no doubles), and there's also a shared kitchen, laundry and luggage storage – note that alcohol is banned and there's a "quiet time" after 10pm. Reserve ahead in high season, and try not to arrive after 8pm, except by prior arrangement.

Gran Hotel Imperial, C 8, Av 0/1 (☏ 222-7899). Near the bus station, the dark and frankly scary entrance belies a secure but basic hotel, popular with backpackers and offering some of the cheapest rooms in San José. The downside is that it's rather noisy, there are no private bathrooms, and there have been reports of people getting ill from the attached restaurant. ❶

Pensión de la Cuesta, Av 1, C 11/15 (☎ & ℻ 255-2896, ✉ ggmnber@racsa.co.cr). Tranquil and good-value rooms – though some are a bit gloomy – in a pink, colonial-style wooden house, with a plant-filled lounge area, gold masks on walls and decorated bedsteads. All rooms have shared bath, plus there's a communal kitchen, laundry service and luggage storage, and staff can also help with tours and car rental. ❸

Ritz, C 0, Av 8/10 (☎ 222-4103, ℻ 222-8849). Very clean and fairly large (25 rooms) central hotel with its own tour service – it's popular with European travellers, and is a good place to meet other backpackers. Management is friendly and the communal areas are pleasant, though rooms are rather dark – those with private bath (❸) are twice the price of those without (❷).

Tica Linda, C 7, Av 6/8 (☎ & ℻ 222-4402). Venerable budget hotel, newly refurbished, with fairly spacious single, double or dormitory rooms, all with shared hot showers, kitchen, and TV. Despite the upgrade, manager José Luis has kept the lowest prices in San José, and the place continues to draw friendly backpackers from around the world. ❶

Toruma, Av 0, C 29/31 (☎ & ℻ 224-4085). Costa Rica's main HI hostel (see p.37), this beautiful establishment with Neoclassical exterior and high ceilings is a good place both to meet people and to make onward hostel, tour and travel reservations. Accommodation is in single-sex dorms ($10 per person for HI members, $13 for non-members – membership is available at the front desk) and a few singles, and there's also luggage storage, a safe, laundry. Book well in advance in high season. Non-smoking.

Moderate

Ara Macao, C 25 bis, Av 0/2, 50m south of *Pizza Hut* in Barrio La California (☎ 233-2742, ℻ 257-6228, ⓦ www.hotels.co.cr/aramacao.html). Small and pleasant B&B with nine rooms and three apartments for longer stays, just outside the city centre, but near the restaurants of Barrio California and Los Yoses. Rooms are airy and have private bath and cable TV. Longer stays are possible: weekly rates are $273 single, $329 double. Breakfast included. ❹–❺

Aranjuez, C 19, Av 11/13 (☎ 256-1825, from the US & Canada call toll-free 1-877/898-8663,

℻ 223-3528, ⓦ www.hotelaranjuez.com). Superb-value hotel in Barrio Aranjuez, a quiet area, but close to the centre. Rooms are arranged in converted houses that have been joined with communal sitting areas throughout, and there's a pretty garden around the back. The 23 rooms either have shared bath (❸) or private bath and TV (❹), and a good buffet breakfast and free local phone calls and email are included. It's often full, so reserve ahead.

Cacts, C 28–30, Av 3 bis (☎ 221-2928, ℻ 221-8616, ⓦ www.tourism.co.cr/hotels/cacts/cacts.htm). Small, quiet and spotless hotel with sunny roof terrace, swimming pool and Jacuzzi. All rooms have ceiling fans, hot shower and TV, and the friendly owners also run a travel agency and can help with tours and reservations. ❹

Casa Hilda, Av 11, C 3 & 3 bis, house no. 353 (☎ 221-0037, ℻ 221-2881, ✉ c1hilda@racsa.co.cr). Small and affordable hotel occupying an old-style wooden house in a quiet street near the city centre. The five rooms are basic but comfortable and have private bath with hot water and fan – rooms with outside-facing windows are best; the others are a bit dark. There's also a patio garden and communal sitting areas with cable TV. Good single rates. ❸–❹

Cinco Hormigas Rojas, C 15, Av 9/11, 200m east of the back of the INS building and then 25m north (☎ 257-8581). Small, quirky but good-value B&B in a private house in quiet Barrio Otoya, decorated with the vibrant paintings of owner Mayra Güell. The bright rooms have shared bath only. Breakfast included. No smoking. ❹

Don Carlos, C 9, Av 7 & 9 (☎ 221-6707, ℻ 255-0828, ⓦ www.doncarlos.co.cr). Elegant landmark hotel filled with replicas of pre-Colombian art and a lovely kitsch breakfast terrace/cocktail lounge with fountain and a pretty tiled mural of the city hand-painted by renowned Costa Rican artist Mario Aroyabe. All rooms have cable TV and safe (some also have private patios) and there's free internet access, plus an excellent souvenir shop and travel agency. ❺

Edelweiss, Av 9, C 13/15 (☎ 221-9702, ℻ 222-1241, ⓦ www.edelweisshotel.com). Small, quiet hotel, situated in pretty Barrio Amón, with clean rooms (all with cable TV), wooden floors and piping hot showers, plus the use of a computer and safe. The excellent *Café Mundo* restaurant is just across the street. Breakfast included. ❹

Europa, C 0, Av 3/5 (☎ 222-1222, ℻ 221-3976, ✉ europa@racsa.co.cr). Good-value mid-range downtown hotel, with a restaurant, bar, indoor pool, and lots of bright communal areas. Outside rooms tend to get street noise but are lighter. Inside rooms are quieter but are less airy. There's a helpful tour desk inside the hotel with good contacts throughout the country. ⑤

Gran Hotel Costa Rica, Av 0/2, C 3 (℡ 221-4000, ℻ 221-3501). Smack in the middle of town, this dowager hotel has a wide variety of spotlessly clean but rather unimaginatively furnished rooms – some are enormous, some are small, though all have TV, phone and 24-hour room service. The location – looking out over the Plaza de la Cultura, and with a popular terrace café below – can be noisy. Discounts are often available in low season. ⑤

La Amistad, Av 11, C 13 (℡ 258-0021, ℻ 221-1407, Ⓦ www.centralamerica.com/cr/hotel/amistad.htm). Good-value hotel in a large house in historic Barrio Otoya. All 32 rooms have cable TV, phone, private bath and queen-sized beds; there are also seven de luxe rooms with a/c and two apartments ($95 for 4 people) with a/c. Upstairs rooms in the original house are quieter. Good single rates ($29). Breakfast included. ④–⑤

La Gema, Av 12, C 9/11 (℡ 257-2524, ℻ 222-1074). South of the centre in a relatively quiet area, this small, light hotel surrounds an open courtyard planted with leafy trees. Rooms are good, though walls are a bit thin – the sunnier upstairs rooms are best. ④

La Rosa del Paseo, Paseo Colón, C 28/30 (℡ 257-3213, ℻ 223-2776). Converted turn-of-the-century house on busy Paseo Colón. Rooms have nice touches – sparkling bathrooms, wooden floors and Victorian fittings – and all come with private bath and cable TV; those with a/c (not really necessary) are on the expensive side at $90; no single rates. Breakfast included. ⑤

Ritmo del Caribe, Paseo Colón, C 32/34 (℡ & ℻ 256-1636). Converted modern house with nicely decorated, good-value singles and doubles, some with TV and balcony; double-glazed windows mean those at the front suffer less from Paseo Colón's round-the-clock traffic. A tasty German breakfast is included, and the helpful owners can advise on tours and travel. ④

Santo Tomás, Av 7, C 3/5 (℡ 255-0448, ℻ 222-3950, Ⓦ www.hotelsantotomas.com). One of San José's best boutique hotels, located in quiet and elegant Barrio Amón, conveniently close to downtown. The hotel occupies an old mansion house decorated with burnished wood, Persian rugs and

soft lighting. Rooms vary widely in size, character and price, though all have TV and telephone, and there's also a gift shop and free internet and email access. ⑤

Vesuvio, Av 11, C 13/15 (℡ & ℻ 221-7586). What this place lacks in decor (long, institutional corridors) it makes up for by being quiet, central and affordable, with friendly management, secure parking and an attached bar-restaurant. Rooms are a bit claustrophobic, though all come with fan, TV, phone and private bath with hot water. Breakfast included. ⑤

Expensive

Brittania, corner of Av 11, C 13 (℡ 223-6667, ℻ 223-6411, Ⓔ britania@racsa.co.cr). Elegant fin-de-siecle mansion-house hotel in Barrio Amón, with large, airy and expensively furnished sitting areas. Standard doubles are located in a new annexe; the more appealing (and expensive) de luxe rooms are located in the original house. All rooms have cable TV and minibar; some also have a/c. There's also a good restaurant in the former wine cellar. Breakfast included. ⑥–⑦

Casa Verde de Amón, corner of C 7 & Av 9 (℡ & ℻ 223-0969, Ⓔ casaverde@racsa.co.cr). Set in a historic turn-of-the century mansion house, this quiet and beautifully restored hotel is loaded with antiques and oriental rugs. Rooms and suites are well furnished, with wooden floors and fittings – some even have Victorian bathtubs. Prices are very reasonable, particularly in low season, and there are weekly discounts. Rooms ⑤, suites ⑦.

Don Fadrique, C 37, Av 8, Los Yoses (℡ 225-8166, ℻ 224-9746, Ⓔ fadrique@centralamerica.com). Upmarket but good-value hotel with restaurant and bar, located in the former home of Don Fadrique Gutierrez, early twentieth-century architect, general and philosopher. The hotel's halls are hung with Costa Rican art, and each of the twenty nicely furnished rooms comes with TV and private bath with hot water. Good low-season discounts. Breakfast included. ⑥

Fleur de Lys, C 13, Av 2/6 (℡ 223-1206, ℻ 257-3637, Ⓦ www.hotelfleurdelys.com). Friendly mansion-house hotel in a pleasant and fairly quiet part of downtown, near the Ticabus stop and the National Museum. Each floor has a sunny and plant-filled atrium, and there's also a recommended restaurant and small bar. Rooms vary: some are a bit dark, some have a bathtub. Good low-season rates (⑤), and under-12s stay free, though high-season prices (⑦) are a bit expensive.

Grano de Oro, C 30, Av 2/4 (℡ 255-3322, ℻ 221-2782, ⓦ www.hotelgranodeoro.com). Elegant converted mansion in a quiet area west of the centre, with 35 comfortable rooms and suites furnished in faux-Victorian-style, with wrought-iron beds and polished wooden floors – they're popular with honeymooners and older Americans. All rooms have cable TV, minibar, phone and fax. An excellent breakfast is served in the highly recommended restaurant. ⑥–⑦

Le Bergerac, C 35, Av 0 (℡ 234-7850, ℻ 225-9103). For luxury without the price tag, this elegant and relaxing top-end hotel is a good bet. The eighteen spacious rooms all have cable TV and phone, and some also have their own private gardens. A superb French restaurant, L'Ile de France, is prettily set in an interior courtyard. Continental breakfast included. ⑤–⑥

Torremolinos, C 40, Av 5 bis (℡ 222-5266, ℻ 255-3167). Now part of the Melia hotel chain, this good-value hotel is in a quiet area just two blocks from Parque la Sabana. Rooms are smallish but nicely furnished, and all have TV, radio and telephone; a/c (not really necessary) costs more. Facilities include a nice pool, Jacuzzi, gym and sauna, and there's a good bar and restaurant too. Good low-season discounts. ⑥

San Pedro and Escazú

Within a ten- to fifteen-minute bus ride either side of the city centre, the suburbs of Escazú and San Pedro are also worth considering as places to stay. To the west of the city is **Escazú**, the stamping ground of American expats, and popularly known as "Gringolandia". The vast majority of B&Bs here are owned by foreign nationals, with higher prices than elsewhere in town. Street names and addresses are particularly confusing in this area: best call ahead to get clear directions or to arrange to be picked up. East of the city and closer to the centre is studenty **San Pedro**, with better connections to downtown and a more cosmopolitan atmosphere. It's a great place to stay, but unfortunately there are only a couple of hotels in the area.

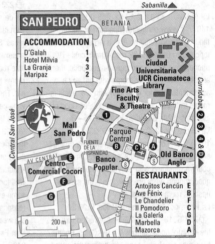

San Pedro

D'galah, opposite the University of Costa Rica, in front of the Facultad de Farmacía (℡ 234-1743). A bit characterless from the outside, though inside there are two plant-filled courtyards, a small swimming pool and bright, quiet and fairly spacious rooms, some with kitchenette (about $10 more). Well priced, and ideal if you want to be near the university. ④

La Granja, off Av 0 in Barrio La Granja, San Pedro, 50m south of the *antiguo higuerón* – the former site of a now disappeared tree which still serves as a local landmark (℡ & ℻ 225-1073). Great budget hotel in a family house with a pretty garden, near the university, bars and restaurants. Most rooms have shared showers. Also has some cheap singles ($12), a TV lounge, communal kitchen and laundry service. ②

Maripaz, 350m southeast of the *antiguo higuerón* tree (℡ & ℻ 253-8456, ⓔ maripaz@racsa.co.cr). Small (5 rooms) B&B in the home of a welcoming Costa Rican family, located in a quiet and pleasant area close to the university and several language schools. Rooms are either with private or shared bath. ③–④

Milvia, 250m northeast of the Muñoz y Nanne supermarket (℡ 225-4543, ℻ 225-7801). One of the city's best-value mid-range hotels, housed in a lovely old historic house in a residential area, beautifully decorated in a variety of styles, including colourful *Caribeña*. There's a soothing fountain, garden, sun terrace and mountain views, plus TV lounge and games room. Lunch and dinner available on request. ❺

Escazú

Casa de las Tias, San Rafael de Escazú (☎ 289-5517, ℻ 289-7353). Quiet, friendly and atmospheric place, with individually decorated rooms complete with private bath and hot water. No under-12s allowed. ❺–❻

Park Place B&B, on the left-hand side of the road up Escazú hill (☎ 228-9200, ℻ 289-8638). Small, nicely decorated B&B with lounge, fireplace, communal kitchen, and a good view from the upstairs verandah. No children allowed. ❹

Posada del Bosque, Belo Horizonte de Escazú (☎ 228-1164, ℻ 228-2006). Very quiet, homely place, in large landscaped grounds, with comfortable no-smoking rooms with shared bath. The friendly owners can arrange tennis, swimming and horse-riding in the area. ❺

Posada El Quijote, Bello Horizonte de Escazú (☎ 289-8401, ℻ 289-8729, ℮ quijote@racsa.co.cr). Eight spacious rooms, all renovated in the style of a Spanish colonial manor and comfortably furnished with bath, hot water and cable TV. Breakfast is served in the lovely garden. ❺

Around San José

Best Western Irazú, off the Autopista General Cañas between San Jose and the airport (☎ 232-4811, in the US 1-800/272-6654, ℻ 231-6485). Big, reasonably priced rooms with TV, telephone, and all the facilities of a resort hotel – swimming pool, sauna, tennis court, restaurants and bars, and a rather tacky casino. If you want to escape San José it's as good a bet as any of the large hotels. Discounts are possible, especially in low season, and there's a free shuttle bus into the city and a daily shuttle service to its sister Best Western at Jacó Beach (see p.332). ❺

Camino Real, 2km north of Escazú, near the Multiplaza shopping centre (☎ 289-7000, ℻ 289-8930, ℮ caminoreal@ticonet.co.cr). If you like big fancy hotels, this is one of the best, with a large pool, pool bar, sauna, gym, two restaurants and a free shuttle bus into town, while rooms come with piping-hot water, cable TV and phone. It doesn't come cheap, however. ❽

Kalexma B&B, in La Uruca, 10min from the airport and city centre (☎ 290-2624, ℻ 232-0115, ℗ www.kalexma.com). The twelve good-value rooms have either shared or private bath (about $5–10 more), plus there's a communal kitchen, two TV lounges and laundry service. Staff can help with arranging transport, tours, Spanish classes and language-based homestays. Breakfast included. ❷ without bathroom, ❹ with bathroom.

The City

Few travellers come to San José for the sights, and going by first impressions it's easy to see why. San José is certainly not a place that exudes immediate appeal, with its nondescript buildings and aggressive street life full of umbrella-wielding pedestrians, narrow streets, noisy food stalls and homicidal drivers. Scratch the surface, though, and you'll find a civilized city, with plenty of places to walk, sit, eat, meet people, go dancing and enjoy museums and galleries. It's also relatively manageable, without the chaos and crowds that plague most other Latin American cities; all the attractions are close together, and everything of interest can be covered in a couple of days.

Of the city's museums, the exemplary **Museo de Oro Precolombino** and the **Museo de Jade**, which houses the Americas' largest collection of the precious stone, are the major draws. Less visited, the **Museo Nacional** offers a brutally honest description of the country's colonization and some interesting archeological finds, while the **Museo de Arte y Diseño Contemporáneo** displays some of the most striking work in the Americas. San José is also a surprisingly green and open city, with paved-over plazas and small, carefully landscaped parks punctuating the centre of town.

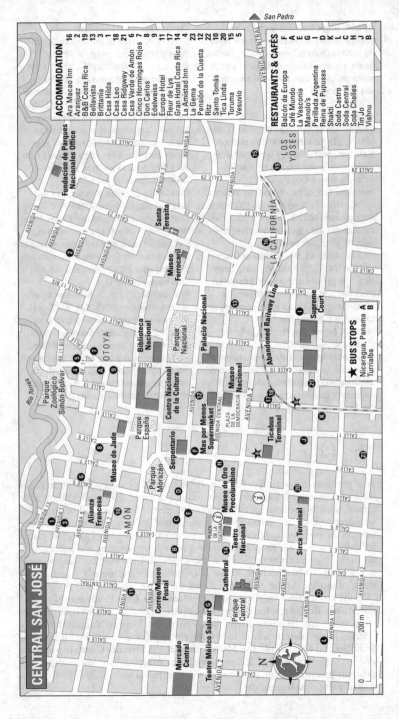

San Pedro

CENTRAL SAN JOSÉ

ACCOMMODATION

Ara Macao Inn	16
Aranjuez	2
B&B Costa Rica	19
Bellavista	13
Brittania	3
Casa Hilda	1
Casa Leo	18
Casa Ridgway	21
Casa Verde de Amón	6
Cinco Hormingas Rojas	7
Don Carlos	8
Edelweiss	9
Europa Hotel	11
Fleur de Lys	17
Gran Hotel Costa Rica	14
La Amistad Inn	4
La Gema	23
Pensión de la Cuesta	12
Ritz	10
Santo Tomás	20
Tica Linda	15
Toruma	5
Vesuvio	

RESTAURANTS & CAFÉS

Balcón de Europa	F
Café Mundo	A
La Vasconia	E
Manolo's	G
Parillada Argentina	I
Reina de Pupusas	D
Shakti	K
Soda Castro	L
Soda Central	C
Soda Chelles	H
Tin Jo	J
Vishnu	B

★ BUS STOPS

Nicaragua, Panama **A**
Turrialba **B**

Fundación de Parques
Nacionales Office

Santa
Teresita

Museo
Ferrocaril

Biblioteca
Nacional

Parque
Nacional

Palacio Nacional

Supreme
Court

Abandoned Railway Line

LA CALIFORNIA

LOS
YOSES

OTOYA

Parque
Zoológico
Simón Bolívar

Río Torres

Museo de Jade

Parque España

Centro Nacional
de la Cultura

Alianza
Francesa

AMÓN

Serpentario

Mas por Menos
Supermarket

Museo
Nacional

Ticabus
Terminal

Parque
Morazán

Museo de Oro
Precolumbino

Sirca Terminal

Mercado
Central

Correo/Museo
Postal

Teatro Mélico Salazar

Cathedral

Teatro
Nacional

PLAZA
DE LA
CULTURA

Parque
Central

PLAZA
DE LA
DEMOCRACIA

AVENIDA CENTRAL

N

0   200 m

The centre itself is subdivided into little neighbourhoods (*barrios*) that flow seamlessly in and out of one another: **Barrios Amón** and **Otoya**, in the north, are the prettiest, lined with the genteel mansions of former coffee barons, while further out, **La California** and **Los Yoses** are home to the *Toruma* youth hostel, most of the embassies and the Centro Cultural Costarricense Norteamericano.

Parque Central

As good a point as any to start a tour of San José is the **Parque Central**, Av 2, C 0/2, a landscaped park punctuated by tall royal palms and centring on a weird Gaudí-esque bandstand. Less frantic than many of the city's squares, it's a nice place to snack on the lychee-like *mamones chinos* or papaya bought from one of the fruit vendors nearby. Directly in front of the Parque Central looms the huge columnar exterior of the **Catedral Metropolitaneo**, newly restored but of little interest inside. The northeast corner is marked by the Neoclassical **Teatro Melico Salazar**, one of Costa Rica's premier theatres, second only to the Teatro Nacional a few blocks further east. The shows (see p.105) here are touristy but well worthwhile. Turning the corner leads to the barely contained hubbub of C 2 and its assorted electronics and shoe shops. One block further on, you'll come to the pleasant, pedestrianized **Avenida Central**, a narrow east–west thoroughfare lined with useful department stores (Universal has a particularly good book department), the cavernous book–stationery shop Librería Lehmann and, further down, a clutch of fast-food outlets.

Plaza de la Cultura

The central **Plaza de la Cultura**, on Av Central at C 3/5, is one of the few places in San José where you can sit at a pleasant outdoor café – the *Café Parisienne,* under the arches of the *Gran Hotel Costa Rica* – and watch the world go by. The plaza's northern edge is taken up by the imposing *Gran Hotel Costa Rica*, while the elegant Neoclassical Teatro Nacional dominates its eastern side. The noisy, ever-busy Avenida 2 marks the plaza's southern border.

Museo de Oro Precolombino

The Plaza de la Cultura cleverly conceals one of San José's treasures, the **Museo de Oro Precolombino**, or Pre-Columbian Gold Museum (Tues–Sat 10am–4pm; $4). The bunker-like underground space is unprepossessing, but the gold on display is truly impressive – all the more extraordinary if you take into account the relative paucity of pre-Columbian artefacts in Costa Rica (compared with Mexico, say, or Guatemala). The exquisitely delicate work on show here is almost entirely the work of the **Diquis** master goldsmiths, ancient inhabitants of southwestern Costa Rica.

Objects are cleverly hung on transparent wires, giving them the impression of floating in space, suspended mysteriously in their perspex cases. Most of the pieces are small and unbelievably detailed, with a preponderance of disturbing, evil-looking **animals**. Information panels (Spanish only) suggest that the chief function of these portents of evil – frogs, snakes and insects – was shamanic. The *ave de rapiña*, or bird of prey, seems to have had particular religious relevance for the Diquis: there are tons of them here, hawks, owls and eagles, differing only fractionally in shape and size. Watch out, too, for angry-looking arachnids, ready to bite or sting; jaguars and alligators carrying the pathetic dangling legs of human victims in their mouths; grinning bats with wings

Costa Rican gold

Little, if anything, is known of the early prehistory of the Diquis, who were responsible for most of the work you see at the Museo de Oro Precolombino. However, the history of gold-working in the New World is fairly well documented. It was first recorded (around 2000 BC) in Peru, from where it spread northwards, reaching Mexico and the Central American isthmus by 700–900 AD. All the ancient American peoples favoured more or less the same methods and styles, using a gold-copper alloy (called *tumbaga*) and designs featuring extremely intricate shapings, with carefully rendered facial expressions and a preference for ingenious but rather diabolical-looking zoomorphic representations – growling peccaries, threatening birds of prey, and a two-headed figure, each mouth playing its own flute. Many of these objects show no sign of having been worn – there are no grooves in the pendant links to indicate they were worn on chains – and were, archeologists believe, intended for ceremonial burial. Some were even "killed" or ritually mutilated before being entombed.

The Diquis would have obtained the gold by panning in rivers, and it is speculated that in Osa, at least, the rivers routinely washed up gold at their feet. Diquis *caciques* (chiefs) and other social elites used their gold in the same way it is used today – to advertise wealth and social prestige. Ornaments and insignias were often reserved for the use of a particular *cacique* and his family, and these special pieces were traded as truce offerings and political gifts between various rulers, maintaining contacts between the *caciques* of distant regions.

Although the Diquis were the undisputed masters of design, archeological digs in the Reventazón valley suggest that gold-working could also be found among the peoples of the Atlantic watershed zone. When Columbus first came ashore in 1502, he saw the local (Talamancan) peoples wearing gold mirror-pendants and headbands and rashly assumed he had struck it rich – hence the country's name. An early document of a subsequent expedition to the Caribbean coastal region of Costa Rica, now housed in archives in Cartago, contains the impressions of native wealth recorded by one gold-crazed Spaniard in Diego de Sojo's 1587 expedition: "The rivers abound with gold . . . and the Indians extract gold with calabashes in very large grains . . . from these same hills Captain Muñoz . . . took from the tombs of the dead . . . such a great quantity of gold as to swell two large chests of the kind in which shoes and nails for the cavalry are brought over from Castile."

spread; turtles, crabs, frogs, iguanas and armadillos; and a few spiny, unmistakable lobsters. The only fish in evidence is the shark. In addition to the animal representations, bell pendants are also common, with two round spheres ("bells") dangling from little squares of gold.

Sharing the building, the marginally interesting **Museo de Moneda** (free with admission to Gold Museum) displays a collection of Costa Rican coins – look out for the old five-colón note, decorated with a delicate, brightly coloured panorama of Costa Rican society.

Teatro Nacional

Reputedly designed as miniature version of the Paris Opéra, San José's heavily colonnaded, grey-brown **Teatro Nacional** sits on the corner of C 5 and Av 2, tucked in behind the Plaza de la Cultura. The theatre's marbled stairways, gilt cherubs and red velvet carpets would look more at home in old Europe than in Central America: you won't find such impressive elegance anywhere else between here and the Manaus Opera House in deepest Amazonia.

The story of the Teatro Nacional is an intriguing one, illuminating the industrious, no-nonsense attitude of the city's coffee bourgeoisie, who demonstrated the national pride and yearning for cultural achievement that came to characterize Costa Rican society in the twentieth century. In 1890 the world-famous prima donna Adelina Patti was making a tour through the Americas, but could not stop in Costa Rica as there was no appropriate theatre. Mortified, and determined to raise funds for the construction of a national theatre, the wealthy coffee farmers responded by levying a tax on every bag of coffee exported. Within a couple of years the coffers were full to bursting; European craftsmen and architects were employed, and by 1897 the building was ready for its inauguration, a stylish affair with singers from the Paris Opéra performing *Faust*.

The theatre itself is done in red plush and gold, while the upstairs "salons" are decorated in mint and jade-green, trimmed by gold, and lined with heavy portraits of former bourgeoisie. All in all, the building remains in remarkably good condition, despite the dual onslaught of the climate and a succession of earthquakes. The latest, in 1991, closed the place for two years – until recently, the huge marble staircases on either side of the entrance still had wooden supports strapped onto them like slings. Above all it is the details that leave a lasting impression: plump cherubim, elegantly numbered boxes fanning out in a wheel-spoke circle, heavy hardwood doors and intricate glasswork in the washrooms.

Even if you're not coming to see a performance, you can wander around the post-Baroque splendour, though you'll be charged about $2 for the privilege. Just off the foyer is a quiet and elegant café serving good coffee, juices, and European-style cakes.

Around the Parque España

Three blocks east and two blocks north of the Plaza de la Cultura, tall-treed **Parque España** is surrounded by a number of the city's most intriguing sights. On the eastern corner, facing Av 5, is the **Edificio Metálica** (Metal Building, also known as the "Escuela Metálica"), so-called because its exterior is made entirely out of metal plates shipped from France at the turn of the century. Though the prospect sounds dour, the effect – especially the bright multi-coloured courtyard as seen from the **Museo de Jade**, high above – is very pretty, if slightly military. Fronting the Edificio Metálica, **Parque Morazón** – more a concrete-paved square than a park proper – is a useful orientation point, centred on the landmark grey-domed bandstand floridly known as the Templo de Música.

Museo de Jade

On the north side of the Parque España rises one of the few office towers in San José: the INS, or Institute of Social Security, building. The eleventh floor of this uninspiring edifice contains one of the city's finest museums, the **Marco Fidel Tristan Museo de Jade** (Jade Museum; Mon–Fri 8am–4pm; $3), home to the world's largest collection of American jade. The museum is currently being renovated, and the displays described below may change, though the impressive amount of jade on show is unlikely to change.

As in China and the East, jade was much prized in ancient Costa Rica as a stone with religious or mystical significance, and for Neolithic civilizations it was an object of great significance and power. It was and is still considered valuable because of its (mineralogically speaking) rarity. Only slightly less hard than quartz, it's well known for its durability, and is a good material for weapons and cutting-tools like axes and blades. As no quarries of the stone have been found in Costa Rica, the big mystery is how the pre-Columbian societies here got hold of so much of it. The reigning theory suggests that it came from Guatemala – where the Motagua valley is home to one of the world's six known jade quarries – or was perhaps traded or sold down the isthmus by the Olmecs of Mexico. This also goes some way to explaining the presence of Maya insignia on some of the pieces – symbols that had no meaning for Costa Rica's pre-Columbian inhabitants.

The museum displays are ingenious, subtly back-lit to show off the multi-coloured and multi-textured pieces to full effect. Jade exhibits an extraordinary range of nuanced colour, from a milky-white green through soft grey and blue to deep green, and was most prized of all by the inhabitants of the Americas around 600 BC. No two pieces in the collection are alike in hue and opacity, though as in the Museo de Oro you'll see a lot of **axe-gods**: anthropomorphic bird-cum-human forms shaped like an axe and worn as a pendant. One entire room is devoted to male fertility symbols, and you'll also see X-shaped objects used to support the breasts of women of standing – a kind of proto-bra.

Incidentally, the **view** from the museum windows is one of the best in the city, taking in the sweep of San José from the centre to the south and then west to the mountains.

Museo de Arte y Diseño Contemporáneo

Sprawling across the entire eastern border of the Parque España, the former National Liquor Factory, dating from 1887, today houses an arts complex including the Centro Nacional de la Cultura, Juventud y Deportes (Ministry of Culture, Youth and Sports), known as CENAC, though many *Josefinos* still refer to the buildings as the old *Liquoría* – indeed you can still see a massive old distilling machine in the grounds, complete with the nameplate of its Birmingham manufacturers. The attraction here is the cutting-edge **Museo de Arte y Diseño Contemporáneo**, or Museum of Contemporary Art and Design (Tues–Sun 10am–5pm; $2), entered from the corner of C 15 and Av 3. Opened in 1994 under the direction of dynamic artist Virginia Pérez-Ratton, it's a highly modern space, with a cosmopolitan, multimedia approach – there's a space especially for outdoor installations. Other exhibits include Costa Rica's entries for the various international biennales and, upstairs, a gallery of industrial and furniture design. There's also a theatre in the CENAC complex; a wander around during the day offers interesting glimpses of dancers and musicians rehearsing.

Serpentario

Lurking on the second floor of a nondescript building on the corner of Av 1 and C 9 is the **Serpentario** (Mon–Fri 9am–6pm; Sat & Sun 10am–5pm; $4), where aghast tourists and fascinated schoolboys wander amid glass cases of snakes, poison dart frogs and the odd lizard. The Serpentario can be an unnerving experience, giving rise to any number of paranoid "escaped snakes" fantasies, but seeing the reptiles in the flesh can help identify them if you see them in the wild; especially handy when it comes to some of the more poisonous species that call Costa Rica home, including the fer-de-lance, bushmaster and jumping and eyelash vipers. Snakes from other countries can also be found here: look out for the Burmese python, who lies curled up in the biggest case doing a deft impression of a large tyre.

Barrios Amón and Otoya

Weaving its way up the hill from the Parque España, the historic **Barrio Amón** leads seamlessly into another old *barrio*, **Otoya**. Chock-full of historic buildings, lined with the former homes of the Costa Rican coffee gentry, these two neighbourhoods are among the most attractive in San José, and after decades of neglect they are currently undergoing something of a rediscovery by hoteliers, café and restaurant owners. More than 100 years old, Amón especially is home to some fine examples of the "neo-Victorian" tropical architectural style, with low-slung wooden houses girthed with wide verandahs and iron railings. Striking examples include the **Alianza Francesa** building (C 5 & Av 7), the turreted **Bishop's Castle** (Av 11 bis & C 3), and the grand old **Casa Verde de Amón** hotel (C 7 & Av 9).

Two blocks north of Parque España, at Av 11 and C 7/9, is the entrance to the **Parque Zoológico Simón Bolívar** (Tues–Fri 8am–4pm, Sat & Sun 9am–5pm; $2). There are plans to move it to a location outside San José sometime in the future, but until then the zoo should be avoided by animal lovers. It's also an unrelaxing place to visit: despite the pitifully cramped conditions it keeps its charges in, continues to draw Tico families on Sundays and great gaggles of schoolchildren on weekdays. If you do visit and want to do something about the facilities, the zoo operates an "adopt-an-animal" scheme – ask at the entrance kiosk or the museum office.

El Pueblo and the Centro de la Ciencia y la Cultura

The cluster of shops, restaurants, bars and discos that make up the **Centro Comercial El Pueblo** – generally known simply as "El Pueblo" – lies about 200m north of the zoo across the Río Torres. For a tourist complex, El Pueblo is well designed, and a sensible initiative to give both tourists and Ticos – who love it – an attractive, atmospheric place to shop, eat, drink and dance, all within virtually the same building. A winding maze of adobe-type edifices, El Pueblo's whitewashed exteriors and wide dark wooden staircases evoke the kind of colonial architecture that has found it hard to survive in Costa Rica, thanks to the knock-down blows of successive earthquakes. The souvenir and crafts shops tend to be a little expensive in comparison to those downtown, but it's still a nice place to wander about and perhaps have lunch. Walking to El Pueblo means running a gauntlet of pedestrian-unfriendly traffic, however, and most people take a taxi, which shouldn't cost more than $2.50 from the Plaza de la Cultura. In the adjacent **Spirogyra Jardín de Mariposas** (daily 8am–4pm; $5) you can see a wide variety of butterflies fluttering about, with daily guided tours pointing out particularly unusual and pretty examples.

Near El Pueblo, at the end of Calle 4, is the **Centro Costarricense de la Ciencia y la Cultura** (Tues–Fri 8am–4pm, Sat & Sun 10am–4pm; $5). Located in a former prison, this complex devotes most of its space to the mildly interesting **Museo de los Niños** (Childrens' Museum), where Costa Rican kids can come to see the interactive displays and learn about their country's history, culture and science. The complex also houses the **Museo Historico Penitenciario** (Penitentiary History Museum), which consists of a number of the original prison cells restored to their nineteenth-century condition, and some rather anodyne accounts of the country's penal history.

The Parque Nacional and around

Bordered by Av 1 and 3 and C 15 and 19, San José's **Parque Nacional** is the finest open space in downtown San José. Almost jungle-like in places, with a tall canopy of mop-headed palms and thick deciduous trees, it's popular among courting couples and older men discussing the state of the nation. After gaining notoriety as a hang-out for muggers and prostitutes, it has recently been equipped with tall lamps to add extra light – a tactic which has apparently succeeded in drawing the courting couples back to its nocturnal benches. Even so, it's still probably not a good idea to wander around here after dark.

Immediately north of the park, the modernist **Biblioteca Nacional** is Costa Rica's largest and most useful library, at least for readers of Spanish (Mon–Fri 8.30am–4.30pm). Anyone can go in to rifle through the newspaper collection to the right of the entrance on the ground floor, or even to use the bathrooms. At the library's southwest corner, the **Galería Nacional de Arte Contemporáneo** (Mon–Sat 10am–1pm & 2–5pm; free) features small and often quirky displays of work by local artists.

You can hear government debates Costa Rican-style at the **Palacio Nacional**, home to Costa Rica's Legislative Assembly, just south of the park at the corner of C 15 and Av Central. The fun starts at 4pm, but check first whether the Legislature is in session. East of the Palacio, at the top end of Av 3 between C 21/23, the **Museo Ferrocarríl**, or Railway Museum (Mon–Fri 9am–4pm; $0.75), was the terminus for the old "Jungle Train" (see p.159). Today it holds a largely photographic collection dedicated to the famed train that once ran from San José to Limón before being dealt two blows in quick succession: one by the April 1991 earthquake and another by the government, who took the decision not to finance its repair. It's worth a look if you're in the area, especially for railway enthusiasts, but doesn't merit a trip in its own right.

Plaza de la Democracía

A block southwest of the Parque Nacional is the concrete **Plaza de la Democracía**, yet another of the city's soulless squares which is just one aesthetic notch up from a paved parking lot. Constructed in 1989 to mark President Oscar Arias's key involvement in the Central American Peace Plan, this expanse of terraced concrete slopes up towards a fountain, with its bottom end being dominated by a line of **artisans' stalls** selling hammocks, chunky Ecuadorean sweaters, leather bracelets and jewellery. You can also buy Guatemalan textiles and decorative *molas* (patchwork textiles in vibrant colours) made by the Kuna people of Panamá here, though at steeper prices than elsewhere in Central America. Other stalls sell T-shirts, wooden crafts and trinkets, and the traders are friendly and won't pressure you; a bit of gentle bargaining is a must.

The Museo Nacional

The top end of the square is crowned by the impressive fortress-like edifice of the **Museo Nacional** (Tues–Sat 8.30am–4.30pm, Sun 9am–4.30pm; $2), occupying the renovated former Bellavista Barracks – bullet holes from the 1948 insurrection (see Contexts) can still be seen on the north side of the building's thick walls. More than a century old (and that *is* old for Costa Rica), the museum's collection, though rather haphazard, gives a fascinating introduction to the story of Costa Rica's **colonization**. A grisly series of drawings, deeply affecting in their simplicity, tells the story of the fate of Costa Rica's **indigenous** people at the hands of the Spanish settlers. Violence, it appears, was meted out in both directions, and beheadings, hangings, clubbings, shooting of priests, the pouring of liquid gold down throats, infanticide and suicide as a means of resistance in the indigenous community are all mercilessly depicted. Displays also explain (in both English and Spanish) how the arrival of the Spanish disturbed forever the balance of social and political power amongst the indigenous groups, and there's also a good explanation of the function of gold in their social hierarchy, describing which objects were used to identify warriors, chiefs, and shamans.

The museum's **colonial-era** section is dominated by the massive but spartan furniture and cheesy religious iconography of the Spanish. Exhibits make clear how slowly culture and education advanced in Costa Rica, giving a lasting sense of a country struggling to extricate itself from terrible cultural and social backwardness – in European terms – until well into the twentieth century. In the same room are examples of **colonial art**, which almost without exception took its inspiration from the Catholic religion and replaced indigenous art forms with scores of lamentable gilt-and-pink Virgin Marys.

Highlights elsewhere include petroglyphs, pre-Columbian stonework, and wonderful anthropomorphic gold figures in the **Sala Arqueológica**. This is the single most important archeological exhibition in the country; the grinding tables and funerary offerings, in particular, show precise geometric patterns and incredible attention to detail, but the really astounding pieces are the "flying panel" **metates**, corn-grinding tables used by the Chorotega peoples of present-day Guanacaste, each with three legs and meticulously sculpted from a single piece of volcanic stone.

Los Yoses and La California

The neighbourhoods of **Los Yoses** and **La California** face one another from opposite side of Av Central as it runs east from the Museo Nacional to San Pedro. Mainly residential, Los Yoses is home to foreign embassies and a few hotels, while commercial La California runs into Barrio Escalante and Barrio Dent, two of San José's nicest residential districts. Walking through Barrio Escalante is the way to go east, and much more pleasant than bus-choked Avenida Central.

Homesick North American tourists should head to the **Centro Cultural Costarricense-Norteamericano**, 100m north of the Am-Pm supermarket on the corner of Av Central and C 37 in Barrio Dent (Mon–Fri 7am–7pm, Sat 9am–noon; ☎255-9433 for library). At the latter you'll find a back stock of English-language publications – the *Miami Herald*, *New York Times* and *USA Today* – as well as all the main Costa Rican dailies. There's also an art gallery, the Eugene O'Neill Theatre, where jazz festivals and English-language theatre performances take place, a good café and CNN beamed out on the communal TV.

About 300m northeast of the Centro Cultural is San José's best bookstore, **Librería Internacional** (Mon–Sat 9.30am–7pm; ☎253-9553), with a well-stocked Latin American literature section, including Costa Rican authors, and a good selection of both fiction and non-fiction in English as well as maps and tourist guides. At the very end of Barrio Dent, where Avenida Central runs into the fountain-roundabout that separates San José proper from San Pedro, is the truly ugly but wildly popular **Mall San Pedro**. A ceramic-coloured multistorey building festooned with plants and simulated waterfalls, inside it's a jumble of largely useless shops and a few dark neon eateries – definitely the place to come to observe upper-class Costa Rican teenage dating rituals and shopping habits.

San Pedro

First impressions of **San Pedro** can be offputting: Avenida Central (known here also as Paseo de los Estudiantes) appears to be little more than a strip of gas stations, broken-up sidewalks and shopping malls. Walk just a block off the Paseo, however, and you'll find a lively university student quarter, plus a few elegant old residential houses. The area has traditionally been home to some of the city's best bars, restaurants and nightlife, but an increasing proliferation of dark bars filled with shouting college students means that it's now not the most relaxing of places to be on a Friday or Saturday night, at least during term time.

Buses to San Pedro from the centre of town stop opposite the small **Parque Central**, with its bubblegum-orange bandstand and monument to John F. Kennedy. Walking north from the *parque*, through three blocks of solid sodas, bars and bookshops you come to the cool, leafy campus of the **University of Costa Rica** (UCR), one of the finest in Central America, and certainly the most prestigious educational institution in the country. Founded in 1940, the university has in the past been accused of being too rigidly academic and elitist, but the overall campus atmosphere is busy, egalitarian and stimulating.

The best places to hang out on **campus** are the frenzied and cheap cafeteria in the building immediately to the right of the library (there's also an excellent **bookstore** across from the back entrance of the cafeteria), the Comedor Universitario, or **dining hall**, and the Faculdad de Bellas Artes, which has a wonderful open-air **theatre** which is used for frequent concerts. Noticeboards around campus, particularly in front of the Vida Estudantíl office (Building A, fourth floor), keep you up to date with what's going on; try also to get hold of a copy of *Semana Universitaria*, the campus newspaper, which is sold in most restaurants and bookshops in the area. The three or four blocks surrounding the university are lined with some lively bars and restaurants, though in most of them you'll feel more comfortable if you're under thirty. For Spanish-speakers this is a great place to meet people, watch movies and browse around the several well-stocked bookstores (one of the best is Librería Macondo, 100m before you come to the university proper; look for the lime-green storefront).

Theoretically it's possible to walk to the campus from Los Yoses, but this entails dealing with the huge, threatening Fuente de la Hispanidad roundabout. This is not recommended, as there are no provisions at all for pedestrians – it's much better to take any bus from Los Yoses.

Around the Mercado Central

Northwest of the Parque Central and the commercial centre between Av Central and 1, and C 6/8 is the **Mercado Central** (Mon–Sat 5am–5pm). Much more orderly than the usual chickens-and-*campesino* Latin American city markets, it is still something of an experience: entering its labyrinthine interior, you're assaulted by colourful arrangements of strange fruits and vegetables, dangling sides of beef and elaborate, silvery ranks of fish. At certain times of the day (lunch time and late afternoon, for example) the Mercado Central can resemble the Eighth Circle of Hell – choking with unfamiliar smells and an almighty crush of people – while at other times you'll be able to enjoy a relaxed wander through wide uncrowded alleys of rural commerce. It's certainly the best place in town to get a cheap bite to eat, and the view from a counter stool is fascinating, as traders and their customers jostle for *chayotes*, *mamones*, *piñas* and *cas*. With a little Spanish, and a pinch of confidence, shopping for fruit and vegetables here can be miles cheaper than in the supermarket.

The surrounding streets, which even in the daytime can look quite seedy (in sharp contrast to the roads just one or two blocks east), are also full of noisy traders and determined shoppers. All this activity encourages **pickpockets**, and in this environment tourists stick out like sore thumbs. Take with you only what you need and be on your guard.

Two blocks east and one block north of the Mercado Central, in the Correo Central, C 2, Av 1/3, the **Museo Postal, Telegráfico y Filatelico** (Mon–Fri 8am–4pm; free) exhibits old relics of telegraphic equipment – of interest to buffs only. Far more appealing is the pretty **flower market** in the square opposite, where carnations, orchids, begonias and scores of lush blooms create a blaze of colour and fragrance. On the C 2 and Av 3 is the **Farmacia Fischel**, one of the oldest pharmacies in the city, with a good stock of both conventional and herbal remedies.

Paseo Colón and Parque la Sabana

Clustered around the main entrance to La Coca-Cola, off C 16, shops selling women's underwear, cosmetics and luggage compete for space with a variety of cheap snack bars and drinks stalls. Two blocks south, however, the atmosphere changes, as Av Central turns into **Paseo Colón**, a wide boulevard of upmarket shops, restaurants and car dealerships. At the very end of the *paseo*, a solid expanse of green today known as **Parque la Sabana** was until the 1940s San José's airport, and is now home to the country's key art museum, the Museo de Arte Costarricense. To get to the *parque*, take the Sabana Cementerio bus from Av 2, or walk (20–30min from downtown).

Parque la Sabana

The bright orange neocolonial edifice of the old air terminal in **Parque la Sabana** has been converted into the attractive **Museo de Arte Costarricense** (Tues–Sun 10am–4pm; $2), with a good collection of mainly twentieth-century Costa Rican paintings. Highlights among the permanent exhibits include the outstanding landscapes of **Teodorico Quirós**, with their Cézanne-inspired palettes of russets and burnt siennas, along with Enrique Echandi, Margarita Berthau, abstract painter Lola Fernández, and a scattershot selection of foreign artists including Diego Rivera and Alexander Calder. The **Salon Dorado** upstairs is remarkable: four full walls of bas-relief wooden carvings overlaid with sumptuous gold, portraying somewhat idealized scenes of Costa Rica's history since pre-Columbian times. On the western wall are imagined scenes from the lives of the indigenous peoples, followed on the north wall by Columbus's arrival, to which the indigenous peoples improbably respond by falling to their knees and praying solemnly. Other golden representations include the Costa Rican agrarian gods of horses, oxen and chickens, and an image of this very building as San José's airport, little biplanes buzzing around it like mosquitos.

On the southwest corner of Sabana Park, across the road in the Ministry of Agriculture and Livestock complex, is the quirky natural science museum **Museo de Ciencias Naturales La Salle** (Mon–Fri 8am–3pm; $1). Walk in, and after about 400m you'll see the painted wall proclaiming the museum; the entrance is at the back. It's an offbeat collection, with displays ranging from pickled fish and snakes coiled in formaldehyde to some rather forlorn taxidermy exhibits – age and humidity have taken their toll. Highlights include the model of the huge **baula**, or leatherback turtle, the biggest reptile on earth, and the **dusky grouper** fish, a serious contendor for first prize in the Ugliest Animal in the World contest. Tons of crumbly fossils and an enormous selection of pinned butterflies (twelve cases alone of titanium-bright Blue Morphos) finish off the collection. Real turtles, virtually motionless, doze off in the courtyard garden. The Sabana–Estadio **bus** (see p.79) stops right outside the museum. Note, on your right as you go by, the futuristic air traffic control tower shape of the **Controlaría de la República**: this is the government's administrative headquarters.

Eating

It used to be said that nobody goes to Costa Rica for the food. However, while it's still true that in most of the country you'll eat nothing more exotic than rice-and-chicken, the standard of cuisine in the capital has improved dramatically in the last few years. For a Central American city of its size, San José has a surprising variety of **restaurants** – Italian, macrobiotic, Thai – along with simple places that offer dishes beginning and ending with rice (rice-and-shrimp, rice-and-chicken, rice-and-meat). For really good *típico* cooking, you'll get the best deals at the more upmarket restaurants that do grills or barbecues (*churrascos*).

Many of the city's best restaurants are in the relatively wealthy and cosmopolitan neighbourhoods of **San Pedro**, along **Paseo Colón**, and in **Escazú**, but wherever you choose, eating out in San José can set your budget back on its haunches. Prices are generally steep, and the 23 percent tax on restaurant food can deliver a real death-blow. The cheapest places are in the centre, especially the snack bars and **sodas**, where the restaurant tax doesn't apply, though sadly the best of these are disappearing at an alarming rate because of competition from fast-food outlets. Those that remain are generally cheap and cheerful – a *plato del día* soda lunch will rarely set you back more than $5. They also have *empanadas* and sandwiches to take out: combine these with a stop at one of the fruit stalls on any street corner and you've got a quick, cheap lunch (the pieces of papaya and pineapple sold in neatly packaged plastic bags have been washed and peeled by the vendors and should be all right, but if in doubt wash again). Snacks sold at the **Mercado Central** are as tasty as anywhere, and there's a good cluster of sodas hidden away in the Galería shopping arcade, Av 2, C 5/7. The sodas along the entrance to the **University of Costa Rica** are all much of a muchness, serving bland lunches eaten with plastic cutlery to the blasting accompaniment of bad 1970s TV shows, but the food is filling and cheap, and the eavesdropping is free.

Fast-food outlets in San José are proliferating so rapidly that at times it can look like a veritable jungle of *Pizza Huts*, *Taco Bells* and *KFCs*, not to mention *McDonald's*. Wildly popular with Tico families and workers for a quick bite, they are cheap and cheerful and, particularly in the case of *Pizza Hut*, not bad value. **Cafés** also abound: some, like *Giacomín*, have old-world European aspirations; others, such as *Spoon*, are resolutely Costa Rican, with *Josefinos* piling in to order birthday cakes or grab a **coffee**. Most cafés serve exclusively export

Costa Rican coffee, with its mild, soft flavour – for something different, try *La Esquina del Café*, which offers numerous blends and roasts (for more on coffee, see Basics, p.41). Wherever you go you're likely to get *café con leche* served in the traditional way – a pitcher of coffee and a pitcher of heated milk, so that you can mix to your liking. As is the case with shops and restaurants, some of the best new cafés are to be found in the new **shopping malls** outside San José – the Multiplaza mall in Escazú, for example, has no fewer than four excellent cafés serving all sorts of cakes and proper coffees – the downside is you'll to take a taxi to get there. **Bakeries** (*pastelería, repostería*) on every corner sell cakes, breads and pastries – most of them thick with white refined flour. Chains to head for include *Musmanni, Spoon, Schmidt* and *Giacomín*. The city's fantastic **ice cream** is another source of woe to dieters: of the major chains, *Pops* is the best, with particularly good fruit flavours.

Working *Josefinos* eat their main meal between noon and 2pm, and at this time sodas especially can get very busy. Many restaurants close at 3pm and open again for the evening. In the listings below we have given a phone number only for places where you might need to **reserve** a table.

Restaurants

Antojitos Cancún, in the Centro Comercial Cocorí, 50m west of the Fuente de la Hispanidad roundabout, Los Yoses. Cheap, filling, Mexican food, not wholly authentic, but good for late-night snacks and cheap all-you-can-eat buffets. Draught beer and an outside terrace where you can sit and watch the 4WDs whizz round the fountain. Mariachi Fri and Sat from 10pm. Daily 11am–midnight.

Ave Fénix, San Pedro, 150m before Parque Central as you come in on Av Central from the west. No-nonsense, dependable Szechuan Chinese place, serving tasty dishes and frequented by the Chinese community. Dinner costs $15 or so.

Balcón de Europa, C 9, Av 0/1 (Ⓣ221-4841). City landmark: the food, largely pasta and Italian staples, is nothing special, but the atmosphere is great. Sepia photos of the early days line the wood-panelled wall, along with annoying snippets of "wisdom". Monster cheeses dominate the dining room, as does the game strummer who serenades each table. Closed Sat.

Cabernet, outside San José in Rancho Redondo, Camino a Las Nubes de Coronado – a taxi will cost about $15 (Ⓣ229-1113). Perched high above San José with breathtaking views, this cosy gourmet restaurant is the place to come for superbly cooked French dishes, with lamb, steak and sea bass figuring prominently on a varied menu. The multilingual proprietor can take you through what is probably the best wine list in San José. About $50 for two with wine and dessert. Closed Mon.

Café Mundo, Av 9, C 15, Barrio Otoya. The best food in San José, served amidst beautiful decor and a relaxed European atmosphere. The subtle and delicately cooked food is Italian influenced, and includes a variety of pasta dishes – the fetuccini with *camarones* ($14) is good – as well as great puddings. The Caesar ($4) and nicoise ($8) salads are large but a bit overpriced – if you're on a budget, go for the pizza, or just come for a cappuccino ($2). At night the bar attracts a largely gay clientele. Closed Sat & Sun.

Cocina de Leña, Centro Comercial El Pueblo (Ⓣ255-1360). *Típico* food, superbly cooked, in rustic surroundings with big wooden tables, gingham tablecloths and menus on paper bags. Most meals are cooked in a wood oven – the succulent chicken dishes are recommended. Good for a quiet, upmarket night out. Dinner for two costs around $35.

Fellini, C 36, A 4 (Ⓣ222-3520). Popular moderate-to-expensive Italian option, with excellent pasta, a good selection of Italian wine, and regular live jazz.

Grano d'Oro, Casa 251, C 3, Av 2/4 (Ⓣ253-3322). Upmarket restaurant with beautifully spare decor and a changing menu. Breakfast (from 6am) includes fresh fruit, eggs benedict and banana macadamia pancakes. Soups are excellent – try the classic black bean or corn chowder. Among the main courses, the beef is consistently delicious, as is white sea bass breaded with toasted macadamia nuts. Amazing desserts – try the tiramisu and strawberry cream cheese. Book ahead and bring plenty of funds.

Il Pomodoro, San Pedro, 150m east of the entrance to UCR. One of the best pizza places in the city, with large pizzas – including a great vegetarian special – and cheap draught beer served in mugs and pitchers in a large and cheerful restaurant popular with the university crowd. Around $18 for two.

La Cascada, behind the Centro Comercial Trejos Montalegre, Escazú (☎ 228-0906). This difficult-to-find-place (there's no sign) with unpromising decor is actually the best steak house in San José. Hugely popular, it's often full of Tico families, especially on Sunday afternoon. The hunks of beef are fantastic, and the terrifically filling plates all come with rice and veg.

La Galería, in Los Yoses, 50m west of *Spoon*, behind the *Aparthotel Los Yoses* (☎ 234-0850). Popular place with *Josefinos* on a special night out (it's expensive), with a range of European cuisines – including fondue – served in rather heavy sauces. Classical music adds to the upmarket atmosphere. Closed Sat & Sun.

La Leyenda, San Rafael de Escazú (☎ 228-6846). This restaurant's Santa Fé-style decor matches its authentic and delicious upmarket Mexican cuisine, with all the ingredients and the 28 different types of tequila being imported from Mexico. Prices are moderate and there are also outdoor tables on an attractive patio overlooking a pool. Popular with San José's fashionable set – look out for the mobile phones and blond highlights.

La Masía de Triquell, Av 2, C 40. Consistently dependable Catalan cuisine – the place to go if the desire for paella hits you. Count on spending at least $35 on dinner for two. Closed Sun.

Le Chandelier, 100m west and 100m south of the ICE building in Los Yoses (☎ 225-3980). Exquisite French food cooked by the restaurant's Swiss owner – try the lobster in pastry or the delicious trout with almonds. The decor is homely, with exposed ceiling beams and a crackling fireplace. Dinner for two costs about $35–45. Closed Sun.

Machu Picchu, C 32, Av 1 (☎ 222-7384). A consistent San José favourite, and the only truly South American place in town (the velvet llamas on the walls help). The appetizers, including *ceviche* and Peruvian *bocas*, tend to be more interesting than the main dishes. Around $30 for two with beer or wine. Closed Sun.

Marbella, in the Centro Commercial Calle Real, San Pedro (☎ 224-9452). Spanish cuisine, specializing in excellent paella ($15 for two) with real rabbit (otherwise unknown in Costa Rica) and veal dishes. Closed Sun evening & Mon.

Mazorca, 200m east and 100m north of San Pedro church. Macrobiotic restaurant just east of the entrance to UCR. Homely, simple decor and menu (lunch is $5; takeaways are also available). The tasty bread, soups, peanut-butter sandwiches and macrobiotic cakes make a welcome change from greasy *arroz con pollo*. Closed Sun.

Tin-Jo, C 11, Av 6/8 (☎ 221-7605). Quiet, popular and fairly formal Chinese-Thai place – the lemongrass soup, bean-thread salad in lime juice and coconut milk curries are particularly recommended. Dinner with wine is around $40 for two; skip the alcohol, or go for lunch, and you'll get away with half that.

Sodas

Castro, Casa 279, Av 10, C 2/4. The 1970s fluorescent vinyl decor and the rough neighbourhood belie the treats inside. Definitely not on the tourist trail, this is where local families take their kids for a Sunday ice-cream treat and to sample the excellent fruit salads.

Central, Av 1, C 3/5. A typical San José soda where you squeeze into small booths to eat massive cheap sandwiches or lunch plates; the lunch specials are very good value at under $2.

Chelles, Av 0, C 9. Open 24 hours, this spartan bar, with bare fluorescent lighting and a little TV blaring away in the corner, is a San José insitution and a great place to sit and watch your fellow customers or the street action outside, while aproned waitresses serve up cold, cheap beer and snacks, as well as lunch-time plates.

Manolo's Churrería, Av 0, C 0/2. A 24hr soda that's become an institution with *Josefinos* as a late-night hangout. It's not cheap, but is safe after hours and serves filling snacks from killer pastries to sandwiches.

La Reina de Pupusas, Av 1, C 5/7, opposite Cine Omni on the corner of Parking Gigante. A Salvadorean foodstall serving great snacks, including tortillas with *frijoles molidos* (refried beans), cabbage, mixed pickles and sausage or meat and cheese. The tortillas are large enough to be a meal in themselves, though very messy to eat.

La Vasconia, Av 1, C 3/5. Enormous menu, featuring cheap breakfasts and lunch specials, including fairly cheap *ceviche*. The place to go to get off the tourist trail and mingle with stressed office workers.

Parillada Argentina, C 21, Av 6, 100m east of the Supreme Court. Watch the Argentine owners prepare exquisite chicken and beef or mozzarella, tomato and oregano *empanadas* to take away (75¢ each), or join the lawyers from the court next door and tuck into a massive lunch – the mini-parillada, with succulent beef, sausage, potato and salad ($4) is quite enough for those with a less than Argentina-sized stomach. Open Mon–Fri lunch only.

Shakti, C 13, Av 8. Fantastically filling *platos del día* include *sopa negra* or salad, a big hearty vegetarian *casado*, a *refresco* and tea or coffee, all for only $2.50. Very friendly and good breakfast specials – granola, fruit juice and coffee or tea for only $2. Popular for lunch, so go early or late for a seat. Open Mon–Fri lunch only.

Tapia, southeast corner of Parque La Sabana. Huge place, open to the street with views of Parque La Sabana. Especially good for late-night snacks, with sandwiches and burgers for those weary of *casados*.

Vishnu, Av 1, C 1/3. Obligatory pit stop for anybody visiting San José, this cheery vegetarian place serves delicious *platos del día* with brown rice, vegetables and soups, while the vegetarian club sandwich is a meal in itself at a bargain $1.50. Fruit plates with yoghurt are a perennial favourite, and a *plato del día*, *refresco* and *café con leche* will set you back about $4.

Cafés and bakeries

Café Parisienne, *Gran Hotel Costa Rica*, Av 2, C 3/5. The closest thing in San José to a European street café, complete with wrought-iron chairs and trussed-up waiters, this is a wonderful place to sit and have coffee and cake on a sunny day. It's also one of the few establishments in the city that does continental breakfast.

El Molino, in the Mall San Pedro, just west of the Fuente de la Hispanidad roundabout. A large variety of italian pastries and every kind of espresso

and macchiato you could want. They also serve tasty sandwiches and pizzas from noon to 3pm.

Expresso Americano, in the Multiplaza Escazú. A place of pilgrimage for true coffee lovers, serving a variety of excellent coffees and desserts. Doubles as a bar on Fridays and Saturdays, staying open until 11pm.

Giacomín, branches next to the Automercado in Los Yoses, in San Pedro, and in Escazú. The place for chocolate and cake lovers, with lots of seasonal cakes such as *Stollen* and *panettone*.

Il Panino, in the Multicentro Paco in Escazú. Classy, modernist European-style café, with a good selection of drinks and high-quality cakes; they also serve breakfast, lunch and dinner.

La Esquina del Café, C 3 bis, Av 9. Small, quiet, aromatic café with excellent coffee, freshly roasted beans and friendly staff who will answer any questions about the entire coffee process, from bean to cup. Also serves good cappuccino with proper frothed milk, tasty desserts (you can try before you buy) and lunches of soups, salads and sandwiches. You can also buy little bags of beans from Costa Rica's various coffee-producing regions.

Ruiseñor, 150m east of the Automercado in Los Yoses. Upmarket restaurant with a pleasant outdoor terrace. The atmosphere and service are European-style and old-fashioned, and the prices are high.

Spoon, Av 0, C 5/7, and other branches throughout San José and the Valle Central. Full of *Josefinos* ordering birthday cakes. Coffee is somewhat bitter but served with mix-it-yourself hot milk; the choice of cookies and cakes is endless.

Teatro Nacional Café Ruiseñor, Av 2, C 3/5. Coffee, fruit drinks, sandwiches and fantastic cakes served in a tranquil mint-green setting: the tables by the window are good for watching the goings-on in the Plaza de la Cultura.

Drinking and nightlife

San José's nightlife is gratifyingly varied, with scores of **bars** and **live music** venues, though note that you need to be at least 18 to drink in Costa Rica, and even if you're well over-age, it's worth carrying a photocopy of your passport. There are a number of places **downtown** with American names that attract gringos in packs, though many are pretty insalubrious, and most *Josefinos* head to Los Yoses or San Pedro. In **Los Yoses**, Av Central features a well-known "yuppie trail" of bars, packed with middle- and upper-middle-class

Ticos enjoying a few beers. It starts roughly at *El Cuartel de la Boca del Monte*, where the crowd is relatively mixed, and reaches its peak at *Río*, a hugely popular American-style bar with an outdoor terrace. **San Pedro** nightlife is geared more towards the university population, with a strip of studenty bars to the east of the UCR entrance. Those looking for local atmosphere should head for a **boca bar**, or seek out places to hear **peñas**, slow, acoustic folk songs from the Andean region which grew out of the revolutionary movements of the 1970s and 1980s.

It's well worth experiencing one of the city's **discos**: even if you don't dance, you can watch the Ticos burn up the floor. For **salsa**, merengue, cumbia and soca try *La Plaza, Cocloco, Las Risas, Infinito, Salsa 54*, and the traditional *El Gran Parqueo* in the working-class suburb of Desamparados. DJs at these places intersperse the Latino playlist with reggae and a bit of jungle from Jamaica, the US, the Dominican Republic and sometimes even Puerto Limón, and then do a house set, usually playing internationally popular, if somewhat out of date, tunes. For **reggae** – hugely popular with young *Josefinos* – head for *Dynasty*. Because locals are usually in couples or groups, the atmosphere at most places is non-"scene"; if you are asked to dance you needn't worry that anyone expects more than that unless you're a woman on your own, which is quite uncommon, and usually taken as a sign of availability. In general, the **dress code** is relaxed: most people wear smart jeans and men need not wear a jacket. **Cover charges** run to about 700 colones ($4), though the big mainstream discos at El Pueblo charge slightly more than places downtown.

Many bars don't offer **music** during the week, but change character drastically come Friday or Saturday, when you can hear jazz, blues, up-and-coming local bands, rock and roll, or South American folk music. That said, activity is not relentlessly weekend-oriented: it's possible, with a little searching, to hear good live music on a Wednesday, or find a packed disco floor on a Monday or Tuesday. People do stay out later on the weekends, but even so, with the exception of the studenty bars in San Pedro, most places close by 2 or 3am, and earlier on Sunday.

San José is one of the best places in Central (possibly Latin) America for **gay** nightlife. Establishments come and go – those in our listings are the best established places – and it helps if you have a local lesbian or gay contact to help you hunt down small local clubs.

For full details of **what's on**, check the *cartelera* in the *Tiempo Libre* section of *La Nación*, which lists live music along with all sorts of other activities, from swimming classes to cultural discussions.

Learning to salsa in San José

One of the best ways to meet people and to prepare yourself for San José nightlife is to take a few salsa lessons at one of the city's many *academias de baile*. You don't necessarily need a partner, and you can go with a friend or in a group. The tuition is serious, but the atmosphere is usually relaxed. The best classes in San José are at Bailes Latinos, in the Costa Rican Institute of Language and Latin Dance, Av 0, C 25/27 (☏ 233-8938, 🖷 233-8670); at Malecón, C 17/19, Av 2 (☏ 222-3214); and at Merecumbé, which has various branches, the most central of which is at San Pedro (☏ 224-3531 or 234-1548).

Bars and live music

Baleares, in San Pedro, 50m west of the Más y Menos supermarket. Live rock (Thurs–Sat) in a dark and cavernous bar popular with students and locals. There's usually a $3 cover charge.

Bar Jazz Café, in San Pedro, next to the Banco Popular (T 253-8933). The best place in San José to hear jazz, with an intimate atmosphere and consistently good groups. The cover charge varies from $5 to $10, sometimes including a glass of wine, but is usually worth it.

Caccio's, 200m east and 25m north of San Pedro church. Insanely popular student hangout with guys wearing baseball caps and singing along to outdated songs – it's a great place to meet people, and the baskets of pizza and cheap cold beer are another bonus. Closed Sun.

Chelles, Av 0, C 9. Round the corner from its namesake (see below), this *Chelles* is a simple, brightly lit bar, with football on the television, cheap beers and *bocas*, and 24-hour service, drawing an eclectic crowd of weary businessmen and late-night revellers.

Chelles Taberna, C 9, Av 0/2 (T 221-1369). More like an English pub than a Latin American tavern, with smooching couples, serious guys in leather jackets and surly waitresses. It has a good range of drinks, though, as well as cheap, tasty *bocas*, and is open 24 hours.

El Cuartel de la Boca del Monte, Av 1, C 21/23. Probably the most popular bar in San José, at least with younger *Josefinos*, with a well-stocked bar, great food (lunch and dinner are served, as well as *bocas*), and some of the best live music in town from up-and-coming bands (Wed only). Dress hip and go early, preferably before 9pm, to get a seat. There's a door policy of sorts, but the bouncers never seem to turn foreigners away. Small cover ($2.50) most nights. Open Wed–Sat 6pm–2am.

La Esmeralda, Av 2, C 5/7. Colourful, landmark institution, being the headquarters of the union of Mariachi bands, who whoosh by your table in a colourful swirl of sombreros and sequins before dashing off in a taxi to serenade or celebrate elsewhere in the city. Closed Sun.

La Maga, inside Centro Commercial Cocorí, just before the Fuente de la Hispanidad roundabout, Los Yoses. Currently one of the most popular places in town day or night, this café-bar doubles as an art gallery, and stocks an enormous array of magazines dealing with Latin American and Spanish art, culture and literature.

La Villa, 150m north of the old Banco Anglo, San Pedro. Located in an atmospheric old house, frequented by students and "intellectuals" and plastered with political and theatrical posters, this is San José's best bar for beer and conversation, with Mercedes Sosa on the CD player, occasional live *peñas* and tasty *bocas*. Closed Sun.

Las Risas, C 1, Av 0/1. One of the best downtown bars, on three floors. The disco at the top is good, with a small dance floor and lively young crowd. Bring ID – a copy of your passport will suffice — or the bouncers won't let you in. The cover charge of $3 will usually get you two drinks or a tequila. Saturday is ladies' night.

Los Balcones, in El Pueblo. Regular *peñas* and other acoustic music and an outdoor terrace make this the nicest bar in the El Pueblo centre (see p.93).

Parillada Los Andes, across the street from the UCR library and cafeteria, San Pedro. University hang-out with a low-key atmosphere, cold beer, good snacks and regular acoustic music, including *peñas*. Closed Sun.

Restaurante Balalaika, in San Pedro, 75m east of the Fuente de la Hispanidad roundabout (T 280-0002). Occasional performances of good live jazz, most frequently on Thursdays (call to confirm), in a rather upmarket new restaurant. Cover charge $3.

Shakespeare, Av 2, C 28. Quiet, friendly place that's popular with people popping in for a drink before seeing a performance at the adjacent Sala Garbo cinema or Laurence Olivier theatre. Also has occasional live jazz.

Soda Blues, C 11, Av 8/10. Quiet, out-of-the-way bar which bursts into life on Thursdays with live *musica latina* and blues, and a beer-and-*boca* special for 75¢; weekends also tend to be busy. Closed Sun.

Tapa Tapa, in the Multicentro Paco in Escazú (T 299-2320). Big, lively tapas bar, situated in a cavernous wooden room and boasting an utterly authentic menu, with manchego cheese, chorizo, anchovies, gazpacho and *calamares a la romana*. Some small tapas are served free with your beer ($1.50); for larger *raciones* you have to order and pay separately.

Boca bars

In Costa Rica, bocas (appetizers) are the tasty little snacks traditionally served free in bars. *Boca* bars are a largely urban tradition, and although you find them in other parts of the country, the really famous ones are all in San José. Because of mounting costs, however, and erosion of local traditions, few places serve *bocas* gratis any more. Several bars have a *boca* menu, among them *Chelles Taberna* in downtown San José and *La Villa* in San Pedro, but the authentic boca bars are concentrated in suburban working- or lower-middle-class residential neighbourhoods. They have a distinctive convivial atmosphere – friends and family getting together for a good night out – and are very busy most nights. Saturday is the hardest night to get a table; get there before 7.30pm. You'll be handed a menu of free *bocas* – one beer gets you one *boca*, so keep drinking and you can keep eating. The catch is that the beer costs about twice as much as elsewhere ($2 as opposed to $1), but even so the little plates of food are generous enough to make this a bargain way to eat out. You'll do better if you speak Spanish, but you can get by with point-and-nod. Typical bocas include deep-fried plantain with black-bean paste, small plates of rice and meat, shish kebabs, *tacos* or *empanadas*; nothing fancy, but the perfect accompaniment to a cold beer.

Among the best *boca* bars are Bar México (Mon–Fri 3pm–midnight, Sat 11am–midnight), opposite the church in Barrio México, northwest of the city, is an old working-class *boca* bar, one of the most authentic and well known in the city. These days Barrio México is a pretty rough neighbourhood, so go by taxi. You'll find a varied clientele – but conspicuously few foreigners – at Los Perales and El Sesteo (both Mon–Sat 7pm–midnight). They're about 100m from each other on the same street in the eastern suburb of Curridabat – hard to find on your own, but taxi drivers will know them.

Gay and lesbian nightlife

Café Mundo, Av 9, C 15, Barrio Otoya. In the restaurant of the same name, this low-key bar attracts a mainly gay clientele.

Déjà Vu, C 2, Av 14/16. A mixed crowd – gay, lesbian and straight – come for the hot and happening atmosphere, mostly house and techno with a few salsa tunes interspersed. There are two large dance floors plus a quiet bar and a café. The neighbourhood is pretty scary though – take a taxi. Cover charge varies from $3 to $5, though drinks are cheap. Closed Sun & Mon.

La Avispa, C 1, Av 8/10. Landmark San José lesbian disco-bar (men are also welcome) with a friendly atmosphere and mainly Latin music. There's a $5 cover charge Thursday to Sunday. Closed Mon.

Discos

Cocoloco, El Pueblo. Smart, well-dressed clientele, small dance floors, and the usual Latin techno-pop/reggae/merengue mix.

Dynasty, in Centro Comercial del Sur, Desamparados, south of central San José next to the old Pacific Railway station. Full of a young, hard-dancing crowd getting down to excellent *caribeña* tunes with reggae, plus the odd bit of garage, soca, merengue and calypso. Open Fri & Sat only.

El Gran Parqueo, Desamparados. Live bands play merengue and salsa at this very traditional venue, packed with older, working-class Costa Ricans who come here to show off their steps. Small cover charge.

Infinitos, El Pueblo. Similar to *Cocoloco*, with three dance floors playing salsa, US and European dance music, and 1970s romantic hits respectively. Attracts an older, smarter crowd, and excellent DJs. Closed Sun.

La Plaza, across from El Pueblo. Archetypical Latin American disco. Designed like a giant bull ring, the huge round dance floor is packed with couples dancing to merengue and superb waiters who twirl in their truncated tuxedos when business is slack. There's also a bar with a big TV screen flashing out a steady diet of music and sport. **Salsa 54**, C 3, Av 1/3. Downtown alternative to the El Pueblo discos, this joint plays the favoured mix of Latin and American tunes but, as the name implies, goes heavy on the salsa and merengue. The best place to dance in San José proper, attracting the most talented *salseros*.

The arts and entertainment

Bearing in mind the decreasing financial support it receives from the national government, the quality of the arts in San José is very high. *Josefinos* especially like **theatre**, and there's a healthy range of venues for a city this size, staging a variety of inventive productions at affordable prices. If you speak even a little Spanish it's worth checking to see what's on.

Costa Rica's **National Dance Company** has an impressive repertoire of classical and modern productions, some by Central American choreographers, arranged specifically for the company – again, ticket costs are low. The city's premier venues are the Teatro Nacional and the Teatro Melico Salazar; here you can see performances by the **National Symphony Orchestra** and **National Lyric Opera Company** (June–Aug), as well as visiting orchestras and singers – usually from Spain or other Spanish-speaking countries.

Going to the **cinema** in San José is a bargain, at around $3 a ticket, though many venues have decamped to the suburbs – particularly to shopping malls, such as the Multiplaza Escazú, which you can only reach by car or taxi. There are still a few good downtown cinemas left, however, several of which retain some original features, along with plush, comfortable seats. Most cinemas show the latest American movies, which are almost always subtitled. The few that are dubbed will have the phrase "hablado en Español" in the newspaper listings or on the posters. For Spanish-language art movies, head to Sala Garbo.

Though obviously geared up for tourists, the **Fantasía Folklórica** held every Tuesday night in the Teatro Melico Salazar is the only forum in which traditional dances and songs of the Costa Rican countryside are performed. Shows vary between representations of, for instance, Guanacastecan dance and music, and historic spectaculars such as the current long-running production *Limón, Limón*. Not nearly as cheesy as they sound, they're generally well staged and good fun if you like musicals.

For **details of all performances**, check the *Cartelera* section of the *Tiempo Libre* supplement in *La Nación* on Thursday and the listings in the *Tico Times*, which also distinguish between English- and Spanish-language films and productions.

Cinemas

Alianza Francesa, Barrio Amón (℡ 222-2283). Occasional French-language films, usually dubbed or subtitled in Spanish.

Capri 1 and 2, C 9, Av 0 (℡ 223-0264). Downtown cinema showing US blockbusters.

Cine San Pedro, Planeta Mall in San Pedro. Blockbuster movies, mostly in Spanish.

Colón, Paseo Colón, C 38/40 (℡ 221-4517). Plush, US mall-style cinema, showing mainstream Hollywood films.

Faculdad de Derecho Cinema, Faculty of Law, University of Costa Rica, San Pedro (℡ 207-5322). Occasional European and arthouse films.

Sala Garbo, Av 2, C 28 (℡ 222-1034). Popular arthouse cinema.

Variedades, C 5, Av 0/1 (℡ 222-6104). Old but well-preserved downtown movie house with rococo-style decor showing good foreign and occasionally Spanish-language films.

Theatres

Aduana, C 25, Av 3/5 (☎ 221-5205). Elegant, medium-sized auditorium which often hosts National Theatre Company productions.

Angel, Av 0, C 11/13 (☎ 222-8258). Musicals and light comedies from a former Chilean company who fled Pinochet's Chile in the 1970s to re-establish themselves in San José.

Arlequín, C 13, Av 0/2 (☎ 221-5485). Popular comedies, well staged and acted.

Bellas Artes, Faculdad de Bellas Artes, University of Costa Rica, San Pedro (☎ 253-4327). Generally excellent and innovative student productions with new spins on classical and contemporary works.

Chaplin, Av 12, C 11/13 (☎ 223-2919). Small space for alternative drama, new plays and mime.

Comedia, Av 0, C 11/13 (☎ 255-3255). As the name suggests, comedy plays only.

Eugene O'Neill, Centro Cultural Costarricense-Norteamericano, Los Yoses (☎ 225-9433). Works by modern playwrights in innovative independent productions.

Laurence Olivier, in the Sala Garbo building, Av 2, C 28 (☎ 223-1960). Modern theatre specializing in contemporary productions, plus occasional jazz concerts and film seasons.

Mascara, C 13, Av 2/4 (☎ 222-4574). Low-brow comedies, farces and burlesques.

Melico Salazar, C Central, Av 2 (☎ 221-4952). San José's "workhorse" theatre, featuring a wide variety of performances, including the *Fantasía Folklórica*.

Nacional, C 5, Av 2 (☎ 221-1329). The city's premier theatre, hosting opera, ballet and concerts, as well as drama.

Shopping and markets

San José's **souvenir and crafts shops** are well stocked and in general fairly pricey; it's best to buy from larger ones, run by government-regulated crafts co-operatives, from which more of the money filters down to the artisans. You'll see an abundance of pre-Columbian gold jewellery copies, Costa Rican liqueurs (of which Café Rica is the best known), T-shirts with jungle and animal scenes, weirdly realistic wooden snakes, leather rockers from the village of Sarchí (see p.129), walking sticks, simple leather bracelets, hammocks and a vast array of woodcarvings, from tiny miniatures depicting everyday rural scenes to giant, colourfully hand-painted Sarchí ox-carts. Look out too for *molas,* handmade and appliquéd clothes, mostly shirts, occasionally from the Bahía Drake region of southwestern Costa Rica, but more usually made by the Kuna peoples of Panamá.

A good place to buy any of these handicrafts is at San José's **street craft-market** in the Plaza de la Democracia (see p.94). Also on sale here is a selection of crafts from other Latin American countres, including Ecuadorian sweaters, and leather and silver jewellery from the region. It's worth bargaining, although the goods are already a little cheaper than in shops.

ANDA, Av 0, C 5/7. Indigenous crafts including wooden masks, colourful *molas* and bags, as well as reproductions of Chorotega pottery.

Atmósfera, C 5, Av 1. Elegant gallery-like outlet selling jewellery, furniture and woodwork.

CANAPI, C 11, Av 1. Big shop with a good stock of wooden bowls, walking sticks and boxes.

Hotel Don Carlos, C 9, Av 9. Good pre-Columbian artefacts and jewellery reproductions.

La Casona, C 0, Av 0/1. A large collection of stalls selling the usual local stuff along with Guatemalan

knapsacks and bedspreads. It's great for browsing, and the traders are friendly, but quality at some stalls is pretty poor, and there's not one good T-shirt in evidence.

Mercado Central, Av 0/1, C 6/8. *The* place to buy coffee beans, but make sure they're export quality – ask for Grano d'Oro ("Golden Bean").

Mercado Nacional de Artesanía, C 22, Av 2 bis. One of the country's largest retailers of souvenirs and crafts, featuring all the usual T-shirts, Sarchí ox-carts, jewellery and woodwork.

Sol Maya, Paseo Colón, C 18/20. Rather pricey indigenous and Guatemalan arts and crafts. Tienda de la Naturaleza, Curridabat, 1km beyond San Pedro on Av 0. The shop of the Fundación Neotropica, this is a good place to buy the posters, T-shirts and other paraphernalia painted by English artist Deirdre Hyde that you see all over the country. She specializes in the landscapes of tropical America and the animals who live there, jaguars in particular.

Listings

Airline offices Aeronica, C 11/13 (☎ 233-2483); Alitalia, C 38, Av 3 (☎ 222-6009); American, Paseo Colón, C 26/28 (☎ 257-1266); Aviateca, at the airport (☎ 255-4949); Continental, C 19, Av 2 (☎ 296-4911); Copa, C 1, Av 5 (☎ 222-6640); Iberia, C 40, Paseo Colón (☎ 257-8266); Lacsa, C 1, Av 5 (☎ 257-9444); Ladeco, C 11, Av 1 (☎ 233-7290); Lufthansa, C 5, Av 7/9 (☎ 221-7444); Mexicana, C 1, Av 2/4 (☎ 257-6334); SAM, Av 5, C 1/3 (☎ 233-3066); Sansa, Av 5, C 1/3 (☎ 221-5774); TACA, C 1, Av 1/3 (☎ 222-1790); United Airlines, Sabana Sur (☎ 220-4844); Varig, Av 5, C 1/3 (☎ 290-5222).

Banks State-owned banks in San José include the Banco de Costa Rica, Av 2, C 4/6 (Mon–Fri 9am–3pm; Visa only) and Banco Nacional, Av 0/1, C 2/4 (Mon–Fri 9am–3pm; Visa only). Private banks include Banco Mercantil, Av 3, C 0/2 (Mon–Fri 9am–3pm; Visa only); Banco Metropolitano, C 0, Av 2 (Mon–Fri 8.15am–4pm; Visa only); BANEX, C 0, Av 1 (Mon–Fri 8am–5pm; Visa only); Banco Popular, C 1 Av 2/4 (Mon–Fri 8.30am–3.30pm; Visa & Mastercard); and Banco de San José, C 0, Av 3/5 (Visa & Mastercard).

Bookstores Mora Books, Av 1, C 3/5, in the Omni building (☎ 255-4136), is a pleasant shop with a good selection of secondhand English-language books, CDs, guidebooks and magazines. Chispas, C 7, Av 0/1 (☎ 223-2240), sells new and second-hand books, and has the best selection of English-language fiction in town. It also sells a good array of guide books and books about Costa Rica (in English and Spanish), plus the *New York Times*, *El País* and several English-language magazines. Lehmann, Av 0, C 1/3 (☎ 223-1212), has a good selection of mass-market Spanish-language fiction and non-fiction, as well as lots of maps and children's books. The Libreria Internacional, with branches 300m west of Taco Bell in Barrio Dent (☎ 253-9553) and in the Multiplaza Escazú (☎ 298-1138), is the classiest of the lot, and has the best selection of international fiction; they also stock travel books and Spanish-language fiction, as well as books in English and German. Macondo, opposite the entrance to the library at the university campus in San Pedro, is probably the best bookshop in town for literature in Spanish, especially from Central America, as well as academic disciplines such as sociology and women's studies. Universal, Av 0, C Central/1 (☎ 222-2222), is strong on Spanish books, fiction, titles on Costa Rica (in Spanish), and maps of the country. Libreria y Bazar Guillen at La Coca-Cola bus terminal is a good place to browse for reading material before leaving on a long trip – if you're away from the capital, you can order books from here by phone and the friendly owners will despatch them to you by bus. 7th street books, C 7 Av 0/1 (☎ 256-8251) has both new and used books; it's good on English literature, and also has a wide selection of books and maps on Costa Rica in English and Spanish.

Car rental see p.31.

Embassies and consulates Argentina, 400m south of *McDonald's* in Curridabat (☎ 234-6520 or 234-6270); Belize, 400m east of the Iglesia Santa Teresita, Rohrmoser (☎ 234-9969 or 234-9445); Bolivia, in Rohrmoser (☎ 232-9455); Brazil, Paseo Colón, C 20/22 (☎ 223-1544); Canada, C 3, Av 1 (☎ 296-4149); Chile, 50m east and 225m west of the Automercado, Los Yoses (☎ 224-4243); Colombia, 175m west of Taco Bell, in Barrio Dent (☎ 283-6871); Ecuador, 100m west and 100m south of the Centro Comercial Plaza Mayor, in Rohrmoser (☎ 232-1503); El Salvador, Av 10, C 33/35, Los Yoses (☎ 225-3861); Guatemala, 100m north and 50m east of *Pizza Hut*, in Curridabat (☎ 224-5721); Honduras, 300m east and 200m north of ITAN, in Los Yoses (☎ 234-9502); Mexico, Av 7, C 13/15 (☎ 257-0633); Nicaragua, Av 0, C 25/27 (☎ 222-2373 or 233-8747); Panamá, C 38, Av 5/7 (☎ 257-3241); Peru, 100m south and 50m west of the San José Indoor Club, in Curridabat (☎ 225-

1786); UK, 11th floor, Edificio Centro Colón, Paseo Colón, C 38/40 (☎ 258-2025); US, opposite the Centro Comercial in Pavas – take the bus to Pavas from Av 1, C 18 (☎ 220-3939); Venezuela, Av 2, C 37/39, Los Yoses (☎ 225-5813 or 8810).

Film processing San José is the only place in the country you should try to get film processed. That said, it's expensive and the quality is low: wait until you get home if you can. Bearing in mind these caveats, try Universal, Av 0, C 0/1, which only processes Fuji; IFSA, Av 2, C 3/5, which only processes Kodak; or Dima, Av 0, C 3/5, which processes both Kodak and Fuji.

Hospitals The city's public (social security) hospital is San Juan de Díos, Paseo Colón, C 14/16 (☎ 257-6282). Of the private hospitals, foreigners are most often referred to Clínica Biblica, Av 14, C 0/1 (☎ 257-5252; emergency and after-hours number ☎ 257-0466), where basic consultation and treatment (for example a prescription for a course of antibiotics) starts at about $100. San José has many excellent medical specialists – your embassy will have a list – and private health care is not expensive.

Immigration Costa Rican *migración* (Mon–Fri 8am–4pm) is on the airport highway opposite the Hospital México; take an Alajuela bus and get off at the stop underneath the overhead walkway. Get there early, if you want visa extensions or exit visas. Larger travel agencies, such as Tikal Tours can take care of the paperwork for you for a fee (roughly $10–25).

Laundry Burbujas, 50m west and 25m south of the Mas x Menos supermarket in San Pedro, has coin-operated machines and sells soap; Lava y Seca, 100m north of Mas x Menos, next to Autos San Pedro, in San Pedro, will do your laundry for you, as well as dry-cleaning. Other places include Lava Más, C 45, Av 8/10, next to *Spoon* in Los Yoses; Lavamatic Doña Anna, C 13, Av 16; and Sixaola (one of a chain), Av 2, C 7/9.

Libraries and cultural centres The Alianza Francesa, C 5, Av 7 (Mon–Fri 9am–noon & 3–7pm; ☎ 222-2283) stocks some French publications; the Quaker-affliated Friends' Peace Center, C 15, Av 6 bis (Mon–Fri 10am–3pm; ☎ 221-8299) has English-language newspapers, plus weekly meetings and discussion groups. Other libraries/cultural centres include the Biblioteca Nacional, C 15, Av 3 (Mon–Sat 9am–5pm) and the Centro Cultural Costarricense-Norteamericano, 100m north of the Am-Pm supermarket in Barrio Dent (Mon–Fri

7am–7pm, Sat 9am–noon).

Pharmacies Clinica Biblica, Av 14, C 0/1 (open 24hr); Farmacia del Este, on Av Central near Mas x Menos in San Pedro (open until 8pm); there are many pharmacies in the blocks surrounding the Hospital Calderon Guardia, 100m northeast of the Biblioteca Nacional, in Barrio Otoya.

Post office the Correo Central (Mon–Fri 7am–5pm, Sat 7am–noon), C 2, Av 1/3, is two blocks east and one block north of the Mercado Central. They'll hold letters for up to four weeks (10 colones per letter; you'll need a passport in order to collect your post).

Sports The Sports Complex behind the Museo de Arte Costarricense on Parque La Sabana has a gym, running track and Olympic-size pool ($3), though it's more often closed than open. Parque La Sabana has tennis courts, and is as good a place as any for jogging, with changing facilities and showers – there are lots of runners about in the morning, though there have been reports of assaults on lone joggers in the evening and it's wise to stay away from the heavily wooded north-eastern corner of the park. Parque de la Paz in the south of the city is also recommended for running; in San Pedro you can jog at the UCR campus. The Club Deportivo Cipresses (☎ 253-0530), set in landscaped grounds 700m north of La Galera in Curridabat offers day membership for $7, which gives access to weights, machines, pools and aerobics classes. The nearest public pool to San José is at Ojo de Agua, 17km northwest of town; you can get a bus there from Av 2, C 20/22 (15min).

Supermarkets The cheapest is Mas x Menos (open daily until 9pm), which stocks mainly Costa Rican brands of just about everything. There are several branches in San José, including one on Av 0 between C 9 and 11, and one on Av 0, 300m north of the church in San Pedro. Branches of the Automercado and the Am-Pm supermarket are springing up all over the place. A more upmarket option is the Muñoz y Nanne complex (open daily until 9pm), on Av Central in San Pedro, where you can buy US brands at high prices.

Telephone offices Radiográfica, C 1, Av 5 (daily 7.30am–9pm; ☎ 287-0087) is the state-run office where you can use directories, make overseas calls, and send or receive faxes – unfortunately, it charges a flat fee of $3 for the use of its phones on top of the price of the call.

Moving on from San José

San José is the **transport hub** of Costa Rica. Most bus services, all express bus services, flights and car rental agencies are located here. Wherever you are in the country, technically you are never more than nine hours by highway from the capital, with the majority of destinations being much closer than that. Eventually, like it or not, all roads lead to San José.

When leaving San José **by bus**, note that thefts from the luggage compartments of long-distance services are becoming more common, especially on the Monteverde and Manuel Antonio routes. The accepted wisdom is, if possible, to take your luggage into the bus with you, and even then to make sure all compartments are locked and that you have nothing valuable inside easily unzipped pockets. If you have to put your bags in the luggage hold, make sure only the driver or his helper handles them, and get a seat from where you can keep an eye on the luggage compartment below during stops.

The tables on the following pages deal with **express bus services** from San José. Regional bus information is covered in the relevant accounts in the Guide. As schedules are prone to change, exact departure times are not given here, though details are given where helpful in the separate accounts of the individual destinations; for a full timetable when you arrive, ask at the ICT office (see p.76).

Bus companies in San José

A bewildering number of bus companies use San José as their hub: the following is a rundown of their head office addresses and/or phone numbers, and the abbreviations that we use in the tables overleaf.

ALF	Transportes Alfaro, C 14, Av 3/5	(℡222-2750)
BA	Barquero	(℡232-5660)
BL	Autotransportes Blanco, C 12, Av 9	(℡257-4121)
BM	Buses Metropoli	(℡272-0651)
CA	CARSOL Transportes, C 14, Av 3/5	(℡224-1968)
CL	Coopelimón, Av 3, C 19/21	(℡223-7811)
CO	Coopecaribeños, Av 3, C 19/21	(℡223-7811)
CPT	Coopetraga, C 12, Av 7/9	(℡223-1276
CQ	Autotransportes Ciudad Quesada, C 16, Av 1/3	(℡255-4318)
EM	Empresa Esquivel	(℡666-1249)
ME	Transportes MEPE, Av 11, C 0/1	(℡221-0524)
MO	Transportes Morales, C 16, Av 1/3	(℡223-5567)
MRA	Microbuses Rapidos Heredianos, C1, Av 7/9	(℡223-8392)
MU	Transportes Musoc, C 16, Av 1/3	(℡222-2422)
PU	Pulmitan, C 14, Av 1/3	(℡222-1650)
S	SIRCA, C 7, Av 6/8	(℡222-5541 or 223-1464)
SA	SACSA, C 5, Av 18	(℡233-5350)
Tica	Ticabus, C 9, Av 4/6	(℡221-8954)
TIL	Autotransportes Tilarán, C 14, Av 9/11	(℡222-3854)
TRA	TRALAPA, C 20, Av 1/3	(℡221-7202)
TRC	TRACOPA, Av 18, C 2/4	(℡221-4214)
TRS	Transtusa, Av 6, C 13	(℡556-0073)
TU	Tuasa, C 12, Av 2	(℡222-5325)
Tuan	Tuan	(℡494-2139)

Domestic bus services from San José

In the table below, the initials in the Ⓣ column correspond to the bus company that serves this route; see p.109 for telephone numbers. Where advance purchase is mentioned, it is advised, and strongly recommended in the high season (HS), or at weekends (WE) – i.e. from Friday to Sunday. You need buy your ticket no more than one day in advance unless otherwise indicated. NP = National Park; WR = Wildlife Refuge; NM = National Monument.

TO	FREQUENCY	BUS STOP	DISTANCE	DURATION	Ⓣ	ADV. PURCHASE
Alajuela (and airport)	every 5min	Av 2, C 10/12	17km	35min	TU	no
Braulio Carrillo NP see Guápiles						
Cahuita	4 daily	C 0, Av 13	195km	4hr	ME	yes (HS)
Caño Negro WR see Los Chiles						
Cartago	every 10min	C 5, Av 18/20	22km	45min	SA	no
Chirripó NP see San Isidro						
Corcovado NP						
see Puerto Jiménez de Osa						
Fortuna	11 daily	C16, Av 1/3	130km	4hr 30min	BA	yes (HS)
Golfito	2 daily	C 14, Av 3/5	339km	8hr	TRC	yes (3 days)
Guápiles	every 45min	C 0, Av 13	30km	35min	CPT	no
Guayabo NM see Turrialba						
Heredia	every 10min	C 1, Av 7/9 & C 12, Av 2	11km	25min	MRA	no
La Selva/Selva Verde						
see Puerto Viejo de Sarapiquí						
Liberia	15 daily	C 24, Av 5	217km	4hr	PU	no
Limón	14 daily	C 0, Av13	162km	2hr 30min	CL/CO	no
Los Chiles	2 daily	C 12, Av 9/11	217km	5hr	CQ	no
Manuel Antonio NP see Quepos						
Monteverde	2 daily	C 12, Av 7/9	167km	3hr 30min	TIL	yes (3–5 days)
Nicoya	6 daily	C 14, Av 3/5	296km	6hr	ALF	no

Nosara	1 daily	C 14, Av 3/5	361km	6hr	ALF	no
Palmar	7 daily	C 14, Av 5	258km	5hr	TRA	no
Playa Brasilito	2 daily	C 20, Av 3/5	320km	6hr	TRA	yes (WE)
Playa Coco	2 daily	C 14, Av 1/3	251km	5hr	PU	yes (WE)
Playa Flamingo	2 daily	C 20, Av 3/5	320km	6hr	TRA	yes (WE)
Playa Hermosa	1 daily	C 20, Av 1/3	265km	5hr	EM	no
Playa Jacó	3 daily	Av 3, C 18/20	102km	2hr 30min	MO	yes (WE)
Playa Junquillal	1 daily	C 20, Av 3/5	298km	5hr	TRA	no
Playa Panamá	1 daily	C 20, Av 1/3	265km	5hr	EM	no
Playa Potrero	2 daily	C 20, Av 3	320km	6hr	TRA	yes (WE)
Puerto Jiménez	1 daily	Av 9, C 14/16	378km	9hr	BL	yes
Puerto Viejo de Sarapiquí	8 daily	C 0, Av 13	97km	4hr	check with ICT	no
Puerto Viejo de Talamanca	4 daily	C 0, Av 13	210km	4hr 30min	ME	yes
Puntarenas	every 40min	C 16, Av 10/12	110km	2hr	PU	no
Quepos	3 daily	C 16, Av 1/3	145km	3hr 30min	MO	yes (3 days)
Sámara	1 daily	C 14, Av 3/5	331km	6hr	ALF	yes (WE)
San Carlos/Ciudad Quesada	14 daily	C 12, Av 7/9	110km	3hr	CQ	no
San Isidro	13 daily	C 14, Av 1/3	136km	3hr	TRC/ MUS	no
Santa Cruz	9 daily	Av 3, C 18/20	274km	5hr	TRA	no
Sarchí	34 daily	C 8, Av 0/1	152km	1hr 30min	Tuan	no
Tamarindo	1 daily	C 14, Av 5	320km	6hr	TRA	yes (WE)
Turrialba	17 daily	C 13, Av 6/8	65km	1hr 30min	TRS	no
Volcán Arenal *see* Fortuna						
Volcán Irazú	1 Sat & Sun	Av 2, C 1/3	54km	1hr 30min	BM	no (but go early)
Volcán Poás	1 daily	Av 2, C12/14	55km	1hr 30min	TU	no (but go early)
Zarcero	14 daily	C 12, Av 7/9	177km	2hr	CQ	no

International bus services from San José

Codes given under the ⓣ column correspond to the relevant bus company (see p.109). Advance purchase – at least a week in advance, particularly for Managua and Panamá City – is necessary for all routes.

TO	FREQUENCY	BUS STOP	DISTANCE	DURATION	ⓣ
David	1 daily	Av 3/5, C 14	400km	9hr	Tracopa
Guatemala City	2 daily	C 9, Av 2/4	1200km	60hr	Tica
(overnight in Managua & El Salvador)					
Managua	2 daily	C 9, Av 2/4	450km	11hr	Tica
Managua	Mon, Wed, Fri, Sun	Av 6, C 7/9	450km	13hr	S
Managua	1 daily	C22, Av 3/5	450km	11hr	Trasnica
Panamá City	2 daily	Av 4, C 9/11	903km	20hr	Tica
Paso Canoas	7 daily	C 14, Av 5	349km	8hr	TRC
(for Panamá)					
Peñas Blancas	5 daily	C 16, Av 3/5	293km	6hr	CA
(for Nicaragua & Santa Rosa NP)					
Sixaola	2 daily	C 0, Av 9/11	250km	6hr	ME
(for Panamá)					
Tegucigalpa	2 daily	C 9, Av 2/4	909km	48hr	Tica
(overnight in Managua)					

Domestic flights from San José are run by Sansa, the state airline, and Travelair, a commercial company. Sansa, who fly from Juan Santamaría International airport, 17km northwest of the city, change their schedules frequently: best phone ahead or double-confirm when booking. Travelair, more reliable in terms of schedules, fly from Pavas airport, 7km west of the city. Although the table opposite gives as accurate a rundown of the routes as possible, flight durations are subject to change at the last minute. Some of the routings, particularly those to Nicoya Peninsula, tend to be roundabout, with one or two stops being quite usual. Note that advance purchase (14 days) is necessary to ensure yourself a seat during the high season, especially for Quepos, Sámara and Tamarindo. Both companies have offices and agents throughout the country in most of the destinations they serve, or you can book and pay for tickets at a travel agent. Sansa check-in is at their San José office one hour before departure; they lay on a free bus to get you to the airport, and in some cases offer free transfers to your hotel at the other end. Fares range from $35 one-way to $70–80 return for most destinations. Travelair is typically $10–15 more expensive.

Domestic flights from San José

Sansa, C 24, Paseo Colón/Av 1
(ⓣ 221-9414, reservations ⓣ 257-9444,
ⓕ 255-2176, Ⓦ www.gruptaca.com)

TO	FREQUENCY	DURATION
Barra del Colorado	1 daily	30min
Fortuna	1 daily	30min
Golfito	2 daily	45min
Nosara	1 daily	1hr 25min
Palmar Sur	1 daily	1hr 30min
Puerto Jiménez	1 daily	1hr 15min
Quepos	4 daily	20min
Sámara	1 daily	1hr 45min
Tamarindo	3 daily	40min
Tambor	2 daily	20min
Tortuguero	1 daily	20min

Travelair, Tobías Bolaños airport,
Pavas (ⓣ 220-3054 or 296-1102, ⓕ 220-0413,
ⓔ reservations@travelair-costarica.com)

Golfito	1 daily	1hr 15min
Palmar Sur	1 daily	1hr 30min
Quepos	1 daily (low season)	20min
	3 daily (high season)	20min
Tamarindo	1 daily	40min
Tambor	1 daily	20min
Tortuguero	1 daily	30min

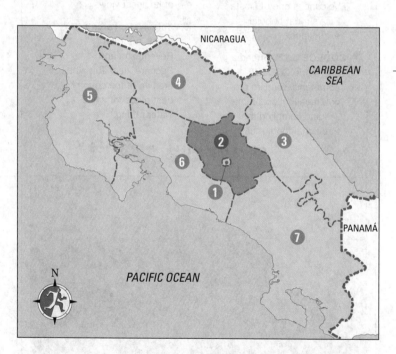

2

The Valle Central
and the highlands

CHAPTER 2   # Highlights

* **Xandari Plantation Hotel
  p.124** Stunning hotel set
  amidst the cool, coffee-
  studded hills of the Valle
  Central.

* **Poás Volcano p.126** An
  easy day-trip from San
  José or Alajuela, the ride
  to the summit of Poás
  Volcano is one of Costa
  Rica's most popular
  excursions.

* **CODECE p.126** Spend a
  day at the CODECE
  community tourism proj-
  ect, meeting local fami-
  lies and sampling the
  traditional food, music

and culture of highland
Costa Rica.

* **Irazú Volcano p.145**
  Dominating the land-
  scape north of Cartago,
  mighty Irazú volcano
  offers some of the coun-
  try's most striking vol-
  canic scenery, and one
  of its finest views.

* **White-water rafting
  p.149** The Ríos
  Reventazón and
  Pacuaré, near Turrialba,
  are two of the country's
  best rivers for white-
  water rafting.

been right there or somewhere exactly like it

2

The Valle Central and the highlands

osta Rica's **Valle Central** (literally "Central Valley") and the surrounding highlands form the cultural and geographical fulcrum of the country. A wide-hipped inter-mountain plateau at a height of between 3000 and 4000m, the area – often also referred to as the Meseta Central, or "Central Tableland" – has a patchwork-quilt beauty, especially when lit by the early-morning sun, with staggered green coffee terraces set in sharp contrast to the blue-black summits of the surrounding mountains. Many of these are **volcanos**: the Valle Central is edged by a chain of volcanic peaks, running from smoking Poás in the north to precipitous Irazú in the east. Though there have been no *bona fide* eruptions since Irazú blew its top in 1963, Poás and Irazú periodically spew and snort, raining a light covering of fertile volcanic ash on the surrounding farmland.

Although it occupies just six percent of the country's total landmass, the Valle Central supports roughly two-thirds of Costa Rica's population. The most fertile land in the country, it is also home to the four most important cities – San José (covered in Chapter One) and the provincial capitals of **Alajuela**, **Heredia** and **Cartago**. The tremendous pressure on land is noticeable even on short forays from San José: urban areas, suburbs and highwayside communities blend into each other, and in places you'll see every spare patch of soil planted with coffee bushes, fruit trees or vegetables.

The area's chief attractions, of course, are the volcanos, especially **Irazú** and **Poás**, both protected by their own national parks, and **Volcán Barva**, sheltered within the huge **Parque Nacional Braulio Carrillo**. In addition, the region

Accommodation price codes

All the accommodation in this book has graded using the following price codes. The prices quoted are for the least expensive double room in high season, and do not include the 18.46 percent national tax which is automatically added onto hotel bills. For more details on accommodation in Costa Rica, see p.35.

❶ less than $10	❷ $10–20
❸ $20–30	❹ $30–50
❺ $50–75	❻ $75–100
❼ $100–150	❽ over $150

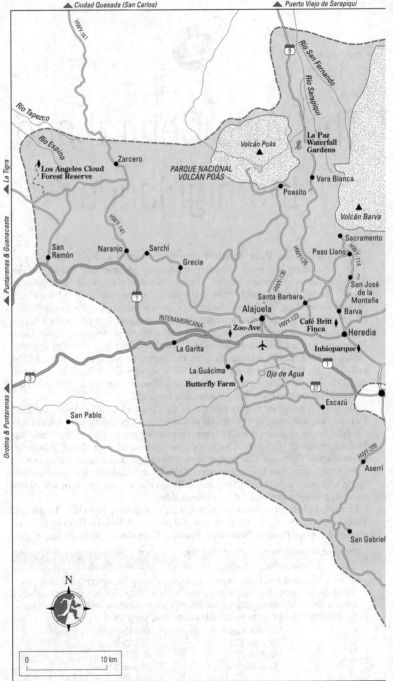

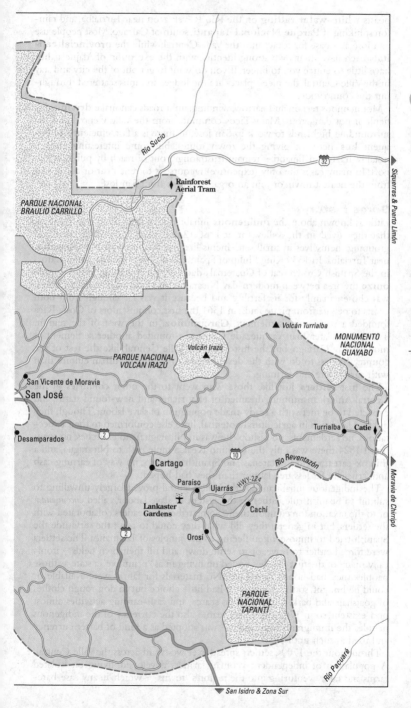

Rainforest
Aerial Tram

PARQUE NACIONAL
BRAULIO CARRILLO

Río Sucio

Siquerres & Puerto Limón

Volcán Turrialba ▲

Volcán Irazú ▲

PARQUE NACIONAL
VOLCÁN IRAZÚ

MONUMENTO
NACIONAL
GUAYABO

San Vicente de Moravia

San José

Moravia de Chiripó

Desamparados

Turrialba   Catie

Cartago

Río Reventazón

Paraíso

Ujarrás   HWY-224

Lankaster
Gardens

Cachí

Orosí

PARQUE
NACIONAL
TAPANTÍ

Río Pacuaré

San Isidro & Zona Sur

boasts **white-water rafting** on the Río Reventazón near Turrialba, and rainforest hiking at **Parque Nacional Tapantí**, south of Cartago. Most people use San José as a base for forays into the Valle Central; while the **provincial capitals** each have their own strong identity, with the exception of Alajuela they have little to entice you to linger. If you do want to get out of the city and stay in the Valle Central, the nicest places are the lodges and inns scattered throughout the countryside.

Mountainous terrain and narrow, winding, unlit roads can make **driving** difficult, if not dangerous. Many Ticos commute from the Valle Central and the surrounding highlands to work in San José, so there is a fast, efficient and frequent **bus** network plying the town routes; but some interesting areas – notably Irazú and Tapantí – remain frustratingly out of reach by public transport. In many cases the only (expensive) recourse is to rent a car or take a taxi from the nearest town, or join an organized tour from San José.

Some history

Little is known about the **indigenous** inhabitants of the Valle Central, except that they lived in the valley for at least 12,000 years, cultivating corn and grouping themselves in small settlements like the one excavated at **Guayabo**, near Turrialba. In 1559 King Philip of Spain and his New World administrators in the Spanish Crown seat of Guatemala decided that it was high time to **colonize** the area between modern-day Nicaragua and Panamá. The Valle Central was chosen mainly for its fertility and because it was far enough from both coasts to be safe from pirate raids; in 1561 the first conquistadors of Costa Rica founded a permanent settlement, **Garcimuñoz**, in the west of the region. Three years later Juan Vazquez de Coronado founded another settlement at modern-day Cartago, but the history of the Valle Central, like the rest of the country, has less to do with the development of towns and urban culture than with agriculture and farming.

The first **settlers**, just like those who went to the other countries of the Central American isthmus, dreamed of easy riches and new-found status, and expected to be met with a ready-made population of slave labour. Though they did find land rich in agricultural potential, little else conformed to their expectations: no settlements, no bishop (he was in Nicaragua), no churches, no roads (until 1824 there was only the Camino Real, a mule path to Nicaragua, and a thin ox-cart track to Puntarenas), no Spanish currency, no way of earning cash and, crucially, far less free labour than they had hoped.

The indigenous inhabitants of the Valle Central proved largely unwilling to submit to Spanish rule, either to the system of slave labour, called *encomienda,* or to the taxation forced upon them. Some tribes and leaders collaborated with the settlers, but in general they did what they could to resist the servitude the Spanish tried to impose, often fleeing to the jungles of Talamanca. The settlers were forced either to leave, or to settle down and till their own fields – ironically, many of the first families ended up living in as "primitive" a state as those peoples they had hoped to exploit. No materials for fabric were available or could be bought, so the immigrants had little choice but to don rough clothes of goatshair and bark. Currency was scarce, and cash-earning activities almost non-existent, so in 1709 the cacao bean – also the currency of the indigenous peoples the immigrants supplanted – was adopted as a kind of barter currency and used as such until 1850.

Throughout the 1700s, settlers spread ever westward across the Valle Central. A population of independent yeoman farmers developed, living on isolated farms and rarely venturing into the region's "towns" – which, in any case, barely existed until well into the eighteenth century. To an extent, Costa Rica's avoidance of the dual society that characterizes other isthmus countries – in which the poor are miserably poor and the rich exceedingly rich – rests upon this initial period of across-the-board poverty and backwardness. Because the Spanish newcomers did not succeed in constructing a properly colonial society, there was an absence of large-scale servitude on big farms in the Valle Central.

Though some twentieth-century historians point to this period as the crucible in which modern-day Costa Rica's largely middle-class society and devotion to the principles of independence and social equality were born, more recent theories (including those expressed in writing by political scientist, former president and Nobel Peace Prize winner Oscar Arias Sánchez) have questioned this depiction of the roots of Costa Ricans' supposedly innate egalitarianism, suggesting that the nascent *criollo* society (*criollo* meaning a Spaniard born in the New World) was quite conscious of social divisions and, in fact, manufactured them where none existed. Though many of the *conquistadors* were from Extremadura, the poorest region in Spain, and had acquired their titles by conquest rather than by inheritance, they and their descendants thought themselves superior to the waves of poor peasants coming from Andalucía. In turn, settled families looked with contempt upon new arrivals, and there is evidence to show that, had economic conditions permitted, they would have imposed a system of indentureship on the local *mestizo* (mixed-race) population, as happened in the highlands of Nicaragua, El Salvador and Guatemala.

In 1808, Costa Rica's governor, Tomás de Acosta, first brought **coffee** here from Jamaica; a highland plant, it flourished in the Valle Central. Legislators, keen to develop a cash crop, offered incentives to farmers – in 1821, San José's town council gave free land and coffee seedlings to the settlers, while families in Cartago were ordered to plant 20 to 25 coffee bushes in their back yards. In 1832 there were enough beans available for export, and real wealth – at least for the exporters and coffee brokers – came in 1844, when the London market for Costa Rican coffee opened up. It was the country's main source of income until war and declining prices devastated the domestic market in the 1930s.

Coffee is still a major earner for Heredia and Cartago provinces – indeed for the whole country – and today the Valle Central remains the most economically productive region in Costa Rica. The huge black tarpaulins you see from the air as you fly in are flower nurseries. Fruits, including mangoes and strawberries, are cultivated in Alajuela; vegetables thrive in the volcanic soil near Poás and Irazú; whilst on the slopes of Irazú and Barva, Holstein cattle, prized dairy stock, provide much of the country's milk. Venture anywhere outside the urban areas and you will see evidence of the continued presence of the yeoman farmer, as small plots and family holdings survive despite the population pressure that continues to erode the available farmland.

Alajuela and around

Alajuela province is vast, extending from **Alajuela** town, 20km northwest of San José, all the way north to the Nicaraguan border and west to the slopes of Volcán Arenal. The account here deals only with that part of the province on the south side of the Cordillera Central, spanning the area from Alajuela itself to the town of Zarcero, 59km northwest, up in the highlands. The **Parque Nacional Volcán Poás** is the area's principal attraction, with some great trails and lakes on its slopes; the ride up to the crater gives good views over the whole densely populated, heavily cultivated province, passing flower-growing fincas, fruit farms and the occasional coffee field. In general the **climate** is good; Alajuela is considerably warmer than San José, and the province contains two towns – Atenas and La Garita – which the National Geographic Society has deemed to have the best climates in the world.

People also head out here to see the crafts factories at **Sarchí**, famous for its coloured wooden ox-carts; **Zoo-Ave**, the exceptional bird sanctuary and zoo just outside town on the way to La Garita; and the **Butterfly Farm** at La Guácima. There's also the little-visited **Los Angeles cloudforest**, a miniature version of the better-known cloudforest at Monteverde, and **Ojo de Agua**, a thermal water-fed swimming and recreation complex near the Juan Santamaría airport, popular with *Josefinos* as a place to escape the city.

Alajuela

Although it has a population of just 35,000, **ALAJUELA** is nonetheless Costa Rica's second city. At first sight there's little to distinguish it from San José, until the pleasant realization dawns that walking down the street you can smell bougainvillea rather than diesel. This is still a largely agricultural centre, with a **Saturday market** that brings hundreds of farmers in from the surrounding area to sell their fruit, vegetables, dairy products and flowers.

Founded in 1657, Alajuela's most cherished historical figure is the drummer-boy-cum-martyr **Juan Santamaría**, hero of the battle of 1856, who sacrificed his life to save the country from the avaricious American adventurer William Walker (see p.256). Today, Santamaría is celebrated in his own **museum**, about the only formal attraction in town. All in all, Alajuela can be seen in half a day, but it makes a convenient base for visiting the arts-and-crafts village of **Sarchí** or the butterfly farm at **La Guácima**. Above all it's a useful place to stay for travellers who have to catch early-morning flights: the **airport** is less than 3km away, about five minutes by bus, compared to 30–40 minutes from San José.

If you're here in mid-October, it's worth stopping to see the **Festival of San Geronado**, the patron saint of Alajuela, which takes place on the 16th. It's a very dignified affair, with well-ordered, flower-strewn parades and performances by schoolkids' orchestras in the Parque Central.

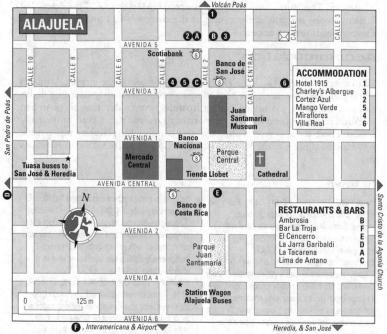

ALAJUELA

Volcán Poás

AVENIDA 5

Scotiabank

Banco de
San José

ACCOMMODATION

Hotel 1915	1
Charley's Albergue	3
Cortez Azul	2
Mango Verde	5
Miraflores	4
Villa Real	6

AVENIDA 3

Juan
Santamaría
Museum

AVENIDA 1

Banco
Nacional

Parque
Central

Mercado
Central

Tienda Llobet   Cathedral

Tuasa buses to
San José & Heredia

AVENIDA CENTRAL

San Pedro de Poás

Santo Cristo de la Agonía Church

Banco de
Costa Rica

RESTAURANTS & BARS

Ambrosia	B
Bar La Troja	F
El Cencerro	E
La Jarra Garibaldi	D
La Tacarena	A
Lima de Antano	C

AVENIDA 2

Parque
Juan
Santamaría

AVENIDA 4

Station Wagon
Alajuela Buses

0   125 m

AVENIDA 6

Interamericana & Airport   Heredia, & San José

Arrival, orientation and information

Red-and-black Tuasa **buses from San José** arrive on C 8, four blocks west of the Parque Central, amongst an inhospitable confusion of bus stops, super-markets and shoe stores. The beige-and-orange Station Wagon Alajuela bus from San José drops you off on Av 4, just west of Parque Juan Santamaría, a few minutes' walk from the centre. If you're **driving**, take the *pista* to the airport (General Cañas Highway), which is also the road to Puntarenas. The turnoff to Alajuela is 17km from San José – don't use the underpass or you'll end up at the airport. For getting around, **taxis** line up on the west side of the Parque Central.

Alajuela's peaceful **Parque Central** (officially called Plaza del General Tomás Guardia), the focal point of Alajuela's grid of streets, is skirted by Avenida Central and Calle Central, the town's main thoroughfares. As in San José, the numbers of *calles* and *avenidas* go up by twos, although no one pays any atten-tion to street numbers, instead giving directions in relation to known **land-marks**, the most popular being the Parque Central; the Mercado Central, two blocks to the west; the Tienda Llobet department store at Av Central and C 4; and the *correo* (see below).

There is no **tourist office** in Alajuela, and the town's **banks** are all clustered around the Parque Central: to change **travellers' cheques**, choose between Banco Nacional on the west side of the parque, Banco de Costa Rica, one block west on Av Central; or the Creditel/Banco de San José on Av 3, oppo-site the entrance to the Juan Santamaría museum. Both the Banco de Costa Rica and Scotiabank on Av 5 have **ATMs** which accept Visa and

Mastercard. The small and efficient **correo** (Mon–Fri 7.30am–5pm, Sat 7.30am–noon) is north of the centre, at the corner of C 1 and Av 5, and has inexpensive **internet access**.

Accommodation

With the opening of the large *Hampton Inn* right beside the airport, Alajuela's few **hotels** are now much less booked up by people with early-morning flights to catch. However, the town's budget **hostels** (better value than those in San José) still fill very quickly, and it's important to reserve ahead even in the rainy season. There are also several attractive and comfortable places to stay outside town including one of the loveliest hotels in Costa Rica, the *Xandari Plantation Inn*.

In town

Hotel 1915, C 2, Av 5/7 (T 441-0495). Easily the nicest hotel in Alajuela, set in an old house arranged around an attractive patio filled with rocking chairs and plants. All rooms have private bath, plenty of hot water and TV. ❹

Charley's Albergue, Av 5 (T & F 441-0115, W www.isacam.com). Some 200m north of Parque Central and attracting a mainly gringo crowd, with 11 large clean rooms, some with private bath and hot running water. Also has a lounge with TV and a kitchen area, and arranges tours to local attractions such as Volcán Poás. ❹

Cortez Azul, Av 5, C 2/4 (T 443-6145, E fabioanchia@latinmail.com). Reasonably priced hostel with 5 small rooms (some with private bath), communal kitchen and laundry facilities. ❷

Mango Verde, Av 3, C 2/4 (T & F 441-6330, E mangover@racsa.co.cr). The best budget option in Alajuela, this small and cheerful hostel has simple rooms, all with private bath, plus a pretty TV lounge and breakfast bar, communal kitchen and attractive blue-walled yard. ❷

Miraflores, Av 3, C 2/4 (T 391-2177, F 441-7116, E mirafloresbb@hotmail.com). Quiet, no-frills hotel with spacious rooms, parking space and tours to nearby attractions by arrangement. ❹

Villa Real, C 1, Av 3 (T 441-4022). Basic backpackers' hang-out with friendly staff – it's often full of travellers just arrived in or about to leave Costa Rica. ❷

Around Alajuela

Orquideas Inn, 5km outside Alajuela on the road to Poás (T 443-9346, F 443-9740, W www.hotels.co.cr/orquideas.html). Spanish hacienda-style country inn with kitsch flourishes, large comfortable rooms, landscaped gardens and attentive service. There's also a pool, barbecue restaurant and coffee shop. Children under the age of ten are not permitted. ❺

Siempreverde Lodge, a well-signed left turn at the school in San Isidro, 8km north of Alajuela on the main Poás road (T 449-5134, F 449-5003). Spotless new B&B with brightly coloured rooms and immaculate gardens. ❺

Xandari Plantation Inn, 6.5km north of Alajuela, clearly signposted from the main road to Poás (T 443-2020, in the US T 805/684-7879, F 442-4847, W www.xandari.com). Beautifully decorated luxury hotel, with 16 spacious villas set in a coffee plantation, wonderful views over the Valle Central and walking trails through the grounds to a series of waterfalls. Facilities include two swimming pools, gym and massage, and free airport pickup. Excellent value. ❽

The Town

Alajuela's few attractions are almost all within a minute's walk of the **Parque Central**, the town's central space, surrounded by colonial buildings, though their aesthetic effect is spoilt somewhat by the storefronts festooned with Pepsi-Cola banners. Most impressive is the sturdy whitewashed former jail that now houses the **Juan Santamaría Cultural-Historical Museum** Av 3, C Central/2 (Tues–Sun 10am–6pm; free), a fortress-like edifice entered through a pretty tiled courtyard lined with long wooden benches. The curiously monastic atmosphere of the exhibition rooms inside is almost more interesting than the small collection they hold, which runs the gamut from mid-nineteenth-century maps of Costa Rica to crumbly portraits of figures involved in the battle of 1856. A modern and comfortable auditorium hosts talks and conferences on topics of regional interest. Flanking the eastern end of the Parque Central is the town's white-domed **Cathedral**, badly damaged in an earthquake in 1990 but now reopened – though of no great architectural merit, it boasts some pretty floor tiles, round stained-glass windows and a large cupola bizarrely decorated with *trompe l'oeil* balconies. One block south of the Parque Central, the small and empty **Parque Juan Santamaría** features a statue of the ubiquitous local hero.

Outside the centre, the town is leafy, quiet and residential, with occasional views of the blue mountain ridges and bright-green carpet of the Valle Central. Five blocks east of the Parque Central is the **Santo Cristo de la Agonía** church, constructed as recently as 1935, though it looks much older. Its exterior is Baroque in style, and painted in two-tone cream, while inside there's a lovely wooden, gilt-edged altar, with naive Latin American motifs, and gilt-painted columns edging the bright tiled floor. Realist murals, apparently painted from life, show various stages in the development of Christianity in Costa Rica, depicting monsignors and indigenous people gathering with middle-class citizens to receive the Word.

Eating, drinking and nightlife

Josefinos often deride Alajuela for its (lack of) **nightlife** – many people still live in and around the centre, so pressure from residents means that bars close relatively early, at around 11pm. Even so, Alajuela has several decent **restaurants**, while the friendly Mercado Central is a particularly good place for delicious *ceviche* and *casados*. In addition, the Juan Santamaría museum occasionally hosts classical or jazz concerts and theatrical events; for more unusual entertainment, the local forty-piece band plays orchestral and local favourites in the bandstand in the Parque Central every Sunday morning.

Ambrosia, Av 5, C 2. Outdoor terrace-café with sticky cakes, an extensive selection of coffees and good-value *casados* at lunch time.

Bar La Troja, a 10–15min walk south from the town centre along C 4. The only vaguely lively place in town, this rooftop bar has a relaxed atmosphere and decent music. Very popular mid-week.

El Cencerro, on the south side of Parque Central. This established steakhouse is an Alajuela institution and specializes in succulent beef dishes ($10–15).

La Jarra Garibaldi, Av Central, ten blocks west of Parque Central. Vast Mexican restaurant with extensive international menu, cocktails and live music at the weekends. Entertainingly cheesy and very popular with a swanky older crowd.

La Tacarena, Av 5, C 2. Quiet corner restaurant with wooden booths and a good varied menu including pizza and Costa Rican dishes ($5–8). One of the few restaurants in Alajuela open on Sundays.

Lima de Antano, Av 3, C 2. Friendly family-run Peruvian café with excellent seafood.

Alajuela doesn't have a main bus terminal. Instead, there's a loose collection of bus stops just south of Av 1 between C 8 and 10. Other than San José and Heredia services, all buses depart from around here, including regular departures for Naranjo, Sarchí, Grecia and La Guácima Abajo, for the Butterfly Farm. It's a confusing area, and the departure points are not well marked, so ask around to make sure you are waiting at the right place.

Fast and frequent Tuasa buses to San José and Heredia leave from a stop on C 8 between Av 1 and Central. Even if the bus says "Alajuela–San José", you'll need to check with the driver if it goes direct to San José or to Heredia first.

Around Alajuela

The most popular excursions in the Valle Central all lie within 30km of Alajuela. Closest to town are the unabashed tourist attractions of **La Guácima Butterfly Farm** and the aviary at **Zoo-Ave**, while slightly further afield in the north of the province are the crafts-making enclave of **Sarchí**, the atmospheric mountain town of **Zarcero**, and **Volcán Poás**, one of the most visited national parks in the country.

Parque Nacional Volcán Poás

PARQUE NACIONAL VOLCÁN POÁS (daily 8am–3.45pm; $6), just 55km from San José and 37km north of Alajuela, is home to one of the world's most easily accessible active volcanos, with a history of eruptions that goes back eleven million years. Poás's last gigantic blowout was on January 25, 1910, when it dumped 640,000 tons of ash on the surrounding area, and from time to time you may find that the volcano is off limits due to sulphurous gas emissions, so it's worth checking conditions with the ICT in San José before you set off.

Codece

Just west of San José, beyond the smart suburbs of San Rafael and San Miguel de Escazú, the mountain town of San Antonio de Escazú is home to an exemplary new agro-ecological community tourism project. Here a group of local families, with help from the Dutch government and a couple of Canadian universities, have established CODECE (Association for the Conservation and Development of the Mountains of Escazú). CODECE offers an authentic experience of Costa Rican *campesino* life, including a visit to a working *trapiche*, or old-fashioned sugar mill, and a trip to a five-acre forest preserve, which includes an organic vegetable garden. Guests get to spend time with community families and are served *típico* food and drink. Depending on your interests, the community can arrange for marimba music to be played, or for retired local schoolteacher Doña Estefania to narrate local history and legends. CODECE works mostly with groups of at least twelve people, but can sometimes accommodate smaller groups or couples. A day tour starts at $15, and accommodation can also be arranged with local families for two-day trips ($50). You need to ring the CODECE office (☎ 228-0183, ✉ codece@racsa.co.cr), preferably several days in advance, and speak to Amalia, the project coordinator.

You need to get to the volcano before the clouds roll in, which they inevitably do, as early as 10am, even in the dry season (Dec–April). Poás has blasted out three craters in its lifetime, and due to the more or less constant volcanic activity, the appearance of the **main crater** changes regularly – it's currently 1500m wide and filled with milky turquoise water from which sulphurous gases waft and broil. Although it's an impressive sight, you only need about fifteen minutes' viewing and picture-snapping.

The park features a few very well-maintained, short and unchallenging **trails**, which take you through a strange, otherworldly landscape, dotted with smoking *fumaroles* (steam vents) and tough ferns and trees valiantly surviving regular scaldings with sulphurous gases (the battle-scarred *sombrilla de pobre*, or poor man's umbrella, looks the most woebegone). Poás is also home to a rare version of cloudforest called **dwarf** or **stunted cloudforest**, a combination of pine-needle-like ferns, miniature bonsai-type trees, and bromeliad-encrusted ancient arboreal cover, all of which has been stunted through an onslaught of cold (temperatures up here can drop to below freezing), continual cloud cover, and acid rain from the mouth of the volcano.

The **Crater Overlook trail**, which winds around the main crater along a paved road, is only 750m long. A side trail (1km; 20–30min) heads off through the forest to the pretty, emerald Botos Lake, which fills an extinct crater and makes a good spot for a picnic. Named for the pagoda-like tree commonly seen along its way, the **Escalonia trail** (about 1km; 30min) starts at the picnic area (follow the signs), taking you through ground cover less stunted than that at the crater. Birds ply this temperate forest: among them the colourful but shy quetzal, the robin, and several species of hummingbird. Although a number of large mammals live in the confines of the park, including coyotes and wildcats such as the margay, you're unlikely to spot them around the crater. One animal you probably will come across, however, is the small, green-yellow **Poás squirrel**, unique to the region.

Getting to Volcán Poás

Most visitors get to the volcano on a pre-arranged **tour** from San José (approximately $35 per person for a 4–5 hour trip, including return transport and guide – see p.33 for details of tour operators). All kinds of combination packages with other Valle Central sites exist: the "Four-in-One" tour organized by Expediciones Tropicales (℡257-4171, ⓦwww.costaricainfo.com) is reasonably priced and very popular, and also takes in the La Paz Waterfall Gardens, the Braulio Carrillo National Park and a boat ride on the Sarapiquí river ($79 per person including breakfast, lunch and guide; 11hr). Otherwise, a Tuasa bus leaves daily from C 12/14, Av 2 in San José at 8.30am, travelling via Alajuela and returning from the volcano at 2.30pm ($3 each way; 2hr). If you want to reach Poás before both tour buses and dense cloud cover arrive, you'll need either to drive or take a **taxi** from Alajuela (roughly $30) or San José ($45–50) – reasonably affordable if split between a group of people.

The park's **visitor centre** shows videos of the volcano and has a snack shop, which also serves hot coffee, though you're probably better off packing a picnic lunch. Make sure you bring a sweater and wet-weather gear with you in the rainy season. No **camping** is allowed in the park.

Accommodation near the park

If you want to get a really early start to guarantee a view of Poás's crater, there are plenty of places to stay in the vicinity, including a couple of comfortable **mountain lodges** on working dairy farms (though you'll need a car to get to

The strawberry trail

You can't fail to notice that the area around Volcán Poás is a **strawberry-growing** region, and it's worth stopping off on your way from Alajuela to the volcano to sample some of this delicious fresh fruit. Two restaurants en route are particularly recommended: *Chubascos* (closed Tues), about 15km from Alajuela on the road to Poás, makes the very best strawberry *refresco* in the country and is also famous for its superlative local cuisine, including succulently cooked *casados* and large lunch plates made with extra-fresh ingredients. *Las Fresas* (closed Wed), a twenty-minute drive from Alajuela on the road to San Pedro de Poás, also specializes in superb strawberry dishes, as well as serving fantastic wood-oven pizzas.

them) and other, more simple and inexpensive places which can be reached on the daily bus to Poás. If you want **to camp**, the *Mountain View Campground* (T 482-2196; $5 per tent per night), just before the *Chubascos* restaurant on the main road to Poas, has a pleasant garden site with hot showers.

La Providencia Ecological Reserve, 1km from the park entrance on the slopes of Poás (T 380-6315). Charming rustic cabinas on a working dairy farm, near the top of Poás, with spectacular views across to Volcán Arenal and the Talamanca mountains. The owners prepare excellent local food, rent out horses for trots up the volcano ($20 for 3 hours) and organize trout fishing trips. ❹

Lo Que tu Quieras ("Whatever you want"), 5km before the park entrance (T 482-2092). The least expensive option in the area, run by a friendly couple, comprising three small cabinas with heated water and fireplaces, and a restaurant serving local dishes with huge picture windows and staggering views across the valley – stop for a drink on your way back from the volcano. There's also a small butterfly garden (Tues–Sun 9am–2.30pm; $3) and horses for hire ($3/hr), while camping is permitted for a nominal fee. ❷

Poás Volcano Lodge, 6km from the small village of Poásito – which is 10km before the entrance to Poás on the main mountain road from Alajuela and San José – take a right fork towards Varablanca (T 482-2194, F 482-2513, W www.arweb.com/poas). A working dairy farm, with patches of private protected forest on the grounds and 9 beautifully furnished rooms evoking a combination of English cottage, Welsh farmhouse and American Shaker. Facilities include a basement games room with pool and ping-pong tables and mountain bikes for hire. Meals ($8–12) by arrangement. ❺

La Paz Waterfall Gardens

A fifteen-kilometre drive east of Poás is one of Costa Rica's newest and most popular attractions, the **La Paz Waterfall Gardens** (daily 8.30am–4pm; $24; W www.waterfallgardens.com), an immaculate series of riverside trails linking five waterfalls on the Río La Paz, all set in a large and colourful garden planted with native shrubs and flowers – there's also a butterfly observatory and a hummingbird garden which is home to sixteen different species. From the reception centre, visitors take one of several self-guided tours which wind prettily through the site and along the river, where viewing platforms mean that at various points you're both above and underneath the waterfalls, the highest of which, **Magia Blanca**, crashes deafeningly almost 40m down into swirling white water. The marked trails conclude at the top of the **La Paz Waterfall**, Costa Rica's most photographed cascade (it can also be seen from the public highway which runs over a large rickety bridge below). The gardens and trails are undoubtedly attractive, though it's all rather sterile – there's little danger of stumbling across any uninvited wildlife here. Still, you could spend a pleasant enough couple of hours exploring the grounds, and if you're feeling hungry there's a decent café in the reception area (set lunch $8), which has an upper level with lovely views over the gardens. Guides are available on request ($25).

There's currently no public transport to the gardens, and most people visit the gardens as part of an organized tour from San José – Expediciones Tropicales (☎257-4171, ℱ257-4124, ⓦwww.costaricainfo.com) include La Paz as part of their "Four-in-One" highlights tour ($79). If you're driving, take a right at the junction in Poasito towardsVara Blanca and, on reaching the village, take a left at the gas station and follow the well-marked signs for 5km.

Sarchí and around

Touted as the centre of Costa Rican arts and crafts, especially **furniture making**, the village of **SARCHÍ**, 30km northwest of Alajuela, is a commercialized place – firmly on the tourist trail but with little or no charm. Its setting is pretty enough, between precipitous verdant hills, but don't come expecting to see picturesque scenes of craftsmen sitting in small historic shops, blowing glass, sculpting marble or carving wood. The **fábricas de carretas** (ox-cart factories) and the **mueblerías** (furniture factories) are large factory showrooms strung out along the main road and, granted that in the larger *fábricas* you can watch the carts and furniture being painted and assembled, there's not much actually to see. Nevertheless, the ox-carts and leather rocking chairs are less expensive here here than anywhere else in the country; most people come on half-day shopping trips from the capital or stop on their way to Zarcero and the Zona Norte.

The **Sarchí ox-cart** was first produced by enterprising local families for the immigrant settlers who arrived at the beginning of the twentieth century to run the coffee plantations. The original designs featured simple geometric shapes, though the ox-carts sold to today's tourists are kaleidoscopically painted square carts built to be hauled by a single ox or team of two oxen. Moorish in origin, the designs can be traced back to immigrants from the Spanish provinces of Andalucía and Granada. Full-scale carts (costing approximately $1000) are rarely sold, but a number of smaller-scale versions are made for tourists ($60–200). Faced with the question "But what, exactly, am I going to do with this at home?" the salespeople in Sarchí deftly whip off the top of the miniature cart to reveal a bar with room for several bottles, a serving tray and an ice section. They sell like hotcakes.

Besides the carts, Sarchí tables, bedsteads and **leather rocking chairs** (about $70) are the most popular items. Other crafts are much the same as you'll see all over Costa Rica: wiggly wooden snakes, hand-polished wooden boxes and bowls, T-shirts and walking sticks, and the ubiquitous hokey "home sweet home" wall hangings. Many of the *mueblerías* will freight-mail your ox-cart if you arrange this in advance.

The village itself is spread out and divided into two halves. Large *fábricas* line the main road from **Sarchí Sur**, in effect a conglomeration of *mueblerías,* to the residential area of **Sarchí Norte**, which climbs the hill. Besides the shops and factories, the only thing of interest is Sarchí Norte's pink-and-turquoise **church**, looking out from atop the hill. Inside, the tiles are delicate pastel shades of pink and green; in the little park fronting the church, stone benches are painted with the same colourful designs you see on the ox-carts.

2

Fábrica Chaverrí, Sarchí Sur, on the left-hand side of the road as you enter the village (☎454-4411, 🖷454-4944). Sarchí's largest ox-cart factory, with a huge showroom. In the back you can wander around the painting workshop and see hundreds of ox-carts in progress. There's a small soda where you can eat lunch outside at picnic tables and a free *Café Britt* kiosk. They will also arrange shipping and transport for souvenirs. Credit cards accepted.

Fabrica Jorge Quesada Alfaro, at the north end of Sarchí Norte, on the main road (☎454-4586, 🖷454-2890, 📧quesada@racsa.co.cr). The classiest selection of rocking chairs and stools in Sarchí, and the only furniture factory where you can watch them being made. There's are children's seats and furry animal hides on sale as well.

Plaza de la Artesanía, Sarchí Sur. Roadside mall-like group of shops and restaurants, arranged in a courtyard. Snazzy and pricey, with boutiques selling everything from Guatemalan vests to gold jewellery. Ox-carts are available from Habanos (☎ & 🖷454-3430, 🖥www.sarchi.freeservers.com/rancho/trabajo.htm), who can arrange freight transport (about $50 for a small cart, $84 for a bigger one, to the US or Europe). There's also an *heladería* and a moderately priced fish restaurant, *La Troja*. The Banco Nacional here can change dollars.

Practicalities

It goes without saying that if you intend to buy a large item, it's best not to come to Sarchí by public transport, as buses are always crowded and seats are tiny. However, if you have no choice, local **buses** from Alajuela run approximately every thirty minutes from 5am to 10pm. Buses back (via Grecia) can be hailed on the main road from Sarchí Norte to Sarchí Sur. From **San José** a daily express service (1hr–1hr 30min) runs from La Coca-Cola every thirty minutes from 5am to 10pm; the return schedule is the same. You could also take the bus to Naranjo from La Coca-Cola, every hour on the hour, and switch there for a local service to Sarchí. Call the Tuan bus company (see p.109) for information.

There's just one small **hotel** in Sarchí Norte, the *Hotel Daniel Zamora* (☎454-4596; ❷), on a sidestreet opposite the soccer field, which has clean rooms and hot water. For **lunch** or a snack, try *Soda Donald* beside the soccer field, which serves decent refrescos and ice cream, or *La Finca* restaurant to the right of the Mercado de Artesanía souvenir shop as you drive north out of town, which serves very good maize soup and grilled steak.

The Banco Nacional on the main road beyond the church changes dollars and travellers' cheques, as does a smaller branch in the Mercado de Artesanía. **Taxis** can be ordered on ☎454-4028, or hailed on the street.

Around Sarchí

If you have time on the way to Sarchí, stop off to see the remarkable *fin-de-siècle* church in the small town of **GRECIA**, some 18km northwest of Alajuela. After their first church burned down, the prudent residents of Grecia decided to take no chances and built the second out of metal, for which pounded sheets were specially made and imported from Belgium. The rust-coloured and white-trimmed result is surprisingly beautiful, with an altar that is a testament to Latin American Baroque froth, made entirely from intricate marble and tottering up into the eaves of the church like a wedding cake. A couple of kilometres outside the centre of Grecia on the Alajuela road is **El Mundo de las Serpientes** (daily 9am–5pm; $11), a small collection of forty species of snakes well housed in large glass boxes. The entrance fee includes a highly informative guided tour (in English or Spanish) during which you are acquainted you with all kinds strange information pertaining to snakes, such as the fact that they are completely deaf, and that they frequently die of stress. From San José there's a **bus** to Grecia every hour on the hour (or when full) from La Coca-Cola (5am–7pm; 1hr).

Four kilometres northwest of Sarchi, at **Llano del Rosario**, (follow a left-fork signposted just south of Naranjo), is Costa Rica's only **bungee jump**: Tropical Bungee (☎233-6455, ⓕ255-4354, ⓦwww.bungee.co.cr; $45) organizes leaps from the bridge over the Río Colorado; they can also arrange pick-ups from San José.

Los Angeles Cloudforest Reserve

Some 40km by road northwest of Alajuela, **LOS ANGELES CLOUD-FOREST RESERVE** (8am–5pm; ⓦwww.villablanca.co.cr) is a less crowded alternative to the Monteverde cloudforest (see p.303), though on nowhere the same scale. Climbing from 700m to nearly 2000m, Los Angeles is home to a number of habitats and microclimates, including dark, impenetrable cloudforest, often shrouded in light misty cloud and resounding with the calls of monkeys.

Two rather short **trails** provide a good introduction to rainforest walking and the cloudforest habitat. Both are easy, along wooden boardwalks covered with non-slip corduroy. A third, much longer, trail (8km), for which a guide is obligatory, takes you to the junction of the rivers Balsa and Espino, through a change in elevation and correspondingly different vegetations, and along paths that are cut but not fitted with corduroy. There's no official puesto in the reserve, and entrance fees ($12 self-guided; $20 with guide) must be paid at the *Hotel Villablanca* reception, which also has details of the **canopy tour** ($38.50; 2hr) – which involves swinging along steel cables stretched between the treetops (not for the faint-hearted) – and horseback rides ($12 per hr) in the reserve.

The hotel grounds also contain a small chapel known as **La Mariana**, built by the reserve's owner, ex-president Rodrigo Corazon, to celebrate his long and happy marriage by honouring the Virgin Mary. The building, plain on the outside, has a unique and colourful ceiling covered with 840 hand-painted tiles depicting traditional and religious ceremonies throughout Latin America. An audiotour in English is available (30 min; $5).

Practicalities

Los Angeles is about 40km northwest of Alajuela by road, and is best reached via San Ramón, 30km from Alajuela on the Interamericana (Hwy-1). From San Ramón, take a right fork opposite the hospital towards La Fortuna and follow the road until you reach the hamlet of Los Angeles Norte, from where the *Hotel Villablanca* and reserve are well signed. If you don't have your own transport, hourly **buses** go from Alajuela to San Ramón; a taxi from here to the reserve costs approximately $10. You can **stay** in the reserve at the *Hotel Villablanca* (☎228-4603, ⓕ228-4004; ⓰), which has 48 comfortable en-suite chalets, plus a restaurant and a TV lounge.

Zarcero

ZARCERO, 52km northwest of Alajuela on Hwy-141, sits almost at the highest point of this stretch of the Cordillera Central in an astounding landscape where precipitous inclines falling into deep gorges and valleys are scaled by contented Holstein cattle. First impressions of Zarcero itself are of a pleasant mountain town, with crisp fresh air and ruddy-faced inhabitants. Head for the central plaza, however, where a pretty white church gleams in the sun, and you'll see the work of Evangelisto Blanco, whose Doctor Seuss-like imagination has manifested itself in a series of fabulous topiary sculptures – an elephant, a light bulb, a strange bird – and vaulting, Gaudí-esque archways from vines and hedges. There's little else to see in town, although **horse-riding tours** through the spectacular surrounding countryside can be organized with Laguna Horseback Riding (☎463-3437, ⓔluisblan@racsa.co.cr; $40 for 3–4hr), situated at *Cabinas la Pradera* in nearby Laguna. Zarcero is also famous for its fresh, white, relatively bland **cheese**, called *palmito* (heart-of-palm, which is what it looks like). You can buy it from any of the shops near the bus stop on the south side of the central plaza.

Practicalities

Buses from San José to Zarcero leave hourly between 5am and 7.30pm from La Coca-Cola (1hr 30min), arriving in Zarcero on the northern side of the Zocaló. The bus stop for San Carlos/Ciudad Quesada and the Zona Norte is on the northwest corner of the central plaza (hourly; 1hr). There is one small and friendly **hotel** on the corner of Zarcero's main square, the *Hotel Don Beto* (☎ & ⓕ463-3137; ❸) and only a few places **to eat**, all of which are around or near the central plaza, including the *Restaurante El Higaron* and *Pizzeria Galeria*, both serving good, inexpensive local food. Next door to the latter, a bakery and sweet shop sells delicious fresh cookies and cakes. **Travellers' cheques** can be changed at the Banco de Costa Rica on Zarcero's main street; it also has an ATM. Oddly, Zarcero is also home to a large, semi-olympic **swimming pool**, Piscinas Apamar ($1.60 entrance), which also has thermal baths and a jacuzzi – it's 450m uphill to the east of the central park.

Southwest of Alajuela

Twelve kilometres southwest of Alajuela, **La Guácima Butterfly Farm** (daily 9.30am–5pm, last tour at 3pm; $15; ☎438-0440, ⓦwww.butterflyfarm.co.cr) breeds valuable pupae for export to zoos and botanical gardens all over the world. Tours begin with an audiovisual exhibit introducing the processes involved in commercial butterfly breeding, after which guides explain all aspects of butterfly life, including their cruelly short lifespans, while flashes of jewel colours flutter prettily around the mesh-enclosed breeding area. The farm also has beautiful views over the Valle Central; in the wet season be sure to go early, as the rain drives the butterflies to hide, and clouds obscure the views. Pick-ups can be arranged from hotels in San José, if you call the farm in advance.

Buses from San José to La Guácima leave from Av 1, C 20/22, daily except Sunday at 11am and 2pm – the trip takes two hours, so get the earlier service. Return buses to the capital leave at 12.15pm and 3.15pm. From **Alajuela**, buses marked "La Guácima Abajo" leave from the area southwest of the area of bus stops at 6.20am, 9am, 11am and 1pm; the Butterfly Farm is practically the last stop, and they will let you off at the gates. Return buses pass the gates of the farm at about 11.45am, 1.45pm, 3.45pm and 5.45pm; get to the stop a little early just to make sure.

The largest aviary in Central America, **Zoo-Ave** (daily 9am–5pm; $9), at Dulce Nombre, 5km west of Alajuela, is just about the best place in the country – besides the wild – to see Costa Rica's fabulous birds. This is an exceptionally well-run exhibition, with large clean cages and carefully tended grounds. Many of the birds fly free, fluttering around in a flurry of raucous colours: look out for the kaleidoscopic *lapas* – **scarlet macaw** – and wonderful blue **parrots**. Other birds include chestnut mandibled **toucans** and the fluffy **tropical screech owls**. There are also some **primates**, from monkeys to marmosets, again in large and well-tended areas. A sign in one of the enclosures says, "There are fifty iguanas in this area. Can you find any?", though you're unlikely to spot even one of these shy creatures. Ideally, you need a minimum of an hour to see everything. The La Garita bus from Alajuela passes right by Zoo-Ave, leaving from the area southwest of the main terminal. The trip takes about fifteen minutes.

Five kilometres west beyond Zoo-Ave, the small hamlet of **LA GARITA** is known for having one of the most clement climates in the world. Fruits, ornamental plants and flowers flourish here, but the only reason to stop, really, is if you happen to be going through to **Playa Jacó** (see p.329) on the weekends when *Restaurante Fiesta del Maíz* ("Corn Party Restaurant") is open. This is a very popular stop for Ticos heading from San José to Jacó, serving inexpensive (under \$5) main courses and snacks, all made from corn. Many have no English translation and are endemic to Costa Rica, but all are pretty tasty, particularly with a cold drink, even if the restaurant itself is disappointingly reminiscent of a fast-food joint, with bolted-down tables and long queues at the till. Open only Friday to Sunday and on holidays, the restaurant is on the left-hand side of the village as you head toward the Pacific coast.

Heredia and around

Heredia province stretches northeast from San José all the way to the Nicaraguan border, skirted on the west by Hwy-9, the old road from San José to Puerto Viejo de Sarapiquí, and to the east by the Guápiles Highway (Hwy-32), which provides access to Braulio Carrillo and to Limón on the Caribbean coast. The moment you leave San José for **Heredia**, the provincial capital, the rubbery leaves of coffee plants spring up on all sides; in the section of the province covered in this chapter, the land is almost wholly given over to coffee production, and there are a number of popular **coffee tours**, especially to the Café Britt finca near Heredia town.

In the Valle Central, the province's chief attractions are the dormant **Volcán Barva**, offering a good day's climb up its dense forested slopes with superb views from the top, and the nearby **Rainforest Aerial Tram**, which allows you to see the canopy of primary rainforest from above, causing minimal disturbance to the animals and birds.

Heredia

Just 11km northeast of San José, **HEREDIA** is a lively city, boosted by the student population of the UNA, the Universidad Nacional, at the eastern end of town, and famed for its **soccer team**, one of the best and most popular in the country. The town centre is prettier than most, though a little run-down, with a Parque Central flanked by tall palms and a few historical buildings. Small and easy to navigate, Heredia is a natural jumping-off point for excursions to the nearby historical hamlet of **Barva** and to the town of **San José de la Montaña**, a gateway to **Volcán Barva**. Many tourists also come to sample the **Café Britt tour**, hosted by the nation's largest coffee exporter, about 3km north of the town centre.

Arrival and information

Tuasa **buses** leave San José for Heredia from C 1, Av 7/9 every 15–30 minutes, and pull into Heredia at the corner of C Central and Av 4, a stone's throw south of the Parque Central. At night, **minibuses** leave San José hourly between midnight and 6am from Av 2, C 12/14. Banco Nacional at C 2, Av 2/4 and Scotiabank at Av 4, C Central/C2 both have ATMs, and change currency and **travellers' cheques**. The **correo** (Mon–Fri 7.30am–5.30pm) is on the northwest corner of the Parque Central, while **taxis** line up on the east side of the Mercado Central, between Av 6 and 8, and on the southern side of the Parque Central.

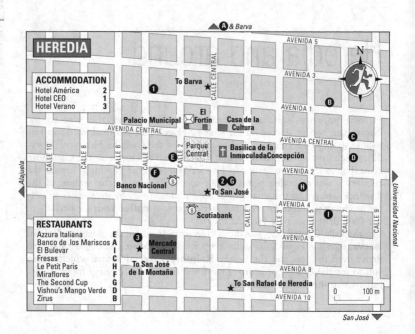

Accommodation

Decent accommodation in downtown Heredia is pretty sparse. It's unlikely, in any case, that you will need to stay in town; San José is within easy reach, and there are several country resort-type hotels nearby, including one of the finest in the country. Although all are accessible by bus, you'll find it handy to have a car once you're there.

Central Heredia

Hotel America, C Central, opposite the San José bus stop (☏ 260-9292, ℱ 260-9293, ⓦ www.hotelamerica.net). Clean if soulless rooms, some of which are rather dark, though all have bathroom, fan, TV and hot water. ④

Hotel CEO, Av 1 (☏ 262-2628, ℱ 262-2639, ⓦ www.hotelamerica.net). Quiet hotel with spotless but no-frills rooms with private bathrooms and hot water. ②

Hotel Verano, Av 6, C 4, at the western entrance to the Mercado Central (☏ 237-1616). Friendly budget option, though the beds and walls are very flimsy. ①

Around Heredia

Chalet Tirol, north of Heredia, well signposted on the road to Los Angeles via San Rafael (☏ 267-6222, ℱ 267-6228, ⓦ www.chalet-tirol.com).

Incredibly kitsch hotel in lovely pine forest on the edge of the Braulio Carrillo National Park, with ten alpine chalets in a grassy clearing plus a reproduction Tyrol village church for concerts and events and a square complete with fountain. Renowned gourmet French restaurant complete with linen napery and well-stocked wine cellar. Guided walking tours available. ⑥

Finca Rosa Blanca, on the road between San Pedro de Barva and Santa Barbara de Heredia (☏ 269-9392, ℱ 269-9555, ⓦ www.finca-rblanca.co.cr). One of the best hotels in the country, like some giant white bird roosting above the coffee fields, with six themed suites and two villas, plus a gorgeous tiled pool which seemingly drips over the hillside. An excellent four-course dinner, prepared from organic produce grown in the lovely gardens, is served family-style round the large table in the fairy-tale hotel foyer. ⑧

The Town

Heredia's layout conforms to the usual grid system, centred on the quiet **Parque Central**, draped with huge mango trees and overlooked by the plain **Basílica de la Inmaculada Concepción**, whose unexcitingly squat design – "seismic Baroque" – has kept it standing through several earthquakes since 1797. North of the Parque, the old colonial tower of **El Fortín**, "The Fortress", features odd gun slats which fan out and widen from the inside to the exterior, giving it a medieval look: you cannot enter or climb it.

East of the tower on Avenida Central, the **Casa de la Cultura**, an old colonial house with a large breezy verandah, displays local art, including sculpture and painting by the schoolchildren of Heredia. The **Mercado Central**, Av 6/8, C 2/4 (daily 5am–6pm), is a clean, orderly place, its wide aisles lined with rows of fruit and veg, dangling sausages and plump prawns.

Eating and drinking

Perhaps because of the student population, Heredia is crawling with excellent cafés, patisseries, ice-cream joints and the best vegetarian/health food **restaurants** outside San José. **Nightlife** is low-key, restricted to a few local salsa spots and some great bars, the best of which are clustered around the four blocks immediately to the west of the Universidad Nacional, in the east of Heredia.

Azzura Italiana, southwest corner of Parque Central. Upmarket café with superior Italian ice cream, excellent *refrescos*, fresh sandwiches and real cappuccino and espresso.

Banco de los Mariscos, in Santa Barbara, 6km north of Heredia (℡ 269-9090). Upmarket restaurant serving delicious fresh seafood, including lobster.

El Bulevar, Av 4, C 5/7. Currently the in place for Heredia's student population, this lively bar is open to the street and does inexpensive beer-and-*boca* specials.

Fresas, C 7, Av 0. Large and popular American-style restaurant with some outdoor seating. Serves upmarket soda food (lunches go for about $6), with an emphasis on strawberries – try the strawberry fruit cups or the fruit salads.

Le Petit Paris, C 5, Av 2/4 (℡ 262-2564). This French-owned oasis of calm has tables set out in a small garden and serves delicious French cui-

sine. The lunch menu changes daily, and there's live jazz on Wednesdays. Expect to pay around $10–15 for a full meal. Closed Sun.

Miraflores, Av 2, C 2/4. Lively disco and bar where Heredians go to dance salsa and merengue; attracts a slightly older crowd.

The Second Cup, foyer of the *Hotel America*, C Central, Av 2/4. Posh café with cappuccino, iced coffee and breakfast, as well as a good-value lunch-time menu ($3). The tables outside on the main street are great spots for people-watching.

Vishnu's Mango Verde, C 7, Av Central/2. One of a chain of vegetarian restaurants, with rustic, plant-filled decor and a pretty back garden. It serves good vegetarian food, including sandwiches made to order, yoghurts, sweets and coffee. Lunch only Mon–Fri.

Zirus, Centro Comercial Plaza Cibeles, Av 1, C 5/7. Popular pizza restaurant with takeaway service (℡ 262-5959) and friendly atmosphere.

Moving on from Heredia

Heredia has no central bus terminal, but a variety of well-signed bus stops are scattered around town, with a heavy concentration around the Mercado Central. Buses to San José depart from C Central, Av 4 (about every 15min during the day). From the Mercado Central, local buses leave for San José de la Montaña, San Joaquín de Heredia, San Isidro de Heredia and the swimming complex at Ojo de Agua. Buses to San Rafael de Heredia depart from near the train tracks at Av 10 and C 0/2. For Barva and Santa Barbara de Heredia the stop is at C Central, Av 1/3. All leave fairly regularly, about every thirty minutes.

Around Heredia

North and east of Heredia the terrain climbs to higher altitudes, reaching its highest point at **Volcán Barva**, at the western entrance of the wild, rugged **Parque Nacional Braulio Carrillo**. Temperatures are notably cooler around here, the landscape dotted with dairy farms and conifers. Though the area in general gives a good picture of coffee-oriented agriculture and provincial Costa Rican life, none of the villages surrounding Heredia town offer much to persuade you to linger. The exception is for aficionados of religious architecture, who could make jaunts out to a number of pretty **churches**, from the old colonial structure in **Barva** to **San Rafael**'s white and silver edifice, set high above the Valle Central, and the jolly twin-towered churches of **Santa Barbara de Heredia** and **San Joaquín de Heredia**.

Parque Nacional Braulio Carrillo

The **PARQUE NACIONAL BRAULIO CARRILLO** (8am–3.45pm; $6), 20km northeast of San José, covers 325 square kilometres acres of virgin rain- and cloudforest, though it's still little visited on account of its sheer size and lack of facilities, and most tourists experience the majestic views of cloud and

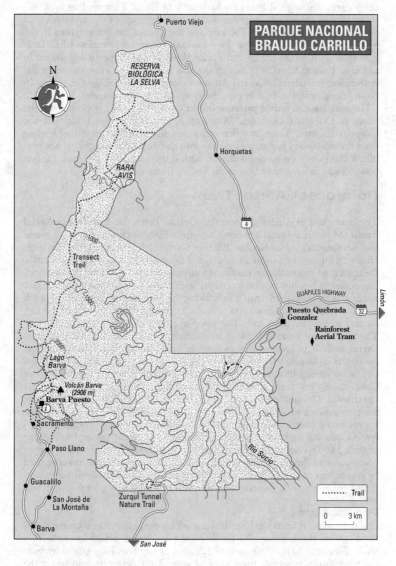

foliage only from the window of a bus on their way to the Caribbean coast. Named after Costa Rica's third, and rather dictatorial, chief of state, who held office in the mid-1800s, the park was established in 1978, mainly to protect the land from the possible effects of the Guápiles Highway, then under construction between San José and Limón, a piece of intelligent foresight without which this whole stretch of countryside might have been turned into a solid strip of gas stations and motels.

Even when only seen from the highway, Braulio Carrillo's dense forested cover gives you a good idea of what much of Costa Rica used to look like about fifty years ago, when approximately three-quarters of the country's total terrain was virgin rainforest. The rare and shy quetzal has been sighted in the higher altitudes of the park, as have toucans, trogons and eagles, while large mammals such as the jaguar and ocelot skulk in the dense undergrowth. In addition, Braulio Carrillo is one of the few places in the country where the bushmaster (matabuey), Central America's largest venomous snake, makes its home, along with the equally poisonous fer-de-lance (terciopelo).

The park has two staffed **puestos**, one at Volcán Barva (see opposite) and the other at Quebrada Gonzalez, 2km east of the Sucio river bridge on the Guápiles Highway. There are picnic facilities and a well-marked trail leading from the puesto at Quebrada Gonzalez into the forest, but camping is not permited and there's no accommodation within this section of the park, though you can stay in very basic huts at the Volcán Barva puesto.

Rainforest Aerial Tram

The brainchild of American naturalist Donald Perry, the **Rainforest Aerial Tram** (Mon 9am–4pm, Tues–Sun 6am–4pm; $50 per person) lies just beyond the northeastern boundary of Braulio Carrillo, 1.5km from the Guápiles Highway. Funded by private investors, and the product of many years' research, the tram is an innovation in rainforest tourism, the first of its kind in the world. Its premise is beautifully simple: twenty overhead cable cars, each holding five passengers and one guide, run slowly along the 1.7km aerial track (45min each way; the entrance fee allows you unlimited rides), skirting the tops of the forest and passing between trees, providing eye-level encounters along the way. The ride affords a rare glimpse of birds, animals and plants, including the epiphytes, orchids, insects and mosses that live inside the upper reaches of the forest and, as it's largely silent, cuts down the chances of animals being frightened by the oncoming thudding of feet. In his book, *Life Above the Jungle Floor* (see Contexts, p.436), Perry tells how he risked life and limb to get the project operational. Committed to protecting the rainforest canopy and the jungle floor, he refused to allow the construction firm erecting the tram's high-wire towers to use tractors; they were unable to secure a powerful enough helicopter in Costa Rica, but Nicaragua's Sandinistas came to the rescue, loaning one of their MI-17 combat helicopters (minus the guns) to help erect the poles.

Surrounding the tram track is a 3.5-square-kilometre **private reserve** used by researchers to study life in the rainforest canopy. There are a few short loop trails here, along with a restaurant, visitor centre and parking area.

Practicalities

Less than an hour from San José, the turn-off for the aerial tram is on the right-hand side of the highway, 5.3 km beyond the (signed) bridge over the Río Sucio. From the turn-off it's another 1.5km walk or drive. To get there **by bus**, catch the Guápiles service from San José and ask the driver to drop you at the turn-off. The return Guápiles–San José bus will stop when flagged down, unless it's full. Alternatively, and much more conveniently, you can organize a **tour** ($65 per person) with the tram's San José office on C 7, Av 7 (☏257-5961, ⊕257-6053, ⊛www.rainforesttram.com), which includes transport to and from your hotel, a guided aerial excursion and hiking on nature trails. Similar trips are offered (at a slightly higher price) by most San José travel agencies. There are also special early-morning bird-watching trips, and torchlit night rides (until 9pm) – many canopy inhabitants become active and visible only in the dark – plus tours combining the tram with other regional attractions, such as La Guácima butterfly farm or Café Britt. These can all be booked through the tram's San José office. It's advisable to wear a hat, insect repellent, and to bring binoculars, camera and rain gear.

North of Heredia: Café Britt and Barva

Just north of Heredia on the road to Barva, you'll see signs off the highway directing you to the **Café Britt finca** (tours daily at 9am & 11am; also at 3pm mid-Dec to April; $15), where you can get an idea of how the modern-day coffee industry works. The finca grows one of the country's best-known coffee brands and is the most important exporter of Costa Rican coffee to the world. Guides take you through the history of coffee growing in Costa Rica, demonstrating how crucial this export crop was to the development of the country, with a rather slick multimedia presentation and thorough descriptions of the processes involved in harvesting and selecting the beans. It all ends with a tasting and, of course, the inevitable stop in the gift shop. The finca (℡ 261-0707, ⓦ www.cafebritt.com) will pick up visitors and return them to most San José hotels ($25, including transport and tour), and also offers day-trips combining a tour of the finca and lunch with visits to La Guácima butterfly farm ($60) and the Rainforest Aerial Tram ($99). They also arrange a "coffee-lover's" tour, including a session on how to make the perfect cappuccino ($50).

A couple of kilometres beyond the finca turning, the unusual **Museo de la Cultura Popular** (daily 8.30am–5pm; $1.50) is worth a browse to find out more about life in Costa Rica in the early part of this century. Set in a large verandah'd house surrounded by coffee fields, the museum has recreated many of the rooms of this coffee finca as they would have been in the late nineteenth and early twentieth century, to give a flavour of life in this era. The museum **restaurant** (closed Sat & Sun) serves authentic food of the period, including *torta de arroz*, *pan casero* and *gallos picadillos*.

A kilometre further on, the colonial village of **BARVA** is really only worth a brief stop on the way to Volcán Barva to have a look at the huge cream Baroque **church**, flanked by tall brooding palms, and the surrounding adobe and tile-roofed houses. Though Barva was founded in 1561, most of what you see today dates from the 1700s. The village also boasts an excellent Mexican restaurant, *El Charro de Fofo,* which serves all the usual Mexican staples like tortillas and refried beans in a cheerful corner spot 300m south of the village's main square on the main road to Heredia. There are several decent sodas near the church; **buses** to San José de la Montaña (for the volcano) stop opposite the soccer field.

Volcán Barva

Just beyond Barva, a turn-off on the right-hand side of the highway heads off towards to **VOLCÁN BARVA**. Although it's not far from Heredia, the volcano is difficult to reach due to the lack of public transport and a bad stretch of unpaved road that's impassable by even the sturdiest of 4WDs, even in the dry season. Daily **buses** (at around 6.30am, 12pm & 4pm) run from Heredia to San José de la Montaña, and on to Paso Llano. From here it's a four-kilometre walk (there's no bus) to the hamlet of Sacramento, followed by another 3km up a steep track to the Barva puesto, where you pay a park fee ($6) which allows you access to the trails that wind up the slope of this long-dormant volcano to a small, pristine crater.

The **main trail** (3km; about 1hr) begins from the puesto, ascending through dense deciduous cover, climbing 3000m before reaching the cloudforest at the top. Along the way you'll get panoramic views over the Valle Central and southeast to Volcán Irazú; if you're lucky – bring binoculars – you might see the elusive, jewel-coloured quetzal (though these nest-bound birds are usually only seen at their preferred altitude of 3600m or more). At the summit, you'll find the green-blue lake that fills the old crater, surrounded by dense forests that are often obscured in cloud. Take a compass, water and food, a sweater and rain gear, and leave early in the morning to enjoy the clearest views of the top. Be prepared for serious mud in the rainy season.

Practicalities

Buses back from Paso Llano to Heredia leave daily at 7.30am, 1pm and (most conveniently, but on weekends only) 5pm. Otherwise it's a case of getting a taxi – ask in either of the restaurants mentioned below, or try ringing local driver Lizandro Cascante (☏ 224-2400).

If you want **to stay** near the volcano, there are basic **huts** ($2/night) and **camping** facilities (reserve in advance on ☏ 283-5906) at the Barva puesto. There are also a couple of surprisingly good places to stay in the hamlet of Guacalillo, 8km south of the volcano. *Hotel de Montaña El Portico* (☏ 237-6022, Ⓕ 260-6002; ❹) has enormous, simply furnished rooms with private bath, and also rents out attractive self-catering cabins ($70 per night for up to 5 people), while the adjacent *Hotel Las Ardillas* (☏ 260-2172, Ⓔ ardillas@racsa.co.cr; ❹) has very pretty cabinas with wall hangings and fireplaces, and a wonderfully cosy restaurant with meat cooked over a coffee-wood fire and a healthy selection of soups and salads. There's also a tiled spa with mud treatments, massage and hypnotherapy ($20–50/hr).

If you want to stock up on energy before climbing, several **restaurants** in the area serve *típico* food, including the *Campesino*, about 3.5km beyond Paso Llano en route to Volcán Barva, and the *Sacramento*, another 500m further on. *Soda El Bosque* in Sacramento, a picturesque little café stuffed full of junk-shop objects collected by its owner, serves up traditional *gallos* with various toppings, as well as breakfast and *casados*.

East and south of Heredia

The small village of **SAN VICENTE DE MORAVIA**, about 7km northeast of San José, is a well-known centre for handicrafts – these mostly consist of ceramics and leather, but you'll also find some wooden bowls and jewellery. There are a dozen or so shops in town, most of them spread along the aptly named Calle de la Artesanía, just north of the Parque Central, with little variety in the price or quality of goods. Most sell the same kind of stuff you find all over the country – wooden walking sticks, snakes, serving bowls, mini oxcarts – but a few specialize in different crafts. Worth a look are Artesanía Bribrí, which sells masks and leather goods made by the **Bribrí** indigenous peoples of the Talamanca coast (see p.179); Magia, specializing in very elegant (and expensive) leather bags; and Artesanías Zurqui, which has a large collection of attractive handmade ceramics with blue glazed finishes.

About 6km east of San Vicente, in a cluster of small villages known commonly as Coronado, lies the hamlet of **DULCE NOMBRE DE CORONADO**. Budding herpetologists will want to stop by the **Instituto Clodomiro Picado**, or "snake farm" (☏ 229-0344; Mon–Thurs 8am–4pm by group reservation only; Fri 2–3pm for the general public; free), where a variety of poisonous species are bred for research, their venom used in the commercial production of antivenin. Most of the action occurs at feeding time, when you can watch live mice and toads being guzzled by the hungry reptiles; Friday-afternoon visitors have a special treat, as this is when the snakes' venom is extracted. The institute also sells pre-prepared antivenin which you can take on the road with you, but in general the serum needs to be refrigerated; ask the staff for instructions. To get to the snake farm **by bus**, a local serviceto Dulce Nombre leaves San José hourly from Av 3, C 3/5. Staff at the institute will know return bus times.

Four kilometres south of Heredia is **INBIOPARQUE** (daily 7.30am–4pm; $18; ⓦwww.inbio.ac.cr/inbioparque), a small educational and recreational centre set up by the Instituto Nacional de Biodiversidad to explain in simple terms how biodiversity works and exactly why it is so important. The park consists of two permanent **exhibitions**, with storyboards explaining biodiversity in action, and three **guided trails** (30min–2hr) through various different kinds of Costa Rican wet and dry forest, with neatly labelled plants and a cultivated area of fruit trees and medicinal plants. Although mostly aimed at schoolchildren and students, the park is a good place for budding naturalists to learn to identify native species. There's a café on site, and transport from San Jose can be arranged ($10); alternatively, take the local bus from San José to the village of Santo Domingo.

Cartago and around

With land made fertile by deposits from Volcán Irazú, **Cartago province** extends east of San José and south into the Cordillera de Talamanca. The section covered in this chapter is a heavily populated, farmed and industrialized region, centred on **Cartago**, a major shopping and transport hub for the southern Valle Central. Dominated by the soaring form of **Volcán Irazú**, the landscape is varied and pretty, patched with squares of rich tilled soil and pockets of pine forest. Though Cartago is home to Costa Rica's most famous church, the fat, Byzantine **Basílica de Nuestra Señora de Los Angeles**, the town itself is not really worth staying in, and many of the region's attractions are best visited on day-trips from San José. The most popular excursion is to the volcano, but there's also the mystically lovely **Orosí valley**, the orchid collection at **Lankester Gardens**, and the wild, little-visited **Parque Nacional Tapantí**.

It takes about forty minutes to reach Cartago on the good (toll) highway from San José. From Cartago there are road connections to Turrialba on the eastern slopes of Irazú, Parque Nacional Tapantí and the Orosí valley, and south via the Interamericana over the hump of the Cordillera Central to San Isidro and the Valle de el General.

Cartago

Founded in 1563 by Juan Vazquez de Coronado, CARTAGO, meaning "Carthage", was Costa Rica's capital for three hundred years before the centre of power was moved to San José in 1823. Like its ancient namesake the city has been razed a number of times, although in this case by earthquakes instead of Romans – two, in 1823 and 1910, conspired practically to demolish the place. Most of the town's fine nineteenth-century and fin-de-siècle buildings were destroyed, and what has grown up in their place – the usual assortment of shops and haphazard modern buildings – is not particularly appealing. Nowadays Cartago's chief function is as a busy market and shopping centre, with some industry around its periphery. Its prize possession is its soaring cathedral, or basilica, dedicated to La Negrita, Costa Rica's patron saint.

Arrival, information and accommodation

SACSA runs frequent local **buses** to Cartago, leaving from its San José terminal on C 5, Av 18/20 (after 8.30pm, buses leave from in front of the *Grand Hotel Costa Rica*), running along Av 2 to C 19, then along Av Central and out through San Pedro – a journey of around 45 minutes. In Cartago, buses sometimes do a bit of a tour of town, stopping at virtually every block; wait to get off at the Parque Central, where you'll be dropped right in front of the ruined church, Las Ruinas.

Like the other provincial capitals in the Valle Central, Cartago has no **tourist office**. Banco de Costa Rica, Av 4, C 5/7, and Banco Nacional, C 1, Av 2, will change **travellers' cheques**, but it'll take a while. The **correo** is ten minutes from the town centre at Av 2, C 15/17 (Mon–Fri 7.30am–6pm, Sat 7.30–12pm). **Taxis** leave from the rank at Las Ruinas.

There's just one decent **hotel** in Cartago, the *Los Angeles Lodge* (℡551-0957; ❸), on the cathedral square. Other accommodation in the town is frequented by commercial travellers and best avoided. In any case, getting stuck in Cartago overnight is an unlikely scenario, as there's a 24-hour bus service to San José.

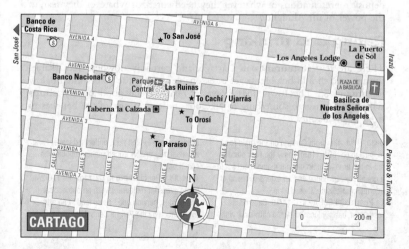

The Town

There's little to see in central Cartago. As usual, the focus of the town is the **Parque Central**, a leafy, tranquil square dominated by the ruined Iglesia de la Parroquía, known as **Las Ruinas**. Originally built in 1575, the church was repeatedly destroyed by earthquakes but stubbornly rebuilt every time, until eventually the giant earthquake of 1910 vanquished it for good. Only the elegantly tumbling walls remain, enclosing pretty subtropical gardens; unfortunately they are locked more often than not, but you can peer through the iron gate at the fluffy blossoms flowering inside. If you inspect the sides and corners of the ruins carefully you'll see where the earthquake dislodged entire rows of mortar, sending them several centimetres beyond those above and below.

From the ruins it's a five-minute walk east to Cartago's only other attraction: the cathedral, properly named the **Basílica de Nuestra Señora de Los Angeles**. Built in a decorative Byzantine style after the previous basilica was destroyed in an earthquake of 1926, this huge cement-grey structure with its elaborate wood-panelled interior is home to **La Negrita**, the representation of the Virgin of Los Angeles, patron saint of Costa Rica. On this spot on August 2, 1635, the Virgin reportedly showed herself to a poor peasant girl in the form of a dark doll made of stone. Each time the girl took the doll away to play with it, it mulishly reappeared on the spot where she had found it; this was seen as a sign, and the church was built soon after. August 2 is now one of the most important days in the Costa Rican religious calendar, when hundreds of pilgrims make the journey to Cartago to visit the tiny black statue of the Virgin, tucked away in a shallow subterranean antechamber beneath the crypt. It is a tradition in this grand, vaulting church for pilgrims to shuffle all the way down the aisle towards the altar on their knees, rosaries fretting in their hands as they whisper a steady chorus of Hail Marys (on August 2, many of them will have shuffled from as far as San José to pay their respects). In the left-hand antechamber of the cathedral you'll see silver *ex votos* of every imaginable shape and size, including horses, planes, grasshoppers (representing plagues of locusts), hearts with swords driven through them, arms, fingers and hands. This is a Latin American tradition stretching from Mexico to Brazil, whereby the faithful deposit representations of whatever they need cured, or whatever they fear, to the power of the Almighty.

Eating and drinking

There are few **restaurants** in Cartago, and certainly nowhere remarkable, though you should be able to get a reasonable meal at the places listed below for around $5. The town does, however, boast several good **pastry shops** where you can grab something to take out and eat on one of the benches in front of the basilica.

Casa Vieja, 4km from Cartago on the main road to Paraíso (⊤ 591-1165). Easily the best place to eat in the area, with an elegant dining room set in a grand colonial house and an extensive menu of international cuisine. Closed Mon.

La Puerta del Sol, Av 4, C 14/16. Cavernous restaurant, handily located by the cathedral, with black-and-white tiled floor, uniformed waiters and a decent, reasonably priced menu. Popular with coach parties.

Taberna y Restaurante la Calzada, Av 1, C 2/4. Large, pleasant restaurant, with an outdoor bar and garden, serving good *típico* food in an attractive location by the Parque Central.

Moving on from Cartago

To get back to San José, hop on whichever bus happens to be loading up in the covered area on Av 4, C 2/4. Buses leave every ten minutes between 5am and midnight, and about every hour otherwise. Local buses are frequent and reliable: for Paraíso, use the stop on Av 3, C2/4 (6am–10pm: Mon–Fri every 30min; Sat & Sun hourly); for Orosí, catch a bus at C 4, Av 1 (6am–10pm; Mon–Fri every 30min; Sat & Sun hourly); for Cachí and Ujarrás, buses leave roughly every hour from C 6, Av 1/2.

Around Cartago

Dominating the landscape north of Cartago is **Volcán Irazú**, part of the mighty Cordillera Central and the most popular excursion in Cartago province. In the opposite direction from Cartago is the less visited **Parque Nacional Tapantí**, one of the closest places to San José for rainforest hiking; if you have your own transport, it makes a good day excursion or weekend trip. The park lies in the pretty **Orosí valley**, which boasts a couple of interesting churches at Ujarrás and Orosí.

On the eastern slopes of the Cordillera Central, the small town of **Turrialba** is a local hub for watersports on the nearby Ríos Reventazón and Pacuaré, two of the best **white-water rafting** rivers in the country. The town is also the gateway to the **Monumento Nacional Guayabo**, the most important ancient site in Costa Rica. A good two hours from San José, both are best reached via Cartago.

Parque Nacional Volcán Irazú

The blasted lunar landscape of **PARQUE NACIONAL VOLCÁN IRAZÚ** (daily 8am–3.45pm; $6) is affectingly dramatic, reaching its highest point at 3432m and giving fantastic views on clear days to the Caribbean coast. Famous for having had the gall to erupt on the day President John F. Kennedy visited Costa Rica on March 19, 1963, Irazú has been more or less calm since; but while its **Diego de la Haya crater** is far less active, in terms of bubblings and rumblings, than that of Volcán Poás, its deep depression and the strange algae-green lake that fills it creates an undeniably impressive sight.

Situated 32km north of Cartago, a journey that is almost entirely uphill, the volcano makes for a long but scenic trip, especially early in the morning before the inevitable **clouds** roll in. Up at the top there is very little vegetation, and what does grow has an otherworldly quality, struggling to survive in this strange environment. There's not much actually to do in the park after viewing the crater from the mirador; there are no official trails, though it's possible to clamber along the scraggly slopes of a few outcrops and scramble amongst the dunes of grey ash. Whatever you do, watch your step, as volcanic ash crumbles easily, and there are a few places where you could end up falling into the ominous-looking lake.

Practicalities

A visit to Irazú is strictly for day-trippers only, since there's nowhere to stay or camp in the park. Only one public **bus** runs to the park, leaving from San José's *Gran Hotel Costa Rica* at 8am on weekends and public holidays only – be there early in high season to make sure you get a seat. The bus stops to pick up passengers at Cartago (from Las Ruinas) at 8.30am. The return fare is about $4.50 ($2.25 from Cartago), which doesn't include the park entrance fee.

There are toilets and an information board at the crater parking area, along with a **reception centre** containing a snack bar serving *tamales*, cakes and hot drinks, and a small gift shop which rents out waterproof ponchos ($2) – it can get cold at the summit, so bring a sweater. The bus returns to San José at about 12.30pm. You can also get to Irazú on any number of half-day **tours** run by travel agencies in San José, which whisk you back and forth in a modern minibus for around $35, not including the entrance fee.

Lankester Gardens

Quite how much you get from a trip to **Lankester Gardens** (daily 8.30am–3.30pm; $4), 6km southeast of Cartago, depends upon the time of year and how strongly you feel about **orchids**, which are the main attraction at this tropical garden and research station. The gardens cover a large, attractively landscaped area housing a bewildering array of plant and flower species, with ostentatious, elaborate blooms thrusting themselves at you out of the undergrowth. While there are always some flowers in bloom at any given time, the wet season (May–Nov) is less rewarding than the dry, and March and April are the best months, when the gardens are alive with virulent reds, purples and yellows.

To get to the gardens by **bus from San José**, take the Cartago service, get off at Las Ruinas, and change to a Paraíso bus. Get off when you see the *Casa Vieja* restaurant, about ten minutes out of town, and take the road off to your right, signposted to the gardens, then turn right at the fork – a total walk of about 1km.

The Orosí valley

West of the small town of **Paraíso**, 8km southeast of Cartago, the road drops down a ski-slope hill into the deep bowl of the **Orosí valley**. Church fans will want to make a trip to the pretty villages of **Orosí** and **Ujarrás**, both accessible by bus via Paraíso; annoyingly, although they lie less than 8km apart, you can't get directly from one to the other, and have to backtrack to Paraíso. Beyond these lies the wildlife-rich, but little-visited, **Parque Nacional Tapantí**.

There are several attractive options if you plan **to stay** around Paraíso, including the *Albergue Linda Vista* (℡ 574-5534; ❷), a friendly B&B with lovely views – coming into Paraíso, turn right at the Parque Central and drive straight on as if to leave town until you see the sign to the *albergue* on your right. A further kilometre out along the same road is the family-run *Mirador Sanchiri* (℡ & ℻ 533 3210, Ⓦ www.sanchiri.com; ❹), whose comfortable cabins sit in a stupendous position high above the valley. There's a good restaurant on site, trail bikes are available for rent and the hotel's friendly staff can help with local information and tours.

Ujarrás

Set in a beautiful corner of the Orosí river valley, in a flat basin at the foot of precipitous hills, the tiny agricultural hamlet of **UJARRÁS**, about 10km southeast of Cartago, is home to the ruins of the church of **Nuestra Señora de la Limpia Concepción**. The church was built in 1693 on the site of a shrine erected by a local fisherman who claimed to have seen the Virgin in a tree trunk, but was abandoned in 1833 after irreparable damage from flooding.

Today the orange-ish limestone ruins are lovingly cared for, with a full-time gardener looking after the landscaped grounds. The ruined interior, reached through what used to be the door, is now a grassy, roofless enclosure fluttering with birds; despite its dilapidated state, you can identify the fine lines of a former altar. There's a small outdoor **swimming pool** across the road, popular with local families, if you fancy the welcoming prospect of a cool swim after a walk around the ruins – Ujarrás has its own microclimate and it can get very hot. Avocados grow nearby, and you'll see plantation workers cycling home at the end of the day with bulging sacks of fruit slung over their backs.

To get to Ujarrás by **bus from Cartago**, take one of the hourly services from Las Ruinas that goes via Paraíso to Cachí. Cachí is some 6km beyond Ujarrás; ask to be dropped at the fork for Ujarrás, from where it's a one-kilometre walk to the ruins. To get back to Paraíso and Cartago just flag the bus down at the same spot – the bus currently passes the fork for Ujarrás at about fifteen minutes past the hour. **Driving**, take Hwy-224 south from Cartago, signed to Paraíso and Cachí, which makes a circular trip around Lake Cachí. Extremely steep and winding, this route affords fantastic views over the valley as you descend the last few kilometres.

There are a couple of **restaurants** near the ruins, though the best, *La Casona del Cafetal,* is at Cachí, several kilometres east on the looped valley road. The Ujarrás **mirador** (entrance $0.50; take a right-hand fork uphill from the road back to Paraíso) is a pretty spot for a cold beer, though the drinks are pricey.

Just past Cachí is the charming **Casa del Sonador**, a wooden and bamboo cottage decorated with local woodcarver Macedonio Quesada's lively depictions of rural people – gossiping women, musicians and farmers – and religious scenes. The house is now used as a workshop by his sons, Hermes and Miquel, from where they sell their wood carvings (about $5), mostly figures carved from coffee-bush roots. If you're interested, they might also take you on an informative walk around the area, explaining the coffee-growing process and the use of local medicinal herbs.

Orosí

One of the most picturesque small villages in Costa Rica, nestling in a little topograpical bowl between gloomy, thick-forested hills, **OROSÍ** also boasts the **church of San José de Orosí** (built 1735). Sitting squat against the rounded pates of the hills behind, this simple, low-slung adobe structure, single-towered and roofed with red tiles, has an interior devoid of the hubris and frothy excess of much of Latin American church decor. The adjacent **Religious Art Museum**, also called the **Museo Franciscano** (Tues–Sat 1–5pm, Sun 9am–5pm; $1) is a fascinating little place, filled with *objetos de culto* such as icons, religious paintings and ecclesiastical furniture, along with a faithful recreation of a monk's tiny room.

If the sun's out, you might want to check out the two **swimming pools** in the village although both are somewhat rundown – Balneario Thermales Orosí (daily 7.30am–4pm; $1.25) has an attractive setting and is the best maintained. There are several lovely **walking trails** around the village, with waterfalls and swimming spots en route; the *Albergue Montana Linda* (see below) offers a wide range of reasonably priced tours, as well as Spanish lessons at its popular language school (see Basics, p.65) and community projects; the knowledgeable owners are an excellent source of general information about the area.

Accommodation in Orosí is surprisingly good: the *Orosi Lodge* (T & F 533-3578, W www.sites.netscape.net/timevelt/orosilodge; ❸), adjacent to the Balneario Thermales Orosí, is a lovely small hotel, all of whose rooms are equipped with coffee-maker, minibar and ceiling fan; the nearby *Cabinas Media Libra* (☎ 533-3838; ❸) has clean rooooms with TV, telephone and private bathroom. For those on a budget, the *Albergue Montana Linda* (☎ 533-3640, ℱ 533-2153, ⓦ www.montanalinda.com) is one of the best hostels in Costa Rica, with pretty dormitory rooms ($6 per person), some private doubles (❷) and the use of a kitchen.

You can grab a bite **to eat** at *Restaurante Coto* on the main road, which serves beer on its outdoor terrace facing the church, while the café in the *Orosi Lodge* has a good breakfast menu, plus decent coffee and cakes and a vintage Costa Rican jukebox. For a **taxi**, ask at the *Restaurante Coto* or go to the rank on the north side of the main square; a 4WD taxi up the hill to Paraíso should cost about $7, or you could hire one to take you to Parque Nacional Tapantí (see below) for about $10.

Regular **buses** leave from the stop on C 4, Av 1 in Cartago for the forty-minute journey to Orosí (6am–10pm; Mon–Fri every 30min, Sat & Sun hourly). The last service back to Cartago via Paraíso leaves at 5pm from the stop on the main street in front of the church. By **car**, take the road from Cartago to Paraíso, then turn right and drive straight ahead until you begin to descend the precipitous hill to the village.

Parque Nacional Tapantí

Rugged, pristine **PARQUE NACIONAL TAPANTÍ** (daily 8am–3.45pm; $6) receives one of the highest average rainfalls (a whopping 5600mm) in the country – if you really want to get wet, go in October. Altitude in this watershed area ranges from 1220m to 2560m above sea level and contains two life zones: low mountain and premontane rainforest. It is chock-full of **mammals** – about 45 species live here, including the tapir (*danta*), the brocket deer (*cabro de monte*), the mountain hare (*conejo de monte*) and wildcats, along with **birds** such as the golden oriole, falcons, doves, hawks and the famous quetzal. Because of the wet, frogs, salamanders and snakes abound.

Tapantí's **trails** are relatively short and densely wooded. The wide, four-kilometre **Camino Principal**, or main road, leads off from the puesto at Quebrada Segunda (Second Creek), 12km from Orosí. Leading off from this are three walks under much denser cover: the **Sendero Natural Arboles Caidos** to the east, and the **Senderos Oropendola** and **Pantanoso** to the west. All provide anywhere from ninety minutes' to three hours' walking. Towards the end of the main trail, **Sendero La Pava** leads to the Río Grande de Orosí and a mirador from where you can see a high waterfall. Whenever you go, bring rain gear and dress in layers. If the sun is out it can be blindingly hot, whereas at higher elevations, when overcast and rainy, it can feel quite cool. Despite its low numbers of visitors, Tapantí has good services, with toilets and drinking water at regular intervals along the trails.

Practicalities

Getting to Tapantí by public transport is difficult. From Cartago, take the bus to Orosí, from where you can catch a jeep taxi ($10) to the park. Alternatively, but less conveniently, stay on the bus until its final stop at the tiny hamlet of Río Macho, from where it's a nine-kilometre walk to the park. **Driving** from Orosí, turn right at the coffee factory Beneficiadora Renex and continue for 10km along a bad road (you'll need a 4WD in the rainy season).

You can **stay** near the park at the *Kiri Mountain Lodge* (☎ & ℱ 284-2024, ⓔ mercatur@hotmail.com; ❸), which has large comfortable rooms, bar and restaurant, and can arrange guided walks, trout-fishing and horse-riding.

Camping is available at the *Finca Los Maestros* (☎533-3312; $1 per person), 800km before the park, which is run by friendly local schoolteacher Mireya Aquilar, who will cook on request ($1.50 for breakfast; $2 for an evening meal). A good place for **lunch** is *Truchas de Purisol,* a trout farm at the end of a bumpy track signposted from the hamlet of Purisol, 3km back from the park towards Orosí. You can catch your own lunch ($5 per kilo) from a series of beautifully landscaped ponds and cook it over one of the picnic area's barbecues; alternatively, the site's restaurant serves a delicious lunch with grilled trout ($8). There are well-signposted trails through the surrounding woods.

Turrialba and around

Though the pleasant agricultural town of **TURRIALBA**, 45km east of Cartago on the eastern slopes of the Cordillera Central, has sweeping views over the rugged eastern Talamancas, it's still little visited. Most tourists are likely to see it as part of a trip to the archeological monument of **Guayabo** or, even more likely, on the way to a **white-water rafting** or **kayaking** trip on the Ríos Reventazón or Pacuaré. Recommended Turrialba rafting operators include Ticos River Adventure (☎394-4479, ⓦwww.ticoriver.com) and Jungla Expediciones (☎556-9525, ⓔjungla@racsa.cr.co), 10km from Turrialba on the old highway to Limón.

The **Proyecto Viborana** (daily 9am–5pm; $5) is a small snake centre run by renowned herpatologist Minor Camacho, who gives fascinating educational talks, focusing on the deadly fer-de-lance snake. Most of the local hotels offer guided walks or horseback rides up the dormant **Volcán Turrialba**, which, with its lack of trails, is otherwise inaccessible to visitors. Finally, Turrialba is the only place in Costa Rica (and indeed all of Central America) with a **hot-air balloon company**, Serendipity Adventures (☎556-2592, ⓦwww.serendipityadventures.com), who also organize pricey but unique holidays in Costa Rica – see Basics (p.34) for details.

There are several decent sodas around the main square in Turrialba and one very good **restaurant**, *La Feria,* next to the *Wagelia* hotel. The Banco Popular on the town's main street has an ATM and changes **travellers' cheques**, as do the Banco Nacional and the Banco de Costa Rica, both opposite the disused railway line; the *correo* is situated north of the centre, directly above the square.

Accommodation in and around Turrialba

Turrialba isn't really a tourist town, but has some perfectly decent places to stay, from simple hotel rooms in town to picturesque mountain lodges Some of the accommodation listed below is at a **higher altitude** than Turrialba's pleasantly refreshing hillside position; bring a sweater or light jacket.

Albergue de Montaña Pochotel, 8km from Turrialba towards Limón (☎384-7292, ℉556-7615, ⓦwww.homestead.com/casalasorquideas). Simple accommodation and traditional mountain fare in a stunning position with volcano views in all directions. Camping also allowed. ❸

Interamericano, southeast corner of Turrialba, near the old train station (☎556-0142, ℉556-7790, ⓦwww.hotelinteramericana.com). Basic, clean and very friendly, this is the best budget deal in town and an excellent place to meet other travellers. There's also a kitchen for guests' use, and

the proprietor organizes kayaking and other tours. ❷

Turrialtico Lodge, 7.5km from Turrialba on the road to Limón (☎ & ℉556-1111, ⓔturrialt@racsa.co.cr). A cosy lodge with 14 wood-panelled rooms, all with private bath and hot water; some have balconies overlooking the gorgeous surrounding countryside. The restaurant is renowned for its barbecued meat and other local specialities. Tours to Irazú and the Río Reventazón are available. ❹

Volcán Turrialba Lodge (☎273-4335, ℉273-

0703, Ⓦ www.volcanturrialbalodge.com). Quiet, modern and simply furnished farmhouse on the flanks of Volcán Turrialba, whose 14 rooms all have woodburning stoves and private bath; diversions include ox-cart rides and horseback tours to Turrialba crater. You can arrange for a pick-up from San José; otherwise you'll need a 4WD to get here over the badly rutted access road (call for directions). ⑤

Wagelia, Av 4, Turrialba, just beyond the gas station on the road from Cartago (Ⓣ 556-1566, Ⓕ 556-1596). Small, clean and comfortable rooms with TV, fridge and phone, though it's popular and often full – ring in advance to reserve a room. ⑥

Monumento Nacional Guayabo

The most accessible ancient archeological site in Costa Rica, the **MONUMENTO NACIONAL GUAYABO** (daily 8am–3.45pm; $6) lies 19km northeast of Turrialba and 84km from San José. Discovered by explorer Anastasio Alfaro at the end of the nineteenth century, the remains of the town of Guayabo were only excavated in the late 1960s. Administered by MIRENEM, the Ministry of Mines and Resources – which also controls Costa Rica's national park system – today Guayabo suffers from an acute shortage of funds, and only a small part of the site has been excavated. With the withdrawal of the annual US aid grant, the prospects for further exploration look bleak.

The site is visually disappointing compared to the magnificent Maya and Aztec cities of Mexico or Guatemala – cultures contemporaneous with that at Guayabo – though it's well to remember that civilizations cannot necessarily be judged on their ability to erect vast monuments. Facing the considerable difficulties posed by the density of the rainforest terrain, the Guayabo managed not only to live in harmony with an environment that remains hostile to human habitation, but also constructed a complex system of water management, social organization, and expressed themselves through the "written language" of petroglyphs.

Archeologists believe that Guayabo was inhabited from about 1000 BC to 1400 AD; most of the heaps of stones and basic structures now exposed were erected between 300 and 700 AD. The central mound is the tallest circular base unearthed so far, with two staircases and pottery remains on the very top. The people of Guayabo brought stones to the site from a great distance – probably from the banks of the Río Reventazón – and petroglyphs have been found on 53 of these stones. Other than this, little is known of the people who lived here, though excavations have shown that they were particularly skilled in water conducting. At the northern end of the site you can see the stone **tanque de captación**, where they stored water conducted by subterranean aqueducts from nearby springs. It's also thought that this community was led by a chief, a *cacique*, who had both social and religious power. There are no clues as to why Guayabo was abandoned, though hypotheses include an epidemic or war with neighbouring tribes.

At the **entrance hut** you can pick up a leaflet, written in the "voice" of Brül, a Bribrí word for armadillo, that points out orchids, a petroglyph and *guarumo* trees; unfortunately, there's no official guided tour available and you'll need to organize your own guide (ask at your hotel or try locally based T.T. Tours Ⓣ & Ⓕ 556-0568, Ⓔ ssalazar@racsa.co.cr, who run a 3.5 hour trip to the monument) to help you interpret what can otherwise look like random piles of stone. There's also a small exhibition space, displaying fragments of pottery and a model showing how the city would have looked.

There are daily **buses** to Guayabo from Turrialba (Mon–Sat at 11am & 5.15pm, returning at 12.30 & 5.30; Sun at 9am, returning at 4pm), though the inconvenient timetable means you may either have not enough or too much time at the site. Alternatively, you could walk back to the main road, a four-kilometre downhill hike, and intercept the bus that goes back from the hamlet of Santa Teresita to Turrialba. It passes by at about 1.30pm, but you should double-check the times with the *guardaparques* or you might be left standing at the crossroads for 24 hours. **Driving** from Turrialba takes about thirty minutes. The last 4km is on a bad gravel road – passable with a regular car, but watch your clearance. **Taxis** charge $13 from Turrialba.

Travel Details

Buses

Alajuela to: La Guácima Abajo, for the Butterfly Farm (4 daily; 20min); San José (every 15min; 20min); Sarchí (hourly; 1hr); Volcán Poás (1 daily; 2hr); Zoo-Ave (every 30min; 15min).

Braulio Carrillo to: San José (every 30min; 35min).

Cartago to: Orosí (every 1hr 30min Mon–Fri, hourly Sat & Sun; 30min); Paraíso (every 30min Mon–Fri, hourly Sat & Sun; 30min); Río Macho, via Orosí, for Tapantí (every 30min Mon–Fri, hourly Sat & Sun); San José (every 20min; 40min); Ujarrás (hourly; 30min).

Heredia to: San José (every 15min; 15min); Volcán Barva, via San José de la Montaña (3 daily Mon–Sat, 2 daily Sun; 1hr).

Orosí to: Cartago (every 30min Mon–Fri, hourly Sat & Sun; 30min).

San José to: Alajuela (constant; 20min); Braulio Carrillo (every 30min; 35min); Cartago (constant; 40min); Heredia (constant; 15min); Sarchí (17 daily; 1hr 30min); La Guacima Abajo for the Butterfly Farm (2 express daily except Sun; 40min); Turrialba (16 daily; 1hr 30min); Volcán Irazú (1 Sat & Sun; 1hr 30min); Volcán Poás (1 daily; 2hr); Zarcero (12 daily; 2hr).

Sarchí to: Alajuela (constant; 1hr); San José (17 daily; 1hr 30min).

Turrialba to: Guayabo (2 daily Mon–Fri; 1hr+).

Ujarrás to: Cartago, via Paraíso (every 1hr 30min Mon–Fri, hourly Sat & Sun; 30min).

Limón province and the Caribbean coast

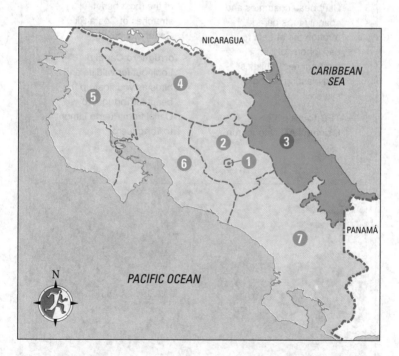

CHAPTER 3

Highlights

✳ **Food** p.158 Sample the region's traditional Caribbean cooking, especially the tasty coconut-flavoured dishes of rice, fish and beans.

✳ **Carnival, Puerto Limón** p.165 Revellers in Afro-Caribbean costumes and spangly tops parade through the streets to a cacophony of tambourines, whistles and blasting sound-systems.

✳ **ATEC tours** p.179 Insightful ATEC tours run from Puerto Viejo to the Bribrí and Cabécar villages of the KéköLdi Indigenous Reserve.

✳ **Playas Cocles, Uvita and Manzanillo** p.180 The idyllic and remote beaches of Cocles, Uvita and Manzanillo dot one of the most beautiful stretches of Costa Rica's Caribbean coast.

✳ **Tortuguero Canal** p.187 Look out for wildlife and birds as you float up the beautiful Tortuguero Canal from Puerto Limón to Tortuguero.

3

Limón province and the Caribbean coast

We were at the shore and travelling alongside a palmy beach. This was the Mosquito Coast ... Massive waves were rolling towards us, the white foam vivid in the twilight; they broke just below the coconut palms near the track. At this time of day, nightfall, the sea is the last thing to darken: it seems to hold the light that is slipping from the sky; and the trees are black. So in the light of this luminous sea, and the pale still-blue eastern sky, and to the splashings of the breakers, the train racketed on towards Limón.

Paul Theroux, *The Old Patagonian Express*

he Miskito coast (in Spanish, Mosquito) is just part of huge, sparsely populated **Limón province**, which sweeps south in an arc from Nicaragua to Panamá. Hemmed in to the north by dense jungles and swampy waterways, to the west by the mighty Cordillera Central – an effective wall that it cost at least four thousand lives to break through during the building of the track for the Jungle Train (see p.159) – and to the south by the even wider girth of the Cordillera Talamanca, Limón can feel like a lost, end-of-the-world place. While the coast is undeniably the main attraction, anyone hoping to find the palm-fringed sands and tranquil crystalline waters that the word "Caribbean" conjures up will be disappointed; Limón has very few really good **beaches** to speak of. Most are battered, shark-patrolled shores, littered with driftwood that has travelled thousands of kilometres, and with huge,

Accommodation price codes

All the accommodation in this book has graded using the following price codes. The prices quoted are for the least expensive double room in high season, and do not include the 18.46 percent national tax which is automatically added onto hotel bills. For more details on accommodation in Costa Rica, see p.35.

❶ less than $10	❷ $10–20
❸ $20–30	❹ $30–50
❺ $50–75	❻ $75–100
❼ $100–150	❽ over $150

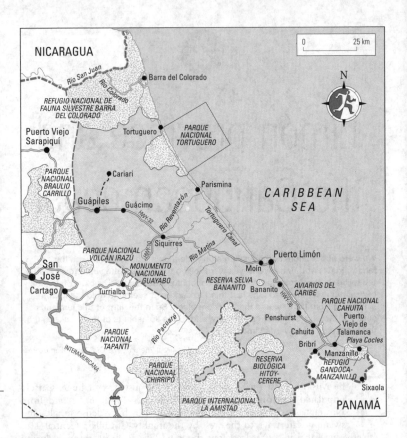

bucking skies stretching out to sea. Here, however, you can watch gentle giant sea **turtles** lay their eggs on the wave-raked beaches of **Tortuguero**; snorkel coral reefs at **Cahuita** or Punta Uva; go surfing at **Puerto Viejo de Talamanca**; or try animal- and bird-spotting in the region's many mangrove **swamps**. The interior of Limón province is crisscrossed by the powerful Río Reventazón and Río Pacuaré, two of the best rivers in the Americas for **white-water rafting**.

Although Limón remains an unknown for the majority of visitors – especially those on package tours – it holds much appeal for eco-tourists and off-the-beaten-track travellers. The province has the highest proportion of **protected land** in the country, from the **Refugio Nacional de Fauna Silvestre Barra del Colorado** on the Nicaraguan border, to the **Refugio Nacional de Vida Silvestre Gandoca-Manzanillo** near Panamá in the extreme south. That said, however, the wildlife reserves and national parks offer only partial resistance to the considerable ecological threats presented by full-scale fruit farming, logging, mining and tourism.

Traditionally neglected and underfunded by Highland-oriented government, Limón suffered a further blow in the 1991 **earthquake**, which heaved the Caribbean coast about 1.5 metres up in the air. Already badly maintained roads, bridges and banana railroads were destroyed, including the track for the famous **Jungle Train** from San José to Puerto Limón, one of the most scenic train rides anywhere in the world. Today, an air of neglect still hangs over much of the province, from housing and tourist infrastructure to basic sanitation. For all its impoverishment, however, the Caribbean coast exudes a greater sense of **cultural diversity** than anywhere else in Costa Rica – a feeling of community and a unique and complex local history. The only town of any size, **Puerto Limón**, is part of a very old community of "black" Central American coastal cities – like Bluefields in Nicaragua and Lívingston in Guatemala. A typical Caribbean port, it has a large, mostly Jamaican-descended **Afro-Caribbean** population. In the south, near the Panamanian border, live several communities of indigenous peoples from the **Bribrí** and **Cabécar** groups. None of these peoples has been well served by the national government: until 1949 blacks were effectively forbidden from settling in the Valle Central or the Highlands, and while the indigenous communities have a degree of autonomy, their traditional territories have long since been eaten up by government-sanctioned mining and banana enterprises.

There are few options when it comes to **getting around** Limón province. From San José to Puerto Limón you have a choice of just two roads, while from Puerto Limón south to the Panamá border at Sixaola there is but one decent route (not counting the few small local roads leading to the banana fincas). North of Puerto Limón there is no public land transport at all: instead, private *lanchas* ply the coastal **canal**, dug in the late 1960s in order to bypass the treacherous breakers of the Caribbean and connecting the port of Moín, 8km north of Puerto Limón, to the Río Colorado near the Nicaraguan border. There are also several scheduled **flights** a week from San José to Barra del Colorado. A good, frequent and quite reliable **bus** network operates in the rest of the province, with the most efficient and modern routes running from San José to Puerto Limón and on to Sixaola. Gas provision is generally poor, except on the highway from San José; take a spare can with you if you plan to do much driving south of Puerto Limón and/or down into Panamá. **Language** can also be a problem: while English is spoken widely along the coast (not just in Limón but also in Tortuguero and Barra del Colorado), do not expect it from everyone. Your best bet is to make your first approaches in Spanish, if you can; people can then choose in which language to answer you.

The area's diverse microclimates mean there is no "best" **time to visit** the Caribbean coast. In Tortuguero and Barra del Colorado, it is very wet all year round, with a small dry spell in January and February. South of Limón, September and October offer the best chance of rain-free days.

Some history

Although the Limón coast has been populated for at least ten thousand years, little is known of the ancient indigenous **Bribrí** and **Cabécar** people who inhabited the area when Columbus arrived, just off the coast of present-day Puerto Limón, on his fourth and last voyage to the Americas in 1502. Well into the mid-eighteenth century the only white people the Limón littoral saw were British **pirates**, rum-runners and seamen from the merchant vessels of the famous Spanish Main, plying the rich waters of the post-conquest Caribbean, bringing with them commerce and mayhem. Nefarious buccaneers often found refuge on Costa Rica's eastern seaboard, situated as it was between the two more lucrative provinces of Panamá and Nicaragua, from which there was a steady traffic of ships to raid. Their presence, along with the difficult terrain, helped deter full-scale settlement of Limón.

Creole cuisine in Limón province

Creole cuisine is known throughout the Americas from Louisiana to Bahía for its imaginative use of African spices and vegetables, succulent fish and chicken dishes, and fantastic sweet desserts. You should make an effort to sample Limón's version by eating at any one of the locally run restaurants dotted along the coast. These are often family affairs, usually presided over by respected older Afro-Caribbean women. Sitting down to dinner at a red gingham tablecloth, with a cold bottle of Imperial beer, reggae on the boombox and a plate full of coconut-scented rice-and-beans is one of the real pleasures of visiting this part of Costa Rica. However, note that many restaurants, in keeping with age-old local tradition, serve Creole dishes like rice-and-beans and rundown on weekends only, serving simpler dishes or the usual Highlands rice concoctions during the week.

Everyone outside Limón will tell you that the local speciality, rice-and-beans (in the lilting local accent it sounds like "rizanbin") is "*comida muy pesada*" (very heavy food). However, this truly wonderful mixture of red or black beans and rice cooked in coconut milk is no more *pesada* – and miles tastier – than traditional Highland dishes like *arroz con camarones*, wherein everything is fried. It's the coconut milk that gives it a surprising lift. Another local speciality, pan bon (not, as is commonly thought, meaning "good bread" – "bon" actually derives from "bun", brought by English-speaking settlers) is sweet bread glazed and laced with cheese and fruit which is often eaten for dessert, as are ginger biscuits and plantain tarts. Rundown (said "rondon" – to "rundown" is to cook) is a vegetable and meat or fish stew in which the plantains and breadfruit cook for many hours, very slowly, in spiced coconut milk. It's harder to find than other creole dishes, mainly because it takes a long time – at least an afternoon – to prepare, and though some restaurants – *Springfields* in Limón, *Miss Junie's* in Tortuguero, and *Miss Edith's* in Cahuita – have it on their menus as a matter of course, it's usually best to stop by on the morning of the day you wish to dine and request it for that evening.

Favoured **spices** in Limonese Creole cooking include cumin, coriander, peppers, chillies, paprika, cloves and groundspice, while the most common vegetables are those that you might find in a street market in West Africa, Brazil or Jamaica. Native to Africa, ackee (in Spanish *seso vegetal*) was brought to the New World by British colonists, and has to be used in knowledgeable hands because its sponge-cake-like yellow fruit, enclosed in three-inch pods, is poisonous until the pods open. The fruit, which is served boiled and looks like scrambled eggs, goes well with fish. Yucca, also known as manioc, is a long pinkish tuber, similar to the yam, and is usually boiled or fried. Local yams can grow as big as 25kg, and are used much like potato in soups and stews. Another native African crop, the huge melon-like breadfruit (*fruta de pan*), is more a starch substitute than a fruit, with white flesh that has to be boiled, baked or grated. Pejiballes (*pejibaye* in Spanish – English-speaking people in Limón pronounce it "picky-BAY-ah") are small green or orange fruits, looking a little like limes. You'll see them sold on the street in San José, boiled in hot water and skinned, but they are most popular in Limón. They're definitely an acquired taste, being both salty and bitter. Better known as heart-of-palm, palmito is served in restaurants around the world as part of a tropical salad. Plantains (*plátanos* in Spanish), the staple of many Highland dishes, figure particularly heavily in Creole cuisine, and are deliciously sweet when baked or fried in fritters. Right at the other end of the health scale, herbal teas are a speciality of the province, available in many restaurants: try wild peppermint, wild basil, soursop, lime, lemon grass or ginger.

The province's development was inextricably linked to two things, themselves related: the **railway** and **bananas**. In 1871 it was decided that Costa Rica needed a more efficient export route for its coffee crop than the long, meandering river journey from Puerto Viejo de Sarapiquí to Matina, midway between Tortuguero and Puerto Limón, from where the beans were shipped to Europe. The other main coffee port was Puntarenas on the Pacific coast (see p.313), from where boats had to go all the way round South America to get to Europe. An American, **Minor Keith**, was contracted to build a railroad across the Cordillera Central from San José to Puerto Limón; to help pay for the laying of the track, he planted bananas along its lowland stretches. Successive waves of Highlanders, Chinese, East Indian (still locally called Hindus) and Italian immigrant labourers were brought in for the gruelling construction work, only to succumb to yellow fever. In the final stages, some ten thousand Jamaicans and Barbadians, who were thought to be immune to the disease, were contracted, many of them staying on to work on the railroad or in the banana plantations. In 1890 the first **Jungle Train** huffed its way from San José via Turrialba and Siquerres to Limón, bringing an abrupt end to the Caribbean coast's period of near-total isolation. This was also the beginning of Costa Rica's **banana boom**. Initially planted as a sideline to help fund the railroad, the fruit prospered in this ideal climate and conditions, leading Keith to found the United Fruit Company, whose monopoly of the banana trade throughout Central America made him far more wealthy than the railroad ever could.

San José to Puerto Limón

There are two land routes from the capital to Puerto Limón. The main route, the **Guápiles Highway** (Hwy-32), is one of the best-maintained roads in the country, though despite its good condition it's only half-jokingly referred to as the "Highway to Heaven", such is its accident and fatality record. Nevertheless, the vast majority of buses and cars take this road, which begins in San José at the northern end of C 3 and proceeds to climb out of the Highlands to the northeast. This opening section of the highway is the most impressive, with Barva and Irazú volcanoes to either side, though in general the road is not as scenic as you might expect, hewn as it is from sheer walls of mountain carpeted with thick, intertwining vegetation. While one side is solid rock, the other is, in places, a sheer phantasmagoric drop that you cannot quite see, with only the enormous huge-leaf common plant known as the "poor man's umbrella" (*sombrilla de pobre*) growing by the roadside to break the monotony.

The older and narrower route, Hwy-10, often called the **Turrialba road**, runs through Turrialba on the eastern slopes of the Cordillera Central before following the old switchbacking San José–Limón train tracks through a dense and pristine mountainous landscape, gutted by the deep cuts of the Pacuaré and Reventazón rivers. It joins the Guápiles Highway near **Siquerres**, about three-quarters of the way to Limón, beyond which the road passes through a final 80km of low flatlands to the coast. Considered dangerous and difficult to drive, the Turrialba road now carries very little traffic, as it takes about four hours as opposed to two-and-a-half to three hours on the Guápiles Highway.

Guápiles

The first town of any size on the Guápiles Highway is **GUÁPILES**, about 50km east of San José, a supply point for the banana plantations of the Río Frío and a waystation for the *bananero* workers. The few **hotels** in town cater mainly to plantation workers and have cold water and thin walls. The one exception is the comparatively swish *Hotel Suerre* (☎710-7551, ℱ710-6376,

Ethnicity in Limón province

"An anthropological Galapagos" is the ingenious term used by journalist and travel writer Peter Ford in his book *Tekkin a Waalk*, to describe the ethnic and cultural oddities encountered in Limón, where the Caribbean meets Central America. There's no doubt that the province provides a touch of multiculturalism lacking in the rest of Costa Rica's relatively homogeneous Latin, Catholic society. Limón is characterized by intermarriage and racial mixing – it's not unusual to find people on the coast who are of combined Miskito, Afro-Caribbean and Nicaraguan ancestry. Though the first black inhabitants of the province were the slaves of the British pirates and mahogany-cutters who had lived in scattered communities along the coast since the mid-1700s, the region's ethnic diversity is largely due to Minor Keith (see p.159), who brought in large numbers of foreign labourers to work on the construction of the Jungle Train – many of whom stayed on after the railway was finished. They were soon joined by turtle fishermen who had settled in Bocas del Toro, Panamá, before migrating north to escape the Panamanian war of independence from Colombia in 1903. The settlers brought their respective religions with them – unlike in the rest of Costa Rica, most Afro-Caribbeans in Limón province are Protestant.

Regardless of race or religion, the coastal settlers were resourceful and independent. Like the pioneers of North America, they not only planted their own crops, bringing seeds to grow breadfruit, oranges, mangoes and ackee, all of which flourished alongside native coconuts and cocoa, but also made their own salt, charcoal, musical instruments, shoes and brewed their own spirits – red rum, *guarapo*, cane liquor and ginger beer.

Limón's diversity has never been appreciated by the ruling and economic elite of the country. Official discrimination against the province's Afro-Caribbean inhabitants only ended in 1949, when a new constitution granted them full citizenship. Black *Limonenses* now make up between 25 and 30 percent of the province's population and are a sharply contrasting and separate entity from the rest of the country.

ⓔ suerre@racsa.co.cr; ⓦ), a country club with pool, gym and exercise room, poolside bar, and a good restaurant (all of which non-guests are welcome to use for a fee). Just outside Guápiles, following a well-marked right turn from the highway at the *Ponderosa* restaurant, is the *Casa Rio Blanco* (ⓣ & ⓕ 382-0957; ⓖ), a rainforest lodge with comfortable cabinas and lush hiking trails down to the river and its waterfalls.

Siquerres

Many of the package tours to Tortuguero (see p.186) make a brief stop at **SIQUERRES**, 1km northeast of the Guápiles Highway at Km-99 from San José, en route to picking up the boat at the small village of Hamburgo de Siquerres on the Río Reventazón. As the rusted hulks of freight cars and track-scarred streets show, Siquerres – which means "reddish colour" in a Miskito dialect – used to be a major railway hub for the Jungle Train, which carted people, bananas and cacao to the Highlands. Along with Turrialba it was a place where black train drivers, engineers and maintenance men would swap positions with their "white" (Spanish, *mestizo*, European or Highland) counterparts, who would then take the train into the Valle Central, where blacks were discouraged from travelling until 1949. Though the Jungle Train no longer runs, trains still haul bananas and machinery to and from Siquerres – mainly servicing the innumerable banana towns or fincas nearby (easily recognizable on maps from their factory-farmed names of Finca 1, 2, a, b, and so forth). There's little to see in town today, though it's worth taking a look at the completely

round church on the western side of the soccer field. Built to mirror the shape of a Miskito hut, its authentic indigenous shape shelters a plain, wood-panelled interior.

From Siquerres it is a relatively easy, flat drive about 60km east to Limón; the road is well maintained and truck and bus drivers love to make up time by speeding and overtaking on these stretches. Outside the window the country-side is home to macadamia nut farms set alongside small banana plots, flower nurseries and bare agricultural land, dotted with humble roadside dwellings.

Puerto Limón and around

To the rest of the country, **PUERTO LIMÓN**, more often simply called Limón, is Costa Rica's *bête noire*, a steamy port raddled with slum neighbour-hoods, bad sanitation and drug-related crime. The traveller is apt to be kinder to the city than the Highland Tico, although Paul Theroux's first impressions in *The Old Patagonian Express* are no encouragement:

> The stucco fronts had turned the colour and consistency of stale cake, and crumbs of concrete littered the pavements. In the market and on the parapets of the crumbling buildings there were mangy vultures. Other vultures circled the plaza. Was there a dingier backwater in all the world?

Not much has changed in the twenty years or so since Theroux went through town, though the vultures have disappeared. Many buildings, damaged during the 1991 earthquake, whose epicentre was just south of Limón, lie skeletal and wrecked, still in the process of falling down. Curiously, however, with its washed-out peeling oyster-and-lime hues Limón can be almost pretty, in a sad kind of way, with the pseudo-beauty of all Caribbean "slums of empire", as St Lucian poet Derek Walcott put it.

There's very little to do. Limón has never been in the same league as the Caribbean ports of Veracruz in Mexico or Cartagena in Colombia, lacking those cities' architecture and dilapidated elegance. It's a working port but a neg-lected one, since the big-time banana boats started loading at the deeper nat-ural harbour of **Moín**, 8km up the headland toward Tortuguero. Generally speaking, tourists come to Limón for one of three reasons: to get a **boat to Tortuguero** from Moín, to get a bus south to the **beach towns** of Cahuita and Puerto Viejo, or to join in the annual **El Día de la Raza** (Columbus Day) carnival during the week preceding October 12.

Arrival, information and orientation

Arriving in Limón after dark can be unnerving – get here in daylight if possi-ble. Coopelimón **buses** (see p.109) run between **San José** and **Limón** rough-ly every hour from 5am until 7pm (2hr 30min–3hr). You should buy your tick-et several days in advance during the El Día de la Raza carnival, even though extra buses are laid on. Buses from San José pull in at the stop on C 2, Av 1/2. Arrivals **from the south** – Cahuita, Puerto Viejo de Talamanca and Panamá (via Sixaola) – terminate at the Transportes MEPE stop at C 3, Av 4, 100m north of the Mercado Central. Buses to Moín leave from beside *Soda La Estrella* at C 5, Av 3–4.

ACCOMMODATION
Acón 7
Albergue Turístico
 Playa Bonita 4
Apartments Cocorí 2
Cabinas Maeva 3
Caribe 8
Maribú Caribe 1
Miami 9
Park 5
Teté 6

RESTAURANTS & BARS
Brisas del Caribe I
Centro Turístico Piuta D
Kimbambu B
Maribú Caribe C
Park Hotel F
Queenies G
Soda La Estrella E
Soda Yans H
Springfield A

PORTETE & PLAYA BONITA

PUERTO LIMÓN

For **information** about the Caribbean coast, you'll need to contact the San José ICT (☎223-1733), as there's no official tourist office in the entire province. The Banco de Costa Rica, on Av 2, C 1, offers **exchange facilities**, as does Scotiabank, on Av 3, C2; both banks have ATMs which accept Visa. The **correo** (Mon–Fri 7.30am–5pm, Sat 8am–12pm) is at Av 2, C 4, though the mail service from Limón is dreadful – you're better off posting items from San José. It does offer **internet access** however, as does the *Edutec Internet Café*, upstairs in the Centro Plaza Caribe on Av 3, C 4. There's a cluster of **payphones** opposite the town hall on Av 2 and on the south side of the Mercado Central. Taxis line up on the corner of Av 2, C 1. Note that during the El Día de la Raza Carnival everything shuts for a week, including all the banks and the post office. Should you need **medical care**, head for Hospital Dr Tony Facio Castro (☎758-2222), at the north end of the *malecón*.

While Limón is not quite the mugger's paradise it is sometimes portrayed to be in the Highland media, standing on the sidewalk looking lost is not recommended, nor is carrying valuables (most of the hotels listed below have safes). When trying to **find your way around**, bear in mind that even more than in other Costa Rican towns, nobody refers to *calles* and *avenidas* in Limón. The city does have street numbers, but there are virtually no signs. To confuse things further, unlike other towns in Costa Rica, *calles* and *avenidas* in Limón run sequentially, rather than in separate even- and odd-numbered sequences. Though the city as a whole is very spread out, central Limón covers no more than about ten blocks.

Accommodation

It's worth shelling out a bit for a **room** in Limón, especially if you're travelling alone; this is a place where the comfort and safety of your hotel makes a big difference to your peace of mind. In midweek, the town's hotels fill up very quickly with commercial travellers; try to get to Limón as early as possible if you're arriving on a Wednesday or Thursday.

Staying **downtown** keeps you in the thick of things, and many hotels have communal balconies, perfect for relaxing with a cold beer above the lively street activity below. The downside of this is noise, especially at night; if you prefer to hear gentle waves lapping in the breeze, your best bet is the *Park Hotel*, which stands alone on a little promontory, close to the sea. There's a group of quieter hotels outside town, about 4km up the spur road to Moín, at **Portete** and the small, somewhat misnamed **Playa Bonita**. A taxi up here costs less than $1.50, and the bus to and from Moín runs along the road every twenty minutes or so. Allow an hour to walk into town. In all but the most upmarket places, avoid drinking the **tap water**, or use a filter or iodine tablets.

Hotel prices rise by as much as fifty percent for **carnival** week, and to a lesser extent during Semana Santa, or Easter week. The least expensive times to stay are between July and October, and December to February, which (confusingly) are considered high season in the rest of the country.

Limón has its share of dives, which tend to fill when there's a big ship in town. None of the places listed below is rock-bottom cheap. If this is what you're after, you'll find it easily enough, but always ask to see the room first and inspect the bathroom, in particular.

In town

Acón, Av 3, C 2/3 (☎758-1010, ℻758-2924). Large central hotel with rather gloomy but well-equipped rooms with TV, a/c and hot water. Private parking. ❸

Caribe, Av 2, C 1 above the restaurant *Brisas del Caribe*, (☎758-0138. Plain but spacious rooms with TV and fan, though they can be noisy at night. ❷

Miami, Av 2, C 4/5 (Ⓣ & Ⓕ 758-0490). Friendly place whose clean rooms all have ceiling fans, cable TV and private bathrooms. ❷

Park, Av 3, C 1, by the *malecón* (Ⓣ 798-0555 or 758-4364). The smartest option in town, popular with Ticos and travellers alike, so you'll have to book in advance. The most expensive rooms come with a sea view, slightly less expensive ones with a street view, and the cheapest, *plana turista*, rooms with no view at all. There's a good restaurant, too. ❹

Teté, Av 3, C4/5 (Ⓣ 758-1122, Ⓕ 758-0707). Clean and well-cared-for hotel, with friendly staff – though nothing special, it's the best-value downtown option in this price range. Rooms on the street have balconies but can be noisy; those inside are a little darker, but quieter. ❷

Portete and Playa Bonita

Albergue Turistico Playa Bonita, Playa Bonita (Ⓣ 793-3090, Ⓕ 798-3612). Good-value family pension with seven simple but clean rooms set round a courtyard. ❸

Apartments Cocori, Playa Bonita (Ⓣ 758-2930; in San José, Ⓣ 257-4674). Beautiful setting with friendly staff and a lively outdoor bar-restaurant right by the sea, with good views. All rooms have basic self-catering facilities; those downstairs have a/c, those upstairs have fans. ❸

Cabinas Maeva, Portete; look for the blue-and-white sign (Ⓣ 758-2024). The best-value accommodation in Limón, with cute, yellow hexagonal cabinas nestling among palm trees, plus a beautiful pool and Neoclassical statues. ❷

Maribú Caribe, Portete (Ⓣ 758-4543, Ⓕ 758-3541). Quiet and very luxurious sea-facing complex of round, thatched-roof huts with 1960s decor with a good pool and a pleasant but pricey bar-restaurant overlooking the sea – a favourite among banana-company executives. ❻

The Town

Fifteen minutes' walk around Puerto Limón and you've seen the lot. **Avenida 2**, known locally as the "market street", is for all purposes the main drag, touching the north edge of Parque Vargas and the south side of the **Mercado Central**. The market is as good a place as any to start your explorations, and at times seems to be full of the entire town population, with dowager women minding their patch while men clutching cigarettes chatter and gesticulate animatedly. The produce looks very healthy: *chayotes*, plantains, cassava, yucca, beans and the odd banana (most of the crop is exported) vie for space with bulb-like cacao fruit, baseball-sized tomatoes and huge carrots. The market's sodas and snack bars are good places to grab a bite.

Limón, often noisy and chaotic, is more pleasantly languid in the heat of the day, with workers drifting at lunch time towards **Parque Vargas** and the *malecón* to sit under the shady palms. A little shabby today, the park, at the easternmost end of C 1 and Av 1 and 2, features a sea-facing **mural** by artist Guadalupe Alvarea, depicting colourful and evocative images of the province's tough history. On the left of the semicircular wall, indigenous people are shown making crafts – later suppressed and destroyed by the Catholic missionaries. Next comes Columbus, ships being loaded with coffee and bananas by women wearing vibrant African cloth, and the arrival of the Jungle Train, with a wonderful Chinese dragon to symbolize the Chinese labourers who came to work on its construction.

The park is also home to nine **sloths**, who live in the tall Royal Palms, though no one seems to know whether they're two-toed or three-toed. There's a shrine to sailors and fishermen at the end of the central promenade, and a dilapidated bandstand which hosts occasional concerts. From here the **malecón** (a thin ledge where it is hardly possible to walk, let alone take a seaside promenade) winds its way north. Avoid it at night, as muggings have been reported. Around the park, you'll see the evocative **Town Hall** (Municipalidad), with its pale facade and peeling Belle Epoque grillework, and

Carnaval in Limón

Though carnivals in the rest of Latin America are usually associated with the days before Lent, Limón takes Columbus's arrival in the New World – October 12 – as its point of celebration. The idea was first brought to Limón by Arthur King, a local who had been away working in Panamá's Canal Zone and was so impressed with that country's Columbus Day celebrations that he decided to bring the merriment home with him. Today, El Día de la Raza (Day of the People) is basically an excuse to party. Ticos from the Highlands descend upon Limón: buses are packed, hotels brim, and revellers hit the streets in search of this year's sounds and style. Rap, rave and ragga – in Spanish and English – are hot, and Bob Marley lives, or at least is convincingly resurrected, for carnival week.

Carnival can mean whatever you want it to, from noontime displays of Afro-Caribbean dance to Calypso music festivals, bull-running, afternoon children's theatre, colourful *desfiles* (parades) and massive firework displays. Most spectacular is the Grand Desfile, usually held on the Saturday before October 12, when revellers in Afro-Caribbean costumes – sequins, spangles, fluorescent colours – parade through the streets to a cacophony of tambourines, whistles and blasting sound systems.

Instead of taking place in Limón's streets as it has in years past – there were some problems with "sanitation" according to the national press, and the whole event was threatened with closure – most of the carnival's night-time activity now occurs within the fences of JAPDEVA's huge docks and parking lot. This might sound like a soulless location, but it's a well-managed affair, and while you may not be dancing in the streets, you're at least dancing. The overall atmosphere – even late at night – is unthreatening, with young bloods and grandparents alike enjoying the music. Kiosks dispense steaming Chinese, Caribbean and Tico food, and on-the-spot discos help pump up the volume. Cultural Street, which runs from the historic Black Star Line (the shipping company that brought many of the black immigrants here) is an alcohol-free zone, popular with family groups, where kids can play games at small fairgrounds to win candyfloss and stuffed toys. Elsewhere, bars overflow into the street, and the impromptu partying builds up as the night goes on.

---

opposite, on the shore, an elegant modern sculpture in the shape of a ship's prow with a small amphitheatre and stage cleverly built into its framework, for occasional concerts or outdoor theatre performances.

The only other building of note in Limón is the landmark **Radio Casino**, on the corner of C 4 and Av 4, which is home to an excellent community-service station, broadcasting by and for *Limonenses* with call-in chat shows, international news and good music, including local and imported reggae. As for **swimming** in town, forget it. One look at the water at the tiny spit of sand next to the *Park Hotel* is discouragement enough; JAPDEVA, the harbour authority, used to run a public pool, but this is now closed. Pollution, sharks, huge banana-carrying ships and sharp, exposed coral make it practically impossible to swim anywhere nearby; the nearest possibility is at **Playa Bonita**, though even that is plagued by dangerous rip tides.

Eating, drinking and entertainment

Though Limón has a surprising variety of places to eat, there's only one restaurant in town, *Springfield*, where you can sample completely authentic **Caribbean or Creole cuisine** (see p.158). It's best to heed warnings not to sit outside to eat at the restaurants in town, especially around the Mercado Central, where tourists are prime targets for often aggressive beggars. Inside the market, however, there's a host of decent sodas serving tasty *casados*. Gringos in

Heading north to Tortuguero, shallow-bottomed private *lanchas* make the trip up the canal from the docks at Moín (3hr). It's best to arrive at the docks early (7–9am) although you ought to be able to find boatmen willing to take you until 2pm. Expect to pay around $50 each return for a group of four to six people; if you are travelling alone or in a couple, try to get a group together at the docks. The bus stop for Moín is at C 4, Av 5/6, 200m north of the Mercado Central, but the bus has no set schedule and leaves when it's full (more or less every thirty minutes), so a taxi ($3) may be a better option.

Buses to San José start running at 5am from the main bus terminal and continue hourly until 7pm. Direct buses to San José are run by Coopelimón (see pp.110–111) and Coopecaribeñéos (see pp.110–111), whose ticket windows are side by side; Coopetraga (T 758-0618) also has services from the main bus terminal to Siquerres and Guápiles, from where there are onward bus connect ions to the capital.

Destinations south of Limón are served from the Transportes MEPE (T 221-0524) office at C 3, Av 4, 100m north of the Mercado Central, from where buses leave four times daily (from 7am until 6pm) to Cahuita (1hr) and eight times (also 7am until 6pm) to Puerto Viejo (1hr 30min–2hr). The Sixaola bus also stops in both places. Two buses (6am & 2.30pm; 2hr) go direct to Manzanillo village in the heart of the Gandoca-Manzanillo Wildlife Refuge, via Puerto Viejo.

Taxis line up on Av 2 around the corner from the San José bus stop: they'll do long-haul trips to Cahuita and Puerto Viejo ($30–40), and to the banana plantations of the Valle de Estrella ($20), from where you can pick up another taxi to the Reserva Biológica Hitoy-Cerere. Prices are per car, so if you're in a group, renting a taxi can be far more convenient than taking the bus.

There are few excursions worth making from Limón. You could make the trip up the canal to Tortuguero and back (see above) in a day, though you would then have to turn round immediately and motor back down without seeing the turtles or the village. A better possibility for a short boat trip is up the Río Matina from Moín; with a guide, you might be able to spot sloths, monkeys, iguanas and caimons. Friendly and knowledgeable local guide Bernardo R. Vargas (T 798 4322, F 758 2683) offers a packed one-day tour which takes in a walk in the rainforest at Aviarios de Caribe, Cahuita National Park, a tour of local banana and coffee plantations and a city tour of Limón ($35; 4–5hr).

general and women especially should avoid most **bars**, especially those that have a large advertising placard blocking views of the interior. If you want to drink, stick to places like *Restaurante Mares* or *Brisas del Caribe*. **Playa Bonita** is a great place for lunch or an afternoon beer if you're tired of town.

In town

Brisas del Caribe, C 1, Av 2, in the same building as the *Hotel Caribe*. Clean bar-restaurant with a good view of Parque Vargas. Except on nights when the sound system is blasting, this is a quiet place to have a hassle-free coffee or beer. For food, there a Chinese menu, sandwiches, snacks and a good *medio casado* (half *casado*) for $2.50.
Park Hotel, Av 3, C 1 by the *malecón*. The only restaurant in town where you feel you might actually be in the Caribbean – sea breezes float in through large slatted windows and all you can see is an expanse of blue sea and cloud. Excellent,

though pricey, breakfast and standard Costa Rican fare.
Queenies, Av 3, C 2. Excellent hole-in-the-wall café with home-made cakes, *tamales* and delicious coffee.
Soda La Estrella, C 5, Av 3/4. The best lunch in town: top marks for soda staples, excellent *refrescos*, coffee, snacks, basic plates and daily specials, all accompanied by cordial service.
Soda Yans, Av 2, C 5/6. Very popular with locals, this vaguely upmarket-looking place has a certain cachet, while the menu, though small, includes some good local dishes.

Springfield, north of the end of the *malecón*, across from the hospital. *The* place in Limón to get coconut-flavoured rice-and-beans with a choice of chicken, beef or fish ($7). It's also one of the few places in Costa Rica to serve turtle, a local delicacy (though illegal). Try to arrive early, as the restaurant gets very full. Credit cards accepted.

Portete and Playa Bonita

Centro Turistico Piuta, Portete. Vast barn-like bar with deafening roots-reggae disco at weekends.

Kimbambu, Playa Bonita. Beach-bar with excellent – though pricey – fresh fish cooked to order. Live music at weekends.

Maribú Caribe, Portete. Peaceful and friendly poolside bar-restaurant high above the sea, offering excellent food and *refrescos*.

South of Puerto Limón

Twenty kilometres south of Limon – reached on an inland road from the main coastal highway through the banana town of Bananito, and then along a very rough track which crosses several rivers (you'll need a 4WD) – the **RESERVA SELVA BANANITO** is a 2000-acre private reserve which runs alongside the Parque Nacional La Amistad and protects an area of mountainous and virgin rainforest. Its owners offer a wide range of activities such as horse-riding, tree-climbing, bird-watching and hiking ($20–50). You'll have to stay in the reserve's **lodge** (①258-8118, ⑤224-2640, ⑩www.selvabananito.com; $100 per person per night, with three meals and at least one tour included), which consists of eleven attractive and spacious cabins with large verandahs overlooking the forest and a main ranch where meals and drinks are served. Owned and run by the environmentally committed children of a pioneering German farmer, the lodge has solar-powered hot water (though no electricity) and is built from secondhand wood discarded by loggers. It's a wonderfully peaceful and relaxing place (once you've recovered from the effort of actually getting there), and a percentage of the lodge's profits goes to the Fundación Cuencas de Limón, which helps to protect the local area and to develop educational programmes. If you haven't got your own transport you can arrange to be picked up from Bananito, which is reachable by bus or taxi from Limón.

Ten kilometres further south along the coast road, and 1km before it crosses the wide Río Estrella, the small wildlife sanctuary **AVIARIOS DEL CARIBE** (8am–5pm; $5), on a small island in the river's delta, is an important rehabilitation and research centre for injured and orphaned sloths, and probably the best place in Costa Rica to see them close up. There are several walking trails in the grounds, with an observation platform for bird-watching (an incredible 318 species have been sighted here – bring binoculars), and you may also spot white-faced, howler and spider monkeys. The three-hour **kayak tour** ($30) through the delta, spotting caimans, river otters and birds is recommended. The sanctuary's lodge (① & ⑤382-1335, ⑩www.members.xoom.com/aviarios; ⑤) is a great place **to stay**, with comfortable B&B accommodation in seven rooms with fans and bath with hot water – it's often full, so book ahead. To reach Aviarios del Caribe by bus from Limón, take the Cahuita service and ask to be dropped off at the entrance, just before the Río Estrella bridge.

Reserva Biológica Hitoy-Cerere

Sixty kilometres, and a three-hour road-trip, south of Limón is one of Costa Rica's least visited national reserves, the **RESERVA BIOLÓGICA HITOY-CERERE** (daily 8am–4pm; $6). Sandwiched between the Tanyí, Telier and Talamanca indigenous reservations, this very rugged, isolated terrain – 91 square kilometres of it – provides no information, campsites or washrooms, though there is a ranger station at the entrance.

The name comes from the Bribrí language: *hitoy* means "woolly" (the rocks in its rivers are covered with algae, and everything else is covered with a soft fuzz of moss); and *cerere* means "clear waters", of which there are many. It is one of the wettest reserves in all Costa Rica, receiving a staggering 4m of **rain** per year in some areas, with no dry season at all. Its complicated biological profile is a reflection of its changing altitude. The top canopy trees are very tall indeed – some as high as 50m – and epiphytes, bromeliads, orchids and lianas grow everywhere under the very dense cover. **Wildlife** is predictably abundant, but most of the species are nocturnal and rarely seen, although you might spot three-toed sloths, and perhaps even a brocket deer. You'll probably hear howler monkeys, and may glimpse some of the whitefaced monkeys which live here too. Pacas and rare frogs abound, many of them shy and little-studied. More visible are the 115 species of **birds**, from large black vultures to hummingbirds, trogons and dazzling blue kingfishers.

Hitoy-Cerere's **Espavel trail** is a tough nine-kilometre hike, leading south from the ranger station through lowland and primary rainforest past clear streams, small waterfalls and beautiful vistas of the green Talamanca hills. Only **experienced tropical hikers** should attempt it, bringing compass, rubber boots, rain gear and water. The trail begins at a very muddy hill; after about 1km, in the secondary forest and open area, you'll notice the white-and-grey wild cashew trees (*espavel*) for which it is named. Follow the sign here; it leads off to the right and cuts through swathes of thick forest before leaving the reserve and entering the Talamanca reservation, which is officially off limits.

From here the trail continues up a steep hill and ends at the Río Moín, 4.5km from the start. All there is to do now is turn back, taking care to negotiate the numerous fallen trees, tumbled rocks and boulders. Many of them were felled by the 1991 earthquake; older casualties are carpeted in primeval plants and mosses. The only possible respite from very dense jungle terrain is along the small dried-up river beds, following streams and tributaries of the Ríos Cerere and Hitoy.

Getting to Hitoy-Cerere is best done with your own car. Take the right fork towards Penhurst from the coastal Limón–Cahuita road and follow the signs to the Reserve. Using public transport, you'll need to take the bus from Limón to Valle de Estrella, and get off at the end of the line at a banana town called (confusingly) both **Fortuna** and **Finca Seis** (Finca Six). It's 15km from here to the reserve, most of it through banana plantation. A local 4WD taxi – ask at the plantation office – can take you there, and will return to pick you up at a mutually agreed time for $15–20. The nearest **accommodation** is at the Selva Bananito lodge or Aviarios del Caribe (p.167).

Cahuita village and the Parque Nacional Cahuita

The tiny village of **CAHUITA**, 43km southeast of Limón, is reached on paved Hwy-36, which runs from Limón to Sixaola on the Panamanian border. Like other villages on the Talamanca coast, Cahuita has become a byword for relaxed, inexpensive Caribbean holidays, with a laid-back atmosphere and great Afro-Caribbean food. The local "dry" season is between March and April, and from September to October, though it's pretty wet all year round.

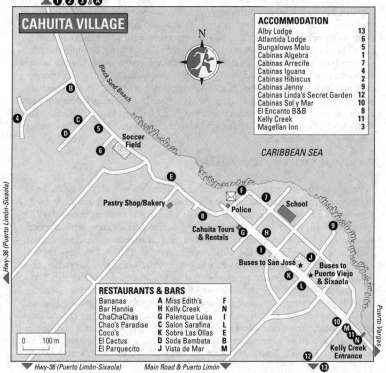

CAHUITA VILLAGE

N

ACCOMMODATION
Alby Lodge	13
Atlantida Lodge	6
Bungalows Malu	5
Cabinas Algebra	1
Cabinas Arrecife	7
Cabinas Iguana	4
Cabinas Hibiscus	2
Cabinas Jenny	9
Cabinas Linda's Secret Garden	12
Cabinas Sol y Mar	10
El Encanto B&B	8
Kelly Creek	11
Magellan Inn	3

Black Sand Beach

Soccer Field

CARIBBEAN SEA

Pastry Shop/Bakery

Police

School

Cahuita Tours & Rentals

Buses to San José

Buses to Puerto Viejo & Sixaola

Hwy-36 (Puerto Limón-Sixaola)

Puerto Vargas

RESTAURANTS & BARS
Bananas	A	Miss Edith's	F
Bar Hannia	H	Kelly Creek	N
ChaChaChas	G	Palenque Luisa	I
Chao's Paradise	C	Salon Sarafina	L
Coco's	K	Sobre Las Ollas	E
El Cactus	D	Soda Bambata	B
El Parquecito	J	Vista de Mar	M

0   100 m

Kelly Creek Entrance

Hwy-36 (Puerto Limón-Sixaola)   Main Road & Puerto Limón

You can swim on either of the village's two **beaches**, although neither is fantastic: the first 400m or so of the narrow **Playa Cahuita** (also known as the White-Sand Beach and as Kelly Creek), just south of the village in the national park, is particularly dangerous on account of rip tides, while the **Black-Sand Beach** (or Playa Negra), at the northern end of the village, is littered with driftwood, although it's safe to swim in most places. Close to the village, the largely marine **Parque Nacional Cahuita** was created mainly to protect one of Costa Rica's few living coral reefs; many people come here to snorkel and take glass-bottomed boat rides. The beach south of Punta Cahuita – sometimes called **Playa Vargas** – is better for swimming than those in the village, as it's protected from raking breakers by the coral reef, but is slightly awkward to get to. Backing the shores, a trail leads through the vast area of thick vegetation and mangrove swamps.

The sheltered bay was originally filled with *cawi* trees, known in Spanish as *sangrilla* ("bloody") on account of the tree's thick red sap – Cahuita's name comes from the Miskito words *cawi* and *ta*, which means "point". Most of the inhabitants are descended from the Afro-Caribbean settlers of the Bocas del Toro area of Panamá and from workers brought to help build the Jungle Train, and older residents remember the days when a little fishing, small-scale farming and some quadrille-dancing formed the mainstay of local life. Now Cahuita, along with the rest of the Talamanca coast, has become very popular with backpackers and surfers, its semi-Rasta culture offering an escape from the cultural homogeneity of highland and Pacific Costa Rican. Yet while tourism has undoubtedly brought prosperity to the village, it has also created problems in its wake – at one point Cahuita was known for its drugs scene, bouts of opportunistic theft and women travellers who came to town looking for a Rasta man of their own for a few days. In recent years, though, the community has made huge and largely successful efforts to clean up the village, with extra policemen drafted in to patrol the sandy streets. Still, it's worth being cautious: lock your door and windows, never leave anything on the beach and avoid walking alone in unlit places at night. Nude or topless bathing is definitely unacceptable, as is wandering though the village in just a bathing suit. With a bit of common sense, though, most travellers really enjoy the community and atmosphere here.

Arrival and information

Until about twenty years ago, Cahuita, like Puerto Viejo and Manzanillo to the south, was cut off from the rest of the country – even from Limón – by the absence of a road. Before the Río Estrella bridge was built in the mid-1970s, a journey from Limón to Cahuita involved a train ride, a canoe ferry across the Río Estrella, and a bus over a dirt road, though things have changed dramatically since the opening of the Guápiles Highway in 1987. Nowadays the easiest way to get to Cahuita from San José is by **bus** on the comfortable direct Transportes MEPE service (4 daily; 4hr) which goes on to Puerto Viejo. Taking a bus from San José to Puerto Limón (3hr) and then changing for Cahuita (4 daily) is only marginally less expensive than taking the direct bus and increases travelling time by at least an hour. In Cahuita, buses stop at the central crossroads opposite the *Salon Sarafina* bar-disco, which has a colourful and detailed map of the village painted on its exterior. Current timetables are posted in front of the Cahuita Tours office, 200m north along the village's main street.

Information

If you're coming to Cahuita **from Puerto Viejo**, be sure to pick up a copy of the free *Costa Rican Caribbean Info Guide*, which unfolds into maps of the local area and a directory of accommodation and businesses in both villages. The only sources of visitor **information** in the village itself are the tour companies: Mr Big J's (☏755-0328), towards the Parque Nacional Cahuita puesto and beach, is particularly friendly and has a book exchange and laundry facilities. Cahuita Tours (☏755-0000) has two public phones outside the office and one inside where you can make international calls, while Turistica Cahuita sells the *Tico Times*. There's internet access at *Cabinas Palmar* (evenings only). There are no banks in town – the nearest are in Bribrí, 20km away, or Limón. Your best bet for **changing money**, travellers' cheques and obtaining cash advances on credit cards is the efficient cambio (7am–4pm) at *Cabinas Safari;* Supermarket Vaz changes cash only. The small police station (*guardia rural*) is on the last beach-bound road at the north end of the village; the **correo** next door (theoretically Mon–Fri 7.30am–5pm) keeps erratic hours, to say the least.

Accommodation

Though Cahuita is popular with budget travellers, it's not especially cheap. If you're travelling in a group, it's possible to keep costs to a minimum, as most **cabinas** charge per room and have space for at least three or four people. Many rooms tend to be of the concrete-cell variety, but facilities are usually good, with fans, mosquito nets, clean sheets and bathrooms. Upstairs rooms are slightly more expensive, due to the sea breezes and occasional ocean views.

The **centre of the village** has scores of options, the best of which are listed below; staying here is convenient for restaurants, bars and the national park. There's also accommodation in all price ranges along the long (3km or so) road that runs by the sea north along **Black-Sand Beach**. It's quieter here, and the beach is not bad, though women (even if travelling in groups) and those without their own car are better off staying in town, since a number of rapes and muggings have been committed along this road, though so far always at night and none recently. You should **book ahead** on weekends during the highland dry season (Dec–April).

There are several **camping** options in the vicinity; the nicest is at the Puerto Vargas ranger station in the national park (see p.174 for details).

In the village

Alby Lodge, down the signposted path behind *Hotel Kelly Creek* at the south end of the village (Ⓣ & Ⓕ 755-0031). A new lodge, set in pleasant grounds, built and run by its Austrian owners. Each of the individual thatched wooden cabins has a porch, hammock and private bathroom. ❹

Cabinas Arrecife, 50m northwest of the school (Ⓣ 755-0081). Good-value option, and a little more luxurious than the village's usual budget rooms, these large and shaded cabinas all come with private bathroom and hot water, while some also have sea views. Friendly management too. ❷

Cabinas Jenny, on the beach (Ⓣ 755-0256). Beautiful rooms, especially the more expensive ones upstairs, with high wooden ceilings, sturdy bunks, mosquito nets, fans and wonderful sea views. Deck chairs and hammocks are provided, and there are good stout locks on all doors. ❷

Cabinas Linda's Secret Garden, near *Alby Lodge* (Ⓣ 755-0327) Good budget choice, set in a charming rock garden, with cosy rooms. Movies shown on request. ❷

Cabinas Sol y Mar, towards Kelly Creek (Ⓣ 755-0237). Small, basic rooms run by friendly locals; clean and safe. ❷

El Encanto B&B, past the police station in the north of the village (Ⓣ & Ⓕ 755-0113, Ⓔ encanto@racsa.co.cr). Highly recommended B&B, with a gorgeous garden, three beautifully decorated doubles, and a delicious breakfast included in the room rate. There's a self-contained house available for rent too. ❹

Hotel Kelly Creek, beside the national park beach (Ⓣ 755-0007, Ⓔ kellycr@racsa.co.cr). Four vast, wood-panelled rooms right by the park entrance, with mosquito nets and a good Spanish restaurant on site. ❹

Black-Sand Beach

Atlantida Lodge, next to the soccer field on the road to Black-Sand Beach, about 1km from the village (Ⓣ 755-0115, Ⓕ 755-0213, Ⓦ www.Atlantida.co.cr). The best of the village's pricier options: friendly, with patio, pretty grounds, good security and the nicest pool in town. The cool rooms are decorated in tropical yellows and pinks, with heated water, and there's free coffee and bananas all day. ❹

Bungalows Malu, beyond the soccer field (Ⓣ 755-0006). Pretty individual cabinas in a large garden facing the sea, with an Italian restaurant on site. ❷

Cabinas Algebra, 2km or so up Black-Sand Beach road (Ⓣ & Ⓕ 755-0057). Funky and attractive cabinas, some distance from town but with the good *Bananas Restaurant* on site. Run by very friendly Austrian couple who offer haircuts, laundry service and free pick-up from the village. ❷

Cabinas Iguana, 200m south of *Soda Bambata* on a small sideroad (Ⓣ 755-0005, Ⓕ 755-0054, Ⓔ iguanas@racsa.co.cr). Some of the best budget accommodation in town, with lovely wood-panelled cabinas set back from the beach and a big screened verandah, plus laundry service, book exchange and a small swimming pool. The friendly owners also rent out two apartments and a three-bedroom house with kitchen. ❷

Chalet Hibiscus, 2.5km north of village on the right (Ⓣ 755-0021, Ⓕ 755-0015). Two luxury houses sleeping six or seven, on a small point by the sea with beautiful views, with good security and friendly owners. The larger house is open and breezy, with a verandah and hammock, rustic wooden decor, an unusual wood-and-rope spiral staircase and comfortable rooms. There's also a swimming pool, games room and a garden down to the sea. ❸

Magellan Inn, 3km up Black-Sand Beach, on a small signposted road leading off to the left (Ⓣ & Ⓕ 755-0035, Ⓔ magellaninn@racsa.co.cr). Very comfortable and quiet hotel, in beautiful gardens dotted with pre-Columbian sculpture and a small pool. The hacienda-style rooms have rattan furniture and running hot water. Rates include continental breakfast, and there's also a bar and very good French creole restaurant. ⑤

The village

Cahuita proper comprises just two puddle-dotted, gravel-and-sand streets running parallel to the sea, intersected by a few cross-streets. Though it seems like anything nailed down has been turned into some kind of small business, you'll still see a couple of private homes among the haphazard conglomeration of signs advertising cabinas and restaurants. Few locals drive (bicycles are popular), so most of the vehicles you see kicking up the dust belong to tourists.

Cahuita's main street runs from the national park's entrance at Kelly Creek to the northern end of the village, marked more or less by the soccer field. Beyond here it continues two or three kilometres north along Black-Sand Beach. The small park at the central crossroads downtown, with its three small busts of Cahuita's founding fathers, is the focal point of the village, where locals wait for buses to San José and catch up on recent gossip. Opposite, *Coco's* disco and bar is *the* place to hang out at night, while at weekends its breezy verandah is crammed full of partygoers from the city and gaggles of young backpackers soaking up the atmosphere.

Pirates and ghosts

According to local history, in the 1800s the coastal waters of the Caribbean crawled with pirates. Two shipwrecks in the bay on the north side of Punta Cahuita are locally believed to be pirate wrecks, one Spanish and one French. You can sometimes see the Spanish wreck on glass-bottomed boat tours to the reef, although it has been (illegally) picked over and the only thing of interest that remains are carbuncled manacles – an indication of the dastardly intentions of the ship's crew.

In her excellent collection of local folk history and oral testimony, *What Happen*, sociologist Paula Palmer quotes Selles Johnson, descendant of the original turtle-hunters, on the pirate activity on these shores:

. . . them pirate boats was on the sea and the English gunboats was somewhere out in the ocean, square rigger, I know that. I see them come to Bocas, square rigger. They depend on breeze. So the pirate boats goes in at Puerto Vargas or at Old Harbour where calm sea, and the Englishmen can't attack them because they in Costa Rican water . . . so those two ships that wreck at Punta Cahuita, I tell you what I believes did happen. Them was hiding in Puerto Vargas and leave from there and come around the reef, and they must have stopped because in those days the British ship did have coal. You could see the smoke steaming in the air. So the pirate see it out in the sea and they comes in here to hide.

Where you find pirates you also find pirate ghosts, it seems, doomed to guard their ill-gotten treasure into eternity. Treasure from the wrecks near Old Harbour, just south of Cahuita, is said to be buried in secret caches on land. One particular spot, guarded by a fearsome headless spirit dressed in a white suit, has attracted a fair share of treasure hunters; no one has yet succeeded in exhuming the booty, however, all of them fainting, falling sick or becoming mysteriously paralysed in the attempt.

The principal daylight activity in Cahuita is taking a boat trip out to the Parque Nacional Cahuita's coral reef to **snorkel** – try the town's three tour companies (see p.170; $15–20) – or you can snorkel off the beach at Playa Vargas (see p.169). Though you can **surf** at Cahuita, Puerto Viejo (see p.176) has better waves – bring your own board, as there's nowhere yet in either village to rent equipment. Wherever you swim, either in the park itself or on Black-Sand Beach, don't leave possessions unattended, as even your grubby T-shirt and old shorts may be stolen. If you don't fancy snorkelling, Mr Big J's organizes **horse rides** along the beach and jungle hikes ($20–30), and all three tour agencies in Cahuita offer combined jeep trips to local villages and the beach ($35).

Eating

Cahuita has plenty of places **to eat** fresh local food, with a surprisingly cosmopolitan selection. As with accommodation, prices are not low – dinner starts at around $5 – and service tends to be laid-back: leave yourself lots of time to eat.

ChaChaChas, next door to Cahuita Tours. Fantastic gourmet cuisine – exotic salads, grilled squid, seafood and Tex-Mex – prepared by French-Canadian chef at very reasonable prices and served in a pretty setting with fresh flowers on the tables and fairy lights at night.

Chao's Paradise, Black-Sand Beach. Groovy little joint serving up posh Creole cooking using the freshest ingredients.

El Cactus, signed down a side street at the northern end of the village. Friendly and informal pizzeria; also has other Italian staples like canelloni and lasagne.

El Parquecito, behind the village park. Best place in the village for breakfast, with fresh juices, pancakes and French toast.

Kelly Creek, beside the hotel of the same name. Classy place with tasty Spanish food such as gazpacho, fried chorizo and paella and a good wine list.

Miss Edith's, northern end of village. The best place in Cahuita for Creole food, *Miss Edith's* is

justifiably popular among tourists, with great rice-and-beans, rundown and *pan bon*, a particularly wide range of vegetarian dishes plus occasional home-made ice cream and herbal teas. The service is notoriously slow, especially at dinner, and no alcohol is served.

Palenque Luisa, in the middle of the village opposite *Bar Hannia*. Good-value and popular restaurant with extensive menu including *casados*, fish and Creole dishes, plus live calypso music on Saturday nights.

Sobre Las Ollas, at the northern end of the village, right on the beach. Atmospheric and classy hangout with first-rate seafood – the lobster is particularly delicious – and the sound of lapping waves in the background, though it's not cheap. Closed Tues.

Vista de Mar (known by the locals as "El Chines"), by Kelly Creek. Barn-sized restaurant with a vast menu featuring inexpensive rice-and-bean combos, fish and Chinese food. It's popular with backpackers, and can get very crowded.

Nightlife and entertainment

Nightlife in Cahuita revolves around having a beer and listening to music. At weekends the village's two discos get very sweaty, with customers spilling out onto the street and cranked-up sound systems playing on until the small hours.

Bar Hannia, in the centre of the village. Small, friendly bar with good cold beer and a relaxed atmosphere.

Coco's, in the centre of the village. *The* place to party in Cahuita, with a pleasant balcony over the main street and a dance floor inside. If you're a single woman you'll inevitably be chatted up by

the resident dreadlocked hustlers, though they're harmless enough.

Salon Sarafina, next to *Coco's*. The village's other disco, used for special occasions, with a large and rather dark interior and huge sound system.

Soda Bambata, Black-Sand Beach. Laid-back reggae bar directly opposite the beach.

Moving on from Cahuita

There are seven buses daily to Limón, where you can connect for San José, but if you're in a hurry to reach the capital, it's faster and easier to take the direct non-stop service (4 daily; 4hr), run by Transportes MEPE. For Puerto Viejo, the local bus leaves Cahuita six times daily, taking forty minutes (first bus at 6am, last at 7pm), and continuing on from Puerto Viejo to Bribri and then Sixaola.

Parque Nacional Cahuita

Occupying just 10.7 square kilometres, **PARQUE NACIONAL CAHUITA** is one of the smallest in the country, covering the wedge-shaped piece of land from Punta Cahuita back to the main highway between Puerto Limón and Sixaola and, most importantly, the **coral reef** (*arrecife*) about 500m offshore. On land, Cahuita protects the coastal rainforest, a lowland habitat of semi-mangroves and tall canopy cover which backs the gently curving white sand beaches of Playa Vargas to the south of Punta Cahuita and Playa Cahuita to the north. Resident **birds** include ibis and kingfishers, along with white-faced (*carablanca*) monkeys, sloths and snakes, but the only animals you're likely to see are howler monkeys and, perhaps, coati, who scavenge around the northern section of the park, where bins overflow with rubbish left by day-trippers.

There are two **entrances** to the park, one at **Kelly Creek** at the southern end of Cahuita village (open during daylight hours; voluntary donation) and another at **Puerto Vargas** (8am–5pm; $6), 4km south of Cahuita along the Limón–Sixaola road. There are good **camping** facilities ($2 per day) here, complete with barbecue grill, pit toilets and showers, but you'll need to bring your own drinking water, insect repellent, and a torch. Be careful, too, not to pitch your tent too close to the high tide line; check with the rangers. Theft is also a problem: don't leave anything unattended and ask the rangers for advice – they may be able to look after your things.

The park's one **trail** (7km), skirting the beach, is a very easy, level walk, with a path so wide it feels like a road, covered with leaves and other brush, and a few fallen trees and logs. Stick to the trail, as snakes abound here. The Río Perzoso, about 2km from the northern entrance, or 5km from the Puerto Vargas trailhead, is not always fordable, unless you like wading through chest-high water when you can't actually see how deep it is. Similiarly, at high tide the beach is impassable in places: ask the ranger at the Puerto Vargas entrance about the tide schedules. Walking this trail can be unpleasantly humid and buggy: best to go in the morning. It's also very likely to rain and, despite the dense cover of tall trees, you'll still get wet.

If you want to go **snorkelling** on your own, you have to enter the

PARQUE NACIONAL CAHUITA

Cahuita Village

Limón (44 km)

Playa Cahuita

Punta Cahuita

Coral

Kelly Creek Entrance

Río Suárez

CARIBBEAN SEA

Playa Vargas

Puerto Vargas Entrance

N

HWY 36

0   1 km

Puerto Viejo (15 km)

Cahuita coral

Arcing around Punta Cahuita, the *arrecife de Cahuita*, or Cahuita reef, comprises six square kilometres of coral, and is one of just two snorkelling reefs to speak of on this side of Costa Rica (the other is further south at the Refugio Nacional de Vida Silvestre Gandoca-Manzanillo; see p.182). Corals are actually tiny animals, single-celled polyps, that secrete limestone, building their houses around themselves. Over centuries the limestone binds together to form a multilayered coral reef. The coral thrives on algae, which, like land plants, transform light into energy to survive; reefs always grow close to the surface in transparent waters where they can get plenty of sun.

Unfortunately, Cahuita's once-splendid reef is dying, soured by agricultural chemicals from the rivers that run into the sea here (the fault of the banana plantations), and from the silting up of these same rivers caused by topsoil run-off from logging, and the upheaval of the 1991 earthquake. The species that survive are common brain coral, grey and mushy like its namesake, moose horn coral, which is slightly red, and sallow grey deer horn coral. In water deeper than 2m, you might also spot fan coral wafting elegantly back and forth.

This delicate ecosystem shelters more than 120 species of fish and the odd green turtle. Lobsters, particularly the fearsome-looking spiny lobster, used to be common but are also falling victim to the reef's environmental problems. Less frail is the blue parrotfish, so called because of its "beak"; actually teeth soldered together. Environmentally incorrect, the parrotfish won't leave the coral as it finds it, and instead gnaws away at its filigree-like structures and spines. Hence the white sand beaches along this part of the coast, formed by shards of excreted coral.

park at the Puerto Vargas entrance and swim the 200 to 500m out to the reef from Playa Vargas. Note the signs indicating treacherous currents, wear shoes (you will have to walk over exposed coral), and watch out for prickly black sea urchins.

Puerto Viejo de Talamanca and around

The 12km stretch between the langorous hamlet of **PUERTO VIEJO DE TALAMANCA**, 18km southeast of Cahuita, and Manzanillo village is one of the most beautiful areas of the country. Though not great for swimming, the **beaches** – Playa Chiquita, Punta Uva and Manzanillo – are the most picturesque on the entire coast; there's also plenty of accommodation, and it's a good deal livelier than Cahuita.

It's **surfing** that really pulls the crowds; the stretch south of *Stanford's* restaurant at the southern end of Puerto Viejo offers some of the most challenging waves in the country and certainly the best on the Caribbean coast. Puerto Viejo's famous twenty-foot wave **"La Salsa Brava"** crashes ashore between December and March and from June to July; September and October, when La Salsa Brava disappears, are the quietest months of the year.

The **village** itself lies between the thick forested hills of the Talamanca mountains and the sea, where locals bathe and kids frolic with surfboards in the waves. It's a dusty little place in daylight hours but reasonably well cared for, with bright hand-painted signs pointing the way to cabinas, bars and restaurants. The main drag through the centre, potholed and rough, is crisscrossed by a few dirt streets and an offshoot road that follows the shore. As in Cahuita,

PUERTO VIEJO DE TALAMANCA

RESTAURANTS, BARS, CAFÉS & NIGHTLIFE

Bambú	E
El Café Rico	H
Johnny's Place	A
Miss Sam's	I
Parquecito	F
Pan Pay	B
Pizzeria Coral	G
Sunset Reggae Bar	D
The Place	C

N

CARIBBEAN SEA

To Cahuita, Limón, Sixaola, Manzanillo

Terraventuras Tours

Police

Puerto Viejo Tours

Comisaratio

ATEC Office

To San José

Black Sand Beach

Manzanillo

Cahuita & Bribri

Laundry

Thunder Love

ACCOMMODATION

Cabinas Casa Verde	2
Cabinas Grant	1
Cabinas Guarana	4
Cabinas Jacaranda	5
Cabinas Tropical	3
Kiskidee	7
Pura Vida	6

0   50 m

Soccer Field

many Europeans have been drawn to Puerto Viejo, and have set up their own businesses; also like Cahuita, most locals are of Afro-Caribbean descent. In recent years Puerto Viejo has become a byword for backpacker and surf-party culture, with a surprisingly vibrant nightlife and its attendant drugs scene, though this is fairly low-key and shouldn't adversely affect your stay. Nevertheless, you should make sure your room is well secured at night and avoid wandering through the quiet fringes of the village alone in the small hours.

Signs of **indigenous culture** are more evident here than in Cahuita; the **KéköLdi** reserve, inhabited by about two hundred Bribrí and Cabécar peoples, skirts the southern end of Puerto Viejo, and ATEC (see p.179) has a strong presence in the town.

Arrival

All buses **from San José** to Puerto Viejo stop first in **Limón** and **Cahuita** (4 daily; 4hr 30min) and then go onto **Sixaola**, with the first one leaving the San José at 6am and the last one at 3.30pm. The last bus back to San José goes at 4pm. Taking a bus from San José to Limón (5 daily) and changing there is only marginally less expensive, and will increase travelling time by an hour at least. Three buses daily go along the coast to **Manzanillo** (7.15am, 3.45pm & 7.15pm; 45min).

Theoretically, you could walk along the beach from Cahuita to Puerto Viejo (a good 15km, and a whole day's walk), but this is not wise. Tides cut you off from time to time, leaving you the grim option of crashing through the jungle that backs the beach; there's also a creek to be forded, and robberies have been reported.

Information

Puerto Viejo has no **tourist information** office but, as with Cahuita, the village's tour operators can give you advice, maps and so on. The most helpful operator is Puerto Viejo Tours (Tues–Sun 8am–12pm & 2–6pm; ℗ & ℉750-0411, ℮puertoviejotours@yahoo.com) on the seafront, who have a wide range of tours, including rafting, snorkelling and bird-watching. They'll also change dollars and travellers' cheques, as will the nearby Comisaratio store. Terraventuras Tours (℗750-0426, ℮terraventuras@hotmail.com) rents out snorkelling equipment at very reasonable rates, while the surf shop Thunder Love rents out surf and boogie boards and can organize surfing lessons. If you're interested in ecology, the proprietor of *Cabinas Tropical,* author and biologist Rolf Blancke, takes people out on excellent trips into the Gandoca rainforest ($35 for a 12hr trip).

There's a large and efficient 24-hour **health clinic** (℗750-0136; $18 per consultation) at Hone Creek, just beyond the crossroads as you turn off the coastal road towards Puerto Viejo. The **correo** (Mon–Fri 7.30am–6pm, Sat 7.30am–12pm) is situated in the small commercial centre three blocks back from the seafront. You can get **gas** at the east end of the village, across the road from *Bambu.* For camera film and other essentials, head for El Buen Precio supermarket, which has two public **phones** in front of it (as does ATEC).

The **ATEC** office on the main road (daily 8am–9pm; ℗ & ℉750-0191, ℗www.greencoast.com/atec.htm) has internet access, telephones for international calls and a fax. They also arrange exemplary tours of the local Bribrí communities (see opposite) plus **Afro-Caribbean tours**, with a historical and educational bent. Locals whose families have been in the area since the eighteenth century take you on walks through the villages and in the jungle, telling you about old farming techniques, and traditional plant remedies. Some tours include time in the Refugio Nacional de Vida Silvestre Gandoca-Manzanillo Wildlife Refuge (see p.182). They can also recommend locals to talk to about diving and snorkelling on the Manzanillo reef, and have a small library of books on the area, plus nature guides, field guides and guidebooks, which they may lend you.

Accommodation

Due to its rapidly increasing popularity, places to stay in and around Puerto Viejo have mushroomed and you shouldn't normally have any problem finding accommodation, although it's still best to reserve a room in advance during high season and surfing-season weekends (Dec–March, June & July). The vast majority of places to stay in the **village** are simple cabinas, usually without hot water (sometimes without water altogether), while more upmarket establishments line the **coast** south of the village. You can **camp** on the beaches, but rock-bottom budget travellers usually forsake their tents and stay at the lovely *Kiskidee*.

Cabinas Casa Verde, one block south of the main drag (℗ & ℉750-0047, ℮cabinascasaverde@hotmail.com). Fourteen fantastic-value cabinas, decorated with shell mobiles and pieces of washed-up coral, with very clean showers, ceiling fans, mosquito nets and space to sling hammocks. ❸

Cabinas Grant, on the main road (℗750-0292). Spotless, locally run hotel with basic but serviceable rooms. ❶

Cabinas Guarana, south of the main drag on the way to the soccer field (℗750-0244, ℗www.hotelguarana.com). Run by a very friendly

About two hundred Bribrí and Cabécar peoples live in the KéköLdi Indigenous Reserve, which begins just south of Puerto Viejo and extends inland into the Talamancas. The reserve was established in 1976 to protect the indigenous culture and ecological resources of the area, but the communities and land remain under constant threat from logging, squatters, tourism and banana plantations. The worst problems arise from poor surveying of the boundaries of the reserve and lax government checks on construction in the area which, inhabitants claim, has led to several hotels being built illegally on their land (the story of all the wranglings surrounding the formation of these reserves is wittily told in Anachristina Rossi's novel, *La Loca de Gandoca* – available, in Spanish only, in San José). The main obstacle to understanding between the indigenous peoples and their neighbours has been, historically, their irreconcilable views of land. The Bribrí and Cabécar see the forest as an interrelated system of cohabitants all created by and belonging to Sibö, their god of creation, while the typical *campesino* view is that of a pioneer – the forest is an obstacle to cultivation (and therefore civilization), to be conquered, tamed and effectively destroyed.

The best way to visit the reserve in on one of the tours ($15 for half a day) organized by the Associación Talamanqueña de Ecoturismo y Conservación, or ATEC, a grassroots organization set up by members of the local community – Afro-Caribbeans, Bribrí indigenous peoples and Spanish-descended inhabitants. If you're spending even just a couple of days in the Talamanca region, an ATEC-sponsored trip is a must; to reserve a tour, go to their Puerto Viejo office (see opposite) at least one day in advance. The organization's main aim is to give local people a chance to demonstrate their pride in and knowledge of their home territory, and to show them how to make a living off tourism without selling their land or entering into more exploitative business arrangements. In this spirit ATEC has trained about fifteen local people as guides, who get about ninety percent of the individual tour price. Whereas many of the hotel-organized excursions to the indigenous reserve take you in cars, ATEC promote horseback and hiking tours. There's a strict maximum of six people, and they visit places on a rotating roster, so that local hamlets do not have to deal with foreigners traipsing through every day.

The tour does not take you, as you might expect, to villages where indigenous peoples live in "primitive" conditions. The Bribrí speak Spanish (as well as Bribrí) and wear Western clothes. But underneath this layer of integration lie the vital remains of their culture and traditional way of life. Although the area has seen some strife between the reserve dwellers, their neighbours, and foreign hotel developments, these altercations remain largely on the level of policy. For the tourist, there is no overtly apparent ill-feeling between the groups. Treks usually last about four hours, traversing dense rainforest and the Talamanca hills. They start near the road to Puerto Viejo – where Bribrí crafts, including woven baskets and coconut shell carvings, are on sale – passing cleared areas, coca plantings and very small homesteads, then into secondary, and then finally primary, cover. In this old forest the guide may take you along the same trails that have been used for centuries by Bribrís on their trips from their mountain homes down to the sea, and point out the traditional medicinal plants (curing everything from malaria to skin irritations). A tour may involve discussions about the permanent reforestation programme in which the Bribrí have been involved, and might perhaps visit the iguana breeding farm the local community have established.

Italian couple, this lovely small hotel has attractive rooms, tiled bathrooms and a communal kitchen for guests' use. Check out the treehouse in the garden, from where there are great views over the village. ❸

Cabinas Jacaranda, just north of the soccer field (☎ 750-0069). Basic but very clean budget option, with lively Guatemalan fabrics and a lush tropical garden. ❷

Cabinas Tropical, on the eastern edge of the village (T & F750-0283, Wwww.cabinastropical.com). Small, quiet and scrupulously clean hotel with five large, comfortable rooms, and pet birds in the garden. ②

Kiskidee, signposted along a path south of the soccer field (T750-0075). Well worth the 15min trek up the hill – bring a torch at night – this is one of the most tranquil lodges in all Costa Rica, and at budget rates. The large verandah is good

for bird- and animal-spotting, and there's spacious bunk accommodation and the use of a kitchen – stock up on food at the pulpería – but no fans and an outdoor toilet only. ①

Pura Vida, near the soccer field (T750-0002, F750-0296). Popular budget hotel which tends to fill quickly, run by friendly owners and their amiable rottweiler. The seven rooms all have private bath, ceiling fans and mosquito nets, and there's a pleasant verandah. ③

Eating, drinking and nightlife

Puerto Viejo has a surprisingly cosmopolitan range of **places to eat**. Good, traditional **Creole food** is served at *Miss Sam's*, and the ATEC can put you in touch with village women who cook typical regional meals on request. Although quiet during the day, Puerto Viejo begins thumping at **night**. If you're after a quiet drink, one of the nicest spots in town is the spacious verandah in front of the Comisaratio store – buy your beer from the shop and drink it from the bottle as you watch the sun slide prettily into the sea.

Bambú, on the eastern edge of town. Beachfront reggae disco which gets absolutely packed on Mondays and Fridays; great fun.

El Café Rico, opposite Cabinas Casa Verde. Dutch-run café with the best coffee in town, tasty sandwiches, crepes and breakfast. Nice rooms (③) also available.

Johnny's Place, on the seafront near the police station. Large airy disco with bonfires on the beach. Very popular at weekends.

Miss Sam's, three blocks back from the seafront. Wonderful Caribbean home cooking at very reasonable prices. Often full at lunchtimes.

Pan Pay, behind Johnny's Place. Popular breakfast spot and bakery with croissants, cakes and delicious Spanish tortilla.

Parquecito, on the edge of town towards Manzanillo. Lively bar-restaurant with sea views, cold beer and good atmosphere – although the food's not up to much.

Pizzeria Coral. Succulent, if pricey, pizzas ($4) served on a lively outdoor terrace.

Sunset Reggae Bar, on the seafront near the bus stop. Groovy little bar with delicious pizza from the wood-fired oven, plus an entertaining Wednesday open-mike session with tables set out on the shore and passing musicians joining in.

The Place, one block back from the bus stop. Attractive café specializing in vegetarian dishes and seafood, popular with tourists sick to death of rice, beans and pizza – try the tasty coconut-flavoured curries.

South from Puerto Viejo to Manzanillo

The 15km south of Puerto Viejo, dotted by the tiny hamlets of **Playa Cocles**, **Playa Chiquita**, **Punta Uva** and **Manzanillo**, the main village, is one of the most appealing on the entire Caribbean coast. All the trappings of a pristine tropical paradise are here, with palm trees leaning over calm beaches, purples, mauves, oranges and reds all fading into the sea at sunset, and a milk-like twilight mist wafting in from the Talamancas. The atmosphere is hassle-free, and there's excellent accommodation along the Puerto Viejo–Manzanillo road, but public transport is infrequent, so you'll find life much easier with a car, especially if you want to explore the **Refugio Nacional de Vida Silvestre Gandoca-Manzanillo**, which borders the area. The road from Puerto Viejo to Manzanillo was only built in 1984 – electricity came five years later – and despite the mini-invasion of hotels and cabinas, local life remains much the same as ever, with subsistence householders fishing for still-abundant lobster and supplementing their income with tourism-oriented activities. **Manzanillo**

Playa has a large shelf of coral reef just offshore which teems with marine life and offers some of the best snorkelling in Costa Rica. The village itself is small and charming, with laid-back locals and a couple of great places to eat and hang out.

Accommodation

Incredibly, there are over 25 places to stay on the road from Puerto Viejo to Manzanillo – mostly mid-range options, plus a couple of elegant boutique hotels and several self-catering places.

Aguas Claras, Playa Chiquita (T 750-0180, F 750-0386, E harbor@racsa.co.cr). The best self-catering option in the area, set in luxuriant gardens just 200m from the beach. Each of the brightly painted wooden chalets has mosquito nets, a sitting area, balcony, clean bathroom, cold water, fully equipped kitchen and electricity. They sleep up to four people, but can only be rented by the week ($240).

Caribbean Casitas, Playa Cocles (T 234-2530, F 225-6143, E helena@novanet.co.cr). Caribbean-style house with gingerbread woodwork and beautiful Spanish-tiled floors set in gardens near the beach. The two large bedrooms ($65) sleep up to four, and the full self-catering facilities include kitchen and fridge – good value for groups or a family.

Cariblue, Playa Cocles (T & F 750-0057, W www.cariblue.com). Comfortable individual cabinas with an Italian restaurant, good souvenir shop and book exchange on site. ❺

Casa Camarona, Playa Cocles (T 750-0151, W www.casacamarona.com). Nineteen rooms, all with private bathroom and a/c, set in a first-class location right on the beach. There's also an attractive restaurant and good *artesanía* shop on site. ❻

La Costa de Papito, Playa Cocles (T & F 750-0080, W www.greencoast.com/papito.htm). Six bungalows with large bamboo beds and balconies, set in pretty gardens and run by an effusive New Yorker. ❹

Miraflores, Playa Chiquita (T & F 750-0038, W www.mirafloreslodge.com). Rustic, comfortable lodge opposite the beach, on an old cacao plantation with tropical flowers in the grounds. The decor is lovely, with Bribrí paintings, carvings and *objets d'art*. The upstairs rooms are brighter – with mosquito nets, mirrors and high bamboo ceilings – and there's an outside breakfast area. The owner has excellent contacts with local KéköLdi Bribrí communities and runs imaginative tours, including trips to Panama in a motorized dugout. ❸

Pangea, Manzanillo (T 224-2400, E pangea@puertoviejo.net). Two beautifully decorated rooms, with private bath and breakfast included. ❹

Shawandha, Playa Chiquita (T 750-0018, F 750-0037, W www.shawandha-lodge.com). Very chic French hotel comprising ten large bungalows with enormous beds and gorgeous tiled bathrooms. Rates include breakfast. ❼

Villas del Caribe, Playa Chiquita (T 750-0202, F 221-2801, W www.villascaribe.net). Actually within the KéköLdi indigenous reserve, this hotel has very comfortable two-storey self-catering accommodation, with terrace, hot water, fan and organic garbage disposal. The grounds are right on the beach, with great sunset views. ❻

Eating and drinking

Elena Brown's, just beyond *Miraflores* lodge, 5km south of Puerto Viejo. This long-established soda-cum-restaurant serves succulent local fish and chicken dishes, as well as inexpensive lunch-time specials and snacks.

El Rinconcito Alegre, Manzanillo. Small, cheerful café with *casados*, fresh fruit juices and seafood.

Maxis, Manzanillo. Large upstairs restaurant with great views over the beach and renowned seafood, including lobster. Gets packed out at weekends.

Selvyn's Restaurant, about 8km south of Puerto Viejo. Long-established restaurant dishing up beautifully cooked local fish (served with coconut-flavoured rice-and-beans at weekends).

Refugio Nacional de Vida Silvestre Gandoca-Manzanillo

In the very southeast corner of the country, bordering Río Sixaola and the frontier with Panamá, the little-visited but fascinating **REFUGIO NACIONAL DE VIDA SILVESTRE GANDOCA-MANZANILLO** incorporates the small hamlets of Gandoca and Manzanillo and covers fifty square kilometres of land and a similar area of sea. The refuge was established to protect some of Costa Rica's last few **coral reefs**, of which **Punta Uva** is the most accessible, with some great snorkelling. There's also a protected **turtle-nesting beach** south of the village of Manzanillo, along with tracts of mangrove forests and the last *orey* **swamp** in the country. More than 358 **bird** species have been identified, many of them rare – ten years ago there were sightings of the endangered harpy eagle, believed to be extinct in the rest of the country due to deforestation. Other species found in the refuge include the *manatí*, tapir and American crocodile, who hang out along the river estuary, though you're unlikely to see them.

If you are interested in exploring the refuge, all Puerto Viejo's tour companies (see p.178) have trips – your best bet, though, is to contact the excellent Aquamor Adventures (☏391-3417, ✉aquamor@racsa.co.cr) in Manzanillo. Although principally a scuba-diving outfit, Aquamor also has a wide range of marine activities including dolphin-spotting and is run by friendly experts who can put you in touch with local guides who know the terrain backwards and can take you on hikes in the refuge. **Camping** is permitted within the refuge, but is really only feasible on the beach, due to the mosquitos, snakes and other biting creatures inland.

Gandoca-Manzanillo has one fairly demanding but rewarding **trail** (5.5km each way), passing primary and secondary forest as well as some pretty, secluded beaches on its way from Manzanillo to **Monkey Point** (Punta Mona). It can get extremely hot, and mosquitos are usually out in force, so carry plenty of water, sunscreen and repellent. Beginning at the northeast end of Manzanillo village, the trail proceeds along the beach for 1km. After crossing a small creek and entering a grove of coconut trees, it becomes poorly marked and easy to lose, but should be just about visible as it climbs up a small bluff. The trail then drops to lower ground and a few small shark-infested beaches before heading inland. Some of these up-and-down sections are quite steep, and if it has been raining (as it invariably has) then mud and mosquitos may combine to make the trip unpleasant.

However, the trail does offer great opportunities for spotting birds and wildlife; you're effectively guaranteed a sight of chestnut-mandibled and keel-billed **toucans**. The tiny flashes of colour darting about on the ground in front of you are **poison dart frogs**; watch where you're stepping, and avoid touching them. Punta Mona, the end of the trail, is flanked by a shady beach, from where you can see across to Panamá, only about 8km to the south. From here you return to Manzanillo the same way.

Four kilometres from Manzanillo down a rough track, **GANDOCA** provides access to the estuary of the Río Gandoca, a bird-spotters' delight, with boat-trips organized from the village. You can get here by walking from Manzanillo, or there's access from the Sixaola road – if you have a 4WD – via the banana fincas of Daytonia, Virginia and Finca 96.

Bribrí and the Panamanian Border

From Puerto Viejo the paved road (Hwy-36) continues inland to **BRIBRÍ**, about 10km southwest, arching over the Talamancan foothills to reveal the green valleys stretching ahead to Panamá. This is banana country, with little to see even in Bribrí itself, which is largely devoted to administering the affairs of indigenous reserves in the Talamanca mountains. Bribrí does, however, have one basic **place to stay**, *Cabinas El Mango* (no telephone; ❶), a couple of simple **restaurants** and a **bank**, the Banco Nacional, which changes money and travellers' cheques, though there's usually a long queue.

There are several **indigenous reserves** near Bribrí. You can't visit them without special permission both from the communities themselves and from the government, but if you're interested, anthropologist Fernando Cortés (☎766-6800) leads small groups through the Talamanca moutnains on officially sanctioned visits to Cabécar communities. Trips begin near Cartago, from where you walk into the Talamanca region, last around a week, and cost about $100 per person.

From here a dusty gravel road winds for 34km through solid banana fincas to **Sixaola**. Locals cross the border here to do their shopping in Panamá, where most things are less expensive. The majority of foreigners who cross into Panamá do so simply because their tourist visa for Costa Rica has expired and they have to leave the country for 72 hours, though the pristine Panamanian island of **Bocas del Toro** just over the border offers an inviting prospect even for those who don't need an extension.

The border and on into Panamá

Sixaola–Guabito is a small crossing that doesn't see much foreign traffic, and for the most part formalities are simple, but you should get here as early in the morning as possible. There's nowhere decent to stay before you get to Bocas del Toro – and you should leave time to look for a hotel once there – and bus connections in Panamá can be tricky.

The Sixaola–Guabito border is open daily from 8am to 5pm Panamá time (one hour ahead of Costa Rica). Tourists leaving Costa Rica need to buy a **Red Cross exit stamp** ($2 from the pharmacy in Sixaola); citizens of some nationalities may require a **tourist card** to enter Panamá (valid for 30 days); the Panamanian consulate in San José issues them, as does the San José office of Copa, the Panamanian airline (see p.107). Immigration requirements often change; check with the Panamanian consulate.

There's nowhere to **stay** in Guabito, the tiny hamlet on the Panamanian side of Río Sixaola, so your best option is to catch the bus to the banana town of Changuinola (7am–5pm; every 30min), further into Panamá, or arrange a taxi (ask at the border post), which will make the thirty-minute trip for about $15. The bus continues on to Almirante – though you may need to change at Changuinola – from where you can get a water taxi to **Bocas del Toro**, the main settlement in a small archipelego of little-inhabited islands, with beautifully clear water, great for snorkelling and swimming. **Hotels** include the friendly *Hotel Angela*, right on the waterfront (❶), and the rather swanky *Swan's Cay* (❻).

Connections with the **rest of Panamá** from this northeast corner are tenuous. From Almirante, you'll need to take the ferry fifty kilometres southeast to the banana town of Chiriquí Grande, from where there are road connections to the rest of the country, and a bus service across the Cordillera Central to Chiriquí on the Interamericana, from where there are bus connections to Panamá City and back to San José.

Refugio Nacional de Fauna Silvestre Barra del Colorado

At the northern end of Costa Rica's Caribbean coast, 99km northeast from San José near the border with Nicaragua, the **REFUGIO NACIONAL DE FAUNA SILVESTRE BARRA DEL COLORADO** was created specifically to preserve the area's abundant fauna. A large, isolated tract, very sparsely populated (by humans, at least), it is crossed by Río Colorado, which debouches into the Caribbean next to the village of Barra del Colorado, while it's northern boundary – which is also the border with Nicaragua – is marked by the grand Río San Juan, which continues north of the border all the way through to the Lago de Nicaragua. Almost all traffic in this area is by water.

BARRA DEL COLORADO is the area's only settlement of any size, a small, quiet village inhabited by a mixed population of Afro-Caribbeans, Miskitos, Costa Ricans and significant numbers of Nicaraguans, many of whom spilled over the border during the Civil War. The village is divided into two halves: Barra Sur and the larger Barra Norte, which stand opposite each other near the mouth of the Río Colorado. Tropical hardwoods are still under siege from illegal logging around here – you may see giant tree trunks being towed along the river and into the Caribbean, from where they are taken down to Limón.

Very few people come to Barra on a whim. As far as tourism goes, **sportsfishing** is the place's *raison d'être*, and numerous lodges offer packages and transportation from San José. Tarpon and snook, two big-game fish prized for

The Río San Juan and the Nicaraguan border

Heading to or from Barra from the Sarapiquí area in the Zona Norte (see p.217) entails a trip along the Río Sarapiquí to the mighty Río San Juan. Flowing from Lago de Nicaragua to the Caribbean, the San Juan marks most of Costa Rica's border with Nicaragua, and the entire northern edge of the Barra del Colorado Wildlife Refuge. Costa Ricans have the right of travel on the river, although it is theoretically in Nicaraguan territory (the actual border is the bank on the Costa Rican side, not the midpoint of the river), but there is no official entry point between the two countries along this stretch and it is technically illegal to attempt to cross here. For details on crossing into Nicaragua see p.214.

One bizarre phenomenon local to this area, and unique in the world, is the migration of bull sharks from the saltwater Caribbean up the Río San Juan to the freshwater Lago de Nicaragua, making the transition, apparently without trauma, from being saltwater to freshwater sharks.

You'll notice much evidence of logging in the area, especially at the point where the Sarapiquí flows into the Río San Juan – the lumber industry has long had carte blanche in this area, due to the non-enforcement of existing anti-logging laws. The Nicaraguan side of the Río San Juan, part of the country's huge Indio Maíz reserve, looks altogether wilder than its southern neighbour, with thick primary rainforest creeping right to the edge of the bank. Partly because of logging, and the residual destruction of banks, the Río San Juan is silting up, and even shallow-bottomed *lanchas* get stuck in this once consistently deep river. It's a far cry from the 1600s and 1700s, when pirate ships used to sail all the way along the Río San Juan to Lago de Nicaragua, from where they could wreak havoc on the Spanish Crown's ports and shipping.

their fighting spirit, ply these waters in droves, as does the garfish, a primeval throwback looking something like a cross between a fish and a crocodile. The season runs from January to May and September to October.

Because of the impenetrability of the cover, there is little for non-fishing tourists to do in Barra other than bird- or crocodile-spotting from a boat in one of the many waterways and lagoons. The usual sloths and monkeys are in residence, and you'll certainly hear the wild hoot of howler monkeys shrieking through the still air. If you are really lucky, and keep your eyes peeled on the water, you might catch sight of a *manatí* (manatee, or sea cow) going by underneath. These large, benevolent seal-like creatures are on the brink of becoming an endangered species. You shouldn't swim here – though you may see locals risking doing so – as this is **shark** territory.

It is very, very **hot**, and painfully **humid** around Barra. Wear a hat and sunscreen and, if possible, stay under shade during the hottest part of the day. February, March and April are the driest months, but there is no season when it does not rain.

Practicalities

In terms of the time it takes you to get there, Barra is one of the most **inaccessible** places in the country. Most people arrive either by **lancha** from Tortuguero (45min) or Puerto Viejo de Sarapiquí (3hr downriver, twice that upriver), both lovely trips – from Puerto Viejo especially, as you come in partly on the Río San Juan. If you do this, be sure to have your passport to show at Nicaraguan border checkpoints. *Lanchas* arrive in Barra Sur, or, if you ask, will take you directly to your accommodation. The **flight** from San José to Barra (landing at Barra Sur) affords stupendous views of volcanos, unfettered lowland tropical forest and the coast. Sansa currently flies from San José daily at 6am, returning at 6.45am.

Accommodation

Because of Barra's inaccessibilty and its emphasis on fishing, hardly anyone comes here for just one night. Most lodges are devoted exclusively to **fishing packages**, although you could, theoretically call in advance and arrange to stay as an independent, non-fishing guest. The lodges can provide details of their individual packages; generally they comprise meals, accommodation, boat, guide and tackle, and some may offer boat lunches, drinks and other extras. One of the few lodges in the area that doesn't cater to sportsfishers, *Samay Laguna*, also brings most of its guests to the area on packages from San José. The only place at all geared up for **independent travellers** is *Tarponland*, which has a few cabinas. While all of the accommodation in this area is comfortable, some tends toward the positively rustic, and you should certainly not expect frills such as air conditioning.

Casamar, across the river from Barra del Colorado (☎ 433-8834, ℻ 433-9287, 🌐 www.casamarlodge.com). Luxurious and elegant cabins set in lovely gardens, with hiking trails through jungle to the beach. Fishing packages only, at around $2500 per week.

Río Colorado Fishing Lodge, Barra Sur (☎ 232-4063, ℻ 231-5987, 🌐 www.sportsmansweb.com/riocolorado). Well-known lodge with lots of character built on walk-

ways over the river, with a/c, comfortable wooden rooms, cable TV, and a dining room with good food and pretty views of Barra Norte. 🌀

Samay Laguna Lodge, 15min by *lancha* south of Barra Sur (☎ 384-7047, ℻ 383-6370, 🌐 www.samay.com). A real away-from-it-all experience, set on the deserted stretch of beach between Barra and Tortuguero, offering simple rooms (take plenty of mosquito repellent) with private bathrooms and hot water, plus boat tours, jungle hikes, horse rides on the beach and tours to Tortuguero. The lodge has several packages with boat or plane transfers, the most popular being a round-trip from San José up the Río Sarapiquí and through southern Nicaragua along the Río San Juan (3 days; $278). The standard room also includes all meals. ❽

Silver King Lodge (☎381-1403, ℱ381-0849, ⓦwww.silverkinglodge.com). Efficient and well-equipped fishing lodge, with big rooms, a bar, restaurant, swimming pool, Jacuzzi and US TV.

Daily rate including fishing $435; without fishing $130 (in the UK, book with Leslies of Luton, ⓦwww.leslies-luton.co.uk). ❽

Tarponland Bar and Restaurant, next to the airstrip in Barra Sur (☎710-1271). Large old lodge, moderately priced, with simple screened rooms with fans and private or shared baths – there are some more basic, budget cabinas attached. It's also one of the few places in town where you can get a cold drink and a meal. ❷

Parque Nacional Tortuguero

Despite its isolation – 254km from San José by road and water, or 83km north-west of Limón – **PARQUE NACIONAL TORTUGUERO** ($6) is one of the most visited national parks in Costa Rica. As the name implies – *tortuguero* means turtle-catcher in Spanish, and turtle-catchers have long flourished in this area – this is one of the most important nesting sights in the world for the **green sea turtle**, one of only eight species of marine turtle in the world. Along with the hawksbill turtle, the green sea turtle, lays its eggs here between July and October.

First established as a protective zone in the 1960s, Tortuguero became a national park in 1975. It's big – 190 square kilometres – protecting not only the beach on which turtles nest, but also the surrounding land, comprising impenetrable tropical rainforest, coastal mangrove swamps and lagoons, and canals and waterways. Except for a short dry season during February and March it's also very wet, receiving over 6000mm of rain a year. This soggy environment hosts a wide abundance of species – fifty kinds of **fish**, numerous **birds**, including the endangered green parrot and the vulture, and some 160 **mammals**, some under the threat of extinction. Due to the waterborne nature of most transport and the impenetrability of the ground cover, it's difficult to spot them, but howler, whitefaced and spider monkeys lurk behind the undergrowth, along with the fishing bulldog bat, which fishes by sonar, and a variety of large rodents, including the window rat, whose internal organs you can see through its transparent skin. Jaguars

Parismina, Moín & Siquerres ▼

used to thrive here, but are slowly being driven out by the encroaching banana plantations at the western end of the park; you may also spot the little-understood West Indian manatee, or sea cow, swimming underwater. It's the **turtles** that draw people here, however, and the sight of the gentle beasts tumbling ashore and shimmying their way up the beach to deposit their heavy load before limping back, spent, into the dark phosphorescent waves can't fail to move.

As elsewhere in Costa Rica, logging, economic opportunism and fruit plantations have affected Tortuguero. Sometimes advertised by package tour brochures as a "Jungle Cruise" along "Central America's Amazon", the journey to Tortuguero is indeed Amazonian, taking you past tracts of **deforestation** and lands cleared for cattle – all outside the park's official boundaries but, together with banana plantations, encroaching on to its western fringes.

The most popular way to see Tortuguero is on one of literally hundreds of **packages** that use the expensive lodges across the canal from the village. These are usually two-night, three-day affairs, although you can go for longer. Accommodation, meals and transport (which otherwise can be a bit tricky) are taken care of, while guides point out wildlife along the river and canal on the way. The main difference between tours comes in the standard of accommodation; check the reviews of the lodges on p.190 for more details.

With a little planning, you can also get to Tortuguero **independently** and stay in cabinas in the village, which is a more interesting little place than initial impressions might suggest. Basing yourself here allows you to explore the beach at leisure – though you can't swim – and puts you in easy reach of restaurants and bars.

Getting to Tortuguero

Until the 1991 earthquake, tour boats and a weekly cargo boat would travel from Moín up the **Tortuguero Canal** towards Nicaragua. Although the earthquake made the canal unpassable in some areas to all but the most shallow-bottomed of boats, *lanchas* still go up the canal from Moín and elsewhere. Expect a three- or four-hour trip (sometimes longer) by *lancha*, depending upon where you embark – if you're on a package tour, it will probably be **Hamburgo de Siquerres** on the Río Reventazón; travelling independently, you'll find it logistically easier to leave from **Moín**. Either way you'll pass palm and deciduous trees, mirror-calm waters, and small, stilt-legged wooden houses, brightly painted and poised on the water's edge – along, of course, with acres and acres of cleared land. Quite apart from the wildlife, the canal is a hive of human activity, with *lanchas*, *botes* (large canoes) and *pangas* (flat-bottomed outboard-motored boats) plying the glassy waters.

If you're travelling **independently**, you ought to be able to find a boat at Moín willing to take you up the canal anytime from 6am until as late as 2pm – see p.166 for full details. You can arrange with your boatman when you would like to be picked up to return (it's really not worth going for the day – if you do you'll have to make the return trip not later than 1.30pm to avoid getting stuck in the dark). Get a phone number from him if possible, so you can call from Tortuguero village if you change plans. The *lanchas* drop you at Tortuguero dock, from where you can walk to the village accommodation or take another *lancha* across the canal to the more expensive tourist lodges. If you haven't booked a hotel, be aware that accommodation in the village can fill up quickly during the turtle-nesting seasons (March–May & July–Oct).

Alternatively, you can do what the locals do and take a 9am bus from San José to **Cariari**, then switch to a bus for the **Geest banana plantation**, from where a boat goes to Tortuguero, arriving in the village at 3.30pm. It's a long journey, but the boat ride costs only $10 each way, and if you're travelling alone it makes sense. The return boat to San José leaves daily at 7am.

If you come **by air** on Sansa's daily flight, which leaves San José at 6am and takes approximately 35 minutes (☎221-9414, ℱ225-2176), you'll arrive at the airstrip some 4km north of the village. There are no taxis from here to the village, though the more upmarket lodges will come and pick you up; otherwise, you'll have to walk.

The village

The peaceful village of **TORTUGUERO** lies at the northeastern corner of the park, on a thin spit of land between the sea and the canal. The exuberant foliage of wisteria, oleander and bougainvillea gives the whole place the look of a carefully tended tropical garden, with tall palm groves and clean expanses of mown grass dotted with zinc-roofed wooden houses, often elevated on stilts. This is classic Caribbean style: washed-out, slightly ramshackle and pastel-pretty, with very little to disturb the torpor until after dark.

A dirt path runs north–south through the village – the "main street" – from which narrow paths go off to the sea and the canal. Smack in the middle of the village stands one of the prettiest churches you'll see anywhere, pale yellow, with a small spire and an oval doorway. Just beyond the church is the colourful **La Crisalida Butterfly Garden** (daily 3–5.30pm; $1), a community initiative manned by volunteers. The Jungle Souvenir Shop (Mon–Fri 8am–7pm), at the northern end of the village across from the small jetty, is very well stocked with T-shirts, wooden souvenirs and cards, with prices more or less the same as in San José. If the sun here is getting to you, this is the place to pick up a hat or sunscreen. The wares are less authentic at the purple Paraíso Tropical souvenir shop, which doubles as the village's Travelair agent, and sells tickets to San José.

Practicalities

A display on the turtles' habits, habitat and history surrounds the **information kiosk** in the centre of the village. Officially you should buy tickets for turtle tours here; the park rangers open the kiosk at 5pm, and this is a good time to find a local guide (see below). In addition, Canadian naturalist and local resident Darryl Loth (①392-3201, ⑤710-0547, ⑥www.safari.jumptravel.com) runs a small information centre in the village and can arrange tours, such as boat trips and hikes up Cerro Tortuguero (see p.192). At the north end of the village, there's also a **Natural History Museum** (daily 10am–5.30pm; $1), with a small but informative exhibition explaining the life-cycle of sea turtles and giving a short history of turtling in the area. The museum is sponsored by the Caribbean Conservation Corporation, the first body in Costa Rica to study and conserve the green turtle.

The *pulpería*, 50m south of the information kiosk, houses a public phone; there's another one at *Miss Junie's* restaurant which you can use for outgoing calls. There are no **bank** or money-changing facilities in Tortuguero – bring all the cash you'll need with you – and though there's a **correo** in the middle of the village, mail may take three or four weeks just to make its way to Limón. If villagers are heading to Limón they might offer to carry letters for you and post them from there, which can be useful if you are staying for any length of time. Tortuguero has a weekly medical service; otherwise emergencies and health problems should be referred to the park's administration headquarters, north of the village, near the airstrip.

Village accommodation

Staying at Tortuguero on the cheap entails bedding down in one of the independent **cabinas** in the village. **Camping** on the beach is not allowed, though you can set up tent at the mown enclosure at the **ranger station** (about $2 per day) at the southern end of the village, where you enter the park. It's in a sheltered situation, away from the sea breezes, and there is water and toilets. Bring a ground sheet and mosquito net, and make sure your tent is waterproof.

Cabinas Aracari, south of the information kiosk and soccer field (in Limón, ①798-3059). New cabinas, all with private bath, cold water and fan, set in a beautiful tree-filled garden and run by a friendly local family. ❶

Cabinas Mary Scar, east of the *pulpería*, before the beach (in San José, ①220-1478). Two new cabins with private bathrooms, plus some older cabins with shared bathroom – they're slightly gloomy but very clean, and the bathroom is spick-and-span. Family atmosphere, with simple meals (about $3) cooked on request. The least expensive option in Tortuguero. ❶

Cabinas Sabina, east of the information kiosk, on the beach (no telephone). Very simple, green cabinas whose main attraction is their setting on a nice strip of sand. The rooms are basic and dark (those upstairs have better ventilation), and the toilet and shower are in an outhouse, though they're perfectly clean. Bar on site. ❶

Cabinas Tortuguero, south of the village, towards the entry to the national park (no telephone). Tortuguero's best option, with 5 simple rooms (all en suite) in a lovely garden and Italian food available on request (one of the owners comes from Bologna; breakfast $3, lunch or supper $5). ❶

Miss Junie's, at the north end of the village, just before you reach the Natural History Museum (①710-0523). Tortuguero's most popular cook (see p.158) also has a few well-decorated and comfortable rooms with private bath (although cold water only) and fan. ❸

The lodges

Staying at Tortuguero's **lodges**, most of which are across the canal from the village, has its drawbacks. You're pretty much duty-bound to eat the set meals included in the package, and – unless you're at the *Laguna* or *Mawamba* – if you want to explore the village and the beach on your own you have to get a *lancha* across the canal (free, but inconvenient). The lodges only rent rooms to independent travellers if they have space, which they rarely do, owing to Tortuguero's perennial popularity, and no official prices are posted for non-package rooms.

El Manatí, 1.5km north of the village, across the canal (T & F 383-0330). Tortuguero's best budget option, this convivial but peaceful family-run lodge has basic but clean rooms with private bath, hot water and fans, as well as several attractive two-bedroom cabinas. Breakfast included. ❸

Jungle Lodge, 1km north of the village, across the canal (T 233-0155, F 233-0778). Owned and operated by Cotur, this friendly, comfortable and unpretentious lodge, set in its own gardens, has en-suite rooms, a good restaurant, games room, a small disco, swimming pool, free canoes and a lagoon. Good value. ❹

Laguna Lodge (T 225-3740, F 283-8031, W www.lagunalodgetortuguero.com). Attractive hotel with driftwood decor, riverside bar and rustic wooden cabins in a convenient village location, with easy access to the beach. Gorgeous pool and butterfly gardens, too, while the peaceful atmosphere and personal service is ideal for those who don't like large touristy lodges. Full tour services. ❹

Mawamba Lodge, 1km north of the village (T 710-7282, F 222-5463, W www.grupomawamba.com). Large, ritzy and gregarious lodge. The well-organized facilities include a gift shop, daily slide-show, environmentally friendly boats and round-the-clock cold beers. The *cabina*-style rooms have ceiling fans and private bathrooms, and there's a large pool and Jacuzzi, while the village and ocean are just a short walk away. ❹

Pachira Lodge, opposite the village (T 256-7080, F 223-1119, E paccira@racsa.co.cr). Tortuguero's newest lodge, this luxurious establishment has spacious and attractive rooms in wood cabins, linked by covered walkways, with large en-suite, hot-water bathrooms, along with a pool, gift shop and imaginative tour options. ❹

Tortuga Lodge, owned by Costa Rica Expeditions (T 257-0766, F 257-1665, W www.costaricaexpeditions.com). The plushest lodge in the area, though it's furthest from the village, with exemplary service, large, attractive en-suite rooms, a riverside swimming pool and elegantly landscaped grounds with walking trails. ❻

Eating, drinking and nightlife

Tortuguero village offers good homely food, typically Caribbean, with wonderful fresh **fish**. The only disadvantage is that prices tend to be high: expect to pay up to twice as much for a meal as you'd pay in other parts of Costa Rica. For entertainment, the Centro Social La Culebra has a nightly **disco**, though the clientele can be a bit rough. *Bar Brisas del Mar* (known to the locals as *El Bochinche*) is better, with a large, semi open-air dance floor and a good sound-and-light system (when it's not visiting Limón). You can hear the sea from your table and the atmosphere is low-key except on Saturday nights, when the lively weekly disco attracts a large local crowd and goes on well into the small hours.

El Dollar, mid-village, on the waterfront. In a great position on the river, with decent local food cooked to order.

El Muellecito, next to the *pulpería*. Tortuguero's best breakfast option, with tasty pancakes and fruit salad.

Miss Junie's, north end of village path, 50m before the Natural History Museum. Solid Caribbean food – red beans, jerk chicken, rice, chayote and breadfruit, all on the same plate – by local cook Miss Junie is dished up here with ice-cold beers in a large dining room with gingham tablecloths and cool white walls. Miss Junie also cooks for the park rangers, so you need to ask a day in advance or in the morning whether she can fit you in.

Miss Miriams, adjacent to village soccer pitch (and a good spot to watch the village teams in action). Cheerful and immaculate restaurant serving Caribbean food at very reasonable prices.

The Vine, opposite the Jungle Souvenir Shop. Café, run by the owners of the souvenir shop, with good coffee, cheesecake and brownies. Closed during the rainy season.

Tropical Lodge Bar, mid-village on the path to the national park entrance. Noisy and entertaining village bar with perfect sunset views over the river.

Visiting the park

Most people come to Tortuguero to see the **desove**, or egg-laying of the turtles. Few are disappointed, as the majority of tours during **laying seasons** (March–May & July–Oct) result in sightings of the surreal procession of the reptiles from the sea to make their egg-nests in the sand. While turtles have been known to lay in the daylight (the hatchlings wait under the cover of sand until nightfall to emerge), it is far more common for them to come ashore in the relative safety of night. Nesting can take place turtle-by-turtle: you can watch a single mother as she comes ashore and scrambles up the beach or, more strikingly, in groups (*arribadas*) when dozens emerge from the sea at the same time to form a colony, marching up the sands to their chosen spot, safely above the high-tide mark. Each turtle digs a hole in which she lays eighty or more eggs; the collective whirring noise of sand being dug away is extraordinary. Having filled the hole with sand to cover the eggs, the turtles begin their course back to the sea, leaving the eggs to hatch and return to the waves under the cover of darkness. Incubation takes some weeks; when the hatchlings emerge they instinctively follow the light of the moon on the water, scuttling to safety in the ocean.

Although Tortuguero is by no means the only place in Costa Rica to see marine turtles nesting (they use the Pacific beaches too), three of the largest kinds of endangered sea turtles regularly nest here in large numbers. Along with the **green** (*verde*) turtle, named for the colour of soup made from its flesh, you might see the **hawksbill** (*carey*), with its distinctive hooked beak, and the ridged **leatherback** (*baula*), the largest turtle in the world, which can easily weigh 300kg – some are as heavy as 500kg and reach 5m in length. The green turtles and hawksbills nest mainly from July to October (August is peak month), while the leatherbacks may come ashore from March to May.

Turtle tours, led by certified guides, leave at 8pm and 10pm every night from the village. If you're not going with an organized group from one of the lodges, you'll need to buy park entrance tickets ($6) from the kiosk in the village, which is staffed by park rangers from 5pm to 6pm every afternoon. There are over a hundred certified guides in Tortuguero; they charge $10 for the turtle tour (roughly half the price of a lodge tour) – if you haven't already sorted one out, they conveniently tend to hang around the ticket kiosk at 5pm in search of custom. Guides are instructed to make as little noise as possible so as not to alarm the turtles, allowing them to get on with their business; everyone must be off the beach by midnight.

A single, generally well-maintained, self-guided **trail** (1km), the **Sendero Natural** starts at the ranger station at the park entrance, passing two ranger huts and skirting west around the *llomas de sierpe* (swamp). As for the long, wild **beach**, you can amble for up to 30km south and enjoy crab-spotting, birds, and looking for turtle tracks, which resemble the two thick parallel lines a truck would leave in its wake. Swimming is not a good idea, due to heavy waves, turbulent currents and sharks. Remember that you need to pay **park fees** to walk on either the beach or along the trail.

Other activities around Tortuguero

Almost as popular as the turtle tours are Tortuguero's **boat tours** through the *caños*, or lagoons, to spot animals and birds, such as dignified-looking herons, cranes and kingfishers. Most lodges have **canoes** you can take out on the canal – a great way to get around if you're handy with a paddle, but do stick to the main canal as it is easy to get lost in the complex lagoon system northwest of

Turtling

For hundreds of years the fishermen of the Caribbean coast made their living culling the seemingly plentiful supplies of turtles, selling shell and meat for large sums to middlemen in Puerto Limón. Initially they were hunted for local consumption only, but around the turn of the century and into the first two decades of the 1900s, the fashion for turtle soup in Europe, especially England, led to large-scale exportation.

Turtle-hunting was a particularly brutal practice. Spears were formed from long pieces of wood, taken from the *apoo* palm or the *rawa*, fastened with a simple piece of cord to a sharp, barbed metal object. Standing in their canoes, fishermen hurled the spear, like a miniature harpoon, into the water, lodging the spear in the turtle's flesh. Pulling their canoes closer, the fishermen would then reel in the cord attached to the spear, lift the beasts into the canoes and take them ashore dead or alive. On land, the turtles might be beheaded with machetes or put in the holds of ships, where they could survive a journey of several weeks to Europe if they were given a little water.

Today, turtles are protected, their eggs and meat a delicacy. Locals around Tortuguero are officially permitted to take two turtles a week during nesting season for their own consumption – the unlucky green turtles are considered most delicious. As the recent sharp decline in the populations of hawksbill, green and leatherback turtles has been linked, at least in part, to poaching, the national parks administration have adopted a firm policy to discourage the theft of turtle eggs within the park boundaries, and rangers are armed. Meanwhile, should you find a turtle on its back between July 10 and September 15, do not flip it over, as in most cases it is being tagged by researchers, who work on the northern 8km of the 35-kilometre-long nesting beach.

It is not just the acquisitive hand of humans that endangers the turtles. On land, a cadre of predators, among them coati and racoons, regularly ransack the nests in order to eat the unborn reptiles. Once the hatching has started – the darkness giving them a modicum of protection – the turtles really have their work cut out, running a gauntlet of vultures, barracudas, sharks and even other turtles (the giant leatherback has been known to eat other species' offspring) on their way from the beach to the sea. Only about sixty percent – an optimistic estimate – of hatchlings reach adulthood, and the survival of marine turtles worldwide is under question.

the village. In the south of the village, Ruben Aragón, 50m north of the ranger station, right by the water, rents traditional Miskito-style boats and canoes for about $8 an hour, or $15 with a guide-paddler.

It is also possible to climb **Cerro Tortuguero**, an ancient volcanic deposit looming 119m above the flat coastal plain 6km north of the village. A climb up the gently sloping side leads you to the "peak", from which there are good views of flat jungle and inland waterways. Accessible only by *lancha*, this is a half-day hike, and you must go with a guide. Some of the lodges offer the guided climb as part of their packages.

Travel details

Buses

Cahuita to: Puerto Limón (4 daily; 1hr); Puerto Viejo de Talamanca (8 daily; 1hr 30min–2hr); San José (4 daily; 4hr); Sixaola (4 daily; 2hr).
Puerto Limón to: Cahuita (4 daily; 1hr); Manzanillo (2 daily; 2hr); Puerto Viejo de Talamanca (4 daily; 1hr 30min); San José (12 daily; 2hr 30min–3hr); Sixaola (1 daily; 3hr).
Puerto Viejo de Talamanca to: Cahuita (8 daily; 1hr 30min–2hr); Manzanillo (3 daily; 45min); Puerto Limón (4 daily; 1hr 30min); San José (4 daily; 4hr 30min); Sixaola (4 daily; 2hr).
San José to: Cahuita (4 daily; 4hr); Puerto Limón (12 daily; 2hr 30min–3hr); Puerto Viejo de Talamanca (4 daily; 4hr 30min); Sixaola (4 daily; 6hr).
Sixaola to: Cahuita (4 daily; 2hr); Puerto Limón (1 daily; 3hr); Puerto Viejo de Talamanca (4 daily; 2hr); San José (4 daily; 6hr).

Boats

Barra del Colorado to: Puerto Viejo de Sarapiquí (private *lanchas* only; 3–4hr). Note that the return trip from Puerto Viejo de Sarapiquí (see p.228) to Barra takes 6hr.
Moín docks to: Tortuguero (private *lanchas* only; 4hr).

Flights

Barra del Colorado to: San José (1 daily; 35min).
San José to: Barra del Colorado (1 daily; 35min); Tortuguero (1 daily; 35min).

LIMÓN PROVINCE AND THE CARIBBEAN COAST

The Zona Norte

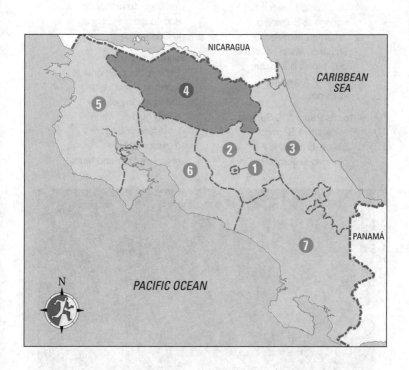

CHAPTER 4 # Highlights

* **Arenal Volcano** p.208
  Stunning by day, and
  even more memorable
  by night, when flows of
  incandescent lava
  illuminate its slopes.

* **Tabacón Hot Springs**
  p.208 Relax with a
  cocktail in the
  volcanically heated hot
  springs at Balneario
  Tabacón, near Arenal
  Volcano, whilst watching
  lava trickle down the
  sides of the erupting
  volcano.

* **Tom's Pan** p.210 Sample
  superlative German
  cakes, bread and
  pastries at Tom's Pan in

  Arenal Town, where you
  can stock up on
  everything from rye
  bread and pumpernickel
  to cakes and
  gingerbread.

* **Rara Avis** p.218 Private
  rainforest reserve
  offering one of the most
  thrilling and authentic
  eco-tourism experiences
  in Costa Rica.

* **Selve Verde** p.224
  Explore the premontane
  forest at Selva Verde in
  the company of top-
  notch guides, who will
  introduce you to the
  mysteries of the
  reserve's flora and fauna.

The Zona Norte

osta Rica's **Zona Norte** (northern zone) spans the hundred-odd kilometres from the base of the Cordillera Central to just short of the mauve-blue mountains of southern Nicaragua. Historically cut off from the rest of the country, the Zona Norte has developed a distinct character, with independent-minded farmers and Nicaraguan refugees making up large segments of the population. Neither group journeys to the Valle Central very often, and many people of the north have a special allegiance to and pride in their region. The **far north**, especially, for years mauled by fighting in the Nicaraguan Civil War, is more Nicaraguan than Costa Rican in feel.

Geographically, the Zona Norte separates neatly into two broad, river-drained plains (*llanuras*), which stretch all the way to the Río San Juan on the Nicaraguan–Costa Rican border. In the west, the **Llanura de Guatusos** is dominated by Volcán Arenal, while to the east the **Llanura de San Carlos** features the tropical jungles of the Sarapiquí area. Less obviously picturesque than many parts of the country, the entire region nonetheless has a distinctive appeal, with lazy rivers snaking across steaming plains, and flop-eared cattle, originally imported from India, languishing beneath riverside trees. The area is vast – at least in Costa Rican terms – and despite huge swathes of empty space, features a number of popular tourist attractions. Most people use the small town of **Fortuna** as a gateway to the active **Volcán Arenal** – which can also be approached from Guanacaste – perhaps staying in one of the lodges around Laguna de Arenal. This and the **Sarapiquí** area, with its tropical-forest eco-lodges and the research stations of **Selva Verde** and **Rara Avis**, are the most heavily visited destinations in the Zona Norte. Further north, the remote flatlands are home to the increasingly accessible **Refugio Nacional de Vida Silvestre Caño Negro**, which harbours an extraordinary number of migratory and indigenous birds. Few visitors venture further, though a steady trickle

Puerto Limón

NICARAGUA

El Castillo de la Concepción

Río San Juan

RESERVA NACIONAL DE FAUNA SILVESTRE BARRA DEL COLORADO

Río Sarapiquí

Puerto Viejo de Sarapiquí

Río Frío

Guápiles

Las Horquetas

Rara Avis

Laguna del Lagarto Lodge

Chilamate

La Virgen

San Miguel

RESERVA BIOLÓGICA LA SELVA

PARQUE NACIONAL BRAULIO CARRILLO

San José

Boca Tapada

Sahino

Pital

La Virgen

Río San Carlos

PARQUE NACIONAL VOLCÁN POÁS

Islas Solentiname

Lago de Nicaragua

San Carlos de Nicaragua

Los Chiles

Llanura de San Carlos

Boca de Arenal

Muelle San Carlos

Platanar

Aguas Zarcas

San Carlos (Ciudad Quesada)

Zarcero

San José

Caño Negro

REFUGIO NACIONAL DE VIDA SILVESTRE CAÑO NEGRO

Llanura de Los Guatusos

San Rafael de Guatuso

HWY-141

Río Frío

Tanque

La Fortuna

La Tigra

San Ramón & San José

Venado Caves

Volcán Arenal (1633 m)

PARQUE NACIONAL VOLCÁN ARENAL

Arenal Town

Balneario Tabacón

Lago Coter

Laguna de Arenal

Santa Elena

Monteverde

Las Juntas

RESERVA BIOLÓGICA BOSQUE NUBOSO MONTEVERDE

Esparza & Puntarenas

Volcán Tenorio (1916 m)

Tilarán

Quebrada Grande

Cañas

INTERAMERICANA

Nicoya

Ferry

Aguas Claras

Fortuna

Bagaces

PARQUE NACIONAL RINCÓN DE LA VIEJA

PARQUE NACIONAL PALO VERDE

Liberia & La Cruz

Santa Cecilia & La Cruz

N

0   20 km

passes through the small border town of **Los Chiles** en route to Nicaragua.

One of the prime agricultural areas in the country, the Zona Norte is carpeted with rice fields, vast banana plantations, dairy-cattle farms and the huge factories of TicoFrut, Costa Rica's major domestic fruit grower. The worst excesses of slash-and-burn **deforestation** are all too visible from the Zona Norte's roadsides and riverbanks, with the matchstick corpses of once-tall hardwoods scattered over stump-scarred fields patrolled by a few desultory cattle. There are plans to establish a transnational park, **Sí-a-Paz** ("Yes to Peace"), which would link the wetlands of Caño Negro with those south of Lago de Nicaragua, about 14km from the Nicaraguan–Costa Rican border, preserving much of the existing rainforest and wetlands in both regions.

The **climate** is hot and wet, more so in the east than in the west near Guanacaste, where there is a dry season. There are regular downpours, but the rain is always warm, and makes an enjoyable respite from the heat. Although many roads in the region are seriously potholed, **getting around** the Zona Norte is easy enough. There's a serviceable bus network, though if you're travelling outside the La Fortuna or Puerto Viejo areas, you'd probably do better with a car. The highway infrastructure is relatively new, and both the western (via Heredia) and eastern (via the Guápiles Highway) routes from San José to Puerto Viejo de Sarapiquí are in good condition, as well as being incredibly scenic. It's possible to travel cross-country between Fortuna and Puerto Viejo in about two hours.

The area around Volcán Arenal is well geared up for tourists, even boasting a couple of excellent five-star **hotels**. Between Boca de Arenal and Los Chiles in the far north, on the other hand, there is a real shortage of accommodation, though other essentials – gas and food – are in good supply.

Some history

For thousands of years before the Conquest, the original inhabitants of the Zona Norte were tribal groups – chief among them the **Corobicí** and **Guatusos** – who made contact with one another via the great rivers. The **Spanish presence** first made itself felt in the early 1600s, when galleons meandered up the Río San Juan and into Lago de Nicaragua, looking for a route to the East. Pirates (mainly British) soon followed, wreaking havoc on the riverside communities. It was two hundred years before the Spanish usurpers made a **settlement** of any size; the Quesada family from San Ramón came down from the highlands of the Valle Central in the nineteenth century to found a village at present-day San Carlos, or Ciudad Quesada, as it's also known. In the meantime, Nicaraguan–Zona Norte communication and commerce carried on as it had for thousands of years via the Ríos San Juan, Frío, Sarapiquí and San Carlos, and the **Río Sarapiquí** remained a more important highway than any road well into the 1800s, carrying coffee for export from the Heredia highlands out to the Caribbean ports of Matina and Limón.

Volcán Arenal and around

That the Arenal region attracts such huge numbers of tourists is largely due to the **volcano** itself, one of the most active in the Western hemisphere. The plain and tranquil village of **Fortuna** sits beneath the volcano, and is now a thriving base for the area's transport, tours and activities: from sportsfishing, windsurfing and boating on **Laguna de Arenal**, to hiking through the pockets of remaining rainforest, soaking in the steamy hot springs of **Balneario Tabacón** or scrabbling through subterranean **caves** to explore ancient geological formations. Another possible base, rather less touristy, is the agricultural town of **San Carlos**, two hours by bus from La Fortuna. It can **rain** a lot in this area, and when it does, prepare to be deluged. The year-round temperature is around 20°C, which accounts for the huge diversity of crops grown here – you'll pass *fincas* growing papaya and oranges, ginger and sugar cane, beans and cassava, and the area is also home to a nascent cut-flower industry. But it's tourism, however, that provides by far the most revenue.

San Carlos

Perched on the northern slopes of the Cordillera Central, 650m above sea level, **SAN CARLOS** (also known as **Ciudad Quesada**, or simply Quesada) has a decidedly rural atmosphere, with fresh produce overflowing from market stalls onto the streets, and *campesinos* with weathered faces hanging out in the main square in front of the church. There's little actually to do: locals only come here to have a drink on Friday night or to sell their wares at the Saturday market, and most tourists base themselves at Fortuna or one of the luxurious resorts nearby (see p.206). The main reason to spend some time here is to get a feeling for what drives the country's still largely agricultural economy: much of Costa Rica's milk, beef, citrus fruit and rice comes from the large-scale agricultural holdings in these parts.

Most travellers arrive here from San José **via Hwy-141**, the switchback road that climbs through Zarcero and over the hump of the Cordillera Central. Another approach is via the spectacular **mountain road** between the town of San Ramón, perched above the Valle Central, and La Tigra, in the lower reaches of the Zona Norte. This winding route passes through isolated and deep-cut valleys, passing the Los Angeles Cloud Forest en route. Though rather indirect – taking you almost to La Fortuna before a right turn heads to San Carlos via El Tanque, Jabillos, and Florencia – it's much less busy than the road to San Carlos via Zarcero. **From San Carlos** it's possible to drive northwest to Fortuna, then around Laguna de Arenal, and connect via Hwy-19 with the Interamericana. To the east you can take the scenic route via Aguas Zarcas, connecting at San Miguel with Hwy-9 to the jungle lodges near Puerto Viejo de Sarapiquí.

The town itself fans out around the **Parque Central**, with just a few streets trailing away on either side. This is where you'll find most of the shops, restaurants and accommodation. On the north side of the square, the cooperative **Mercado de Artesanía de San Carlos** (T 460-1613) sells leatherwork and other crafts, with many of the same items, but in a less touristy atmosphere, than in the big Sarchí souvenir shops (see p.129). San Carlos is also a **saddlery** centre, and you can see local leatherworkers making intricate Costa Rican saddles in any of the *talabarterías* dotted around town.

Practicalities

Buses for San Carlos depart from San José's La Coca-Cola bus terminal daily every hour on the hour from 5am until 7.30pm. It's quite a long haul; even the so-called *directo* services take three hours or more, and stop frequently. The **tourist office** (T 460-1672) at the southern entrance to town, 200m from the Parque Central, stocks a map of the Zona Norte and can give advice on road conditions and help with hotel reservations in the area. You can change cash

> ## Moving on from San Carlos
>
> San Carlos is a transport hub, with frequent buses to a range of destinations. All buses leave from the station, 50m south and 50m east of the southeast corner of the Parque Central. Autotransportes Ciudad Quesada buses leave for San José every hour on the hour until 7pm. Ten buses a day leave for Los Chiles, while three buses daily (6am, 10am & 3pm; 3hr) run along Hwy-9, via Aguas Zarcas and Varablanca, to Puerto Viejo (sometimes signed Río Frío). There are six buses daily to La Fortuna, the first leaving at 6am and the last at 6pm. The journey takes just over an hour. For other destinations, ask at the bus station.

and **travellers' cheques** at the Banco Nacional, the Banco de Costa Rica and the Banco Popular – they're all within about a hundred metres of the Parque Central. For **medical emergencies**, the Hospital de San Carlos (T 460-1176) is the best in the Zona Norte.

Accommodation in the centre of San Carlos is adequate but nothing special; if you're looking for luxury you'd be better off outside town. Of the options in town, *Hotel del Valle*, 200m north of the northwest corner of the Parque Central and 50m east (T 460-0718; ❷) is small and plain but comfortable, with hot water and a TV lounge. Though undeniably basic, *Hotel La Central*, on the north side of the Parque Central (T 460-0766, F 460-0391; ❶), has over forty rooms, all en suite with hot water, and a serviceable restaurant downstairs – though light sleepers may not appreciate the new casino. It's also conveniently situated around the corner from the bus station. *Hotel Don Goyo* (T 460-1780; ❷) has thirteen clean and quiet brightly painted rooms in a modern building 100m south of the southwest corner of the Parque Central; the single and double rooms here all have private bath and hot water. *Balneario San Carlos*, 600m north of the Parque Central (T 460-0747; ❸) has clean, basic cabinas with nice views, and a pool. There are no **restaurants** of any note in town, but the bar/restaurant *La Jarra*, 100m south and 25m east of the church cooks tasty *churrascos*, as does the steakhouse *Coca Loca* on the west side of the Parque Central, while the *Marisquería Tonjibe* on the south side of square serves decent *corvina* and *camarones*.

Around San Carlos

The country **around San Carlos** is beautiful, still largely untouristed territory, with the precipitous slopes of the Cordillera Central hiding pockets of rainforest before gradually giving way to the flatlands of the Llanura de San Carlos and the wide rivers that arc through them. Volcán Arenal dominates, and there are stupendous views of it from the northern slope of the Cordillera Central. Driving through, the small villages of **Muelle**, **Platanar** and **Aguas Zarcas** have nothing worth stopping for, other than to pick up a snack at one of the roadside restaurants or to fill up on gas. If you want to spend more time here enjoying the wonderful scenery, there are plenty of good options: two good **resort hotels** lie within thirty minutes' drive of San Carlos, and there are some very pleasant cheaper choices nearby.

Accommodation

La Garza, in Platanar, 15km northeast of San Carlos (T 475-5222, F 475-5015). Named for the herons (*garzas*) that nest around the hotel grounds, this good-value hotel is part of a working dairy farm, with rustic and comfortable rooms sporting nice details like Guatemalan fabrics and verandahs overlooking the river. There's also a restaurant and pool. ⑤

La Mirada, 4km north of San Carlos (☏ 460-2222). Good-value cabinas on a hillside overlooking the northern plains, with some of the most beautiful vistas in the area – the views from the open-air restaurant are no less impressive. Parking, hot water, private baths and phone. ③

La Quinta, 15km north of San Carlos in the village of Platanar (☏ & ℻ 475-5260 or 761-1052). The best budget option hereabouts, family-run and accessible by bus from San Carlos. It has smart, dorm-like cabinas, a fully equipped self-catering apartment, and a huge pool. The helpful English-speaking owners are very knowledgeable about the area. ②

Melia el Tucano Hotel and Country Club, 8km east of San Carlos on the road to Agua Zarcas (☏ 460-6000, ℻ 460-1692,

Ⓔ meliatuc@racsa.co.cr). The plushest accommodation in the San Carlos area, this upmarket European-style resort complex sits amidst a series of thermal springs in beautifully landscaped grounds full of tropical flowers. There's also a swimming pool, and tennis and horse-riding are available. The spa treatments and natural saunas attract a mainly older-European clientele; non-residents can use the springs for $5. ⑥

Tilajari Resort Hotel, 1km west of Muelle, 22km north of San Carlos (☏ 469-9091, ℻ 469-9095, Ⓦ www.tilajari.com). A quiet and beautifully situated resort hotel on an out-of-the-way working cattle ranch by the Río San Carlos (which many of the rooms overlook). Iguanas roam the landscaped grounds, which also offer great bird-watching. There's a restaurant, conference room, pool and tennis courts, and horse-riding and rainforest walks can also be arranged. ⑥

Fortuna

FORTUNA (or La Fortuna de San Carlos to give it its correct title) was until recently a simple agricultural town dominated by the majestic conical form of Volcán Arenal, just 6km away. Nowadays, true to its name, Fortuna is booming. Looming 1633m above town, Arenal seems to sit directly on top of the town. If the day is clear – and many, unfortunately, are not – you can sometimes see smoke wisps drifting from the crater, although the summit can often be obscured by a little sombrero of cloud. When it's rainy and foggy the volcano is almost totally obscured, but its brooding presence remains palpable, and even if you can't actually see it, you'll almost certainly hear it. Residents, used to Arenal's rumblings and splutterings, seem generally unperturbed when the earth trembles before one of its larger eruptions.

While there's nothing much to do in the town itself except book tours, bed down and have a meal or a beer, the atmosphere is jolly enough, with legions of tourists threatening to outnumber the Tico farmers going about their everyday business. As it struggles to accommodate the tourism boom, Fortuna can sometimes look like an extended construction site, with people rushing to build cabinas and cafés and add to the already overwhelming number of "tourist information offices". It's still a friendly place, however, with plenty of reasonably priced accommodation and excellent bus connections, as well as being one of the main bases for tours to the remote wildlife refuge of **Caño Negro** (see p.212).

Arrival and information

There are three daily direct services from **San José to Fortuna** (4hr), currently leaving La Coca–Cola at 6.15am, 8.40am and 11.30am. Alternatively, you could take a direct bus from **San José to San Carlos** (see p.110), where you can change for frequent buses to Fortuna (1hr). Buses from San José, San Carlos and Tilarán all stop by the soccer field.

Fortuna comprises a small grid of streets centred on the soccer field in front of the modern stucco church. It's never hard to orient yourself – the volcano is west. Most hotels will change money for about the same rate as the Banco

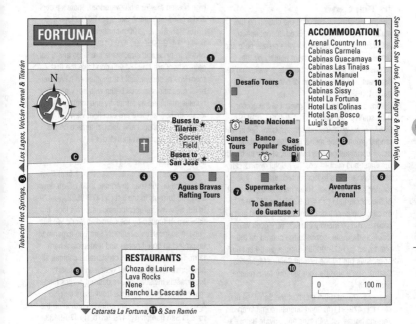

FORTUNA

N

Los Lagos, Volcán Arenal & Tilarán ◀

Tabacón Hot Springs, ③ ◀

①

②

Desafío Tours

Ⓐ

Buses to
Tilarán ★

Ⓒ

Soccer
Field

Buses to
San José ★

🕏 Banco Nacional

Sunset   Banco   Gas
Tours   Popular   Station

Ⓑ

✉

④

⑤ Ⓓ

Aguas Bravas
Rafting Tours

⑦ Supermarket

To San Rafael
de Guatuso ★

⑧

⑥

Aventuras
Arenal

⑨

RESTAURANTS

Choza de Laurel	C
Lava Rocks	D
Nene	B
Rancho La Cascada	A

⑩

| 0 | 100 m |

ACCOMMODATION	
Arenal Country Inn	11
Cabinas Carmela	4
Cabinas Guacamaya	6
Cabinas Las Tinajas	1
Cabinas Manuel	5
Cabinas Mayol	10
Cabinas Sissy	9
Hotel La Fortuna	8
Hotel Las Colinas	7
Hotel San Bosco	2
Luigi's Lodge	3

▼ Catarata La Fortuna, **⑪** & San Ramón

Nacional opposite the soccer field; apart from a few of the more expensive hotels, this is the only place to change **travellers' cheques**. There are **phones** scattered about town, most of which purport to take local and international phonecards, but only one or two of them actually work – they're the ones with the queues. There's **internet access** at the Desafío Tours office, across from *Rancho La Cascada*, and the Aguas Bravas tour agency, on the main road opposite the soccer field, sells *La Nación*, *Tico Times* and the *New York Times* – this is also the best place to **rent bikes** (around $10/day for sturdy mountain bikes).

Taxis line up on the south side of the Parque Central – they rarely (if ever) use their meters, so agree a price before getting in and beware of overcharging. Try to negotiate a lower price than the first one you're quoted, or ask locals what they currently pay.

Accommodation

People with their own transport and a bit of money tend to stay in the **lodges** either on the road between Fortuna and La Tigra/San Ramón, on the road linking Fortuna and the Parque Nacional Volcán Arenal, or in one of the many pleasant hotels that border Laguna de Arenal (see p.210). Budget travellers tend to stay in town – really the only option if you don't have your own transport. Most of the simple **cabinas** sprouting up all over town are pretty similar, with a few plain rooms and cold showers. Competition means that Fortuna is also one of the few places in the country where you might encounter **hotel touts** as you stumble off the bus. There's no hard-and-fast rule about taking them up on their recommendations, but be aware that if they are not the actual owner, they'll be on commission, which you'll end up paying yourself in the form of a higher room rate. Prices drop significantly in the wet season; conversely, during the dry season you should try to reserve in advance.

In Fortuna

Cabinas Carmela, opposite the church on the main road (T 479-9010). Good budget option, with ten spacious rooms (all with private bath and hot water) made slightly more homely by the wooden – as opposed to concrete – walls. You can hang out in a rocking chair or hammock on the patio, too. ❸

Cabinas Guacamaya, 200m east of the soccer field, south of the school (T 479-9393, F 479-9087, W www.cabinasguacamaya.com). Set in well-tended grounds, the rooms in these comfortable and rather upmarket cabinas have a/c, private bath with hot water and mini-fridge. The helpful owners can also organize tours to local attractions. ❹

Cabinas Las Tinajas, 100m north and 25m west of the soccer field (T 479-9308, fax 479-9145). Small complex of four clean, well-furnished and airy cabinas, run by friendly owners; very good value. ❸

Cabinas Manuel, opposite the church on the main road (T 479-9069). Simple, well-kept budget cabinas run by the helpful Señora Mercedes Castro. She'll also do your laundry for a reasonable price. ❷

Cabinas Mayol, 50m south of the San José bus stop (T 479-9110). Good budget rooms in an old Fortuna house, all with fans and private bath. ❶

Cabinas Sissy, 100m south and 125m west of the soccer field (T 479-9256). Basic budget traveller's hangout, friendly and clean, with eight good-sized rooms with hot-water showers. You can also camp here for $3. ❶

Cabinas Villa Fortuna, on the main road, 500m east of the soccer field (T 479-9139). Slightly outside of town, but quieter because of it. The large clean rooms come with fridge and private bath with hot water. ❹

Hotel La Fortuna, 75m south and 100m east of the soccer field (T 479-9197). Basic but good-value hotel – the ten rooms come with shared or private bath. It's very popular with budget travellers, so book in advance. Breakfast included. ❷

Hotel Las Colinas, 50m south of the soccer field (T 479-9107). A bit pricey for what you get, although the clean and comfortable rooms have hot water and fans – the upstairs ones are airier and some have views of the volcano. There's a silence-after-9pm rule. The hotel is popular and fills quickly, so book in advance. ❸–❹

Luigi's Lodge, 200m west of the church (T & F 479-9898, W www.luigislodge.com). Rooms here all come with a/c, private bath and hot water, and look directly out onto the volcano, though the decor is nothing special and at the upper end of the high season they're a bit overpriced. There's a pool and a good restaurant, too. Breakfast included. ❺

Hotel San Bosco, 100m northeast of the soccer field (T 479-9050, F 479-9109). Rooms vary widely in price and size; some are large and a bargain, others are tiny – if you don't like the first room you're shown, ask for another. All have overhead fans and spacious baths with hot water. The hotel is managed by a friendly and informative local family, and there are excellent views of Arenal from the pool and Jacuzzi terrace on the upper level. Breakfast included. ❹

Around Fortuna

Alberge Ecotouristico la Catarata, 1.5km from of Fortuna on the road to Arenal, then 1.5km down a signed turn-off to the left (T 479-9522, F 479-9168, W www.agroecoturismo.net). This local initiative, part funded by the Canadian World Wildlife Fund, also includes a butterfly farm, an experimental project to breed pacas and a medicinal herb farm. The eight rustic but comfortable cabinas all have private bath with hot water, and a hearty breakfast is included; the restaurant serves food made with organic produce from its garden. ❸

Arenal Country Inn, 1km outside Fortuna on the road to San Ramón (T 479-9670, F 479-9433, W www.costaricainn.com). Quiet and fairly upmarket – for the area – hotel in spacious grounds with good views of the volcano and twenty bright rooms set in small bungalows. A superb breakfast is included. ❺

Hotel Arenal Paraíso, 5km outside Fortuna en route to the volcano (T 460-5333, F 460-5343, W www.arenalparaiso.decostarica.co.cr). Attractive hotel with expensive-looking wooden cabinas, all with private bath with hot water (some also have fridges) and huge porches looking out directly onto the volcano. The adjacent restaurant serves good meals. ❺

Hotel Arenal Rossi, 2km west of La Fortuna (T & F 479-9414, W www.hotelarenalrossi.com). Twenty-five simply but attractively furnished rooms, some with a/c, all painted bright blue and white. Good rates for the more-than-adequate standard singles and doubles, though the deluxe rooms and suites cost considerably more. ❹

Las Cabañitas, 1km from Fortuna, on the road to El Tanque/San Carlos (T 479-9400, F 479-9408). Nicely made wooden cabinas with their own balconies and rocking chairs, though they get quite hot during the day; there's also a pool and a restaurant. It's within walking distance of Fortuna, though a car's preferable. ❺

Tours from Fortuna

It seems that every business in Fortuna, even the hardware store, sells tours, and you'll see "tourist information office" signs sprouting from every surface – but be aware that though information may be given, the real raison d'être of these places is to sell their tours. Price competition between tour agencies in Fortuna is fierce, but bear in mind that while you may save a few dollars by going with the cheapest agency, you could end up on a badly organized tour with under-qualified guides, or no lunch – get as many details as you can before you put down your cash. In general, it's worth going with a reputable tour operator, such as those listed below, and not with one of the freelance "guides" who may approach you; one was recently convicted of the rape of a female tourist whilst on a tour.

By far the most popular excursion is the late-afternoon hike around Volcán Arenal, followed by a night-time soak in the thermal pools at Balneario Tabacón (see p.209), though few tours include the admission fee ($15) in their prices. The volcano hike involves a walk through rainforest, much of it uphill, and a final scramble over lava rocks – take care, as they're particularly sharp, and few guides carry a medical kit. Bring a torch, too. The actual sight of the volcano – if you're lucky enough to be there on a clear night when there's activity – is amazing. Scarlet rivers of lava pour from the top, and you can hear the crunch of boulders landing as they are spewed from the mouth of the volcano.

Also popular are horse-rides to the Catarata de la Fortuna (see p.207), boat trips to Caño Negro (see p.215), and rafting down the Río Sarapiquí. A popular new trip is the transfer to Monteverde (4–5hr), using a combination of taxi, boat and horse – it's faster and much more interesting than taking the local bus. This tour has been conceived as a more humane alternative to the five-hour horse-ride to Monteverde by which tourists used to make the transfer – see p.311 for more details.

Sunset Tours (⊤479-9415, Ⓕ479-9099, ⓌWww.sunset-tours.com), on the main road, to the east of the soccer field, is pricier than other tour operators, but has professional, well-qualified guides. Their volcano tours ($25) include the entrance fee to the national park, but not to Balneario Tabacón. They have a good day-trip to Caño Negro ($45), as well as taxi ($30) transfers to Monteverde. Trips run by the professional Aventuras Arenal, 150m east of the soccer field (⊤ & Ⓕ479-9133), are almost identical and slightly cheaper, and they can also offer transport to just about anywhere in the country.

Desafío Tours (⊤479-9464, Ⓕ479-9178, ⒺDesafio@racsa.co.cr) across from Rancho La Cascada are friendly, efficient and helpful rafting specialists and run half- and full-day tours ($65–70) for all levels on the Ríos Toro, Peñas Blancas and Sarapiquí. They also offer the jeep-boat-horse-jeep transfer to Monteverde for an economical price (and they take good care of their horses), and can sort out flights, tours and accommodation anywhere in the country.

Jacamar (⊤479-9767, Ⓕ479-9456, ⒺJacamar@racsa.co.cr), next to the Lava Rocks restaurant, does an Arenal night tour ($25), trips to the Venado caves (see p.211; $35) and Caño Negro ($45) and gentle rafting excursions on the Río Peñas Blancas. Their boat-and-taxi (no horses) transfer to Monteverde costs $25 and takes (they claim) just two hours. Aguas Bravas (⊤479-9025, Ⓕ229-4837), on the main road opposite the soccer field, offers white-water-rafting trips on the Río Sarapiquí.

Eating and drinking

Fortuna lacks a really good **restaurant**. Though food is generally fresh and served in generous portions, it's pretty much the same everywhere, with the usual *casados*, *platos del día* and *arroz-con*–whatever. Considering the number of tourists passing through, however, **prices** are quite fair, catering for locals as much as visitors – you'll be able to get dinner for around $5–7 per person.

Breakfasts have become more Americanized, with some places offering pancakes and continental breakfasts. There's no evening activity to speak of; *Rancho la Cascada* and *Choza de Laurel* are where people head for a beer.

Choza de Laurel, 100m west of the soccer field, on the road to Volcán Arenal. Very reasonably priced Tico food roasted in an outside wood oven. Breakfasts are particularly good value – $2 for *gallo pinto*, $3 for continental breakfast – and *casados* ($3) are similarly cheap. In the evening beers are served with good free *bocas*.

Lava Rocks, by the soccer field. Popular place run by two brothers (one of whom also manages the recommended Jacamar tour agency next door). Breakfasts are reasonably priced and huge – the pancakes are particularly good – and evening meals are equally generous and well cooked. If nothing else, try their flavoured coffee ($1.25) – a rarity around here.

Nene, two blocks east of the soccer field. Nothing much to look at – it's just a small terrace looking out onto a parking lot on a muddy side street – but

Fortuna residents like it, and it's about the only place in town where you'll eat entirely among locals rather than tourists. The draw is large portions of good food, including tender steak and nicely cooked fish dishes, all served with rice and vegetables. The *refrescos naturales* are good, too.

Pizza Luigi's, in *Luigi's Lodge*. A sort of upmarket pizza place, with pizza and pasta dishes for $5–10, plus a good wine list.

Rancho La Cascada, northeast corner of the soccer field. This gigantic open-air restaurant is particularly popular with tour groups at lunch time, and is the only place in Fortuna that gets remotely lively at night. The menu is not particularly cheap, but is more varied than most places in town, with Tico fare, Italian dishes and good fish soup. Good beer and *bocas* too.

Around Fortuna

The area west of Fortuna offers a variety of outdoor activities, from fishing and windsurfing on the **Laguna de Arenal** to hiking forested trails and bathing in steaming hot springs at **Tabacón**. Between Fortuna and Laguna de Arenal the landscape is as picturesque as you could desire, and spectacularly varied, with pockets of rainforest-like vegetation opening up into wide grassy fields, with the mauve-grey summit of **Volcán Arenal** dominating the scene.

Many scenic **lodges and hotels** dot the Laguna de Arenal area. They're hugely popular, and it's best to book ahead in the dry season: some hotels require advance booking all year round. Most of the more expensive places can be arranged on all-in package tours from San José, including meals and outdoor activities. If you are staying at any of the lodges below you'll find life much easier if you have a car, as they are quite remote and public transport is erratic. Wherever you stay, almost every hotel can fix you up with tours of the volcano and other local attractions.

Accommodation

Arenal Lodge, 14km west of La Fortuna or 2km beyond the entrance to the national park (☎ 228-3189, ⓕ 289-6798, ⓔ arenal@racsa.co.cr). Less than 2km from the shore of Lake Arenal, this lodge specializes in rainbow bass (*guapote*) fishing (fishing packages can be arranged). A range of rooms, with and without volcano views, are situated in pleasant landscaped tropical gardens with trails and a startling view of Arenal. The lodge has a pool table and library. Breakfast included. ⑥

Arenal Observatory Lodge, about 8km down the road to the park entrance, past the visitor's centre – follow the signs (☎ 257-9489, ⓕ 257-4220,

ⓔ arenalob@racsa.co.cr). Just 1.8km from the crater, this is considered the area's best base for serious volcano watchers. The extensive grounds include primary rainforest with trails – in some rooms only a vast pane of glass separates you from the sights and sounds of the forest. Standard rooms are rustic and comfortable; budget rooms are in the La Casona farmhouse. There's a restaurant too, though the food is unremarkable. ⑤–⑦

Montaña de Fuego Inn, 8km west of La Fortuna, on the road to Tabacón (☎ 382-0759, ⓕ 479-9579, ⓔ monfuego@asstcard.co.cr). Individual cabins built out of dark wood, each with a huge glassed-in porch from where, on clear nights, you can watch the spectacular light shows from the volcano opposite. The surrounding grounds are a bit bare; you have to be comfortable with being face to face with the volcano here – it seems very close. The cabins have fridges, a/c and fans. Breakfast included. ⑤

La catarata de La Fortuna

The higher of Río Fortuna's two **cataratas** (waterfalls) is the epitome of the picturebook cascade – a tall, thin stream plunging prettily from a narrow aperture in the rocky heights 75m above, and forming a foaming pool among rocks and rainforest vegetation below. Just 6km south of Fortuna, it's an easy day's hike (though make sure you wear sturdy waterproof shoes), or a half-day horse-ride.

To get to the waterfalls, take the road heading south from Fortuna, then turn west down a gravel track (it's the only turn-off in sight). This track is not really driveable, except by the hardiest 4WDs, though some jeep owners seem to make it a point of honour to do it anyway, leaving behind the best part of their undercarriage on their way up. If you walk along this track in the morning there are plenty of birds to be seen, if you have the patience to stop and look for them – bring binoculars.

The waterfalls used to be free; there's now a kiosk where you pay a $2 entrance fee, which seems to go to a community association. A sign points to the *cataratas*; enter the woods on the left to hike the steep trail leading down to the waterfall – it's tricky when wet, and not that easy when dry, either, although ropes are provided to help you scrabble down. The river's current has to be traversed before you reach the base of the falls. You'll see the first of the waterfalls at the head of this stream; the higher, more spectacular one is another minute's walk along the trail. If in doubt, just follow the roar. Swimming is not recommended, due to flash floods, although a lot of people do. There's a *mirador* (signposted) for those who would rather look from a distance, giving great views across the steep valley and its heavily forested floor to the thin finger of the cascade.

Moving on from Fortuna

Despite its small size, Fortuna is something of a transport hub, and with a little planning you can get from here to Guanacaste, Puntarenas, Monteverde and Puerto Viejo de Sarapiquí without backtracking to San José. For Puerto Viejo de Sarapiquí, take a bus to San Carlos (6 daily; 1hr), where you can pick up a service east to Puerto Viejo. Buses currently leave San Carlos at 6am, 10am and 3pm, but double-check these times, since if you miss your connection you'll need to stay the night. For Monteverde, there are two daily buses from Fortuna to Tilarán, at the head of Laguna de Arenal (3hr). The bus currently leaves at 8am and 5pm – if you take the later one you'll have to stay the night in Tilarán. You can connect in Tilarán with the Santa Elena service (for the Monteverde Cloudforest Reserve), which currently leaves at 1pm (3–4hr). There are also frequent local services from Tilarán to Cañas and the Interamericana, where you can pick up buses north to Liberia and the beaches of Guanacaste, or south to Puntarenas. To get back to San José from Fortuna, take the Garaje Barquero *directo* service (3 daily; 4hr 30min), which currently departs at 2.45pm, or head to San Carlos (see above) from where you can connect with hourly buses to the capital.

For those driving, the roads are good, with the exception of a perenially difficult patch between Fortuna and Arenal Town. For a full rundown of routes within the Zona Norte, see pp.200 & 228–229.

4

THE ZONA NORTE | Around Fortuna

Parque Nacional Volcán Arenal

Volcán Arenal was afforded protected status in 1995, becoming part of the national parks system as the **PARQUE NACIONAL VOLCÁN ARENAL** (daily 8am–4pm; $6). The park has some good **trails**, some of them across lava fields, while the four-kilometre "Tucanes" trail takes you to the part of the forest which was flattened by the 1968 eruption; you may also see some wildlife – birds (including oropendolas and tanagers) and agoutis are particularly common. Although the park has a simple café, it's best to take a picnic lunch and plenty of water if you intend to spend some time walking. Hiking any distance up the volcano's sides has always been energetically discouraged, and fences now stop you doing so. If you arrive on a cloudy or rainy day (which is most of the year, unfortunately) and can't see the summit, the park's visitor's centre has video displays of the volcano's more spectacular activity.

You can't stay in or visit the park after dark except by taking one of the **night tours** which leave Fortuna every afternoon at about 3–4pm. Most operators run them even when it is cloudy, in the hope that the cloud will lift or the opposite side of the volcano will be clear. None offers you a refund if you don't see anything, so you might want to wait for a clear evening before signing up. Aventuras Arenal runs a sunset **boat tour**, on which you can watch the action from Laguna de Arenal.

The park entrance is 12km from Fortuna; look for the well-signed driveway off to the left. If you don't have your own vehicle, you can take a **taxi** from Fortuna to the west side of the volcano (around $35 return per car, including waiting time of a few hours), but unless you're in a large group, it's cheaper – and less bother – to take a tour. The **bus** from Fortuna will drop you off at the entrance to the park and is much the cheapest option, though the return journey can be a bit tricky – unless you manage to connect with the bus coming from Tilarán or Arenal Town, your only option is to try to get a ride back with other park visitors.

The geological history of Volcán Arenal

Volcán Arenal is the youngest stratovolcano – the term for a steep, conical volcano created by the eruption of thick lava flows – in Costa Rica, and also the most active. Stratovolcanoes are responsible for nearly half the planet's volcanic activity – of the 1511 volcanoes known to have erupted in the past 10,000 years, 699 are stratovolcanoes. Geologists have determined that Arenal is no more than 2900 years old; by comparison, Volcán Chato, which flanks Arenal to the south, is much older, and last erupted in the late Holocene period, around 10,000 years ago. Arenal is so active because – geologists speculate – it directly taps a magma chamber located on a fault about 22km below the surface.

Arenal's growth over the ages has been characterized by massive eruptions every few centuries. It is thought to have erupted round about 1750, 1525, and 1080 AD, and 220 and 900 BC. The most recent eruption occurred a quarter of a century ago. At that time, Arenal seemed to be nothing but an unthreatening mountain, and locals had built small farms up its forested sides (take a look at Volcán Chato and you get the idea). On July 29, 1968, an earthquake shook the area, blasting the top off Arenal and creating the majestic, lethal volcano you see today.

Arenal killed 78 people on that day: fatalities were caused by a combination of shockwaves, hot rocks and poisonous gases – what volcanologists describe as "Strombolian activity", a volcanic eruption characterized by fountains of fluid basalt lava being ejected from a central crater. The explosion created three craters, and Arenal has been continuously active ever since, with almost daily rumblings and shakings.

You can also see the volcano (but not the nocturnal lava) from **Volcán Chato**, 3km southeast of Arenal, though you'll need a guide to ascend it – Sunset Tours offer a day hike up to the summit and crater lake for around $65.

Los Lagos and Balneario Tabacón

LOS LAGOS (8am–4pm; $2), set beneath the volcano about 6km northwest of Fortuna on the road to Tilarán, is an affordable park and recreation centre designed for Costa Ricans rather than foreign tourists. Within the park are two pools, a Jacuzzi, a couple of small lakes and several well-signed, untaxing trails, all of which offer great views – on a clear day at least – of Volcán Arenal, although several of those closest to the volcano have been closed in the wake of the pyroclastic flows in August 2000 (see below); ask for a map at the entrance. It can be muddy in the wet season, so bring rubber boots. Within the park there's also a restaurant and some basic but comfortable **cabinas** (T & F 479-9126; ④) with private bathroom and hot water; camping is permitted for $3 per day.

The majority of foreign tourists, however, bypass Los Lagos and continue down the road for 4km to **BALNEARIO TABACÓN** (Tabacón Hot Springs; daily 10am–10pm; $15). Fed by a magma-boiled underground thermal river, originating in the nether parts of Volcán Arenal, the hot-springs complex comprises five pools, some with natural Jacuzzis, slides and sculpted waterfalls, as well as several artificial hot tubs, warm streams and ponds. The water in the warmest of the pools is about 40°C, while the others are closer to swimming-bath temperature. There's also a small system of trails winding up through the grounds, some of which are lit at night. If it's a clear night, you can watch the erupting volcano's fireworks from the restaurant, one of the many terraces or, best of all, from the bar inside one of the hot pools whilst sipping

---

Tragedy at Volcán Arenal

Just before 10am on August 23, 2000, Volcán Arenal emitted larger than usual pyroclastic flows (lava flows accompanied by clouds of hot gas and ash). The toxic, superheated cloud surprised and engulfed a Costa Rican tour guide and his two charges, an American woman and her 8-year-old daughter, who were on a walking tour in the Los Lagos tourist complex only 2.3km from the crater. Despite having suffered severe burns, the tour guide, 28-year-old Ignacio Protti, managed to get his clients off the volcano. All three were taken to hospital in San José, where Protti died that same night. The young girl succumbed to her injuries after being airlifted to hospital in the US.

This was the first time since 1988 that the volcano had claimed a life. The tragedy highlights the fact that Arenal is an active volcano, and gas emissions, incandescent avalanches, and ash columns are all regular occurrences. Despite being constantly monitored by geologists and volcanologists, volcanos are notoriously unpredictable, a fact reiterated by the August 2000 tragedy: previous eruptions had always taken place to the west, in the direction of Laguna de Arenal, and the Los Lagos trails where Protti and his charges were walking that day face the east, and were thought to be totally safe. Those trails are now closed, choked by the lava flows that streamed down Arenal's flanks in the wake of that outburst.

Danger is part of the appeal: the atavistic thrill of a night-time lava flow or merely the sound of its deep, planetary rumble is undeniable. It's imperative, though, that you never veer from trails or guided tours, and do not to attempt to hike anywhere near the crater, since lethal gases, ballistic boulders and molten rock can appear or change direction without warning.

a cocktail – all in all, the atmosphere, with cocktail bar and bikini-clad tourists, combines to make you feel like you've just stepped into a 1970s James Bond film.

Day packages (for four people or more) are available for about $20 per person including lunch, and the complex also offers individually priced spa remedies, such as massage ($26/hr) and mud masks ($10). Don't leave valuables in your car in the car park – despite having a guarded parking lot, thefts from cars are common. If you want to stay, the upscale **Tabacón Lodge** (Ⓣ 256-1500, Ⓕ 221-3075, Ⓦ www.tabacon.com; ❻–❼), 100m down the road from the springs, has 42 modern rooms with TV, air-conditioning and volcano views (though it's so close here it would be difficult not to have one). Rates include unlimited access to the hot springs.

A cheaper, unnamed **thermal spring** ($3) has been opened across the road – look for the sign or for the cars parked along the verge. It's much more basic and there's only one creek, but it's at a pleasant temperature, and there are showers and changing rooms; the disadvantage is that you can't see the volcano from here. There have also been reports of assaults on tourists here, so it's probably not the place to go alone for a night soak.

Laguna de Arenal

The waters of **Laguna de Arenal** make what would otherwise have been a pretty area into a very beautiful one – a fact exploited by the tourist board's promotional posters which show a stately and serene Volcán Arenal rising preternaturally out of the lake. Actually a man-made body of water created when the original lake was dammed, the resulting Arenal Dam, built in 1973, now generates much of the country's hydroelectricity. The lake is also very good for fishing rainbow bass (*guapote*), an irridescent fish found only in freshwater lakes and rivers in Costa Rica, Nicaragua and Honduras, and windsurfing (Dec–March only) – many of the hotels in the area rent boards. Tourism in the area is on the rise, bringing with it a sizeable colony of year-round foreign residents, many of them Germans or Austrians, perhaps attracted by the combination of a rather European-looking landscape with the added benefit of a volcano and year-round tropical temperatures.

You can't actually make a full circuit of the lake, but you can drive along its northeast and west sides, from where there are beautiful views of the volcano and of gentle hills, some of them given over to wind-farming – look for the giant white windmills on the hills above the north edge of the lake. About midway between Fortuna and Tilarán is the lakeside **ARENAL TOWN**, also known as **Nuevo Arenal** (the original Arenal was flooded when the dam was built). One of the biggest treats here is the superlative German cakes, bread and pastries at *Tom's Pan* on the main road through town (daily 6.30am–6pm), where you can stock up on everything from rye and pumpernickel to cakes and gingerbread, or just enjoy the good coffee and lakeside view from their outdoor terrace. For lunch and dinner, the *Restaurante Tramonti* (closed Mon) serves good-value traditional thin-crust pizzas ($4–8), cooked in a wood oven. **Arenal Botanical Gardens** (daily 9am–5pm, closed Oct; $5), 5km east of Arenal Town, is a pretty collection of tropical plants, featuring orchids of all shapes and sizes.

Accommodation around Arenal Town

Chalet Nicholas, 2km northwest of Arenal Town, on the road to Tilarán (Ⓣ & Ⓕ 694-4041). Small, beautifully kept hotel with just three rooms – all with private bathroom and hot water – looking out to the lake and distant volcano. Horse-riding and bird-watching tours can be arranged (there are lots of birds in the hotel grounds too). Breakfast included. Non-smoking. ⑤

La Ceiba Lodge, 6km from Arenal Town on the road to La Fortuna, (☎694-4297, ☎ & ⓕ385-1540, ⓔceibalodge@hotmail.com). Very reasonably priced lodge located just above Lake Arenal, with good views. The four rooms have private bath and hot water, and there's a big communal terrace for sunset viewing – in front of the lodge you'll notice the enormous ceiba tree from which the lodge takes its name. There are walking trails in the hotel grounds, and mountain-biking, horse-riding, fishing and sailing can be arranged. ④

Lago Coter Ecoadventure Lodge, on Lago Coter, 4km north of Arenal Town (☎257-5075, ⓕ257-7065). The rooms are simple, but facilities – including telescopes for volcano-watching and guided bird-watching walks – are outstanding. Well-maintained nature trails in a small section of cloudforest and lake activities, including windsurfing and watersports, make this a great place for outdoor types. ⑦

Los Héroes Hotel and Restaurant, 30km west of Fortuna on the road to Arenal Town (☎ & ⓕ441-4193). Small Swiss-style hotel perched

right above Laguna de Arenal, with a Jacuzzi, pool, alpine decor with gingerbread woodwork, and a restaurant serving rösti and cheese fondue. ⑤

Marina Hotel, 40km west of Fortuna on the road to Tilarán (no phone, ⓕ479-9178). Simple, nicely furnished tiled and hardwood rooms, right on Laguna de Arenal, with good views. ④

Mystica Resort, 45km west of Fortuna, on the road to Tilarán (☎382-1499, ⓕ695-5387). Small motel-style hotel, with six comfortable rooms (some with bunk beds) set in pretty landscaped gardens with stupendous views. The friendly Italian/Tico owners make tasty pizza in a wood oven, and can organize windsurfing on the lake, as well as giving advice on other activities in the area. ③

Villa Decary, 2km east of Arenal Town, on the lake (☎383-3012, ⓕ694-4330). These nicely furnished rooms with balconies and lakeside views are fairly expensive, but a good place to stay if you fancy a spot of self-indulgence. There's lots of bird life in the grounds, and a good hike to the rear of the hotel. A delicious and healthy breakfast using some of the owners' home-made jams is included. No credit cards. ⑥

The Venado Caves

About 30km northwest of Fortuna, on a paved road near the tiny mountain town of **Venado** ("Deer"), are the **Venado Caves** ($2, though there may be no one to collect it). A small network of subterranean caverns, these are quite accessible – provided you don't mind getting wet and aren't afraid of bats. Inside is a tangle of stalactites and smoothed-out rock formations: spooky and unique, but not for claustrophobes. Some of the passages from cave to cave are so narrow that you should measure whether or not you are going to fit before you begin the crawl. Using the services of a guide is a very good idea – the caves are labyrinthine – and you should bring a torch and rubber boots (you may be able to rent them from your hotel if you're staying locally).

One of the nicest places **to stay** hereabouts is the isolated and beautifully rustic *Magíl Forest Lodge* (☎221-2825, ⓕ233-5991; ⑧), 20km west of San Rafael de Guatuso, in a private reserve amidst rolling fields not far from a protected rainforest and the Venado Caves. The lodge is remote and difficult to find, and access is difficult and sometimes only possible with a 4WD, so phone ahead for road conditions and directions; the lodge owners can sometimes arrange transport from San José.

There's a daily **bus** from San Carlos via Fortuna to Venado, but it leaves at 2pm and returns at 4.30pm, which doesn't give enough time to explore the caves. More frequent buses from Fortuna to Guatuso will drop you off at a private farm (owned by Sr Solis). From here to the mouth of the caves it's a walk of several kilometres along a gravel road and marked trail.

San Rafael de Guatuso

Historically part of the Corobicí tribal group, the present-day Guatusos are a community of interrelated clans that have inhabited northwestern Costa Rica and southern Nicaragua for thousands of years. Now numbering about four hundred, their history and the story of their steady decimation is a familiar one for tribal peoples in the area: the victims of disease, intertribal kidnapping and slavery to Spanish settlers in Nicaragua, in the 1700s and 1800s they were dealt further blows by the efforts of the Nicaraguan and Costa Rican Catholic Churches to convert them to Christianity.

The Guatuso communities today live on three **reserves**, established by the government in the 1960s. The reserves are not obviously demarcated, and you will pass through them en route to the village of **SAN RAFAEL DE GUA-TUSO** – known locally as **Guatuso** – 10km north of Venado. Though they speak their own language – Maleku, broadcast by Radio Sistema Cultural Maleku and taught in schools – don't expect to see native dress or any outward signs of tribal identity: the locals wear western clothes and the town looks much like any other in Costa Rica. There are, however, several places to buy Guatuso **crafts** – rather folksy, with a preponderance of decorated drums covered in snakeskin and small wooden carvings. Excavations of old Guatuso **tombs** in the area every now again turn up jade and pottery artefacts, which you can see in San José's Museo Nacional (see p.94).

The only place **to stay** around here is the *Magíl Forest Lodge*, 20km west of San Rafael de Guatuso (see above). Irregular **buses** (about 2 daily) from Fortuna to Guatuso leave from the stop next to the *Hotel La Fortuna* and around the corner from *El Jardín* restaurant.

The far north

The **far north** of the Zona Norte is an isolated region, culturally as well as geographically, closer to Nicaragua than to the rest of the country. Years of conflict during the Nicaraguan civil war made the region more familiar with CIA men and arms runners than with tourists, but most of the area, and certainly all the tourist destinations, are quiet now. Los Chiles, near the Nicaraguan border, is the only village of any size: the drive up here, along the stretch of good tarmac road from San Carlos, takes you through a flat landscape broken only by roadside shacks – many inhabited by Nicaraguan economic migrants. Tourist facilities are practically non-existent, and between the small village of Muelle, 8km from San Carlos, and Los Chiles there's 74km of virtually empty highway, with the Llanura de Guatusos stretching hot and interminably to the west.

Most tourists come here to see the **Refugio Nacional de Vida Silvestre Caño Negro**, a vast wetland, and one of the most remote wildlife refuges in the country. No longer a well-kept secret, it's possible to visit Caño Negro on a day-trip from the capital, on an excursion from Fortuna or one of the larger hotels in the Zona Norte, or to go independently.

During the Nicaraguan civil war, **Los Chiles**, right next to the border, was a Contra supply line. Nowadays, though, there is a climate of international co-operation, helped by the fact that many of the residents are of Nicaraguan extraction, and the area is gently opening up to tourism. A committed group of local hoteliers, restaurateurs and boatmen have formed a local tourism association with help from the national tourist board, and crossing the border is straightforward so long as your documents are in order. Despite these initiatives, bear in mind that you will have a hard time finding people who speak English; the further north you head, the more Spanish you'll need.

Incidentally, the **Río San Juan** is technically Nicaraguan territory – the border is on the Costa Rican bank – though Costa Rica is allowed free use of the river under the terms of a treaty between the two countries.

Los Chiles

Few tourists make it to **LOS CHILES**, a border settlement just 3km from the Nicaraguan frontier, and other than soaking up the town's end-of-the-world atmosphere, there's little to do, except perhaps try to rent a boat or horse to go to **Caño Negro**, 25km downstream on the Río Frío (see p.215). The only other reason you might come to Los Chiles is to cross the Nicaraguan border, although the majority of travellers still cross at Peñas Blancas, further west on the Interamericana.

Arrival

Until 1982, when the current highway was built, Los Chiles was cut off from the rest of Costa Rica. Nowadays two buses daily run from La Coca-Cola in **San José** to Los Chiles. Although known as "*directo*" buses, they always stop in San Carlos (and frequently in other places too) and, despite the highway being in good condition, the journey takes more than five hours. From **San Carlos** to Los Chiles, there are ten services daily between 5am and 7pm, and ten returning in the opposite direction between 4.45am and 4pm (2hr 30min). The San José bus stops right outside the Mercado Central, while buses arriving from San Carlos often stop close to the docks, in town.

Driving from San Carlos, Hwy-141 heads north along a poor, potholed road through the tiny settlements of Florencia and Muelle, and then along the 66km stretch, potholed in places, from Boca de Arenal through to Los Chiles. There are few gas stations north of Muelle: make sure you have lots of petrol. The only other way to get there is to charter an **air-taxi** from San José (see p.32); the airstrip is next to the *guardia civil* post on the edge of town.

Information

Although Los Chiles has no official **tourist information**, the travel agency Servitur (see below) offers good advice, and everyone in town knows the current bus schedules and the times of the river-boat to the Nicaraguan border, though you'll need Spanish to ask around. **Migración** (officially Mon–Fri 8am–5pm; ℡471-1153) can answer more detailed enquiries, but it often closes before 5pm – get there by 3pm to be safe.

Los Chiles might seem like the last place on earth, but it has most of the facilities you'll need: you can supposedly change dollars and **travellers' cheques** at the Banco Nacional on the north side of the soccer field (Mon–Fri 8am–3.30pm), though it's safest to bring an adequate supply of colones. Full postal services, including fax, are offered at the **correo** in the Mercado Central (Mon–Fri 8am–4pm). For **supplies**, head for the Dos Piños general store 50m east of the docks. There's even a small **travel agency**, Servitur (Mon–Sat 8am–6pm; ℡471-1055, ℱ471-1211), based at the *Cabinas Jabirú*, 200m north of the centre. Nelson Leitón, the owner and long-time local resident, can arrange boat tours to Caño Negro for about $35 per person. They also have an affiliated office in Granada, in Nicaragua, and are very knowledgeable about visiting the Lago de Nicaragua area, the Solentiname Islands, or indeed anywhere else in Nicaragua.

Accommodation

If you're intending to cross the border, you may well need to **stay the night** in Los Chiles. The most comfortable accommodation in town, the cool and spotless *Cabinas Jabirú* (T 471-1055; ❶), 200m north of the centre, offers rooms with private bath, hot water and fan, plus a laundry service. Other good options include the long-established *Cuajipal Lodge*, 1km south of town (T 471-1197; ❷), which has simply furnished rooms, with private bath and hot water, along with an on-site restaurant. If you have a bit more to spend, check out the *Complejo Turístico El Gaspar* (T 460-0124, F 460-3150; ❹), next to the *Cuajipal Lodge*. The rustic-style rooms here are airy and clean, with cold water and table fans only – nothing special, and a bit pricey for the area, though the complex also has three small pools (the only public ones in Los Chiles) and a small restaurant.

Crossing into Nicaragua

The border at Los Chiles between Nicaragua and Costa Rica has a turbulent history. During the Nicaraguan civil war, US-sponsored Contras were supplied through here, and it was not unusual to see camouflaged planes sitting on the airstrip, disgorging guns. In the past the border was closed to foreigners, and even for a while to Nicaraguans and Costa Ricas, though it's now possible for anyone to enter Nicaragua by boat from here. The service usually leaves the docks at 8am (Mon–Fri), but it's always worth checking first with officials in either Los Chiles or at the Nicaraguan consulate in San José (see p.107). The Los Chiles *migración* officials are relatively friendly, and you may be able to confirm current boat times with the groups of Nicas or Ticos who hang around the office.

Some nationalities need tourist visas to enter Nicaragua. Requirements are constantly in flux, so always check with the consulate in San José, which is the only place in the country that can issue the necessary documentation (allow at least 24hr for processing). Make sure that the Nicaraguan border patrol, 3km upriver from Los Chiles, stamps your passport, as you will need proof of entry when leaving Nicaragua. There is also a police check south of Los Chiles on the highway to San Carlos and Fortuna. Don't worry if they signal you over – this is mainly to guard against Nicaraguans entering or staying in Costa Rica illegally.

From the border control point it's a 14km trip up the Río Frío to the small town of San Carlos de Nicaragua, on the southeast lip of the huge Lago de Nicaragua. You'll need some cash upon arrival; change a few colones for cordobas at the Los Chiles bank. From San Carlos de Nicaragua it is also possible to cross the lake to Granada and on to Managua, but again check with the consulate in San José; this is an infrequent boat service and without forward planning you could end up stuck in San Carlos for longer than you'd hoped.

In the current atmosphere of relative political stability in Nicaragua, there are tentative plans for one-day river tours from Los Chiles to Nicaraguan San Carlos, Lago de Nicaragua, and even the Solentiname islands in the lake. Visitors may even be able to see the fortress San Juan – also called the Castillo de la Concepción or Fortaleza – which is one of the oldest Spanish structures (1675) in the Americas, built as a defence against the English and pirates (often one and the same) plying the Río San Juan. Bear in mind, however, that there is some controversy about Costa Rican tour operators taking tourists into Nicaraguan territory without informing Nicaraguan officials, and it is currently in dispute whether tourism constitutes the "trade" purposes for which Costa Rica is allowed to use the river.

The Town

Los Chiles is laid out on a small grid of dusty and uneventful streets. The highway peters out just beyond the town in the direction of the Río San Juan, leaving nowhere to go but the river. There's no traffic to speak of – just a few *campesinos* ambling along on their horses, huge workhorse trucks rumbling by caked with the red dust of the tropical forest soil, and children nipping past on creaky bikes – probably the most excitement you'll encounter will be the clumps of youths sitting in the middle of the road idly chatting.

There is little to see around the usually deserted **main square** (more accurately, an ill-kempt soccer field), although the faded, tumbledown houses lining the right-hand side of the road to the river have a certain atmospheric melancholy, embellished with wooden latticework of surprising delicacy and French doors opening off tall, narrow porches. Some of the first buildings to be built in the area, forty to fifty years ago, they now evoke a forlorn, France-in-the-tropics feel. The only sign of any activity is at *migración* and the adjacent docks, where children frolic in the river, and at the bunker-like **Mercado Central**, 200m northeast of the soccer field – apart from the Dos Piños store, this is the only place in town to buy fresh food.

Though less well known in this respect than Barra del Colorado (see p.184), Los Chiles is a great spot for **tarpon-fishing**, with locals offering fishing trips in their own *lanchas* (except during Jan–April, when fishing is not permitted) – enquire at the dock or with Servitur. Provision of rods and tackle varies, and you need a licence – again, ask at Servitur.

There's just one **bar** in town, not far from the dock. Dingy and uninviting it may be, but it does at least serve ice-cold beers – very welcome in this steamy climate. For **eating**, you're limited to the *Restaurante El Parque* in the centre of town, which is OK, though nothing special.

Refugio Nacional de Vida Silvestre Caño Negro

The largely pristine **REFUGIO NACIONAL DE VIDA SILVESTRE CAÑO NEGRO** ($6), 25km west of Los Chiles, is one of the best places in the Americas to view huge concentrations of both migratory and indigenous **birds**, along with mammalian and reptilian **river wildlife**. Until recently its isolation kept it well off the beaten tourist track, though nowadays, more and more tours are being offered to the area.

Caño Negro is created by the seasonal flooding of the Río Frío, so, depending on what time of year you go, you may find yourself whizzing around a huge broad lake in a motorboat or walking along mud-caked riverbeds. There's a three-metre difference in the water level between the rainy season (May–Nov), when Caño Negro is at its fullest, and the dry season (Dec–April); note that the rainy season is not necessarily the best time to see wildlife, because while the mammalian population of the area stays more or less constant, the birds vary widely (see p.217). In the dry season you'll see enormous flocks of birds mucking about in the mud together or washing their feathers; the **best time** of all to visit for birders is between January and March, when the most migratory species are in residence.

Unless you're an expert in identifying wildlife, the most rewarding way to enjoy the diverse flora and fauna of Caño Negro is to use the services of a **guide** who knows the area and can point out animals and other features of river life. However, it is not always possible to find trained guides, and the prices of organized tours can be prohibitive for many travellers. Usually, though, the locals will know quite a bit about wildlife in the area and, if you're travelling in one of the *lanchas* from Los Chiles, you may be lucky enough to hook up with a boatman who can identify many animals. They may not be as stimulating as a professionally trained guide (and they usually will not speak English), but they'll improve your trip nonetheless. Asking at the docks or Servitur in town might turn up someone.

Getting to Caño Negro

An increasing number of **tour companies** run trips to Caño Negro from San José, Fortuna and the more upmarket Zona Norte hotels. Prices vary widely, but in general the trip to Caño Negro is a little more expensive than many expeditions because of the distances involved and – in the wet season – the amount of time spent in the boat simply getting there. Horizontes, at C 28, Av 1/3 in San José (☏ 222-2022) runs three-day/two-night tours from the capital to Caño Negro, including a stop at Volcán Arenal, with accommodation at the *Tilajari Resort Hotel* (see p.202), with all meals, accommodation, transport and guides included. Tours from Fortuna, including transport in air-conditioned minibus, launch, bilingual guide, and lunch by the river, cost around $40 with Aventuras Arenal, a little more with Sunset Tours.

The journey to Caño Negro from Los Chiles varies according to season. In the wet months you'll be transported by boat all the way into the lake that forms the main part of the refuge. The rest of the year, boats, vehicles or horses (itineraries vary – check with your tour operator) travel down the Río Frío or along the dirt road to the entrance of the refuge, from where it's possible to walk (if the water is very low) or take a horseback tour.

You can also get to Caño Negro **independently**. Driving is easy enough in the dry season, while in the wet season a boat leaves from the Los Chiles docks (Tues & Thurs only at 7.30am; for information call ☏ 460-1301). On other days you can take your pick from several *lanchas*: get there early in the morning, compare prices and expect to pay at least $65 per boat for the five-hour return trip – the people at Servitur in Los Chiles can also recommend someone reliable. Note that the first 25km of the trip down the Río Frío (taking an hour or more by *lancha*) does not take you through the wildlife refuge, which begins at the mouth of the large flooded area and is marked by a sign poking out of a small islet. Make sure your boatman takes you right into Caño Negro.

If you take a tour, the **entrance fee** is included. If not, you should pay at the **ranger station** on the north side of the lake, provided you can find someone to collect the money. You can also stay at the ranger station (☏ 460-1301; ❶) – call from the public telephone at Caño Negro to reserve – though facilities are variable: you may be able to buy a meal, but bring your own supplies just in case. **Camping** is permitted in Caño Negro, but no formal facilities are provided and there's a charge of around $4, payable to the ranger.

La Laguna del Lagarto Lodge

Poised midway between Caño Negro and Tortuguero, 70km from either, **La Laguna del Lagarto Lodge** (☏ 289-8163, ☏ 289-5295, ⓦ www.adventure-costarica.com/laguna-del-lagarto; ❺) is one of the most remote in the country. Set in an extensive area of virgin tropical rainforest, the lodge is home to an incredible variety of trees, plants and animals and offers some of the best bird-watching in the country – it's one of the very few places in Costa Rica where you might still see the highly endangered great green macaw, as well as a large resident colony of more common oropendolas. The lodge is only 16km from

Migratory birds such as storks, ducks, herons and cormorants join an abundance of permanent residents including iguanas, snakes, osprey eagles, kingfishers, "Jesus Christ" lizards, yellow turtles, "yellow-footed" birds (*patas amarillas*) and egrets (*garças*). The largest colony of the Nicaraguan **grackle** also makes regular appearances here, the only place in Costa Rica where it nests. Large animals including **pumas, jaguars** and **tapirs** have also been spotted – there are thought to be considerable numbers in the reserve, though it's very rare to see them.

Among the more unusual inhabitants of Caño Negro in the wet season is the **garfish**, a kind of in-between creature straddling fish and mammal. This so-called "living fossil" is a fish with lungs, gills and a nose, probably looking its oddest while it sleeps, drifting along in the water; again, it's rare to see one. The **tarpon** can grow to truly huge dimensions – up to 2m in length – and you'll often see its startling white form splashing out of the water, arcing its huge fin and long body.

Other creatures to watch out for include the ubiquitous pot-bellied **iguanas**; **swimming snakes**, heads held aloft like periscopes, bodies whipping out behind (don't get too close and do not touch – in most cases they will be fleeing from you); the elegant, long-limbed **white ibis** that rests on river-level branches and banks; and the sinuous-necked **anhingas** (snakebirds), who impale their prey on the knife-point of their beaks before swallowing. **Crocodiles** and **caimans** also live here, although the latter being far more common than the former.

Howler monkeys (*monos congos*) will often sound the alarm as you approach. To see them, look up into the taller branches of riverside trees. It helps to have binoculars to distinguish their black hairy shapes from the densely leaved trees. Equally, the **sloth's** resemblance, from a distance, to a dense clump of leaves makes them very difficult to spot. Not only do they move very little during the day, they are also very well camouflaged by the green algae that often covers their brown hair. For the best chances of catching sight of one, use binoculars to scan the middle and upper branches of Eucalyptus trees (the ones with the big, light-green leaves growing in umbrella-patterns) and especially the V-shaped intersections between branches, keeping an eye out for what will initially look like a dark mass. The rows of small grey triangles you might see on riverside tree trunks are **bats**, literally hanging out during the day.

the Nicaraguan border and can arrange horse-riding tours and river excursions on the Río San Juan – not usually very accessible to tourists – as well as hiking and canoeing.

Rooms are rustic but comfortable, and have peaceful views from their balconies; rates include breakfast. To reach the lodge **by car** from San José or Ciudad Quesada you have to drive east through Aguas Zarcas, then turn left (signed) to Pital. From there head northwest to Sahino and Boca Tapada on good gravel roads. The lodge is 10km to the east of Boca Tapada, also on a reasonable road, although 4WD is recommended. **Buses** leave from Av 9, C12 in San José daily at 12.30pm, and hourly from San Carlos to Pital, from where you can connect with buses north to Boca Tapada. The lodge will pick you up from here.

The Sarapiquí region

Northwest of the Las Horquetas turn-off on the Guápiles Highway, the **Sarapiquí area** stretches around the top of Braulio Carrillo National Park

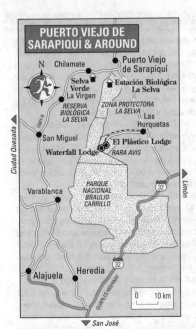

PUERTO VIEJO DE SARAPIQUÍ & AROUND

Chilamate
Puerto Viejo de Sarapiquí
Selva Verde
Estación Biológica La Selva
La Virgen
RESERVA BIOLÓGICA LA SELVA
ZONA PROTECTORA LA SELVA
Ciudad Quesada
Hwy 4
San Miguel
Las Horquetas
El Plástico Lodge
Waterfall Lodge
RARA AVIS
Limón
Varablanca
PARQUE NACIONAL BRAULIO CARRILLO
32
Alajuela
Heredia
32
GUÁPILES HIGHWAY
0   10 km
San José

(see p.136) and west to the village of San Miguel, from where Volcán Arenal and the western lowlands are easily accessible by road. Steamy, tropical and carpeted with fruit plantations, the area bears more resemblance to the hot and dense Caribbean lowlands than the plains of the north and, despite the large-scale deforestation, still shelters some of the best preserved **premontane rainforest** in the country.

South of Puerto Viejo de Sarapiquí, the area around the small town of **Las Horquetas** is home to the biggest *palmito* (heart-of-palm) plantations in the world. This and banana cultivation form the core of the local economy, alongside more recent ecotourism initiatives such as the research station **La Selva**, and the rainforest lodges of **Rara Avis** and **Selva Verde**. The region's chief tourist attractions, these lodges offer access to some of the last primary rainforest in the country. The largest settlement, sleepy **Puerto Viejo de Sarapiquí** attracts few visitors and is primarily a river transport hub and a place for fruit-plantation workers to stock up on supplies and have a beer or two.

There are two options when it comes to getting **from San José or the Valle Central** to Puerto Viejo. The western route, which takes a little more than three hours, goes via Varablanca and La Paz waterfall, passing the hump of Volcán Barva. Characterized by winding mountain roads and plenty of potholes, this route offers great views of velvety smooth green hills clad with coffee plantations, which turn, eventually, into rainforest. Faster (1hr–1hr 30min) and less hair-raising – although less scenic – is the route via the **Guápiles Highway** through Braulio Carrillo National Park, heading off to the left at the Las Horquetas/Puerto Viejo turn-off at the base of the mountain pass. If you're on an all-in package to one of the lodges and have transport included, your driver will take this route.

Unsurprisingly the region receives a lot of **rain** – as much as 4500mm annually, and there is no real dry season (although less rain is recorded from January to May), so rain gear is essential.

Rara Avis

RARA AVIS, a private rainforest reserve 17km south of Puerto Viejo and about 80km northeast of San José, offers one of the most thrilling and authentic ecotourism experiences – if not *the* best – in Costa Rica, featuring both primary rainforest and some secondary cover dating from about thirty years ago. This general area, bordering the northeast tip of pristine Braulio Carrillo National Park, is home to a number of unique **palm species**, while huge, ancient hardwood trees, smothered by lianas, "walking" palms (that shift a metre or so in their lifetime), primitive ferns and mosses, orchids and other flowering plants are also common.

Established in 1983 by American Amos Bien (a former administrator of the Estación Biológica La Selva) and Trino (a local squatter *campesino*), Rara Avis combines the functions of a tourist lodge and a private rainforest reserve, and is dedicated to the conservation, study and farming of the area's biodiversity. Its ultimate objective is to show that the rainforest can be profitable for an indefinite period, giving local smallholders a viable alternative to clearing the land for cattle. Rara Avis supports a number of endemic plants that have considerable economic potential, including *geonoma epetiolata*, or the stained-glass palm, which was until recently believed to be extinct. Another significant part of the Rara Avis mandate is to provide alternative sources of employment in Las Horquetas, 15km away, where most people work for the big fruit companies or as day-labourers on local farms.

Rara Avis also functions as a **research station**, accommodating student groups and volunteers whose aim is to develop rainforest products – orchids, palms and so forth – as crops. A further objective to create sustainable hardwood forests has been dropped, however, as there is no longer sufficient forest in the Las Horquetas area. For more on rainforest management and sustainability, see Contexts.

Getting to Rara Avis

Because of its isolation, you'll have to spend at least one night in the reserve, though two or three would be preferable. If time is short, a **package** to Rara Avis including transport from San José may be worth considering (see p.33 for tour agents), but with a little planning it is perfectly possible – and more economical – to get there **independently**. To do this you need to take the bus from San José to near the small village of Las Horquetas, then a taxi to the village, from where a tractor-pulled cart makes the final 15km of the journey. You'll need to reserve accommodation at the reserve in advance, however you arrive.

As the tractor for Rara Avis leaves daily at 9am, you have to take the 7am bus to Río Frío/Puerto Viejo de Sarapiquí from San José. Make sure you get the express (*directo*) service via the Guápiles Highway (the bus via Heredia leaves thirty minutes earlier and takes the long western route to Puerto Viejo). It takes between an hour and ninety minutes from San José to reach the turn-off (*cruce*) for Las Horquetas – ask the driver to let you off. From here, a five-minute **taxi** ride will take you to the **Rara Avis office** in Las Horquetas (since all accommodation at the lodges must be pre-booked, they'll know you are coming, though it's worth calling ⊕ 253-0844 to double-check that a taxi will be waiting for you). From the office, the tractor-cart will take you to Rara Avis. If you come with your own transport, there's a car park at the office, where you can leave your vehicle.

Getting to Rara Avis from Las Horquetas is at least half the fun, though not exactly comfortable. The uphill flatbed-tractor journey to the lodges takes two to four hours depending both on the condition of the "road" (actually a muddy rutted track) and on where you're staying. The pluses of this mode of transport include the sheer excitement – there's much multilingual cheering when the driver revs up the tractor and, squelching and spluttering, gets to the top of each slippery hill – and an exhilarating open-air view of the surrounding landscape, with plenty of time for toucan-spotting. Minuses include bumps and bruises, choking diesel fumes and a few worrying moments as the tractor slithers and slides up pitted hills.

What to see at Rara Avis

Rara Avis's flora is as diverse as you might expect from a premontane rainforest. The best way to learn to spot different flowers, plants, trees and their respective habitats is to go on a walk with one of the knowledgeable guides, most of whom have lived at Rara Avis or nearby for some time. Especially interesting plants include the stained-glass palm tree, a rare specimen much in demand for its ornamental prettiness, and the walking palm, whose tentacle-like roots can propel it over more than a metre of ground in its lifetime as it "walks" in search of water. Orchids are numerous, as are non-flowering bromeliads, heliconias, lianas, primitive ferns and other plants typically associated with this dense rainforest cover.

A mind-boggling number of bird species have been identified at Rara Avis, and it is likely that more are yet to be discovered. As well as the fearsome black, turkey and king vultures and the majestic osprey eagle, you might see four types of kites, ten types of hawk owls, hummingbirds, pretty Amazon and green kingfishers, woodpeckers, both chestnut-mandibled and keel-billed toucans, robins, warblers, great-tailed grackle, and the unlikely named black-crested coquette, great potoo and tiny hawk. The endangered great green macaw also nests here.

Among the more common mammals are monkeys, tapirs, ocelots and jaguars, though the last three are rarely seen. Along with other vipers, the fer-de-lance and bushmaster snakes, two of the most venomous in the world, may lie in wait, so take extra care on the trails, and look everywhere you step and put your hand.

Rara Avis's butterfly farm (for which a nominal entrance fee of $2 is asked – you don't have to pay, but it goes towards the farm's upkeep) is at *El Plástico Lodge*. Boa constrictors hang out around here; ask if any have been spotted lately. If you do see one, be careful: boas are generally quite torpid, but can get aggressive if bothered.

If you miss the tractor, **horses** are available for hire from the villagers until noon ($15) – any time after that is too late, as the trip takes several hours. Ask at the Rara Avis office when you arrive. The horses can get as far as the *El Plástico Lodge* (see below), but if you're staying at the *Waterfall Lodge* or the *Riverside Cabin*, you'll have to walk the last 3km on a rainforest trail.

Leaving Rara Avis, the tractor departs at about 2pm from the *Waterfall* lodge, passing the *Plástico* lodge at around 3pm. This means that it often arrives in Horquetas too late to rendezvous with the last bus for San José, which passes through at 5.15pm daily. If you miss this bus, the Rara Avis office in Horquetas can arrange for a taxi (about $25 per carload) to the Guápiles Highway, from where you can flag down a Guápiles–San José bus, which pass by hourly until 7pm.

Accommodation

There are three **places to stay** at Rara Avis, all bookable on ⓣ253-0844 or 764-3131, ⒻF257-4876, Ⓔraraavis@racsa.co.cr. Rates at all three include all meals, transport by tractor from and to Las Horquetas, and guided walks. The cheapest is the HI-affiliated *El Plástico Lodge* ($45 per person in a dormitory; $35 for students and HI members), in a cleared area 12km from Las Horquetas. *Plástico*, as it is known, is named after a convicts' colony that used to stand on the site, in which the prisoners slept underneath plastic tarpaulins. It has dirt floors downstairs, bunk-style beds and hot water, a covered but open-view communal dining table and a sitting area. Despite its rusticity, it's all very comfortable, and the only way to see Rara Avis on the cheap. *Plástico* maintains radio contact with the outside world, but there's no phone at the lodge itself.

The road from here to the more comfortable *Waterfall Lodge* (Ⓞ) is only 3km, but it's uphill, through dense rainforest, and takes at least an hour by tractor

from *Plástico*. If you are in good shape, the best way to get there is to hike the (fairly obvious) trail through the rainforest – you can pick up a map at the Rara Avis office in Las Horquetas. This should take about an hour: do not, under any circumstances, leave the trails, which are in good condition despite year-round mud.

Set above a picture-perfect cascade, the *Waterfall* has rooms with running hot water, private baths, spacious balconies with hammocks, and fantastic views of utterly pristine rainforest and the hot, flat lowland plains stretching towards the Caribbean. It's an idyllic place to stay; the only sounds heard at five or six in the morning are the echoing shrieks of birds and *monos congos* (howler monkeys), and the light, even first thing, is sheer and unfiltered, giving everything a wonderfully shimmering effect. Meals, cooked by local women and served three times a day, are delicious: breakfasts consist of heaped platters of eggs and cheese, *gallo pinto*, corn muffins, fresh fruit and wonderful coffee, while lunches and dinners are filling, delicately flavoured dishes with a variety of meat and vegetables. Vegetarians are well catered for, and beer and snacks are kept in a small "tuck shop": you take your own and keep track of your bill. There's no electricity (but plenty of kerosene lamps), though there is a phone from which you can make international calls.

The third accommodation option is the still more isolated still *Riverside Cabin* (➑), about 500m from the *Waterfall* – if you stay here you'll have to be unfazed by walking through the forest at night with only a torch or a lamp. Even more isolated, in a vertical sense, is the **tree-top cabin** which has been built on a platform 30m up a rainforest tree – strictly for hardy outdoor types. Guides show you how to climb up using ropes and pulley-type gadgets. Once up, there are beds for two people and water (although this too has to be winched up the tree) and a chemical toilet. The prices are the same as the *Waterfall*, and the restrictions of staying here are obvious: once you're up the tree for the night, you're up.

Rara Avis activities

Rara Avis also has a network of very good **trails**: there are at least four around *Plástico*, not including the two ("Atajo" and "Catarata") that lead up to the *Waterfall Lodge*. From the *Waterfall*, nine or so trails weave through fairly dense jungle cover. All are well marked, and give walks of thirty minutes to several hours depending upon the pace. While guided walks are fun and informative, guests are welcome to go it alone: you'll be given a map at the lodge reception, but you should always let the staff know which trail you are following and how long approximately you intend to be. Rain gear is essential at all times.

Just below the *Waterfall Lodge*, a fifty-metre-high waterfall on the Río Atelopus plummets into a deep pool before continuing the river's slide down towards lower ground. **Swimming** in the icy-cold pool, shrouded in a fine mist, is a wonderful experience, but don't even consider it without a guide. Occasional *cabezas de agua* (flash floods) up in the highlands swell the river and cause sudden rushing torrents, with potentially fatal consequences – three people were swept to their deaths here some years ago.

Estación Biológica La Selva

A fully equipped research station, **ESTACIÓN BIOLÓGICA LA SELVA**, 4km southwest of Puerto Viejo and 93km northeast of San José, is owned and operated by the Organization of Tropical Studies (OTS), a group of international institutions dedicated to the study of rainforest and tropical areas. La Selva is probably the best place to visit in the Sarapiquí region if you are a botany student or have a special interest in the scientific life of a rainforest and, like Rara Avis, it is a bird-watcher's paradise, with more than four hundred species of indigenous and migratory birds. An equally staggering number of tree species – some 450 – have been identified, as well as 113 species of mammals. Many leading biologists from various countries have at one time studied here, and its facilities are extensive – a large swatch of pre-montane rainforest shouldering the northern part of Braulio Carrillo National Park forms the natural laboratory, while the research facilities comprise lecture halls and extensive labs along with accommodation for the scientists and students who make up the majority of its residents.

La Selva is impressively geared up to cope with its many visitors, with a reception, dining room, shop and visitors' centre. The ground cover extends from primary **forest** through abandoned plantations to pastureland and brush, and is crossed by an extensive network of about 25 **trails**. Varying in length from short to more than 5km long, most are in very good condition, clearly and frequently marked. Some, however, are "real" trails, with no corduroy, cement blocks or wire netting to help you get a grip, and many can get very muddy indeed. Tourists tend to stick to the main trails within the part of La Selva designated as the Ecological Reserve, next to the Río Puerto Viejo. These trails, the **Camino Circular Cercano**, the **Camino Cantarrana** and the **Sendero Oriental** (each about a four-hour hike), radiate from the river research station and take you through the dense, primary-growth tropical forest for which the Sarapiquí area is famous.

The simple **map** they hand you at reception leads you adequately around the main trails, but for more detail the OTS booklet, *Walking La Selva,* sold at the station shop, gives a comprehensive, annotated trail-by-trail account.

Practicalities

Though tourists are very much secondary to research at La Selva, visitors are welcome, providing there's space – it's impossible to overstate La Selva's popularity, and in the high season (Nov–April) you need to book by fax months in advance (ⓣ766-6565, ⓕ710-1414, ⓔlaselva@ns.ots.ac.cr; $20, including entrance to the reserve and half-day guided tour). Visiting in the low season (roughly May–Oct) is easier, but even then you should call first; if you come on spec, staff will simply turn you away.

To get to La Selva **from San José**, the least expensive option is to take the Río Frío/Puerto Viejo bus (see below), which, if you ask, will drop you off at the station's entrance road, a two-kilometre walk from the station itself. The OTS (ⓣ240-6696, ⓕ240-6783) also lays on a thrice-weekly bus (Mon, Wed and Fri; $10 one-way) from its office in Curridabat, San José; though mainly reserved for researchers and students, it's worth asking if they can fit you in. Taxis make the four-kilometre trip **from Puerto Viejo** for about $5.

The simple but comfortable **accommodation** (in San José ⓣ240-6696, ⓕ240-6783; in La Selva ⓣ740-1515, ⓕ740-1414; ⓺) at La Selva isn't cheap, but proceeds go towards the maintenance of the station. Researchers and students with scientific bona fides stay for less (ⓞ). Rates include three meals a day, served in the communal dining hall.

Many people unaccustomed to the rainforest approach it with the kind of awe reserved for great architectural or engineering feats. The idea that a rainforest is like a cathedral, to be admired in hushed and humbled voices, is strangely intermingled with its metaphorical role as the epitome of the pristine, a latter-day Eden. Regeneration and decay is quick in tropical climes, but it has always been assumed that the highly complex and intertwined mechanisms that make a rainforest take centuries, even millennia, to regenerate themselves.

The tropical rainforest in the Sarapiquí region, and especially that within La Selva's natural laboratory, has long been thought to be representative of premontane, or ancient and relatively untouched, rainforest cover. But recent research into the history of La Selva's forests has raised new theories about the regenerative capacities of rainforests – ideas that are bound to be considered controversial by conservationists.

Unlike temperate-zone deciduous trees, those that make up the tropical rainforest do not form rings, so traditionally scientists have had to resort to other tactics, like examining the soil layer for clues, to determine the age of a given piece of forest. Recent findings – pottery pieces, two thousand year-old charcoals, burial sites, an ancient hearth, and tools used to cultivate crops like maize and yucca – unearthed in La Selva suggest, in the broadest sense, that early rainforests around here may have been slashed, burned and inhabited by generations of indigenous peoples. Meanwhile, contemporaneous evidence provided by scientists working in the Darién Gap and in the Amazon basin presents the possibility that rainforests throughout the Americas may be more resilient to disturbances than previously thought.

At the 1993 Ecological Society of America conference, La Selva researchers announced new data illustrating that between about 2000 and 800 years ago the reserve's forest was put under the scythe by indigenous people to make space for, typically, corn plantations, small villages and patches of *pejibaye* (a kind of miniature coconut). For rainforest scientists the chief benefit of this information is that certain puzzles surrounding seemingly natural patterns of plant distribution may be solved. But in a wider sense it suggests that, far from being static repositories of untouched biodiversity, rainforests may be the products of constant change and adaptation.

Scientists at La Selva and elsewhere are quick to say that these findings do not sanction clear-cutting or any other modern form of rainforest destruction. Whilst admitting that it may be possible to cultivate the land in a sustainable or regenerative fashion, the scientists insist that the kind of agriculture they believe pre-Columbian people to have practised in the rainforest in no way resembles the massive plantation-style cultivation, logging, large squatter settlements, and other threats to the rainforest that we witness today.

Selva Verde Lodge

One of the premier rainforest lodges in Costa Rica, if not the Americas, **SELVA VERDE LODGE** sits amid two square kilometres of preserved forest alongside the Río Sarapiquí, near the village of Chilamate, 5km west of Puerto Viejo and 103km from San José. Owned and operated by a US-based company which specializes in ecological and adventure holidays, Selva Verde comprises an impressive complex of accommodation blocks, dining hall, lecture rooms and a lovely riverside bar-patio where monkeys chatter above and the Sarapiquí bubbles below. The lodge is set in landscaped tropical gardens rather than dense overgrowth, and appears to have mastered its environment to the extent that even the animals – among them the dreaded fer-de-lance snake – behave themselves and don't bother the tourists. And while it's run by very friendly, dedicated staff, and has some of the most knowledgeable naturalist guides in Costa Rica, the atmosphere is rather *Sheraton*-in-the-jungle, with super-comfortable rooms and very tasty food. The hiking, wildlife-spotting and bird-watching opportunities, however, are undeniably excellent, as are the refreshing swims in the Sarapiquí. White-water rafting, horse-riding, riverboat rides and visits to a banana plantation are among the many other activities offered.

Getting to Selva Verde

Taxis from Puerto Viejo to Selva Verde cost about $5 per car. If you're driving, watch for a green gate and a large orange building (the lodge's library and community centre) on the left-hand side of the road from Puerto Viejo. Coming from the west on Hwy-9 via Heredia, look out for a large pasture field (with the Río Sarapiquí visible beyond), after which the shallow driveway with its "Selva Verde" sign comes into view. If you reach the village of Chilamate (signed), you've gone too far.

Accommodation

Accommodation at the **Selva Verde Lodge** (⊤766-680, in the US ⊤1-800/451-7111, ⓕ766-6011, ⓦwww.holbrooktravel.com; ⓢ) is in two complexes of elevated bungalows: the *River Lodge* – from which the Sarapiquí's gentle chatter can be heard – and the *Creek Lodge*, named for a dried-up creek nearby. The former is slightly more expensive because of its tranquil location; the rooms with river views are best. Each room has a hammock and electric light after dark, so night owls at least have the option of reading (everybody at Selva Verde seems to go to bed early – the bar and barbecue area empties out by 9pm). Bear in mind that much of the time the lodge, which has a long-established link with the *Elderhostel* organization in the US, is full of tour groups or study groups (it's often possible to join one of their fascinating evening talks – recent topics have included a discussion of the position of Blacks in Costa Rica, and a lecture by a Costa Rican anthropologist who spent two years living with the indigenous peoples of the Talamanca region). Rates include all meals, good showers with hot water, and full mosquito netting. Reservations should be made at least thirty days in advance, and the first night must be pre-paid. Children under 12 stay for free.

Selva Verde activities

Selva Verde's expanse offers an excellent variety of walks along well-marked trails through primary and secondary forest, riverside, swamps and pastureland. Unless you've come as part of a pre-paid, all-inclusive package, you'll need to pay for the activities below: these cost from $15 (for guided walks) to $45 (for a half-day white-water rafting); there's also a free bird-watching tour daily at 6am.

You can take a **self-guided walk** in the section of secondary rainforest across the road from the lodge – ask for a map at reception. While you might not see much in terms of animal life, birding is rewarding here – recent sightings have included a family of toucans. For experienced rainforest walkers or botany enthusiasts, the **guided walks** through the denser section of premontane forest across the Río Sarapiquí are more rewarding. The guides are absolutely top-notch and will point out poison-dart frogs, primitive ferns, complex lianas, make uncannily authentic bird calls to get the attention of trogons and toucans, and generally give you a very good and informative time.

The most popular activity at Selva Verde, however, is **white-water rafting** on the Class III (easy–moderate) Río Sarapiquí (May–Nov only). The trip is exciting enough, though experienced rafters might regret the lack of any really scary rapids. You can also take **riverboat rides** from Puerto Viejo, which give a good introduction to wildlife in the area – though, admittedly, animal-watching is better in more pristine spots like Caño Negro or Tortuguero (see p.217 & p.186). The banks of the Sarapiquí are, at least in Costa Rican terms, heavily populated, and on one side are packed for long stretches with banana plantations – you'll be able to observe at first hand the problems caused by the plastic pesticide bags used in the plantations, which get caught up in the water or tangled around the lower branches of trees, poisoning the river and its wildlife.

Puerto Viejo de Sarapiquí

Just under 100km northeast of San José, **PUERTO VIEJO DE SARAPIQUÍ** (known locally as Puerto Viejo, though not to be confused with Puerto Viejo de Talamanca on the Caribbean coast) is the epitome of the steamy jungle town. The Río Sarapiquí is the focal point for the six thousand local inhabitants, and most cargo, both human and inanimate, is still carried by river to the Río San Juan and the Nicaraguan border in the north, and to the canals of Tortuguero and Barra del Colorado in the east. Though an important hub for banana plantation workers and those who live in the isolated settlements between here and the Caribbean coast, Puerto Viejo is of little interest to independent travellers except as a jumping-off point to visit the nearby jungle lodges.

Arrival

Numerous **buses** leave from Av 11, C 0/1 in San José for Puerto Viejo and the small settlement of Río Frío (they'll be marked "Río Frío"). The fast service, **via the Guápiles Highway and Las Horquetas**, currently departs at 7am, 9am, 10am, 1pm, 3pm and 4pm; the 97-kilometre trip takes just ninety minutes. Buses from San José to Puerto Viejo **via Heredia** (ask the driver if you're unsure which bus you're on – there's nothing on the front indicating which route it takes) take more like three hours and leave at 6.30am, noon and 3pm, returning from Puerto Viejo at 8am and 4pm – although the 4pm bus sometimes only goes as far as La Virgen, some 12km west of Puerto Viejo.

Accommodation

The **accommodation** situation in Puerto Viejo de Sarapiquí is pretty good considering the town's size, though Friday and Sunday nights can get booked up with plantation workers. To really get to know the dense rainforest in the region, however, you may prefer to stay at one of the nearby **jungle lodges**, or at one of the good, privately owned hotels near the town (see below).

Mi Lindo Sarapiquí (℡766-6074; ❷), on the main street, is the best-known spot in town, with a good restaurant that doubles as a bar at night – ask behind the counter in the restaurant for rooms, as there's no reception. Rooms are clean, fairly spacious and have private bath. The downside is that you're in the middle of town, and cooking smells might drift up from the restaurant, but it's fairly quiet nonetheless, and handy for the bus stop across the street. A good fall-back, *Cabinas Monteverde* (℡766-6236; ❶), on the main street next to the *Monteverde* restaurant, has small and very basic (though clean) rooms with cold-water shower and fans. Also on the main street is *El Bambú* (℡766-6005,

Ⓕ 766-6132, Ⓦ www.elbambu.com; Ⓢ), the plushest accommodation in town, with nicely decorated rooms (all with fans, colour TV and hot water), pretty potted tropical plants and a restaurant, bar and full tour service.

The town

A strange mixture of tropical langour and industriousness, Puerto Viejo is a relatively clean and well-ordered place, though it gets a bit more lively on Friday evenings, when the banana and palmito plantation workers are paid. The town's one main street runs from the Cruz Roja at the entrance to the town and curves around towards the river and the small dock. The town centre lies across from the large, well-manicured soccer field, where well-dressed school-children gather to watch the local team practise. The best source of general **information** is Souvenirs Río Sarapiquí (daily 8am–5.15pm; Ⓣ 766-6727), diagonally across from the Banco Nacional. It's run by the knowledgeable and affable Luis Alberto Sanchez, who can make reservations for lodges and hotels in the area, arrange transfers to La Fortuna, rafting trips and boat rides on the Río Sarapiquí ($25 per person for 2hr), plus tours to the Tortuguero/Barra del Colorado area staying at the *Samay Lagoon Lodge* (see p.185). He also sells bespoke gold jewellery and other well above average souvenirs, some made by local craftspeople.

There's an efficient **Banco de Costa Rica** on the main street, a **Banco Nacional** on the corner of the little road heading to the docks, and a **correo** (Mon–Fri 7am–5pm) on the corner where the main street joins the road to the dock. Locals hang out around the **taxi rank** next to the soccer field (there is a taxi line-up sign). If none is parked you'll see plenty roving around the area – look out for tough-looking red four-wheel drives. They'll theoretically take you anywhere, and prices are more or less fixed: it's about $2.50 per person to La Selva, and around $8 per person to Rara Avis.

Eating and drinking

Mi Lindo Sarapiquí on the main street is the place **to eat**, with an extensive menu of good *típico* food and what may well be the best hamburgers and fries in the country. At night it becomes a laidback **bar**, and is the best place in town to sit and have a beer. The busy and surprisingly smart bus station has an excellent cheap **snack bar**, while the soda near the dock by the river serves drinks, *empanadas* and other snacks – a pleasant spot to while away an hour with a cold beer, watching the activity at the docks. A few **fruit stalls** on the main street sell seasonal treats such as *mamones chinos*, the spiky lychees that look like vivid sea anemones. Considering Puerto Viejo is on the fringes of one of the biggest **banana**-producing zones in the country, if not in all Central America, bananas are something you won't see much of around town – they're all exported.

Accommodation around Puerto Viejo de Sarapiquí

Although La Selva, Selva Verde and Rara Avis are the prime tourist destinations in this area, there are also a number of very attractive **hotels** and **lodges** dotted around Puerto Viejo that allow you to experience something of the **rainforest**. In general they're reasonably priced and accessible, and some offer packages from San José. If you're travelling by bus and the accommodation is west of Puerto Viejo, you could also take the San José–Río Frío bus via Heredia (see above). Anything in Puerto Viejo itself or east of it can be reached more quickly by the service to Río Frío/Puerto Viejo via the Guápiles Highway.

Moving on from Puerto Viejo

Puerto Viejo is a transport hub for the entire Zona Norte and eastern side of the country. From here it's possible to travel back to the Valle Central, either via the Guápiles Highway (1hr 30min or more) or via Varablanca and Heredia (3hr or more). You can also cut across country west to San Carlos (3 hr) and on to Fortuna (3–4hr) and Volcán Arenal, from where it's easy to continue, via Tilarán, to Monteverde and Guanacaste.

By river it's possible to continue north from Puerto Viejo along the Río Sarapiquí to the Nicaraguan border then east along the Río San Juan to Barra and Tortuguero on the Caribbean coast. You'll have to rent a private *lancha* to do this pleasant journey, which can take anywhere between four and seven hours (you're going upstream). It's fairly pricey, unless you're in a group of eight or so – about $300 (8–10 maximum capacity). Ask at Souvenirs Río Sarapiquí or at the docks.

For a full rundown of routes within the Zona Norte, see opposite.

Ara Ambigua, 400m down a signed gravel road just to the right as you leave Puerto Viejo (T & F 766-6971, mobile 393-5026). Lovely rustic cottages, nicely furnished and impeccably clean. Rooms come with private bath, hot water and fan, and prices are frankly a steal, with singles for just $10. It's worth a visit just for the splendid food – try the chicken brochettes – dished up by owners Lisbeth and Delfin in the pseudo-Baroque restaurant, complete with giant gold-painted wooden chandelier. ❸

Islas del Río Adventure Center, 6km west of Puerto Viejo, 2km west of Chilamate (T 766-6574). Occupying a singular location on two islets in the Rio Sarapiqui, the pleasant, rustic rooms here have heated water, and there's a small network of on-site trails for walking and riding, plus a restaurant with riverside patio. Discounts (30 percent) are available for IYHF members; reserve at the *Toruma* hostel in San José (see p.84). Breakfast included. ❹

La Quinta, 7km west of Puerto Viejo, and 5km east of La Virgen (T & F 761-1052, W www.quintasarapiqui.com). On the banks of the Río Sardinal, near Selva Verde, this comfortable lodge has 23 rooms, all with ceiling fans and hot water, set in bungalows scattered throughout the property. Activities include swimming in the pool or river, exploring the lodge's own cultivated lands, its butterfly garden and the new on-site exhibition, "Jewels of the Rainforest", featuring a massive collection of butterflies and insects. The owners have also set up ingenious riverside "frog-watching posts" where you're virtually guaranteed to see colourful little poison-dart frogs. There's a pleasant outdoor restaurant, and biking, horse-riding and bird-watching can all be arranged. ❹

Posada Andrea Cristina, 1km west of Puerto

Viejo (T & F 766-6265). Simple rooms with fan and private bath – try the nice A-frame cabins, with high wooden ceilings – along with the best breakfasts, coffee and conversation in the area. Many people stay here for the family atmosphere and use it as a base to explore the area, including Tortuguero; the owners can advise on and arrange trips throughout the area. ❹

Rancho Leona, La Virgen, 12km west of Puerto Viejo (T 761-1019 or 269-9410, W www.rancholeona.com). Set right by the river in landscaped gardens, with comfortable rustic bunk-bed rooms, some with verandas, and a homely atmosphere – guests really do feel part of the family. The lodge specializes in kayaking, offering good-value two-night packages and river trips, though you don't have to kayak to enjoy it here. You can cook for yourself in the communal kitchen or try the restaurant's wholesome vegetarian cooking. ❸

Sarapiquí Ecolodge, 4km south of Puerto Viejo, across the river from the La Selva Biological Station (T 766-6122; F 253-8645). The home and working farm of the Murillo family, offering many of the same facilities and activities as La Selva, including horse-riding, bird-watching excursions, boat trips and hiking (all cost extra). No luxury accommodation here, but the dormitory bunk-beds are comfortable enough, and prices include generous meals. $15 per person.

Sarapiquis Centro Neotrópico, 2km east of La Virgen (T 761-1004, F 761-1415, W www.sarapiquis.org). Part-funded by the Belgian government, this unique place – half hotel, half educational centre – has its own rainforest reserve, botanical garden and greenhouse, all contained in a replica of a fifteenth-century pre-Columbian village. The 24 rooms are housed in large *palenques* (round buildings based on an indigenous design); all have a private terrace and bath with solar-heated hot water (waste water is recycled, and there's even an organic biological sewage treatment, the only one in Costa Rica). A museum to the Votos, the ancient people of the area, is being created, and a pre-Colombian grave has recently been unearthed in the grounds. There's a bar and restaurant, too (meals not included in room rate).

⑥

Travel details

Buses

Fortuna to: San Carlos (6 daily; 1hr); San José (3 daily; 4hr 30min); San Rafael de Guatuso (2 daily; 1hr); Tilarán (2 daily; 2hr).

Los Chiles to: San Carlos (10 daily; 2hr 30min).

Puerto Viejo de Sarapiquí to: San Carlos (3 daily; 3hr); San José (via Guápiles Highway, 7 daily; 1hr 30min–3hr; via Heredia, 3 daily; 3–4hr).

San Carlos to: Fortuna (6 daily; 1hr); Los Chiles (10 daily; 2hr 30min); Puerto Viejo de Sarapiquí (3 daily; 3hr); San José (14 daily; 3hr); San Rafael de Guatuso (5 daily); Tilarán (1 daily; 2hr).

San José to: Fortuna (3 daily; 4hr 30min); Los Chiles (2 daily; 5hr); Puerto Viejo de Sarapiquí and Río Frío (via Guápiles Highway, 7 daily; 1hr 30min–3hr: via Heredia, 3 daily; 3–4hr); San Carlos (14 daily; 3hr); Tilarán (4 daily; 4–5hr).

Tilarán to: Fortuna (2 daily; 2hr); San Carlos (1 daily; 2hr); San José (4 daily; 4–5hr); Santa Elena, for Monteverde (1 daily; 3–4hr).

Guanacaste

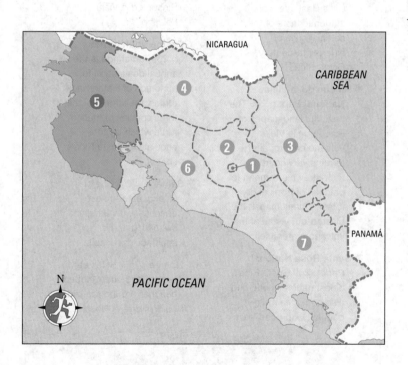

CHAPTER 5

Highlights

＊ **Cowboys** p.235 Skilful and self-reliant, Guanacastes' cowboys – or *sabaneros* – encapsulate the history of Costa Rica's vibrant rural communities.

＊ **Calle Real, Liberia** p.247 The recently restored Calle Real offers an authentic taste of the colonial style of nineteenth-century Costa Rica.

＊ **Rincón de la Vieja National Park** p.249 The beautiful landscapes of Rincón de la Vieja Volcano encompass terrains varying from rock-strewn savannah to patches of tropical dry forest, culminating in the blasted-out vistas of the volcano crater itself.

＊ **Santa Rosa National Park** p.253 Costa Rica's oldest national park, and also one of its most popular, with good trails, great surfing and plenty of turtle-spotting opportunities.

＊ **Albergue Buenavista** p.251 Ride with the cowhands at this working cattle ranch or explore the marvellous trails around the flanks of Rincón de la Vieja Volcano.

＊ **Leatherback turtles** p.268 Tamarindo is the annual destination for hundreds of leatherback turtles, the largest of the three species of marine turtle which lay their eggs along Costa Rica's shores.

＊ **Sámara** p.278 One of Guanacaste's finest beaches, with excellent swimming and spectacular sunsets.

＊ **Nosara** p.281 Relax at the remote and undeveloped beaches around the laid-back village of Nosara.

5

Guanacaste

Those features in which the inhabitants of Guanacaste resemble Nicaraguans and differ from the rest of Costa Rica, so far as I could learn, are: their racial character, the Indian element being furnished by the Chorotegan tribe not found east of the Cordillera de Tilarán; many peculiar idioms not in use elsewhere in Costa Rica; a farm life of different character; the use of the marimba as a musical instrument; and certain peculiar dances . . .

Amelia Smith Calvert and Philip Powell Calvert,
A Year of Costa Rican Natural History

Considering it was written in 1910, biologist Smith Calvert's description of the cultural profile of Guanacaste is still remarkably apt. For the inhabitants of the Valle Central – whom *Guanacastecos* still sometimes call "*Cartagos*", an archaic term dating back to the eighteenth century when Cartago was Costa Rica's capital – **Guanacaste province**, hemmed in by mountains to the east and the Pacific to the west, and bordered on the north by Nicaragua, is distinctly Other. Though little tangible remains of the dance, music and folklore for which the region is famous, there is undeniably something special about the place. Granted that much of the **landscape** has come about essentially through the slaughter of tropical dry forest, it is still some of the prettiest you'll see in the country, especially in the wet season, when wide-open spaces, stretching from the ocean across savannah grasses to the brooding humps of volcanos, are washed in a beautifully muted range of earth tones, blues, yellows and mauves. Its **history**, too, is distinct. If not for a very close vote in 1824, it might have been part of Nicaragua, which would have made Costa Rica very small indeed.

Accommodation price codes

All the accommodation in this book has graded using the following price codes. The prices quoted are for the least expensive double room in high season, and do not include the 18.46 percent national tax which is automatically added onto hotel bills. For more details on accommodation in Costa Rica, see p.35.

❶ less than $10	❷ $10–20
❸ $20–30	❹ $30–50
❺ $50–75	❻ $75–100
❼ $100–150	❽ over $150

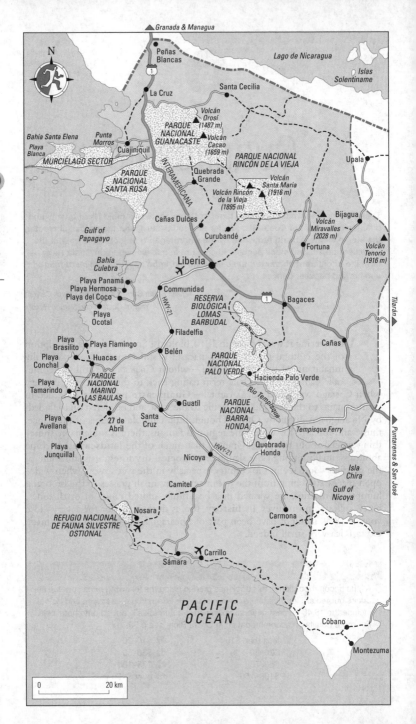

0   20 km

The dry heat, relatively accessible terrain and panoramic views make Guanacaste the best place in the country for **walking** and **horse-riding**, especially around the mud pots and stewing sulphur waters of **Parque Nacional Rincón de la Vieja**, and through the tropical dry forest cover of **Parque Nacional Santa Rosa**. For many travellers, however, Guanacaste means only one thing: **beaches**. Most of these are found where the **Nicoya Peninsula** joins the mainland (roughly two-thirds of the mountainous peninsula is in Guanacaste, with the lower third belonging to Puntarenas province, covered in Chapter 6), and they range from simple hideaways to huge mega-resorts aimed at the North American winter market. That said, however, many of the province's beaches are not particularly beautiful, nor are all of them great for swimming, though some are used as nesting grounds for several species of **marine turtles**. The only **towns** of any significance for travellers are the provincial capital of **Liberia**, and **Nicoya**, the main town on the peninsula. If you are overnighting on the way to **Nicaragua**, La Cruz makes a useful base.

Highland Ticos tend to describe Guanacaste as a virtual desert, liberally applying the words *caliente* (hot) and *seco* (dry). Certainly it is dry, in comparison to the rest of the country: parts of it receive only 500mm of rain a year, ten times less than on the Caribbean coast. To some extent irrigation has helped, but in summer (Dec–March) Guanacaste still experiences some drought. This is when you'll see an eerie landscape of bare, silver-limbed trees glinting in the sun, as many trees shed their leaves in order to conserve water. The province is significantly greener, and prettier, in the wet season (May–Nov), which is generally agreed to be the **best time** to come, with the added benefit of fewer travellers and lighter rainfall than the rest of the country receives during these months.

Today, Guanacaste is a province on the verge of great change, with the opening of a new international **airport** near Liberia and growing numbers of hotel mega-developments. To date, the airport receives mostly winter charters and

Cowboy culture in Guanacaste

Much of Guanacaste has long been turned into pasture for cattle ranching, and a huge part of the region's appeal is its sabanero (cowboy) culture. As in the US, the *sabanero* has come to be seen as a mythical figure – industrious, free-spirited, monosyllabic, a skilful handler of animals and the environment – and his rough, tough body, clad in jeans with leather accoutrements symbolizes "authenticity" (women get assigned a somewhat less exciting role in this rural mythology: the *cocinera*, or cook). In reality, however, the life of the *sabaneros* is hard, working often in their own smallholdings or as *peones* (farm workers) on large haciendas owned by relatively well-off ranchers.

To witness the often extraordinary skills of the *sabaneros*, head for the smaller towns – particularly on the Nicoya Peninsula – where during the months of January and February weekend fiestas are held in the local *redondel de toros* (bullring). Unlike in Spain, no gory kills are made: the spectacle comes from amazing feats of bull riding and roping. You'll see cowboys riding alongside the Interamericana, too, often towing two or three horses behind them as big transport trucks steamroller past on their way to Nicaragua. This dependence on cattle culture has its downside, however: much of Guanacaste is degraded pastureland, abandoned either because of its exhaustion by grazing or as a result of continually poor domestic and foreign markets for Costa Rican meat. Although impressive efforts to regenerate former tropical dry forest are under way – at Parque Nacional Santa Rosa and Parque Nacional Guanacaste, for example – it is likely that this rare lifezone will never recover its original profile.

has not had the explosive effect on a culturally fragile area which had been feared, although the appearance of *Burger King* and *McDonald's* in the dignified streets of Liberia is jarring. There seems no getting away from "progress", however, and the province may become many tourists' first, and perhaps only, glimpse of the country.

For now, **access** to most of Guanacaste from the Valle Central by road is easy, via the Interamericana, which runs right through to the Nicaraguan border at Peñas Blancas – though hazards such as falling mangos, dead monkeys, iguanas, cyclists, school children and traffic cops are all common along this road. Modern, comfortable **buses** ply the highway, with good services to Cañas, Liberia and the border. The national parks of Rincón de la Vieja and Santa Rosa are trickier to reach, however, and bus travellers should reckon on some walking, taxi-ing and hitching. All the beaches are accessible by bus and car, although the roads are not in fantastic shape, and journeys from San José can take at least five hours – those on the top half of the Nicoya Peninsula are the easiest to get to.

Some history

Due to significant excavations in the area and some contemporaneous Spanish accounts, Guanacaste's **pre-Columbian** history is better documented than in the rest of Costa Rica. Archeologists have long been interested in the **Chorotegas** – considered to have been the most highly developed of all Costa Rica's scattered and mutually isolated pre-Columbian peoples, but whose culture predictably went into swift decline after the Conquest – and in the entire area of Guanacaste. In archeological terms it belongs to the **Greater Nicoya Sub-area**, a pre-Columbian designation that includes some of western Nicaragua, and which continues to throw up buried clues to the extent of communication between the Maya and Aztec cultures to the north and smaller groups inhabiting Mesoamerica from the fifth to fifteenth centuries.

Following the conquest, the region became part of the administrative entity known as the **Captaincy General of Guatemala**. Guanacaste was annexed to Nicaragua in 1787, but in 1812 the Spanish rulers about-faced and donated the province to Costa Rica, so that its territory became large enough for it to be officially represented in the Captaincy. When the modern-day Central American nations declared independence from Spain, and the Captaincy was dissolved in 1821, Guanacaste found itself in the sensitive position of being claimed by both Costa Rica and Nicaragua. In an 1824 vote the province's inhabitants made their allegiances clear: the *Guanacastecos* in the north, traditionally cattle ranchers with familial ties to Nicaragua, voted to join that country, while the inhabitants of the Nicoya Peninsula wished to maintain links with Costa Rica. The peninsular vote won out, by a slim margin.

As the nineteenth century progressed, **cattle ranching** consolidated and began to dominate the landscape, providing the mainstay of the economy until well into the 1900s. Despite the continuing presence of the cattle culture and the *sabanero* in Guanacaste, however, beef prices have been dropping in Costa Rica for some years now: in 1993–94 meat exports declined 17 percent. In contrast, as in the rest of the country, the **tourist industry** is becoming increasingly important to the local economy.

Part of Guanacaste's prettiness is due to the pastel puffs of colour which the province's many flowering trees give to the landscape. Trees blossom in a strange way in the dry lands of Guanacaste, flowering literally overnight and then, just as suddenly, shedding their petals to the ground, covering it in a carpet of confetti colours. The **corteza amarilla** bursts into a wild Van Gogh-like blaze of colour in March, April and May, all the more dramatic for being set against a landscape of burnt siennas, muted mauves and sallow yellows.

In November the deciduous **guachipelín** tree blooms, with its delicate fern-like leaves; in January it's time for the pastel-pink floss of the **poui**, followed in March by the equally pretty **tabebuia rosea**. By the end of the dry season the red flowers of the **malinche** explode into colour.

The Río Tempisque area: north to Liberia

From San José the Autopista General Cañas leads 95km to the Puntarenas turn-off and the Interamericana (Hwy-1). For Guanacaste and Nicaragua, you turn off to the right, heading north. Eventually, neat white fences of cattle *fincas* begin to appear, with stretches of cleared land on both sides of the highway. Heading north to Liberia you pass the turn-off for Las Juntas de Abangares on your right, one possible route to Monteverde and Santa Elena (see p.293), while on the left is the road to the Río Tempisque, Guanacaste's principal drainage river, and the ferry across its estuary. Beyond Cañas, protected areas administered by the **Area de Conservación Tempisque** (ACT) encompass **Parque Nacional Palo Verde**, an important site for migratory birds, **Reserva Biológica Lomas Barbudal**, and the deep underground caves of **Parque Nacional Barra Honda** on the Nicoya Peninsula, just across the Río Tempisque (see p.284).

The **ACT head office** (Mon–Fri 8am–4pm; ☎671-1062), on the Interamericana across from the turn-off to Parque Nacional Palo Verde, is not set up for tourists, though staff can advise on current road conditions. For general information, it's best to head to Palo Verde itself.

Volcán Miravalles and Volcán Tenorio

North of the Interamericana beyond the town of Cañas, the two peaks of Volcán Miravalles and Volcán Tenorio are clearly visible from the hot Guanacaste lowlands, but merit closer inspection if you're adventurous and have a bit of time to kill. From the Reserva Biológica Privada La Pacifica, 7km north of Cañas, turn north off the Interamericana onto the road to Upala, a paved and reasonably maintained 58-kilometre stretch which runs between the two volcanoes, and from which you can contemplate the spectacular colour changes and cloud-shadows on their flanks. **Miravalles**, the highest volcano in Guancaste, is home to an important forest reserve, containing abundant wildlife and birds, though it's not open to the public. An active volcano, although so far without spectacular eruptive displays, **Tenorio** has recently been designated a national park, although there are no services or hiking trails as yet. Indeed, it's advisable not to walk around in this area, especially in places where you can see

Greater Nicoya (modern-day Guanacaste) was an archeological and cultural buffer zone between the complex cultures of the Aztecs and the Maya to the north, and the simpler agrarian cultures to the south, who had more in common with the prehistoric peoples of the Amazon basin. Greater Nicoya was occupied from an indeterminate date by the **Nicoyans**, about whom little is known, but most of the historical and archeological facts discovered about the region relate to the peoples known as the **Chorotegas**, who arrived in Nicoya in 800 AD, though some sources date their arrival as late as the fourteenth century, fleeing social and political upheavals far to the north.

The central Mexican empire of Teotihuacán, near the Mexico City of today, had fallen into disorganization by about 650 AD, and was abandoned about one hundred years later, at the same time that the Classic Maya civilizations of modern-day Yucatán and northern Guatemala also collapsed. New **fragmented groups** were created, some of whom forged migratory, militaristic, bands. In the eighth century, harassed by their territorial enemies the Olmecs, groups of Maya and Aztecs migrated south. Among them were the people who would become known as Chorotegas. The word Chorotega derives from either their place of origin, Cholula, or from two words in the Chorotegan language: *cholol* (to run or escape) and *teca* (people – "the people who escaped").

Evidence of immediate and long-term cultural upheaval in the area after 800 AD includes a significant increase in the number of Nicoyan **burial sites** found dating from around this time. The use of objects associated with elites – like ceremonial skulls, jades and elaborate metates – suddenly declined almost to the point of disappearing completely, and populations seem to have migrated from the interior toward the coasts. While this evidence could suggest a natural disaster (a volcanic eruption, perhaps) it also bears the hallmarks of what could be termed an invasion.

The Chorotegas' first contact with the **Spanish** was not fortuitous. The 1522 Spanish expedition from Panamá up the Pacific coast to Nicaragua brought smallpox, the plague and influenza to the indigenous people of Greater Nicoya. Imprisonment and slavery followed, with coastal peoples raided, branded and sold into slavery in Panamá and Peru. The demise of the Chorotegas from the sixteenth century was rapid and unreversed.

Excavations in Guanacaste and the Nicoya Peninsula reveal something of the

fumaroles (little columns of hot vapour escaping from the ground), and certainly not anywhere near mud pots – one false move and you could step into skin-stripping volcanic superheated soil. The ICE (Costa Rican Electricity Institute) signs hereabouts point towards several geothermal plants where geologists are successfully exploiting heat vents far below the surface to tap much-needed new sources of energy.

About 35km along the road to Upala is the small hamlet of **BIJAGUA**, where you can **stay** in the *Las Heliconias Ecotourist Lodge* (☎259-3605, Ⓦwww.toursexplore.com; ❹). The lodge is located on a private forest reserve set right between the volcanos, with hiking trails, waterfalls and natural hot springs. Rooms are in six cabins, all with private bath, and there's a restaurant and stunning views throughout. Bijagua itself is an impressively enterprising community, home to a number of ecotourism projects, including an ecology centre, organic farms and a collective of women artisans. The lodge can arrange trips to the Refugio Natural Caño Negro (see p.215), travelling via the spectacular road to Upala, from where you can glimpse Lago Nicaragua, and the Solentiname islands shimmering in its blue waters.

The new **La Carolina Lodge**, 6km east from Bijagua, in the hamlet of San

Chorotega's belief systems and social arrangements. Excavations near Bahía Culebra unearthed pottery shards, utensils and the remains of hearths, along with a burial ground holding twenty females, children and infants. Chorotega villages were made up of longhouse-type structures – common to many indigenous cultures of the Americas – inhabited by entire extended families, and centred on a large square, site of religious ceremonies and meetings.

Like the Maya and Aztecs, the Chorotegas had a belief system built around blood-letting and the sacrifice of animals and humans. Although it is not known whether beating hearts were ripped from chests, virgins were definitely thrown into volcano craters, all in order to appease their gods, about whom little is known. Chorotegas also believed in yulios, the spirit alter ego that escaped from their mouths at the moment of death to roam the world for ever. Although pagan, Chorotega priests shared a number of duties and functions with the Catholic priests who worked to destroy their culture. Celibate, they may also have heard confessions and meted out punishments for sins.

The Chorotega economy was based on maize (corn). They also cultivated tobacco, fruit, beans and cotton, using cacao beans as currency, and the marketplace was run by women. All land was held communally, as was everything that was cultivated and harvested, which was then distributed throughout the settlement. This plurality did not extend to social prestige, however. Three strata characterized Chorotega society: at the upper echelon were chieftains (caciques), warriors and priests; in the middle were the commoners, and at the bottom were the slaves and prisoners of war. The Chorotegas were the only indigenous peoples in Costa Rica to have a written language, comprising hieroglyphs similar to those used by the Maya, and were also skilled artisans, producing ornamental jewellery and jade, and colouring cotton fabrics with animal and vegetable dye. They also made the bulk of the distinctive ceramics so celebrated in the country today, many of which can be seen in San José's Museo Nacional (for more on Chorotega pottery, see p.276).

Few Chorotega rituals are documented. One known practice was the formation of a kind of human maypole, consisting of voladores, or men suspended "flying" (actually roped) from a post, twirling themselves round and round while descending to the ground. Originating with the Aztecs, the display is no longer seen in Costa Rica, though it is still performed in the Mexican state of Veracruz and in certain villages in Guatemala.

Miguel (T 380-1656, W www.lacarolinalodge.com; ©), is a rustic lodge set in a working farm well off the beaten path in extremely quiet surroundings. There's a (swimmable) river by the lodge, where toucans, green parrots, and hummingbirds nest, while you might also see sloths and anteaters. There are four rooms (one sleeping up to seven people), and home-style meals are included in the very reasonable price. The owners offer transport from Liberia (about $75 per carload); alternatively, there are also three buses daily from Cañas to Bijagua, from where a taxi to the lodge costs about $12.

You can also stay near Volcán Miravalles on the side facing Rincón de la Vieja volcano (see p.251).

Parque Nacional Palo Verde

About 30km west of Cañas on the northern bank of the Río Tempisque is the **PARQUE NACIONAL PALO VERDE** (daily 8am–4pm; $6), created in 1982 specifically to preserve the habitat of the **migratory birds** which nest in the estuary of the Tempisque and a large patch of relatively undisturbed lowland dry forest. With a distinctive topography featuring ridged limestone hills

– unique to this part of the country, and attesting to the fact that certain parts of Guanacaste were once under water – the park shelters about fifteen separate ecological habitats. From December to May, Palo Verde can dry out into baked mud flats, while in the wet season, extensive flooding gives rise to saltwater and freshwater lakes and swamps. Following the wet season, the great floodplain drains slowly, creating marshes, mangroves and other habitats favoured by migratory birds. Little visited by tourists, the park is mainly of interest for serious **birders**, but what you see depends on the time of year – by far the **best months** are at the height of the dry season (Jan–March), when most of the 250 or so migratory species are in residence. In the wet season, flooding makes parts of the park inaccessible.

The park is home to one of the largest concentrations of **waterfowl** in Central America, both indigenous and migratory, with more than three hundred species of birds, among them the endangered Jabirú stork and black-crowned night herons. Further from the river bank, in the tree cover along the bottom and ridges of the limestone hills, you may spot toucans, and perhaps even one of the increasingly rare scarlet macaws. At evening during the dry season, many birds and other species – monkeys, coatis and even deer – congregate around the few remaining waterholes; bring binoculars and a torch. Note, though, that you shouldn't swim in the Río Tempisque (or anywhere else), as it's home to particularly huge crocodiles – some, according to the park rangers, are as much as five metres long.

From the administration building (see below), two **trails** lead up to the top of hills, from where you can see the expansive mouth of the Río Tempisque to the west and the broad plains of Guanacaste to the east. A number of other **loop trails**, none more than 4km long, run through the park. The shortest of the trails, at just 300m, is **Las Calizas**; others include **El Manigordo** ("ocelot"; 1.5km), **El Mapache** ("racoon"; 2km) and **Venado** ("deer"; 2km), all of which give you a good idea of the landscape and a chance of sighting the animals after which they're named. You've also got a good chance of seeing a collared peccary, which are abundant in this area, while another common mammal you may see or hear foraging in the undergrowth is the coatimundi; white-tailed deer also live here, but they're very shy and likely to dart off at the sound of your approach.

For longer treks, try the **Bosque Primario** trail (about 7km), through, as the name suggests, primary forest cover, or walk the 6km (dry season only) to the edge of the Río Tempisque from where you can see the aptly named **Isla de los Pájaros** (Bird Island). Square in the mouth of the river, the island is chock-full of birds all year, with black-crowned night herons swirling above in thick dark clouds. Many hotels and tour agencies in the province offer boat trips around the island, but landings are not permitted, so you have to content yourself with bird-spotting and taking photographs from the boat.

Check with rangers regarding conditions before walking on any of the trails: access is constantly subject to change, due to flooding (and sometimes bee colonies), and the Río Tempisque walk in particular can be muddy and unpleasantly insect-ridden in all but the driest months. You should bring plenty of water, as the heat and humidity are considerable. A note on **safety** in Palo Verde: in recent years swarms of **Africanized bees** – sometimes sensationally termed "killer bees" – have taken to colonizing the area. Africanized bees are aggressive, and may pursue – in packs – anyone who unwittingly disturbs one of their large, quite obvious, nests. The usual advice is to cover your head and run in a zigzag pattern so that you can dodge the cloud of pursuing bees. Although, luckily, this occurs very rarely, you should take special care if you are

sensitive to stings, and ask the rangers about the presence of nests on or around trails. Bees are also to be found in the Lomas Barbudal Reserve (see below).

Practicalities

Getting to Palo Verde takes a while, though it is possible with a regular non-4WD vehicle in the dry season. From the well-signed turn-off from the Interamericana at Bagaces (opposite the ACT head office, where you can check out current road conditions) it's a thirty-kilometre drive to the entrance hut, and a further 9km to the administration building. There are signs all along the road to the park, but at long intervals, and the road forks unnervingly from time to time without indicating which way to go. If in doubt, follow the tyre tracks made by the rangers.

The Organization for Tropical Studies (OTS) has a field station at Palo Verde, originally set up for comparative ecosystem study and research into the dry forest habitat. If you contact their San José office (℡240-6696 ℻240-6783, ℮reservas@ns.ots.ac.cr) in advance you may be able to stay in their rustic **field station**, next door to the administration building (⑤), providing it's not full of scientific researchers. There's also a rustic but perfectly comfortable **albergue** at the ranger station, about 10km from the entrance. The six rooms here each contain six bunk beds ($12 per person), including mosquito nets and fans, and meals are available (breakfast $3; lunch and dinner $5). You can also **camp** ($2 per day) at the small site next to the administration building, where there are lavatories, but it's best to call ahead on ℡671-1290 or 671-1062 and check there's space.

Reserva Biológica Lomas Barbudal

Created by locals for locals, the **RESERVA BIOLÓGICA LOMAS BAR-BUDAL** (daily 8am-4pm; $6) is an impressive, though small-scale, initiative about 20km west of Bagaces. Home to some of the last vestiges of true **tropical dry forest** in the region, the reserve's vegetation still looks a bit ravaged from the terrible El Niño-inspired drought of 1997. Lomas Barbudal means "bearded hills" and that's just what they look like – although less so since the drought – with relatively bare pates surrounded by sideburns of bushy decid-uous trees. Stretches of savannah-like open grassland are punctuated by the thorny-looking **shoemaker's tree** and crisscrossed by rivers and the strips of deciduous woods that hug their banks. The reserve also features isolated exam-ples of the majestic **mahogany** and **rosewood** trees, whose deep blood-red timber is coveted as material for furniture.

Lomas Barbudal is also rich in **wildlife**: you'll hear howler monkeys, at least, even if you don't spot one, and this is practically the only place along the entire Guanacaste coast where you have a reasonable chance of seeing the **scarlet macaw**. Like Parque Nacional Santa Rosa to the north, Lomas Barbudal hosts an abundance of **insects** – some 200 to 300 **bee species** alone, around 25 per-cent of the species of bees in the entire world. Those allergic to stings or oth-erwise intolerant of the insects might want to give Lomas Barbudal a miss; they're everywhere, including the aggressive Africanized bees (see p.240).

Practicalities

Although you could take a **taxi** (about $30 return) to Lomas Barbudal from Bagaces, it is best reached with your own transport. Take the road north from Bagaces, and after about 7km follow the road off to the left. The administra-tion office lies 6km further, prettily set on the banks of the Río Cabuyo. You can **camp** ($2.50 per night), but bring your own water and food; there are no lavatories. There are also two swimmable rivers, a small network of trails designed and cleared by local volunteers, and a visitor centre.

Tropical dry forest

With its mainly deciduous cover, Guanacaste's tropical dry forest, created by the combination of a Pacific lowland topography and arid conditions, looks startlingly different depending upon the time of year. In the height of summer (approximately Nov–March), almost no rain falls on lowland Guanacaste, the trees are bare, having shed their leaves in an effort to conserve water, and the landscape takes on a melancholy, burnt-sienna hue. In April or May, when the rains come, the whole of Guanacaste perks up and begins to look comparatively green, although the dry forest never takes on the lush look of the rainforest.

The story of the demise of the tropical dry forests in Mesoamerica is one of nearly wholesale destruction. In all, only about two percent of the region's pre-Columbian dry forest survives, and what was once a carpet stretching the length of the Pacific side of the isthmus from southern Mexico to Panamá now exists only in besieged pockets. Today, dry forests cover just 518 square kilometres of Costa Rica, almost all in Guanacaste, concentrated around the Río Tempisque and, more significantly, north in the Parque Nacional Santa Rosa. Due to deforestation and climatic change, tropical dry forests are considered a rare life zone. Their relative dryness means they are easily overrun by field fires, which ranchers light in order to burn off old pasture. Hardy grasses spring up in their wake, such as the imported African jaragua, which gives much of Guanacaste its African, savannah-like appearance.

Along with the leafy trees, tropical dry forest features palms and even a few evergreens. At the very top of a good thick patch of dry forest you see the umbrella form of canopy trees, although these are much shorter than in the tropical rainforest. Dry forest is a far less complex ecosystem than the humid rainforest, which has about three or four layers of vegetation (see p.418). Like temperate-zone deciduous forests, the tropical dry forest has only two strata. The ground shrub layer is fleshed out by thorn bushes and tree ferns, primitive plants that have been with us since the time of the dinosaurs. Unlike rainforest, dry forest has very few epiphytes (plants growing on the trees), except for bromeliads (the ones that look something like upside-down pineapple leaves). The most biologically diverse examples of tropical dry forest are in the lower elevations of Parque Nacional Santa Rosa, where the canopy trees are a good height, with many different species of deciduous trees. There are also some pockets of mangroves and even a few evergreens in the wetter parts of the park.

Tropical dry forests can support a large variety of mammal life, as in the Parque Nacional Santa Rosa–Parque Nacional Guanacaste corridor. Deer and smaller mammals such as the coatimundi and paca are most common, along with large cats, such as the jaguar and ocelot, provided they have enough room in which to hunt. You may see the endangered scarlet macaw, who likes to feed on the seeds of the sandbox tree, in a very few remaining pockets of Pacific dry forest, including Lomas Barbudal and, further south, around Río Tarcoles and Carara (see p.327), itself a transition zone between the dry forests of the north and the wetter tropical cover of the southern Pacific coast. In addition, a staggering number and diversity of insects makes the tropical dry forests of northern Guanacaste of interest to biologists and entomologists: there are more than two hundred types of bee in Lomas Barbudal, for example, and a large number of butterflies and moths in Parque Nacional Santa Rosa.

Liberia and around

True to its name, the spirited provincial capital of **LIBERIA** (from *libertad*, meaning liberty) has a distinctively free-thinking feel, its wide clean streets the legacy of the pioneering farmers and cattle ranchers who founded it. Known colloquially as the "Ciudad Blanca" (white city) due to its whitewashed houses, Liberia is the only town in the country that seems truly colonial in style and character, and many of the white houses still have their **puerta del sol** – corner doors that were used, ingeniously, to let the sun in in the morning and out in the late afternoon, thus heating and cooling the interior throughout the day – an architectural feature left over from the colonial era and particular to this region.

At present most travellers use Liberia simply as a jumping-off point for the national parks of **Rincón de la Vieja** and **Santa Rosa** or as an overnight stop-off en route either to the beaches of Guanacaste or to the Nicaraguan border. It's worth getting to know it better, however, for Liberia is actually one of the most appealing towns in Costa Rica, with everything you might need for a relaxing stay of a day or two – well-priced accommodation, a couple of nice places to eat and drink, and a cinema showing unusual English-language films. It's also a great place to do essential things like visiting the tourist office, checking your email and changing money. This may all change, of course, if the nearby international airport ever starts delivering passengers in large numbers, but for now Liberia is still the epitome of dignified (if somewhat static) provincialism, with a strong identity and atmosphere all its own.

Liberia also boasts several lively local **festivals**, the most elaborate of which is on July 25, **El Día de la Independencia**, celebrating Guanacaste's independence from Nicaragua with parades, horseshows, cattle auctions, rodeos, fiestas and roving marimba bands. If you want to attend, make bus and hotel reservations as far in advance as possible. The last week in September is known as the **Semana Cultural Liberia Ciudad Blanca**, offering similar goings-on but without the wild patriotic revelry of July's celebration; there's no need to book buses and hotels in advance.

Arrival and information

Liberia's international **airport** is connected to San José by regular Sansa and Travelair flights; you'll have to take a taxi from here into town ($5). **Buses** from San José pull in at Liberia's clean and efficient bus terminal on the western edge of town near the exit for the Interamericana – it's a ten-minute walk at most from here to the centre of town. **Drivers** enter from the Interamericana at an intersection with traffic lights and four gas stations – known as "La Esquina de las Bombas", or **Gas Station Corner** – and turn right into **Avenida Central**, lined with floppy mango trees. No one refers to *calles* and *avenidas* in Liberia: almost everything is described in terms of distance from the **church** or the **Gobernación**, the white house on the south side of the **Parque Central**.

Liberia's supremely helpful **tourist office** (Mon–Sat 9am–noon & 1–5pm, Sun 9am–1pm; ☎666-1606) is on C 1, five minutes' walk south of the Parque Central, in the same building as the Museo de Sabanero. Staff will make phone calls to book hotels or ask directions, and will even place international calls and faxes at cost. In the high season, especially, they also function partially as a **tour service**, using local operators. Staff speak some English and give unbiased

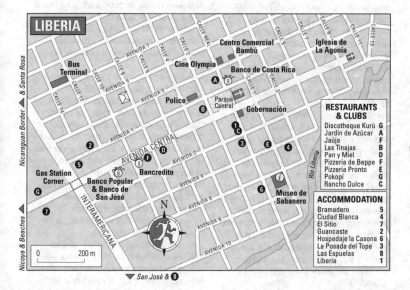

advice and information. The office is a non-profit-making service, and any donations are appreciated.

The efficient **correo**, Av 3, C 8 (Mon–Fri 7.30am–6pm, Sat 7.30am–noon), is a bit hard to find: it's the low-slung white house across from an empty square field bordered by mango trees. Liberia's one **internet café**, *Cybermania* (daily 8am-10pm), located in a small business centre on the north side of the Parque Central, is efficient, friendly, air-conditioned and cheap. There are plenty of **banks** in Liberia, many of them on Av Central, leading into town. The Banco de San José deals with Mastercard and Cirrus, while the Banco Popular next door does VISA and Plus cards – both have ATMs. The next one along, Bancredito seems to take both. The Banco de Costa Rica across from the Parque Central will change travellers' cheques, but its ATM only accepts Costa Rican-issued cards.

You can pick up the *Miami Herald* and *New York Times* **newspapers** from the Librería Universitaria on Av 1, 100m east of the Parque Central. For **souvenirs**, head to the Sabanero Art Market, 50m south of the *gobernación*, where you'll find a good selection of Chorotega-inspired copies of archeological pieces, local brands of coffee, T-shirts, beachwear and a selection of American magazines.

Accommodation

Liberia is the most convenient place to spend the night along this northern stretch of the Interamericana. Standards are generally very high and, though dirt-cheap places are scarce, the ones that do exist are good. Because of tourist traffic to and from the beaches, Liberia is chock-full in the dry season, especially weekends, and it is imperative to have a **reservation**. At other times, midweek especially, there's no problem with space.

Hotel Bramadero, Gas Station Corner (☎ 666-0371, ℻ 666-0203, ℮ bramadero@racsa.co.cr). The setting, beside the fuel pumps on the Interamericana, isn't the loveliest, but it's convenient for the beaches and popular with Ticos. Nondescript, basic rooms, good restaurant, plus pool. Try to get a room at the back, away from the highway. A good bet if everything else is full. ③–④

Hostal Ciudad Blanca, 200m south and 150m east of the *gobernación* (☎ 666-2715). Spotless hotel with a small breakfast terrace/bar, and twelve modern, a/c rooms with TV, private bath and ceiling fans. Popular with American travellers bedding down before heading out to the beach. ⑤

Hotel El Sitio, on the Nicoya road, 200m west of Gas Station Corner (☎ 666-1211, ℻ 666-2059, ℮ htlsitio@racsa.co.cr). Now part of the Best Western chain, this large motel-style hotel, shaded by huge Guanacaste trees, is a good option for families (despite a brash new casino on site), with an on-site pool and restaurant, and large rooms with a/c, TV and private bath. Buffet breakfast included. ⑤

Hotel Guanacaste, Av 1, 300m south of the bus station (☎ 666-0085; ℻ 666-2287, Ⓦ www.hostelling-costarica.com). Popular, HI-affiliated hotel, with a traveller-friendly cafeteria-restaurant. The rooms are simple, clean and dark; all but two have private bath. The hotel fills up quickly, so book ahead. If you have a HI card you get 15 percent discount; you might wangle a further 10 percent with student ID. The management organizes a daily transfer (small charge) to Rincón de la Vieja, and sells bus tickets to Nicaragua. Visa and Mastercard accepted. ①–②

Hospedaje La Casona, 300m south of the Parque Central (☎ 666-2971). Six basic and rather dark rooms with shared bath, arranged on either side of a long corridor. It's clean, cheap – and consequently often full – and there's a cable-TV lounge. ②

La Posada del Tope, 150m south of the *gobernación*, on C 0 (☎ 666-3876, ℻ 385-2383, ℮ hottope@racsa.co.cr). Popular, cheap budget option in a beautiful historic house. The six basic rooms with fan and shared showers in the old part of the hotel are a bit stuffy, but clean. The modern rooms across the street in a new annexe with cable TV cost about the same. There's a courtyard cafeteria-bar, plus free email, bike rental, and a rooftop telescope for star-gazing. The manager runs transport to Rincón de la Vieja for $11 per person roundtrip. Visa and Mastercard accepted. ②

Hotel Las Espuelas, 2km south of town, on the right (☎ 666-0144, ℻ 666-2441, ℮ espuelas@racsa.co.cr). The most upmarket hotel in the region, this low-slung hacienda-style building has friendly staff, a nice pool with poolside bar, a restaurant serving good steaks, and rooms with a/c and cable TV. ⑦

Hotel Liberia, C 0, 75m south of the Parque Central, (☎ & ℻ 666-0161). Established, friendly youth hostel-type hotel located in an historic house – look for the jolly papaya orange exterior. Rooms are set around a sunny but bare courtyard: the newer rooms in an annexe to the rear are better than the old ones, though they cost an extra $5. Popular with vacationing foreigners and Costa Ricans alike – a reservation and deposit are required in the high season – and they also organize transport to Rincón de la Vieja. Visa accepted. ①–②

The Town

Liberia's wide streets, used more by cyclists and horsemen than motorists, are shaded by mango trees that plop ripe fruit at your feet in March and April. The town is arranged around a large **Parque Central**, properly called Parque Mario Cañas Ruiz and dedicated to *el mes del annexion*, the month of the annexation (July), celebrating the fact that Guanacaste is not in Nicaragua. On the eastern edge of the Parque is the town **church**, a modern structure whose startlingly modernist – some would say downright ugly – form looks a little out of place in this very traditional town.

About 600m away down Avenida Central at the eastern end of town, the colonial **Iglesia de la Agonía** is more interesting, with a mottled yellow facade like a peeling, washed-out banana. On the verge of perpetual collapse – it has had a hard time from successive earthquakes – it's almost never open, but you could try shoving the heavy wooden door and hope the place doesn't collapse around you if it gives way.

The most interesting street in town is the **Calle Real** (marked as Calle Central on some maps). In the nineteenth century this street was the entrance to Liberia, and practically the entire thoroughfare has now been restored to its original colonial simplicity. Next to the *Posada del Tope* hotel is the home of Doña Emilia, which often has its door open to the street. If your Spanish is good, you might chat to the venerable Emilia, who comes from a old local family and who may show you around her stately living room, filled with antiques and old photographs, as her grown-up *sabanero* sons troop in and out.

Museo de Sabanero

Dusty mementoes of daily life on the old cattle ranches can be seen at the **Museo de Sabanero**, or Cowboy Museum (Mon–Sat 9am–noon & 1–5pm, Sun 9am–1pm; donation appreciated), housed in the same building as the tourist office. The small but interesting exhibition shows well-worn examples of objects that would have been found in the big ranch houses, or *casonas*, that formed the nucleus of the ranch communities. Entering the museum from the tourist office, you pass an enormous wooden hacienda table then come into the musty, low-lit world of the old adobe house. Here you'll see the taut skins of former cattle: bridles, chaps, boots and the *sabanero's* distinctive high-backed saddle, kept in place by a lariat wound around the horse's tail. Also on show are twirling spurs, old hacienda chairs, lariats smoothed with age, elaborate whips, branding irons and several unidentifiable tools which look like instruments of bovine torture.

> ### Tours from Liberia
>
> Guanacaste Tours in the *Hotel Bramadero*, Gas Station Corner (T 666-0306, F 666-0307), run various day-trips from Liberia and the surrounding area (they can provide pick-ups from hotels) to Río Tempisque and Palo Verde ($80) or the *casona* at Parque Nacional Santa Rosa – although these are relatively easy to get to even if you don't have a car. They also do turtle-watching tours – destinations and turtles depend on the time of year. Outside town, Safaris Corobicí, 5km before Cañas on the Interamericana (T 669-1091 or 669-2091, F 669-0544, W www.nicoya.com), specialize in floating trips on the Río Corobicí – guides row while you watch the howler monkeys, huge iguanas and caimans who inhabit the environs. They also do good 2–3hr bird-watcher's tour ($35–45) – mot-mots, cuckoos, laughing falcons, osprey eagles and herons, including the endangered Jabirú stork, have all been spotted along the Corobicí.

Eating, drinking and entertainment

Liberia has several **restaurants** serving local dishes such as **natilla** (soured cream) eaten with eggs or *gallo pinto* and tortillas. For a real feast, try the various **desayunos guanacastecos** (Guanacastecan breakfasts, consisting of tortillas, sour cream, eggs, rice and beans, and sometimes meat too). This is *sabanero* or, more properly, **criollo** food, made to be worked off with hard labour. For rock-bottom cheap **lunches**, head for the stalls in the bus terminal, Las Tinajas or Rancho Dulce in town, or at a number of fried chicken places. You can pick up Guanacastecan **corn snacks** from stalls all over town and at Gas Station Corner.

For **drinking**, places like *Las Tinajas* and *Pizzería Pronto* are good for a quiet beer. The town's one **disco**, *Kurú*, next to the *Pokopí* restaurant, gets lively with salsa and merengue, especially on weekends and holidays. The main Saturday evening activity, however, involves the locals parading around the Parque Central in their finery, hanging out, having an ice cream, and maybe going to the movies at the **Cine Olympia**, 100m north of the church, which shows a variety of English-language movies, including the latest art-house releases, as well as the usual action–adventure blockbusters.

La cocina Guanacasteca: corn cooking

Corn is still integral to the regional cuisine of Guanacaste, thanks to the Chorotegas, who cultivated maize (corn), to use in many inventive ways. One pre-Columbian corn concoction involved roasting, then grinding the maize, and combining the meal-like paste with water and chocolate to make the drink *chicha*. Although you can't find this version of *chicha* any more you can still get grain-based drinks in Guanacaste, such as *horchata* (made with rice or corn and spiced with cinnamon), or *pinolillo* (made with roasted corn), both milky and sweet, with an unmistakably grainy texture.

Corn also shows up in traditional Guanacastecan snacks such as tanelas (like a cheese scone, but made with cornflour) and rosquillas, small rings of cornflour that taste like a combination between tortillas and doughnuts. You can buy these at roadside stalls and small shops in Liberia, and from hawkers at both ends of the Tempisque ferry. Served throughout the country, chorreados crop up most often on menus in Guanacaste: they're a kind of pancake made (again) with cornflour and served with natilla, the local version of sour cream.

Restaurants, bars and sodas

Jardín de Azúcar, 100m north of the *gobernación* on C 0. Big breakfasts include the "Americano" (ham, egg, toast, plus coffee or tea) and the "Guanacasteco" (*gallo pinto, natilla*, tortillas and eggs), while later on you could opt for Liberia's cheapest grilled fish in garlic, all unfortunately accompanied by ear-splitting Latinopop and the cries of children in the adjacent play area.

Jauja/Pizzeria Da Beppe, Avenida Central. Good breakfasts and pizzas served in a pleasant outdoor garden setting.

Las Tinajas, west side of Parque Central. The outdoor tables on the verandah of this old house make a good spot for watching the goings-on in the Parque while enjoying a *refresco* or beer. Basic *casados* and excellent hamburgers ($3) are also served. There's live music on Thursdays and Sundays.

Pan y Miel, next to the *Restaurante Jauja* on Avenida Central. More a cafeteria than a restaurant, with buffet breakfasts, good cakes and coffee.

Pizzería Pronto, C 1, 200m south of the church. Situated in an old adobe house, with wooden tables and decor and a covered garden patio, the friendly *Pronto* serves excellent – if smallish – pizzas ($4–5) cooked in a giant wood oven. The restaurant's bar is popular with gringos.

Pokopí, 100m west of Gas Station Corner, on the road to Nicoya opposite *Hotel el Sitio*. Fastidiously clean (they mop the floor every two seconds) and decorated with colourful toucans, this pleasant restaurant serves huge, dripping burgers for $3, and very tasty snapper in garlic butter (*pargo en ajillo*) for about $7. Eat early on weekends, though: the *Kurú* disco starts up around 9.30, and might drown out your supper.

Rancho Dulce, 50m south of the *gobernación*. Tiny soda serving *casados*, sandwiches, *empanadas* and *refrescos*: great for a cheap lunch. You can sit at the tiny outdoor stools (if you have a small bottom) or tables.

As well as having good connections with San José (8 direct Pulmitan de Liberia buses daily), Liberia is also the main regional transport hub, providing easy access to Guanacaste's parks and beaches, and the Nicaraguan border. All buses leave from the terminal.

For the Parque Nacional Santa Rosa, take a La Cruz or Peñas Blancas (Nicaraguan border) bus (hourly) from the bus terminal. Take the earliest bus you can to give yourself time for walking, and ask the driver to let you off at Santa Rosa. If you want to get to the park's Murciélago sector, however, take the Cuajiniquil service (daily 3.30pm; 1hr 30min). The return bus is at 7.30am, so, allowing for a day in the Murciélago sector, it's a three-day trip. The Parque Nacional Guanacaste isn't really reachable by bus; you could theoretically take the 3pm bus to Quebrada Grande village, from where it's a walk of at least two hours – you'd arrive after closing time. If you're heading for the border, take one of the hourly buses to La Cruz or Peñas Blancas (the border's official name) (1hr). Services to Bagaces and Cañas leave the terminal at 5.45am, 1.30pm and 4.30pm, taking about forty minutes to an hour.

Colectivo taxis, shared between four or five people, can be good value if you're heading for Parque Nacional Rincón de la Vieja or the lodges near Las Espuelas ranger station. They line up at the northwestern corner of the Parque Central, and charge about $25 for four people; to Parque Nacional Santa Rosa the price is $15 per taxi. Arguably the best way to get to Rincón de la Vieja is to travel with one of the various Liberia hotels – *Posada del Tope*, *Hotel Liberia* and *Hotel Guanacaste* – which arrange transport to the park. All services are open to non-residents though hotel guests get first option. In each case, drop by beforehand to check if it's going.

There are direct services to the more northerly of Guanacaste's beaches: for Playas Hermosa and Panamá, two buses leave daily (11.30am & 7pm; 1hr). Playa del Coco is served by three or four services per day (5.30am, 12.30pm, 4.30pm and, high season only, 2pm; 1hr). You can also get to Santa Cruz (hourly 5.30am–7.30pm; 1hr), from where you can hook up with buses to Tamarindo, Junquillal and beaches further south. Buses for Nicoya leave on the hour from 5am to 7pm (2hr). Buses to Puntarenas leave at 5am, 8.30am, 10am, 11am and 3pm (3hr).

Parque Nacional Rincón de la Vieja

The beautifully dry landscape of **PARQUE NACIONAL RINCÓN DE LA VIEJA** (daily 8am–4pm; $6), about 30km northeast of Liberia, encompasses terrains varying from rock-strewn savannah to patches of tropical dry forest, culminating in the blasted-out vistas of the volcano crater itself. The land here is actually alive and breathing: Rincón de la Vieja's last major eruptions took place in 1995 and 1998, and were serious enough to cause some local residents to be evacuated. The danger has always been to the northern side of the volcano, facing Nicaragua (i.e. the opposite side from the two entrance points), and the most pressing **safety** issue for tourists is to be aware that rivers of lava and hot mud still broil beneath the thin epidermis of ground. While danger areas are clearly marked with signs and fences, you still have to watch your step: walkers have been seriously burned from crashing through this crust and stepping into mud and water at above-boiling temperatures.

With the right amount of caution, however, this is an enchanted place: brewing **mud pots** (*pilas de barro*) bubble, and puffs of steam rise out of lush foliage, signalling sulphurous subterranean springs. This is great terrain for **camping, riding** and **hiking**, with a comfortable, fairly dry heat – although it can get

damp and cloudy at the higher elevations around the crater. **Birders**, too, get excited about Rincón de la Vieja, as there are more than two hundred species in residence.

Getting to the park

The local dry season (Dec–March especially) is the **best time** to visit Rincón de la Vieja, when the hiking trails and visibility as you ascend the volcano are at their best. To make management of the forest more efficient, the park has been split into two **sectors**: Sector Pailas ("cauldrons") and Sector Santa Maria, each with its own **entrance** and ranger station. From Liberia most people travel through the hamlet of Curubandé, about 16km northeast, to the **Las Pailas** sector. The other ranger station, **Santa María**, lies about 25km northeast from Liberia. The **casona** that houses the ranger station here is a former retreat of US president Lyndon Baines Johnson, and, at more than 110 years old, is ancient in Costa Rican terms.

Both routes to the park are along stony roads, not at all suitable for walking. People do, but it's tough, uninteresting terrain, and it is really more advisable to save your energy for the trails within the park itself. Options for getting here from Liberia include either renting a *colectivo* **taxi** or taking the private transport which is laid on by several hotels in Liberia (see p.245); **hitching** is also an option if you can find a truck driver making a delivery, possibly at one of the gas stations at Gas Station Corner on the Interamericana at Liberia. Alternatively, you could **rent a car** (you'll need a 4WD), and stay in one of the upmarket tourist lodges, such as the *Hacienda Guachipelín* or *Rincón de la Vieja Lodge*.

To get to the **Las Pailas sector** and the lodges, take the Interamericana north of Liberia for 6km, then turn right to the hamlet of Curubandé – you'll see signs for the *Guachipelín* and *Rincón de la Vieja* lodges. A couple of kilometres before the *Guachipelín* there's a barrier and toll booth, where you'll be

Border checks in Guanacaste

Driving along the Interamericana north of Liberia, do not be surprised to see a blue-suited *policía de transito* (traffic cop) or a light-brown-suited *guardia rural* (border policeman) leaping out, kamikaze-like, into the highway directly in front of you – you'll need to stop and show your driver's licence and passport (which you must have on you at all times). These are routine checks, mainly to deter undocumented Nicaraguans from entering Costa Rica. The nearer the border you get, the more frequent the checks become. Make sure you drive carefully: knocking over a policeman is not a good move.

charged $2 to use the road. If you don't have your own transport, both lodges will pick you up from Liberia for an extra charge ($10–25 return); they also offer **packages** from San José, with transport included. The **Santa María sector** and the *Rincóncito* lodge are reached by driving through Liberia's *barrio* La Victoria in the northeast of the town (ask for the *estadio* – the soccer stadium – from where it's a signed 24km drive to the park).

Accommodation

The Rincón de la Vieja area boasts some very good **lodges**, most of which offer their own tours, either on horseback or by foot; some go into the national park itself and some don't. Staying at the *Buenavista* you can take tours to the crater without paying the park fees, as they own the land from which the crater is accessed. There's a basic **campsite** near the Las Pailas *puesto*, and another slightly better equipped one at the Santa María *puesto* ($3 per person), where there are lavatories and water, though you should take your own cooking utensils, food and water. If you have a sleeping bag, and ask in advance, you can also stay inside the musty bunk rooms in the Santa María ranger station (phone the ACG office at Santa Rosa for permission on ☎695-5598).

Albergue Buenavista, 31km northeast of Liberia (☎ & ⓕ661-8158 or 666-2069, ⓦwww.buenavistalodge.net). A working cattle ranch – you can even ride with the cowhands – with stupendous views over Guanacaste and trails through pockets of rainforest on the flanks of the volcano. Has good-value dorm beds and singles ($15–20), plus double rooms in individual bungalows, many set around a small lake in which you can swim. The restaurant serves up wholesome meals, and there are reasonably priced horseback and hiking tours available. If you're driving here, a 4WD is recommended; alternatively, you can arrange to be picked up from Cañas Dulces (accessible from Liberia by bus). ⑤

Albergue Nueva Zealanda, in Quebrada Grande (marked as García Flamenco on many maps), about 35km northeast of Liberia (☎666-4300, 666-3804, ⓦwww.tourism.co.cr/hotels/nzelandia). Rustic and comfortable lodge located on the northwest flank of Rincón de la Vieja park, with abundant bird- and animal-life. ⑤

Borinquen Mountain Resort (☎666-5098, ⓕ666-2931 ⓔborinquen@racsa.co.cr). Top-notch new lodge with its own mudpools and sauna,

set in stunning lanedscape at the skirts of Rincón de la Vieja volcano. Packages with meals included (⑦–⑧) are good value, though extras are pricey.

Hacienda Guachipelín, 5km beyond Curubandé on the edge of the park (☎284-2049, ☎ & ⓕ256-6995, ⓦwww.guachipelin.com). A working ranch, the historic *Guachipelín* looks every inch the old cattle hacienda, with comfortable doubles in the main house and bargain dorm beds ($10). Meals are extra – portions can be a bit mean, considering the cost. Attractions include a nearby waterfall, mud pots and some well-marked trails, while guides are available for a variety of tours, including riding and hiking to the volcano. Pick-ups from Liberia can be arranged, for a fee. ④

Rincóncito, in San Jorge (☎666-2764, mobile 380-8193). The cheapest option close to the park, this farm is owned by a friendly family, and has plain but good-value cabinas with cold water and no electricity. The owners are a good source of advice on local transport, guides and directions, and can also arrange horse-riding, guided tours and pick-ups from Liberia (about $35 return per car). Meals available (breakfast $3, lunch and dinner $5). ①–②

Rincón de la Vieja Lodge, 5km northwest of the *Guachipelín* and 3.5km from the Las Pailas park entrance; follow the signs (ⓣ & ⓕ 661-8198, ⓦ www.rincondelaviejalodge.com). Popular lodge with simple, rustic accommodation, including doubles with private bath and hot water (⑤), and dorm beds with communal bathrooms and cold water ($20 per person). There's a pool, reading area, and restaurant serving tasty and filling meals. Horse-riding, mountain-biking, a canopy tour and swimming in nearby waterfalls can all be arranged, and packages are available, with meals and some activities included. ⑥

Visiting the park

Massive and majestic, Rincón de la Vieja volcano utterly dominates the landscape. The most direct approach to the crater and summit of the volcano is via the Las Pailas entrance, along a marked trail. In all but the worst weather, it's hard to lose your way, at least on the lower parts of the trail. Whether or not you choose to go all the way to the crater, this is quite simply one of the best hikes in the country. A variety of elevations and habitats reveals hot springs, sulphur pools, bubbling mud pots, fields of purple orchids – the *guaria morada*, the national flower – plus a great smoking volcano at the top to reward you for your efforts. **Animals** in the area include all the big cats (but don't expect to see them), the shy tapir, red deer, collared peccary, two-toed sloth, and howler, white-faced and spider monkeys. There's a good chance you will see a brilliant flash of fluttering blue – this is the **blue morpho** butterfly, famous for its electric colours. **Birders** will have a chance to spot the weird-looking three-wattled bellbird, the Montezuma oropendola, the trogon and the spectacled owl, among others.

Rincón de la Vieja is becoming more and more popular, and it is likely that the trails will soon become over-walked. If you stay at one of the lodges (see above) and take their summit tours, either by horseback or foot, you may pass through areas not covered in this section. Also, bear in mind that Rincón de la Vieja is an active volcano, and the trails described here may have been altered due to periodic **lava flows**. Before setting out, you should always check current conditions at one of the ranger stations, or call the Area de Conservación de Guanacaste (ACG) headquarters at the Santa Rosa National Park (ⓣ666-5051, Spanish only). It's also advisable to carry all your drinking **water** – streams might look inviting, but often carry high concentrations of minerals (like sulphur) which can lead to extreme stomach upset if drunk.

The trails

From the Las Pailas puesto the summit is 7.7km away. Theoretically, if you start out early in the morning you could get to the top and back down before nightfall, but only if you don't mind rushing. The Las Pailas sector is where you find the fumaroles and mud pots, and you can also hike to two waterfalls, the *cataratas escondidas*.

The hike up to the summit from Las Pailas takes you through forest similiar to lower montane rainforest, densely packed, and lushly covered with epiphytes and mosses. Cool mist and rain often plague this section of the trail: if you are anywhere near the top and lose visibility, which can happen very suddenly, you're advised to stay away from the crater, whose brittle and ill-defined edges became more difficult to see, and consequently more dangerous, in cloudy weather.

At the **summit**, Rincón de la Vieja presents a barren lunar landscape, a smoking hole surrounded by black ash, with a pretty freshwater **lake**, Lago los Jilgueros, to the south. Quetzals are said to live in the forest that surrounds the lake, though you're unlikely to see them. When clear, the **views** up here are ample reward for the uphill sweating, with Lago de Nicaragua shimmering silver-blue to the north, the hump of the Cordillera Central to the southeast and the Pacific Ocean and spiny profile of the Nicoya Peninsula to the west. You can get hammered by wind at the top; bring a sweater and windbreaker.

Back down at the Las Pailas entrance, look for the "Pilas de Barro" sign to the **mud pots**; listen out for strange bubbling sounds, like a large pot of water boiling over. Mud pots, which should be treated with respect, are formed when mud, thermally heated by subterranean rivers of magma, seeks vents in the ground, sometimes actually forcing itself out through the surface in great thick gloops. It's a surreal sight: grey-brown muck blurping and blopping out of the ground like slowly thickening gravy. Another trail leads to the geothermal **hornillas** (literally, "stoves") – mystical-looking holes in the ground exhaling elegant puffs of steam. You almost expect to stumble upon the witches of Macbeth, brewing spite over them. Make sure not to go nearer than a metre or so, or you'll be steamed in no time. The combined effect of all these boiling holes is to make the landsape a bit like brittle Swiss cheese – tread gingerly and look carefully where you're going to avoid the ground crumbling underneath you. Many hikers have been scalded by blithely strolling too close to the holes.

From the Santa María entrance it's a more difficult and longer walk to the crater, although you can hike several other trails. These include the three-kilometre **Bosque Encantado** (Enchanted Forest) trail, which leads to a small forest and some hot springs next to a creek, which hikers love to leap into after a wallow in the springs, imitating a sauna effect. The temperature is usually about right for soaking, but you should never jump into any thermal water without first checking current temperatures at the ranger station.

Parque Nacional Santa Rosa

Established in 1971, **PARQUE NACIONAL SANTA ROSA** (daily 7.30am–4.30pm; $6), 35km north of Liberia, and 260km from San José, is Costa Rica's oldest national park, and also one of its most popular. Established to protect a stretch of increasingly rare dry tropical forest, the park boasts good trails, great surfing (though poor swimming), prolific turtle *arribadas*, and historical and cultural interest in the form of **La Casona**, a fortress-cum-farmhouse whose proximity to Nicaragua made it a prime target for would-be interlopers. It's also, given a few official restrictions, a great destination for **campers**, with a couple of sites on the beach.

Santa Rosa has an amazingly diverse topography for its size, ranging from mangrove swamp to deciduous forest and savannah. Home to 115 species of mammals (half of them bats), 250 species of **birds** and 100 of **amphibians** and **reptiles** (not to mention 3800 species of **moths**), Santa Rosa is a rich biological repository, attracting researchers from all over the world. Jaguars and pumas prowl the park, though you're unlikely to see them; what you may spot – at least in the dry season – are coati, coyotes and peccaries, often snuffling around watering holes.

The appearance of the park changes drastically between the **dry season**, when the many streams and small lakes dry up, trees lose their leaves, and thirsty animals can be seen at known waterholes, and the **wet months**, which are greener, but afford fewer animal-viewing opportunities. From August to November, however, you may be able to enjoy the sight of hundreds of **Olive Ridley turtles** (*llora*) dragging themselves out of the surf and up Playa Nancite by moonlight; September and October are the months when you are most likely to see them arrive. You need a permit to watch the "*arribadas*", when the

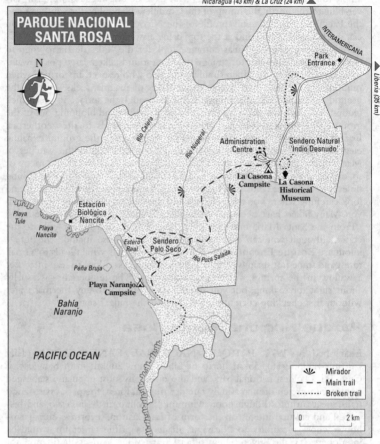

PARQUE NACIONAL
SANTA ROSA

Nicaragua (43 km) & La Cruz (24 km) ▲

INTERAMERICANA

Liberia (35 km) ▲

N

Park
Entrance

Río Calera

Río Nisperal

Administration
Centre

Sendero Natural
'Indio Desnudo'

La Casona
Campsite

La Casona
Historical
Museum

Estación
Biológica
Nancite

Playa
Tule

Playa
Nancite

Estero
Real

Sendero
Palo Seco

Río Poza Salada

Peña Bruja

Playa Naranjo
Campsite

Bahía
Naranjo

PACIFIC OCEAN

〰 Mirador
– – – Main trail
· · · · · · Broken trail

0   2 km

turtles arrive en masse to lay their eggs: in an attempt to avoid the disturbance caused by big tour groups à la Tortuguero (see p.188), permits are only given to individuals or small groups, up to a maximum of 25 people daily; ask at the administration centre when you arrive.

Though too rough for swimming, the picturesque **beaches** of Naranjo and Nancite, about 12km down a bad road from the administration centre, are popular with serious **surfers**. They're also great places to rest out for a while, or do a little camping and walking on the nearby trails.

Visiting the park

Many of Santa Rosa's **trails** are intended for scientific researchers rather than tourists, and so are not well signed. If you do set off to walk, it's a good idea to hire a ranger as a guide ($10–15) – ask at the administration centre. If you walk only one trail in the entire park, make it the very short (1km) and undemanding *sendero natural*, which provides an introduction to the unique features of the tropical dry forest. Curving round from the road just before the *casona*, it is signed as the **Sendero "Indio Desnudo"**, after the peeling-bark trees of the same name (also tongue-in-cheekily called "sunburnt tourists trees"). Along the trail you'll see acacia and **guapinol** trees, whose colloquial name is "stinking toe" on account of its smelly seed pods. Look out for monster iguanas hiding innocuously in tree branches, and for the ubiquitous bats.

From the administration centre a rough (signposted) track leads past *La Casona* camping area, with several trails branching off on the way. Some of these may be restricted at any one time for research purposes; check first at the administration centre, however, as you can usually walk where you want as long as you let someone know. After about 5km you come to a fork, bearing left to Playa Naranjo, and right to Playa Nancite, both of them about 3km further on.

A lovely grey sand beach, **Playa Nancite** is as lustrous as a wet seal's skin when the tide has just gone out. It is also the nesting home of the **Olive Ridley turtles**, a species which nests only here and at Ostional near Nosara on the Nicoya Peninsula. With none of the large tour groups you find at other Costa Rican turtle beaches, it's a great place to watch the **arribadas**, during which around eight thousand turtles – weighing on average around 40kg each – come ashore on any given evening, virtually covering the beach. According to estimates, more than eleven million eggs can be deposited by the turtles during a single *arribada*.

Due to rip tides, Playa Nancite is no good for swimming but, as is usually the case, it's good for **surfers**, with huge rolling, tubular waves. For the best surf, though, you should head for Playa Naranjo. Theoretically you can hike between the two (2hr) on a narrow trail across the rocky headland, which opens out on top into hot, dry scrub cover, but you have to watch the tide, since the trail crosses the deep Estero Real, the drainage point for two rivers. Ask for the *marea* (tidal times) from the administration centre before setting out.

La Casona

About 400m from the administration building, **La Casona** (Big House), one of Costa Rica's most famous historical sites, was for many years the centre of a working hacienda until the land was expropriated for the national park in 1972. This formidable wooden and red-tiled country fortress is an impressive sight, and **plaques** (in Spanish) outside the house recount the various instances of derring-do which have occurred at the *casona*, with resumés of the battles of March 20, 1856 (the confrontation of William Walker's filibusters and the Costa Rican forces; see p.256), of 1919 (against the Nicaraguans), and of 1955, against another Nicaraguan – the dictator Anastasio Somoza, whose hulk of a tank can still be seen, rusting and abandoned, along a signed road just beyond the entrance hut.

Like all old houses, the *casona* has the fragrant, slightly musty odour of wood comfortable in itself. It is now entirely given over to **exhibitions**, and you are free to clamber up and down the worn steps and wander around the dark rooms. One wing concentrates on archeology, with plaques explaining the unique history of Guanacaste, some lovely **petroglyphs**, and the dusty skulls of long-dead animals. In the main house are formal oil portraits of hacienda owners and presidents, and old family **photographs** of peones who worked on the hacienda over the years: fine-looking sepia-toned *sabaneros* and *cocineras* lined up together, staring rigidly at the camera. Most interesting is the **kitchen**, showing a table set for the *sabaneros'* morning coffee, a stone kiln-like hole used for cooking, and the *choreador de café* (like a cafetière) among other domestic relics. The **barn** is also worth a look, filled with harnesses and saddles quietly gathering dust.

The great pretender: William Walker

Born in Tennessee in 1824, William Walker was something of a child prodigy. By the age of 14 he had a degree from the University of Nashville, notching up degrees in law and medicine just five years later before setting off to study at various illustrious European universities. However, upon his return to the US, Walker proceeded to fail in his chosen professions of doctor and lawyer and, somewhat at a loose end, landed up in California in 1849 at the height of the gold rush. Here he became involved with the pro-slavery organization Knights of the Golden Circle, who financed an expedition, in which Walker took part, to invade Baja California and Mexico in a kind of *Lebensraum* manoeuvre to secure more land for the United States. Though this expedition failed, Walker, undeterred, soon put his mind to another plan. Intending to make himself overlord of a Central American nation of five slave-owning states, and then to sell the territory to the US, in June 1855 Walker invaded Nicaragua. The next logical step was to secure territory for the planned eleven-kilometre long canal between Lago de Nicaragua and the Pacific. Gaining much of his financial backing from Nicaraguan get-rich-quick militarists and North American capitalists who were quick to see the benefits of a waterway along the Río San Juan from the Pacific to the Atlantic, in 1856 William Walker, and several hundred mercenary troops, invaded Costa Rica from the north.

Meanwhile, Costa Rican president Juan Rafael Mora had been watching Walker's progress with increasing alarm and, in February 1856, declared war on the usurper. Lacking military hardware, Costa Rica was ill-prepared for battle, and Mora's rapidly gathered army of nine thousand men was a largely peasant-and-bourgeois band, armed with machetes, farm tools and the occasional rusty rifle. Marching them out of San José through the Valle Central, over the Cordillera de Tilarán and on to the hot plains of Guanacaste, Mora got wind that Walker and his band of three hundred filibusters were entrenched at the Santa Rosa casona, the largest and best-fortified edifice in the area. Although by now Mora's force was reduced to only 2500 (we can only guess that, in the two weeks that it took them to march from San José, heat exhaustion had left many scattered by the wayside), on March 20, 1856 they routed the filibusters, fighting with their *campesino* tools. Mora then followed Walker and his men on their retreat, engaging them in battle again in Nicaraguan territory, at Rivas, some 15km north of the border, where Walker's troops eventually barricaded themselves in another wooden *casona*. It was here – and not, as is commonly thought, at Santa Rosa – that Juan Santamaría, a lowly nineteen-year-old drummer boy, volunteered to set fire to the building in which Walker and his men were barricaded, flushing them out, and dying in the process. Walker, however, survived the fire, and carried on filibustering, until in 1857 a US warship was dispatched to put an end to his increasingly embarrassing antics for the US government, who had covertly backed him. Undeterred after a three-year spell in a Nicaraguan jail, he continued his adventuring until being shot dead by the Honduran authorities the same year.

Meanwhile, Mora, no devotee of democracy himself, rigged the 1859 Costa Rican presidential election so that he could serve a second term – despite his military victories against Walker, there was strong popular opposition to his domestic policies – and was deposed later that year. He attempted a coup d'état, but was subsequently shot in 1860, the same year that his former adversary met his Waterloo in Honduras.

Murciélago sector

Few tourists go to Santa Rosa's **Murciélago sector**, an area of reserve to the northwest of – and entirely separate from – the main sector of the national park. It's a kind of reforestation labaratory in which former cattle pasture is slowly being regenerated, though there's also a beach that's safe for swimming. To get there, drive along the Interamericana from the main Santa Rosa entrance about 10km north to the hamlet of **Cuajiniquil**. The road is poor, with two creeks to cross in the wet season; it's practically impossible to get there without your own vehicle, and even then you'll need high clearance. Two roads head on from Cuajiniquil: be sure to take the dirt road and not the paved one, which heads north to Punta Morros. After another 15km, the road ends in the **Area Recreativa Junquillal** (not to be confused with Playa Junquillal on the west of the Nicoya Peninsula; see p.273) and the pretty **Playa Blanca**. A small, white-sand beach where you can swim safely, Playa Blanca is one of the most isolated and least visited in the country, with a ranger station and camping area with water and toilet facilities. **Border checks** (see p.251) are particularly vigilant in this area. As usual, have your passport and all other documents in order.

Just 30km from the border, Murciélago is home to the remains of the training grounds used by the CIA-backed **Contras** during the Nicaraguan civil war. They're overgrown and scrubby today, with no sign that anything was ever there. It was also the location of the famous "secret" airstrip built, on Oliver North's orders, in direct violation of Costa Rica's declared neutrality in the conflict. Originally given the go-ahead by President Alberto Monge, the airstrip was eventually destroyed under President Oscar Arias's subsequent administration – a unilateral action that led to the US reducing its financial and political support for Costa Rica.

Practicalities

Santa Rosa's **entrance hut** is 35km north of Liberia, signed from the Interamericana. After paying the park fee, pick up a map and proceed some 6km or so, taking the right fork to the **administration centre** (☎666-5051, ℱ666-5020), which also administers Guanacaste and Rincón de la Vieja national parks. As well as checking road conditions and getting your camping/turtle-watching permits, you could ask to join the rangers on patrol and make reservations (at least 3hr in advance) for a simple lunch in the *comedor*. The food – *casados* with fish, chicken or meat and salad – is good, and this is a great place to get talking to rangers or other tourists. From here a rough road lead to the beaches; to drive these, even in the height of the dry season, you need a sturdy 4WD. The administration discourages any driving at all beyond the main road; nevertheless, people – surfers, mainly – insist on doing so, and survive. Most people park their vehicle at the administration centre and walk. One thing is for sure: don't try to drive anywhere in the park (including the Murciélago sector to the north, and the road to Cuajiniquil) in the rainy season without asking rangers about the state of the roads. You could get bogged down in mud or stopped by a swollen creek. Before setting off, you could always phone the Area de Conservación de Guanacaste (ACG) headquarters (☎666-5051, Spanish only) to check the current state of the roads in the park.

If you're walking, a ranger or fellow tourist will probably give you a ride, but on no account try walking down without **water** – a couple of litres per person, at least, even on a short jaunt. The easy-to-carry bottles of water with plastic handles sold at the gas stations on the road outside Liberia, are particularly good for walkers: stock up before you come. You can also buy **drinks** at the administration centre.

Camping facilities at Santa Rosa are some of the best in the country. There are two sites, each costing $2 per person, which is payable as you arrive at the administration centre. The shady **La Casona** campsite has bathrooms and grill pits, while **Playa Naranjo**, on the beach (and only open outside the *arribada* season), has picnic tables and grill pits, and a ranger's hut with outhouses and showers plus, apparently, a boa constrictor in the roof. Wherever you camp, watch your fires (the area is a tinderbox in the dry season), take plastic bags for your food, do not leave anything edible in your tent (it will be stolen by scavenging coati) and, of course, carry plenty of water.

Parque Nacional Guanacaste

Located 36km north of Liberia on the Interamericana, much of **PARQUE NACIONAL GUANACASTE** (daily 7.30am–4.30pm; $6) not long ago was nothing more than cattle pasture. Influential biologist D.H. Janzen, editor of the seminal volume *Costa Rican Natural History*, who had been involved in field study for many years in nearby Santa Rosa, was instrumental in creating the park virtually from scratch in 1991. Raising over $11 million, mainly from foreign sources, he envisioned creating a kind of biological corridor in which animals, mainly mammals, would have a large enough tract of undisturbed habitat in which to hunt and reproduce.

The **Santa Rosa–Guanacaste** (and, to an extent, Rincón de la Vieja)

corridor is the result of his work, representing one of the most important efforts to conserve and regenerate tropical **dry forest** in the Americas. Containing tropical wet and dry forests and a smattering of cloudforest, Parque Nacional Guanacaste also protects the **springwell of the Río Tempisque**, as well the Ríos Ahogados and Colorado. More than three hundred species of **birds** have been recorded here, while mammals lurking behind the undergrowth include jaguar, puma, tapir, coati, armadillo, two-toed sloth and deer. It's also thought that there are about five thousand species of **butterflies** and moths alone.

Few people come to Parque Nacional Guanacaste, and you may hear from the administration at Santa Rosa (see p.253) that there's nothing to see. It's true in a way, as the only primary rainforest exists at the upper elevations and, of the three biological stations, you are currently allowed to visit only the one on Volcán Cacao. **Trails** are being cut, however, and there are pre-Columbian **petroglyphs** lying around at a place called El Pedregal, near the Maritza field station at the bottom of Volcán Orosí. Ask the rangers at the entrance about the best way to see them; they are not on any currently existing trail, nor are they marked.

Practicalities

Facilities at Guanacaste are still minimal. **Access** is very difficult, unless (as usual) you've got a Range Rover or some other tank of a vehicle. While the dirt and gravel road from the highway is passable most of the way, the boulders from hell appear 3km from the entrance; at this point you have to ditch non-4WD vehicles and walk. To get there, take the exit for Potrerillos on the right-hand side of the Interamericana, 10km south of the Santa Rosa turn-off. At Potrerillos turn right for the hamlet of Quebrada Grande (on some maps called Garcia Flamenco) and continue for about 8km. You can **camp** at the main ranger station and there's a rustic, simple **lodge** at Cacao field station. Call the Santa Rosa administration (℡666-5051, ℱ666-5020) to check if it's open and how much they're charging for people to stay.

La Cruz, the haciendas and the border

Set on a plateau north of Parque Nacional Guanacaste, overlooking Bahía Salinas and the Pacific Ocean to the west, the tiny town of **LA CRUZ** is the last settlement of any size before the border, just 20km away, and makes a useful refuelling stop if you're heading up to Nicaragua. There are a couple of good **places to stay** and eat in town, although if you're staying any length of time in the area you'd do better at one of the nearby tourist lodges (see below). The friendly and good value *Villa Amalia* (℡ & ℱ679-9181; ❸–❹), 100m south of the town's Parque Central, is quirky and homely, and has a pool and stupendous views over the Pacific. The best budget bet is the friendly *Cabinas Santa Rita*, across from the courthouse (℡679-9062, ℱ679-9305), offering clean, simple rooms (❷) with private bath (cold water only), along with more upmarket rooms with air conditioning and private bath in a new annexe at the back (❸). Across the street from the bus station, *Cabinas Maryfel* (℡679-9096; ❶) is even more basic, with dark, clean rooms. For a proper **meal**, go where the locals go: *Ehecatl*, well known throughout the province for its seafood and lovely views over Bahía Salinas.

Hacienda accommodation around La Cruz

Las Colinas del Norte Ecolodge, 5km beyond La Cruz on the Interamericana (☎ 679-9132, ℱ 679-9064). Once a simple, friendly family cattle ranch, now transformed by its Italian owners into a small (24 rooms) resort with a pool and disco. Horseback trips on the ranch are available, and the restaurant does good pizza with home-made mozzarella. ④.

Los Inocentes, about 17km along the right turn (for Santa Cecilia), 3km before La Cruz (☎ 679-9190, ℱ 265-4385, ℮ orosina@racsa.co.cr). Stunningly located hacienda, built in 1890, with lots of wildlife in the grounds and ample bird-watching opportunities. Horse-riding is the thing to do here – you can ride up Volcán Orosí, which hovers prettily above – and there's also a pool, small bar and restaurant with excellent food (around $25 a day for three meals). You can get

here by bus; contact the owners for current bus schedules from La Cruz. ⑤.

Santa Clara Lodge, 7.5km south of the entrance to the Parque Nacional Guanacaste on the side road that goes to the park; follow the signs (☎ 666-4054, ℱ 666-4047). This small and charming IYHA-affiliated lodge (HI members get a discount) makes a convenient base for visiting Guanacaste and Santa Rosa national parks. It's set on a working ranch and dairy farm, with resident *sabaneros* and lots of horses and cattle around. The rooms are tiny and sparsely furnished, but the atmosphere and authenticity of the place make up for this. Horse-riding trips to nearby Volcán Orosí are available, and the owners can advise on transport to Santa Rosa. ④.

The border: Peñas Blancas

Peñas Blancas (8am–noon & 1–4pm) is emphatically a border post and not a town, with just one or two basic sodas and no hotels. Frontier-crossing procedures here are ponderous; you'll be lucky to get through the whole deal in less than ninety minutes. If you come on a Ticabus, things are smoother – all passengers are processed together and have some priority. Both Costa Rican and Nicaraguan border officials are quite strict, and there are many checks to see that your paperwork is in order, so make sure that you have any necessary visas before you come.

Exit stamps are given and the fee (75 colones) paid on the Costa Rican side, where there is a restaurant and a helpful, well-organized Costa Rican **tourist office** (Mon–Sat 8am–12.30pm & 1.30–3pm, Sun 8am–noon). Money changers are always on hand and can change colones, córdobas and dollars. After getting your Costa Rican exit stamp you walk north to the barrier and get one of the regular shuttle buses ($2), 4km north to the Nicaraguan shantytown of Sapoá, where you go through Nicaraguan *migración*. If you are one of those nationalities (Canadians, Australians and New Zealanders, for example) who need **visas** for Nicaragua, you should have already obtained them in San José (around $25, or $15 for a 72-hour transit visa).

An **alternative** way to cross into Nicaragua from Liberia is to take a Peñas Blancas service, then pick up a local bus to **Rivas**, the first Nicaraguan town of any size, 37km beyond the border. This might not be convenient if you are going all the way to Managua, but the formalities are far less cumbersome than on the Tica and SIRCA services. As there's so much regular local traffic and fewer (potentially visa-holding) foreigners on these buses, they are generally processed much more quickly.

Whichever route you take, you should aim to get to the border as **early** as possible. Buses on the border routes leave early in the morning, and fizzle out completely by 2 or 3pm. If you arrive any later than this you'll be left with no alternative but to take a costly taxi into Nicaragua or back to Liberia.

The Guanacaste beaches

The **beaches of Guanacaste** are scattered along the rocky coastline which runs from Bahía Culebra in the north near Liberia to Sámara on the west of the Nicoya Peninsula. Few of those in the north could truthfully be called beautiful, and most are quite small, located in coves or sheltered bays which makes them good for swimming, and relatively safe – though they lack the impressive expanse of Playas Flamingo and Tamarindo a bit further down the coast. The waters in the **Bahía Culebra** (marked on some maps as Playa Panamá) are some of the clearest and most sheltered in the country, with good snorkelling.

The landscape of the Nicoya Peninsula is changing rapidly as Costa Rica tries to attract more package tourists during the North American winter. The relatively new airport in Liberia exists mainly to service the package and charter market along this coast, while Playa Panamá, on the southern stretch of Bahia Culebra, is the site of the **Papagayo Project** (see box on p.263), the country's largest tourist development. The signs of mass tourism lessen as you head further south towards **Parque Nacional Marino Las Baulas**, where droves of leatherback **turtles** come ashore to lay their eggs between October and February. If it's a good swim you want, however, best head down to **Tamarindo**, or better still to **Sámara** or **Nosara**, on the Nicoya Peninsula. The beaches here have drawn pockets of foreign expatriates in pursuit of paradise, and the cosmopolitan enclaves – and inflated prices – are in sharp contrast to the rest of the region. Inland, the small towns of **Nicoya** and **Santa Cruz** are of little interest in themselves, but do have some reasonably priced accommodation and places to eat; also, as the main transport hubs for the area, they're pretty much unavoidable. The beaches of the southern part of the Nicoya Peninsula are covered in Chapter 6.

It can take a long time to get to the Guanacaste coast from San José (5hr minimum by car or bus), and in some places you can feel very remote from civilization indeed. Outside the large tourist developments there are few settlements of any size, and only a desultory scattering of hotels. **Getting around** can take time, too, as the beaches in the northern part of the peninsula tend to be separated by rocky headlands or otherwise impassable formations, with barren hilly outcroppings coming right down to the sea, carving out little coves and bays, but necessitating considerable backtracking inland to get from one to the other. Although bus connections with the capital are good, travelling from beach to beach on the peninsula by **bus** is can be tricky, and you'll to ask locals to figure out the peninsular services, whose schedules are not formally published, but which locals will know. By far the most popular option is to explore with a **rental car**, which allows you to beach-hop with relative ease. Roads are not bad, if somewhat pothole-scarred, and you'll do best with a 4WD, though this can work out a bit expensive. Another possibility for couples or small groups is to **hitch**, as there's a fair amount of tourist traffic around here.

Bahía Culebra

Once a quiet area washed by the sheltered, clear blue waters of **Bahía Culebra**, the sparsely populated Gulf of Papagayo was the perfect candidate for Costa Rica's first big mega-development (see box on p.263). The waters around here are some of the best in the country for swimming and snorkelling, as they are sheltered from the full force of the Pacific.

The northernmost beach of the bay, **Playa Panamá**, with its grey volcanic sand, is still a nice quiet spot, although there is no shortage of upmarket hotels being built here, many of them by Italians. The resort-style hotel *Costa Smeralda* (T672-0070, F670-0379, E smeralda@racsa.co.cr; 8) has a nice pool, good restaurant and efficient management, while the new *Giardini di Papagayo* (T & F670-0476, F290-6195, E carpag@racsa.co.cr; 8), well situated on a plateau overlooking Playa Hermosa, has spanking new rooms decorated in the Californian-Spanish colonial vein favoured by upmarket hoteliers hereabouts. Another large new development is the *Blue Bay Resort* (T233-8566, F670-0033, E costarica@bluebayresorts.com; 8), an attractive, all-inclusive resort situated at the north end of Playa Panamá. Luxuriously furnished, with all the amenities you would expect (three pools, a gym, tennis courts and watersports), this is as upmarket as you'll get in Costa Rica. Two **buses** daily do the hour-long trip from Liberia, on a good paved road, leaving Liberia at around 11am and 7pm. The turn-off for Playa Panamá is 3km beyond the Playa del Coco turn-off.

Playa Hermosa lies on the southern edge of the Bahía Culebra, 10km north of the nearest beach to the south, Playa del Coco. The water here is relatively calm, clean and good for swimming. Unusually for this dry, hot zone of Guanacaste, the beach is blessed with good shade, and the view out to the Pacific and the islets hovering offshore is gorgeous, especially at sunset. Hermosa is wonderfully quiet, in the wet season at least, and you may find that, apart from the odd cow, you have the beach to yourself. Playa Hermosa is easily accessible by **car** from Liberia. Take the turn-off to the right just after the hamlet of Comunidad – signposted to Playas Hermosa, Panamá and Coco – and continue for several kilometres over the good paved road. There's another turn-off to Hermosa and Panamá on the right.

Playa Hermosa practicalities

Hermosa is experiencing its own mini development boom, with quite a few (mainly upmarket) **hotels** having sprung up in the past few years. All Playa Hermosa's hotels are signed and easy to find in the small village. The best places **to eat** are the restaurant at the *Hotel El Velero*, with the usual grilled fish dishes served in pleasant surroundings, and the open-air restaurant at the *Villas del Sueño*, again with unremarkable food, but in a nice beachside location.

Cabinas/Hotel Playa Hermosa (T & F672-0046). Basic rooms with private bath and ceiling fans in a new block – fairly spartan for the price. 4

Condovac la Costa (T672-0150, F672-0151, E condovac@racsa.co.cr). Without doubt the plushest place in Hermosa, with large, attractive villas with kitchenette, cable TV and a nice view of the ocean, plus a pool, restaurant and disco. Tours are available, including sports-fishing and snorkelling. 8

Hotel El Velero (T670-0036, F670-0016, E elvelerocr@yahoo.com). Popular and friendly hotel, with two-level rooms with balconies and sea views in lovely gardens filled with birds and lizards. There's also a good restaurant and a small pool, while a short path leads from the hotel down to the beach. 6–7, but with hefty low-season discounts.

Rancho Vallejo (T672-0108). One of the few places left in Playa Hermosa that could conceivably be described as budget, with simple, clean rooms with private (cold-water) bath. 2

Villas del Sueño (T & F670-0026, W www.villadelsueno.com). Good-value small hotel with eight large and lovely rooms, all attractively furnished and with pretty tiled floors; there's also a small pool and a nice open-air restaurant. 4

The Papagayo Project

For several years now the entire Bahía Culebra area, encompassing Playas Panamá and Hermosa, has been under threat from the Papagayo Project, originally intended to be the largest tourist development in Central America, with no less than 14,000 rooms (there are currently a total of 13,000 hotel rooms in the whole of Costa Rica). Needless to say, the environmental impact of such a project on a relatively undeveloped region would have been – and may still be – catastrophic. In 1994, the entire project ground to a halt, though it's now rumoured that the development will go ahead, featuring a number of hotels with golf courses (a total of four or five are rumoured), the latest craze of the moneymen behind the project, albeit a seemingly mad idea in this semi-arid landscape. Environmentalists fear that the enormous amount of water needed to maintain these golf courses will be taken from nearby wetlands, mangroves and other delicate habitats, whilst the locals are worried that their water supplies may be curtailed, too.

Playa del Coco

Some 35km west of Liberia, with good road connections, **Playa del Coco** was the first Pacific beach to hit the big time with weekending Costa Ricans from the Valle Central. The beach itself is nothing special, but it's kept nice and clean by rubbish-collecting brigades organized by local residents, and the town's accessibility and good budget accommodation make it a useful base to explore the better beaches nearby. It also has many good restaurants, all within walking distance, and is a good place from which to take a snorkelling or diving tour.

Arrival and information

Direct **buses** (5hr) leave San José for Coco daily at 10am, returning at 9.15am. You can also get to Coco on local services from Liberia (see p.249), returning to Liberia at 7am, 9.15am (high season only), 2pm and 6pm (1hr). The town itself spreads out right in front of the beach, with a tiny **parquecito** as the focal point. Minimal services include a tiny **correo** (Mon–Fri 7.30am–5pm), and public **telephones** on either side of the *parquecito*. The Banco Nacional, will change dollars and travellers' cheques; otherwise you can **change money** at *Flor de Itabo* (see below). **Taxis** gather in front of the *Restaurante Cocos* by the beach.

Playa del Coco is a popular **snorkelling** and **diving** centre: try Mario Vargas Expeditions (T & F670-0351, @mvexped@racsa.co.cr) in Coco itself, or Bill Beard's Diving Safaris (T & F672-0012, @diving@racsa.co.cr) in nearby Playa Hermosa. The staff at Rich Coast Diving (T670-0176, @dive@rich-coastdiving.com), about 300m from the Coco beach on the main road, speak English, and can organize snorkelling and scuba trips and rent out mountain bikes. Expect to pay $65–80 for a two-tank dive.

Accommodation

Coco has lots of fairly basic **cabinas**, catering to weekending nationals and tourists. In the high season, you should **reserve** for weekends, but can probably get away with turning up on spec midweek, when rooms may be a little cheaper. In the low season, too, bargains abound. There's **camping** ($4 a night) at the *Ojo Parqueo*, 75m from the beach on the main road; they sell water and will also keep an eye on your belongings while you go for a swim or a meal.

Cabinas Catarina, 100m before you reach the *parquecito* (☎ 670-0156). The most basic budget cabinas in town, and a very good deal. Each *cabina* has a private bath with cold water only, and the friendly management will let you do laundry and cook meals in the small kitchen. ❶

Cabinas Chale, 500m up the road branching off to the right as you approach the beach (☎ 670-0036). Very plain a/c lodgings, but just 50m from the beach, with big rooms plus fridges (useful if you don't want to walk into town for a beer) and a pool. ❹

Cabinas El Coco, on the beach, 200m north of the *parquecito* (☎ 670-0167). Comfortable, clean and friendly cabinas right on the beach. The rooms on the second floor are best, and come with shared or private bath, and fans. On Saturday nights, noise from the nearby disco can be troublesome. ❸

Flor de Itabo, on the main road coming into town, about 1km before you reach the beach (☎ 670-0011, ℱ 670-0003). This long-established hotel, for many years the best in Coco, is tasteful and friendly, decorated with lovely dangling shell mobiles and Guatemalan bedspreads. All rooms have private bath, a/c, hot water and TV. Non-residents can change money here, and use the pool for about $3. There's also an excellent on-site Italian restaurant, *Da Beppe*. ❺

Hotel/Cabinas Luna Tica, 100m south of where the road ends at the beach (☎ 670-0459). Rooms with private bath and cold water: those in the hotel are a bit airier than those in the cabinas, and some have fans or a/c. ❸

Pato Loco Inn, on the road coming into town, about 300m before the village (☎ & ℱ 670-0145, ⓦ www.accommodations.co.cr/patoloco.htm). The "Crazy Duck" has nice airy rooms with private bath and either fan or a/c, and there are a couple of longstay apartments fitted out with kitchens too. Email and internet service for guests. ❹

Villa del Sol, 1km north of the village; turn right off the main road 150m before the beach (☎ & ℱ 670-0085, ⓦ www.villadelsol.com). Small new hotel in a quiet location with five rooms set around a large plain grassy space – all have private bath with hot water and ocean views. The hotel has been pleasantly decorated by its friendly French-Canadian owners, and also has its own large pool. ❹–❺

Villa Flores, on the road leading to the right before you reach the beach (☎ 670-0787, ℱ 670-0269). Quiet and comfortable, this hotel has rather dark rooms each with private bath and hot water – some have ceiling fans, others a/c (about $10 more). The second-storey balcony is a great place to catch sea breezes. There's a pool, Jacuzzi, small gym, and dives can be arranged. ❺

Vista Mar, signposted turn 1km north of the village (☎ & ℱ 670-0753, ⓦ www.arweb.com/vistamar). A good-value and nicely maintained option, with eight spacious and pleasantly decorated rooms, either with shared or private bath with hot water, plus fan or a/c. There's a nice palm-fringed pool and a good restaurant serving Italian- and French-themed food. Breakfast included. ❹–❺

Eating, drinking and nightlife

Coco has two very distinct types of places to eat and drink: those catering to Ticos and those that make some sort of stab at cosmopolitanism to attract the gringos. The Italian presence in town makes itself felt in a plethora of eateries offering pizza and spaghetti, all at quite reasonable prices compared to other resort areas nearby. Nightlife is generally quiet during the week, but things get livelier at the weekend, when the **disco** starts up.

Bar Coco, opposite the *parquecito*. A popular place in a prime position. Good for seafood lunches and dinners or just a beer in the evening.

Bar El Bohio, in the centre of the village. Extensive, gringo-friendly fare, running from Chinese to tacos, with menus in English.

CocoMar Bar and Disco, right on the beach, about 100m north of the *parquecito*. Coco's only disco can be very loud at weekends, when it plays a mixture of salsa and reggae. On weekday evenings it's a quiet bar unless someone decides to crank up the powerful sound system. Open until midnight; later at weekends.

Da Beppe in the *Flor de Itabo* hotel. The most ambitious food in town, with prices to match; the fillet of beef and fresh shrimp are recommended if you feel like splashing out. The popular *Havana Bar* is in the same building.

Pizzería Pronto, 500m before the beach on the right-hand side as you enter Coco. Green salads and large pizzas (the *jalapeña* is good) for about $7, served beneath a pleasant canopy. Closed Tues.

Sambuka, right on the beach, opposite the park. Doubles as a seafood-restaurant and bar, with good fruit-based cocktails.

San Francisco Treats, 200m from the beach. The San Francisco crowd who run this cheery melon-coloured restaurant offer treats such as home-made lasagne and roast beef sandwiches.

Desserts – brownies and pies – are especially good.

Spaghettería L'Angoletto di Roma, at the *Pato Loco*. Good Italian pasta.

Playa Ocotal to Conchal

Past the rocky headland south of Coco, the upmarket enclave of **Playa Ocotal** is reached by taking the turn-off to the left (signed) at the *Don Humo* restaurant. Ocotal and its surrounds have lovely views over the ocean and off to the Papagayo Gulf from the top of the headland, and the small beach is better for swimming than Coco, but the real attraction are the marlin and other "big game" fish that buzz through these waters. Ocotal **hotels** are usually tied in with sports-fishing packages – one of the most highly rated is *El Ocotal* (T670-0321, F670-0083, Wwww.resortocotal.com; ❻), whose elegantly furnished rooms have TV, air conditioning and fridges. Set on top of a hill, it has stunning views over the Pacific, and offers tennis and swimming as well as sports-fishing packages. The best **mid-range** place to stay is *Villa Casa Blanca* (T670-0518, F670-0448, Wwww.ticonet.co.cr/casablanca; ❺), a small, quiet B&B that offers boat tours, deep-sea fishing, scuba diving to the Islas Murciélago near Santa Rosa, and horse-riding trips. There's a pool and a tennis court in the grounds, and rates include breakfast.

Playas Flamingo and Brasilito

Despite its name, there are no flamingos at the upmarket and expensive gringo ghetto of **Playa Flamingo**, a place which feels more Florida or Cancún than Costa Rica – some of the big beach houses lining the white sands are reputedly owned by the odd movie star. It does, however, have a the best beach on this section of the coast, and great **sports-fishing**: almost all the resort-style hotels in the area cater to fishing enthusiasts or sun-worshippers on packages. It's approached along the road to small, unappealing **Playa Brasilito**, a scruffy beach with darkish sand; about 5km beyond it you see Playa Flamingo's marina. This is more or less the centre of the community, with the larger **hotels** spread out along the beach. The *Flamingo Beach Resort* (T654-4011, F654-4060, Wwww.ticonet.co.cr/flamingo; ❽) is one of the largest places to stay, with a good pool, several restaurants and a casino, while the *Flamingo Marina Resort* (T654-4141, F654-4035, Wwww.flamingomarina.com; ❻) has fully equipped suites with Jacuzzis, a restaurant and tour service. Both hotels can arrange air charter service and will pick you up from the airstrip.

If you want to enjoy the beach but avoid the static and stand-offish atmosphere of Flamingo, nearby **Playa Potrero** is a small cove which opens onto a decent crescent-shaped beach whose calm waters are good for swimming. The friendly Italian-run *Bahía Esmeralda* (T654-4480, F654-4479; ❸) is a good option here, with rooms located in a complex of cabins, plus a pool and a small restaurant. The only budget options are nearer Brasilito: the *Hotel Brasilito* (T654-4237; ❸) is well priced, with friendly German owners, though the rooms are sparsely furnished and have cold water only. There's a good restaurant attached.

To reach Playas Flamingo and Brasilito by **car**, take the Liberia–Nicoya road to Belen, then turn right off the main road and follow a side road to the hamlet of Huacas, 25km beyond Belen, from where the beaches are signposted. Getting to Flamingo **from San José**, Tralapa runs direct buses (2 daily; 6hr). There are two buses daily from **Santa Cruz** (see p.274), arriving at Brasilito,

Flamingo and Potrero beach, several kilometres north, early in the morning or mid-afternoon.

Playa Conchal

Playa Conchal ("Shell Beach"), set in a steep broad bay and protected by a rocky headland, is an appealing pink-coloured beach, with mounds of tiny shells and quiet waters which are good for swimming and snorkelling. Set back from the beach between Playas Brasilito and Conchal, is the huge *Melia Conchal Resort*, a plush Spanish-owned tourist complex, whose recent arrival has dramatically changed the character of the area from a sleepy low-key beach community to an exclusive resort. If you're looking for somewhere **to stay**, however, a much better option is *Casa Blanca* (T654-4259; ❺), a small, German-run complex of spacious rooms with private bath (hot water) and balcony, plus a swimming pool. To get to Conchal from Flamingo, you have to backtrack inland, turning right at the village of Matapalo.

Parque Nacional Marino Las Baulas

On the Río Matapalo estuary between Conchal and Tamarindo, **PARQUE NACIONAL MARINO LAS BAULAS** (8am–4pm, though open until late at night for guided tours in season; $6, including tour) is less a national park than a reserve, created in 1995 to protect the nesting grounds of the critically endangered **leatherback turtles**, which come ashore here to nest from October to February. Leatherbacks have laid their eggs at **Playa Grande** for quite possibly millions of years, and it's now one of the few remaining such nesting sites in the world. The beach itself offers a beautiful sweep of light-coloured sand, and outside laying season you can surf and splash around in the waves, though swimming is rough, plagued by crashing waves and rip tides. Despite its proximity to an officially protected area, someone seems to have given developers carte blanche to build at Playa Grande. What effect this will have on the millennia-old nesting ground of the turtles remains to be seen. Meanwhile, the new *Rancho Las Colinas Golf and Country Club*, which includes an eighteen-hole golf course and over two hundred separate villas, is symptomatic of the lack of planning, the short-termism and the plain daftness (the golf course is located in an area with a long, hot dry season and a history of water shortages) that characterizes so much recent tourist development in Costa Rica.

Turtle nesting takes place only in season and at **night**, with moonlit nights at high tide being the preferred moment. Note that you are not guaranteed to see a nesting turtle on any given night, and it's definitely worth calling in at El Mundo de la Tortuga (see opposite) before your visit, both to see the informative exhibition and to ask if tides and weather are favourable for nesting – alternatively you could ask the rangers at the entrance hut.

Those who see a nesting are often moved both by the sight of the turtles' imposing bulk, and also by their vulnerability, as they lever themselves up on to the beach. Each female can nest up to twelve times per season, laying a hundred or so eggs at a time, before finally returning to the sea – after which she won't touch land again for another year. Eggs take about sixty days to **hatch**, and the female turtle hatchlings that make the journey from their eggs to the ocean down this beach will (if they survive) return here ten to fifteen years later to nest themselves.

While it's worth seeing a nesting, it's difficult not to feel like an intruder. Groups of up to fifteen people are led to each turtle by guides (some of them "rehabilitated" former poachers), who communicate via walkie-talkie – and if it's a busy night there might be several tour groups after the same turtle. When the guide locates a turtle ready to lay her eggs you trudge in a group along the beach and then stand around watching the leatherback go through her procreative duty, while from time to time the turtle will cast a world-weary glance in the direction of her fans. It's hard not to think it would be better for the turtle if everyone just stayed away and bought the video, although the viewing is well managed and fairly considerate, and the revenue does help to protect the turtles' habitat.

Around 200m from the park entrance, the impressive and educational **El Mundo de la Tortuga** exhibition (early Oct to mid-March daily 4pm to late; $5) includes an audioguided tour in English and some stunning photographs of the turtles. You'll gain some insight into the leatherback's habitats and reproductive cycles, along with the threats they face and current conservation efforts. There's also a souvenir shop and a small café where groups on turtle tours are often asked to wait while a nesting turtle is located. It's open late at night – often past midnight – depending on demand and nesting times.

Practicalities

There are two official entrances to Playa Grande, though **tickets** can only be bought at the southern entrance, where the road enters the park near the *Villa Baulas*. Playa Grande has in the past has been a magnet for tour groups from upmarket Guanacaste hotels as well as day-trippers from Tamarindo and Coco. Nowadays, however, visitor numbers are regulated and you are no longer allowed to walk on the beach during *arribadas* (get the rangers to tell you stories of what people used to do to harass the turtles and you'll see why).

There are no bus services to the park. To **drive to Las Baulas**, take the road from Huacas to Matapalo, and turn left at the soccer field (a 4WD is recommended for this stretch during the wet season). Most people, however, visit the park by **boat** from Tamarindo, entering at the southern end rather than from the Matapalo road.

Accommodation

Although most visitors to Las Baulas stay in Tamarindo, a few kilometres to the south, there are a few very good **hotels** at Playa Grande.

Cantarana, between Playa Grande and the river that runs behind the beach (T 653-0486, F 653-0491, W www.unicaribbean.com; ⑤). One of the area's best-value hotels, in a spectacular situation, five minutes from Playa Grande. There are just ten rooms, plus some bungalows (sleeping 4–6 persons). Excursions offered include kayaking, sportsfishing, horse-riding and golf. The restaurant serves fantastic food, particularly the large continental and Costa Rican breakfasts (included in room rate).

Las Tortugas, right on the beach (T 653-0423, F 653-0458, W www.cool.co.cr/usr/turtles; ⑤). The area's longest established hotel, with pool, restaurant and luxurious a/c rooms. The conscientious owners have kept the light the hotel throws onto the beach to a minimum (turtle hatchlings are confused by light coming from land), and even showed the foresight to build so that the structure will block light from any future developments to the north. They also rent surfboards and can advise on turtle tours and horse-riding.

Villa Baula, on Playa Grande (T 653-0493, F 653-0459, W www.hotelvillabaula.com; ⑤). Twenty-five beachfront rooms with ceiling fans, plus some attractive private bungalows, all with private bath and hot water (some also have fridge). There are two lovely pools on the grounds and a good restaurant serving Indonesian cuisine.

Playa Tamarindo

Perennially popular **Playa Tamarindo** is one of the nicest beaches in Guanacaste, stretching for a couple of kilometres over a series of rocky head

The leatherback turtle

Leatherback turtles (in Spanish, *baula*) are giant creatures. Often described as a relic from the age of the dinosaurs, they're also one of the oldest animals on Earth, having existed largely unchanged for 120 million years. The leatherback's most arresting characteristic is its sheer size: reaching a total length of about 2.4m and a weight of 540kg. Its front flippers are similarly huge – as much as 2.7m long – and it's these which propel the leatherback on its long-distance migrations (they're known to breed off the West Indies, Florida, the northeastern coasts of South America, Senegal, Madagascar, Sri Lanka, and Malaysia). Leatherbacks are also unique among turtles in having a skeleton that is not firmly attached to a shell, but which consists of a carapace made up of hundreds of irregular bony plates, covered with a leathery skin. It's also the only turtle that can regulate its own body temperature, maintaining a constant 18°C even in the freezing ocean depths, and withstanding immense pressures of over 1500 pounds per square inch as it dives to depths of up to 1200m.

Since the 1973 Convention on the International Trade of Endangered Species, it is illegal to harvest green, hawksbill, leatherback and loggerhead turtles. Unlike Olive Ridley or hawksbills, Leatherbacks are not hunted by humans for food – their flesh has an unpleasantly oily taste – though poachers still steal eggs for their alleged aphrodisiac powers. Even so, leatherbacks still face many human-created hazards. They can choke on discarded plastic bags left floating in the ocean (which they mistake for jellyfish, on which they feed), and often get caught in longline fishing nets or wounded by boat propellers – all added to a loss of nesting habitats caused by beachfront development and the fact that, even in normal conditions, only 1 in every 2500 leatherback hatchlings makes it to maturity.

The number of nesting females at Las Baulas alone dropped from 1646 in 1988 to 215 in 1997, although numbers are reportedly up slightly for 2000–01. At Las Baulas, authorities have established a hatchling "farm" to allow hatchlings to be born and make their trip to the ocean under less perilous conditions that would normally prevail, though this will not affect adult mortality, which is believed to be the root cause of the drop in leatherback numbers. The population drop has been particularly blamed on longline fishing, while large-scale rubbish dumping, ocean contamination and other factors contributing to fertility problems are also cited.

You can **volunteer** on two leatherback conservation projects: Earthwatch have run conservation vacations on Playa Grande for a number of years. On the Caribbean side of the country, the Culebra Leatherback Project concentrates on saving its Caribbean nesting habitat. Contact **Earthwatch** (in the US: 3 Clock Tower Place, Suite 100, Box 75, Maynard, MA 01754, ☏1-800/776-0188, ✉info@earthwatch.org; in the UK: 57 Woodstock Road, Oxford OX2 6HJ, ☏01865/318838, ⦿www.earthwatch.org) or the **Leatherback Sea Turtle Research Project** (Bahia Culebra, CRESLI, Campus Box 1764, Southampton College of Long Island University, Southampton, NY 11968, ☏631/287-8223).

lands. **TAMARINDO** village, which has a sizable foreign community, boasts a great selection of restaurants, has a lively beach culture (for which read beautiful young things parading up and down the sand), and a healthy nightlife. There's a price to pay for the cosmopolitan atmosphere, however, as everything costs that bit more here. Even by its own popular terms, Tamarindo is booming, with small complexes of shops springing up in the concrete mini-mall-style favoured hereabouts, while internet cafés, restaurants and real-estate agents have now colonized the entire centre of the village, as foreigners rush in to snap up their plots in paradise, even if they're no longer the bargain they once were.

Though **fishing** still plays a large part in the local economy, Tamarindo's transformation from village to beach resort has been rapid, with the usual associated worries about drugs and the loss of community. The beach attracts a combination of enthusiastic surfers and well-to-do Costa Ricans, who maintain vacation houses in the vicinity. The **swimming** isn't great, as the waves are fairly heavy, rip tides are common, and there are a number of submerged rocks – ask around regarding conditions. Most people are content to paddle in the rocky coves and tide-pools south of the town. The Tamarindo area has always been a **surfing** paradise, and its credibility was upped several notches when Bruce Brown's seminal surfing docudrama *Endless Summer II* was partly filmed here. Enthusiasts ride the waves at Tamarindo, Playa Grande and adjacent Playa Langosta. For a more general form of locomotion, *Tito's Camping*, at the south end of the beach, hires out **horses** for reasonable prices.

North of the Tamarindo river estuary begins the long sweep of Playa Grande (see p.266), where the **leatherback turtles** lay their eggs. Turtles also come ashore at Tamarindo, but in much smaller quantities. Officially, Tamarindo is within the boundaries of Las Baulas national park, in so far as the ocean

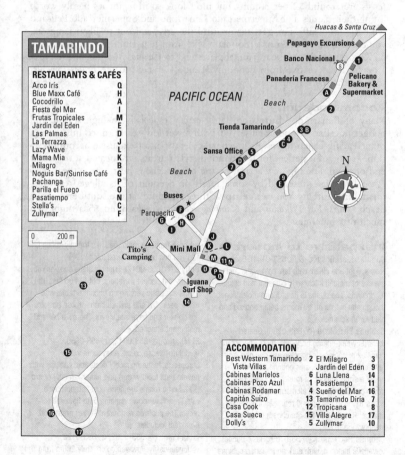

TAMARINDO

Huacas & Santa Cruz

RESTAURANTS & CAFÉS

Arco Irís	Q
Blue Maxx Café	H
Cocodrillo	A
Fiesta del Mar	I
Frutas Tropicales	M
Jardín del Eden	E
Las Palmas	D
La Terrazza	J
Lazy Wave	L
Mama Mia	K
Milagro	B
Noguis Bar/Sunrise Café	G
Pachanga	P
Parilla el Fuego	O
Pasatiempo	N
Stella's	C
Zullymar	F

PACIFIC OCEAN

Papagayo Excursions

Banco Nacional

Panadería Francesa

Pelicano Bakery & Supermarket

Beach

Tienda Tamarindo

Sansa Office

Beach

Buses

Parquecito

Tito's Camping

Mini Mall

Iguana Surf Shop

0   200 m

N

ACCOMMODATION

Best Western Tamarindo Vista Villas	2	El Milagro	3
Cabinas Marielos	6	Jardín del Eden	9
Cabinas Pozo Azul	1	Luna Llena	14
Cabinas Rodamar	4	Pasatiempo	11
Capitán Suizo	13	Sueño del Mar	16
Casa Cook	12	Tamarindo Diriá	7
Casa Sueca	15	Villa Alegre	17
Dolly's	5	Zullymar	10

covered by the protected area extends out in an arc, encompassing Tamarindo beach. The SPN has bought up the beach south of Tamarindo to Playa Langosta, too, preventing further hotel development and allowing turtles to continue coming ashore along this entire stretch.

Other than picking up the many pretty pastel-coloured shells that wash up on the beach, eating well, swimming and maybe doing a bit of surfing, there's little to keep you occupied in the village itself. In the evening, the main activity is watching the typically opulent **sunsets**, as the sun disappears into the Pacific just beyond the rocky headland that marks the southern end of the beach.

You can **fly** into Tamarindo on Travelair and Sansa, and both have offices in town; **buses** arrive by the village loop at the end of the road. The loop effectively constitutes Tamarindo's small centre, with a *parquecito* populated by new age jewellery-sellers – and even the odd pecking chicken – surrounded by restaurants. The small Banco Nacional, about 1km north of the loop, across from Supermercado Pelicano, will probably be able to **change dollars**; there are **public telephones** on the *parquecito*. There are several **internet cafés** (costs are around $2 per 30min), but most look so itinerant it's hardly worth listing their names. The Supermercado Tamarindo and Supermercado Pelicano sell basic foodstuffs. For **getting around** the area, and out to Playa Langosta, you could rent a scooter or a mountain bike from Tamarindo Rental Tours (see p.272) or from the surfboard/rental place next to *Cabinas Marielos*, or even rent a car for a day or two from Economy Rent a Car, next to the *Frutas Tropicales* soda on the main road.

Accommodation

Many of Tamarindo's **hotels** are fairly pricey, especially in high season, and budget travellers are not well served, with fewer low-season discounts than in other Pacific beach towns. As a general rule, the most exclusive accommodation – some of it perfect for honeymoon-style retreats – is located at the south end of town. The big new arrival on the hotel scene is near here – the *Barceló Playa Langosta* – resented by some locals on account of its alleged environmental insensitivity. You can **camp** at three campsites at the south end of the beach: *Tito's*, *Los Pelicanos* and *Camping Rancho* – all around $5 a night and much of a muchness.

Inexpensive to moderate

Cabinas Marielos (☎ & ℉ 653-0141). Basic rooms, light and clean, with fan, cold water and the use of a small kitchen, in pleasant and colourful grounds. The *dueña* is helpful and professional, though she insists on all rooms being booked and paid for in advance. ❹

Cabinas Pozo Azul (☎ 653-0280). Geared towards week-ending nationals, this rather worn complex of cabinas is nonetheless one of a very few budget-to-inexpensive options in town. It offers a small kitchen, a murky pool, and run-down but clean rooms, all managed by Jesus – who's trying to sell up and retire, so things may change. Rooms with fan are cheap; price rises steeply for a/c. ❷

Cabinas Rodamar (☎ 653-0109). Basic budget traveller's hangout, with dark and spartan cabinas

set back from the main road. It's friendly, though, and you can use the shared kitchen. ❷

Dolly's (☎ 653-0017). Friendly place popular with surfers and budget travellers, but fills up fast. The rooms are basic verging on uncomfortable, with flimsy beds, fan and private bath – those upstairs are quieter and have sea views. There's a bar and restaurant attached. ❸.

El Milagro (☎ 653-0042, ℉ 653-0050, ✉ flokiro@racsa.co.cr). A favourite with Europeans, featuring nicely decorated cabinas with private bath (cold water) and either fan (❺) or a/c (❻). Some rooms are generously proportioned, with French windows opening onto flowered terraces. The poolside restaurant serves great food. Breakfast included.

Luna Llena (☎ 653-0082, ℉ 653-0120, ✉ lunallena@yellowweb.co.cr). Only 200m from the beach, with unusual two-floor thatched cabinas arranged around a pool and filled with wooden carvings and ceramics. All have fridge and private bath with hot water. Breakfast included. ⑥

Tropicana (ⓣ & ⓕ 653-0261, 653-0503, ⓦ www.tropicanacr.com). Solid and clean hotel built around a good-sized pool. Rooms are simple, without TV or phone – those on the second storey get more air and have nicer views. Better value in low-season than in high. ⑤

Zullymar (ⓣ 653-0140). Clean, spacious and – for Tamarindo – reasonably priced cabinas, set in pleasant grounds scattered with reproductions of pre-Columbian art. The rooms with fan and cold water are about half the price of than those with fridge, a/c and "hot" showers. ③ .

Expensive

Best Western Tamarindo Vista Villas (ⓣ 653-0114, ⓕ 653-0115, Etamvv@racsa.co.cr). Villa complex which has been taken over by the Best Western chain, though not too much branding is in evidence so far: villas are large, brightly decorated and most have some sort of sea view. Facilities include a pool, Jacuzzi and restaurant. ⑥–⑦

Capitán Suizo (ⓣ 653-0075, ⓕ 653-0292, ⓦ www.hotelcapitansuizo.com). Popular and upmarket Swiss-run hotel set in spacious landscaped grounds on the beach. The *cabina*-style rooms all have a balcony or terrace, fridge, ceiling fans or a/c, bathtub, hot water and an outside shower. The pool is bigger than most, and the atmosphere friendly and relaxed. There's also a cocktail bar, beautiful beach views and a buffet breakfast. Good low-season discounts. ⑦–⑧

Casa Cook (ⓣ 653-0125, ⓕ 653-0753, ⓦ www.tamarindo.com). Intimate hotel right on the beach, with four tasteful cabins (each sleeping up to four, but often occupied by couples) arranged around a pool, each with a fully-equipped kitchen, a/c and cable TV. Howler monkeys congregate in the surrounding trees in the mornings and evenings. Strict reservations policy – book early. ⑦

Casa Sueca (ⓣ & ⓕ 653-0021). Beautifully appointed and cosy apartments, all artistically decorated, with private bath, hot water and fans. (It may be called something else by the time you arrive, however, since the Swedish owner is reportedly selling up.) ⑥

Jardín del Eden (ⓣ 653-0137, ⓕ 653-0111, ⓦ www.jardindeleden.com). Discreetly upmarket hotel in an exclusive hilltop position, with fine views over Tamarindo. Villas have all the usual amenities – a/c, fans, satellite TV, telephone and fridge – plus nice touches like tiled bathrooms and wicker chairs on the large balconies. There's also a nicely landscaped pool, Jacuzzi, bar and restaurant. ⑦

Pasatiempo (ⓣ 653-0096, ⓕ 653-0275). Popular hotel with a relaxed and friendly atmosphere. The spotless rooms have ceiling fans and hot water – the larger rooms (sleeping 5) are a particularly good deal. The atmosphere is homey, with hammocks strung outside the rooms and around the nice pool, and there's also a lively restaurant and very popular bar (though it can get a bit loud in high season). ⑦

Sueño del Mar, 1km from Tamarindo on the road heading south to Playa Langosta (ⓣ 653-0284, ⓦ www.tamarindo.com/sdmar). Swing in a hammock on the ocean-facing verandah of this beautiful house, designed in Spanish-hacienda style with tiled roofs and adobe walls. The three rooms and one *casita* all come with pretty tiled showers, and rates include a tasty and filling breakfast. ⑦

Tamarindo Diría (ⓣ & ⓕ 653-0031, ⓦ www.tamarindodiria.co.cr). Tamarindo's oldest large hotel, set in shady palm groves on the beach, and though it might look a bit worn, it obviously nabbed the village's prime location. Arranged around a good-sized swimming pool looking out to the ocean, the large – if slightly dated – rooms all have a/c, cable TV, telephone and private bath. Breakfast included. ⑦

Villa Alegre (ⓣ 653-0270, ⓕ 653-0287, ⓔ vialegre@racsa.co.cr). A new Californian-owned B&B, set in a quiet location on the beach just south of Tamarindo. Each of the four rooms and two suites has a private garden and patio; you can choose between ceiling fans or a/c and private or shared bath. There's a pool, too, and a good breakfast (included in rate) is served on the verandah with a lovely ocean view. ⑥

Playa Tamarindo activities

A number of outfitters in Tamarindo rent **surfboards**, **windsurfers** and **snorkelling equipment**; most charge $15–20 a day for a surfboard and $12 a day for snorkelling gear. You can also rent **bikes** and **boogie boards** (both about $8 per day). Agua Rica Diving (ⓣ & ⓕ653-0094) have a good reputation and do certification courses and **dive trips** in the area – their trip to the Islas Catalinas is recommended. The Iguana Surf Shop, south of the village (ⓣ & ⓕ653-0148), has a larger selection of surfboards, boogie boards and snorkelling gear. In addition, numerous operators, such as Papagayo Excursions at the northern entrance to the village (ⓣ653-0254, ⓔpapagayo@racsa.co.cr), offer **turtle tours** to Las Baulas in nesting season (about $15 per person). Ask about tours to the **Río Corobicí** to see birds, crocodiles and marshlands. Tamarindo Rental Tours (ⓣ & ⓕ653-0078) will take you furthest afield; as well as turtle tours they offer excursions to Rincón de la Vieja and Santa Rosa national parks.

Eating, drinking and nightlife

Tamarindo has an astounding number of good-quality, cosmopolitan restaurants – in fact, it's well on its way to becoming the gourmet capital of Costa Rica, if not Central America. The town's large Italian population means that this cuisine is perhaps over-represented, but French, Mexican, Costa Rican (and fusions of all these) can also be found. **Nightlife** focuses on the restaurants and bars – a couple of them with pleasant beachfront locations – in the centre of the village.

Arco Iris Impressively large vegetarian menu. Closed Mon.

Blue Maxx Cafe Good, filling American breakfasts, served with real cappuccino or espresso, and tasty fresh sandwiches and salads at lunch – a nice place to go for a coffee at any time of day.

Cocodrillo Well-cooked, healthy fare, including reasonably priced pizzas, salads and sandwiches, though breakfasts ($4.50) are a bit expensive. The back opens onto the beach, where you can sit at tables parked underneath the palms. Not open for dinner.

Fiesta del Mar Recommended by locals for good quality "surf n' turf" (meat dishes served with seafood) at slightly above-average prices ($10–12 for most main dishes). Good selection of non-alcoholic fruit drinks and fruit cocktails, too.

Frutas Tropicales One of the few genuinely cheap places in Tamarindo. As the name says, there's plenty of tropical fruit in this little snack bar – try the fruit *refrescos*. Otherwise, the menu is the usual soda fare, with *casados* ($3.50) and hamburgers ($3) both good bets. They also rent out a couple of cabinas (❸).

Jardín del Eden, at the *Jardín del Eden* hotel. Upmarket but reasonably priced restaurant serving high-quality cuisine, mostly French and Italian, using top-notch ingredients – the lobster, seafood brochettes and *pargo* (snapper) are all recommended. A romantic setting in tropical gardens

adds to the appeal. Count on around $30 per person.

Las Palmas Tasteful alfresco dining in shady beachside palm groves with candlelit tables; the menu is inventive and favours clever fruit combinations including *dorado* fillet with papaya ($10), jumbo shrimp with coconuts and banana curry cream ($12).

La Terrazza Good, authentic Italian pizzas, with an impressive view of the village and beach from the upstairs dining room.

Lazy Wave This outdoor restaurant may look casual, but it dishes up some of the best cooking in the area, if not the country, with a very fairly priced menu (changes daily) distinguished by the delicacy and inventiveness of its ingredients and flavours. The bakery-patisserie is worth a visit too.

Mama Mia Pasta and other Italian dishes, served up by the extremely competent resident chef, though it's not cheap – the tagliatelli with shrimp and mascarpone, while delicious, will set you back $14. It's the only place to come if you want to settle that *tartuffo* craving, however, and the staff and chef are very friendly.

Milagro, in the *Hotel El Milagro*. Respected restaurant with a changing menu of European dishes and a pleasant poolside setting, though the bar is rather expensive.

Noguis Bar/Sunrise Cafe Serves excellent breakfasts, with good breads, pastries and coffees, which you can either eat at the breezy seaside tables or take away.

Pachanga Intimate, candlelit restaurant, tastefully decorated, and with dependable a menu including *dorado* curry ($8) and BBQ ribs ($10). No credit cards.

Panadería Francesa (although the sign still says "Johan's Bakery"). Small bakery serving delicious fresh croissants, *pan dulce*, *pain au chocolat*, banana cake, pizza, waffles and apple flan for breakfast.

Parilla el Fuego Reasonably priced meals, including local favourites *ceviche, mahi-mahi* (grouper; $6.50) and lobster, as well as breakfast specials. The atmosphere is pleasantly laidback, with tables, hammocks and armchairs, plus soothing music, thankfully not cranked up too loud.

Pasatiempo, in the hotel of the same name. Perenially good restaurant serving crowd-pleasers like caesar salad ($4) and a wonderfully succulent blackened fish with greens, or try the chicken breast with mango stuffing ($8). Very reasonable prices, too, which isn't always the case in Tamarindo. If nothing else, try the superlative fruit cocktails and a few nibbles. Live music twice a week in high season.

Pelicano Bakery and Supermarket Tasty, high-quality sweets and sandwiches, with wholewheat sandwiches, coffee, desserts, bagels and takeout lunches.

Stella's One of Tamarindo's best restaurants, with good Italian pasta and fresh fish cooked in excellent, inventive sauces. A large menu encompasses wood oven-baked pizzas and even – rare for Costa Rica – veal. Main courses $8–12. Closed Sun.

Bar/Restaurante Zullymar Unbeatable beachfront location – everybody seems to come here for a drink whilst watching the sun go down – and good food, with main dishes for $5–7. Breakfasts are tasty and (for Tamarindo) good value, while the *típico* dishes – *pargo* and *dorado* fish *casados* in particular – are always well prepared.

Moving on from Tamarindo

There's a direct bus to San José daily at 6am (6hr), and one to Liberia daily at 6am (1–2hr). Alternatively, you could take one of the daily buses to Santa Cruz (see p.274) at 10am and 3pm, from where you can connect with local services to Liberia or San José (call ☏221-7202 for schedule information). As always, bus timetables are likely to change. Buses currently stop at the town circle, in front of the *parquecito*.

Continuing down the west coast of the peninsula is only really possible if you have your own transport, preferably a 4WD, although you can pick up occasional services to Sámara or Nosara from Santa Cruz and Nicoya. A more convenient, if expensive, option is to take a long-distance taxi – you'll see numbers and names of local people who act as taxi drivers posted at the supermarkets and other businesses in town: destinations include Nicoya, Santa Cruz, Liberia, Nosara and Sámara. Fares run between $30 and $80. Travelair and Sansa both have daily flights to San José; Sansa also operate a daily flight to San José via La Fortuna in the Arenal area ($60). You can buy tickets from the Sansa office, on the road into town on the right-hand side, about 400m before you reach the village loop. The airstrip is located 2.5km north of town.

South from Tamarindo to Playa Junquillal

It's not possible to continue straight on down the coast from Tamarindo: to pick up the road south you have to return a couple of kilometres inland to the hamlet of Villareal. Don't head south in the rainy season without a 4WD, and not at all unless you like crossing creeks – there are plenty on this stretch, and they can swell worryingly fast in the rain. In the dry months you should be all right with any vehicle as far as the surfing beach of **Playa Avellana**, 11km south of Tamarindo, and then to Junquillal, 10km beyond, but it may not do the car any good, and further south the roads become discouragingly rough. There are a few surfers' hangouts where you can **stay** at Avellana, with spartan but good-value accommodation, though if you're not a surfer, you'll feel a bit out of it, and may prefer the more upscale option of the *Lagartillo Beach Hotel* (☎225-5693, ℻253-0760; ④) with rooms attractively arranged in quiet grounds, and a pool and restaurant on hand.

Playa Junquillal is a lovely if expensive spot, with a long, relatively straight beach. It's ideal for **surfing**, pounded by breakers crashing in at the end of their thousand-kilometre journeys, but far too rough for swimming. If you're looking for seclusion and quiet, however, it's a great place to hang out for a few days – there's precious little to do, and nothing at all in the way of nightlife. There are several very good **hotels**, many perched up above the beach on a small cliff, with stupendous views. The friendly *Hotel Iguanazul*, 3km north of Playa Junquillal (☎653-0123, ✉iguanaazul@ticonet.co.cr; ④), has a great setting overlooking the sea, with bright rooms decorated with indigenous art, plus its own pool, bar and restaurant with a lovely view of the beach. It offers fishing, diving and horseback tours, as well as excursions to Las Baulas. Call ahead to reserve and ask about road conditions, especially in the rainy season. The quiet *Guacamaya Lodge*, 2km south of Junquillal (☎ & ℻653-0431, ✉ailbern@ racsa.co.cr; ④), is exceptionally good value, with very comfortable, semicircular rooms, lovely views, friendly management and a pool. The cheapest accommodation at Junquillal is the US-owned *Hotel Playa Junquillal* (☎ & ℻653-0432, ◍www.playa-junqillal.com; $30). The rooms are basic, but reasonably furnished, with private bath and hot water. There's a small bar and restaurant, and the friendly management is very knowledgable about good walking and camping in the area.

One **bus** daily arrives in Junquillal from San José (via Santa Cruz). This service currently gets you to Junquillal after dark: as with all the places along the west coast of Nicoya, make sure you book a room in advance. The bus returns to San José at 5am.

Santa Cruz

Generally seen by travellers as little more than somewhere to pass through on the way from Liberia or San José to the beach, the sprawling town of **SANTA CRUZ**, some 30km inland from Tamarindo and 57km south of Liberia, is actually "National Folklore City". Much of the music and dance that are considered quintessentially Guanacastecan originate here, like the various complex, stylized local dances, including the "Punto Guanacasteco" ("*el punto*"), which rivals Scottish country dancing for its complexity and has been adopted as the national dance. That said, however, they're not exactly dancing in the streets in Santa Cruz; life is actually rather slow, much of it lived out in contemplative fashion on the wide verandahs of the town's old houses.

Santa Cruz has little of interest to keep you in town any longer than it takes to catch the bus out. There isn't much in the way of services, either, apart from the **Banco Nacional** on the way into town. In the unlikely event that you need a **hotel**, choose from the *Diriá* (☎680-0080, ℻680-0442; ④), which has a pool and rooms with TV; or *Hotel La Estancia* (☎680-1033; ③), whose rooms have TV, private bath and fans, but can be stuffy. For **food**, join the locals at the popular *Coopetortilla*, a tortilla factory just off the central plaza that has its own restaurant selling chicken, Guanacastecan *empanadas* and sweet cheese bread, as well as, of course, tortillas.

Santa Cruz is something of a regional **transport** hub, with good connections inland and to the coast. Tralapa runs five buses daily from the bus terminal, 400m east of the Parque Central, to **San José** (4.30am, 6.30am, 8.30am, 11.30am & 1pm; 5hr), and there are numerous **local services** to Liberia

Dance and music in Guanacaste

In their book *A Year of Costa Rican Natural History*, Amelia Smith Calvert and Philip Powell Calvert describe their month on Guanacaste's fiesta circuit in 1910, starting in January in Filadelfia, a small town between Liberia and Santa Cruz, and ending in Santa Cruz. They were fascinated by the formal nature of the functions they attended, observing: "The dances were all round dances, mostly of familiar figures, waltzes and polkas, but one, called '*el punto*' was peculiar in that the partners do not hold one another but walk side by side, turn around each other and so on."

At Santa Cruz, "All the ladies sat in a row on one side of the room when not dancing, the men elsewhere. When a lady arrived somewhat late then the rest of the guests of the company, if seated, arose in recognition of her presence. The music was furnished by three fiddles and an accordion. The uninvited part of the community stood outside the house looking into the room through the open doors, which as usual were not separated from the street by any vestibule or passage." The Calverts were also delighted to come across *La giganta*, the figure of a woman about 4m high; actually a man on stilts "with a face rather crudely moulded and painted". What exactly *La giganta* represented isn't known, but she promenaded around the streets of Santa Cruz like an Edwardian goddess, long white lace trailing, while her scurrying minders frantically worked to keep her from keeling over.

Outside of the occasional local fiesta, today the only places you'll come across many of the dances of Guanacaste, as well as its music, are in specialist, Spanish-only publications. For enthusiasts, *La danza popular costarricense* by Bonilla and Guayacán, comes complete with diagrams. *La musica en Guanacaste* is a collection of tunes and lyrics, collected by Jorge Luis Acevedo, who has also written a more accessible publication, *Antología de la música guanacasteca*. For a good overall description of musical and dance styles search out *Santa Cruz Guanacaste: una approximación a la historia y la cultura popular* by Roberto Cabrera, which includes accounts of hacienda life in the eighteenth and nineteenth centuries, plus vivid descriptions of bull-riding and other Guanacastecan cultural events. All these titles are available in San José's Librería Universal (see p.107).

(hourly 5.30am–7.30pm). A number of buses leave for **Tamarindo**, including a direct service at 8.30pm (about 1hr), returning at 6.45am. For **Junquillal** a bus leaves at 6.30pm and returns to Santa Cruz at 5am. You can also get to **Playas Flamingo** and **Brasilito**, via Tamarindo, with two services leaving daily at 6.30am and 3pm (1hr 30min) and returning to Santa Cruz at 9am and 5pm (call ☏221-7202 in San José or ☏680-0392 in Santa Cruz for schedule information).

Guaitíl

The one place in Guanacaste where you can see crafts being made in the traditional way, **GUAITÍL**, 12km east of Santa Cruz, is well known throughout the country for its **ceramics**, and is the best place in the country to buy them. On the site of a major Chorotega potters' community, the present-day artisans' co-operative was founded more than twenty years ago by three local women whose goal was to use local traditions and their own abilities as potters and decorators for commercial gain. Today the artisans are still mainly women, keeping traditions alive at the distinctive, large, dome-shaped kilns, while the men work in agricultural smallholdings.

Potters in Guaitíl use local resources and traditional methods little-changed since the days of the Chorotegas. To make the clay, local rock is ground on ancient metates, which the Chorotegas used for grinding corn. The pigment

Chorotega pottery

The chief characteristics of Chorotega pottery are the striking black and red on white colouring, called *pataky*, and a preponderance of panels, decorated with intricate anthropomorphic snake, jaguar and alligator motifs. Archeologists believe that pieces coloured and designed in this way were associated with the elite; possibly as mortuary furniture for *caciques* (chiefs) or other high-ranking individuals. In the Period VI (an archeological term for the years between 1000 BC and 500 AD) the *murillo appliqué* style emerged, an entirely new, glossy, black or red pottery with no parallel anywhere else in the region, but curiously similar to pottery found on Marajó Island at the mouth of the Amazon in modern-day Brazil, thousands of kilometres away.

After the Conquest, predictably, pottery-making declined sharply. The traditional anthropomorphic images were judged to be pagan by the Catholic Church and subsequently suppressed. Today you can see some of the best specimens in San José's Museo Nacional, or watch them being faithfully reproduced in Guaitíl.

used on many of the pieces, *curiol*, comes from a porous stone that has to be collected from a local natural source, a four-hour walk away, and the ceramic piece is shaped using a special stone, also local, called *zukia*. *Zukias* were used by Chorotega potters to mould the lips and bases of plates and pots; treasured examples have been found in Chorotega graves.

Every house in Guaitíl seems to be in on the trade, with pottery on sale in front of people's homes, on little roadside stalls, and in the Artesanía Co-op on the edge of the soccer field. Some of the houses are open for you to wander inside and watch the women at work. Wherever you buy, don't haggle and don't expect it to be dirt cheap, either. A large vase can easily cost $20 or $25. Bear in mind, too, that this is decorative rather than functional pottery, and may not be that durable.

Guaitíl is on the old road to Nicoya; **to get there** from Santa Cruz, head east on the smaller road instead of south on the new road; turn off to the left where you see the sign for Guaitíl.

Nicoya

Bus travellers journeying between San José and the beach towns of Sámara and Nosara need to make connections at the country town of **NICOYA**, the peninsula's main settlement. Set in a dip surrounded by low mountains, it's a hot place, permeated by an air of infinite stasis; but undeniably pretty nonetheless, with a lovely **Parque Central** and its white adobe church (earthquake-battered, structurally unstable and currently closed), cascading bougainvillea and aggressive-looking plants. There's a considerable Chinese presence in the town, with many restaurants, hotels and stores being owned by descendants of Chinese immigrants.

Practicalities

Eight **buses** a day arrive in Nicoya from San José, a journey of around six hours. Some take the slightly longer way round via the road to Liberia, but most take the Tempisque ferry. In addition, buses arrive from a number of regional destinations, including Liberia (10 daily), Santa Cruz (16 daily), Sámara (3 daily) and Nosara (1 daily). Most buses arrive at Nicoya's spotless bus station on the southern edge of town, a short walk from the centre. The Liberia service, however, pulls in across from the *Hotel Las Tinajas*. As usual, you'll find

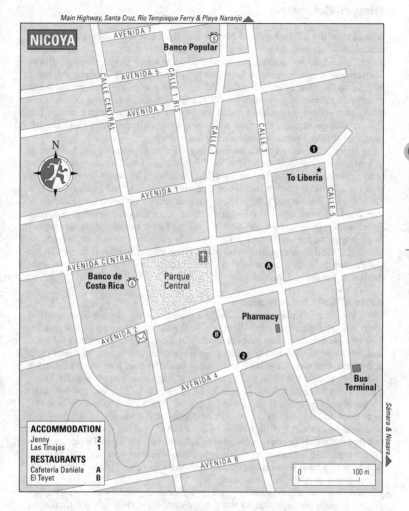

Sámara & Nosara

ACCOMMODATION
Jenny   2
Las Tinajas   1
RESTAURANTS
Cafetería Daniela   A
El Teyet   B

most **services** around the Parque Central, including the *correo* (Mon–Fri 7.30am–5.30pm) and the Banco de Costa Rica. The Banco Popular has an ATM that accepts foreign-issued cards – it's 100m east and 300m north of the Parque Central on the main road out of town. **Taxis** line up by the Parque, or call Coopetico (☎658-6226).

The friendly *Hotel Jenny* (☎685-5050; ❷), 200m south of the Parque Central, is the cheapest **place to stay**, with old, basic rooms with air conditioning, TV and phone. The similarly priced *Hotel Las Tinajas* (☎685-5081; ❷), 100m northeast of the Parque Central, is nicer, with dark rooms inside the main building and lighter cabinas around the back. Good **restaurants** include the *Cafetería Daniela*, 100m east of the Parque, for breakfast and pastries; the sodas by the Parque for large *casados*; and, for Chinese food, the *Restaurant El Teyet*, across from the *Hotel Jenny*.

Playa Sámara

A road runs the 35km between Nicoya and the coast at Nosara, via Caimital, though it's only negotiable with a 4WD. Most drivers, and all buses, take the longer, paved route (marked as Route 150 on some maps) through **Playa Sámara**, from where you can loop north back up the coast. The scenery from Nicoya to Sámara, 30km south, is rolling, rather than precipitous, although there are a couple of particularly nasty corners, marked by crosses commemorating the drivers who didn't make it. As you approach Sámara at the *Bar Rancho* and gas station, the road splits into two, with the right-hand branch heading off into a creek, which is sometimes deep.

For sheer size and safety for **swimming**, Sámara is probably the best beach in Costa Rica, especially now that local residents and visitors have tackled the litter problem that once plagued its wide, flat sands. The waves break on a reef about a kilometre out, so the water near the shore is actually quite calm – a rarity for the Pacific coast. It's a great place to relax – midweek, especially – as even at the busiest times there's little action other than weekenders tottering by on stout criollo **horses** (available for rent at $5 per hour) and the occasional dune buggy racing up the sand. On Sundays the town turns out in force to watch the local **soccer** teams who play on the village field as if they're Brazil and Argentina battling it out for the World Cup – even weekending Ticos shun the beach for the sidelines.

Arrival and information

Sansa and Travelair **planes** from San José come in at the airstrip 6km south of town at Carrillo, from where 4WD taxis make the trip to Sámara for about $6. The express **bus** from San José leaves daily at 12.15pm, 12.30pm and 6.15pm, and gets in some six hours later, stopping about 50m in front of the beach right at the centre of the village. The express bus **back to San José** currently leaves at 4.30pm and 9am Monday to Friday, and at 7am and 1pm on Sunday. There are buses **to Nicoya** at 5am, 7am, 1.30pm and 4.30pm (2hr). You can buy tickets for some bus services from the Transporte Alfaro office (daily 7am–5pm), next door to the *Pulpería Mileth* in the centre of the village, which also sells potato chips, suntan lotion, bottles of cold water, and has the village's public **telephone**. Sámara's **correo** (Mon–Fri 7.30am–6pm) – a small shack really – 50m before the entrance to the beach, offers minimal services, and there is nowhere to **change money** (other than at the large hotels), so bring plenty of colones, especially in low season.

There aren't as many **tours** or other activities at Sámara as around other places on the peninsula, due to the sheer distance and driving time it takes to get anywhere. Jorge Gonzalez does **taxi tours** (☏656-0081, mobile 390-4198) to Guatíl for pottery (see p.275) for $40 per day, and Rincón de la Vieja ($70 per day, including park entrance). You could try Sámara Adventures (☏656-0655, ✉j_esqui@yahoo.com), 100m south of the soccer field at the Super Samara, for tours to Ostional Wildlife Reserve (see p.284), and **white-water rafting** and **sports-fishing** anywhere in the country. They also arrange transfers. An unusual adventure is offered by the Flying Crocodile, just north of Samara at Esterones – follow the copious signs (☏656-0483, ℱ656-0196, ⓦwww.flying-crocodile.com). Guido, the highly experienced pilot, can fly you along the area's stunning coastline in an **ultra-light aircraft** ($60), skimming the treetops – or you could even stay a while and train as an ultra-light pilot yourself.

Accommodation

Staying in Sámara is getting pricier, with few cheap cabinas. Though during the low season most hotels offer better rates than the ones listed here, at high-season weekends you should have a **reservation** no matter what price range you aim for. The best budget option is to **camp** – this is especially popular at weekends with weekending Costa Rican families (read: loud radios). *Camping Coco*, on the beach, is clean and well run, with cooking grills, as is *Camping Playas Sámara*, at the north end of the beach, with toilets and showers (both $3 a night).

Belvedere B&B, 100m down the road to Carillo (Ⓣ & Ⓕ 656-0213, Ⓔ belvedere@samarabeach.com). Wonderfully pleasant and excellent-value hotel. The ten rooms and two apartments come with either a/c or fan ($8 less), and all are brightly furnished in light wood, with mosquito nets and solar-heated water. There's also a Jacuzzi and whirlpool, and a good German breakfast is included. ❹

Casa del Mar, 50m north of the entrance to beach on the left (Ⓣ 656-0264, Ⓕ 656-1029). Good-value, although a bit sparsely furnished, rooms close to the beach. The downstairs rooms are clean and white, but rather dark; ask for an upstairs room with shared bath and palm-fringed sea view. ❺

Casa Naranja, in the centre of the village (Ⓣ 656-0220). Owned by Suzanne, an energetic ex-chef from Paris, this small, central hotel has three rooms (one with a/c) in a modern building. The very fair price includes a good French break-fast, and the attached bar-restaurant-creperie is highly recommended. VISA accepted. ❹

Giada, about 100m before you come to the beach, on the left (Ⓣ 656-0132, Ⓕ 656-0131, Ⓦ www.hotelgiada.net). Small hotel set round a compact pool, with spotless banana-yellow rooms, good beds, overhead fans, private baths and tiled showers – the upstairs rooms are better for views and breeze. The friendly management also offer good-value dollar exchange (for guests only) and sell Sansa air tickets. ❹

Isla Chora Inn, 400m down the Nosara road (Ⓣ 232-3087, Ⓕ 296-1873). Slightly pricey hotel with cabinas attractively set around a swimming pool; some also have their own kitchens (about $50 extra). There's a restaurant, bar, Italian ice-cream parlour and a disco on site, and the owners can arrange tours and activities. ❼

Magica Cantarana, Playa Buena Vista, 1km north of Sámara on the road to Nosara (Ⓣ 656-0071, Ⓕ 656-0260). In a quiet beachside setting, with plain but comfortable rooms in a modern two-storey building with swimming pool – the upstairs rooms with balconies are best. ❹

Hotel Marbella, first left as you come into town from Nosara (Ⓣ & Ⓕ 656-0122). Fairly cheap hotel, with a tiny pool – for plunging rather than swimming – and fourteen rather dark but brightly painted rooms. The helpful management can advise on transport in the area and also rent out bikes. ❹

Hotel Mirador de Sámara, 100m up the hill from the *Marbella* (Ⓣ 656-0044, Ⓕ 656-0046, Ⓦ www.miradordesamara.com). Huge apartments ($80) sleeping five to seven people, with large bathrooms, bedrooms, living rooms, kitchen and terrace, all with panoramic views over the town and beach. The bar is in an impressive tower with a 360° view for watching the spectacular sunsets, and there's a new pool with nice wooden sun-decks. Good low-season and long-stay discounts, but the price means it's better value for four or more people, rather than couples.

Villas Playa Samara, on the road to Carillo (Ⓣ 656-0102, Ⓕ 221-7222, Ⓔ htlvilla@racsa.co.cr). Upmarket resort, wildly popular amongst wealthy Costa Rican families, with both all-inclusive ($150) and accommodation-only ($80) tariffs. The well-built villas come with large, spacious kitchens and sitting rooms, outside terrace and hammock, but the whole effect (golf carts for your luggage; see-your-neighbour prox-imity) is a bit suburban, and the management could be more efficient – although the beachside setting at the quiet south end of the beach is love-ly. ❺

Eating, drinking and nightlife

There are a couple of very nice places to **eat** in Sámara, where you can enjoy a cold beer by the lapping waves. **Nightlife** is quiet, though things can get a bit loud on Friday and Saturday nights in high season, when the *Tutti Fruti* disco at the old *Hotel Playa Sámara* comes into its own.

Ananas, in front of the beach. Bar-restaurant, nicely set in a small rancho, serving incredibly tasty fruit salads, juices, breakfasts and coffee-and-cake combinations. Open for breakfast, lunch and afternoon coffee only.

Colochos, next to the *Hotel Sámara Beach*. Moderately priced seafood (around $4 a dish) – try the *pargo* (snapper) or *corvina* (bass).

Creperie Naranja, in *Casa Naranja* in the centre of the village. Authentic French cuisine (the owner is a former Paris chef) served in a small outdoor garden lit with candles in the evening. The wide menu offers, among other things, crepes ($3.50), French favourites like *duck à la orange* ($5) and some incredible traditional cakes and desserts, flan, tartes and sweet crepes from $3 to $4 – pricey, but worth every penny.

Delfín, about 100m along the beach towards

Playa Carillo. Bar-restaurant with a large, seafood-dominated menu and tables set under the palm trees right on the beach – by far the best place to nurse a cold Imperial in the evening.

Dorado, opposite the soccer field. German-run establishment with good fish dishes, particularly the filet of its namesake *dorado* (sea bass), although the *pargo* (snapper) is also very good – both are a real bargain at $3 each with tasty vegetables.

El Ancla, next door to the *Delfín*. Relatively new restaurant on the beach, with a long menu of fish dishes and a pretty setting close to the water.

Isla Chora Inn, 400m down the Nosara road. Run by an Italian couple, with superb ice cream and thin-crust pizza – the *pizza con mariscos* ($7) is spectacular – as well as good pasta dishes and attentive service.

South of Sámara

Aficionados of Pacific sunsets will want to head 6km south of Sámara to **Playa Carillo**, a ninety-minute walk along good flat sands. Known for its spectacular evening light and colours, Carillo is also safe for swimming, though the fact that more and more people are buying plots here and setting up hotels and restaurants means that the beach no longer has the sleepy, end-of-the-line feel it once had. For **food**, try the *Mirador* restaurant, just behind Playa Carillo up on a hill, where you can have a drink and a meal (though the food is rather plain) to the sound of crashing waves and watch the pastel mauves, pinks and oranges blend into each other as the sun goes down. Just behind the *Mirador* is a good new budget **accommodation** option, the *Cabinas Colibri* (☎656-0056; ❸) – rooms have tiled floors, hot showers and above-average beds, and breakfast is included.

The stretch south of Carillo is for off-road driving nuts only, and should not be attempted without a 4WD (make sure the clearance is high). You need a good **map**, because roads go haywire in this part of the peninsula, veering off in all directions, unsigned and heading to nowhere, some ending in deep creeks (unpassable even by Range Rovers and Land Rovers at high tide). The further south you go, the tougher it gets, as dirt roads switch inland and then through the hamlets of Camaronal, Quebrada Seca and Bejuco, all just a few kilometres apart but separated by frequent creeks and rivers. It's best not drive down here alone, as there's a very good chance you'll get stuck (rising to a virtual certainty in the rainy season, whatever vehicle you have) and settlements are few and far between. There are **gas stations** in Sámara and Cobano: bring a spare can with you, just in case, because the distance between the two, in total, is about 70km. Be sure also to carry lots of drinking water and food, and, if possible, camping gear. You can **camp** on the deserted beaches, or you might be able to rent a room in someone's house. There is one **hotel**, the rather expensive *Hotel Punta*

Islita, 8km south of Playa Carrillo (☎231-6122, ⓕ231-0715, ⓔptaisl@racsa. co.cr; ❼); the atmosphere is exclusive, with snorkelling, mountain-biking and fishing trips arranged by the management.

North of Sámara: Nosara and around

The drive from Sámara 25km north to the village of **NOSARA** is pretty, following a shady, secluded stretch of coast along dirt and gravel roads, punctuated by a few creeks. It's passable with a regular car (low clearance) in the dry season (though you'll still have to ford two creeks except at the very driest times of year), but you'll need a 4WD or high clearance in the wet. The road follows a slightly inland route; you can't see the coast except where you meet the beach at **Garza**, about ten minutes before Nosara. This little hamlet is a good place to stop for a *refresco* at the *pulpería*, and perhaps take a dip in the sea. Though most people drive to Nosara; you can also come on the daily **bus** from Nicoya.

Nosara itself is set some 3km inland, between a low ridge of hills and the sea. Usually grouped together as **Playas Nosara**, the three beaches in the area – Nosara, Guiones and Pelada – are fine for **swimming**, although you can be buffetted by the crashing waves, and there are some rocky outcroppings. Playa Guiones is the most impressive of the beaches: nearly 5km in length and with probably the best swimming, though there's precious little shade. The whole area is a great place to go beachcombing for shells and driftwood, and the vegetation, even in the dry season, is greener than further north. Some attempts have been made to limit development, and a good deal of the land around the Río Nosara has been designated a wildlife refuge.

In contrast to the busier Sámara, the vast majority of people who come to Nosara are North Americans and Europeans in search of quiet and natural surroundings. Much of the accommodation is slighly upmarket, and the owners and managers are more environmentally conscious than at many other places on the peninsula. A local civic association keeps a hawkish eye on development in the area, with the aim of keeping Nosara as it is, rather than having it become another Tamarindo or Sámara.

Nosara village, properly called **Bocas de Nosara**, has an appealing setting about 5km inland from the ocean, with the low ridge of the Nicoya hills backing it to the east and tree-lined beaches to the west. The atmosphere is shady and slow, with the sweet smell of cow dung in the air and excitable voices drifting out from the local Evangelical church. People are friendly, and Nosara is still low-key, though it does get busy in the high season when foreigners flock here in search of seclusion. The area around the village can be very confusing, with little dirt and gravel roads radiating in all directions. To counter the lost-tourist effect locals have erected copious signs – though there are so many at certain intersections that they simply add to the confusion. Resign yourself to driving around looking lost at least some of the time.

Travelair and Sansa **fly** daily except Sunday to Nosara from San José, usually via Sámara, landing at the small airstrip. The San José **bus** comes in at the Abastecedor general store. There isn't much to the village itself but a soccer field, a couple of restaurants and a gas station (the latter is little more than a shack, with no pumps to show what it is – gas is siphoned out of a barrel). The Nosara Office Center (Mon–Fri 9am–noon & 1.30pm–5pm, Sat 9am-2pm), on the left as you enter the village, can send faxes and have the only **internet access** south of Tamarindo ($3 for 15 min – pricey, but then there's no competition). They also reconfirm flights and sell tickets to San José on the private

The recorrido de toros

If you're in Nosara on a weekend in January or February, or on a public holiday like the first of May, be sure not to miss the **recorrido de toros** (rodeo). *Recorridos*, held in many of the Nicoya Peninsula villages, are a rallying point for local communities, who travel long distances in bumpy communal trucks to join in the fun.

Typically, the village *redondel* (bullring) is no more than a rickety wooden circular stadium, held together with bundles of palm thatch. Here local radio announcers introduce the competitors and list the weight and ferocity of the bulls, while travelling bands, many of them from Santa Cruz (see p.274), perform oddly Bavarian-sounding oom-pah-pah music at crucial moments in the proceedings. For the most fun and the best-seasoned rodeo jokes, sit with the band – usually comprising two saxophones, a clarinettist, a drummer and the biggest tuba known to man – but avoid the seat right in front of the tuba.

The *recorrido* usually begins in the afternoon, with "Best Bull" competitions, and gets rowdier as evening falls – after dark, a single string of cloudy white light bulbs illuminates the ring – and more beer is consumed. The *sabanero* tricks on display are truly impressive: the mounted cowboy who gallops past the bull, twirls his rope, throws it behind his back and snags it as desultorily as you would loop a garden hose, has to be seen to be believed. The grand finale is the bronco bull-riding, during which a sinewy cowboy sticks like a burr to the huge spine of a Brahma bull who leaps and bucks with increasing fury. During the intervals, local men and boys engage in a strange ritual of wrestling in the arena, taking each other by the forearm and twirling each other round like windmills, faster and faster, until one loses his hold and flies straight out to land sprawling on the ground. These displays of macho bravado are followed by mock fights and tumbles, after which everyone slaps each other cordially on the back.

The *recorrido* is followed by a dance: in Nosara the dance floor takes up the largest flat space available – the airstrip. The white-line area where the planes are supposed to stop is turned into a giant outdoor bar, ringed by tables and chairs, while the mobile disco rolls out its flashing lightballs and blasts out salsa, reggae and countrified two-steps. Wear good shoes, as the asphalt is super-hard: you can almost see your soles smoking after a quick twirl with a hotshot cowboy.

The atmosphere at these events is friendly and beer-sodden: in villages where there's a big foreign community you'll be sure to find someone to talk to if your Spanish isn't up to conversing with the *sabaneros*. Food is sold from stalls, where you can sample the usual *empanadas* or local Guanacastecan dishes such as *sopa de albondiagas* (meatball soup with egg).

---

charter service Pitts Aviation. The **correo** (Mon–Fri 7.30am–6pm) is next to the air strip and public **phones** are in front of the police station, next to the Cruz Roja. You can rent **bikes** at Souvenirs Tuanis in the ramshackle old house on the corner of the village. If it's long-term accommodation or taxis to the Ostional refuge you're after, check out their notice board.

Accommodation

If you want to stay **on the beach** you've got two options: posh gringo-run accommodation or camping. There's a group of economical cabinas and hotels **in the village**, but you'll need to rent a bike or count on doing a lot of walking to get to the ocean.

Almost Paradise Café and Cabinas (☎ 682-0173, ✉ almost@nosara.com). Unpretentious, hospitable and tranquil accommodation in a pink wooden bungalow perched above the village with stupendous views. The six spacious and very comfortable rooms have private bath with hot water; there's also pool in the grounds, with howler monkeys and birds roaming around, and a restaurant serving healthy, mainly vegetarian food. ❹

Cabinas Agnell, in the village (no phone). Basic,

dark, thin-walled rooms with fans, and newer cabinas with private bath and cold water only. No great shakes for view – you're basically in a driveway – but clean, and with friendly management. ❶

Cabinas Chorotega, in the village (Ⓣ 682-0105). Small, ten-room complex of pleasant cabinas with large rooms – those upstairs are best, though they're reached by an extremely steep staircase. There's a communal terrace with rocking chairs where you can sit with a beer and watch the scenery. ❷–❸

Café de Paris, south end of Nosara, at the entrance to Playa Guiones (Ⓣ 682-0087, Ⓕ 682-0089, Ⓦ www.cafedeparis.net). Well-appointed rooms set in bungalows arranged around the pool, all with private bath and hot water, and a choice of ceiling fans or a/c. Rooms range from standard doubles to suites with a/c, kitchen, fridge and a small rancho with hammocks. ❹

Casa Romantica, behind Playa Nosara (Ⓣ 682-0019, Ⓦ www.nosara.com/casaromantica). Clean and well-kept family-run hotel, right on the beach, with bright rooms, all with hot water, fridge and terrace (along with a family room sleeping five people). There's also a pool and a fantastic on-site restaurant (see p.284). If you fly or take the bus in the owners will pick you up with advance notice. ❺

Casa Tucan, 200m east from Playa Guiones (Ⓣ & Ⓕ 682-0113, Ⓔ casatucan@nosara.com). Small, eight-room hotel, with brightly decorated rooms (four with kitchen, $70), sleeping up to five people; all have private bath and hot water, and fan or a/c ($10 extra). There's a good restaurant and bar, including a new juice bar, on the premises. Good low-season or long-stay discounts. The owner will pick you up if you fly in on Sansa or Pitts Aviation. ❺

Estancia Nosara, set back about 1km from Nosara beach; follow the signs (Ⓣ & Ⓕ 682-0178, Ⓔ estangis@racsa.co.cr). Quiet, upmarket hotel set in landscaped grounds, with a restaurant and tennis court. The comfortable rooms all come with refrigerators, private bath and hot water; a couple also have cooking facilities. ❹

Giardino Tropicale, at the south end of Nosara, as you enter from Sámara (Ⓣ 682-0035, ask for Myriam). Cabinas with private bath, hot water, set back from the beach in lush tropical gardens, open to the forest, with lots of wildlife. ❹

Lagarta Lodge, signed from the village (Ⓣ 682-0035, Ⓕ 682-0135, Ⓦ www.nosara.com/lagarta). Set in a small private nature reserve, this lodge has excellent bird-watching and stunning coastal views – the rooms above the pool looking out onto the ocean have one of the best panoramas in the country. Rooms have private bath, hot water and fridges. A healthy buffet breakfast (not included) and evening meals are also available. ❻

Playas Nosara, on the hilltop, between Playas Guiones and Pelada; follow the signs (Ⓣ 682-0121, Ⓕ 682-0123, Ⓦ www.nosarabeachhotel.com). Dramatically situated hotel on a headland overlooking the beach and pine-clad coastline. The large, clean, cool rooms with fans are priced according to the quality of the view (not all rooms overlook the beach). Unfortunately, ongoing building works can make the place look like a construction site. ❹.

Villa Taype, 200m east from Playa Guiones (Ⓣ 682-0333). Family-managed hotel, with thirty rooms ($60, sleeping up to five) in bungalows, all with satellite TV, a/c or fan, and a little terrace with hammock out front. ❺

Eating and drinking

The Nosara area has experienced a mini-explosion of restaurants in the past few years. Many of them are very good, and prices are not as high as you might expect, given the area's relative isolation. There are a number of places in the **village**, most of them around the soccer field or on the road into town, though most of the better restaurants are huddled together near **Playa Guiones**, which is where the majority of tourists eat.

Nosara village

Bambú Bar, next to the Abastecedor general store. A bit dark, and with pounding music, though it's still a decent place to have a beer and watch the kids kick balls around the soccer field.

Iguanas Locas, across from the airstrip. Reasonable bar-restaurant, and an OK place to sit under the rancho and have a cold beer.

Soda El Tico, across from the airstrip. Geared toward locals, though budget travellers might want to check out its *comida típica*, served in a small diner-type room.

Soda Vanessa, next to *Cabinas Agnell*. Recommended by locals for its cheap and well-prepared *casados*.

Playa Guiones and Pelada

Almost Paradise Café, in the hotel of the same name. Vegetarian food served on an outside terrace with wonderful views.

Bar-restaurant Tucan, next to the *Casa Tucan* hotel. The menu features seafood in adventurous fruit-based sauces, lobster, chicken, pasta and steaks (all $7–12), served in a pleasant rancho strung with inviting hammocks and coloured lights. A new juice bar offers "create-your-own" drinks.

Café de Paris, at the southern entrance to Playa Guiones. The brioche and *pain au chocolat* confirm this bakery as a bona-fide overseas *département* of France, while the pleasant poolside restaurant serves sandwiches and pizzas for lunch ($4–9).

Casa Romantica, in the hotel of the same name. The most ambitious food in town, featuring a changing menu of fish, steak and pasta dishes ($7–10). There's a good wine list, too – possibly the only one in Nosara. Dining is in a small outdoor area, lit with candles at night.

Giardino Tropicale, south end of Nosara, on the road towards Sámara. Superior-quality pizza cooked in a wood oven and served in a pretty plant-strewn dining area.

Gilded Iguana, behind Playa Guiones. Upmarket bar with Mexican food that attracts the local expats, and well-priced lunch specials including filet of *dorado* ($4) and fish and chips ($3). Closed Mon, Tues & Sun.

Lagarta Lodge, in the hotel of the same name. Although the changing menu is perfectly good, it's the setting rather than the food which makes this place special, as you dine to the sound of the Pacific crashing gently below. The sociable seating arrangement has all guests sharing space round a big mahogany table – a good way to meet people. Closed Tues.

Marlin Bill's, Playa Guiones. Fairly pricey but well-prepared seafood dishes served in a setting just above the growing village near Playa Guiones. Closed Sat & Sun.

Olga's, on Playa Pelada. Cold beer, good *casados* and fish, and ocean views, but watch the bill – they don't itemize your food and drinks.

Refugio Nacional de Fauna Silvestre Ostional

Eight kilometres northeast of Nosara, **Ostional** and its chocolate-coloured sand beach make up the **REFUGIO NACIONAL DE FAUNA SILVESTRE OSTIONAL**, one of the most important nesting grounds in the country for **Olive Ridley turtles** who come ashore to lay their eggs between May and November. You can't swim here, though, since it's too rough, and is plagued by sharks.

If you're in town during the first few days of the *arribadas* you'll see local villagers with horses, carefully stuffing their big, thick bags full of eggs and slinging them over their shoulders. This is quite legal: villagers of Ostional and Nosara are allowed to harvest eggs, for sale or consumption, during the first three days of the season only. Don't be surprised to see them barefoot, rocking back and forth on their heels as if they were crushing grapes in a winery; this is the surest way to pick up the telltale signs of eggs beneath the sand. It takes about fifteen minutes to drive the gravel-and-stone road from Nosara to the refuge; alternately you can bike it or take a taxi.

Parque Nacional Barra Honda and around

The **PARQUE NACIONAL BARRA HONDA** (Dec–April daily 8am–4pm; $6), about 40km east of Nicoya and 13km west of the Río Tempisque, is popular with spelunkers for its forty-odd subterranean **caves**. A visit to Barra Honda is not for claustrophobes, people afraid of heights (some of the caves are more than 200m deep) or anyone with an aversion to creepy crawlies. They are only open to visitors in the dry season (Dec–April).

The landscape around here is dominated by the **limestone plateau** of the Cerro Barra Honda, which rise out of the flat lowlands of the eastern Nicoya Peninsula. About seventy million years ago this whole area – along with Palo Verde, across the Río Tempisque – was under water. Over the millennia, the porous limestone was gradually hollowed out, by rainfall and weathering, to form caves.

The caves form a catacomb-like interconnecting network under the limestone ridge, but you can't necessarily pass from one to the other. Kitted out with a rope harness and a helmet with a lamp on it, you descend with a guide, who will normally take you down into just one. The **main caves**, all within 2km of each other and of the ranger station, are the Terciopelo, the Trampa, Santa Ana, Pozo Hediondo and Nicoa, where the remains of pre-Columbian peoples were recently found, along with burial ornaments and utensils thought to be over two thousand years old. Most people come wanting to view the huge needle-like **stalagmites** and **stalactites** at Terciopelo, or to see subterranean wildlife such as bats, blind salamanders, insects and even birds.

Down in the depths, you're faced with a sight reminiscent of old etchings of Moby Dick's stomach, with sleek, moist walls, jutting rib-like ridges, and strangely smooth protuberances. Some caves are big enough – almost cathedral-like, in fact, with their vaulting ceilings – to allow breathing room for those who don't like enclosed spaces, but it's still an eerie experience, like descending into a ruined subterranean Notre Dame inhabited by crawling things you can barely see. There's even an "organ" of fluted stalagmites in the Terciopelo cave; if knocked, each gives off a slightly different musical note.

Above ground, three short **trails**, not well marked, lead around the caves. It's easy to get lost, and you should walk them with your guide or with a ranger if there is one free, and take water with you. A few years ago two German hikers attempted to walk the trails independently, got lost and, because they were not carrying water, died of dehydration and heat exhaustion.

The endangered **scarlet macaw** sometimes nests here, and there's a variety of ground mammals about – including anteaters and deer – as usual, you'll be lucky to see any, though you'll certainly hear howler monkeys.

Practicalities

You need to be pretty serious about caves to go spelunking in Barra Honda. Quite apart from all the planning, what with the entrance fee, the payment to the guide and the price of renting equipment ($25), costs can add up. It's obligatory to go with a guide, who will also provide equipment; to do otherwise would be foolhardy, not to mention illegal. Before setting out, ring the national parks information line (☏192) for up-to-date details about permits and which times of year it's safe to go into the caves, and visit the ACT regional headquarters (see p.237) for names of their approved guides. You should also tell them the date and approximate time of your arrival. Anyone who wants to follow the **trails** at Barra Honda has to tell the rangers where they are intending to walk and how long they intend to be gone for.

Cave architecture

Created by the interaction of water, calcium bicarbonate and limestone, the distinctive cave formations of stalagmites and stalactites are often mistaken for each other. Stalagmites grow upwards from the floor of a cave, formed by drips of water saturated with calcium bicarbonate. Stalactites, made of a similar deposit of crystalline calcium bicarbonate, grow downwards, like icicles. Both are formed by water and calcium bicarbonate filtering through limestone and partially dissolving it. In limestone caves, stalagmites and stalactites are usually white (from the limestone) or brown; in caves where copper deposits are present colours might be more psychedelic, with iridescent greens and blues. They often become united, over time, in a single column.

Moving on from the Nicoya Peninsula

There are three alternatives when it comes to leaving the peninsula by bus or car from Nicoya. One is to drive north through Santa Cruz and around the cleft of the peninsula, picking up the Interamericana at Liberia. This drive takes two hours at most and, except for a few bad stretches between Nicoya and Santa Cruz, is fairly easy.

The most popular way to leave the peninsula, however, is on the Río Tempisque ferry. Some bus services between Nicoya and San José take this ferry, which can cut the trip to Nicoya or San José by about an hour, and saves a 110-kilometre drive up and over the cleft of the peninsula via Liberia. If you're driving, leave yourself plenty of time. The queues, even in midweek, are substantial, while on weekends (Fridays and Sundays especially) and holidays, the pile-up of traffic can mean waits of four to five hours – you're unlikely to save as much time as you do gas. Bus passengers don't have a problem, however, as buses have priority over cars on the ferry. Unless curtailed by bad weather in the wet season, eastbound crossings depart on the half-hour between 6.30am and 8.30pm, westbound crossings every hour on the hour from 6am to 8pm – the trip takes twenty minutes.

The third and least common way to leave the peninsula is to go from Nicoya by bus (year-round) or car (4WD essential) and continue southeast for about 72km to Playa Naranjo, from where a vehicle and passenger ferry sails to Puntarenas. However, the road to Playa Naranjo, especially after the Tempisque turn-off, is currently in such bad shape that even locals dissuade you from trying it. It can take as long as three hours, and it's a somewhat featureless journey, probably only of any interest to hardened explorers who will find satisfaction in the fact that barely any gringos come this way.

If you speak Spanish, another good way to hook up with guides is to call Sr Olman Cubillo, president of the local community development association, at the Complejo Ecoturistico Las Delicias (☏685-5580) in **Santa Ana**, the nearest hamlet to the caves. Recommended by both the SPN and the ACT, he can also give you **local information** about food, lodging, camping and horseback tours.

Driving to Barra Honda is possible even with a regular car. From the Nicoya–Tempisque road, the turn-off, 13km before the ferry, is well signed. It's then 4km along a good gravel road to the hamlet of Nacaome (also called Barra Honda), from where the park is, again, signed. Continue about 6km further, passing the hamlet of Santa Ana until you reach the ranger station, where most people arrange to meet their guide.

There's a **campsite** inside the park, with picnic tables and drinking water ($2 per person), and good basic **rooms** at *Proyecto Las Delicias* (❶), in Santa Ana. Most people who come to Barra Honda, however, stay in Nicoya (see p.276), or across the Río Tempisque on the mainland.

Travel details

Buses

Cañas to: Liberia (3 daily; 50min); San José (6 daily; 3hr 30min).

Junquillal to: San José (1 daily; 5hr); Santa Cruz (1 daily; 1hr 30min).

Liberia to: Bagaces (3 daily; 40min); Cañas (3 daily; 50min); Cuajiniquil (1 daily; 1hr 30min); La Cruz (14 daily; 1hr); Nicoya (10 daily; 2hr); Parque Nacional Santa Rosa (5 daily; 1hr); Peñas Blancas (5 daily; 2hr); Playa del Coco (3–4 daily; 1hr); Playa Hermosa (6 daily; 1hr); Playa Panamá (6 daily; 1hr); Puntarenas (5 daily; 3hr); San José (11 daily; 4hr); Santa Cruz (14 daily; 1hr); Tamarindo (1 daily; 1–2hr).

Nicoya to: Liberia (10 daily; 2hr); Nosara (1 daily; 2hr); Playa Sámara (4 daily; 2hr); San José (6 daily; 6hr); Santa Cruz (16 daily; 40min).

Nosara to: Nicoya (1 daily; 2hr); Playa Sámara (1 daily; 40min); San José (1 daily; 6hr).

Peñas Blancas to: Liberia (5 daily; 2hr); San José (3 daily; 6hr).

Playa Brasilito to: San José (2 daily; 6hr); Santa Cruz (2 daily; 1hr 30min).

Playa del Coco to: Liberia (3–4 daily; 1hr); San José (1 daily; 5hr).

Playa Flamingo to: San José (2 daily; 6hr); Santa Cruz (2 daily; 1hr 30min).

Playa Hermosa to: Liberia (6 daily; 1hr); San José (1 daily; 5hr).

Playa Panamá to: Liberia (6 daily; 1hr); San José (1 daily; 5hr).

Playa Potrero to: San José (2 daily; 6hr); Santa Cruz (2 daily; 1hr 30min).

Playa Sámara to: Nicoya (4 daily; 2hr); San José (2 daily; 6hr).

San José to: Cañas (6 daily; 3hr 30min); Junquillal (1 daily; 5hr); Liberia (11 daily; 4hr); Nicoya (6 daily; 6hr); Nosara (1 daily; 6hr); Peñas Blancas (3 daily; 6hr); Playa Brasilito (2 daily; 6hr); Playa del Coco (1 daily; 5hr); Playa Flamingo (2 daily; 6hr); Playa Hermosa (1 daily; 5hr); Playa Panamá (1 daily; 5hr); Playa Potrero (2 daily; 6hr); Playa Sámara (2 daily; 6hr); Santa Cruz (5 daily; 5hr); Parque Nacional Santa Rosa (4 daily; 6hr); Tamarindo (1 daily; 6hr).

Santa Cruz to: Junquillal (1 daily; 1hr 30min); Liberia (14 daily; 1hr); Nicoya (16 daily; 40min); Playa Brasilito (2 daily; 1hr 30min); Playa Flamingo (2 daily; 1hr 30min); Playa Potrero (2 daily; 1hr 30min); San José (5 daily; 5hr); Tamarindo (2 direct daily; 1hr).

Tamarindo to: Liberia (1 daily; 1–2hr); San José (1 daily; 6hr); Santa Cruz (2 direct daily; 1hr).

Flights (Sansa)

San José to: Liberia (1 daily); Nosara (Mon–Sat 1 daily); Playa Sámara (Mon–Sat 1 daily); Tamarindo (3 daily).

Flights (Travelair)

San José to: Liberia (1 daily); Nosara (Mon–Sat 1 daily); Playa Sámara (1 daily); Tamarindo via Liberia (1 daily), Tamarindo via Fortuna (1 daily).

6

The Central Pacific and southern Nicoya

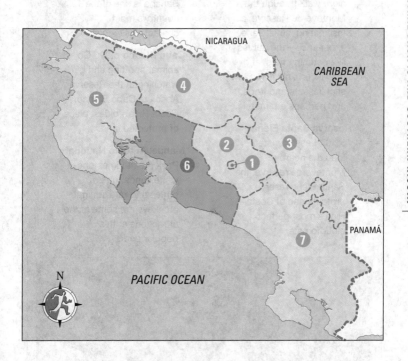

CHAPTER 6

Highlights

＊ **Arco Iris Eco-lodge**
p.297 One of Costa Rica's most attractive eco-lodges, the Arco Iris makes the perfect base from which to explore Santa Elena.

＊ **Monteverde Reserve Night Walk** p.307 Take a night walk through the Monteverde Reserve, a fascinating, albeit eerie, experience – the guides like catching bats, and they'll certainly find a few stick insects and frogs, and perhaps a tarantula.

＊ **Reserva Santa Elena** p.307 Less touristed than the nearby Monteverde reserve, the Santa Elena reserve protects one of Costa Rica's most perfect cloudforests.

＊ **Sky Walk** p.310 Walk through the rainforest canopy on high-level walkways and suspension bridges.

＊ **El Sano Banano** p.323 Close to the relaxed beach hang-out of Montezuma, El Sano Banano is one of the country's most characterful lodges.

＊ **Cabo Blanco** p.325 Go animal-spotting and bird-watching at the Reserva Absoluta Cabo Blanco, Costa Rica's oldest piece of protected land.

＊ **Manuel Antonio National Park** p.344 Limestone-white sands, green turtles and rare squirrel monkeys are some of the attractions at this popular park.

6

The Central Pacific and southern Nicoya

While Costa Rica's **Central Pacific** area is less of a geographical or cultural entity than other regions of the country, it does contain several of its most popular tourist spots, among them the number-one attraction, the **Reserva Biológica Bosque Nuboso Monteverde** (Monteverde Cloudforest Reserve), draped over the ridge of the Cordillera de Tilarán. Along with the nearby **Reserva Santa Elena**, Monteverde protects some of the last remaining pristine **cloudforest** in the Americas. **Southern Nicoya**, effectively cut off by bad roads and a provincial boundary from the north of the peninsula (covered in chapter 5), is part of **Puntarenas** province, whose eponymous capital, a steamy tropical port across the Gulf of Nicoya on the mainland, is the only town of any size in the entire area.

Along with those of Guanacaste, the region's **beaches** are some of the best known in the country. **Montezuma** , a former fishing village near the southwest tip of the Nicoya Peninsula, is surrounded by a series of coves that, while picturesque in the extreme, are not great for swimming, though if you just want to hang out and sunbathe they can't be bettered. On the mainland coast, the steady waves at **Playa Jacó** make it one of the best places to surf in the country, while further south, **Parque Nacional Manuel Antonio** has several extraordinarily lovely beaches, with the kind of white sand and azure water normally equated with the Caribbean islands, though only one of them is safe for swimming. The rugged natural beauty of the surrounding Manuel Antonio area – roughly from the park itself to the sports-fishing town of **Quepos**, 7km to the north – continues to be one of the most heavily touristed areas in the country.

Accommodation price codes

All the accommodation in this book has graded using the following price codes. The prices quoted are for the least expensive double room in high season, and do not include the 18.46 percent national tax which is automatically added onto hotel bills. For more details on accommodation in Costa Rica, see p.35.

❶	less than $10	❷	$10–20
❸	$20–30	❹	$30–50
❺	$50–75	❻	$75–100
❼	$100–150	❽	over $150

With the exception of the cool cloudforest of Monteverde, the region is trop-ical, hot and rather drier than in the south of the country. Temperatures can be uncomfortably high all over the region, with a dry-season average of about 30°C. It's not that much cooler in the wet months, when Quepos and Manuel Antonio, in particular, often receive torrential afternoon rains. Further north, the wet season is less virulent, though high in the clouds of Monteverde it can bucket down, especially in the afternoons. Even so, given the number of visi-tors who descend on the Central Pacific during the dry season, visiting during the wet is a definite possibility. Hotels in Monteverde actually have space at this time, while prices in the Manuel Antonio area come down from the strato-sphere – and although you might have to put up with a couple of hours' rain in the afternoon, it won't keep you indoors all day.

There are two **routes from San José** to Puntarenas and points south. The main road is the Interamericana, which climbs over the Cordillera Central before dropping precipitously into the Pacific lowlands, levelling out at the town of Esparza, a few kilometres before the turn-off for Puntarenas – a total trip of about two hours. Many travellers who are aiming for Playa Jacó and Manuel Antonio choose the older road, Hwy-3, which passes Atenas and Orotina before heading south, skirting the **Reserva Biológica Carara**. This is the nicer route, overall, with great scenery and good roadside stalls at Orotina, where you can buy fudge, nuts, *galletas* (cookies) and crafts. The road is in very good condition for most of the way between Orotina to Jacó, and offers some of the least stressful driving in the country. By contrast, driving up **to Monteverde** is always a bit of an expedition. Although it's not far – just 180km – from San José, the final 35km is unpaved and in bad condition. Most car rental agencies won't allow you to take a regular car on this road – as in much of Costa Rica, you'll need a 4WD.

Though it's possible to reach the southern third of the Nicoya Peninsula overland by private transport, most people cross over from Puntarenas on the ferries or *lanchas* **to Naranjo** or **Paquera**. From Naranjo you can continue west to Carmona and then up to Nicoya and Santa Cruz (though you'll need 4WD), while from Paquera public transport runs to Tambor and Montezuma. It's best to inquire about the condition of the roads beforehand and be pre-pared to turn back, especially in the rainy season, since even with a 4WD the various creeks that cross the road might be too high or the road too rutted.

The Monteverde area

Though it's generally associated only with the eponymous cloudforest reserve, **Monteverde** is, properly speaking, a much larger area, straddling the hump of the Cordillera de Tilarán between Volcán Arenal and Laguna de Arenal to the east and the low hills of Guanacaste to the west. Along with the reserve, you'll find the spread-out **Quaker** community of Monteverde, the neighbouring town of **Santa Elena** – which has its own cloudforest reserve – and several small hamlets for which Santa Elena is the regional hub.

The area's huge popularity stems in part from the **Reserva Biológica Bosque Nuboso Monteverde** (Monteverde Cloudforest Reserve), and also from the cultural and historical uniqueness of the Monteverde community, which was colonized in the early 1950s by a number of Quaker families, most-ly from Alabama, some of whom had been jailed for dodging the draft. The

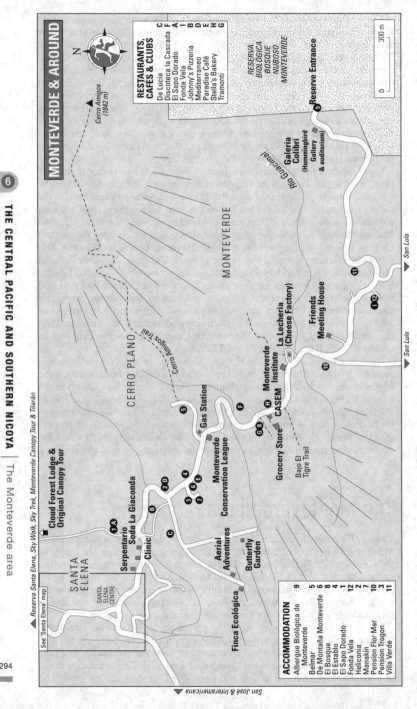

MONTEVERDE & AROUND

▲ Reserva Santa Elena, Sky Walk, Sky Trek, Monteverde Canopy Tour & Tilarán

■ Cloud Forest Lodge & Original Canopy Tour

▲ San José & Interamericana

▼ San Luis

Cerro Amigos (1842 m)

RESTAURANTS, CAFÉS & CLUBS
De Lucia — C
Discoteca la Cascada — F
El Sapo Dorado — A
Fonda Vela — I
Johnny's Pizzeria — B
Mediterraneo — D
Paradise Café — E
Stella's Bakery — H
Tramonti — G

RESERVA BIOLÓGICA BOSQUE NUBOSO MONTEVERDE

Reserve Entrance

0   300 m

Galería Colibrí (Hummingbird Gallery & auditorium)

Río Guacimal

MONTEVERDE

Friends Meeting House

La Lecheria (Cheese Factory)

Monteverde Institute

CASEM

Grocery Store

Bajo El Tigre Trail

Gas Station

Monteverde Conservation League

Cerro Amigos Trail

CERRO PLANO

Serpentario
Soda La Giaconda
Clinic

Aerial Adventures

Butterfly Garden

Finca Ecológica

SANTA ELENA

SANTA ELENA CENTRE

See 'Santa Elena' map

ACCOMMODATION
Albergue Biológica de Monteverde — 9
Belmar — 5
De Montaña Monteverde — 6
El Bosque — 8
El Establo — 4
El Sapo Dorado — 1
Fonda Vela — 12
Heliconia — 2
Manakin — 7
Pension Flor Mar — 10
Pension Trogon — 3
Villa Verde — 11

settlers first arrived in this remote area – at that time peopled only by a few Costa Rican farming families – in 1950–51. Monteverde's isolation suited the Quakers well in their desire for autonomy and, to a degree, isolation – there was no road, only an ox-cart track, and it was a journey of several days to San José, 180km away. The families bought and settled on some twelve square kilometres of mountainside, dividing the land and building their houses, meeting house and school. The climate and terrain proved ideal for **dairy farming**, which fast became the mainstay of the economy with the building in 1954 of the local cheese factory (*la lechería*). The area is now famous in Costa Rica for its dairy products – you'll see various Monteverde **cheeses** sold in most Costa Rican supermarkets – though abroad the area is better known as the home of several pioneering **private nature reserves**. Of these, Monteverde is by far the best known, although the less-touristed **Reserva Santa Elena** is just as interesting, with an equally pristine cloudforest cover. Because it receives fewer visitors you may spot more animal and bird life here, and you will certainly have a quieter walk through the forest than at Monteverde. More or less adjacent is the **Bosque Eterno de los Niños** (Children's Eternal Rainforest), established with funds raised by schoolkids from all over the world. More difficult to describe than the charms of the cloudforest reserves, though, is the Monteverde area's nameless quality of enchantment – a combination of tranquil beauty, invigorating weather and the area's weird mix: part tidy Swiss farming community, part tropical botanical garden. For a comprehensive preview of the area, visit the **website** Ⓦwww.monteverdeinfo.com, which has background information on the flora and fauna of the cloudforest, plus details and current prices of tours and hotels.

If there's a downside to the Monteverde area, it's the **expense**. Admission fees to the reserves are between $6 and $8, and if you want to take a guided tour, you're looking at shelling out at least another $15. Accommodation near the reserve tends to be expensive, though the further away from the entrance you get, the better value lodgings become. Eating, too, is pricey, owing in part to the distance involved in trucking in food from San José, and partly, perhaps, to the captive audience. The **rainy season** (May–Nov) is the best time to visit Monteverde if you want to avoid the crowds, although the weather can stay rainy and grey for days on end. Ideally, try to come at the beginning or end of the wet season, when you get the double benefit of fewer visitors but good weather.

The road to Monteverde

Dazed travellers, stumbling off the bus from San José, often wonder why the roads to Monteverde are so bad. The obvious reasons are the terrain – mountainous, with a large run-off of soil in the wet season – and the fact that these roads, like so many in Costa Rica, were built to serve small rural communities. The difference with Monteverde, though, is that tens of thousands of visitors make the journey up and down to see the reserve, passing through villages that elsewhere in the country would not expect to see more than a handful of tourists each year.

In fact, Monteverde has become more popular than anyone every really imagined, but although tour operators regularly bemoan the state of the roads up to the reserve, the Monteverde Conservation League (MCL) and the community in general have resisted suggestions that the road(s) up to Monteverde be paved, arguing that easier access would increase visitor numbers to unsustainable levels and threaten the integrity of the local communities. In any case, Monteverdeans are fully aware that local businesses, especially hotels, benefit from the fact that people have to spend at least a night in the area. Whatever the future holds, it's unlikely that Monteverde will be ruined: the community is too articulate and organized to let itself be overrun by its own success.

Arrival

Getting to Monteverde independently **from San José**, especially in the dry season, entails some pre-planning. There are only two bus services daily: buy your ticket as far in advance as possible, and buy your return ticket as soon as you arrive. In the wet season you should be able to get away with buying your ticket just a day in advance. **From Puntarenas**, or travelling from La Fortuna de San Carlos in the Zona Norte via Tilarán (see p.313), demand is somewhat less strained, and you can probably get away with not booking. Wherever you arrive from, in the dry months you should **book a room** in advance – the larger and plusher hotels are often full for weeks at a time with tour groups, and the cheaper ones are also much in demand. In the wet season, especially midweek, you can probably get away with turning up on spec. Give yourself at least three days in the area; one to get up there, at least one to explore (two is better), and another to descend.

All the major operators offer **tours** to Monteverde from San José, usually comprising two or three nights with accommodation, and sometimes meals, pre-paid – a smooth but rather pre-packaged way to experience the area. Transport (generally in a private minibus) to and from the capital and between your accommodation and the reserve is included, and the operators may even lay on wildlife-spotting treks with a private guide. The main difference between tours is the hotel they use, and whether or not the reserve entrance fee is covered in the price.

By car

Driving from San José to Monteverde takes some three and a half hours via the Interamericana – two hours to the turn-off (there's a choice of three – see below), then around another ninety minutes to make the final mountainous ascent. The question most drivers face is which **route** to take, and hardened two-day 4WD veterans argue endlessly about which way is more exciting and entails shifting into four-by-four mode more often.

One route, sometimes called the Sardinal route, follows the Interamericana north from Puntarenas towards Liberia, branching off at the **Rancho Grande** turning to Monteverde. Buses go a shorter route, continuing past Rancho Grande to the **Río Lagarto** turn-off – just before Río Lagarto itself – which is signed to Santa Elena and Monteverde. The least-known route, which local *taxistas* will swear on a book of lottery tickets is the best, is via **Las Juntas de Abangares**, a small town reached from a small road, labelled "145" on some maps, off the Interamericana. Once you've reached Las Juntas, drive past the main square, turn left and continue over a bridge; turn right, and follow the signs. The first 7km of this 37-kilometre road, via Candelaría, are paved, but have some spectacular hairpin bends – drive slowly. Higher up are a few magnificent viewpoints where the whole Gulf and Peninsula of Nicoya can be seen in the distance. You can also reach Monteverde from **Tilarán**, near Laguna de Arenal. The road (40km) is often very rough, but provides spectacular views over the Laguna de Arenal and Volcán Arenal (both covered in chapter 4).

Whichever route you take, you'll need a **4WD** in the rainy season, unless you are very good at fishtailing up and down hills while dodging large stones. Indeed, some agencies will refuse to rent you a regular car to drive up to Monteverde in the rainy season, no doubt through long experience with cars breaking down or foundering in mud.

By bus

All **buses** arrive first in Santa Elena. Some then continue along the road to Monteverde, making their last stop at the Lechería (cheese factory). Most people arrive on one of the two direct services from **San José**'s Tilarán terminal. Note that with the afternoon service you'll arrive after dark (it takes three-and-a-half hours minimum – more like five, especially in the rainy season). From **Tilarán**, you can catch the 1pm bus (3hr). This service is only dependable in the dry season; in the rainy months you may have to walk for as long as an hour with your gear after the bus gives up. From **Puntarenas**, a bus leaves for Santa Elena at 2.15pm and arrives three hours later (note that this bus doesn't continue beyond Santa Elena).

The **Santa Elena bus stop** is at the top of the "triangle", next to the Banco Nacional, the local landmark from which all directions are given. From here, it's no more than 200m to anything you might need. If you are booked in to one of the hotels on the road to the reserve, stay on the bus and ask the driver to drop you off or, if you arrive on the bus from Puntarenas, arrange with your hotel to have a taxi meet you ($5–6).

Accommodation

The cheapest place to stay in the Monteverde area is **Santa Elena**. With the exception of the well-appointed *Arco Iris*, all the accommodation here is basic, but you'll get a bed and heated water at least, and almost certainly a warm welcome. Many small *pensiones* are run by local families or couples and offer an array of services, from home cooking – the prices quoted below are for room only – to laundry and horse hire. Some of the hotels "downtown" in the village triangle, like *Pensión Santa Elena* and *Pensión El Tucán*, are convivial places to meet up with other travellers. Santa Elena is also one of the few places in Costa Rica where you will be met off the bus by **hotel touts** scrambling to get you to stay at their budget *pensión* – their pitch is a little more fierce in the wet season, when there are fewer paying customers.

By contrast, most hotels in and around the **Monteverde** community aspire to European mountain-resort facilities and atmosphere and, with the exception of a couple of cheap *pensiones*, tend to be expensive and packaged, appealing to those who like their wilderness de luxe. You'll certainly be comfortable in the majority of these places – large rooms, running hot water, orthopedic mattresses, even saunas and Jacuzzis, are the norm. Most hotels have a restaurant and, if you come on a package, meals may be included. Many of the larger places are set in extensive grounds and have their own private trails in the surrounding woods. Most have a small library and show slides of local flora and fauna; aside from illustrated nature talks, nightlife within the hotels is low-key to non-existent – some have a small bar, and that's about it. You can check out many of the hotels listed below at ⓦ www.monteverdeinfo.com.

Wherever you stay, if you haven't come on a tour or with private transport, you are going to have to do a lot of **walking** – at least 5km uphill from Santa Elena to either reserve, or about 2km from the nearest hotels in Monteverde to the Monteverde reserve. Despite reports that people will give you a lift at least partway to either reserve if you stick out your thumb, nobody seems to be that obliging.

Santa Elena and around

Albergue Ecológico Arco Iris, up a side street just behind the *Pensión Santa Elena* (ⓣ 645-5067, ⓕ 645-5022, ⓔ arcoiris@racsa.co.cr). The best-value mid-range accommodation in the area, with well-decorated and spacious cabins in quiet landscaped gardens in a central location; they also have cheaper rooms with bunk beds (③) plus a family cabin (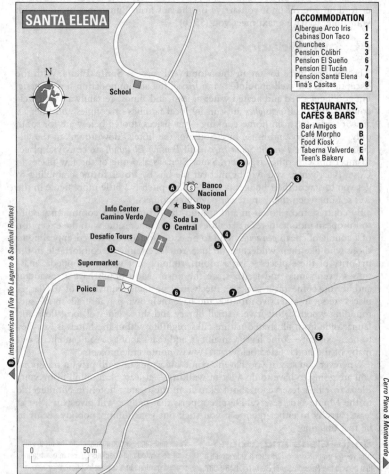). There's a pleasant family atmosphere, with a resident pet goat and the owner's horses nearby, and the delicious breakfast ($5) with German bread, granola, fresh fruit and eggs and toast is unequalled. ⑤

Cabinas Don Taco, 300m north of the Banco Nacional (☎ 645-6023). Pleasantly furnished individual cabinas with private bath; some have good views over the area and, on a clear day, the Gulf of Nicoya. Breakfast included. ①–②

Monte Los Olivos, 4km from Santa Elena on the road to Tilarán (☎ & ⓕ 283-8305, ⓕ 283-9116, ⓔ wwfcii@.racsa.co.cr). Ecotourist lodge with accommodation in authentic, rustic and simple cabins (some en suite), with porches and bunk beds. Tasty home-cooked meals ($3–5) are served in a large communal dining hall, and the extensive grounds include a small lake where you can swim, trails through the surrounding forest and opportunities for horse-riding. You'll need a car to get here, and try to reserve ahead. ②–③

Pensión Colibrí (☎ 645-5682). Simple, family-run accommodation in small rooms with shared bath and heated water. Cooked breakfasts (not included in room rate) and lunch-time *casados* are available, and the owner's also rent out horses. ①

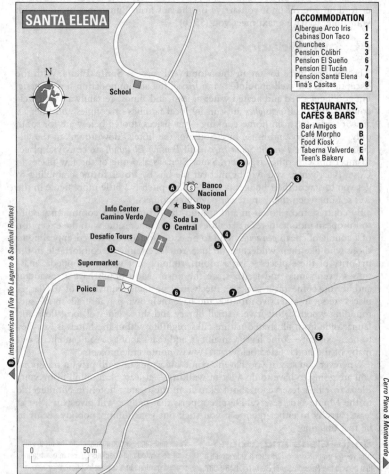

Reserva Santa Elena (5 km), Tilarán ▲ (Fortuna, Laguna de Arenal)& Las Juntas (for the Interamericana; 40 km),

SANTA ELENA

N

School

Banco Nacional

Info Center Camino Verde

★ Bus Stop

Soda La Central

Desafío Tours

Supermarket

Police

Ⓐ Ⓑ Ⓒ Ⓓ

❶ ❷ ❸ ❹ ❺ ❻ ❼

Ⓔ

ACCOMMODATION

Albergue Arco Iris	1
Cabinas Don Taco	2
Chunches	5
Pensión Colibrí	3
Pensión El Sueño	6
Pensión El Tucán	7
Pensión Santa Elena	4
Tina's Casitas	8

RESTAURANTS, CAFÉS & BARS

Bar Amigos	D
Café Morpho	B
Food Kiosk	C
Taberna Valverde	E
Teen's Bakery	A

⑧ Interamericana (Via Río Lagarto & Sardinal Routes)

Cerro Plano & Monteverde ▶

0   50 m

Pensión El Sueño, 25m east of the *correo* (T 645-5021). Fourteen cosy rustic wooden rooms right in the heart of Santa Elena; the cheaper ones, in the main building, have shared bath, while for around $10 more there are nicer en-suite rooms out the back. There's also a small lounge with Sarchí leather rocking chairs for stargazing, a kitchen for guests' use and friendly *dueños* who cook a good breakfast ($3) on request. Good low-season discounts. ②–③

Pensión El Tucán, 100m south of the Banco Nacional (T 645-5017, F 645-5462). The best rock-bottom budget rooms in town, with shared bath and heated water. Most rooms are located above the (good) restaurant of the same name: those with private bath cost a few dollars more, while the new cabins set away from the main building in quiet grounds come with private bath and balcony. ①–②

Pensión Santa Elena, 50m south of the Banco Nacional (T 645-5051, F 645-6060, W www.monteverdeinfo.com). HI-affiliated place (members get ten percent discount) right in the centre of things, with bargain rooms with shared bath for just $5, though they're small, basic and sometimes dark, and the owner has been known to "forget" reservations. It's also a great place to meet other travellers, plus there's a kitchen, a pleasant candlelit dining area, email, international phone and fax, laundry service, and the owners can fix up horse-riding tours with Sabina (see p.312). ①–②

Tina's Casitas, walk past the supermarket, and down the steps following a dirt track for 200m – it's clearly signed (T 645-5641, E tinas_casitas@hotmail.com). Friendly German owner Tina has built three small cabins, simply furnished and clean, although the walls are a little thin. ①–②

Monteverde and around

Albergue Reserva Biológica de Monteverde, at the entrance to the Monteverde reserve (contact the Monteverde Conservation League on T 645-5122, F 645-5034). Accommodation right in the reserve, though it's often packed with researchers and students – tourists have second priority. Reservations are essential, and you'll need to pay half your room cost 45 days in advance. $10 per person; $23 with meals.

Belmar, Cerro Plano (T 645-5201, F 645-5135, E belmar@racsa.co.cr). The oldest of the area's many Swiss-style hotels, the perenially popular *Belmar* has 34 rooms, some of them enormous – those at the front benefit from astounding views out over the Gulf of Nicoya. Reception is well

meaning but understaffed. ④–⑤

Cloud Forest Lodge 500m northeast of Santa Elena (T 256-0096 or 645-5058, F 645-5168). Set in 70 acres of primary and secondary forest high above Santa Elena, on a steep road, this secluded hotel is now the classiest in the area. The eighteen well-appointed wood-panelled rooms all come with cable TV, a large private bathroom, and terraces with dizzying views over the Gulf of Nicoya. The hotel has its own 5km system of trails, plus a bar, restaurant, horse-riding tours and a 25 percent discount off the Original Canopy Tour, which is located here. It's best if you have your own transport, since it's a bit of a walk to Santa Elena or Monteverde. ⑥

Hotel El Bosque, in Monteverde, about 3km from the reserve entrance (T 645-5221, E elbosque@racsa.co.cr). Twenty-eight rooms, rather prefab looking, but affordably priced, with private bath, hot water and a good range of sizes from singles to triples. Some have views over the hills out towards the Gulf of Nicoya. ④

Hotel El Establo, 500m beyond Santa Elena on the road to Monteverde (T 645-5110, F 645-5041). Rapidly expanding hotel (there are currently 20 rooms, with 30 more under construction) which when finished will also house a large restaurant, conference centre and heated pool. The existing rooms are simply furnished, and some are much lighter than others – ask to see a selection. New rooms will cost double or triple the current standard room rate ($40). There's also a nice games area and TV room. ④

Hotel El Sapo Dorado, 500m east of Santa Elena (T 645-5010, F 645-5180, E elsapo@racsa.co.cr). Twenty rooms housed in ten spacious, rustic wooden chalets on a hill with stupendous views of the Gulf of Nicoya; the "mountain suites" are set higher than the others, while the "sunset suites" lower down come with minibar, fridge, and a terrace with views over the gulf. There's also a good restaurant. ⑥–⑦

Hotel Fonda Vela, Monteverde (T 645-5125, F 645-5119, E fondavel@racsa.co.cr). Set in quiet grounds fairly close to the reserve, the *Fonda Vela* is probably the best hotel in the area, expertly managed, with attentive staff, beautiful touches and a range of good-value rooms – plus a highly recommended restaurant. New rooms ("suites") aim for de luxe, with huge bathrooms and beautiful fixtures and furniture. Older rooms are more rustic but have greater charm, with wood-panelled walls and huge windows – most giving astonishing views, especially at sunset. The owner's father is an artist and classical musician, and sometimes gives concerts in the hotel. ⑤–⑥

Hotel Heliconia, Cerro Plano (☎ 645-5109, ℻ 645-5007). Unpretentious and comfortable hotel, with friendly management and the very good *Mediterraneo* restaurant on site. Rooms have private bath and hot water, but are quite simply furnished for the price. ❺

Hotel de Montaña Monteverde, 500m south of Santa Elena (☎ 645-5046, ℻ 645-5320, ⒺＭ monteverde@ticonet.co.cr). One of the oldest hotels in the area, in a beautiful setting overlooking the Gulf of Nicoya. Rooms are housed in cabins, some with views to the Gulf, and the hotel has its own private forest preserve with a few trails, plus a Jacuzzi and sauna. ❻

Pensión Flor Mar, about 2km before the reserve entrance (☎ 645-5009, ℻ 645-5088). One of the area's older *pensiones*, offering basic and good-value (though small) rooms, some with private bath. The Nicaraguan owners serve tasty vegetarian food in the pleasant restaurant, and breakfast is included. ❸–❹

Pensión Manakín, Cerro Plano (☎ 645-5080). Friendly family pension with some of the best budget rooms in the area, including basic dorm accommodation ($10–15 per person), a couple of singles and a lovely double room which opens out onto the forest behind the house. There's a communal kitchen, and breakfast is included. ❹

Pensión Trogon, in Cerro Plano, next to *Pensión Manakín* (☎ & ℻ 645-5130). Good-value budget pension with lots of animals, including monkeys, around. Cheaper rooms have shared bathroom; a private bath costs an extra $10. There's a collective cooking area, and breakfast ($3) and dinner ($4) are also available. Freddy Mejías, the friendly and energetic owner, also offers a wide range of services including local transport and a laundry service. You can also camp in the grounds for $3. ❷–❸

Villa Verde Hotel, in Monteverde, near the reserve entrance (☎ 645-5025, ℻ 645-5115, ⒺＭ estefany@racsa.co.cr). Simply furnished rooms in quiet grounds, all with private bath with hot water, though some are a little dark; there are also villas for two people with fireplace and fridge ($90). Breakfast included. ❺

The villages

In recent years the tiny town of **SANTA ELENA** has benefited – economically, anyway – from the influx of visitors to the Monteverde reserve and, increasingly, to the Santa Elena reserve, 5km northeast. The centre of the village is a triangle, formed by three streets on which you'll find most of the businesses and services, and a number of the *pensiones*. Here you'll also find the only bank, *correo* and large grocery store for miles.

There is, however, no source of unbiased **information**. In Santa Elena, a father-and-son team (a frighteningly professional 12-year-old, in this case) run the Info Center Camino Verde in the centre of Santa Elena (☎ 645-5916, ℻ 645-6305), which sells tickets to the Santa Elena reserve, the Sky Walk, Sky Trek, and the Monteverde Canopy Tour; they can also arrange guided tours to the Monteverde reserve and guides for the Sky Walk. Friendly and efficient Desafío Tours next door offers a similar range of services, plus **internet access** ($5/hr); they can also hook you up with white-water rafting in the Fortuna area (see p.205) and run a speedy and enjoyable transfer from Monteverde to Fortuna and vice versa using horses, boat-taxi, and jeep-taxi, which gets you to Fortuna in about 4–5 hours and costs about $25. For a one-page handout with a map of the area and a helpful run-down of bus times and other transport details, head to the Pensión Santa Elena, 50m south of the Banco Nacional.

Travellers hang out at *Chunches* (Mon–Sat 8am–6pm; ☎ 645-5147), opposite the *Pensión Santa Elena*, which has a fax service, laundry, a small secondhand bookstore, a café serving espresso and snacks, US newspapers, and a useful notice board with details of tours, rooms and just about everything else. Banco Nacional can give advances on VISA and change **travellers' cheques**, a service also offered to guests by many of the upscale Monteverde hotels.

Essentially a group of dairy farms and smallholdings strung out alongside the dirt road between Cerro Plano and the Monteverde reserve, **MONTEVERDE** is a seemingly timeless place where milk cans are left out at the

Many people who come to Monteverde don't quite know what to expect from a Quaker (*cuáquer*) community. Quakerism does not impose any obvious standards of dress or appearance upon its followers – you're not going to see the jolly old man on the oatmeal box walking by – nor does it manifest itself in any way that is immediately obvious to visitors, save, of course, for the lack of bars.

Also called the Society of Friends, Quakerism, an altruistic, optimistic belief system, was founded by George Fox (1624–91), an Englishman born near Manchester. He instilled in his followers the importance of comporting themselves in the best way to encourage the goodness in others. Quakers are encouraged to see God in everybody, even those who are doing evil. Another cornerstone of Quaker belief is pacifism. All war is seen as unlawful, as it impedes the call to bring out people's "inner light". From the beginning, Quakers placed themselves in opposition to many of the coercive instruments employed by the state and society, and they continue to embody a blend of the conservative, the non-conformist and absolute resistance to state control.

In 1656 Quakerism arrived in the New World, where followers were initially subject to severe discrimination. It was a deeply felt pacifism that led to the exodus of several Alabama Quaker families from the USA in the early 1950s to settle in the Monteverde area. Harassed to the point of imprisonment for refusing the draft, the Quakers were convinced by Costa Rica's abolition of its army a few years earlier in 1948 – an extraordinary move under any circumstances, but particularly in the context of Central America – that they could live as they wanted, unmolested, in this remote corner of a remote country.

Quakers manage their meeting houses individually; there is no officiating minister and most meetings confine their agendas to the purely local. Gatherings are for the purpose of meditation, but anyone who is moved to say a few words or read simply speaks up, out of the silence. All verbal offerings in context are considered valid. Outsiders are welcome at the meeting houses, and there is no question of trying to convert them. In Monteverde visitors are invited to join the meetings at the Friends Meeting House, held on Sundays and Wednesdays (look for announcements on the various community noticeboards). San José's Centro de los Amigos para la Paz (Friends Peace Centre; ☎233-6168), C 15, Av 6 bis, is an excellent source of material on Quakers and other pacifist groups in Central America. They have leaflets, newsletters, newspapers and a small library, plus a café and weekly meetings and discussion groups.

end of small dairy-farm driveways to be collected, modest houses sit perched above splendid forested views, and farmers trudge along the muddy roads in sturdy rubber boots. The focal points of the community are the **lechería** (cheese factory), the **Friends Meeting House** and school, and the cluster of services around **CASEM**, the women's arts and crafts collective.

Eating, drinking and entertainment

Many visitors to **Monteverde** eat in their hotels, or in other hotels along the main road. Choices are wider in **Santa Elena**, where a few restaurants offer an alternative to hotel dining. One way to avoid eating endless *casados*, although you won't necessarily save any money, is to buy your own supplies in the **supermarkets** in Santa Elena or at the Coop Santa Elena store next to CASEM in Monteverde.

Santa Elena

Surprisingly, given the captive audience, Santa Elena is short on **restaurants** and, perhaps because of the lack of competition, prices are a bit high. On the main street in front of the church, Doña Laura's **food kiosk**, popular with the locals, serves up good, cheap *casados* – clamber up on a wooden stool and chat to the regulars. For **coffee and cakes**, *Chunches* is the best place to sit down with a cappuccino, although the cakes and pastries are better at *Teen's Bakery* opposite the bank, which is open from 5am – a good place to pick up breakfast if you're headed off to the Monteverde reserve on the 6.15am bus. If it's a **beer** you're after, *Bar Amigos* is the local gathering spot; the lighting can be a bit garish, but the beer is cheap and cold, and they often have live music from 8 to 11pm at weekends. After the music at *Bar Amigos* stops, there's usually a mass exodus to the *Taberna Valverde* just outside Santa Elena on the road to Monteverde, or the *Discoteca La Cascada* in Monteverde (Thurs–Sat), both of which keep going until 2 or 3am.

Café Morpho, in the centre of Santa Elena, across from the church. The best bet in Santa Elena itself, with well-prepared, healthy – if not particularly cheap – food, with a pleasant candlelit ambience in the evening.

El Mediteraneo, at the *Hotel Heliconia*, Cerro Plano. A varied menu of expertly cooked Italian/international food with very fresh shellfish and fish, grilled meats and pizza, though the red wine is scandalously overpriced.

El Sapo Dorado, 1km east of Santa Elena. Good vegetarian *casado* (although the rest of the menu isn't particularly distinguished) served in a nice atmosphere, with classical music on the stereo and jaw-dropping views out over the gulf from the open-air terrace in front. Open evenings only.

Johnny's Pizzeria, Cerro Plano. One of the most popular restaurants in the area, both among tourists and locals, and it's not hard to see why, with superior cocktails, pizza ($5) cooked in an open wood oven and superb service in a candlelit colonial decor. There's pasta, meat and fish on the menu too, but everybody seems to come for the pizza. During the day you can sometimes see hummingbirds in the quiet garden from the window and outside tables.

Miramontes, in the *Miramontes Hotel*, 2km from Santa Elena on the road to Tilarán. If it's Swiss food and atmosphere you're craving, this is the place to tuck into tasty cheese fondue and strudel in a cosy setting.

Paradise Café, opposite the *Hotel El Establo*, between Santa Elena and Cerro Plano. The portions are grudging and the service lacks charm, but if it's a bagel you want, this is the only place outside of San José you're likely to get it. They also hold a weekly salsa class and show films a few evenings a week. Closed in the afternoons and for the whole of Sunday.

Pensión El Tucán, 100m south of the Banco Nacional. Open to non-guests, the restaurant at the *Pensión El Tucán* serves very tasty and cheap local food, especially *casados*. They're probably the best bet for breakfast in the village, with good gringo fare – the banana pancakes are recommended. Closed lunch time and the whole of Sunday.

Soda La Central, in the centre of Santa Elena. New soda, strategically placed in front of the bus stop to San José, Puntarenas and other points, with above-average *casados* ($3) and tasty hamburgers with fries ($2).

Soda La Gioconda, on the outskirts of Santa Elena on the road to Monteverde, next to the clinic, Good local food at local prices.

Monteverde

Cuisine in many of the top-end **Monteverde** hotels is very good indeed, and most of them open their restaurants to the public. Menus are usually fixed, and meals are served at set times – drop round in person to book for dinner and see what's on the menu. Apart from that, as it's a Quaker community there's not much **drinking** in the village. Most restaurants do have alcohol on the menu, and several have an above-average selection of red wine, but you might still notice a whiff of temperance in the air. *Stella's Bakery* (daily 6.30am–4.30pm), opposite CASEM, offers delicious chocolate-chip cookies, strudels, brownies and coffee in a pleasant café-like atmosphere – although service is brusque, to say the least.

Fonda Vela, in the *Hotel Fonda Vela*, Monteverde. Two restaurants at the hotel of the same name – a fairly formal and intimate fireside restaurant and a larger, slightly less staid one – with lovely views out over the property and a varied (though fairly expensive) menu including good, generous breakfasts and succulent dinner specialities – try the chicken in white wine and almonds ($11).
Restaurante de Lucia, Cerro Plano. One of the area's most upmarket restaurants, with an elegant atmosphere and good wine list; the grilled meats are particularly succulent, and the sea bass ($9) is simply delicious. Prices are not always written on the menu, though – an awkward situation where you're forced to ask, or get a larger-than-expected bill.
Restaurante El Bosque, in Monteverde, about 3km from the reserve entrance. Now under Italian management and specializing in authentic and tasty thin-crust Italian pizzas (about $6). The spaghetti marinara ($8) is good too, but you can't help feeling that the real attraction is the pizza.

Art and entertainment

If you're around during January, February or the first half of March, you can enjoy the **Monteverde Music Festival**, which attracts all sorts of groups from chamber orchestras to big bands. Performances are held at the Monteverde Institute, near the cheese factory in Monteverde, daily at 5pm, and there's sometimes a shuttle bus from Santa Elena to performances – ask at your hotel. **Monteverde Studios of the Arts** (℡645-5435, in the US ℡800/370-3331, ⒲www.mvstudios.com) offers workshops from January to August in, among other things, batik, ceramics, storytelling, travel writing, photography and yoga. Nearby, the women's arts and crafts cooperative **CASEM** (Mon–Sat 8am–5pm, Sun 10am–4pm) sells embroidered T-shirts, blouses and dresses, and some hand-painted T-shirts – lovely but expensive. Cards emblazoned with various representations of the quetzal are also popular. Various **art galleries** have opened recently in the area, including several beyond CASEM on the way to the reserve. All represent the work of local artists, of which there is a strong community in the area.

Reserva Biológica Bosque Nuboso Monteverde

By 1972, homesteading in the Monteverde area had spread to the surrounding cloudforest. At the behest of two visiting American biologists and a number of local residents, plans to establish a reserve were initiated. Funds provided by the World Wildlife Fund enabled the community to buy an additional five-and-a-half square kilometres, bringing the total protected area of the **RESERVA BIOLÓGICA BOSQUE NUBOSO MONTEVERDE** (Monteverde Cloudforest Reserve; daily 7am–4pm; $10; ℡645-5112, ⒲www.monteverde-info.com/monteverde_conservation_league) to ten square kilometres. Administered by the non-profit-making organization Centro Científico Tropical (Tropical Science Centre) based in San José, today the reserve is hugely popular with both foreigners and Costa Ricans, who flock here in droves – especially during Easter week and school holidays – to walk the trails through one of the last sizeable pockets of primary cloudforest in Mesoamerica.

Few people fail to be impressed, either by the sheer diversity of **terrain** – from semi-dwarf stunted forest on the more wind-exposed areas to thick, bearded cloudforest vegetation – or by the truly moving **views** from the reserve's various miradors, where you find yourself looking out over a world of dense, uninterrupted green, the unimpeded wind whistling in your ears, with no sign of human habitation as far as the eye can see. The Monteverde reserve supports six different **life zones**, or eco-communities, hosting an estimated 2500 species of plants, more than 100 species of mammals, some 490 species of butterflies, and over 400 species of birds, including the **quetzal**.

The cloudforest

Many visitors are enchanted with the primeval, otherworldly feel of the cloud-forest, often described as a disturbingly impenetrable terrain of quetzals, jaguars and other near-mythical animals. The cloudforest's most obvious property is its dense, dripping wetness, and even in the morning or in the dry season it looks as if everything has just been hosed down. Cloudforests are formed by a perennial near-100 percent humidity created by mists, produced here by the northeasterly trade winds from the Caribbean that drift across to the high ridge of the continental divide, where they cool to become dense clouds which settle over this high-altitude forest.

The cloudforest can also be rather eerie, due to the sheer stacking and layering of vegetation, and the preponderance of epiphytes. Everything seems to be growing on top of each other, and you will notice, walking the Monteverde and Santa Elena trails, that many trees seem to be wholly carpeted by green mosses and other guests, while others seem to be choked by multiple layers of strangler vines, small plants, ferns and drooping lianas.

The leaves of cloudforest plants are often dotted with scores of tiny holes, as though they have been gnawed by insects that have given up the ghost after only a few millimetres. This is, in effect, exactly what happens. Many cloudforest plants have the ability to produce toxins to deter insects from eating an entire leaf or plant, producing the poisons from the excess energy conserved by not having to protect themselves against adverse weather conditions, such as a prolonged dry season and heavy winds and rain. Insects in turn guard themselves against being poisoned by eating only a very little of any one leaf at any time, and by sampling a wide variety, thus juggling the different toxins consumed so that they are not overwhelmed by any one.

It's important to remember, however, that the cloudforest cover – dense, low-lit and heavy – makes it difficult to see, and many visitors leave the reserve disappointed that they have not spotted more wildlife. Plant-spotting at Monteverde, however, is never unrewarding, especially if you take a **guided walk**, which will help you identify thick mosses, epiphytes, bromeliads, primitive ferns, leaf-cutter ants, poison dart frogs and other small fauna and flora – not to mention directing you towards the fantastic views. Serious rainforest walkers should plan on spending at least a day in the reserve, and many people spend two or three days quite happily here.

Temperatures are cool, as you would expect at this altitude: 15° or 16°C is not uncommon, though in the sun it will feel more like 22° to 25°. The average **rainfall** is 3000mm per year, and mist and rain move in quickly, so dress in layers, and be sure to carry an umbrella and light rain gear, especially after 10 or 11am. You should also bring binoculars, fast-speed film and insect repellent. It's just about possible to get away without **rubber boots** in the dry season, but you will most definitely need them in the wet. The reserve office (see below) rents them out for $1, as do some hotels.

Practicalities

The reserve **entrance** is a walk of 45 minutes to an hour from most of the hotels and about a two-hour (7.5km) walk from Santa Elena – despite reports that people will pick you up and give you a lift at least partway, this is often not the case. Except on Sundays, a **bus** leaves Santa Elena twice daily for Monteverde (Mon–Sat 6.15am & 1pm; $0.80); alternatively, a **taxi** will set you back $6 per carload – try to get a group together to share. If you decide **to walk**, be aware that the road is uncomfortably dusty in the dry season, and that there's a surprising amount of traffic, though nearer the reserve it becomes quieter and gives good views over the area. Because the vegetation is more open along the road, opportunities for **bird-spotting** are often just as good if not better than on the reserve trails, especially early in the morning.

The **reserve office**, right at the entrance, is very well geared up for tourists, with a **visitor centre** where you can pick up maps (including a contour map of the area, also covering Volcán Arenal) and buy useful interpretative booklets for the trails. There's also a good souvenir shop and a small soda, which dishes out coffee, cold drinks and snacks plus vegetarian *casados* at lunch time. Also at the reserve's entrance, the **Galería Colibrí**, or Hummingbird Gallery (Mon–Sat 9.30am–4.30pm, Sun 10am–2pm), named after the birds that buzz in and out to feed at the sugared water fountains, sells nature slides, cards, jewellery and the like, as well as hosting slide shows on cloudforest topics.

You can stay inside the reserve in bunk-bed **dormitory** accommodation ($10 per person, or $23 including three meals daily), although it's often full with students, researchers or volunteers (telephone the reserve office on ☏645-5112 or 645-5122 for information). The accommodation is spartan, with just a bed and a sheet, but it gets you right inside the reserve and is a good place to meet people. For overnight and long-distance hikers, there are three simple **shelter facilities** along the trails – the closest is upwards of four hours' hike from the reserve entrance – which cost $4 per person per night, plus the entrance fee for each day you're in the reserve (for example, if you stay in the reserve for one night, you'll pay two days' entrance fees plus accommodation, a total of $24). Shelters have beds and foam mattresses, drinking water, a basic shower, a small number of cooking utensils and, crucially, electricity. You must bring a sleeping bag, torch and food. The reserve office will give you the key and explain trail conditions and hiking times to each shelter.

The reserve imposes **a quota**, with a maximum of 120 people allowed in the reserve at any given time. Although you're unlikely to be turned back because the quota has been reached – even in the dry season – it's another good reason to get there early. If you can't or don't want to go on the official **tours** organized by the reserve (see "Tours and talks" on p.307), a number of local people act as excellent and experienced **guides** for the reserve and the entire Monteverde area. Ask at your hotel or *pensión*.

The reserve strongly advises that serious birders, wildlife spotters and those who would prefer to walk the trails in quiet avoid the **peak hours** of 8 till 10am, when the tour groups pour in. If you arrive at this time in the dry season you are very unlikely to have trails to yourself.

The trails

Most of the reserve's **trails** are contained in a roughly triangular pocket known as **El Triángulo**. They're clearly marked and easily walkable (at least in the dry season), and many of them are along wooden or concrete wiremesh-netted pathways – though this somewhat mars the feeling that you are hiking in a real wilderness, at least it means you're not slipping and sliding around in seas of mud.

The visitor centre at the reserve office gives out a good map of El Triángulo, with accurate distances, and shows roughly where you pass the continental divide – there's no obvious indication when you're on the ground. If you're keen to plunge straight into the cloudforest, the self-guided **Sendero Bosque Nuboso** (2km) is the trail to make for, armed with the interpretive booklet sold at the visitor centre. Cover along this trail is literally dripping with moisture, each tree thickly encrusted with moss and epiphytes. You'll hear howler

What to see in Monteverde

Seeing a quetzal is almost a rite of passage for visitors to Monteverde, and many zealous, binocular-toting birders come here with this express purpose in mind. A member of the trogon family, this slim bird, with sweet face and tiny beak, is extraordinarily colourful, with shimmering green feathers on the back and head, and a rich, carmine stomach. The male is the more spectacular, and it is he who has the long, picturesque tail and fuzzy crown. About a hundred pairs of quetzals mate at Monteverde, in monogamous pairs, between March and June. During this period they descend to slightly lower altitudes than their usual stratospheric heights, coming down to about 1000m to nest in dead or dying trees, hollowing out a niche in which to lay their blue eggs. However, even during nesting season you are not guaranteed a glimpse of them; the best chance is on a guided tour. If you want to try your luck, however, it's best to arrive at the reserve between 5.30 and 6am – experienced birders know the hour just after dawn is the most fruitful. Even though the office is closed, you can enter the reserve trails and pay your entrance fee when you leave.

Other birds to look out for at Monteverde are the bare-necked umbrella bird and the bizarre-looking three-wattled bellbird (March–Aug especially), with three black "wattles", or skin pockets, hanging down from its beak. Even if you don't see one, you'll almost certainly hear its distinctive metallic call, which has been likened to a pinball machine. There are also some thirty types of hummingbird. Several types of cats, all of them considered endangered, live in the reserve, which gives them enough space for hunting; among them are the puma, jaguar, ocelot, jaguarundi and margay. As with all rainforest and cloudforest habitats, however, you should not expect to come face to face with a jaguar. If you are lucky you might hear the growl of a big cat coming at you out of dense forest, which is usually unnerving enough to cure you of your desire to actually see one.

Another famous resident of the Monteverde area – though it may now be extinct – is the sapo dorado, or golden toad, a vibrant red-orange-gold toad discovered in Monteverde in 1964. However, it has not been spotted since 1989. Ithomiid butterflies, better known as clearwings, have just that: transparent wings, fragile as the thinnest parchment. They abound in the reserve, especially on the Sendero Bosque Nuboso, feeding on dead insects, flower water and bird droppings.

monkeys and a few flutters, but it is quite difficult to spot birds in this dense, dark cover. Your best bet is around the beginning of the trail, where the three-wattled bellbird and the bare-necked umbrella bird hang out. The spongy terrain efficiently preserves **animal tracks** – in the morning you may be able to see the marks of the agouti and coati.

El Camino (2km), higher in elevation, is a mini-version of the road up to Monteverde: stony, deeply rutted in spots, and muddy. There's a small mirador, La Ventana (on the trail signed to Peñas Blancas), looking out to the thickly forested hills on the other side of the continental divide. It's reached via a virtual staircase of cement-laid steps which lead to a high, wild, wind-sculpted garden, empty and pristine, dotted with stunted vegetation, and suspended over an amazingly green expanse of hills – a surreal place, the only sound being the wind whizzing past your ears.

Clambering up and down both sides of the continental divide, the **Río, Pantanoso** and **Chomogo** trails are all fairly long, some steep, and more apt to be muddy than the others. A new trail, **Sendero El Puente**, links Sendero El Camino with Sendero Roble in El Triángulo. It features, as the name suggests, a 100-metre suspension bridge which takes you high up into the trees, and allows you to observe the cloudforest canopy.

Tours and talks

Whatever sort of **guided nature walk** you go on in Monteverde – or anywhere else in the country, for that matter – it's worth realizing that you are more likely to be looking at plants, smaller animals and insects rather than staring into the eyes of pumas or tapirs. Bearing this in mind, the reserve itself runs excellent guided walks, including a slide show of photographs by world-renowned photographers and long-time Monteverde residents Michael and Patricia Fogden. Walks start at 8am sharp (or at 7.30am and 8pm if demand is high), last three to four hours and cost $15 (plus the $10 entrance fee). Ask in your hotel or call the reserve office a day in advance on ℡645-5112 or 645-5122 to secure a place, since there's a maximum of just nine people – and make sure to arrive on time, too, or they'll set off without you. It might seem like a pricey tour, but the guides are informative and the experience supremely educational.

Another highly recommended way to experience another side of the rainforest – though not for those who are put off by the dark or by creepy crawlies – is the **night walk** ($13), which leaves at 7.30pm each evening – you don't have to book for this tour, but turn up at the reserve office by 7.15pm to buy a ticket. Many of the reserve's animal are nocturnal, and your chances of seeing one of the mammals – albeit only as two brilliant eyes shining out of the night – are vastly increased after dark. These are fascinating, albeit eerie, experiences, and recommended if you want to see a maximum of amphibian, reptile and insect life and you don't spook easily – some guides like catching bats, and they will certainly find a few stick insects and frogs, while it's not uncommon to see tarantulas. Also fairly easy to spot are the hosts of (sleeping) birds, including toucans with their beaks tucked between their feathers. Although the guides carry a powerful torch, it's useful to bring your own, as well as rain gear. Walks last about two and a half hours.

There are also occasional **orchid walks** – ask at the visitor centre. **Discussions** are sometimes held at 7.30pm in the Galería Colibrí (Hummingbird Gallery) auditorium, covering such broad themes as "gender issues in sustainable development" and "sex lives of lesser-known insects", usually given by visiting academics and researchers. Look for notices posted at the hotels, at the Galería Colibrí or in *Chunches* in Santa Elena.

Reserva Santa Elena

Less touristed than Monteverde, the **RESERVA SANTA ELENA** (daily 7am–4pm; $7; Ⓦwww.monteverdeinfo.com/reserve.htm), 6km northeast of

Santa Elena, offers a no-less illuminating experience of the cloudforest, with 3.1 square kilometres of mainly primary forest cover, poised at an elevation of 1650m. Santa Elena reserve was established in 1992 as a separate entity from the Monteverde reserve and the MCL, and is owned by the local high school, whose students sometimes work in the reserve during school holidays, and who help to maintain the trails year-round. It strives to be self-funding, assisted by donations and entrance fee revenue, and gives a percentage of its profit to local schools. For maintenance and building projects it depends greatly on **volunteers**, usually foreign students (see box above).

There's a **visitor centre** at the entrance, with washrooms and an information booth where staff hand out maps of the twelve-kilometre network of trails. Highly recommended guided tours can be arranged for between one and four hours (about $20, including entrance fee); the reserve also rents out boots ($6.50) and issues a succinct six-page leaflet discussing rainforests, cloudforests, epiphytes, seed-dispersal patterns and some of the mammals you might see within the reserve. A small interpretative display written and illustrated by local schoolchildren documents the life of the cloudforest ecosystem and the history of the reserve itself. A cafeteria serving coffee, cold drinks and sandwiches is open in high-season (Nov–April).

Walking to the Santa Elena reserve involves an arduous six-kilometre trudge, much of it uphill from the village; if you walk it, take lots of water and sunscreen and be advised you might not have much energy left to explore the reserve when you get there. **Jeep-taxis** ($6) can be arranged by your hotel or can be picked up on Santa Elena's main street; the reserve can call a taxi to come and pick you up to take you back into town. More economically, a **collective taxi** ($2) leaves for the reserve from in front of the Banco Nacional daily at 6.45am, 11am and 3pm, returning at 10.30am, noon and 3.30pm; make reservations a day in advance at the Info Center Camino Verde.

The trails

Santa Elena's four **trails**, covering a total distance of 12km, are confined to a roughly square area east of the entrance. The easiest (and fastest) to walk is the hour-long **Youth Challenge** trail, which has an observation tower near its end from where, occasionally, you might be able to see Volcán Arenal – though it's usually too cloudy. With the map from the visitor centre – which clearly states distances between points and the estimated time needed to walk them – you should be able to tackle even the more difficult trails such as the Sendero del Bajo, Sendero Caño Negro and Sendero Encantado. If you want to be on your own and have the best chance of views toward Volcán Arenal, get to the reserve as early as possible, especially in the wet season, before cloud, mist and fog roll in to obliterate the views of the volcano.

Some trails are covered in cut wood and mesh, while others are unmade. In the wet season bring rubber boots (or rent them at the entrance), rain gear or an umbrella, and even a light sweater. Though the average temperature is 18°C, it can feel cooler once the clouds move in. **Guided nature walks** ($15) are offered at 7.30am and 11.30am daily; **night tours** ($15, inclusive of entrance fee) leave at 7pm daily. A line of **hummingbird** feeders has been strung along the entrance path, where you can watch these tiny, many-coloured birds zooming in and out of the nectar-dishes.

Other attractions around Monteverde

A number of attractions have sprung up around Monteverde in recent years, some of which have come to rival visits to the reserves themselves in popularity – among the latest activities are various "adventure" experiences, with canopy tours in particular seemingly mushrooming from every available tree. Generally, though, for serious walkers and birders these activities are useful fallbacks should you need to fill an afternoon before heading off to the reserves in the early morning.

Canopy tours and the Sky Walk and Sky Trek

The **Original Monteverde Canopy Tour** (℡645-5243 or ℡257-5149, Ⓦwww.canopytour.co.cr; $45), pioneered here by locals and now copied all over the country, is based at the *Cloud Forest Lodge* near Santa Elena. Using techniques developed by spelunkers (cavers) and canyon rapellers, the Canopy Tour allows you to experience the rainforest from a bird's-eye view. Having grappled up strangler figs to reach the top – which gives great views of life in the forest canopy – you can whizz from platform to platform via pulleys strung on horizontal traverse cables. It's not a particularly educational experience, nor do you normally see much plant, animal or bird life – you're moving too fast – but it's a nice little thrill. You have to reserve in advance for the tour, something a number of businesses in Santa Elena will do for you; the Info Center Camino Verde in Santa Elena also lays on free transportation, leaving daily at 7.15am, 10.15am and 2.15pm.

Three other places in the area offer canopy tours: the **Monteverde Canopy Tour** office on the road to the *Reserva Santa Elena* (℡645-5929, Ⓕ645-5822, Ⓦwww.canopytours.com; $35) is a well-equipped outfit whose tour comprises a 1600-metre ride through the canopy via fourteen platforms; their brochure's translation unfortunately refers to "casualties" – let's hope they mean "accidents". They'll pick you up from your hotel; make reservations a day in advance, either directly with the office, through your hotel, or with the Info Center Camino Verde, who also lay on free transport if you book through them, leaving at 8am, 10.30am, 12.30pm and 2pm.

The **Sky Trek** (℡642-5238), located at the Sky Walk office on the road to the Santa Elena reserve, charges the same price ($35) as the Monteverde Canopy Tour and has an extensive network of trails, platforms, suspension bridges and "ziplines" – the ropes you slide along from platform to platform. The longest zipline is 427m in length, at a height of nearly 130m – thrilling or scary, according to taste. Tours leave at 7.30am, 9.30am, 11.30am, 1.30pm and 2pm; reserve at least a day in advance.

It's worth noting that, while most canopy tour operators take considerable precautions to make sure the experience is a safe one, as with any kind of adventure tourism, **accidents** do happen, less from equipment failure than from people not listening properly to the advice given before they are strapped in.

A more sedate ride through the forest is offered by **Aerial Adventures** (daily 6am–6pm; $10; ℡645-5960), on the road to the *Finca Ecológica* in Cerro Plano. Rather like a rainforest ski lift, the ninety-minute trip consists of a slow journey above the rainforest in hanging chairs. You're given a guide to tree and plant species and there are lots of opportunities for bird-watching, especially in the early morning – a pleasant, contemplative experience, and reasonably priced.

A different bird's-eye view of the forest can be had from the unique **Sky Walk** (daily 7am–4pm; $12; Ⓦwww.skywalk.co.cr), an impressive series of

Horse-riding tours in the area attracted controversy a few years ago following reports of widespread mistreatment of horses by outfitters running trips between Monteverde to Fortuna. The trip consisted of at least five hours riding on steep, muddy, slippery and boulder-strewn trails, and there were many stories of abuse, and even of horses dying on the trail, as competition became fierce and some outfitters felt the only way they could make money was to buy cheap – meaning old or unfit – horses, and work them literally to death.

Fortunately, increased awareness of the plight of local horses means that this trail is no longer used. Several companies now offer a less arduous (both for people and horses) journey between Monteverde and Fortuna, and at least one, Desafío (in Monteverde ⓣ645-5874, ⓕ645-5904, ⓔrivers@racsa.co.cr; in La Fortuna ⓣ479-9494, ⓕ479-9463, ⓔdesafio@racsa.co.cr), has instigated a rota of veterinary inspections and days of rest for their horses. Their transfer from Monteverde to La Fortuna comprises a ninety-minute jeep-taxi ride down to Río Chiquito, a three-hour horse-ride around Lake Arenal, a trip in a motorized *lancha* across a narrow part of Lake Arenal, followed by a 25-minute taxi ride to Fortuna.

This transfer has proved a popular alternative to the otherwise lengthy drive or bus journey down from Monteverde and around Lake Arenal (if you have a rental car you can still do the trip: Desafío will take out secondary driver insurance and drive your vehicle around the lake to Fortuna for you). Quite apart from being a fast way to get from A to B, the transfer is fun, although not necessarily comfortable – it's meant to be "adventurous", after all. Desafío makes sure the trails used are safe for the horses, and the trip offers a fairly quiet and undemanding ride in a nearly uninhabited area, with spectacular views of the volcano (when it's clear).

As a general note, horse lovers may find the physical state of some horses in Costa Rica very distressing. It's difficult to know, though, whether the remedy is to boycott the offending horseowner – making clear why – or simply to pay up and hope that some of your money makes its way into the horses' feed bin.

bridges and paths built by Fernando Valverde, a biologist from Monteverde and world authority on the construction of rainforest suspension bridges. Located 3.5km along the road towards the Santa Elena reserve, the Sky Walk consists of a network of suspension-style footbridges, stretching from the ground to canopy level between acres of virgin rainforest. Bridges provide some really spectacular views, plus there's the added thrill of walking along the wobbly structures over serious heights. Several of the bridges take you right alongside the canopy of tall trees – indeed some of them have colonized the bridges, draping woody lianas over the ramparts. If you're lucky and bring binoculars you can spot **birds** at their own level, rather than craning your neck as usual. You'll have to be much more sharp-eyed to see the howler monkeys who, judging from their enthusiastic grunting, live around the trails. It's worth visiting even in rainy or cloudy weather – take waterproofs – and can be combined with the Sky Trek tour (see above).

Other trails and walks

For a smaller-scale rainforest walking experience, the **Reserva Sendero Tranquilo**, a private reserve in the grounds of a local farm behind the cheese factory in Monteverde, offers informative guided tours (book on ⓣ645-5010; around $13 per person) through primary- and secondary-growth forest. The only part of the **Bosque Eterno de los Niños** (Children's Eternal Rainforest; part of the Reserva Santa Elena) that you are currently permitted to walk is the **Bajo El Tigre trail** (daily from 8am, last entrance at 4.30pm, though you can stay in the reserve until dusk; $5), a short, unchallenging trek at lower elevations than in the cloudforest reserves with great views out to the Gulf of Nicoya; sunsets from here can be spectacular. The **Finca Ecológica** (daily 7am–5pm; $6), south of Santa Elena, is, as the name suggests, an ecological farm where bananas and coffee are grown. Animals in the area frequently come to snack at feeders the farm has set up; the most frequently sighted creatures are agoutis and coatis, as well as a resident sloth. A system of trails leads to a quiet waterfall, and you can also take a guided night walk here ($13), leaving daily at 5.30pm and 7.30pm.

Other attractions and activities

Unlike most such places in Costa Rica, the **Monteverde Butterfly Garden**, near Santa Elena (daily 9.30am–4pm; $7), is geared to research rather than the exporting of pupae. The entrance fee includes an hour-long talk by knowledgeable staff on the life cycle of butterflies. The best times to visit are between 11am and 1pm, especially on a sunny day – butterflies tend to hide when it's raining. You can volunteer here; contact ⓔ wolfe@racsa.co.cr.

Just east of Santa Elena, Fernando Valverde's **Serpentario** (daily 8am–5pm; $3) has a range of unnerving vipers in residence; informative talks are available for groups with advance notice. About 2km from the Monteverde reserve entrance, **La Lechería** (Cheese Factory; Mon–Sat 7.30am–noon & 1–4.30pm, Sun 7.30am–12.30pm) sells various types of Monteverde cheese and *cajeta*, a butterscotch fudge, as well as delicious ice cream. Guided tours (book on ⓣ645-2850; $8) give you a behind-the-scenes glimpse into the world of cheese.

Other good options for a rainy afternoon are the **Orchid Gardens** in Cerro Plano (daily 9am–5pm; $5; ⓣ645-5510), run by orchid enthusiast Gabriel Barboza, with over 400 different species of orchids on show, including the world's smallest. A **slide show** of Patricia and Michael Fogden's rainforest photos takes place year-round at the Monteverde reserve auditorium (daily 4.30pm; $3).

You can't **ride horses** on the trails in the Monteverde or Santa Elena reserves, but a number of local outfitters hire them for trips through the surrounding countryside – as always in Costa Rica, the state of the horses varies wildly. In Santa Elena ask at the *Pensión Santa Elena* for Sabine Hein (ⓣ645-5051, ⓦwww.horseback-riding-tour.com), who has several healthy, well-cared for horses and who knows the stunning countryside around Santa Elena well – you can stop at several look-out points with panoramic views out to the Pacific and the Nicoya Peninsula. On the road to Monteverde, Meg's Stables (ⓣ645-5052), next to Stella's Bakery, hires out horses for around $10/hr.

Moving on from Monteverde

Buses to San José leave Santa Elena daily at 6.30am and 2.30pm, and there's sometimes an extra bus on Friday, Saturday and Sunday at 2pm. For Tilarán, one bus leaves daily at 7am; for Puntarenas, the daily service departs at 6am. Two buses also leave daily at 5am and 6am for the two-hour journey to Las Juntas, from where you can get to Liberia and points north in Guanacaste. Check in the office beside the bus stop in Santa Elena; tickets are sold here too.

Around Monteverde

TILARÁN, 40km northeast of Monteverde and roughly the same distance west of Fortuna, is not an attraction in itself, but is a pleasant, clean town and a useful stop-off between Guanacaste to the west and the Zona Norte to the east. It is also about the best place in the country for **windsurfing** – the Tilawa Viento Surf & High Wind centre (℡695-5050, ℻695-5766) can arrange all kinds of rentals and advise on conditions on the Laguna de Arenal. There are also a few **cabinas** in Tilarán: two good options are *Cabinas El Sueno,* 150m from the northwest corner of the central plaza, with good rooms and private bath and a nice patio (℡695-5347; ❷), and *Hotel Naralit* (℡695-5555; ❷), opposite the church, whose comfortable and spotless rooms have TV and private bath. The best restaurant in town is **La Carreta**, behind the church, North American-owned but offering nicely cooked Italian food, along with pizzas and sandwiches to eat in or take away. In addition to the service to Santa Elena (see p.302), Tilarán has good **bus** connections with Cañas and the Interamericana, from where you can head on to Liberia and the Guanacaste beaches, or south to Puntarenas. The bus station is 100m north of the Parque Central.

Some 37km southwest of Santa Elena and 10km off the Interamericana, **LAS JUNTAS DE ABANGARES** was a small gold-mining centre in the late nineteenth and early twentieth centuries. Just off the road to Monteverde, 5km outside town on a rough (4WD only) little road, its **Ecomuseo Oro**, or "Gold-Mining 'Ecological' Museum", is one of the more bizarre uses of the "eco-" prefix in Costa Rica – gold mining is not known for respecting environmental integrity. Commemorating the activities of the Abangares Gold Fields Company, the small-scale exhibition features dusty photographs of the area's mini-gold boom, along with a ragbag collection of mining artefacts. The museum is meant to be open daily between 6am and 5pm, but is often closed; donations are gratefully accepted. Surrounding the building, short trails pass through pockets of tropical dry forest.

You can ask to be dropped off the bus from Santa Elena (see p.302) at the entrance to the Ecomuseo, although you'll have a hot thirty-minute walk from the fork (follow the signs). If you're driving down the road from Monteverde, look for a fork on the left just before you hit the outskirts of Las Juntas, and the museum is signed from here. You'll need 4WD, or could drop your car in Las Juntas and hop in one of the 4WD **taxis** waiting at the rank around the corner from the church.

Puntarenas

Heat-stunned **PUNTARENAS**, 110km west of San José, has the look of raffish abandonment that haunts so many tropical port cities. What isn't rusting has long ago been bleached out to a generic pastel, and the town's cracked, potholed streets, shaded by mop-headed mango trees, are lined with old wooden buildings painted in faded tutti-frutti colours. It's hard to believe now, but in the 1800s this was a prosperous port – the export point for much of Costa Rica's coffee to England – and a popular resort for holidaying Ticos. Today most vacationing Costa Ricans have abandoned its dodgy beaches and somewhat tawdry charms in favour of the ocean playgrounds of Manuel Antonio and Guanacaste,

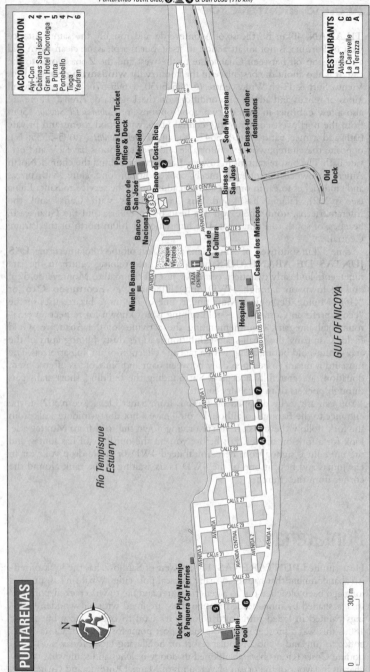

Puntarenas Yacht Club, ③, ▲ ④ & San José (116 km)

PUNTARENAS

N

0   300 m

ACCOMMODATION

Ayi-Con	2
Cabinas San Isidro	4
Gran Hotel Chorotega	1
La Punta	5
Portebello	7
Tioga	4
Yadran	6

RESTAURANTS

Alohas	C
La Caravelle	B
La Terazza	A

Río Tempisque Estuary

GULF OF NICOYA

Paquera Lancha Ticket Office & Dock

Mercado

Banco de Costa Rica

Banco de San José

Banco Nacional

Parque Victoria

Muelle Banana

Casa de la Cultura

Casa de los Mariscos

Soda Macarena

Buses to all other destinations

Buses to San José

Old Dock

Plaza Central

Hospital

Paseo de los Turistas

Dock for Playa Naranjo & Paquera Car Ferries

Municipal Pool

CALLE 10
CALLE 8
CALLE 6
CALLE 4
CALLE 2
CALLE CENTRAL
CALLE 1
CALLE 3
CALLE 5
CALLE 7
CALLE 9
CALLE 11
CALLE 13
CALLE 15
CALLE 17
CALLE 19
CALLE 21
CALLE 23
CALLE 25
CALLE 27
CALLE 29
CALLE 31
CALLE 33
CALLE 35
CALLE 37

AVENIDA 3
AVENIDA CENTRAL
AVENIDA 1
AV 4 BIS
AVENIDA 2
AVENIDA 4

and foreign tourists, who never spent much time here anyway, come only to catch a *lancha* or ferry across to southern Nicoya or to go on a boat trip to pristine **Isla Tortuga** – although in recent years the town's tourist trade has been somewhat revived by the daily visits of the giant **cruise ships** that call at the site of the old docks. Puntarenas carries on, however, as a working fishing town and a regional hub, with banks, businesses, hotels and transport facilities serving the populations of the southern Nicoya Peninsula and the Pacific coast.

Arrival and orientation

Puntarenas means "sandy point", and that's what it is: a thin, island-like finger of sand pointing out into the Gulf of Nicoya, just five blocks across at its widest point, but more than sixty streets long, and attached to the mainland only by a narrow isthmus. You come into town from the east, on the narrow isthmus road that follows the old train tracks, eventually becoming the **Avenida Central**. It seems to take for ever to get into the centre; if you're driving, look for the orange colonial-style building on your right. This is the **Casa de la Cultura**, and marks the centre of town.

Scores of **buses** arrive from San José every day. The bus stop is on the corner of C 2 and Paseo de los Turistas, near the old train tracks and the old dock that juts out into the gulf. **Local services** from Manuel Antonio and Quepos arrive just across the street from the San José bus stop, as does the daily service from Liberia, which arrives at about 11am, and the daily run from Santa Elena, which currently arrives at about 9.30am.

The **north shore** is the estuary side, where the Gulf of Nicoya narrows into the Río Tempisque. The *lancha* to Paquera on the Nicoya Peninsula – from where you can head on to Playa Tambor and Montezuma – leaves from the busy docks here. The **south shore** is the site of the old docks, long abandoned by the container ships for the deeper harbour of Puerto Caldera, but now used by the cruise ships that dock here daily in the dry season. This side of town is worth a visit, if only for the sere, uninterrupted views out over the wide mouth of the Gulf of Nicoya and across to the Pacific. To the right is the southern tip of the Nicoya Peninsula; to the left, Costa Rica's long western coast.

The town centre is just a few blocks northwest of the San José bus stop. Here you'll find banks, the municipal market, and a slew of cheap hotels. The Banco de Costa Rica, Banco de San José and the Banco Nacional, virtually next to each other on the north shore near the docks area, offer **currency exchange**. If you get stuck, hotels like the *Gran Hotel Chorotega* can probably help you out, or you could try the more upscale ones like the *Tioga*, although these normally only change dollars for their own guests. Though it's easy enough to get around on foot, **taxis** scoot through the town, and can be flagged down. You can also wave down the **buses** that ply Avenida Central – the last stop is in front of the Playa Naranjo ferry dock at the western end of town.

Accommodation

The **cheap hotels** around the docks are useful if you want to catch an early *lancha* to Paquera. It's not a great area at night, however, and most cheap hotels in this neighbourhood not listed below are specifically to be avoided – the clientele may be drunk and/or not be there for sleeping. In a hot area, Puntarenas stands out as an exceptionally hot town. Wherever you stay, make sure your room has a **fan** that works, otherwise you'll be as baked as a ceramic pot by morning.

Ayi-Con, 50m south of the *mercado* on C 2
(☎661-0164 or 661-1477). Venerable budget
option near the Paquera *lancha* dock, catering
mainly to Costa Ricans. Rooms are depressing
cells with cold water, but it's cheap, clean, safe
and central. ②

Caribbean Village Fiesta, on Playa Doña Ana,
10km southeast of Puntarenas (☎663-0808,
Ⓕ663-1516, Ⓔfiesta@racsa.co.cr). There's little
of the Caribbean village about this all-inclusive
hive of organized activity, but it's undeniably popu-
lar with Costa Rican familes and good for those
travelling with small children or who just want a
break. It's situated on brown-sand Playa Doña Ana,
which isn't that clean, though nicely landscaped
pools – including a large children's wading pool –
help make up for it. Management is friendly and
prices are inclusive of everything, including alco-
hol. Rooms have cable TV and a/c, and the buffet-
style food is quite good. If you get bored you can
join the grannies in a salsa class. ⑥–⑦

Costa Rica Yacht Club, 3km east of the town
centre, next to the *Portobello* (☎661-0784,
Ⓕ661-2518). Accommodates non-members if
there's space. Rooms are nothing special but the
ambience is very nice, and you get a/c, private
bath with hot water; and a swimming pool. ④

Gran Hotel Chorotega, C 1, Av 3 (☎661-0998).
Very basic downtown hotel near the docks. Rooms
have a table fan, just about adequate for this cli-
mate, and private or shared bath. Well run and
very popular, it's often full of dockers and refinery
workers at weekends. ①–②

La Punta, Av 1, C 35 (☎661-0696). Looks a bit
abandoned, but it's close enough to the ferry for
the Nicoya Peninsula for you to park your car in
the line the night before, and stumble out of bed
and onto the boat the next morning. Rooms are
nothing special, but are reasonably priced, and
there's a small, leaf-strewn pool. ③

Portobello, 3km east of the town centre on the
estuary (north) side (☎661-1322, Ⓕ661-0036).
The plushest place in Puntarenas proper, set in
landscaped gardens, with swimming pools, a
restaurant and good en-suite rooms with hot water
and a choice of a/c or sea breezes. ④

Tioga, Paseo de los Turistas, C 17/19 (☎661-
0271, Ⓕ661-0127). The nicest downtown hotel,
with an elegant atmosphere, extra-friendly man-
agement and a/c rooms – those on the sea-facing
side get the best views. There's also a soothing
interior courtyard and a very pretty indoor pool.
Rates include breakfast in the cafeteria-style
restaurant. ④–⑤

Yadran, Paseo de los Turistas, C 35/37 (☎661-
2662, Ⓕ661-1944). Drab and institutionalized
tourist-complex atmosphere, with lots of concrete,
but the carpeted rooms are comfortable enough,
with TV, a/c and bath, and the quiet situation, with
uninterrupted views over the gulf, is pleasant.
There's also a swimming pool and restaurant. ⑦

The Town

By far the best thing in town is the clean, cheap and underused **municipal
pool** (daily except Tues 9am–4pm; $2), at the western edge of town, perched
on the very point of the sandspit. From the pool's landscaped terrace and gar-
dens you have an uninterrupted view over the whole gulf and off to the brown
humps of the Nicoya Peninsula in the distance.

Otherwise, there's little to see, though the place does have a certain sad
charm. Even if Puntarenas does look as if it is slowly expiring in the Equatorial
sun, it is doing so with an affecting elegance. The southerly promenade is opti-
mistically called **Paseo de los Turistas**, though nowadays the only *turistas* to
be seen are off the cruise ships or on high-season weekends. A wide avenue, it's
bordered on the town side with hotels and restaurants and a couple of discos,
while the sea-facing side is home to a long painted promenade – the colours,
of course, long since faded by the sun. The **beach** itself used to be polluted;
these days the sand at least looks quite clean, backed by sparse landscaped
greenery, but there's an unsettling, metallic whiff coming off the water, and the
breezes do little to mitigate the intense heat. It's pleasant enough, however, to
sit at one of the beachside restaurants or kiosks, where you can dig into good
pargo (snapper) and other fresh fish while watching clouds drift in across the
Gulf of Nicoya.

By ferry

Puntarenas is a jumping-off point for the southern Nicoya Peninsula. The Playa Naranjo and Paquera car ferries, run by Coonatramar (ⓣ661-1069, ⓕ661-2197), currently leave from the docks at the western end of the northern side of town for Paquera (3 daily at 8.45am, 2pm & 8.15pm; 1hr–1hr 30min; $10). A private ferry company, Naviera Tambor, also runs car ferries from here to Paquera at 5am, 12.30pm and 5pm. In summer (Dec–April), especially, arrive ninety minutes before sailing to be sure of a space. Bear in mind that, though it's possible to drive to Paquera from Naranjo in about an hour, the roads are not in great shape, and you'll need a 4WD. A much better option if you've got a car is to take one of the ferries to Paquera. Buses meet each Coontramar car ferry in Paquera (but not the Naviera Tambor ferry; best to get a taxi or try to hitch a lift) – it's a drive of about 45 minutes to Tambor and about an hour to Montezuma.

The passenger ferry (*lancha*) to Paquera currently leaves from behind the *mercado*, three times daily in the high season, twice in low season (1hr 30min; $1.50). Schedules are posted outside the blue kiosk where you buy tickets. Buses for Tambor and Montezuma are timed to meet the Paquera *lancha* and leave once everyone is on board. Be quick to get off the ferry when it docks and you'll have a better chance of getting a seat on the bus. The only buses meeting the Playa Naranjo car ferry go north to Nicoya, a dusty and uncomfortable two-hour trip over horrible roads.

By bus

Buses leave at least every hour on the hour for San José from the San José bus terminal just off the Paseo de los Turistas on C 2. Services to Liberia (6 daily; 3hr) and Santa Elena (daily 2.15pm; 3hr 30min) depart from just across the road. For Manuel Antonio, take the Quepos service from the same place (3 daily; 2hr). This bus will also drop you off just 2km from Jacó.

From the eastern end of the Paseo, the long, skinny finger of the **old dock** crooks out into the gulf. This is where the bananas and coffee were loaded, before all the big shipping traffic shifted 18km down the coast to the deeper harbour of Puerto Caldera. The docks on the northern, **estuary** side, however, are a quite different matter, with a jungle of ketches and sturdy mini-trawlers testifying to a thriving fishing industry. Despite the aura of hot lassitude, a lot of business is done in the few blocks surrounding the docks, especially in the hectic **mercado**, a cacophony of noise, people and pungent smells. Safe enough during the day, the docks area is best avoided at night.

West of the docks, the **Parque Victoria** is one of the least park-like *parques* in the country, little more than a long, thin strip of green, bordered by red benches and an unusual and pretty stone **church**, which looks like it might be more at home in England. A few metres south, the **Casa de la Cultura** (officially Mon–Fri 8am–noon & 1–4pm) exhibits evocative *fin-de-siècle* photographs documenting Puntarenas' lost prosperity – sepia images of tough fishermen clash with upright, white-clad Edwardian ladies, their husbands made wealthy from coffee exports.

Eating, drinking and nightlife

Perhaps because of its history as a bona-fide resort, eating out in Puntarenas is expensive. Even fish – which have probably been caught no more than a couple of hundred metres away – is pricey, and you'll be lucky to get *casados* or *platos del día* for less than $6. As usual, the **mercado** is a good place to pick up a cheap meal and a *refresco*, although the atmosphere is pretty frantic, and you should avoid drinking anything made with the local water. The beachside sodas and kiosks near the **old dock** are more appealing places to linger over a quiet drink or a seafood lunch.

For **evening meals**, if you've got money to spend, head for one of the well-above-average restaurants that line the western end of the **Paseo de los Turistas**. For **nightlife**, the Casa de Cultura hosts concerts on summer weekends (Dec–April), and there are sometimes discos at the larger hotels, especially on Saturday nights and holiday weekends.

Restaurante Alohas, Paseo de los Turistas, C 19/21. The most popular place in town for an evening drink, with an extensive and expensive menu, and nice breezy outdoor tables where you can sit looking out to sea. Live music on Tues.
Casa de los Mariscos, Paseo de los Turistas, C 7/9. Good seafood, though it's not cheap ($6–10).
Restaurante La Caravelle, 100m west of the *Restaurante Alohas* on the Paseo. Good, honest French cuisine – not cheap, but a change from *casados* and burgers. Closed Mon.

Restaurante La Terraza, Paseo de los Turistas, C 21/23. All in all the nicest place in town, with a reasonably priced menu concentrating on seafood, pizza and pasta. The marinated mussels are a bargain at $4, and the seafood salad is also good.
Soda Macarena, at the bus stop. A small soda with ocean views and cheap and delicious food, including all kinds of fruit plates and toasted sandwiches; try their "Churchills" – similar to a crushed-ice granizado, but made with ice cream.

The southern Nicoya Peninsula

The hour-long ferry trip from Puntarenas across the Gulf of Nicoya is soothing and slow-paced, with the boat purring through usually calm waters and past island bird sanctuaries, while the low brown hills of the Nicoya Peninsula, ringed by a rugged coastline and pockets of intense jungly green, rise in the distance. Much of the southern peninsula has been cleared for farming, cattle grazing or, in the case of **Tambor**, given over to tourism. **Cóbano**, 6km inland from Montezuma, is the main town in the southwest of the peninsula, with gas station, *correo*, *guardia rural* and a few bars, though most tourists pass straight on their way to **Montezuma**, one of the most popular beach hangouts in the country. Montezuma is reached by a reasonable and partly paved road lined by cattle pasture which gives you – like many parts of the Osa Peninsula (see p.374) – a startling vision of the future of the deforested tropics. Once covered with dense primary Pacific lowland forest, today the fields are dotted with stumps, the red soil cutting rivulets down hills as it runs off, unimpeded by the natural drainage of the felled forest cover.

Refugio Nacional de Vida Silvestre Curú

The small, privately owned **REFUGIO NACIONAL DE VIDA SIL-VESTRE CURÚ** (⊕661-2392; $6), 8km southwest of Paquera, protects a wide variety of flora, including many endangered **mangrove** species. Also within its grounds are some pretty white-sand **beaches**, dotted with rocky coves – a kind of mini-Montezuma. Deciduous forest areas are home to a great variety of **wildlife** which, due to the small number of people allowed in each day, have not become too shy. You are most likely to see or hear monkeys and agoutis – live deer and wildcats also live here but are less forthcoming. At low tide the rocky tidal pools can yield crabs and assorted shellfish. All in all there

One of the most popular day-trip destinations in Costa Rica, Isla Tortuga is actually two large (over three square kilometres in total) uninhabited islands, just off the coast of the Nicoya Peninsula near Paquera. Characterized by its poster-perfect white sands, palm-lined beaches and lush, tropical deciduous vegetation, it's certainly a picturesque place, offering quiet – during the week, at least – sheltered swimming and snorkelling. At the weekend, however, a number of tour operators and boats disgorge their loads of passengers, roughly at the same time and the same place, somewhat marring the islands' image as an isolated pristine tropical paradise.

Cruises to Isla Tortuga usually leave from Puntarenas and take between one and three hours' sailing time each way. There's plenty of opportunity for spotting marine animals, including large whale sharks, depending upon the season. You also pass by Negritos and Guayabo island sanctuaries, where swarms of sea birds nest. On the island there's time for lunch (usually included in the tour price) and snorkelling, followed by sunbathing or a little walking. Swimming in the warm water is perfectly safe.

The majority of visitors to Tortuga actually come on day-trips from San José. All in all, tours from the capital – including transport to and from Puntarenas – cost about $100, which is fairly steep, especially as you only get two to two-and-a-half hours on the island itself. One of the biggest operators is Calypso Tours (℡256-2727, 🖶 233-0401, 🌐 www.calypso.com), who also run one-day catamaran cruises around the Gulf of Nicoya ($150, including all meals). A slower-paced and less regimented option is to take a tour from Tambor or Montezuma on the Nicoya Peninsula (see pp.319–320).

is a network of seventeen **trails**; you can ask the owners for a map and directions, and some are signposted.

Practicalities

A number of **restrictions** govern visits to Curú. You cannot arrive here on your own, unannounced, but must call the owner, Sra Schutz, a week in advance, and let her know when to expect you, so she can make sure the gate is unlocked. Only thirty people are allowed in at any one time – students and field researchers have priority, and Curú's association with the University of Massachusetts means that it is often booked solid. Guides are available for about $15 for a few hours – ask when you telephone, or talk to the Schutz family when you arrive. No **camping** is allowed, but you could ask if there is space at the accommodation reserved for students and researchers. However, it's far easier to use Tambor as your base and travel here by taxi or bus.

Tambor

Since 1992, when the Spanish hotel group Barceló completed its 400-room *Hotel de Playa Tambor*, the small village of **TAMBOR**, set in Bahía Ballena, has become synonymous with big-time tourist-resort development. The hotel is one of the largest single hotel developments in Costa Rica and has been plagued by controversy since even before it opened. In a drawn-out legal case, the Costa Rican government is still suing the developers for breaches of the law and degradation of the environment.

The Playa Tambor project sparked much discussion from the outset. At times the backers seemed wilfully bent on acting out every environmental and social gaffe possible. Barceló was accused of both illegally draining and filling ecologically valuable mangroves, similar to those protected by the nearby Curú Wildlife Refuge, and also of violating the Costa Rican law that states that the first 50m of any beach is public property, with no development or habitation allowed. Continual complaints about the group's working and management style were aired both locally and in the national press. Despite an order issued by the Costa Rican supreme court in 1992, ruling that the project be stopped, the government appeared unwilling to enforce the ruling. Barceló went ahead as planned and the hotel was opened in November the same year – Grupo Barceló now owns several other hotels elsewhere in the country.

Despite the presence of the mega-hotel, set off by itself in the bay, with its own road, grounds and guards, the whole area remains rather remote in feel, and the **village** itself, surrounded on two sides by rising, thickly forested hills, is friendly and laid-back. There's not a lot to do other than go to the seal-grey, sandy beach, which stretches along a narrow horseshoe strip at the western end of the sheltered Bahía Ballena. Swimming is good, and whales are sometimes seen in the bay (hence the name – *ballena* means whale). The setting is pretty and the beach broad and calm. If you fancy a trip out to Isla Tortuga (see p.319), enquire at the hotels or ask one of the local boatmen.

Tambor has an **airstrip** which, apart from being used by guests of the *Hotel de Playa Tambor*, is also served by scheduled Sansa flights. The **Montezuma–Paquera bus** stops outside.

Accommodation

Dos Lagartos, by the beach (☎683-0236). Beautifully situated hotel with friendly staff and unremarkable rooms with fans and a choice of private or shared bathroom – the latter are particularly good value. Also has a good restaurant. ②–③

Tambor Tropical, by the beach (☎683-0011, ☎683-0013). Small, beachside, resort-type hotel, with comfortable hexagonal cabinas with kitchen, set in very scenic grounds centred on a pool and

Jacuzzi. It's all very nice and very expensive – not to say overpriced. ⑧

Tango Mar, by the beach (☎683-0002, ☎683-0003). Large resort-type hotel which hasn't yet perpetrated any major ecological disasters, with swimming pool, tennis court and a small golf course. The comfortable cabins with private bath are nice, if overpriced, though weekly discounts and low-season bargains can make them more affordable. ⑦–⑧

Montezuma and around

The popular beach resort of **MONTEZUMA** lies some 25km southwest of Paquera, near the southwestern tip of the Nicoya Peninsula. Some twenty-five years ago a handful of foreigners fell in love with the place and settled here. Then it was just a fishing village, largely cut off from the rest of the country; nowadays it's definitely been discovered: lights twinkle, music pours out of restaurants and bars peopled by tattooed boys and batik-clad girls. Some who knew it when it was still primarily a fishing village complain that it has become commercialized and touristy, and certainly, compared to the other small towns around the peninsula, Montezuma comes as a shock. For a place that didn't even have electricity until ten years ago, and which only received a working telephone exhange in 1995, the village has grown quickly, developing from a haunt of younger backpackers into a destination for groups as diverse as honeymooners and ecotourists, complete with a full complement of tourist facilities ranging from vegetarian restaurants to internet cafés. But its remote location and community of conscientious foreign residents will probably contain over-development, at least for the time being.

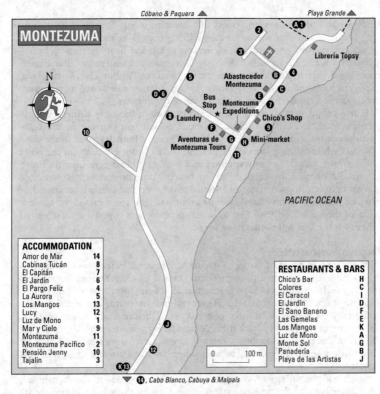

Cóbano & Paquera ▲   Playa Grande ▲

A1

Librería Topsy

Abastecedor
Montezuma

Bus
Stop   Montezuma
               Expeditions

Laundry   Chico's Shop

Aventuras de   Mini-market
Montezuma Tours

PACIFIC OCEAN

ACCOMMODATION

Amor de Mar	14
Cabinas Tucán	8
El Capitán	7
El Jardín	6
El Pargo Feliz	4
La Aurora	5
Los Mangos	13
Lucy	12
Luz de Mono	1
Mar y Cielo	9
Montezuma	11
Montezuma Pacífico	2
Pensión Jenny	10
Tajalín	3

RESTAURANTS & BARS

Chico's Bar	H
Colores	C
El Caracol	I
El Jardín	D
El Sano Banano	F
Las Gemelas	E
Los Mangos	K
Luz de Mono	A
Monte Sol	G
Panadería	B
Playa de las Artistas	J

0   100 m

▼ **14**, Cabo Blanco, Cabuya & Malpaís

What brings everyone here is the astounding beauty of the setting. Montezuma and the coast south to Cabo Blanco feature some of the loveliest coastline in the country: white sand, dotted with jutting rocks and leaning palms, and backed by lush greenery, including rare Pacific lowland tropical forest. The village itself is surrounded by thickly forested hills, and there are uninterrupted views out into the Pacific – especially arresting on nights when there's a full moon or when the occasional lightning storm illuminates the horizon and silky waters.

Arrival and information

From where you get off the bus, at the bottom of the hill, you can see pretty much the entire centre of "town". *Chico's Bar* is straight ahead, as is the grocery store and the souvenir shop. To the right are two of the village's places for health-food and smoothies, the *Sano Banano* and the *Soda Monte Sol*.

Nearly everyone in town claims to be able to fix you up with tours. On the main drag, the helpful multilingual people at **Aventuras de Montezuma** (℡ & 🖷 642-0050, 🖂 avenzuma@racsa.co.cr) have the largest range of tours, services and information in town, including trips to Isla Tortuga ($40) and horseriding on the beach and to local waterfalls ($25). They also have an internet café, international phone service, arrange car and motorbike rental, sell tickets for Travelair flights from Tambor to San José, and have information on current bus, ferry and flight times to and from Montezuma.

In the centre of the village, the **Montezuma Expeditions** kiosk rents out bicycles and motorbikes, and offers full-day trips to Isla Tortuga ($40; including breakfast and time for snorkelling); diving trips ($80, including equipment rental); four-hour horse-rides to waterfalls ($25); and boat transfers to Jacó – though this can be a rough ride. They also arrange transfers to Cabo Blanco reserve and act as the local Sansa agent for flights to Tambor. The *Sano Banano*, adjacent to Aventuras de Montezuma, has an internet café above its restaurant with satellite connection for about $3 for thirty minutes.

Chico's shop, next to the bar and grocery store of the same name, sells sunscreen, film, clothing and telephone cards, which you can use in the **telephones** outside (if the lines are working). There's a **laundry** next to the *Sano Banano*, while for nice **souvenirs**, head to the El Jardín gift shop (in the hotel of the same name). For **newspapers** and a lending library, try Librería Topsy, about 20m before the entrance to the beach. Some businesses in town close down between noon or 1pm and 4pm. Almost everyone seems to change dollars, or will accept **travellers' cheques** (but will give you a rate slightly below that of the banks). Still, it's best to bring some colones – you'll certainly need them for the bus and the ferry or *lancha*.

Accommodation

There's a good range of places to stay in Montezuma. **Prices** are moderate, as the village still caters to a young, studenty crowd who can't afford the rates of, say, Manuel Antonio, and even prices in some of the more upscale hotels drop in low season, by about $10–15. **Reservations** are useful in the dry season, especially on weekends, and are essential over Christmas and Easter when, as elsewhere in the country, both nationals and foreigners are on holiday and want to go to the beach. Most times, though, if you arrive on a late bus without a reservation, there is bound to be somewhere to stay, even if it's not your first choice.

Staying in the **village** is convenient, but can be noisy, due to the shenanigans at *Chico's Bar* and the odd car pulling in and out of the village. Elsewhere it's wonderfully peaceful, with choices out on the **beach**, on the road that heads southwest to the Cabo Blanco Refuge, and on the sides of the steep hill about 1km above the village. If you get bitten by the Montezuma bug (and many do) and decide you'd like to stay **long-term**, you'll see notices around town advertising houses for rent; most are located between Montezuma and Cabo Blanco, or Mal Pais. Try the noticeboard at the *Restaurante El Capitán*, the restaurant at the *Hotel Amor de Mar*, or ask in the Aventuras de Montezuma tour and information agency.

Camping is, according to various sources, either grudgingly permitted or vigorously frowned upon, so ask around – there have been problems with beach campers killing palm trees by building fires too close to their trunks, while the lack of sanitary facilities available also raises hygiene questions. You would be better advised to stay at one of the organized camping sites between Montezuma and Cabuya, on the road to the Reserva Absoluta Cabo Blanco, where there are toilets, showers and barbecues.

In the village

Cabinas Tucán (℡ 642-0284). Basic, good-value accommodation in a clean and well-run two-storey wooden house, though rooms can get hot and are a little airless during the day; upstairs rooms are marginally better. Shared cold-water baths and table fans, but no curtains. ❸–❹

Hotel El Capitán (℡ 642-0069). Plain, rather dark rooms, with cold water only, in an old wooden house close to the beach. It's cheap, though, and the first-floor veranda is a good place from which to watch the town's goings on. ❷

Hotel El Jardín (℡ & ℻ 642-0074). Attractive, spacious cabins with wooden ceilings, tiled bathrooms, and verandas or terraces with leather rocking chairs from Sarchí. Some rooms come with fridges, while those upstairs have views over the town and sea. ④

El Pargo Feliz (☎ 642-0065). Plain but reasonable value cabinas, very close to the beach, with fan and private bath (cold water). There's a good restaurant attached, too. ③.

Hotel La Aurora (☎ 642-0051, Ⓔ aurorapacific@hotmail.com). Pleasant, friendly and environmentally conscious *pensión*, with 16 varied rooms – the older budget rooms are good value, especially in low season, with fans, communal fridge, coffee- and tea-making facilities and shared bath. Upstairs rooms are a little more expensive but still very good value, while the new cabinas come with a/c and private bath with hot water; there's also an apartment with its own kitchen and terrace. ②–④

Hotel Lucy (☎ 642-0273). A Montezuma stalwart (the government once attempted to have torn down as it violates the *zona marítima*, which prohibits building on the first 50m of beach) containing ten clean and basic rooms with cold-water showers and a nice seaside veranda upstairs. It's one of the village's best cheapie options, if a little quirky – weirdly, pictures of autumnal New England adorn the walls. The owner also offers a reasonable laundry service. ①–②

Hotel Luz de Mono (☎ 642-0090, Ⓕ 642-0010, Ⓦ www.luzdemono.com). New hotel with friendly management offering well-appointed rustic stone villas and rooms, all with private bath, hot water, fridge, coffee maker and CD player (complete with CDs of Costa Rican music). There's also an excellent restaurant attached. Good value for groups, although it's expensive for couples. ⑤–⑦

Mar y Cielo (☎ 642-0261). Nice beachfront cabinas (sleeping 2–6 people), a cut above the basic category, with private bath, fan, cold water and sea breezes. As the name suggests, your view here is of sea and sky, though local sound effects might include nearby *Chico's Bar*, in addition to the crashing waves. ④–⑤

Hotel Montezuma (☎ & Ⓕ 642-0258). Popular with budget travellers, and one of the cheapest places in town, with rooms offering either shared or (considerably more expensive) private bath and ceiling fans. Management is not that friendly, however, and there's noise from *Chico's Bar* next door. Go for the upstairs rooms if you want to sleep. ②–③

Hotel Montezuma Pacífico (☎ 642-0204). Rooms are rather characterless, but good value, considering you get a/c, hot water and breakfast included in the price; there are good low-season discounts too. Try to get a room at the front, with something of a view, or one with a balcony. ④

Hotel Tajalin (☎ 642-0061, Ⓕ 642-0527). Reasonably priced rooms in a quiet location near the centre of the village – those with fan are better value than those with a/c, while the ones with top floor are airier and have sea views. ⑤

Around the village

Amor de Mar, 600m southwest of the village on the beach (☎ & Ⓕ 642-0262, Ⓔ shoebox@racsa.co.cr). Upmarket (for Montezuma) seafront hotel, well managed by its German owners, set in pretty landscaped gardens on a rocky promontory, with hammocks swinging between giant mango trees. There's a good selection of rooms, with and without bathroom – those upstairs and facing the sea are best – and most come with veranda and ocean views. Good low-season discounts, plus there's a small restaurant downstairs serving healthy breakfasts. ④–⑤

Horizontes de Montezuma, 1.8km before Montezuma on the road from Cóbano (☎ & Ⓕ 642-0534, Ⓔ collina@racsa.co.cr). Small and distinctive hotel in tropical-Victorian style, perched in the hills above Montezuma. Rooms are spacious and airy; all have private bath with hot water and balcony with jungle or ocean views. There's a pool and a good restaurant as well, and the owners offer intensive private Spanish lessons. ⑤

Hotel Los Mangos, about 500m down the road to Cabo Blanco (☎ 642-0076, Ⓕ 642-0259). Expensive-looking but slightly dark bungalows, with large (hot water) showers and fan. The cheaper rooms – the best are upstairs – in the main building down by the road are good value, particularly for groups of four or six; some have their own verandas complete with rocking chairs. There's also a pool, Jacuzzi and a restaurant. ③–⑤

Nature Lodge Finca Los Caballos, 4km before Montezuma on the road from Cóbano (☎ 642-0124, Ⓦ www.centralamerica.com/cr/hotel/caballos.htm). Eight comfortable rooms with private bath and hot water, set in tropical gardens with a small pool. The owners offer highly recommended horse tours, as well as advice on birdwatching and local fauna and flora, while the restaurant serves international food with organic vegetables. ⑤

Pensión Jenny, on the beach (☎ 642-0306). The cheapest place in town, with dorm beds ($5) and basic clean singles ($10) with shared bath in a house on the side of the road, overlooking the beach. ②

Sano Banano, a 15min walk north of the village along the beach (☎ & Ⓕ 642-0638, Ⓕ 642-0068, Ⓔ elbanano@racsa.co.cr); not to be confused with the café in the village centre. A truly special place, one of the most characterful in country, with secluded circular cabinas, all featuring beachfront balconies and outside showers (some also have kitchenettes); there's also a lovely freeform swimming pool with a waterfall, sun terrace and beautifully landscaped gardens. You have to not mind being close to nature – cabins are unscreened and there's lots of wildlife about. Bring a torch. ④–⑤

The village and around

It's Montezuma's atmosphere, rather than its activities, which draw visitors, and other than hanging out and sipping smoothies, there's not much to do in the village itself, Despite the inviting palm-fringed, white-sand beaches, **swimming** isn't very good on the beaches immediately to the north of Montezuma – there are lots of rocky outcroppings, some hidden at high tide, and the waves are rough and currents strong. It's better to head north along the lovely **nature trail** (1.5km; 30min), which dips in and out of several coves before ending at **Playa Grande**. There's reasonable swimming here, decent surfing, and a small waterfall at its eastern edge; some people also come here to sunbathe topless or nude, though this isn't particularly appreciated by local people.

Montezuma and its environs are laced with a number of **waterfalls** – the closest is about a kilometre down the road towards Cabo Blanco and then another 800m on a path (signposted to the *catarata*) through the dense vegetation. Bring your swimsuit if you want to bathe, but always take care, especially in the wet season, on account of flash floods, and also be careful on the rocks by the fall – people slip and have accidents here every year, and one person was killed a few years ago.

Isla Tortuga (see p.319), off the coast of the peninsula near Curú, is a popular place to snorkel, swim safely in calm, warm and shallow waters, and sunbathe. Local boatmen can take you there and back for quite a bit less than you'd pay with one of the "cruise ship" companies doing the run from San José or Puntarenas, although tours from Montezuma are less posh – drinks, for instance, may be included, although lunch is usually not. It's best to stock up in the village and ask the boatmen if they have a cooler you can use.

The single most popular excursion in town, however, is probably to the **Cabo Blanco** reserve for a morning's walking. Although you can do this independently if you have your own (4WD) transport, most people take a tour. If you like **mountain biking** you could ride the 9km down to Cabo Blanco, walk the trails and bike back in a day. Mind the height of the two creeks en route, though, as you might not get through them on your bike at high tide.

Eating, drinking and nightlife

Just a few years ago all you could get to eat in Montezuma was fantastically fresh **fish**, practically straight off the hook, though nowadays this is complemented by tourist favourites like vegetarian pizza, granola, mango shakes and paella, not to mention more exotic dishes. Eating three meals a day will set you back a few colones, though: Montezuma's accommodation may still be moderately priced, but food is on the expensive side. If you're staying somewhere with a kitchen you can cut costs by grabbing food from Chico's grocery store in the centre of the village.

Nightlife in Montezuma centres around *Chico's Bar*, an interesting mix of local kids, who arrive packed in the back of pickups, and tourists guzzling from a surprisingly wide bar stock and shouting above the music. More retiring types can take in the very popular nightly video shows (in English) at the *Sano Banano* at 7.30pm; you have to spend at least $6 in the restaurant to get in.

Amor de Mar, at the hotel of the same name. Enjoy beautiful ocean-front views whilst sampling a range of light snacks, smoothies (made with homemake yoghurt) and superb, healthy breakfasts using delicious home-baked German bread.

Colores Good, varied menu of well-prepared food served up in a garden setting near the beach – try the *fajitas de pollo* ($5). Closed Mon.

El Caracol Unpretentious soda serving tasty local food, chilled drinks and hearty lunches; the fish *casado* ($3) is particularly good value.

El Jardín Espresso, good fruit drinks and some veggie dishes, including stuffed zucchini and burritos. The spaghetti and shrimp is good value, as is the fish fillet in ranchera sauce.

El Sano Banano Excellent North-American-style breakfasts and filling lunch and dinner specials – the fillet of fish ($6) makes a good evening meal – plus crepes, vegetarian pizzas and vegetarian canelloni with spinach; organic produce is used where possible. If you have nothing else, try the incredible smoothies made with fresh fruit and yoghurt. Films are shown in an intimate candlelit atmosphere nightly at 7.30 (you have to spend a minimum of $6 in the restaurant to get in) – arrive before 7pm for a table.

Las Gemelas One of the most economical places to eat in Montezuma, this small soda serves filling and cheap Costa Rican food. Lunch-time *casados* ($3.50) are especially good value, or splash out a bit more and try the lobster with garlic.

Los Mangos Nice poolside location with cosmopolitan food, much of it Mediterranean-style, including pastas, salads and seafood.

Luz de Mono The village's most upmarket restaurant, with gourmet dining in a large airy rancho. The jumbo shrimp ($15) are beautifully cooked, while the "American" breakfasts ($7.50) are similarly pricey but undeniably delicious. If you can't afford to eat, try the happy hour cocktails (4–7pm). Credit cards accepted.

Monte Sol A fair imitation of the *Sano Banano*, with healthy fare and a good selection of breakfasts and smoothies, plus pizza, served at popular outdoor tables in a central location.

Montezuma Beautifully situated upstairs restaurant, looking out to sea from beneath the palm trees. The Spanish chef cooks great paella and seafood – grilled or garlic fish seems to be the plate of choice, and is good value at $5 – and there's delicious fresh bread too.

Playa de las Artistas Classy Italian-owned restaurant, with tables set romantically among the palm trees and nice touches like lampshades made out of coconut. The menu features exquisitely prepared Mediterranian cuisine with a local twist – the spaghetti with lobster and white wine sauce ($11) is superb. Closed Sun.

Panadería Good coffee, ice cream and lovely cakes – if you want to take lunch to the beach, try the takeaway avocado, vegetable and hummous sandwiches on brown bread. Closed Sun.

Cabuya

Nine kilometres south of Montezuma, close to the Cabo Blanco reserve, **CABUYA** is home to a growing permanent community of foreign residents, drawn by the slow pace of life, relative isolation and unspoiled scenery. Some 4km north of Cabuya, *Fernando Morales'* house (☎642-0351) is a good place to stay, with **rooms** (❶–❷) and a pleasant **campsite**. The *Hotel Cabo Blanco* (☎ & ℻ 642-0332) is set right on a gentle beach with good swimming; the nine reasonable rooms cost a flat rate of $50 and can sleep up to four, so are more economical for groups than for singles or couples.

Just down the road in Cabuya, *El Ancla de Oro* dishes up dinner nightly, including delicious **lobster** served in garlic butter ($11) and cheaper but equally good red snapper. They also have two comfortable rustic **cabins** (❶). The road to Cabuya can be in very bad shape: you're only guaranteed to get there in the dry season (Dec–April), and even then only with 4WD.

Reserva Natural Absoluta Cabo Blanco

RESERVA NATURAL ABSOLUTA CABO BLANCO (Wed–Sun 8am–4pm; $6), 9km southwest of Montezuma, is Costa Rica's oldest protected piece of land, established in 1963 by Karen Morgenson, a Danish immigrant to Costa Rica, and her Swedish husband Olof. Its name – the "absolute" bit – derives from until 1989, no visitors were allowed here. Even now, scientific researchers have priority, and attempts are made to keep the number of visitors down.

Cabo Blanco occupies an area of around 12 square kilometres – almost the entire southwestern tip of the Nicoya Peninsula – and the natural beauty of the setting is complemented by its unique biodiversity, with pockets of **Pacific lowland tropical forest** of a type that is found nowhere else in the country. It's hard to believe now, but most of today's reserve was pasture and farmland until the early 1960s. Since its inauguration, the reserve has been allowed to regenerate naturally – with a small area of original forest that had escaped destruction serving as a "genetic bank" for the re-establishment of the complex tropical forest that now fills the reserve.

It used to be said that **animals** in Cabo Blanco were less shy than in any other protected area in Costa Rica, perhaps due to the lack of visitors, though these days, as Montezuma's popularity increases, so do pressures on the reserve, to a degree few expected. The more people that have flooded in, the shyer the animals have become, and there's now talk of imposing daily limits on visitors – about forty, probably. The most frequently seen animals are howler monkeys, deer, sloths and squirrels, while agoutis and coati are also common, as are snakes – watch your step. The margay and the tamandua (anteater) are among the species that live here, but which you're unlikely to see. The best times for animal-spotting is any morning around 8am, or on Wednesday mornings, after the reserve has been closed for two days. **Bird life** is astonishingly plentiful down by the shore – you'll often see scores of pelicans and clouds of frigate birds, while brown boobies nest on the islands off the tip of the peninsula.

Practicalities

The **roads** down to Cabo Blanco are bad; you'll need 4WD to get there yourself, and watch the two creeks, which are deep at high tide. An old, road-hardened **bus** runs between Montezuma and Cabo Blanco, leaving from the side of Montezuma's *parqueo* at 8am, noon, 2pm and 7pm, returning to Montezuma at 7am, 9am, 1pm and 4pm daily except Sunday; this service may not run in the rainy season if it has been very wet. **Jeep-taxis** make the trip from Montezuma to Cabo Blanco for $10 per person.

You pay your entrance fee ($6) at the ranger hut, where they'll supply you with a map of the trails, which also outlines the history of the reserve and species found in it. A **trail** (5km; 2hr) leads from here through tropical deciduous forest to **Playa Cabo Blanco** and **Playa Balsitas** – two very lovely, lonely spots, through they're not great for swimming. Be wary of the high tide (*marea*) – ask the ranger at the entrance when and where you're likely to get cut off if walking along the beach. It's very **hot**: 30°C is not uncommon, so bring a hat, sunblock and five litres of water per person. There's no real need to take a **guide** – ask at Aventuras de Montezuma in Montezuma if you do decide you want one. No camping is allowed in the reserve, but you can stay in simple **rooms** just outside the reserve in the house or campsite at *Lila's* (call the *Soda Fin de Luna* on ☎642 0327 and ask for Lila; ❶); she'll also cook meals on request. From here it's less than a kilometre to the ranger station, convenient for keen early morning animal spotters.

Malpaís and around

On the other side of the peninsula from Cabuya, **MALPAÍS** ("Bad Country") is more attractive than its name suggests: a lonely, lovely spot which for a few years now has been attracting a growing community of foreigners. The most established place is the basic but clean *Cabinas-Restaurant Mal País*, near the beach (☎642-0096; ❶–❷); a couple of kilometres before Malpaís proper is the *Star Mountain Eco-Resort* (☎ & ℱ642-0024, ✉info@starmountaineco.com;

⑤), a quiet hotel with nicely decorated rooms built – according to the owners – without felling a tree. There are also some comfortable dormitory beds ($25 per person including breakfast) and a pool, too. Most people drive here, though there's also a daily **bus** from Cóbano.

Surfers with 4WD can try heading to **Manzanillo**, a great surfing beach on the western side of the peninsula with long waves similar to Playa Junquillal in the north (see p.274). There are few facilities, though, and the beach is likely to be deserted. In the rainy season the drive really isn't recommended, however: the creeks – at least a dozen of them – that cut the dirt road between Malpaís, Manzanillo and Sámara are likely to be so high that you'll be pushing it in anything less than a Land Rover or a large truck.

Roads all over this part of the peninsula are confusing, in bad shape, and liable to be nearly impassable in the rainy season. It's just about possible to get around in the dry season in a 4WD, however, with a good road map, some Spanish and camping gear. Some people, certainly locals, drive from Cóbano up to **Carmona** in the north, or from Manzanillo northwest to **Sámara**, but neither is an interesting enough drive to make it worth the trouble.

South of Puntarenas

South of Puntarenas on the mainland, the coast road, sometimes signposted as the **Costañera Sur**, leads down to Quepos and continues, in various states of paving, south to Dominical (covered in Chapter 7). At first the landscape is sparse and hilly, with the coast coming into view only intermittently. The road improves considerably once you're past the huge trucks heading to the container port and refineries at Puerto Caldera. About 30km southeast of Puerto Caldera, just across the wide mouth of the Río Tárcoles, is the **Reserva Biológica Carara**, known for its rich birdlife. There are a number of lovely old places to stay nearby, and you're probably better off staying here than at the run-of-the-mill hotels in the resort town of **Jacó**, especially for birders who want to get going early on the trails. South of here, running down the coast from the hamlet of Parrita to Quepos, you enter a long corridor of African oil palm plantations, a moody landscape of stout, brooding palms.

Reserva Biológica Carara and Río Tárcoles

The **RESERVA BIOLÓGICA CARARA** (daily 7am–5pm; $6), 90km west of San José, occupies a transition area between the hot tropical lowlands of Guanacaste and the humid, more verdant climate of the southern Pacific coast. Consequently, Carara teems with **wildlife**, much of it of the unnerving sort: huge crocodiles lounge in the bankside mud of the Río Tárcoles, and snakes (19 out of Costa Rica's 22 poisonous species) go about their business. Mammals include monkeys, armadillos, agoutis and most of the large felines, including the jaguar, puma, ocelot and margay – the latter, of course, are very rarely seen. **Birding** is very good, and this is one of the best places in the country to see the brightly coloured **scarlet macaw** in its natural habitat. Most nights at twilight, anytime between 3pm and 5.30pm, they migrate from the lowland tropical forest areas to the swampy mangroves, soaring off in a burst of red and blue against the darkening sky. Among other birds that frequent the treetops, you may see toucans, trogons and guans, while riverside birds include herons, anhingas and storks. The best time to see **migratory birds** is, as usual, the dry season, from December to April.

Whatever time of the year you're here, it's a good idea to hire a **guide**. Some travellers have reported seeing more wildlife on a guided tour in Carara than at other, better-known, national parks, and guides can also take you into restricted areas where tourists aren't allowed on their own. Be aware, though, that many day-tours from San José come here, as it's only two-and-a-half hours' drive from the capital. Serious birders are advised to stay overnight in the area, as early mornings are notoriously more fruitful for bird-watching than other times of day.

Practicalities

Carara is reached **from San José** by taking the Orotina highway and turning left at the long bridge over the Río Tárcoles. You'll see many cars parked at the entrance, just past the bridge, and even on the bridge itself, with birders training their binoculars on the river, or croc-spotters pointing at the lazing reptiles. There have been robberies on this bridge and some people advise that it is no longer safe to stop, although plenty of people do. It's 3km from the bridge to the **ranger station**, where there are toilets and picnic tables, and where you pay your entrance fee. Staff give out basic maps and will answer questions about the reserve's resident wildlife. The car park here has recently become a magnet for **thieves** breaking into unattended cars, and vehicles should be left in the guarded *parqueo* at the ranger station at the entrance. It's extremely **hot** at Carara, especially at midday, when temperatures of 30°C are common, and it receives a good amount – 3000mm – of rain per year, most of it in the wet season. Take a hat, sunscreen and waterproof clothing.

Carara is on the itineraries of a number of tour operators, and is included in most of the serious **birding tours** from North America and the UK. In San José, Geotur (T & F227-4029) and Costa Rica Expeditions (T257-0766) offer all-inclusive tours with trained guides, transport and lunch for about $75. Another option, if you're staying there, is to take one of the boat tours from the *Dundee Ranch Hotel* (see below), on which you can spot crocodiles and river-borne bird life.

Although camping is not allowed, there are a number of very good **accommodation** options near Carara (see below). They all offer **birding tours** – *Tarcol Lodge* is one of the premier birding destinations in the country – and a couple of them are great destinations for horse-riding and hiking. All are accessible to independent travellers, although it's best to phone ahead and ask to be met off the buses from San José; if you don't have a car you could also ask if transport from the capital, or from nearby Jacó or Quepos can be provided.

Dundee Ranch Hotel, Cascajal, near Orotina (T267-6222, F267-6229). Lovely former cattle ranch – guests stay in the old ranch house – recommended for enthusiastic riders and hikers, as the *peones* who work on the mango farm can take you riding through rivers, rainforest, beautiful dry-forest and mango plantations, with abundant of wildlife all around. They also run trips to Carara, and have their own lake, fitted out with decks for great bird-spotting. The good restaurant serves food grilled to your liking, and there's a lovely pool. 6

Hacienda Doña Marta, Cascajal, near Orotina (T253-0853, F234-0958). Family-run, working dairy farm with accommodation in new cabinas, surrounding a pool, and home cooking. The hacienda has its own areas of forest and riverside land and offers horse-riding, birding trips, and tours to Carara, which is only ten minutes away. Good-value packages are available, with meals, farm tours and horse-riding included. 6

Tarcol Lodge, 5km north of Tárcoles village on the south bank of the Tárcoles river (T & F267-7138, in the USA 800/593-3305,

ⓔ johnerb@racsa.co.cr). Though pre-eminently dedicated to the needs of bird-watchers, the *Tarcol* is a pleasant rustic lodge in its own right. At high tide it's surrounded on three sides by water; the birds really come out, however, when the tide retreats and the sandflats attract literally hundreds of species. Local tours, all meals and transport from San José are included in the lodge's prices. The owners also run the *Rancho Naturalista Lodge* near Turrialba (see p.149) and offer week-long packages split between here and Turrialba. ⑧

Villa Lapas, 500m east of the turn-off to Tárcoles village, signed from the Costañera Sur just past the Río Tárcoles bridge (ⓣ 284-1418, ⓔ fiesta@racsa.co.cr). Large, pleasant rooms with private bath; the rooms with ceiling fan are brighter than those with a/c. The complex is set in landcaped gardens near the river; the owners have established a small network of trails in a private reserve which offer good early morning bird-watching. The Río Tárcoles and Carara entrance are both within walking distance, and there's a swimming pool and restaurant too. ⑥

Jacó

Less than three hours from San José, the resort town of **JACÓ** sits in a hot coastal plain behind the broad **Playa Jacó**, the closest beach to the capital and an established seaside attraction that nowadays draws a mix of surfers, week-enders and holidaying Ticos, from party-hearty students to working-class families (the other major presence – you'll notice the ingratiating flags flown everywhere – are Canadians, who descend during the winter on package tours). If you dream of swimming in the Pacific off pristine white sands, how-

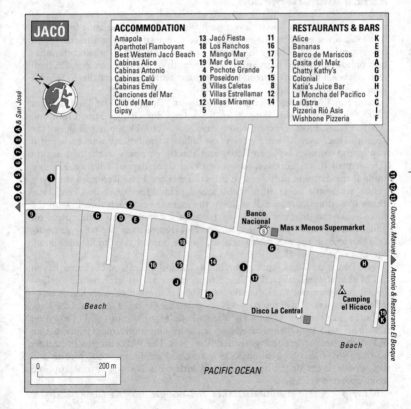

JACÓ

ACCOMMODATION

Amapola	13	Jacó Fiesta	11
Aparthotel Flamboyant	18	Los Ranchos	16
Best Western Jacó Beach	3	Mango Mar	17
Cabinas Alice	19	Mar de Luz	1
Cabinas Antonio	4	Pochote Grande	7
Cabinas Calú	10	Poseidon	15
Cabinas Emily	9	Villas Caletas	8
Canciones del Mar	6	Villas Estrellamar	12
Club del Mar	12	Villas Miramar	14
Gipsy	5		

RESTAURANTS & BARS

Alice	K
Bananas	E
Barco de Mariscos	B
Casita del Maíz	A
Chatty Kathy's	G
Colonial	D
Katia's Juice Bar	H
La Moncha del Pacifico	J
La Ostra	C
Pizzeria Rió Asis	I
Wishbone Pizzeria	F

Banco Nacional

Mas x Menos Supermarket

Beach

Camping el Hicaco

Disco La Central

Beach

0   200 m

PACIFIC OCEAN

ever, Jacó is not the place to come: the water is reported to be polluted in places, and can also be dangerous due to rip tides – locals advise that the southernmost part of the beach is the best place to swim. Having said that, when covered in mist and backed by a spectacular Pacific sunset, the beach's wide, chocolate-coloured sands can look quite attractive, and they're now a lot cleaner than they used to be, thanks to conscientious locals who organize clean-up brigades after heavy high-season weekends.

Despite the caveats, Jacó continues to grow in popularity, with good-value hotels and restaurants opening every year – you'll need reservations during the high season, especially at weekends. Jacó is also the place where many **surfing** afficionados stay, not only to surf the steady waves of Jacó, but also to visit the more challenging nearby beaches of Playa Hermosa, and Esterriollos Este and Oeste, among others. For surfing lore and the company of other similarly wave-obsessed folk, *Los Ranchos* hotel is the place to stay. Staff and other surfing guests will have information on current conditions, transport and surfboard rental.

Locals advise against walking on the beach at night: hold-ups by knife-wielding characters have been reported. Otherwise, walking around town, even at night, should be safe, especially since a special contingent of bike-riding police have taken to patrolling the streets.

Arrival and orientation

Jacó straggles along a three-kilometre main road, little more than a strip of shops, restaurants and hotels. Turning off from this main drag are a few streets that head for the sea but never quite make it, petering out in attractive palm groves or the beach. This is the **centre** of town, although many accommodation options are found to the north or the south of this little nucleus. On high season weekends the main road becomes busy with traffic; bear this in mind if your hotel backs onto it.

From San José **buses** leave for Jacó daily at 7.30am, 10.30am and 3.30pm (2hr 30min–3hr). From Puntarenas, buses leave for Jacó at 5am, 11pm and 2.30pm (1hr). From Quepos, buses leave at 4.30am, 11.30pm and 3pm (1hr 15min). There may be extra services on holidays and holiday weekends, but if you intend to travel between Friday and Sunday, especially in the high season (Dec–April) or on holidays, buy your ticket three days in advance. The bus stops at the extreme north end of the village at the Plaza Jacó mini shopping centre, where the ticket office is also found, behind the Banco de Costa Rica. Buses sometimes continue 3km down the main street which runs behind the town – ask the driver; if you know more or less where you want to get off and/or have gear, it's best to stay on. The *Best Western Irazú* (see p.87), just outside San José on the way to Alajuela, has shuttle buses that go to its sister hotel, the *Best Western Jacó Beach*, daily.

The Banco de Costa Rica, in the Plaza Jacó at the north end of town, has an **ATM** that theoretically takes Visa, although as with all state banks, foreign-issued cards may not work (see Basics, p.26). The bank itself will change **travellers' cheques**, as will the Banco Nacional in the centre of town and the larger hotels, like the *Best Western*. The Banco Popular at the south end of town on the main road also changes travellers' cheques but, more importantly, has an **ATM** that will accept foreign-issued Visa cards. The ICE office in the centre of town (Mon–Sat 8am–noon & 1–5pm) offers an international **phone** and fax service. Next door, the self-serve **laundry** has hot water, free soap and coin-operated machines.

Many places rent **mountain bikes** and **boogie boards** (about $2/hr or

$10/day – though note that bikes aren't allowed on the beach) and **surfboards** ($5/hr or $20/day). You can also rent scooters, for which you'll need your licence and passport – try Señor Bill's (daily 7am–10pm) on the main road near the south end of town.

Accommodation

The listings below give the places offering the best value or location amidst the forest of cheap **cabinas** which fill Jacó and which historically catered to week-ending *Josefinos* or surfers; typically they can err on the depressing side of "basic", with cement walls, rickety beds and cold water only. Jacó is the sort of place where budget travellers might want to consider shelling out an extra $10–20 a night for more comfortable mid-range accommodation, much of which is **self-catering** – useful if you're in town for more than a couple of days. Jacó is also well served at the upper end of the market. With some notable exceptions, be prepared to pay a bit more than either the town or, in some cases, the accommodation, merits. At the larger hotels you can expect some sort of **discount** – up to fifty percent on the prices we've listed – for low-season (May–Nov) weekends. Keep an eye on the *Tico Times* and *La Nación* for big splashy adverts. You'll need to **reserve** at holiday times, like Easter and Christmas, and weekends, for most of the places listed below. Jacó is a growing town, and staying on the main road can mean **traffic noise**, particularly on busy weekends. Beach-front hotels and cabinas on the beach (but not near bars and discos) are better bets for those wanting peace and quiet, as are accommodation options at either the extreme north or south ends of town.

Jacó is well endowed with **campsites** – all charge about $3 a night to pitch a tent and have showers, toilets and beach access. Sites include *Camping and Cabinas Mariott* (nothing at all like its hotel-chain namesake), set in level, clear grounds at the north end of town; the shaded *Camping Madrigal*, at the southern end of the beach; and the newer *Camping El Hicaco*, in the centre of town, with nice grounds dotted with picnic tables.

Budget

Cabinas Antonio, at the north end of Jacó, near the San José bus stop (T 643-3043). Friendly establishment whose basic but well-priced cabinas come with fans and private bathrooms with hot water; there's also a restaurant. Low-season discounts. ③

Cabinas Calú, in the centre (T 643-1107). Large, good-value rooms, if a bit dark, with hot water, although the central location can get noisy at weekends. The friendly owners also offer a laundry service. ③

Cabinas Emily, on the main road on the north side of town (T 643-3513). Filled with surfers on a budget, these friendly, rock-bottom cabinas sport green cement walls and come with private bath (cold water only). A bit pricey for single travellers, but good value for 2–4 sharing. There's a restaurant of the same name attached. ②

Gipsy, north end of town (T & F 643-3448). Well-maintained cabinas, only 250m from the beach, in nice grounds with a small swimming pool – the cheaper cabinas with fan and hot water are especially good value. Breakfast included. ③

Hotel Poseidon, in the centre (T 643-1642, F 643-3558, E poseidon@racsa.co.cr). New hotel right in the centre of Jacó, set in a two-storey white stucco building, with 14 good-sized rooms including excellent-value singles, doubles and triples, all with hot water and fans, although the lower rooms are a bit dark. There's a small pool and a restaurant attached. Credit cards accepted. ③–④

Moderate

Aparthotel Flamboyant, in the centre in front of the beach (T 643-3146, F 643-1068). Good-value, well-kept apartments sleeping two people, with hot water, kitchen and ceiling fans. There's a pool and a good restaurant attached. ⑤

Cabinas Alice, on the beach towards the southern end of town (T & F 643-3061). Twenty-two super-clean cabinas set in beautiful beachfront grounds with little to disturb the peace except the crashing of waves. All cabins come with fan and hot water, while some also have a small kitchen plus fridge and a small terrace; the older and more basic cabinas are slightly cheaper. Good restaurant attached. Visa accepted. **4**

Canciones del Mar, near the north end of town, just off the main road (T 643-3273, F 643-3296, W www.cancionesdelmar.com). The swankiest place in Jacó, this small (10 rooms) beachfront hotel has a pool and oceanfront apartments with Spanish colonial decor, kitchens, cable TV, a/c and telephone. Good weekly and off-season rates available on request. **5**

Club del Mar, southern end of town (T & F 643-3194). Tastefully decorated, English-owned apartments on a quiet section of beach south of town, with a friendly family atmosphere and a range of amenities – there's also a pool, restaurant, a small library and a games room. **5**

Los Ranchos, in the centre (T & F 643-3070). Arranged in attractive gardens around a pool, this welcoming hotel offers good value for single travellers and groups alike, with a variety of rooms and prices from upstairs loft rooms (some with kitchenettes) to two-storey bungalows with kitchens sleeping two to four people. **4–5**

Mango Mar, in the centre, off the main drag towards the sea (T 643-3670). Small modern hotel set in beachside grounds, with a small pool and a Jacuzzi. The spotless en-suite rooms (those upstairs have good views) come with hot water and a/c; some also have kitchenettes. **5**

Mar de Luz, in the centre, on the landward side of the main drag (T & F 643-3259). Well-kept hotel set in landscaped grounds away from the road, with thirty generous-sized rooms arranged around two large pools – plus a good security system in the form of the friendly Dutch owners' alert dachshunds. There's TV in the rooms, plus a communal TV, games area and a small library. Credit cards accepted. **4–5**

Pochote Grande, at the very northern end of town (T 643-3236, F 220-4979, E pochote@racsa.co.cr). Nicely kept rooms, with hot water, fridges and ceiling fans, set around a pool in landscaped grounds. Good restaurant attached. **5**

Villas Estrellamar (T 643-3102, F 643-3453). Get-away-from-it-all place, with twenty bungalows (all with bath, hot water, fan, TV, kitchen and fridge) in quiet tropical gardens with a large pool. Good low-season prices. **5**

Villas Miramar, in the centre, off the main drag towards the sea (T 643-3003). One of the nicer mid-range places, with landscaped gardens, a pool, and quiet, clean rooms with kitchenettes and bathrooms with hot water. **5**

Expensive

Amapola, a 2min walk from the beach (T & F 643-3668, E amapola@racsa.co.cr). One of Jacó's newer and classier hotels, the good-value rooms have a/c, cable TV and minibar; there are also larger suites and three villas ($100–150) that can sleep up to six people. The large pool has a swim-up bar, and the restaurant serves tasty Italian food. Good low-season rates. **6**

Best Western Jacó Beach, north end of town (T 643-3246, F 643-1000, E jacohotel@racsa.co.cr). Well-established resort hotel, recently acquired by the Best Western chain and refurbished to a good standard. It's not the cheapest place in Jacó, but it has lots of facilities, including a big clean pool, restaurant, casino and disco, plus kayaking, sports-fishing and sailing lessons. Rooms are decorated in anonymous chain-hotel style, but are perfectly comfortable, and come with private bath, a/c and cable TV. **7**

Jacó Fiesta, southern end of town (T 643-3147, F 643-3148). Located at the quiet southern end of the beach, this is a smaller and older hotel than the *Best Western*, though the rooms are clean and have private bath with hot water, a/c, well-equipped kitchenettes and cable TV. There are also several swimming pools and a good restaurant attached. **6**

Villas Caletas, 8km north of Jacó, off the Costañera Sur (T 257-3653, F 222-2059, E caletas@ticonet.co.cr). Perched on a clifftop above the Pacific, this is one of Costa Rica's finest boutique hotels, offering luxurious accommodation in a quiet atmosphere. Accommodation is in beautifully decorated individual villas spread around the landscaped grounds, from where there are stunning views, especially at sunset. A daily shuttle takes guests down the precipitous one-kilometre trail to the beach. Cuisine is of a gourmet standard, with prices to match ($30pp for dinner). **7–8**

The Town and around

Jacó is very much a beach town, and other than sunbathing, surfing and a little cautious swimming, there's not much to do. The combination of beach-crazed weekending *Josefinos* and surfers – not known for their sobriety or quietness – can also make Jacó too much of a party beach for many travellers.

That said, it can be eerily quiet in the **low season**, with only a few ecstatic French Canadians, recently liberated from the northern winter, scooting about on motor bikes. Jacó also makes a good base for the many surfing beaches nearby (most of them better than Jacó). Little **Playa Herradura**, 7km north, deserves a particular mention, if only for its good beach breaks. Most visitors come to Herradura on day-trips, as there's nothing much in the way of accommodation.

A sequence of wild and wave-crashed beaches begins a couple of kilometres **south of Jacó**, starting with Playa Hermosa and continuing through Esterillos Oeste, Esterillos Este and Bejuco. They're of interest only to surfers – swimmers will get clobbered by waves and harassed by rip tides – and you'll need a 4WD to get to them, as the little roads leading off the Costañera Sur can be tricky in the rainy season (which is the best time for surfing). Don't leave belongings locked in your car at Playa Hermosa; cars parked behind the beach are frequently broken into.

Surfers can **rent boards** at a number of places in town (ask at *Los Ranchos* hotel for recommendations); alternatively, you could rent a **mountain bike** (about $10 per day) or a **moped** (about $35 per day) to explore the spread-out town and the surfing beaches described above. A number of operators in town offer **tours** – those to the nearby Carara Biological Reserve are popular, while trips to the Damas estuary offer a good chance to spot lots of monkeys, although there are surprisingly few birds. The biggest range of tours can be found at Jacó Adventures (☎643-1049, ✉jacoadventures@playajaco.com), 100m south of the *Restaurante Colonial*. Their day-long tours to **Manuel Antonio** ($35) are popular, and they also run rafting trips on the **Rio Savegre** ($89) and **kayaking** and **snorkelling** tours for $55; day-trips to **Isla Tortuga** ($70) are another perennial favourite. Their real speciality, however, is **sports-fishing**, and Argentine capain Marcelo offers some of the best value half and full-day sports-fishing tours on the coast – a half-day for four people starts at $240.

Eating

Considering how much local accommodation is geared toward self-catering, there's a good selection of **eating** establishments in Jacó. Many of the best hotels have very good restaurants, though as always in Costa Rica, if you're on a budget, make the lunch-time *casado* or *plato del día* your main meal.

Alice, at the *Cabinas Doña Alice*. Good family-run restaurant, serving fresh seafood and shellfish from a varied menu.

Bananas, in the centre. Popular for its reasonable breakfasts, including tasty pancakes, for $3.

Barco de Mariscos, in the centre on the main drag. New venue specializing, as its name suggests, in well-prepared fresh shellfish.

Casita del Maíz, north end of town. One of Jacó's better sodas, popular with locals, with good *casados* made with fresh ingredients.

Chatty Kathy's, opposite the *Max x Menos* supermarket. One of the best places in town for breakfast, this Canadian-owned upstairs café serves pancakes, cooked breakfasts and delicious cinnamon rolls, as well as light lunches.

Colonial, on the main drag. Tastefully designed new bar-restaurant popular with travellers for drinks as well as main meals.

Katia's Juice Bar, next to Señor Bill's bicycle rental on the main drag. Small kiosk serving delicious melon, pineapple and papaya drinks ($1.25).

La Moncha del Pacifico, in the centre. Tasty smoothies and chicken fajitas, though its poetry-spouting owner can be a bit tiresome.

La Ostra, on the main drag. Long-established *marisquería* (seafood restaurant) set in a quiet rancho next to a creek, and good for both fish and shellfish. Credit cards accepted.

Rio Asis, in the centre. Good cheap pizza.

Wishbone Pizza, in the centre. One of the most popular places in town, serving good pizza and home-made vegetarian pitta sandwiches for $4. Closed Wed.

Drinking and nightlife

Sedate during midweek in low season, Jacó can transform itself into a beer-drinking-contest hell during weekends and holidays. For **drinking**, bar *Zarpe* at the north end of town is recommended for cold beer and good, if slightly pricey, Mexican *bocas*. *Bar y Restaurante Bohio*, right on the beach, is a great place for a sunset drink – check out the church-pew benches and tables under a ranch roof. They sometimes lay on a very loud **disco**. Other discos include that at the *Best Western Jacó Beach*, the swankiest in town, though it's only open on weekends, and *Disco La Central*, on the beach right in the centre of town – popular with gringos, though again it only really gets going at weekends.

> ### Moving on from Jacó
>
> Buses for San José leave the bus stop at the north end of Jacó daily at 5am and 3pm (2hr 30min–3hr). It's also possible to continue to Quepos and the Manuel Antonio area by walking 2km out to the Costañera Sur and flagging down the Puntarenas–Quepos or San José–Manuel Antonio buses that pass on the highway. Buses from Puntarenas to Quepos (see opposite) pass by about ninety minutes after leaving Puntareanas – it's a good idea to check times with locals and to get out onto the highway a few minutes early, just to be sure.

Quepos and Parque Nacional Manuel Antonio

The small corridor of land between the old banana-exporting town of **Quepos** and the little community of **Manuel Antonio**, outside the **Parque Nacional Manuel Antonio**, has experienced one of the most dramatic tourist booms in the country. The stunning, picture-postcard setting, with its spectacular white-grey sand beaches fringed by thickly forested green hills, is the main attraction, and there's also a huge variety of things to do – including walking the park's easy trails, white-water rafting, ocean-cruising and horse-riding, to name but a few. The beauty of the area is due in part to the unique "*tómbolo*" formation of **Punta Catedral**, which juts out into the Pacific from the park. A rare geophysical phenomenon, a *tómbolo* results when an island becomes joined, slowly and over millennia, to the mainland through accumulated sand deposits. Other smaller islands, some of them no more than rocky outcroppings, straggle off from Punta Catedral and, from high up in the hills, watching a lavish sunset flower and die over the Pacific, it does seem as though Manuel Antonio is one of the more charmed places on earth.

That said, the huge tourist influx has undeniably taken its toll on the area. The tiny village of Manuel Antonio has been practically drowned in a sea of hotels, cabinas, restaurants and bars and, in particular, there has been concern over an inadequate-to-nonexistent sewage system, and fears that the area's waters are being polluted. In the last few years the area has been perceived as overpriced, and budget travellers have headed instead to Montezuma or Samara on the Nicoya Peninsula. Falling demand has caused some hotels in Manuel Antonio to drop their prices, so that where they were once overpriced, they are now merely expensive.

Then there's the road: sometimes it's in good condition; at other times, deep potholes puncture the asphalt. Beyond the nondescript town of **Parrita**, the road runs through a surreal landscape of brooding African oil palm plantations owned by United Brands. Bridges along this stretch are very rudimentary and periodically washed out, however, and driving is subject to delays as you wait to cross yet another makeshift bridge. Along with the forests of oil palms, you'll pass a series of "company" villages, with identical two-storey bungalows on stilts, arranged around soccer fields. Bright blue once, but long since bleached to a uniform grey-green, the bungalows were originally built for the banana workers, before the onset of Panamá disease in the 1950s ravaged the fruit plantations. Today they're bunkhouses for oil-palm workers and managers.

Quepos

Arriving at the town of **QUEPOS** it's immediately apparent that you've crossed into the lush, wetter southern Pacific region. The vegetation is thicker and greener than further north, and more often than not it has just started or just finished raining. Backed up against a thick hill, with a muddy – and polluted – beach in front (obscured by the seaside road out to the old dock), Quepos can look pretty ramshackle. It's good place to meet fellow travellers, however, with plenty of hotels, bars and restaurants, and the presence of the town's burgeoning community of foreigners does have its advantages, especially on the gastronomic front.

The name "Quepos" derives from the indigenous language of the Quepoa people, part of the larger Borucas (or Bruncas, as they are sometimes called) group, who occupied this area for at least a thousand years before the arrival of Juan Vásquez de Coronado in 1563. After the invasion the Quepoa went into predictably swift decline due to disease and enslavement. Once a banana-exporting town, Quepos was severely hit by Panamá disease, which caused United Fruit to pull out in the 1950s. It's had something of a resurgence in recent decades, with the establishment of the African oil palm plantations, and has also developed into one of the country's prime **sports-fishing** destinations. The waters around these parts are stuffed with big, hard-fighting fish, with Spanish mackerel, sailfish, wahoo, yellowfin tuna, dorado, blue marlin, white tip shark and cubera snapper all to be found in the local waters. Posh sports-fishing boats anchor in Blue Bay in front of town, and you'll see drawings of marlin and other big-game fish all around the place, as well as many small tour agencies that cater more or less exclusively to sports-fishers.

Most important to the average visitor is the town's proximity to the Parque Nacional Manuel Antonio and its beaches, 7km south. Compared to most of the establishments along the road to the park entrance, lodgings and restaurants in Quepos are affordable, and there are frequent buses to the park, making it the most useful base in the area. That said, there's little to do in the town itself – illustrated by the disaffected youth who linger out on the stone benches along the main drag or whizz their mountain bikes back and forth to the old banana docks.

Arrival

Buses leave San José's La Coca-Cola for Quepos four times daily (at 7am, 10am, 2pm & 4pm; 4hr); there's a faster service, also leaving from La Coca-Cola, to Manuel Antonio (daily at 6am, noon & 6pm; 3hr 30min) which calls at Quepos en route to the park entrance. At weekends, holidays and any time during the dry season, you'll need to buy your bus ticket for the Manuel Antonio service at least three days in advance, and your return ticket as soon

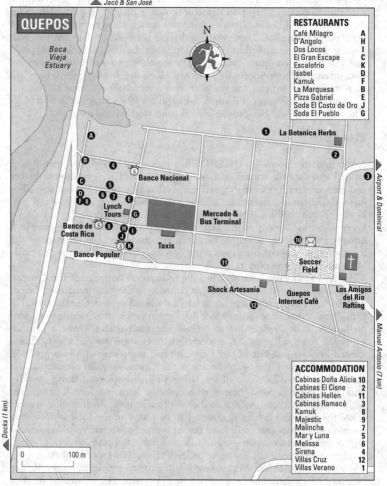

QUEPOS

Boca Vieja Estuary

N

Jacó & San José

Airport & Dominical

Manuel Antonio (7 km)

Docks (1 km)

RESTAURANTS

Café Milagro	A
D'Angolo	H
Dos Locos	I
El Gran Escape	C
Escalofrío	K
Isabel	D
Kamuk	F
La Marquesa	B
Pizza Gabriel	E
Soda El Costo de Oro	J
Soda El Pueblo	G

1 La Botanica Herbs

2

3

Banco Nacional

Lynch Tours

Banco de Costa Rica

Banco Popular

Mercado & Bus Terminal

10

Soccer Field

Taxis

11

Shock Artesanía

12

Quepos Internet Café

Los Amigos del Río Rafting

0   100 m

ACCOMMODATION

Cabinas Doña Alicia	10
Cabinas El Cisne	2
Cabinas Hellen	11
Cabinas Ramacé	3
Kamuk	8
Majestic	9
Malinche	7
Mar y Luna	5
Melissa	6
Sirena	4
Villas Cruz	12
Villas Verano	1

as you arrive. All buses arrive in Quepos at the busy **terminal**, which doubles as the *mercado*, just one block east of the town "centre". In addition to these two buses, Interbus's new **shuttle service** (see Basics, p.29) makes the trip between San José and Quepos daily using air-conditioned Mercedes minibuses ($25 each way). They leave San José at 8am, returning from Manuel Antonio at 1.30pm, and will pick you up from your hotel at each end. For reservations, call ☎283-5573 in San José, or contact Lynch Tours in Quepos (☎777-0161, ✉lyntur@racsa.co.cr).

Driving to Quepos, it's easy to miss the town and find yourself out on an old abandoned dock with nowhere to go but the Pacific. The entrance is actually on the left-hand side, down a narrow slip road, just after you cross the bridge into town. From there, continue straight ahead until you reach the last street where you can turn left – about 1km further down this road the winding uphill road to Manuel Antonio branches off to the right; it's signed, but easy to miss.

Due to the long drive and the condition of the roads, it's a good idea to **fly** from San José: this takes only fifteen minutes and, as Quepos residents like to point out, there are no potholes in the sky. Keep in mind that Sansa or Travelair flights are often booked weeks in advance, however, especially in the dry season. Alternatively, you could charter your own plane (see Basics, p.32). The airstrip is about 5km north of town.

Orientation and information

The town itself is tiny, three blocks or so by four – "downtown" consists of the main road along the front (sea-side) and the three blocks that run around it. Quepos's streets do have numbers, but nobody uses them. Quepos has no official **tourist office**, although Lynch Tours (see box on p.338) is a good source of information. Shock Artesanía, on the south side of the soccer field, sells **maps** and laminated wildlife guides. *Quepolandia*, a free bimonthly English newsletter, has information about the area and can be picked up at many local businesses.

To change **money and travellers' cheques**, head for the Banco Popular, just southwest of the bus terminal; the attached ATM accepts Visa and Mastercard. The Banco de Costa Rica and Banco Nacional also change travellers' cheques, but may be slower. The Banco de San José/Credomatic is the only place you can get cash advances on Mastercard, and is also open on Saturday mornings. Many businesses in town will change dollars, and there's a branch of Western Union (Mon–Fri 9am–noon & 1pm–6pm, Sat 9am-2pm) next to the *Café Milagro* just as you enter Quepos.

The **correo** (Mon–Fri 8am–5pm) is at the eastern end of town. There's a plethora of places with **internet access**, including Los Amigos del Rio, next to the church; *Internet Tropical*, in front of the *Hotel Malinche*, which also has an international phone service, plus good fruit *batidos* and toasted sandwiches; and *Quepos Internet Café*, opposite the soccer field, which has a happy hour and student discounts.

Take precautions against **theft** in the Manuel Antonio area. Rental cars left on the street have become a favourite target – never leave anything in them. Some hotels have secure parking or can point you towards a safe place to leave your vehicle. Never leave anything on the beach when swimming and, if you take the bus, don't let anyone else handle your luggage: best to keep it with you in the bus if possible. People waiting for the Manuel Antonio bus in Quepos bus station have also lately become targets for theft: watch your back. Wherever you stay, ensure your hotel room is locked at all times. It's also unwise to walk around at night in Quepos – especially alone – as the seawall area is a hangout of the local drug users. Drugs, especially crack cocaine, have become a problem in the area and are blamed on the more frequent robberies from hotel rooms and cars. In case of medical emergencies, Quepos has an excellent **hospital**, the Hospital Dr Max Teran (⊕777-0200).

Accommodation

Budget travellers will have a hard time in the Manuel Antonio area, especially in the dry season, when hotels are full and charging their highest prices. The area's few budget options can be found in Quepos, which is more economical overall than Manuel Antonio both for accommodation and eating. Wherever you plan to stay, book well ahead in high season – as ever, things are cheaper and easier in the wet.

Tours in the Quepos area

There's a good range of tours in the Quepos area. If you're staying at one of the upmarket hotels in town or on the road to Manuel Antonio, many have their own tour-service desk. Most day-trips include equipment rental and guides where necessary, along with lunch and/or snacks. Note that though you can theoretically visit Bahía Drake and the Osa Peninsula – including Isla del Caño just off the coast of Osa – from Quepos, it's far cheaper to get there from Palmar (see p.365) or Golfito (see p.369) in the Zona Sur.

In the town centre, the friendly and reputable Lynch Tours (☎ 777-0161, ⓕ 777-1571, ⓦ www.lynchtravel.com) is a good source of unbiased information. They can get you to Dominical, Corcovado, and Bahía Drake either by bus or plane, and arrange transfers to nearly all parts of the country in air-conditioned Mercedes shuttle buses; they also arrange airport transfers ($3) and handle plane ticket sales and reservations. Their many local tours include horse-riding trips to a local waterfall ($55), sports-fishing ($500–1000 for a full day's offshore fishing), sea kayaking ($60), white-water rafting ($75–$90), rainforest canopy tours ($80), and ever-popular day-time or sunset cruises, some specifically to see dolphins ($60).

Equus Stables (☎ 777-0001, ⓔ havefun@racsa.co.cr), on the road to Manuel Antonio, can take you horse-riding on the beach – sunset is the time to go – and up into the mountains behind on a two-hour tour ($35). As elsewhere in the country, it's worth having a look at how the horses are treated and stabled before you ride, since overwork and abuse of horses is fairly widespread and a thorny issue among travellers and riding outfitters (see box on p.311). The area's best established sports-fishing outfitter is Costa Rica Dreams (☎ & ⓕ 777-0593), while Isabel Guillen's Boutique El Pescador (☎ & ⓕ 777-1596) is also recommended; a day's fishing will cost up to $950. Rafting outfitters Los Amigos del Río (☎ & ⓕ 777-1262) have offices in Quepos itself, next to the church, and between Quepos and Manuel Antonio (look for a large orange building on the left with inflatable rafts outside).

One of the most popular activities hereabouts are the cruises along the coast to Manuel Antonio. Sunset Sails (☎ & ⓕ 777-1304; or book through Lynch Tours) offer dolphin-watching or sunset cruises (Dec–April only) in a classic wooden yacht, with stunning views of the coastline and offshore islands ($60 for a 4hr cruise); they claim that whales and sea turtles are sometimes spotted. The cruise includes lunch and snorkelling, and there's time for a swim off the boat. Another popular excursion is the day-trip to Hacienda Barú, a private hacienda-cum-nature-reserve near Dominical (☎ 787-0003, ⓕ 787-0004, ⓔ sstroud@racsa.co.cr). They have a canopy observation platform from where you get a bird's-eye view of the upper rainforest canopy, and also offer horse-riding.

Cabinas Doña Alicia, on the northwest corner of the soccer field (☎ 777-0419). Good budget choice: the hot rooms (with comfortable double beds) all sleep up to four people, apart from a few good-value singles, a rarity in Quepos. All have private bath (cold water only), and the friendly owners keep everything spotlessly clean. ❷

Cabinas El Cisne, 200m north of the church (☎ 777-1570). Good-value rooms, with refrigerator, TV and standing fans, and friendly owners who keep everything clean. ❸

Cabinas Hellen (☎ 777-0504). Clean cabinas in the back of a family home, with private bath, hot water, fridge, fans, small table and chairs, a small patio and a laundry service. Secure, and recom-mended for those travelling with children. Good single rates too. ❸

Cabinas Ramacé, opposite Cabinas El Cisne (☎ 777-0590). Similar to other cheap cabinas in Quepos, with clean – if bare – rooms with hot water and refrigerator in somewhat sterile sur-roundings. ❹

Hotel Kamuk, just west of the mercado (☎ 777-0379, ⓕ 777-0258). Now part of the Best Western chain, though it's still a basic hotel, and fairly pricey even for Quepos. There's a small pool, how-ever, and a decent restaurant with airy views over the sea wall. ❺

Hotel Majestic, in the centre (no phone). Clean and friendly place with the cheapest rooms in town, though they're extremely basic – little more than concrete cells – and bathroom facilities are shared. **1**

Hotel Malinche, just west of the *mercado* (Ⓣ & Ⓕ 777-0093). Modern, "American"-style a/c rooms (**3**–**4**) with carpet, TV and balcony, and cheaper, older rooms (**2**) with ceiling fans and cold water – the latter are better value, especially for singles. Rooms vary, so if you don't like the first one they show you, ask to see another – those upstairs are better.

Hotel Mar y Luna, just northwest of the *mercado* (Ⓣ 777-0394). Central, friendly budget hotel. Rooms are dark, but have private bath, heated water and fans, and there's a small plant-filled communal balcony, shared fridge and free coffee. **4**

Hotel Melissa, just west of the *mercado* (Ⓣ 777-0025). Characterless but very clean budget rooms with cold water and fans – the small balcony and

conscientious management makes it stand out from the town's other concrete-box-style accommodation. Good low-season rates, though during high season it's a bit expensive for what's on offer. **2**

Hotel Sirena (Ⓣ 777-0528, Ⓕ 777-0165). Simple rooms – the nicest are upstairs – with private bath, hot water and a/c, and there's also a small pool, plus poolside bar, and restaurant. Breakfast included. **5**.

Villas Cruz, 50m east of *Cabinas Hellen* (Ⓣ 777-0271). Basic but comfortable cabinas, all with ceiling fans, kitchen and TV. **3**

Villas Verano, 250m northeast of the *mercado* (Ⓣ 777-0271). Small cabinas arranged near the home of the friendly owner, who will also serve breakfast in her dining room. All cabinas have private bathroom (cold water only), and a few have their own refrigerators. **2**–**3**

Eating and drinking

As in other tourist towns in Costa Rica, Quepos' eating scene divides into places owned by and geared towards gringos, and those owned by locals and frequented by Ticos; it's usually pretty obvious which is which. As a rule, **fish** is predictably good – order grilled *pargo* or *dorado* and you can't go far wrong.

Cafe Milagro, on the sea wall. Sells English-language newspapers and magazines and serves tasty coffee (they have a real espresso machine) and cakes – try the vanilla nut chill or iced raspberry mocha. Drinks, including the "Queppuccino" ($2), are fairly expensive but well made. Buy a bag of roasted beans to take home: the coffee here is among the best in the country. Accepts US dollars and travellers' cheques, and has a sister restaurant on the road to Manuel Antonio (see below).

D'Angolo, across from the *Restaurante Dos Locos*. Small Italian deli with a couple of tables. This is the place to come if you crave fettuccini with real gorgonzola cheese ($6), or if you're self-catering – buy some fresh bread, Emmenthal, *mortadela* and Italian wine for a picnic lunch at the beach.

Dos Locos, just southwest of the *mercado*. Moderately priced restaurant with a cosmopolitan menu, popular with travellers, including large, healthy sandwiches and Mexican cuisine, in a nice dining area open to the street.

El Gran Escape, on the sea wall. Recently expanded bar-restaurant catering to an overwhelmingly American crowd – weekend nights can get rowdy. There's a good selection of drinks at the bar and a pleasant, plant-filled seating area, open to the street, where you can sample the restaurant's fairly pricey Mexican food and American-style breakfasts.

Escalofrío, opposite the Banco Popular. Delicious Italian ice cream – certainly the best in the area, possibly in the whole of Costa Rica – owned by a member of Quepos's growing Italian community.

Isabel, on the main street. Pleasant wooden house with soft wicker chairs and friendly and fast service from a menu of American and continental breakfasts, salads, pasta and rice dishes.

Kamuk, beneath the hotel of the same name. Small restaurant open to the street and popular with travellers, with a good choice of breakfasts.

La Marquesa, on the seawall front. Large *casados* for $2.50; the *tipico* breakfasts are also good value.

Pizza Gabriel, west of the *mercado*. Small, quiet restaurant with gingham tablecloths, serving nice, simple and fairly economical pizzas.

Soda El Costo de Oro, next to the Banco Popular. "The Price of Gold" really is gold-dust, with lunches that are well cooked and also the cheapest in town (just over $2 for a fish *casado*), while the busy lunch-time crowd features both locals and tourists, for once under the same roof.

Soda El Pueblo, west of the *mercado*. Spotless soda, with huge menu; good if you've got a craving for *arroz con pollo* at 3am – it's open 24 hours.

6

Moving on from Quepos

Buses to Manuel Antonio leave from the terminal at the *mercado* (15 daily; 20min) between 5.30am and 9.30pm; there are slightly fewer in the rainy season. The service to San José (3hr 30min) departs at 5am, 8am, 2pm and 4pm. Buses to Puntarenas (3hr) leave at 4.30am, 10.30am and 3pm; the Puntarenas bus will also drop you at the entrance to Jacó (1hr 30min). There are usually two buses daily to San Isidro in the Zona Sur at 5am and 1.30pm (3hr 30min), depending on the condition of the roads. Taxis line up at the rank at the south end of the *mercado* and will take you to the park for $3. You can get to San Isidro, Golfito and the Osa Peninsula, and other points in the Zona Sur via Dominical, 44km south of Quepos – although the road is usually in terrible condition and a sturdy 4WD is needed, it beats going all the way back to San José and taking the Interamericana south. For plane tickets and schedules to San José, visit Lynch Tours (see box on p.338).

Quepos to Parque Nacional Manuel Antonio

Southeast of Quepos, the road winds for 7km over the surrounding hills, pitching up at the village of **MANUEL ANTONIO** and the entrance to Parque Nacional Manuel Antonio. Manuel Antonio was one of the first places in the country to feel the effects of the tourism explosion in the 1990s. Hoteliers and businesses rushed into the area, drawn by its lavish beauty, and driving along the road from Quepos to the park you come upon some sort of accommodation every few metres. The most exclusive – and expensive – places are hidden away in the surrounding hills, with wonderful ocean and sunset views. The very best overlook Punta Catedral ("Cathedral Point"), which juts out picturesquely into the Pacific. Though there are some reasonably affordable places near the park entrance, and the occasional low-season discount, prices are high compared to the rest of the country.

The Manuel Antonio **bus** from San José continues beyond Quepos, dropping people off along the seven-kilometre stretch of road between the town and the park entrance, and is convenient if you're staying at one of the hotels between the two – ask to be dropped off at you hotel. **La Buena Nota** souvenir shop, on the road to Manuel Antonio between the *Hotel Karahé* and *Cabinas Piscis* (℡777-1002), functions as an information centre for the area, as well as selling camera film, foreign papers and magazines, and locally made hand-crafted clothing, including some featuring *molas* (designs from the Panamanian Kuna peoples). There's **internet access** in the unlikely setting of a restored railway car – brought all the way from northern Chile – in front of *La Cantina* restaurant across from the *Costa Verde* hotel. For **shopping**, the Sí Como No artesanía shop in Manuel Antonio stocks the work of local painters and craftsmen; while La Buena Nota (see above) has an impressive range of swimwear, beach-bags, sandals and batik clothing at reasonable prices.

There are several **language schools** in Manuel Antonio, and a few San José schools offer a week's study here as part of their curriculum. Local schools include the Escuela de Idiomas d'Amore (℡777-1143, ℻777-0233, ℇdamore@racsa.co.cr), which offers all levels of tuition and has a good reputation, and the *Escuela del Pacífico* (℡777-0010, ℠www.escueladelpacifico.com), housed in the *Cabinas Pedro Miguel*, whose Canadian owner offers personalized classes.

The privately run animal sanctuary, **Jardín Gaia Wildlife Rescue Center** (℡ & ℻777-0535), on the road to Manuel Antonio between hotels *Sula Bya*

Bya and *Las Tres Banderas*, offers small group tours (daily at 9am, 11am, 2pm & 4pm; $7; maximum 20 people per day) during which you can see some of the animals – mostly birds and monkeys – they have rescued from neglect or found hurt in the wild. The guides are entertainingly frank about the habits of the animals, all of which are eventually returned to the wild. The centre also operates a volunteer programme – contact them directly for further information.

Accommodation

The hotels below are listed **in the order you encounter them from Quepos** – all are well signed from the road. More than anywhere else in this guide our choice is partial, representing the best value in each price range. Prices quoted are high season prices and generally include tax and breakfast; in the low season, midweek and for a long stay some of these hotels will give good discounts – it's worth asking. You should make sure to **reserve** well in advance – in the highest season, from December 1 to January 15, you'll have to reserve as much as four months ahead to secure a place in many of these hotels.

Between Quepos and Manuel Antonio

Cabinas Pedro Miguel (T 777-0035, F 777-0279). One of the friendliest places in the area, Costa Rican-owned and managed and currently home to the Escuela del Pacífico language school. The family rent two little *casitas*, backed up against the rainforest, with mosquito nets, kitchenette and basic furnishings. There's also a small pool and great cook-your-own restaurant (see p.343). Low-season and midweek discounts are available, but book ahead. ⑤

Hotel Plinios, (T 777-0055, F 777-0558, W www.hotelplinio.com). Good selection of rooms (though some are a bit dark), all well screened and nicely decorated with Guatemalan prints – the highest rooms give spectacular sunset views which you can watch from the raised platform beds. The landscaped tropical gardens feature a pool and a four-kilometre nature trail, with stupendous views from the top. There's a very good restaurant too, and off-season discounts. ⑥

Aparthotel Mimo's (T 777-0054, F 777-2217, W www.hotelmimos.com). Big double rooms and one suite – all with fan, hot water, and hammocks outside – situated around a large pool. There's also a good Italian restaurant attached. Reasonable rates, especially in low season. ⑤–⑥

El Mono Azul (T & F 777-1954, W www.monoazul.com). One of the best-value places in Manuel Antonio, with ten small but bright and clean rooms with fans (two have a/c), hot water and outside terrace. A lovely pool and an excellent restaurant (see p.343) add further lustre. Book in advance. ④

Villa Teca (T 777-1117, F 777-1578). Affordable mid-range accommodation, with big low-season discounts, in smallish but brightly painted bungalows surrounded by bougainvillea in a beautifully tranquil hillside setting, with a good-sized pool and on-site restaurant. Breakfast included. ⑤–⑥

Hotel Las Tres Banderas (T 777-1284, F 777-1478, E Banderas@centralamerica.com). Situated in a quiet wooded area, this is one of the area's best hotels, though moderately priced. The large double rooms open onto a terrace or balcony, while the even more spacious suites are furnished with kitchenette and sofa bed. There's also a large swimming pool and a good restaurant. ⑤–⑥

La Colina (T 777-0231, E lacolina@racsa.co.cr). Located on the near-vertical incline locals call "cardiac hill", this lovely hotel offers rare, good-value mid-range rooms, all with private bath and ceiling fans or a/c; the suites with kitchenettes are good value for groups of three or more. There's a nice pool too, and breakfast is included. ⑤–⑥

Flor Blanca (T & F 777-1633). The only "budget" option on the road to Manuel Antonio, with plain, thin-walled rooms and a choice of ceiling fan or a/c. It's overpriced for what you get, though there are good off-season discounts. ②

Tulemar (T 777-0580, F 777-1325, W www.tulemar.com). A great hideaway, and slightly cheaper than the area's other top-end hotels, with fourteen beautiful octagonal bungalows, many with panoramic views over Punta Catedral, built on stilts and set into the hillside. All are luxuriously furnished with a/c, VCR and TV, phones and well-equipped kitchenettes, and there's also a large swimming pool and nature trails in the grounds. Breakfast included. ⑥

Hotel La Mariposa (T 777-0355, F 777-0050, E mariposa@racsa.co.cr). Manuel Antonio's oldest luxury hotel, complete with prestigious (and overpriced) restaurant. Rooms are arranged in villas set in lovely gardens around a pool, but the real highlight is the views out to Punta Catedral. Breakfast included. **7**

Makanda-by-the-Sea (T 777-0442, F 777-1032, E makanda@racsa.co.cr). Manuel Antonio's best top-range choice, with a friendlier atmosphere than at some other luxury establishments in the area. Accommodation is in elegant villas, all with kitchenettes and outside balconies or terraces, set in quiet gardens with ocean views. Breakfast included. **8**

El Parador (T 777-1414, F 777-1437, W www.hotelparador.com). Stuffed with hundreds of specially imported antiques and suits of armour quietly oxidizing in the tropics, the *Parador* has entered local legend for the scale of its luxuriousness. The sumptuous hillside villas, many with staggering views, come with cable TV, a/c and bathtubs, and there are further spectacular vistas from the pool and (expensive) restaurant. Reached down a long rough road, the hotel is enviably secluded, though expensive to reach without a car – taxis can charge up to $10. A lavish breakfast buffet is included. **7–8**

Villas El Parque (T 777-0096, F 777-0538, E vparque@racsa.co.cr). Good self-catering rooms, suites and duplex villas, all with kitchen, balcony and screened dining area. Some also come with a/c, and many have views of the Pacific and Punta Catedral. **5–7**

Villas Nicolas (T 777-0481, F 777-0451, E nicolas@racsa.co.cr). Friendly, classy and reasonably priced accommodation set high above the surrounding landscape – rooms with views go for about $20 more than those without. All rooms have private bath, hot water and ceiling fans; some have kitchens, too. There's also a small pool. Good value. **6**

Si Como No (T 777-0777, F 777-1093, E sicomono@racsa.co.cr). Architectural award-winning complex set on a hill overlooking the Pacific and Punta Catedral – there are beautiful views from nearly every room. The hotel has solar-heated hot water, Jacuzzi, pool, swim-up bar and waterslide, as well as a small cinema with nightly screenings (free to guests). Rooms (and prices) vary from well-appointed doubles to fully equipped villas. The poolside *Rico Tico* grill serves excellent food, and breakfast is included. **8**

Casitas El Eclipse (T & F 777-0408, W www.casitaseclipse.com). A variety of rooms, nicely set around three swimming pools, ranging from nicely decorated standard doubles to split-level (but expensive) *casitas* that can sleep up to five people. All rooms have refrigerator, telephone

and private balcony, and rates include continental breakfast. It's advertised as a gay-friendly hotel – *Bar Cocatoa*, popular with the gay crowd, is next door. **6–8**

Hotel Villa Nina (T 777-1221 or 777-128, F 777-1497, W www.hotelnina.com). One of Manuel Antonio's best-value lower mid-range hotels. Most rooms have refrigerator, telephone, coffee-maker, a/c and a private balcony or terrace; those upstairs have ocean views. Breakfast is included, and there's a pool, a great rooftop bar, and sloths and monkeys in the trees. **4–5**

Costa Verde (T 777-0584, in the US T 1-800/231-RICA, F 777-0560). Friendly and professionally run hotel in a quiet area, with spacious rooms and studio apartments constructed from beautiful hardwood, rustic in feel but with all amenities and nice details such as decorative tiles and balconies with terrific ocean views. The best-value rooms are in D block, looking out directly onto Punta Catedral and offering the most stunning views in Manuel Antonio. There's a separate air-conditioned area for families, along with a restaurant, bar, and a swimming pool with impressive views. **4–6**

Manuel Antonio Village

Cabinas Piscis (T 777-0046). One of the few budget places left in Manuel Antonio: rooms are dark and basic, with cement floors and private bath with cold water. Even so, they're clean and are connected to the beach by a pleasant garden, where a little restaurant serves juices and sandwiches (high season only). Student and group discounts are available, but it's popular, so book ahead. **3–4**

Cabinas Espadilla (T 777-2135, T & F 777-0903, W www.espadilla.com). The nicest place in Manuel Antonio village, although slightly over-priced – the cabinas with fan, sleeping three or four people, are the best value. Each room has private bath with hot water and kitchen, and the complex is set in attractive gardens with a nice pool. **6**

Villabosque (T 777-0463, F 777-0401, E andrea@racsa.co.cr). Clean, bright and nicely furnished rooms, with wicker chairs, private bath with hot water, and a choice of a/c or ceiling fan. There's also a pleasant outdoor reading and TV area, a good restaurant and bar, and a small swimming pool. **4–5**

Los Almendros, (T 777-0225). Moderately priced option close to the beach and park. Rooms with fan and cold water are cheaper than those with a/c and hot. Good restaurant attached. **4–5**

Hotel Vela Bar (T 777-0413, F 777-1071,

@ velabar@maqbeach.com). Small and reasonably priced hotel offering basic but pleasant rooms with private bath and fan or a/c – those with fan are better value. Close to the beach and park. ⑤

Cabinas ANEP (T 777-0565). By far the most basic accommodation in the area, with dark and spartan – but clean – cabinas with fans and private bath set in quiet landscaped grounds close to the park and beach. Though technically reserved for members of the Costa Rican Public Employees Association, they'll take foreign tourists when there's space – usually midweek and in low season. ②

Eating and drinking

Eating in Manuel Antonio is notoriously expensive and the area's few good-value restaurants, like *El Mono Azul* and *Mar y Sombra*, are understandably popular. The more upmarket hotels all have restaurants attached; some are very good, though most are expensive, or simply overpriced. Some restaurants in Manuel Antonio, including several of the best, close or have restricted hours in the rainy season – ask at La Buena Nota (see p.340) for information. For the more popular places – *Plinios*, *Karola's* and *Vela Bar* among them – you should call or stop by to make a reservation, especially on weekends and during high season. Locals warn against eating at the cheap but largely unlicensed **sodas** (you can spot them by their itinerant look) in the village near the park entrance, which have dubious hygiene standards.

Between Quepos and Manuel Antonio

Anaconada, at the *Costa Verde* hotel. Pleasant dining in an enormous *rancho*, with a menu ranging from American-style breakfasts to good-value eggplant Parmesan (a bizarrely popular local favourite) and tasty grilled fish ($5.50).

Barba Roja, next to the *Divisimar Hotel*, on the road to Manuel Antonio, about 2.5km from the park entrance. Friendly and perennially popular place for high-quality American cuisine, including burgers and desserts.

Bar Cocatoa, next door to the *Casitas El Eclipse*. Very popular gay bar with a nice rooftop location and a good selection of drinks – women are welcome, so long as they don't mind being surrounded by boys who are more beautiful than they are. Open from around 10.30pm until "who knows" – about 3 or 4am.

Café Milagro, one of the best local places for breakfast (from 6.30am), with excellent locally roasted coffee and superlative cappuccino, pastries and cooked food served up in a pleasant environment.

El Mono Azul, in *El Mono Azul* hotel. Generous and reasonably priced plates of well-cooked chicken, fish, hamburgers and sandwiches. Check out the shop next to the restaurant – all proceeds go to a local project run by children to preserve the rainforest and the habitat of the squirrel monkey.

Gato Negro, next to *Cabinas El Eclipse*. Expensive but classy Italian dining, ranging from a pricey Caesar salad ($6) to fettucine with truffle cream ($13). Breakfast – marginally less expensive – is served from 6.30am.

Karola's, near the *Barba Roja*. Mexican cuisine, with burritos, seafood, vegetarian dishes and a macadamia-nut pie that has entered local food legend. Closed Wed and in low season.

La Cantina, across from the *Costa Verde* hotel. American-style open-air bar with live music most nights and fresh but pricey seafood (fish for $7 or jumbo camarones for $15). If you're not flush, just go for a beer and the music. The enterprising owner is soon to open a bar just up the hill, housed inside an old American bomber plane he rescued from former drug traffickers.

La Cocina de mi Abuela, at the *Hotel Dorado Mojado*. Tasty, filling gringo-style breakfasts, with huge plates of fruit and pancakes, but so-so coffee. Open from 7am.

Pedro Miguel, in the *Cabinas Pedro Miguel*, signposted as soon as you leave Quepos,. Wonderful, open-air do-it-yourself barbecue restaurant with rough-hewn wooden tables and chairs, set right next to the forest. Choose your cut of meat or fish, then cook it to your liking on the big outdoor grill. Extremely popular, and lots of fun. Dec–April only.

Plinio's, opposite *Pedro Miguel* (T 777-0055, F 777-0558). Quite simply one of the best restaurants in the country, open for breakfast, lunch and dinner. It's famous locally for its eggplant parmesan, though it's also worth trying the pot roast in red wine, the tiramisu, and the selection of reasonable Chilean wine. There's a nice and relaxed bar, too, with good music.

Rico Tico Grill, at the *Si Como No*. Poolside dining with a view over the ocean and superbly cooked food – try the succulent fish brochettes – only slightly marred by excessively obsequious service. Try an exceptional cocktail or chilled fruit drink. Breakfast is also good, with the added entertainment – if you're lucky and up early – of watching the squirrel monkeys and coatimundi that live in the trees in front of the restaurant.

Villabosque, at the *Hotel Villabosque*. Upmarket by Mantuel Antonio village standards, with a nice atmosphere and good service. The seafood is overpriced ($20 for shrimp), though the sandwiches and hamburgers are reasonable.

Manuel Antonio village

Los Almendros, at *Los Almendros* hotel, Manuel Antonio village. Nothing special, but reasonably priced local food plus the usual offerings of hamburgers. Good for lunch before or after visiting the park.

Manuel Antonio, Manuel Antonio village, close to the park entrance. Friendly and popular place, with *típico* food, rice dishes and good *refrescos*.

Mar y Sombra, Manuel Antonio village, on the beach 500m from the park entrance. In a grove of shady palm trees, this cheap, sprawling place is the most popular in the village, with *típico* food including good *casados* and fried fish of the day ($4.50), simply done in garlic and butter, with fried plantains and salad. Drinks include superlative *batidos en agua*, and there's also a disco here at weekends

Vela Bar, Manuel Antonio village. The swankiest food in the village, with dishes (starting from around $7) featuring good grilled fish, plus some vegetarian choices and paella.

Playa Espadilla

Playa Espadilla (also sometimes called Playa Primera or Playa Numero Uno) is outside the park, immediately north of the entrance. It's not hard to see why it's one of the most popular beaches in the country, with wide, smooth, light-grey sands and stunning sunsets. It is also very dangerous, however, and plagued by **rip tides** that travel between six and ten kilometres per hour. Even so, lots of people do swim here – or rather, paddle and wade – and live to tell the tale, and now there are professional lifeguards on hand during high season (see box below), it's considerably safer.

Lifeguards at Playa Espadilla

Until recently very few of Costa Rica's beaches had lifeguards (in Spanish, *guardavivas*). Like most South and Central American countries graced with good beaches, the nation lacks the resources to make them safe for swimmers – which goes some way to explaining why two hundred people drown in Costa Rica every year – one of the highest rates in the world, and the country's second leading cause of accidental death after car crashes.

In 1993, members of the Quepos and Manuel Antonio business community contributed funds to form Costa Rica's first professional surf rescue lifeguards. This eleven-strong team of professionally trained locals who know the currents well, has reduced the number of drownings to nearly zero. Before the lifeguards, the beach usually claimed between five to ten lives a year. Funds, donated by local businesses dependent on tourism, the US Lifesaving Association and the University of California's Ocean Initiative Group, are currently sufficient only to guard the beaches in the high season, between December and April.

Parque Nacional Manuel Antonio

Though it's by far the smallest national park in Costa Rica, the **PARQUE NACIONAL MANUEL ANTONIO** (Tues–Sun 7am–4pm; $6; ⓦwww.manuelantonio.com) fights it out with the Parque Nacional Volcán Poás in the Valle Central for the title of the most popular park in the country. It's hard not to appreciate the foresight that went into its creation in 1972; considering the number of hotels and restaurants that line its approaches, it's all too easy to imagine the fate that would have otherwise have overtaken the lime-stone-white sands of Playa Espadilla Sur. Even so, the park is a victim of its own popularity, and the current system of closing the park on Mondays is an attempt to give the animals a rest and the rangers and trail maintenance staff a chance to work.

Covering an area of just 6.8 square kilometres, Manuel Antonio preserves not only the lovely **beaches** and the unique *tómbolo* formation (see p.334) of Punta Catedral, but also **mangroves** and humid tropical **forest**. Visitors can only visit the section of the park facing the sea. The eastern *montaña*, or mountain section, off limits to the public, is regularly patrolled by rangers to deter poaching, which is rife in the area, and incursions into the park from surrounding farmers and *campesinos*.

Rangers at Manuel Antonio know their terrain well and are happy to talk to you about the park if they are not too busy – telling fond stories about boa constrictors, and the antics of the *monos tití*, or **squirrel monkeys**. Manuel Antonio is one of the few remaining natural habitats for the squirrel monkeys, whose cuteness is their own nemesis – highly sought after as pets and for zoos, they used to be prime targets for poachers. Smaller than their primate cousins – the howler, white-faced, spider and capuchin monkeys – they have close-set bright eyes and a delicate, white-haired face. According to rangers, their numbers are still quite low. Still, you might well see the squirrel monkeys on the trail or outside the park in the Manuel Antonio area. Local schoolchildren have set up a project to build overhead wooden "bridges" for the monkeys to cross the increasingly busy road from Manuel Antonio to Quepos, rather than risk being run over on the ground, and to allow them to increase their area of habi-

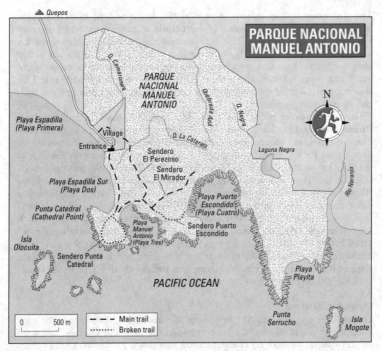

tation. Contributions are welcome – ask Jennifer at the *Mono Azul* for details. Besides being quiet, you can also help the squirrel monkeys – and other resident animals – by not feeding them (an action for which you can be fined) or leaving any litter.

You also have a good chance of seeing other **smaller mammals**, such as the racoon, the coati, the agouti, the two-toed sloth and white-faced capuchin monkey. **Birdlife** is also abundant, including the shimmering green **kingfisher**, the brown pelican, who can often be seen fishing off the rocks, and the laughing falcon. Beware the snakes that drape themselves over the trails and look for all the world like vines – be careful what you grab onto. Big iguanas hang out near the beaches, often standing stock-still for ten minutes at a time, providing good photo opportunities.

The **green turtle**, or llora, has probably nested in the Manuel Antonio area for thousands of years. At low tide at the south end of Playa Manuel Antonio, rangers can show you stones that they believe were used as turtle traps by the indigenous peoples of the area. Rangers have recently set up a project to preserve the area as a nesting ground for the green turtle, and to try to increase the species' dangerously low numbers. Volunteers are needed: contact Délio or Denis on ☏ 777-0644 (Spanish only).

The **climate** is hot, humid and wet, all year round. Though the rains ease off in the dry season (Dec–April), they never disappear entirely. The average year-round temperature is 27°C, and it can easily get to 30°C and above – take lots of water on the trails. If you run out, you can buy water and fizzy drinks at the canteen at Playa Manuel Antonio, the first beach inside the park (see box opposite).

Trails

The **entrance** to the park is located at the south end of Playa Espadilla. Manuel Antonio has a tiny system of short **trails**, all easy, except when it's rainy and they can get slippery. The trail nearest the entrance is the short **La Catarata** trail (The Waterfall; 500m), which takes to you a small but pretty waterfall, after which you can continue towards Playa Manuel Antonio on the main trail – watch out for the massive giant bamboo on the left hand side. This area is fairly good for spotting sloths in the eucalyptus trees that line the trail, and occasionally monkeys.

The most popular trail is the small loop around Punta Catedral, **Sendero Punta Catedral** (1.4km) – although the hilly terrain means it can get treacherous at times, and rangers sometimes close it completely. There's a wonderful view of the Pacific, dotted with jagged-edged little islands, from the mirador at the very tip of the point. If you loop round this trail you come to the beachside trail that rings **Playa Manuel Antonio** (also known as Playa Tres or Playa Blanca), the best beach for swimming. At the end of Playa Manuel Antonio you can either go inland on the **Sendero El Mirador** (1.3km) or take a beachside trail, **Sendero Playa Gemalas y Puerto Escondido** (1.6km), which heads through relatively dense humid tropical forest cover, crossing a small creek before eventually reaching rocky Playa Puerto Escondido. You can clamber across Playa Puerto Escondido at low tide – but check tide times with the rangers before leaving to avoid getting cut off. All in all it's pretty untaxing walking, although the views are fabulous.

Practicalities

Buses from Quepos and San José drop off passengers 200m before the park entrance. If you're staying at a hotel between the park and Quepos, and want to go to either by **taxi**, it's cheaper to flag one down on the road rather than

Manuel Antonio beaches

Beaches in the Parque Nacional Manuel Antonio can be confusing, since they're called by a number of different names. Because some are not safe for swimming, however, it is important to grasp which one is which. Follow the rangers' advice and swim only at Playa Manuel Antonio (also called Playa Tres), which is where everyone else will be, anyway. From the north to the south they are as follows:

Playa Espadilla, outside the park; see box p.344 (also called Playa Primera or Playa Numero Uno).

Playa Espadilla Sur (also called Playa Dos or Playa Segunda) is the first beach inside the park, on the north side of Punta Catedral. The park rangers take a dim view of people swimming here, and the surf can be rough.

Playa Manuel Antonio (also called Playa Tres or Playa Blanca) is by far the best swimming beach. Immediately south of Punta Catedral, it's in a deeper and more protected bay than the others, though you can still get clobbered by the deceptively gentle-looking waves as they hit the shore – be careful getting in and out. Unfortunately it's quite narrow and can get crowded. Early morning before 10am is the best time to come.

Playa Puerto Escondido (also called Playa Cuatro) is a pretty, white horseshoe-shaped beach which can be reached along the Puerto Escondido trail, but don't set out here without checking with the rangers about the *marea* (tide) first, since at high tide you can't get across Puerto Escondido, nor can you cross it from the dense forest behind. At best it will be a waste of time; at worst you'll get cut off on the other side for a few hours. Rangers advise against swimming here, as the currents can be dangerous.

ringing from the hotel – you'll be charged a per-person fare, and the taxi may pick up more people. If you're driving, note that there isn't much **parking** at the road loop at the end of Manuel Antonio village; arrive early in the morning for the best (shaded) spots, the going rate for guard cars is about $1.50 per day. The entrance hut is on the other side of the bridge. Here you can pick up a colour map of the park which shows the beaches and trails and also gives information on the local climate and flora and fauna. There are toilets and showers at Playa Tres. There have been problems with **theft** in Manuel Antonio, usually as a result of people leaving valuables (like cameras) on the beach: the rangers, who often sit at the picnic tables, might be able to look after your stuff, but ask nicely, as it's not actually part of their job.

Guided **tours** are available with park-accredited guides for $15 per person. The guides are informative and bring binoculars, telescopes, and speak Spanish and English. Ask at the park entrance, or ask your hotel to ring the park office to reserve a guide. Be aware that when you leave your car in the parking area in Manuel Antonio village that you may be approached by "guides" offering their services at the same price as the official park guides. These "guides" have been known to rob their clients while in the park; though it's more likely that they simply won't be able to show you anything you couldn't see with your own eyes, as they're not trained. If in doubt, the park-accredited guides carry photo ID. Rangers advise against walking alone in remote areas of the park. Although rangers are very often on patrol and can nearly always be found near Playa Tres, by law they can't deny entrance to the park to anyone, even suspicious-looking characters.

Travel details

Buses

Jacó to: Quepos (3 daily; 1hr); San José (3 daily; 2hr 30min–3hr).

Montezuma to: Paquera, for ferry to Puntarenas (3 daily; 1hr).

Paquera to: Montezuma (3 daily; 1hr); Tambor (3 daily; 40min).

Puntarenas to: Liberia (1 daily; 3 hr); Quepos (3 daily; 3hr 30min); San José (14 daily; 2hr); Santa Elena (1 daily; 3hr 30min).

Quepos to: Jacó (3 daily; 1hr); Puntarenas (3 daily; 3hr 30min); San Isidro (2 daily; 3hr 30min); San José (5 daily; 3hr 30min–5hr).

San José to: Jacó (3 daily; 2hr 30min–3hr); Manuel Antonio (express service, 3 daily; 3hr 30min–4hr); Puntarenas (14 daily; 2hr); Quepos (5 daily; 30hr 30min–5hr); Santa Elena (2 daily; 4–5hr).

Santa Elena to: Las Juntas (2 daily; 2hr); Puntarenas (1 daily; 3hr 30min); San José (2 daily; 4–5hr); Tilarán (1 daily; 3hr).

Tilarán to: Santa Elena (1 daily; 3hr).

Ferries

Naranjo to: Puntarenas (car/passenger ferry, 4–5 daily; 1hr 30min).

Paquera to: Puntarenas (passenger ferry, 3–4 daily; 1hr 30min).

Puntarenas to: Montezuma (passenger ferry, via Paquera, 3–4 daily; 1hr 30min; car/passenger ferry, via Naranjo, 4–5 daily; 1hr 30min).

Flights (Sansa)

Quepos to: San José (4 daily; 20min).

San José to: Quepos (4 daily; 20 min); Tambor (1 daily; 20min).

Tambor to: San José (1 daily; 20min).

Flights (Travelair)

Quepos to: San José (4 daily high season, 1 daily low season; 20min).

San José to: Quepos (4 daily high season, 1 daily low season; 20min).

7

The Zona Sur

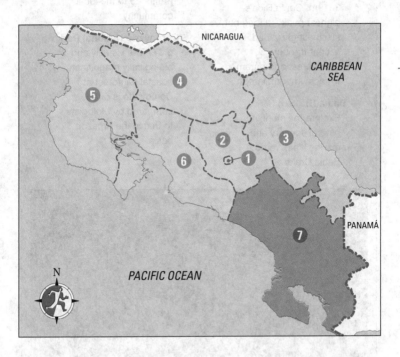

CHAPTER 7

Highlights

✳ **San Isidro p.356** A quiet and beautiful agricultural town where Costa Rica's countryside traditions live on, especially during the agricultural fair in February.

✳ **Chirripó p.357** Climb Cerro El Chirripó – at 3819m, Costa Rica's highest peak – a long but fascinatingly varied ascent through cloudforest and páramo to rocky mountaintop.

✳ **Bahía Drake p.366** Explore the stunning natural scenery and marine life of remote Bahía Drake.

✳ **Esquinas Rainforest Lodge p.371** Stay in primary rainforest at the friendly Esquinas Eco-lodge, part of a model project combining development aid, nature conservation and rainforest research – all profits go to the local community.

✳ **Corcovado National Park p.377** The visually and biologically magnificent coastal rainforest at Corcovado is often compared by biologists to that in the Amazon basin.

The Zona Sur

osta Rica's **Zona Sur** (southern zone) is the country's least-known region, both for Ticos and for travellers. Geographically it's a diverse area, ranging from the high mountain peaks of the Cordillera de Talamanca at its northern edge, via the agricultural heartland of the nearby Valle de el General, to the river-cut lowlands of the Valle de Diquis around Palmar and the coffee-growing Valle de Coto Brus, near the border with Panamá. The region is particularly popular with hikers, many of whom come to climb Cerro el Chirripó in the Talamancas – at 3819m one of the highest peaks in Central America – set in the chilly, rugged terrain of the **Parque Nacional Chirripó**, while a few experienced walkers venture into the giant neighbouring **Parque Internacional la Amistad**, a UNESCO Biosphere Reserve and World Heritage Site which protects an enormous but largely inaccessible swathe of land along Costa Rica's southern border.

Halfway down the region's Pacific coast is the **Playa Dominical** area, originally a surfing destination, whose tropical beauty is beginning to draw other visitors, especially since road improvements made it accessible without a 4WD. Further south down the coast, the **Osa Peninsula** is the site of the both the **Parque Nacional Corcovado** – one of the country's prime rainforest hiking destinations, whose soaring canopy trees constitute the last chunk of tropical wet forest on the entire Pacific side of the Central American isthmus – and the remote and picturesque **Bahía Drake**, from where tours depart to the nearby **Reserva Biológica Isla del Caño**, scattered with the lithic spheres fashioned by the local Diquis. On the opposite side of the Golfo Dulce from the Osa Peninsula, near the border with Panamá, is **Golfito**, the only town of any size in the region, and one which suffered from an unsavoury reputation for years after the pull-out of the United Fruit Company's banana operations in 1985. It has been attacting more visitors of late since being made a tax-free zone for

---

Accommodation price codes

All the accommodation in this book has graded using the following price codes. The prices quoted are for the least expensive double room in high season, and do not include the 18.46 percent national tax which is automatically added onto hotel bills. For more details on accommodation in Costa Rica, see p.35.

❶ less than $10	❷ $10–20
❸ $20–30	❹ $30–50
❺ $50–75	❻ $75–100
❼ $100–150	❽ over $150

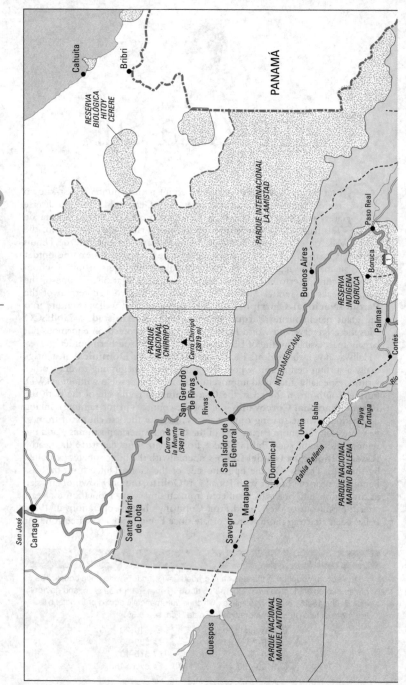

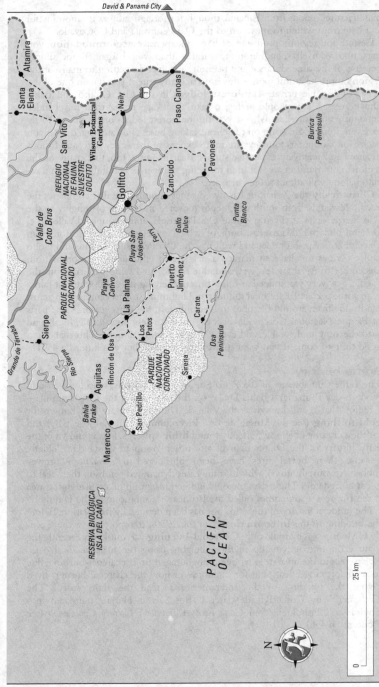

Santa Elena

Altamira

San Vito

Neily

Paso Canoas

Wilson Botanical Gardens

REFUGIO NACIONAL DE FAUNA SILVESTRE GOLFITO

Golfito

Zancudo

Pavones

Burica Peninsula

Valle de Coto Brus

Playa San Josecito

Golfo Dulce

Punta Blanco

PARQUE NACIONAL CORVOVADO

Playa Cativo

La Palma

Puerto Jiménez

Ferry

Grande de Térraba

Sierpe

Río Sierpe

Rincón de Osa

Los Patos

Carate

Osa Peninsula

Aguijitas

PARQUE NACIONAL CORCOVADO

Sirena

Bahía Drake

San Pedrillo

Marenco

RESERVA BIOLÓGICA ISLA DEL CAÑO

PACIFIC OCEAN

N

0   25 km

manufactured goods from Panamá, though for foreign visitors it's more useful as a base from which to move on to the Osa Peninsula and Corcovado.

Despite the region's profusion of basic, inexpensive **accommodation**, you may find yourself spending more money than you bargained for simply because of the time, distance and planning involved in getting to many of the region's more beautiful spots – this is particularly true if you stay in one of the very comfortable private **rainforest lodges** in the Osa, Golfito and Bahía Drake areas. Many people prefer to take a package rather than travel independently, and travellers who stay at the rainforest lodges often choose to fly in. Even doing Corcovado on the cheap, taking buses and camping, can set you back a bit, as the bus journeys are more expensive than elsewhere, and food is in short and relatively expensive supply. Bear in mind, too, that many of the region's communities are not used to seeing strangers – certainly women travelling alone will attract some curiosity.

Climatically the Zona Sur has two distinct regions. The first comprises the Pacific lowlands, from south of Quepos (covered in chapter 6) roughly to the Río Sierpe delta at the top of the Osa Peninsula, and the upland Valle de el General and the Talamancas, both of which experience a dry season from December to April. The second region – the Osa Peninsula, Golfito and Golfo Dulce – does not have so marked a dry season (although the months from December to April are less wet) and, due to localized wind patterns from the Pacific, gets very wet indeed at other times, receiving up to 5000mm of rain a year, with spectacular seasonal thunder and lightning storms cantering in across the Pacific from around October to December. In the rainy season, some parts of Parque Nacional Corcovado become more or less unwalkable, local mud roads become undriveable, and everything gets more difficult. This makes it a good time to come if you want to avoid the crowds, but you'll need a 4WD.

Some history

The earliest inhabitants of the Zona Sur were the **Diquis**, who lived around modern-day Palmar and Bahía Drake, on the shoulder of the Osa Peninsula – a region that is still known as the Valle de Diquis. They are best known for **goldsmithing** (see the Museo de Oro Precolumbiano in San José, p.89) and for their crafting of almost perfectly round **lithic spheres**. Less is known of the early history of the Diquis than of any other group in Costa Rica, chiefly because their burial sites have been plundered by *huaqueros* (grave-robbers/treasure hunters), who in some cases dynamited tombs in their zeal to get at buried gold. These days the only indigenous group of any size in the area is the Borucas – sometimes called the Bruncas – a subgroup of the Diquis.

The modern history of the Zona Sur has been defined by its isolation. Before the building of the **Interamericana** in the 1950s, transport across the Cerro de la Muerte was by mule only. **Charcoal-burning** was until very recently the main economic activity up in these heights, using the majestic local oaks. *Campesinos* in the area are now being discouraged from charcoal-burning, due to its deforesting effects, but for a glimpse of how the charcoal-burners lived before the building of the Interamericana, read the short story "The Carbonero" by Costa Rican writer Carlos Salazar Herera, translated into English and anthologized in *Costa Rica: A Traveller's Literary Companion* (see Contexts, p.438).

San José to San Isidro

The ease of travel from San José, via Cartago, 136km southwest to the market town of **San Isidro de el General** depends on the current condition of the Interamericana, which winds its way about 2000m up from the bowl of Cartago's enclosing valley to the chilly heights of the 3491-metre **Cerro de la Muerte** ("Death Mountain") pass. Rock- and mudslides are frequent along the highway, and there have been isolated reports of drivers being flagged down and robbed by bandits, although this normally happens to intercontinental truckers rather than tourists. Still, it's not a good idea to drive at night – not just because of the chance of robbery, but more crucially because of reduced visibility. Fog, mist, rain are a constant threat at all times, and the road lacks shoulder or meridian markings. The biggest problem you're likely to face, though, are the long tailbacks caused by lack of overtaking opportunities. Ticos frequently risk life and limb passing large trucks on blind corners, but don't be tempted to follow suit – Costa Rica has one of the world's highest road-accident rates. Remember, too, that if you have just arrived in Costa Rica, you may be prone to a bit of altitude or **mountain sickness** caused by too quick an ascent to the pass.

This whole area is defined by the Interamericana (also known here as Hwy-2), heaving with international transport trucks and other large vehicles. Yellow-topped kilometre markings line the highway, and villages and hamlets are often referred to by these numbers (Briseño, for example, is usually called "kilómetro treintesiete"). Ardent **quetzal** spotters should note that the chilly approaches to the Cerro de la Muerte pass are the most reliable place to spot the birds, who like these untouched high-altitude cloudforests. Several places are well set up for spotting, which is best in nesting season (March–June).

About 60km south of San José, the *Albergue de Montaña Tapantí* (℡290-7641, ℱ232-0436; ❺) enjoys a fantastic setting high on a ridge, with warm and comfortable bungalow-like chalets with private bath and hot water. The lodge also hosts unique small-scale **cultural tours** of the area, where for $10 you can spend the morning with a local *campesino* family (who receive the entire fee). If your Spanish is good, this can be a worthwhile encounter for both parties; you can find out about local farming methods, tour smallholdings, perhaps do a bit of trout fishing and watch milk being churned into cheese.

Ten kilometres further on, on a side road to the right at kilometre 70, is the *Albergue Mirador de Quetzales* (℡381-8456; ❸), run by a local family who have many of the quetzals' favourite trees on their land. They offer guided hikes and special quetzal-spotting outings at 6am daily ($6 per person). The *albergue* itself is cosy and reasonably priced, with wooden cabinas including private bath, and smaller rooms with shared facilities. You can have delicious home-cooked meals included for about $10 extra.

A little less than 20km further on, a turn-off leads to the lovely hamlet of **SAN GERARDO DE DOTA** – you'll need a 4WD to get there, since the road down from the Interamericana is treacherously steep in parts. In the village, the *Hotel de Montaña Savegre* (℡ & ℱ771-1732, ⓦwww.ecotourism.co.cr; ❺ including all meals) is well known among birders for the number of quetzals that nest on or near its property. The very friendly *dueños* have trail maps, can arrange guides (which cost extra) and offer bird-spotting tips; they also offer trout-fishing in the Río Savegre and horse-riding through the village. Close by, the *Trogon Lodge* (℡223-2421, ℱ222-5463, ⓦwww.grupomawamba.com; ❺) has comfortable cabins (although, despite being heated, they can get chilly at

The Diquis

Very little is known about the history of the Diquis region before 1000 BC, though culturally it appears to have formed part of the Greater Chiriquí region, which takes its name from the province in southwestern Panamá. Archeologists date the famous lithic spheres (see box on p.366) from some time between 1000 BC and 500 AD; between around 700 and 1600 AD the Diquis began fashioning gold pendants, breastplates, headbands and chains, becoming master goldsmiths within a hundred years or so. Between 500 and 800 AD drastic changes occurred in the culture of the Diquis. Archeologists posit the impact of the arrival of sea-going peoples from Colombia or possibly the Andes – a theory borne out by their metates and pottery, which show llama or guanaco figures, animals that would have been unknown on the isthmus. In the Diquis's own artisanry, both the ingenious – often cheeky – goldwork and the voluptuous pottery display a unique humour as well as superlative attention to detail.

The Diquis were in a state of constant warfare among themselves and with foreign groups. Like the Chorotegas to the north in Greater Nicoya (see p.238), they seem to have engaged in sacrifice, ritually beheading war captives. Huge metates unearthed at Barilles in Panamá show images of these rituals, while smaller crucible-like dishes – in which coca leaves, yucca or maize may have been crushed and fermented – suggest ritual inebriation.

The indigenous peoples of the Zona Sur first met the Spaniards in 1522 when the *cacique* of the Térraba group graciously hosted Captain Gil González for a fortnight. González was on his way from near the present-day Panamá border, where his ship had run aground, to Nicaragua. Despite infirmity (he was in his fifties), he was walking all the way. The Diquis seem to have declined abruptly after this initial contact, most likely felled by influenza, smallpox, the plague, and other diseases brought by Spanish settlers.

night) and immaculate grounds, with several trout ponds and marked trails through the woods – there are also normally many quetzals to be seen around here (Marcelina Mata Martinez is a recommended birding guide). Both hotels offer a transfer service from San José. If you're on a tight budget, *Cabinas El Quetzal* (no phone; ❷) in the centre of the village has simple rooms in a family home.

San Isidro and the Valle de el General

The spectacular descent into **SAN ISIDRO DE EL GENERAL**, just 702m above sea level, brings you halfway back into tropical climes after the chilly ride over Cerro de la Muerte. In Costa Rica, San Isidro is seen as an increasingly attractive place to live, with its clean, country-town atmosphere. While the Talamancas are a non-volcanic range – and the Valle de el General therefore lacks the incredibly fertile soils of the Valle Central – there is still considerable local agricultural activity, with pineapples growing particularly well. The town hosts an **agricultural fair** in the first week in February, when farmers don their finery, put their produce up for competition and sell great fresh food in the streets. May is the **month of San Isidro** – patron saint of farmers and animals – and is celebrated by fiestas, ox-cart parades, dog shows, and the erection of gaudy ferris wheels. The town's one museum, the **Museo Regional del Sur** (Tues–Sat 8am–4.30pm in theory, though it's often closed), 75m northwest of the church, is devoted to the *campesino* history of the area.

If you're travelling south from San Isidro to Palmar, Golfito or Paso Canoas, it's better to get a bus that originates in San Isidro rather than one that's coming through from San José, as they're often full and you could find yourself standing all the way to Panamá. If you want to try for one of the through-services, visit TRACOPA's ticket office (Mon–Sat 7am–4pm) at C 3 and the Interamericana; you can buy tickets if there are seats available, and schedules are posted telling you what time the buses pass through town. Buses for Quepos (4 daily; 3hr 30min) and Dominical (4 daily; 40min–1hr) leave from the terminal known locally as Y Griega, at the corner of C 2 and the Interamericana. Buses for San Gerardo de Rivas leave at 5am and 2pm (1hr 40min) from the El Mercado bus terminal at Av 6, C 0/2. For all local services, buy your ticket on the bus.

Practicalities

Rival **bus** services from San José to San Isidro (continuing to Golfito, Palmar and Paso Canoas) are run by MUSA and TRACOPA. San Isidro's main bus terminal is adjacent to the town's central market at Av 6, C 0/2, but most buses from here head to local destinations. To and from San José, TRACOPA buses stop right on the Interamericana at the corner of C 2, while MUSA buses pick up passengers across the road. The Banco Nacional on the main square changes **travellers' cheques**, while the Banco de Costa Rica on Av 4, C 0 has an ATM. There's an **internet café** next door to the Banco Nacional; the *correo* is on Av 4.

Of the budget choices in town, the best **accommodation** is at the large *Chirripó*, C 1, Av 2/4 (☎771-0529; ❶), which has simple rooms with private bath and hot shower and a decent restaurant. The *Hotel del Sur* (☎771-3033, ☏771-0527, ⓦwww.hoteldelsur.co.cr; ❹) is set in quiet, pleasant grounds about 6km southwest of San Isidro on the Interamericana and has en-suite rooms, tennis courts, a swimming pool and a good restaurant.

San Isidro also has a few good places to **eat**, where the fresh and amazingly varied local produce is put to good use – and because it's not on the tourist trail, food also tends to be inexpensive. The best place for breakfast is the café at the *Hotel Chirripó*, which serves *gallo pinto* and toast and eggs with excellent local coffee daily from 6.30am. Almost next door is the *Taquería Mexico Linda,* a brightly decorated and cheerful little café with excellent Mexican food.

Information about the Parque Nacional Chirripó and Parque Internacional La Amistad is available from the regional office of the parks service at C 2, Av 4/6, south of the Parque Central (Mon–Fri 8am–4pm; ☎771-3155, ☏771-3297, ⓔacla-p@ns.minae.go.cr). It's worth stopping off here to ask about current conditions and, if possible, to make reservations for Chirripó (see below). On C 4, Av 1/3 are the offices of **CIPROTUR** (☎771-6096, ☏771-2003, ⓦwww.ecotourism.co.cr), a non-profit organization which promotes tourism in the Zona Sur – the helpful staff can book hotel rooms and answer queries, while their website is an informative noticeboard for the region, worth checking out before you set off.

Parque Nacional Chirripó

PARQUE NACIONAL CHIRRIPÓ, some 20km northeast of San Isidro, is named after the Cerro el Chirripó, which lies at its centre – at 3819m the

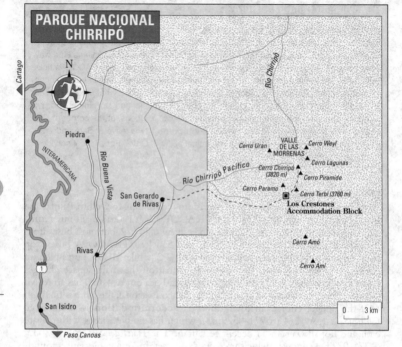

highest peak in Central America south of Guatemala. Ever since the conquest of the peak in 1904 by a missionary priest, Father Agustín Blessing (local indigenous peoples may of course have climbed it before), visitors have been flocking to Chirripó to do the same.

The park's terrain varies widely, according to altitude, from cloudforest to rocky mountaintops. Between the two lies the interesting alpine **páramo** – high moorland, punctuated by rocks, shrubs and hardy clump grasses more usually associated with the Andean heights. Colours are muted yellows and browns, with the occasional deep purple. Below the *páramo* lie areas of **oak forest**, now much depleted through continued charcoal-burning. Chirripó is also the only place in Costa Rica where you can observe vestiges of the **glaciers** that scraped across here about thirty thousand years ago: narrow, U-shaped valleys, moraines (heaps of rock and soil left behind by retreating glaciers) and glacial lakes, as well as the distinctive **crestones**, or heavily weathered fingers of rock, more reminiscent of Montana than Costa Rica. The land is generally waterlogged, with a few bogs – take care where you step, as sometimes it's so chilly you won't want to get your feet wet.

Many **mammals** live in the park, and you may see spider monkeys as you climb from the lower montane to the montane rainforest. Your best bet for **bird-spotting** is in the lower elevations: along the oak, mixed and cloudforest sections of the trail you may spot hawks, trogons, woodpeckers and even quetzals, though in the cold and inhospitable terrain up high, the most you'll see are robins and hawks.

The **weather** in Chirripó is extremely variable and unpredictable. It can be hot, humid and rainy between May and December, but is clearer and drier between January and April (the peak season for climbing the mountain). Even then, clouds may roll in at the top and obscure the view, and rainstorms move in very fast. The only months you can be sure of a dry spell are March and April. **Temperatures** may drop to below 0°C at night and rise to 20°C during the day, though at the summit, it's so cold that it's hard to believe you're just 9° north of the equator.

San Gerardo de Rivas

The tiny town of **SAN GERARDO DE RIVAS**, 17km from San Isidro and 3km from the park, is home to a park puesto and several very reasonably priced, friendly **places to stay**, and most climbers spend a night here before heading into the park – but try to get somewhere with **hot water**, as it can get very cold at night. There are also a couple of attractive family-run hotels a few kilometres further back down the road towards San Isidro in the village of **Rivas**. Many of the places listed below also rent out camping equipment like sleeping bags and cooking stoves. There are also several decent places **to eat** in San Gerardo, the best of which is the *Restaurante El Bosque*, which has tasty *bocas* as well as *casados*, table football and gorgeous views over the river below.

Albergue de Montaña El Pelicano, San Gerardo de Rivas (T 382-3000). Lovely Alpine chalet-style hotel with small but attractive wood-panelled rooms with shared bath and hot water. The restaurant below houses a small collection of owner Rafael Elizondo's coffee-root sculptures, including an amazing wooden motorbike. Also has horses for hire and arranges tours; special rates for groups. ❶

Albergue de Montaña Talari, Rivas (T & F 771-0341, E talaripz@racsa.co.cr). Eight neat en-suite rooms, set in twenty acres of tranquil riverside forest, with walking trails, a swimming pool and an excellent restaurant – they also offer good-value packages to Chirripó ($215 for four nights). ❹

Albergue Vista al Cerro, San Gerardo de Rivas (T 373-3365 or 771-1866). Very friendly guesthouse with immaculate dormitory accommodation and shared bathroom with hot water, plus a restaurant which opens at 3am for climbers

wishing to make an early start; also arranges tours. ❶

Cabinas El Descanso, San Gerardo de Rivas (T 771-1866). Private house close to the ranger station with 12 basic rooms, a shared bathroom with hot water and free transport to the park entrance, 3km away. ❶

Rancho La Botija del Sur, Rivas (T & F 770-2146, E ciprotur@racsa.co.cr). Four cabinas with pretty bamboo ceilings, plus a swimming pool and a viewing tower overlooking the farm's coffee and banana plantations. Several large stones carved with indigenous patterns have been discovered on the property, and can be seen on a daily tour (7am–9am; $5 per person). ❺

Hotel y Restaurante Roca Dura, San Gerardo de Rivas (T 225-2500). Seven smallish but clean rooms (one of which is built into a large slab of rock), some with private bath and hot water. The café and restaurant are quite a hive of activity, even in such a small village. ❶–❷

Visiting the park

Visiting the Parque Nacional el Chirripó requires advance planning. First you have to **reserve a place**, since no more than forty hikers are allowed in the park at any one time, and demand far outstrips capacity at the most popular times (around March and April, especially Easter, and Christmas) – although there are sometimes cancellations. When making reservations you should state your preferred dates, bearing in mind that it's not possible to book for the high season (which starts in January) before November 1. Most hikers find two or three nights sufficient. You may have to pay in advance and in full – $6 per day, plus $6 per night for accommodation.

To reserve a place, call or visit either the Fundación de Parques Nacionales office in San José (see p.77) or the regional parks office in San Isidro (see p.357). You can't officially make a reservation at the park's puesto in San Gerardo and if you turn up without one, you'll most likely be turned away. Even with a reservation you're required to check in at the puesto; this regulation also applies if you're heading for the camping trail which starts from Herradura. If you're not camping (see below) you must stay in the **accommodation block** at Los Crestones, which has fifteen rooms, each sleeping four people, cold showers, a cooking area and a big sink where you can wash clothes. It's also now possible to **camp** in the park, although this takes a bit more planning. You'll need to make a special reservation, hire a local guide (obligatory; $25 per day for up to 10 people; $50 for groups of 10–16) in the nearby hamlet of Herradura (ask at the *pulpería* for recommendations or the puesto in San Gerardo) and enter the park from Herradura. The trail to the summit of Chirripó via the campsite is longer and more arduous than the more common trek via the accommodation block at Los Crestones – you'll need a minimum of three days. Note if you're camping that no fires are allowed in the park – forest fires frequently devastate the area, some caused by improperly put-out campfires.

While Chirripó is hot at midday, it frequently drops to freezing at the higher altitudes at night. You should bring **warm clothing** (temperatures can fall to −7°C at night) and a proper **sleeping bag** (though these can be rented on site), a blanket, water, food and a propane gas stove. A short list of clothing and other essentials might include a good pair of boots, socks, long trousers, T-shirt, shirt, sweater, woolly hat and jacket, lots of insect repellent, sunglasses, first aid (for cuts and scratches), gloves (for rocks and the cold), binoculars and a torch – the accommodation huts only have electricity between 5.30pm and 8.30pm.

Detailed contour **maps** of the park are available from the Instituto Geográfico (see p.24) in San José, who sell four maps covering the entire climb. Otherwise, the staff at the entrance puesto can supply you with an adequate map of the park, showing some altitude markings. You can also hire a horse to carry your gear up to the accommodation huts, while the services of a **guide** can be useful and interesting in helping to identify local species and interpreting the landscapes you pass through – again, ask at the entrance puesto for recommendations.

The hike

Almost everyone who climbs Chirripó goes up to the accommodation huts first, rests there overnight, and then takes another day or two to explore the summit, surrounding peaks and *páramo*. During high season, you'll have company on the path up the mountain, and the trail is well marked with signs stating the altitude and the distance to the summit. Watch out for **altitude sickness**, though; if you have made a quick ascent from the lowland beach areas, you could find yourself becoming short of breath, experiencing pins and needles, nausea and exhaustion. If this happens, stop and rest; if symptoms persist, descend immediately. The main thing to keep in mind is **not to go off the trail** or exploring on your own without telling anyone, especially in the higher areas of the park. Off the trail, definite landmarks are few, and it's easy to get confused.

The **hike** begins at 1219m and ends at 3819m – the summit. It's almost entirely uphill and so exhausting that you may have trouble appreciating the scenery. On the first day most hikers make the extremely strenuous fourteen-kilometre trek to the accommodation huts – reckon on a minimum of seven hours if you're very fit (and the weather is good), up to twelve hours or more if you're not. You may be able to hire a horse to carry your gear for you (around $60 per 20kg). On the second day you can make the huts your base while you hike to the summit and back, which is easily done in a day, perhaps taking in some of the nearby lagoons.

The walk begins amidst cow pasture, before passing through thick, dark cloudforest, a good place to spot **quetzals** (March–May are the best months). Next comes a relatively flat stretch of several kilometres, where you're likely to be plagued by various biting insects. About halfway to the accommodation huts is a **rest station**; some people stay here, splitting the hike into a less-taxing two days, but conditions are extremely rustic, with three sides open to the wind. The **Cuesta de los Arrepentidos** ("Hill of the Repentants", meaning you're sorry at this point that you came) is the real push, all uphill for at least 3km. At **Monte Sin Fé** ("Faithless Mountain"), about 10km into the trail, is another patch of tropical montane forest, more open than the cloudforest. Keep your eye out for the *refugio natural*, a big cave where you can sleep in an emergency, from where it's just 3km to the **accommodation huts**. At the huts, the land looks like a greener version of Scotland: bare moss cover, grasslands, and a waterlogged area where the lagoons congregate. There are no trees, and little wildlife in evidence.

The **rangers** based up here are friendly, and in the high season (Jan–April) you can ask to accompany them on walks near the summit, thus sidestepping the possibility of getting lost. Do not *expect* this, however, as it is not their job to lead guided walks. It's just ninety minutes' walk from the accommodation huts along a well-marked trail to **the summit** – there's a bit of scrambling involved, but no real climbing. You'll need to set off by dawn, as clear weather at the peak is really only guaranteed until 9am or 10am. There's also a little book in a metal box that you can sign with your "I did it" message; bring a pen. From the top, if it's clear, you can see right across to the Pacific. However, you're above the cloud line up here, and the surrounding mountains may often be obscured by drifting milky clouds.

Dominical

The once quiet fishing village of **DOMINICAL**, 44km south of Quepos and 29km southwest of San Isidro, has for several years now been home to a small (mostly North American) surfing community, who claim it to be of Costa Rica's top surf spots. It's still a pleasantly laid-back and low-key place, with sandy streets, a long windy beach, and not much else other than a couple of decent bars and restaurants.

Nowadays any vehicle *should* be able to make the trip to Dominical, from either approach, although it makes sense to rent a 4WD if you want to explore the surrounding area. **From San José** it is more convenient and faster to come via San Isidro; **from Guanacaste** and the Central Pacific, you'll do best to take the road south from Quepos. **Buses** from Quepos arrive daily at around 6.30am and 3pm, and continue to San Isidro (2hr). Buses from San Isidro go on to Uvita. You can **change money** at the San Clemente Bar and Grill, which also acts an informal information centre and post office.

Dominical activities

Backed by a wall of palms, Dominical's dark-sand **beach** can, at sunset especially, look postcard-pretty. It is often deserted, and rarely crowded, except occasionally with surfers. As is usual with surfing beaches, the **swimming** varies from not great to downright dangerous, and is plagued by rip tides and crashing surf. About twenty minutes' walk south along the beach brings you to a small cove, where the water is calmer and you can paddle and snorkel.

The most popular activity here, other than exploring the beach and surrounding forest, is **Don Lulo's Nauyaca Falls Tour** (⊤771-3187, Ⓦwww.ecoturism.co.cr/NauyacaWaterfalls; $35), one of Costa Rica's best days out. The tour begins with a horseback ride to Don Lulo's (real name Señor Braulio Jiménez) home and small private zoo for breakfast, before continuing on horseback through lush rainforest with knowledgeable guides to the two cascades that make up the Nauyaca Falls – the principal one drops 150ft into a sparkling pool where you can swim. A *típico* lunch cooked over an open flame completes the day. You'll need to reserve a place on the tour as far in advance as possible.

Also popular is the private rainforest reserve at **Hacienda Barú** (see opposite for details), which features tree-climbing trips during which you winch yourself up extremely tall trees, as well as guided walks and an exhilarating canopy tour ($30), which involves swooping from platform to platform through primary rainforest on long steel cables, accompanied by guides who impart a wealth of forest folklore. Also recommended is **Kayak Joe's South Zone Psycho Tours**, a half-day guided kayak tour exploring the nearby sea caves ($50 per person; minimum of 2 people). You can find Joe at his bar, *Zona Libre*, in the Plaza Pacifica mall just south of Dominical.

Accommodation

There's a surprising range of good **accommodation** in the Dominical area. Some is basic and caters mainly for surfers, but there are also a number of more upmarket places, usually owned by foreigners, with more springing up all the time. The most expensive hotels include some wonderful hideaways, good for honeymooners, romantics and escapists. Aside from accommodation in the village itself there's a string of hotels and self-catering cottages along the coast road towards the next hamlet and its beach, **Dominicalito**, and in the surrounding hills.

Dominical

Cabinas San Clemente, down the main street and on the beach to the right (⊤787-0026). Attractive en-suite rooms plus basic but very clean dormitories for the surfer crowd a stone's throw from the sea. Surf and boogie board rental available. ❶–❷

Posada del Sol, on the main street opposite *San Clemente Bar* (⊤ & Ⓕ787-0085). Lovely hotel with four very good-value double rooms, all with private bath, and a two-bedroom apartment ($500 per month) for rent. ❷

Río Lindo, on the right as you enter Dominical (⊤787-0078). Ten comfortable rooms with private bathroom, some with a/c; there's also a pool, bar and whirlpool in the grounds. ❹

Tortilla Flats, next to *Cabinas San Clemente* on the beach (⊤787-0033). Popular small hotel with brightly decorated en-suite rooms overlooking the sea, plus on-site restaurant. ❸

Villas Río Mar, down a track to the right as you enter the village (⊤787-0052, Ⓕ787-0054, Ⓦwww.villasriomar.com). Upmarket accommodation with swimming pool, bar, tennis court and Jacuzzi. Comfortable rooms in individual chalets, set in extensive terraced gardens. ❻

Around Dominical

Cabinas el Coquito del Pacifico, 10km north of Dominical in the village of Matapalo (⊤222-4103, Ⓕ222-8849). Comfortable rooms with private bath and fan, a bar-restaurant and direct access to a wide and mostly deserted white-sand beach, good for bathing (but ask about currents). **❹**

Coconut Grove, 2km south of Dominical (☎ & ☏ 787-0130, ✉ coconutgrove@pocketmail.com). Comfortable self-catering units ($500 per week for 4 people) with all facilities, plus a barbecue area, pool and a lovely deserted beach.

Finca Brian y Milena, 3km south of Dominical, on the road to Escaleras – take a steep left fork away from the coast (☎ 771-4582, ✉ selvamar@racsa.co.cr). A nice small-scale family farm, doubling as a wildlife sanctuary, experimental fruit farm, botanical garden and guest lodge. There's also good bird-watching, and volunteer programmes. Most people arrive on packages, which include hikes in the surrounding rainforest and meals. Camping is also available. **❸**

Hacienda Barú, 1km north of Dominical on the road to Quepos (☎ 787-0003, ☏ 787-0004, ⓦ www.haciendabaru.com). Good-value, comfortable self-catering chalets set in a beautiful private reserve comprising over three square kilometres of rainforest, mangrove and protected beach. Good

for birders and orchid lovers – there are 250 varieties scattered around – plus there's a butterfly farm, turtle nursery and a fixed canopy platform on site; horse-riding tours are also available. Try to talk to the hacienda's owner, Jack Ewing, a committed environmentalist with a vast amount of local knowledge. **❺**

Pacific Edge, 3km south of Dominical – follow the signed left-hand fork (☎ 381-4369, ☏ 771-8841, ✉ pacificedge@pocketmail.com). Secluded, simple and comfortable, on a ridge above the sea, with beautiful mountain and beach views. The four roomy chalets each have private shower and hammocks, and delicious meals, including bangers and mash (one of the owners is English), can be ordered in advance. **❹**

Roca Verde, 1.5km south of Dominical (☎ 787-0036, ☏ 787-0013, ⓦ www.hotelrocaverde.com). Ritzy small hotel in a wonderful position right on the beach. All rooms have en-suite bath, a/c and balcony, and there's also a swimming pool, table tennis and a restaurant with Tex-Mex and American food. **❻**

Eating and drinking

If you're self-catering there's a small **supermarket** in Dominical as well as another just outside town in the pink Plaza Pacifica mall. Otherwise there's a handful of decent places to eat in and around the village.

Jazzy's River House, opposite the football field. Private house which hosts join-in musical evenings (bring your instrument) on Wed with delicious, healthy, home-cooked food.

La Capanna, on the right-hand side as you enter Dominical (☎ 787-0072). Excellent Italian restaurant with daily specials and delicious pizza. Often full, so you may need to book. Closed Mon and in autumn.

Punta Dominical, 5km south of Dominical (take a signed right fork down to the beach, which then winds up onto the rocky point above). Fancy

Italian-run restaurant with wonderful food and great sea views. Also has cabinas for rent.

San Clemente Bar and Grill, on your left as you enter the village, just past the football pitch. Large, breezy Tex-Mex restaurant popular with the surf crowd, with pool table and half-price cocktails on Tuesdays.

Thrusters, towards the beach on the left. Large, barn-like bar with TV, pool tables, darts board, table football and an extensive range of drinks. Hots up at weekends.

South of Dominical

The stretch of coast which runs south from Dominical to the lovely shallow bay at **Playa Tortuga** is one of the most pristine in Costa Rica, and as a consequence is currently under siege from real-estate agents, who buy and sell plots of land as fast as they can persuade local fishermen and farmers to part with them. In addition, plans to reroute a section of the Interamericana so that it runs along the shore from Quepos to Palmar mean that it is probably only a matter of time before beach resorts rivalling those in Guanacaste start to take shape. For the moment, though, the area south of Dominical takes in a string of gloriously empty beaches as well as **Parque Nacional Marino Ballena** –

56 square kilometres of water around Uvita and Bahía which was created to safeguard the ecological integrity of the local marine life.

Bahía Ballena and the Parque Nacional Marino Ballena

In the last decade or so, access to the lovely **Bahía Ballena**, south of Dominical, has become relatively easy (albeit by sturdy 4WD), but the tiny hamlets of **Bahía** and **Uvita** are still little-visited, and hardly geared up for tourism. Efforts to get here are amply rewarded, however, with wide beaches washed by lazy breakers, palms swaying on the shore, and a hot, serene and very quiet atmosphere. This will no doubt change, as more people discover Bahía Ballena, but for the time being it's extremely unspoilt.

There's not a lot to do. If you like hanging out on the beach, surfing and walking through rock shoals and along the sand, you'll be happy. At certain times of year (usually May–Oct), Olive Ridley and hawksbill **turtles** may come ashore to nest, but nowhere near to the same extent as elsewhere in the country. The beach is now regulated by volunteers working for the Parque Nacional Marino Ballena, who patrol the beaches at night warning off poachers. If you want to see the turtles, it's best to talk to the rangers at the park's puesto in Bahía village – whatever you do, remember the ground rules of turtle-watching: come at night with a torch, watch where you walk (partly for snakes), keep well back from the beach, and don't shine the light right on the turtles. You may also see **dolphins** frolicking in the water. Ask around about **boat tours**, making sure that the boat has a good outboard motor and life-jackets on board, as you'll be out on the open Pacific; tours include snorkelling and sports-fishing trips, and visits to the Isla del Caño. With your own equipment you can snorkel to your heart's content directly off the beach.

There are two villages on Bahía Ballena. **UVITA**, which winds inland at the crossroads just north of the Uvita river, has a decent roadside soda, *El Viajero*, but otherwise little to offer tourists other than a visit to the local waterfall (ask for directions at *El Viajero*) and a renowned Indonesian restaurant, *El Balcon de Uvita* – take a left fork as you enter Uvita, though you'll need a 4WD to get there (cabinas are also available; ❹). The tiny village of **BAHÍA**, right next to Uvita, is better situated, on the lovely beach next to the national marine park, although tourist infastructure is limited as yet. There are, however, a couple of **places to stay**: *Villas Hegalua* (no phone; ❶) and *Cabinas Punta Uvita* (no phone; ❶) both have basic rooms; the latter is next door to an excellent café, and there are also a couple of good village sodas. From San Isidro, **buses** leave C 1, Av 4/6 twice daily, heading for Uvita and Bahía via Dominical (1hr 30min).

Parque Nacional Marino Ballena

Created in 1990, the **PARQUE NACIONAL MARINO BALLENA** protects an area of ocean of the coast by Uvita containing one of the biggest chunks of **coral reef** left on the Pacific coast. It is also the habitat of **humpback whales** – although they are spotted very infrequently (Dec–April is best) – and **dolphins**. The main threats to the ecological survival of these waters is the disturbance caused by shrimp trawling, sedimentation caused by deforestation – rivers bring silt and pollutants into the sea and kill the coral – and drag-net fishing, which often entraps whales and dolphins. On land, 1.1 square kilometres of sandy and rocky beaches and coastal areas are protected, as is **Punta Uvita** – a former island connected to the mainland by a narrow land bridge.

There are minimal **services** to speak of: though there are park rangers, there are no trails.

Playa Tortuga

Heading south on the coastal road, the Costanera Sur, you'll come to **Playa Tortuga**, about halfway between Dominical and Palmar. A few years ago this beach won an award as the cleanest in Costa Rica: no wonder, as practically nobody made the bone-shaking trip out here then. Not too many people venture here even now, since the road is still frequently impassable by ordinary car. There are, however, a couple of very good **hotels** close to the beach: *Posada Playa Tortuga* (☎ 220-2410, ⓦ www.turtlebeachinn.com; ❹), which has comfortable rooms, a large swimming pool and an amazing view; and *Villas Gaia* (☎ & Ⓕ 256-9996, ⓦ www.villasgaia.com; ❹), with eleven brightly coloured cabinas, a pool and an attractive restaurant. *Villas Gaia* is also the headquarters for Mambo Tours, which has an imaginative list of activities (from $30), including microlight plane trips and visits to a local ranch to play at cowboys for a day.

Inland from Playa Tortuga is the pretty Quebeçois community of **Ojochal**, which has several decent eating places, including *Gringo Mike's*, a top-notch pizza joint.

Palmar to Bahía Drake

Back on the Interamericana some 30km beyond Playa Tortuga, and about 100km north of the Panamá border, the small, prefab town of **PALMAR** is the hub for the area's banana plantations. This is a good place to see **lithic spheres** (see box on p.366), which are scattered on the lands of several nearby plantations and on the way to **Sierpe**, 15km south, on the Río Sierpe. Ask politely for the "esferas de piedra"; if the banana workers are not too busy they may be able to show you where to look. Palmar is also a useful jumping-off point for the beautiful **Bahía Drake** – accessed via Sierpe – and for the Marenco/San Pedrillo entrance to the **Parque Nacional Corcovado** on the Osa Peninsula.

The town is divided in two by the Río Grande de Térraba. **Palmar Sur** is where the airport is located; most of the services, including hotels and buses, are in **Palmar Norte**. Osa Tours, in the Centro Comercial del Norte, Palmar Norte (☎ 786-6534, Ⓕ 786-6335, Ⓔ osatours@racsa.co.cr), offers **tourist information**, help with reservations and transport, as well as selling stamps; you can make international telephone calls and receive Western Union money transfers here too. The town's **accommodation** is very basic. *Casa Amarilla*, 300m east of the TRACOPA bus stop (☎ 786-7251; ❶), has clean rooms with private bath and fan; the upstairs ones have balconies and better ventilation. *Hotel Osa*, on Calle Principal, has very simple budget rooms (☎ 786-6584; ❶).

From San José, TRACOPA **buses** run to Palmar Norte seven times daily, with the last one returning to the capital at 4.25pm. Buses for **Sierpe** leave Palmar Norte from the Supermercado Térraba (5 daily; 30min), with the first bus leaving at 7am.

Lithic spheres

Aside from goldworking, the Diquis are known for their precise fashioning of large stone spheres, most of them exactly spherical to within a centimetre or two – an astounding feat for a culture without technology. Thousands have been found in southwestern Costa Rica and a few in northern Panamá. Some are located in sites of obvious significance, like burial mounds, others are found in the middle of nowhere; they range in size from that of a tennis ball up to about two metres in diameter.

The spheres' original function and meaning remains obscure, although they sometimes seem to have been arranged in positions mirroring those of the constellations. In many cases the Diquis transported them a considerable distance, rafting them across rivers or the open sea (the only explanation for their presence on Isla del Caño), indicating that their placement was deliberate and significant. (Ironically, some of the posher Valle Central residences now have stone spheres – purchased by the inhabitants at great price – sitting in their front gardens as lawn sculpture.)

As well as in the area around Palmar, you can see lithic spheres most easily by visiting Isla del Caño. Tours are available from the Quepos/Manuel Antonio area (see p.338) and Dominical hotels (see p.362).

Bahía Drake and around

BAHÍA DRAKE (pronounced "Dra-kay") is named after Sir Francis Drake, who anchored here in 1579. Today a favourite of yachters, the calm waters of the bay are dotted with flotillas of swish-looking boats. This is one of the most stunning areas in Costa Rica, with the blue wedge of Isla del Caño floating just off the coast, and fiery-orange Pacific sunsets. The bay is rich in marine life, and a number of **boat trips** offer opportunities for spotting manta rays, marine turtles, porpoises and even whales. You can also go hiking or horse-riding, or take a tour to **Isla del Caño**, about 20km off the coast of the Osa Peninsula (and easily visible from Drake).

Bahía Drake and the tiny hamlet of **AGUJITAS** make a good base from which to strike out for the Parque Nacional Corcovado on the northwest of the Osa Peninsula – the park's San Pedrillo entrance is within a day's walk, and hikers can combine serious trekking with serious comfort at either end of their trip by staying at one of the upscale rainforest eco-lodge-type hotels (see opposite) that have sprung up in recent years. Other than the lodges and a couple of inexpensive, locally run hotels in Agujitas, there are very few facilities here, though the village has a small *pulpería* and there's a medical clinic on the beach.

Getting to Corcovado from Agujitas

From Agujitas you can follow the beachside trail via Marenco to the San Pedrillo entrance of Parque Nacional Corcovado (see p.377) – a walk of around eight to twelve hours. You can camp at San Pedrillo, although the Fundación de Parques Nacionales much prefer that you let them know in advance if you want to do this by contacting the Puerto Jiménez office. If you are staying at any of the Bahía Drake lodges, they should be able to contact the Puerto Jiménez office of Corcovado and make a reservation for you to stay and eat in San Pedrillo with the rangers.

Getting to Bahía Drake along the Río Serpe

Like many other places in the Zona Sur, **getting to Bahía Drake** requires some planning. There are three choices: the really tough way, hiking in from Corcovado; the cheap way, by bus from San José and then by boat along the Río Sierpe; and the luxury way, by flying from San José to Palmar or Sierpe, and taking one of the many **packages** offered by hotels in the area. If you do this, transport to your lodge is taken care of.

Travelling **independently**, you'll need to get a bus from San José to Palmar (7 daily; 5hr 30min); depending on what time you get in, you can then either bed down in Palmar Norte for the night or get a local bus (see p.365) or taxi to **Sierpe** (about $12), where there are a few cabinas. In Sierpe, you must find a **boatman** to take you the 30km downriver to Bahía Drake, a journey of two hours. You need someone with experience, a motorized *lancha*, and lifejackets: Chichu Mora is recommended – ask Sonia Rojas at the *Fenix pulpería* to help you find him (and any other general advice you may need). You can also hook up with a boatman in *Bar Las Vegas*, a rendezvous for tourists and boat captains – try out the ancient jukebox while you wait. The going rate for a one-way trip to Drake is currently about $20 per person or around $65–85 per boat-load (maximum usually eight); ask around for the best rates.

The trip down the Río Sierpe is calm enough, with mangroves lining either side of the bank (you can spot monkeys, sloths and sometimes kingfishers), until you see the Pacific rolling in at the mouth of the river. The Sierpe is very wide where it meets the sea, and huge breakers crash in from the ocean, making it a turbulent and treacherous crossing (sharks reportedly wait here for their dinner). If the tide is right and the boatman knows his water, you'll be fine. All the *lanchas* used by the lodges have powerful outboard motors, and there's little chance of an accident; all the same, some find this part of the trip a bit disconcerting. Once you are out in Bahía Drake the water is calm.

Accommodation

Accommodation is clustered either in the tiny village of Agujitas itself, or on Punta Agujitas, the rocky point on the other side of Río Agujitas. Virtually all the eco-lodges listed below do a range of **tours**, from accompanied excursions to Corcovado to boating in Bahía Drake and trips to Isla del Caño. The larger lodges are accustomed to bringing guests on packages from San José and can include transport from the capital, from Palmar, or from Sierpe. The packages (and the prices we give below) usually include three meals a day – there are few eating options in Bahía Drake otherwise. Although hoteliers will tell you you can't **camp** in the Drake area, people do – if you want to join them, pitch your tent considerately and be sure to leave no litter.

Aguila de Osa Inn, at the end of the village on Río Agujitas (℡ 296-2190, ℻ 232-7722, ⓦ www.aguiladeosa.com). Very posh sports-fishing lodge with a smart restaurant, landscaped gardens and 13 beautifully decorated rooms, all with large tiled bathrooms. Tours are also available. ❽

Cabinas Jade Mar, in the village (℡ 284-6681, ℻ 786-7366). One of the few village cheapies, and a good place to stay if you want to get a taste of local life, with extremely well priced and pleasant, if basic, cabinas, kept very clean by the informative Doña Martha. All cabins have private bath, and hearty meals are included in the price.

Inexpensive tours to Corcovado and Isla de Caño are also available. ❹

Cocalito Jungle Resort, Punta Agujitas (℡ 495-6821, ℻ 290-1280, ⓔ conexion@racsa.co.cr). Small, family-run, Canadian-owned cabinas (with and without en suite) scattered around a main lodge, where delicious meals are served by candlelight in the restaurant. There's also safe swimming on the resort's small beach, mountain bike rental and solar-heated water; all accommodation is well screened. You can also camp here, and tents can be rented. ❺

Corcovado Adventures Tent Camp, 2km south of Agujitas (☎384-1679, in San José ☎284-3595, ⓦwww.corcovado.com). On an isolated beach en route to Corcovado National Park, with well-screened and furnished tents (complete with beds and tables) on platforms facing the sea. ❺

Delfin Amor Eco Lodge, just beyond Punta Agujitas (☎394-2632, ⓦwww.divinedolphin.com). Tent-style accommodation, vegetarian food and a friendly community atmosphere in a small lodge specializing in encounters with wild dolphins ($85 for a full-day tour; $35 for sunset tour). ❺

Drake Bay Wilderness Resort, Punta Agujitas (☎ & ⓕ770-8012, in San José ☎256-7394, ⓦwww.drakebay.com). The most established lodge in the area, providing a buffer zone between tourist and wilderness with rustic, comfortable cabinas or, if you want to rough it a bit, well-appointed tents – both options are well screened. There's hearty local food, and the camp also has its own solar-heated water supply, night-time electricity, laundry service, plus excellent snorkelling and canoeing. It's popular, so best book and pay in advance. Packages include direct flights from San José to Bahía Drake. ❼

Jinetes de Osa, between Punta Agujitas and Agujitas (☎385-9541, ⓦwww.costaricadiving.com). One of the less expensive options in Bahía Drake, right on the area's main beach – there's an on-site PADI dive school and most guests come here on good-value dive packages. Accommodation, some of it en suite, is simple but comfortable, and prices include three meals a day. ❹

La Paloma Lodge, Punta Agujitas (☎239-2801, ⓦwww.lapalomalodge.com). Beautiful, rustic rooms in thatched hilltop bungalows, with private bath, balconies and hammocks – the airy, two-storey bungalows are best, being surrounded by forest and boasting spectacular views, particularly at sunset. *Pangas* (traditional canoes) are available for guests to paddle on the Río Agujitas behind the lodge, and there's also an attractively tiled swimming pool. Excellent service, with friendly and helpful staff. ❼

Poor Man's Paradise, Playa San Josecito, just beyond the San Pedrillo entrance on the way to Bahía Drake (in the US ☎ 715/588-3950). Accommodation in tents, set in gardens and with ocean views – the tents have beds and shared bath and are comfortable enough, and rates include three good meals daily. Open Dec–May only. ❹

Proyecto Campanario, near Sierpe (☎282-5898, ⓕ282-8750, ⓔdirector@campanario.org). Established in 1991 by ex-Peace Corps volunteers, this remote field station offers courses in tropical ecology and tour "packages" for hardy ecotourists not fazed by the isolation (it's only reachable by boat from Sierpe). Tours can consist of short walks, long hikes, or all-day expeditions to the Campanario Biological Reserve, Corcovado National Park, deforested and impacted areas, local communities and the Isla del Caño, as well as snorkelling, scuba-diving, sports-fishing or canoeing. Basic four-night packages start at $327 and include accommodation, all meals and activities. Contact Proyecto Campanario, S.J.O. 2827, Unit C101, PO Box 025216, Miami, FL 33102-5216, USA, or Apdo 56-6151, Santa Ana 2000, Costa Rica.

Rancho Corcovado, on the beach in front of Agujitas (☎384-1457, 240-4085 or 786-7059). Good-value, family-run hotel with beautiful views over the bay and simple, clean en-suite rooms. Rates all include full board, and camping and horse-riding tours are also available. ❹

Isla del Caño

The tiny **RESERVA BIOLÓGICA ISLA DEL CAÑO** sits placidly in the ocean some 20km due west of Bahía Drake. Just 3km long by 2km wide, the island is the exposed part of an underwater mountain, thrown up by an ancient collision of the two tectonic plates on either side of Costa Rica. It's a pretty sight in the distance, and going there is even better – if you can afford it. You can't get there on your own, but a **tour** is usually included in the package price of the Bahía Drake lodges. Alternatively, tours are run by many operators in the Manuel Antonio area (see p.338) and, increasingly, from Dominical (p.361).

The island is thought to have been a burial ground of the Diquís, who brought their famed **lithic spheres** here from the mainland in large, ocean-going canoes. Your guide can take you hiking into the thick rainforest interior to look for examples near the top of the 110-metre high crest, and you'll certainly come across some as you wander around – they're lying about all over the place. Caño is also a prime **snorkelling** and diving destination. Under water you'll see coral beds and various **marine life**, including spiny lobsters and sea cucumber, snapper, sea urchins, manta rays, octopus and the occasional barracuda. On the surface, porpoises and Olive Ridley marine turtles are often spotted, along with less frequent sightings of humpback and even sperm whales.

Golfito and around

The former banana port of **GOLFITO**, 33km north of the Panamanian border, straggles for 2.5km along the water of the same name (*golfito* means "little gulf"). The town's setting is spectacular, backed up against steep, thickly forested hills to the east, and with the glorious Golfo Dulce – one of the deepest gulfs of its size in the world – to the west. The low shadow of the Osa Peninsula shimmers in the distance, and everywhere the vegetation has the soft, muted look of the undisturbed tropics. It is also very **wet** – even if you speak no Spanish, you'll certainly pick up the local expression *va a caer baldazos* – "it's gonna pour".

Golfito's history is inextricably intertwined with the giant transnational **United Brands** company – known locally as "La Yunai" – which first set up in the area in 1938, twenty years before the Interamericana hit town. The company built schools, recruited doctors and police, and brought prosperity to the area, though "problems" with labour union organizers began soon afterwards, and came to characterize the relationship between company and town. What with fluctuating banana prices, a three-month strike by workers and local social unrest, the company eventually decided Golfito was too much trouble and pulled out in a hurry in 1985. The town died and, in the public eye, became synonymous with rampant unemployment, alcoholism, abandoned children, prostitution and general unruliness.

Today, at the big old *muelle bananero*, container ships are still loaded up with bananas processed further up towards Palmar. This residual traffic, along with tourism – Golfito is a good base for getting to the Parque Nacional Corcovado by *lancha* or plane, as well as a major **sports-fishing** centre – have combined to help revive the local economy. The real rescue, though, came from the Costa Rican government, who in the early 1990s established a Depósito Libre – or tax-free zone – in the town, where Costa Ricans can buy manufactured goods imported from Panamá without the 100 percent tax normally levied. Ticos who come to shop here have to buy their tickets for the Depósito 24 hours in advance, obliging them to spend at least one night, and therefore colones, in the town.

Golfito straggles for ages without any clear centre, through stretches where the main road is hemmed in by hills on one side and the lapping waters of the *golfito* on the other. The town is effectively split in two – by a division in wealth as well as architecture. In the north is the **Zona Americana**, where the banana company executives used to live and where better-off residents still reside in beautiful wooden houses shaded by dignified palms. Here you'll find the **Depósito Libre**, an unaesthetic outdoor mall ringed by a circular concrete wall. Some two kilometres to the south of the Depósito, the **Pueblo Civil** (civilian town), is a very small, tight nest of streets; hotter, noisier and more crowded than the *zona*. It's here you'll find the good-value hotels and sodas, as well as the *lancha* across the Golfo Dulce to Puerto Jiménez and the Osa

GOLFITO

ACCOMMODATION
Cabinas El Vivero	5
Cabinas Isabel	1
Cabinas Koktsur	4
Delfina	2
Esquinas Rainforest Lodge	8
La Purruja Lodge	7
Las Gaviotas	6
Pensión El Tucán	9
Samoa del Sur	3

RESTAURANTS
La Eurekita	B
Soda El Barco	A

GOLFITO

& Interamericana (26 km)

Land-Sea Tours

Parquecito

Gas station

Muellecito
(Boats to Playa Cacao & Puerto Jiménez)

PUEBLO CIVIL

0   500 m

Peninsula. Although the Pueblo Civil is perfectly civil in the daytime, it's best to be careful at night.

Arrival and information

Buses from San José to Golfito currently leave the TRACOPA terminal at 7am and 3pm (8hr) – you should book your ticket in advance, particularly in December, when hoards of bargain hunters descend on the Depósito to do their Christmas shopping. Buy your return ticket as soon as you disembark. You can also **fly** here with Sansa; the airstrip is in the Zona Americana. The Banco Nacional opposite the TRACOPA terminal changes **travellers' cheques** and gives cash advances on credit cards, but it's a tediously slow process. The **correo** (Mon–Fri 7.30am–5pm, Sat 8am–noon) is right in the centre of the Pueblo Civil and has internet access. Land-Sea Tours (☎ & ℻775-1614, ⓔ landsea@racsa.co.cr), on the waterfront at the southern end of the *pueblo*, organizes a wide range of tours, has a book exchange and is an excellent source of information.

Accommodation

Accommodation in Golfito tends to cater for Costa Ricans visiting the Depósito Libre and is both basic and good value. There are a couple of slightly smarter hotels too. Be warned that the sheer number of people coming to Golfito to shop, especially at Christmas, means that rooms are often booked out in advance – if you don't have reservations try to get to the town as early in the day as possible.

Cabinas El Vivero, just south of the Depósito (☎775-0217). Big, simply furnished rooms, shared kitchen and a friendly family atmosphere.

Dueño Don Bob grows orchids and other plants in his nursery next door, and is a one-man history of the area. Very good value. ①

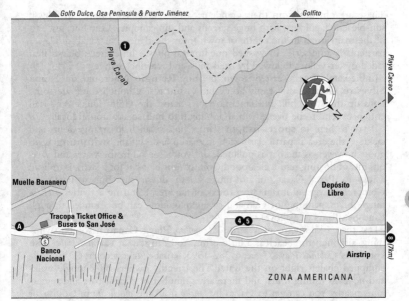

Cabinas Koktsur, next to *Cabinas El Vivero*
(☎ 775-1191). Basic but clean double rooms and
friendly staff. No hot water. ❶

Delfina, in the Pueblo Civil (☎ 775-0043). Old
house converted into a warren of widely varying
rooms. Some are good value, others are dark;
those at the back are quieter and overlook the
water. The budget rooms (shared bath, ceiling fan)
are better value than those with private bath and
ancient, groaning a/c. Fills up at weekends with
visitors to the Depósito. ❶

Esquinas Rainforest Lodge, La Gamba, approx
7km from Km-37 on the Interamericana (☎ &
🖷 775-0901, 🖳 www.regenwald.at). Friendly eco-
lodge run by the Government of Austria as part of
a model project combining development aid,
nature conservation and rainforest research – all
profits go to the local community. It's set in pri-
mary rainforest, with resident wildlife and on-site
hiking trails. There's a wide range of packages
available, plus a variety of tours, including ones to
Corcovado and the Wilson Botanical Gardens.
Fantastic meals are included in the room rate. ❼

La Purruja Lodge, 4km south of Golfito towards
the Interamericana (☎ 775-1054, 🖳 www.purru-
ja.com). Small family-run hotel set in lovely gar-
dens, with spacious rooms, pool table and darts
board. Camping is also available. ❷

Las Gaviotas, at the southern entrance to town
(☎ 775-0062, 🖷 775-0544, 🖳 www.costaricas-
ur.com/lasgaviotas). Golfito's most upmarket
accommodation, set in lovely gardens, and with
the town's only pool. The good rooms all have pri-
vate bath with hot water, a/c and cable TV, and the
waterside rancho restaurant serves great local
seafood. ❹

Pensión El Tucán, on the main road between the
Zona Americana and the Pueblo Civil (☎ 775-
0553). Good, inexpensive rooms. Most are quite
dark, so look around, but all have private bath, fan
and cold water only. The very friendly dueña will
throw in breakfast for $2.50. ❶

Samoa del Sur, on the main road between the
Zona Americana and the Pueblo Civil (☎ 775-
0233, 🖷 775-0573, 🖂 samoasur@racsa.co.cr).
Fourteen spacious though slightly gloomy rooms
on the waterfront, with a large boat-shaped bar
and on-site restaurant. ❸

The Town

Though there's little to do in Golfito, be sure to check out the old homes of
the banana company execs in the Zona Americana near the Depósito Libre.

These are obvious from their grandeur: wide-verandah'd, painted in jolly, if sun-bleached, colours, with huge screens and sun canopies. One line, just east of the main street in the centre of town (near the Banco Nacional) displays a particularly fine series of washed-out tropical hues – lime-green blends into faded oyster-yellow, followed by tired-pink and metallic-orange.

Immediately to the east of town, the tiny **Refugio Nacional de Fauna Silvestre Golfito** isn't easily accessible to tourists, although there are some trails up the steep hill, and fantastic views across the Golfo Dulce. The trail entrances tend to be overgrown and difficult to find, so ask around locally.

If you're here to **sports-fish**, the larger hotels can help arrange tours and tackle – the area is particularly rich in marlin and sailfish. **Swimming** is no good, however, as the bay is polluted, and you'll see oil in the water and various bits of floating refuse all around Golfito. Your best bet for a swim is to head across to Playa Cacao, or to move south down the Burica Peninsula. Comprehensive and imaginative **tours** of the area, featuring activities such as jungle hikes, panning for gold and cave exploration, can be arranged through Land-Sea Tours (see above).

Less than a kilometre away across the *golfito*, **Playa Cacao** has good swimming, although the beach is a little grimy. You can stay at *Cabinas Isabel* (also known as *Cabinas Playa Cacao*; ☎382-1593, ⓔisabel@racsa.co.cr; ❸) in well-equipped chalets right on the water. The friendly owners offer jungle walks and no-frills fishing tours, and there are a number of decent bars and restaurants nearby. You can get to Cacao by *lancha* from the *muellecito* in Golfito, or in the dry season drive a rough unfinished track from the turn-off right in front of the *guardia*, bearing left.

Eating and drinking

There's no shortage of **places to eat** in Golfito. For *casados* and *platos del día* there are two groups of simple **sodas**: one near the Depósito Libre, catering to Ticos who have come to Golfito on shopping trips, and another, slightly better value bunch on the main drag of the Pueblo Civil and in the surrounding streets. *Soda El Barco*, on the sea-facing side of the main road between the Zona and the Pueblo, is a nice place for beer or a *refresco*, while *Restaurante La*

Moving on from Golfito

Buses to San José leave daily at 5am and 1.30pm, and there are also flights daily to San José on Sansa and Travelair, bookable through Land-Sea Tours. For Corcovado, you can either take the ferry across the Golfo Dulce to Puerto Jiménez (daily at 11am from the *muellecito*; 1hr 30min; $3), or a small plane to Jiménez (approx $99 for up to 5 people) – contact Alfa Romeo Aero Taxi's office at the airstrip, or call ☎755-1515. Daily buses to Neily and San Vito leave from in front of the *muelle bananero* where, in the dry season only, you can also pick up buses south to Playas Zancudo and Pavones (2hr 30min–3hr).

There are two ferry piers in Golfito, the old *muello bananero* and the municipal dock, called the *muellecito*, near the Pueblo Civil. All boats are motorized *lanchas*, and prices seem to be about the same from either place. Whoever you go with, make sure there are lifejackets on board: the Golfo Dulce is usually calm, but winds can come up suddenly and waves are unexpectedly high. To Puerto Jiménez, there's a *lancha* from Golfito daily at 11.30am (1hr 30min). Alternatively, Land-Sea Tours organize transport in their boats to almost anywhere in the Golfo Dulce area, including Playa Cacao, Playa Cativo, Playa Zancudo and Puerto Jiménez – costs are competitive, but you'll get a much better price if you gather a group together.

Eurekita, in the Pueblo close to the post office, serves solidly *típico* food, very good burgers, and has a nice breezy view of the water.

Of the **hotel-restaurants**, *Hotel Las Gaviotas* has an all-you-can-eat barbecue ($10) on Friday and Saturday evenings from 6pm, with good meat and even a reasonable wine list, though its best feature is the waterside location on the *golfito*. The beachside bar and restaurante at the *Samoa del Sur* hotel is a nice place for an evening beer or meal, with a menu featuring seafood and reasonable pizza ($5–8).

Around Golfito

There are some luxurious accommodation options along the coast **north of Golfito**. **Playa San Josecito**, 10km northwest of Golfito and accessible only by boat, has two upmarket eco-lodges: *Golfo Dulce Lodge* (☎222-2900, ℱ222-5173, ⓦwww.golfodulcelodge.com; ❼) and *Dolphin Quest* (☎775-1742, ℱ775-0373, ℮dolphinquest@email.com; cabinas ❹, suites ❼), both of which have extensive grounds with trails and tours, including horse-riding, kayaking and fishing. Book in advance and you'll be picked up by *lancha* from Golfito. Further north along the coast at **Playa Cativo**, thirty minutes by boat from Golfito, *Rainbow Adventures* (☎1-800/565-0722, ⓦwww.rainbowcostarica.com; ❽) is one of the premier places of its kind in Costa Rica, with luxurious, tastefully decorated individual chalets next to a beautiful, pristine beach and excellent food. They also offer tours in the surrounding rainforest, as well snorkelling and bird-watching.

South of Golfito

South of Golfito are a couple of very isolated **beaches** en route to the **Burica Peninsula** – a thin, pristine finger of land that is shared with Panamá. Ask anyone in town where you can swim, and they'll direct you to black-sand **Playa Zancudo**, 15km southwest of Golfito, facing the Golfo Dulce and bordered on one side by the Río Coto Colorado. During summer weekends from December to April you may be joined by Zona Sur Ticos taking a beach break, but otherwise it's fairly low-key, except for a small colony of mainly US expats. It's a friendly place, perfect for unwinding, and there are several decent **places to stay**. *Los Cocos* (☎776-0012, ⓦwww.loscocos.com; ❹) is the most upmarket, while *Sol y Mar* (☎776-0014, ⓦwww.zancudo.com; ❸) has groovy little huts in a garden by the beach and *Maria's* (☎776-0131; ❶) offers very basic but good-value rooms above a restaurant. For **food**, there's a good Italian restaurant, *Macondo*, the usual sodas serving tasty *casados*, and gourmet French cuisine at *Sol y Mar*, which also has a lively bar with popular volleyball competitions on Saturday afternoons. Zancudo also hosts a couple of professional sports-fishing outfits; other local activities include surfing, river trips and excursions (run by *Los Cocos* hotel) across the bay to the unique Casa Orchideas botanical gardens, reachable only by boat.

About 12km further south is **Playa Pavones**, famed among surfers for having the longest continuous wave in the world – exactly how long, they do not divulge. The waves are biggest and best from May to November. Needless to say the water's too rough for anything else and the community here largely consists of avid surfers. There are few facilities in Pavones other than basic cabinas for rent and a couple of nondescript bars.

You can reach both Pavones and Zancudo from Golfito by **lancha** or, in the dry season only (Jan–Sept), by **bus** from in front of the *muelle bananero* (2hr 30min–3hr). **Driving** to the beaches takes a little over two hours from Golfito and entails crossing the Río Coto Colorado on a tiny ferry. You need a 4WD, whatever the time of year; during the wet season it's worth checking the levels of the creeks and fords that you'll have to pass before you set out.

After another 10km or so you come to **Punta Banco**, site of the beautiful *Tiskita Lodge* (☎233-1511, ℱ233-6890, ⓦwww.tiskita-lodge.co.cr; ➐), a friendly, extremely comfortable rainforest lodge – which doubles as a biological research station – with cabinas overlooking the beach and a swimming pool in the grounds. Trails weave through the surrounding forest, bird-watching is good, and you can tour their fruit farm (the owner is an agronomist). They also offer good-value packages, including flight from San José and three high-quality meals a day.

The Osa Peninsula

In the extreme southwest of the country, the **Osa Peninsula** is an area of immense biological diversity, somewhat separate from the mainland. In the early years of the twentieth century, Osa was something of a **penal colony**; a place to which men were either sent forcibly or went, machete in hand, to forget. Consequently, a violent, frontierlands folklore permeates the whole peninsula, and old-time residents of **Puerto Jiménez** – the only town of any size – are only too happy to regale you with hosts of gory tales. Some may be apocryphal, but they certainly add colour to the place.

It was on the Osa Peninsula that the Diquis found **gold** in such abundant supply that they hardly had to pan or dig for it, and gold can still be found, as can the odd *orero* (goldminer/panner). When **Parque Nacional Corcovado** was established, in the mid-1970s, substantial numbers of miners were panning within its boundaries, but the heaviest influx of *oreros* stemmed directly from the pull-out of the United Brands Company in 1985. Many were laid-off banana plantation workers with no alternate means of making an living: a case of the pull-out of a large-scale employer leading to immediate and serious environmental threat. In 1986 the *oreros* were forcibly deported from the park by the Costa Rican police. Today, several well-known international conservationist groups are involved in protecting and maintaining Osa's ecological integrity, and were recently successful in fighting off an attempt to establish a wood-chip mill here.

Few will fail to be moved by Osa's beauty. Whether you approach the peninsula by *lancha* from Golfito or Bahía Drake, on the Jiménez bus, or driving in from the mainland, you will see what looks to be a floating island, an intricate mesh of blue and green, with tall canopy trees sailing high and flat like elaborate floral hats. You'll also see a revealing picture of *precarista* (squatter) life on the country's extreme geographical margins. Since the mid- to late 1980s the improvement of the road between Jiménez and Rincón has brought many families seeking land. Most have built simple shacks and cultivated a little roadside plot, burning away the forest to do so. They plant a few vegetables and a banana patch and may keep a few cattle. Soil here is classically tropical, with few nutrients, poor absorption and minimal regenerative capacity. In a few years it will have exhausted itself and the smallholders will have to cultivate new areas or move on.

You could feasibly explore the whole peninsula in four days, but this would be rushing it, especially if you want to spend time walking the trails and wildlife-spotting at Corcovado. Most people allot five to seven days for the area, taking it at a relaxed pace, and more if they want to stay in and explore Bahía Drake (see p.366). Hikers and walkers who come to Osa without their own car tend to base themselves in Puerto Jiménez – a place where it's easy to strike up a conversation, people are relaxed, environmentally conscientious, and not yet overwhelmed by tourism.

Puerto Jiménez

The friendly town of **PUERTO JIMÉNEZ** – known locally simply as Jiménez – has plenty of places to stay and eat and good public transport connections. From Jiménez you can also take the truck to **Carate**, 43km southwest, from where it's possible to enter Corcovado (see p.377). Drivers shouldn't try going further south – including to Carate – in anything less than a 4WD, at any time of year. What looks like a good, patted-down dirt road can turn into a quagmire after a sudden downpour.

Arrival and information

Two **buses** arrive daily from San José via San Isidro (6am & noon; 10hr) returning at 5am and 11am. The ticket office in Jiménez is open daily (7–11am & 1–5pm). There's a **lancha** from Golfito daily at 11.30am (1hr 30min); another *lancha* returns to Golfito daily at 6am. You can **fly** in from San José with Sansa or Travelair, or from Golfito with Travelair or the charter company Alfa Romeo (☏735-5112 in Puerto Jiménez; ☏775-1515 in Golfito). The tiny Banco Nacional changes **travellers' cheques** and dollars. The *correo*, opposite the soccer field, has public phones and internet access, as does *Café Net El Sol* on the main street – you can phone abroad from here.

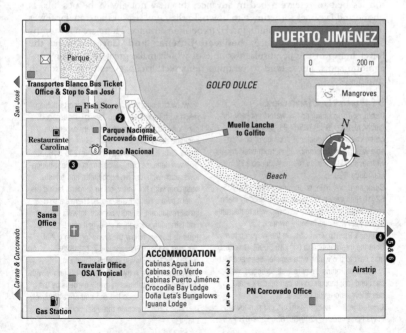

PUERTO JIMÉNEZ

0   200 m

GOLFO DULCE

Parque

Transportes Blanco Bus Ticket Office & Stop to San José

San José

Fish Store

Mangroves

Parque Nacional Corcovado Office

Muelle Lancha to Golfito

Restaurante Carolina

Banco Nacional

N

Beach

Sansa Office

Carate & Corcovado

Travelair Office OSA Tropical

ACCOMMODATION
Cabinas Agua Luna	2
Cabinas Oro Verde	3
Cabinas Puerto Jiménez	1
Crocodile Bay Lodge	6
Doña Leta's Bungalows	4
Iguana Lodge	5

PN Corcovado Office

Airstrip

Gas Station

For **tourist information**, try one of the several tour companies in town – the helpful Osa Tropical (℡735-5062, ℻735-5043, @osatropi@racsa.co.cr), on the main road 50m north of the gas station, doubles as the local Travelair and Sansa agent, handles accommodation reservations and has phone and fax services. Escondido Trex (℡ & ℻735-5210, @osatrex@racsa.co.cr) offers a wide range of tours and has an office in the *Restaurante Carolina*. For something more unusual, contact biologist Andy Pruter of Everyday Adventures (℡ & ℻735-5138, ⊛www.psychotours.com), who takes people on high adrenalin "psycho" tours ($50) to nearby waterfalls – not for the faint-hearted. Joseph Chestnut takes people out for tours – one at a time obviously – on the back of his motorbike ($20; contact *Cabinas Oro Verde*).

If you're planning a **trip to Corcovado**, the Oficína de Area de Conservación Osa (Mon–Fri 8am–noon & 1–4pm; ℡735-5036, ℻735-5276), facing the airstrip, is staffed by friendly rangers who can answer questions and arrange accommodation and meals at the park puestos (though you're advised to sort this out before you arrive – see p.379 for details). The main form of transport from Jiménez to Corcovado, the **truck to Carate** ($5 one way), goes daily except Sundays in the dry season at about 6am, but you'd do best to confirm this locally; try asking staff at *El Tigre* supermarket, from where it leaves. Departures are less frequent in the wet season, about three weekly. The truck will drop you off at at any of the lodges between Jiménez and Carate, and will also pick you up on its way back to town if you arrange this in advance – ask the driver. If you don't get a place on the truck, a number of local taxi drivers have 4WDs; try Orlando Mesen (℡735-5627; approx $60 return to Carate).

Accommodation

Jiménez's **hotels** are reasonably priced, clean and basic. Though in the dry season it's best to reserve a bed in advance, this may not always be possible, as phone and fax lines sometimes go down. In the rainy season there are far fewer people about and you shouldn't need to book in advance. There are a few comfort-in-the-wilderness places **between Jiménez and Carate** around the lower hump of the peninsula, a couple of which make great retreats or honeymoon spots. These tend to be quite upmarket; backpackers tend to stay in Jiménez.

In Puerto Jiménez

Cabinas Agua Luna, on the waterfront near the *lancha* pier (℡ & ℻735-5393, ⊛www.costaricasur.com/agualuna). A range of comfortable waterfront accommodation, from basic rooms with fans (❷) to luxury rooms with cable TV, a/c and fridge (❺).

Cabinas Oro Verde, on the main street (℡735-5241). Nine very good-value and spotlessly clean rooms right in the middle of town, with restaurant, laundry service and friendly owners. ❶

Cabinas Puerto Jiménez, on the way into town from the Interamericana (℡735-5090). Quiet cabinas next to the water, with simple, clean and nicely furnished rooms. They're well screened, with bath and fan, though some can be dark – ask to see a few before you choose. ❶

Crocodile Bay Lodge, 4km out of town towards Playa Platanares (℡209-9976, ℻209-6177, ⊛www.crocodilebay.com). Luxury sports-fishing resort with swimming pool, Jacuzzi, landscaped gardens and its own large pier. Very expensive package deals only. ❽

Doña Leta's Bungalows (℡ & ℻735-5180, ⊛www.donaleta.com). Nice group of eight bungalows, each with its own kitchenette and private bathroom with hot water, set in gardens facing the hotel's own small private beach. There's also a small restaurant, laundry service, kayaks for rent and (strangely enough) a volleyball court. ❺

Iguana Lodge, follow the signs for 5km out of Jiménez to Playa Platanares (℡735-5205, ℻735-5436, ⊛www.iguanalodge.com). Wonderful hotel run by very friendly US family with four two-storey cabinas in lovely gardens by the beach – all rooms face the sea and are attractively decorated. Rates include three delicious meals a day. ❺

Between Puerto Jiménez and Carate

The following are listed **in order of their distance from Puerto Jiménez**. The first, *Lapa Ríos*, is 20km south of the town. The last, the *Corcovado Tent Camp*, is right next to the park entrance. All are signed from the road and include three meals a day in their room rates.

Lapa Ríos, 20km south of Puerto Jiménez (ⓣ 735-5130, ⓕ 735-5179, ⓦ www.laparios.com). One of the country's most comfortable and impressive jungle lodges, set in a large private nature reserve with excellent bird-watching. Rooms have big beds and mosquito nets, and blend nicely into surrounding forest. There's also a huge thatched restaurant, complete with spiral staircase, and a swimming pool. ❽

Bosque del Cabo, above Playa Matapalo, down a private road to the left off the Carate road (ⓣ & ⓕ 735-5206, ⓦ www.bosquedelcabo.com). Very secluded, beautifully decorated bungalows with stupendous views out to the Pacific and a good restaurant. There's also a waterfall and swimming hole nearby, along with lots of scarlet macaws (the owners are helping to repopulate the local area). ❼

Lookout Inn, just north of Carate, and very convenient for its airstrip (no phone, ⓦ www.lookout-inn.com). Three large rooms in a beach house set on rainforested hillside, with swimming pool and beautiful ocean views. Informal and fun atmosphere; tours available. ❻

Luna Lodge, set in the hills above Carate – call for a pick-up from the nearby Carate airstrip (ⓣ 380-5036, ⓦ www.lunalodge.com). Remote, tranquil and beautiful lodge with welcoming owners and staggering views over the surrounding virgin rainforest. Healthy home-grown food and yoga classes available. ❼

Corcovado Tent Camp, about a 45min walk along the beach from Carate (book via Costa Rica Expeditions, see p.33). Twenty self-contained and fully screened "tent-camps" elevated on short stilts in an amazing beachside location, with bedrooms and screened verandahs, communal baths and good local cooking. Very good value, with packages available (some including flights right to Carate) plus guided tours around Corcovado National Park ($38–68) and horse-riding. ❺

Eating and drinking

There's not much choice when it comes to **eating** in Jiménez, but you certainly won't starve. The most popular place in town (particularly with tourists and expats) is the funky little *Fish Store*, which does very good fish tacos, fish and chips and proper home-made burgers – a great place to hang out with a cool drink even if you're not in the mood for food – while another good meeting place is *Restaurante Carolina*, on the main drag, which has a *comida típica* menu. *Soda La Parada*, beside the Transportes Blanco bus stop, is as good a place as any to have a *casado* or *plato del día*, or try *Soda El Ranchito*, next to the post office. For evening meals, try the restaurant *Agua Luna*, across the creek on the way to the *lancha* dock; the seafood is good and the light breezes coming off the *golfito* more than welcome.

Parque Nacional Corcovado

Created in 1975, **PARQUE NACIONAL CORCOVADO** ("hunchback"), 368km southwest of San José (daily 8am–4pm; $6), protects a fascinating and biologically complex area of land, most of it on the peninsula itself. It also covers one mainland area just north of Golfito, which may soon be made into a national park in its own right. It's an undeniably beautiful park, with deserted beaches, some laced with waterfalls, high canopy trees and better-than-average wildlife-spotting opportunities. Many people come with the express purpose of spotting a **margay**, **ocelot**, **tapir** and other rarely seen animals. Of course, it's all down to luck, but if you walk quietly and there aren't too many other humans around, you should have a better chance of seeing some of these creatures here than elsewhere.

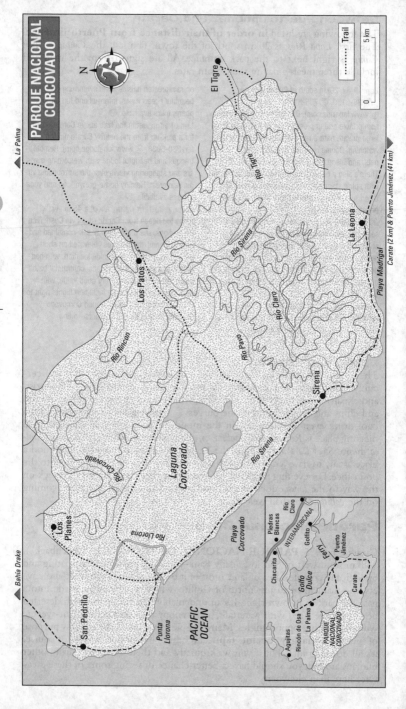

PARQUE NACIONAL
CORCOVADO

N

La Palma

Bahía Drake

Los Planes

San Pedrillo

Punta Llorona

Playa Llorona

PACIFIC OCEAN

Laguna Corcovado

Río Corcovado

Playa Corcovado

Río Rincón

Los Patos

Río Sirena

Río Claro

Río Pavo

Río Sirena

Río Tigre

El Tigre

Sirena

La Leona

Playa Madrigal

Carate (2 km) & Puerto Jiménez (41 km)

· · · · · · Trail

0   5 km

Chacarita
Río Claro
Piedras Blancas
INTERAMERICANA
Golfito
Golfo Dulce
Aguitas
Rincón de Osa
La Palma
Puerto Jiménez
Ferry
Carate
PARQUE NACIONAL CORCOVADO

Serious walking in Corcovado is not for the faint-hearted. Quite apart from the distances and the terrain, **hazards** include insects (*lots* of them, especially in the rainy season: take a mosquito net, tons of repellent, and all the precautions you can think of), herds of peccaries – who have been known to menace hikers – rivers full of crocodiles (and, in one case, sharks), and nasty snakes, including the terciopelo and bushmaster, which can attack without provocation. That said, most of these are present elsewhere in the country anyway, and everybody seems to make it through Corcovado just fine. But you must at least be prepared to get wet, dirty and incredibly hot – bear in mind that the sea does contain **sharks**, though everyone swims in it and no attacks have ever been recorded.

The **terrain** in Corcovado varies from beaches of packed or soft sand, riverways, mangroves and *holillo* (palm) swamps to dense forest, although most of it is at lowland elevations. Hikers can expect to spend most of their time on the beach trails that ring the outer perimeters of the peninsular section of the park. Inland, the broad, alluvial Corcovado plain contains the **Corcovado lagoon**, and for the most part the cover constitutes the only sizable chunk of tropical **premontane wet forest** (also called tropical humid forest) on the Pacific side of Central America. The Osa forest is as visually and biologically magnificent as any on the subcontinent: biologists often compare the tree heights and density here with that of the Amazon basin cover – practically the only place in the entire isthmus of which this can still be said.

The coastal areas of the peninsular section of the park receive at least 3800mm of **rain** a year, with precipitation rising to about 5000mm in the higher elevations of the interior. This intense wetness is ideal for the development of the intricate, densely matted cover associated with tropical wet forests; there's also a dry season (Dec–March). The inland lowland areas, especially those around the lagoon, can be amazingly **hot**, even for those accustomed to tropical temperatures.

Practicalities

Unless you're coming to Corcovado with Costa Rica Expeditions and staying in their tent camp (see p.377), in the dry months, at least, you have to **reserve** in advance – this will include meals, camping space or lodging at the puesto of your choice (see below). The best way to do this is to fax the park's Puerto Jiménez office directly on 735-5276 or, if you're already in the country, visit the Fundación de Parques Nacionales in San José (see p.77), who will fax or telephone Corcovado on your behalf. You'll have to specify your dates and stick to them. In the rainy season or off-peak times (generally between Easter and Christmas), it's possible to do all this at the park's office in Jiménez (see p.376), but the Fundación prefer that you go through their San José office. Be warned that the park is one of Costa Rica's most popular, and you'll need to book at least six weeks in advance or risk not getting in. It currently costs $2 per night to camp at the puestos, or $6 to sleep in the comfortable accommodation block at Sirena. You can either take **meals** with the rangers ($3 for breakfast, $6 for lunch and dinner – you pay in colones at the puesto) or bring your own food and utensils and use their stove. Food is basic – rice and beans or fish – but filling.

It's suggested that you come in a group of at least two people, that you bring your own mosquito net, sleeping bag, food and water – though you can fill up at the beachside waterfalls and at the puestos – and be more or less experienced in hiking in this kind of terrain. If you can afford it, your best option is to hire a local guide – particularly useful in helping you to spot the recalcitrant wildlife (ask at the Puerto Jiménez office for advice; Oscar Cortes Alfaro is highly recommended). You should plan to hike early in the day – though not before dawn, due to snakes – and take shelter at midday. Corcovado is set up so that the rangers at each puesto always know how many people are on a given trail, and how long they are expected to be. If you are late getting back, they will go looking for you. This gives a measure of security but, all the same, take **precautions**. There have been no mishaps (like people getting lost) in the park of late, but always check with the rangers or ask around in Jiménez regarding current conditions. A few years ago things were tense between the *oreros* who still mine, some of them illegally, in and around Corcovado, and the rangers, whose job it is to stop them. Though no tourist has been hurt, the *oreros* may well be suspicious of strangers, and it's best not to walk alone just in case.

Incidentally, it's especially important when coming to Corcovado to brush up on your **Spanish**. You'll be asking the rangers for a lot of crucial information and few, if any, of them speak English. Bring a phrase book if you're not fluent.

The puestos

The *pulpería* in the village of **Carate**, about 43km from Jiménez, sells basic foodstuffs, though it's not cheap. You can also pitch your **tent** right outside; there's a minimal charge ($2 per tent per night) which covers the use of toilets and showers. From here it is a ninety-minute walk along the beach to enter Corcovado at the **La Leona** puesto. It's then a sixteen-kilometre hike to **Sirena**, where you can stay for a day or two in the simple lodge, exploring the local trails around the Río Sirena. Sirena, the biggest puesto in the park, is also a research station, and often full of biologists. Hikers coming from the Bahía Drake area enter at **San Pedrillo** and walk to Sirena from there.

The small hamlet of **La Palma**, 24km northwest of Puerto Jiménez, is the starting point for getting to the **Los Patos** puesto. It's a twelve-kilometre walk to the park, much of it through hot lowland terrain. You need to arrive at Los Patos soon after dawn; if you want to stay in La Palma and get up early, *Cabinas Corcovado* (**❶–❷**) is a good bet. The relatively new **El Tigre** puesto, at the eastern inland entrance to the park, is a good place to take breakfast or lunch with the ranger(s) before setting off on the local trails. To get there from Jiménez, drive 10km north and take the second left, a dirt track, signed to El Tigre and Dos Brazos.

Local guides

In recent years a programme to train local men and women between the ages of 18 and 35 as naturalist guides has been initiated at Rincón de Osa, a village about 35km north of Jiménez, snug in the curve of the Golfo Dulce. The programme is typical in Costa Rica – Rara Avis and Selva Verde in Sarapiquí, among others, have similar schemes – enabling people not only to make a living from their local knowledge, but also to appreciate the many ways in which a rainforest can be sustainable. Guides are taught to identify some of the 367 or more species of birds recorded in the area, the 177 amphibians and reptiles, nearly 6000 insects, 140 mammals and 1000 trees – Corcovado's biodiversity makes for a lot of homework. They are also given lectures in tourism and tutored by working professional guides. If you wish to hire a local guide, ask in Rincón or at the Fundación Neotrópica office in San José for details. This arrangement works best if you are planning to hike around the Los Patos–Sirena trail, as this has the nearest entrances to Rincón.

All puestos have camping areas, drinking water, information, toilets and telephone or radio-telephone contact. Wherever you enter, jot down the details of the **marea** (tide tables) which are posted in prominent positions. You'll need to cross most of the rivers at low tide – to do otherwise is dangerous. Rangers can advise on conditions.

The trails

The sixteen-kilometre trail from **La Leona to Sirena** runs almost entirely along the beach. You can only walk its full length at low tide; if you do get stuck, the only thing to do is wait for the water to recede. If you can avoid problems with the tides, you should be able to do the walk in five to six hours, taking time to look out for birds. The walking can get a bit monotonous, but the beaches are uniformly lovely and deserted, and you may be lucky enough to spot a flock of **scarlet macaws** in the coastal trees – a rare sight. You will probably see (or hear) monkeys, too. Take lots of sunscreen, a big hat and at least five litres of water per person – the trail gets very hot, despite the sea breezes.

The really heroic walk in Corcovado, all 25km of it, is from **Sirena to San Pedrillo** – the stretch along which you'll see the most impressive trees. It's a two-day trek, so you need a tent, sleeping bag and mosquito net, and you mustn't be worried by having to set up camp in the jungle. Fording the **Río Sirena**, just 1km beyond the Sirena puesto, is the biggest obstacle: this is the deepest of all the rivers on the peninsula, with the strongest out-tow current, and has to be crossed with care, and at low tide only (sharks come in and out in search of food at high tide). Get the latest information from the Sirena rangers before you set out.

About half of the walk is spent slogging it out on the beach, where the sand is more tightly packed than along the La Leona–Sirena stretch. Some hikers do the beach section of the walk well before dawn or after dark; there are fewer dangers (like snakes) at night on the beach and as long as you have a good torch with lots of batteries and/or the moon is out, this is a reasonable option. The second half of the walk – a seven-hour stint – is in the jungle, just inland from the coast. Beyond the jungle you come once more to the beach, at which point you are only about an hour away from the Río San Pedrillo and just 10km from Bahía Drake, easily walkable along the coast.

A third walk is the twenty-kilometre inland trail from **Los Patos to Sirena**, generally less frequented than the track around the edge of the peninsula. From Los Patos a well-marked trail takes you steeply uphill for some 5km, after which the rest of the walk is flat, but extremely hot. There are crude shelters en route where you can rest in the shade (but not camp), and quite a lot of wildlife – tapirs and peccaries especially – has been spotted hereabouts.

The trail across the peninsula from **Los Patos to Sirena** is 20km long. You may want to take a rest at the entrance, as this is an immediately demanding walk, continuing uphill for about 6–8km and taking you into high, wet and dense rainforest – and after that you've still got 14km or so of incredibly hot lowland walking to go. This is a trail for experienced rainforest hikers and hopeful **mammal**-spotters: taking you through the interior, it gives you a reasonable chance of coming across, for example, a margay, or the tracks of tapirs and jaguars. That said, some hikers come away very disappointed, having not seen a thing. It's a gruelling trek, especially with the hot inland temperatures (at least 26°C, with 100 percent humidity) and the lack of sea breezes, and is best avoided if you've not done much rainforest hiking before.

The **El Tigre** area, at the eastern inland entrance to the park, is gradually becoming more developed, with short walking trails being laid out around the

What to see at Corcovado

Walking through Corcovado you will see many lianas, vines, mosses and spectacularly tall trees – some of them 50m or 60m high, and a few more than 80m high. All in all, Corcovado's area is home to about a quarter of all the tree species in the country, including the silkwood (or *ceiba pentandra*), characterized by its height (it is thought to be the largest tree in Central America) and its smooth grey bark. One silkwood, near the Llorona–San Pedrillo section of the trail, is over 80m high and 3m in diameter. You'll also notice huge buttresses: above-ground roots shot out by the silkwoods and other tall canopy species. These are used to help anchor the massive tree in thin tropical soil, where drainage is particularly poor.

Corcovado supports a higher volume of large mammals than most other areas of the country, except perhaps the wild and rugged Talamancas. Jaguars need more than 100 square kilometres each for their hunting; if you are a good tracker you may be able to spot their traces within the park, especially in the fresh mud along trails and riverbeds. Initially they look identical to those made by a large dog, but the four toes are of unequal size – the outermost one is the smallest – and the fore footprint should be wider than its length. You might, too, see the margay, a spotted wildcat about the size of a large domesticated house cat, which comes down from the forest to sun itself on rocks at midday. The ocelot, a larger spotted cat, is even shyer; rarely seen for more than a second, poking its head out of the dense cover and then melting away into the forest again immediately.

With a body shape somewhere between a large pig and a cow, the Baird's tapir is an odd-looking animal, most immediately recognizable for its funny-looking snout, a truncated elephant-type trunk. Tapirs are very shy – and have been made even more so through large-scale hunting – and not aggressive, and you would have to be exceptionally lucky to see one here or anywhere. More threatening are the packs of white-collared peccaries, a type of wild pig, who in Corcovado typically group themselves in packs of about thirty. They are often seen along the trails and should be treated with caution, since they can bite you. The accepted wisdom is to climb a tree if they come at you threateningly, clacking their jaws and growling – though this, of course, means you have to be good at climbing trees, some of which have painful spines.

More common mammals that you will almost certainly catch a glimpse of are the ubiquitous agoutis (also called pacas), foraging in the underbrush. Essentially a large rodent with smooth, glossy hair, the agouti looks similar to a large squirrel. The coati, a member of the racoon family, with a long ringed tail, is also sure to cross your path. Another mammal found in significant numbers in the park – and all over the peninsula – is the tayra (*tolumuco*), a small and swift mink-like creature. They will in most cases run from you, but should not be approached, as they have teeth and can be aggressive.

Among the park's resident birds is the scarlet macaw, around 300 of which live in the park – more, in terms of birds per square kilometre, than anywhere else in the country. Macaws are highly prized as caged birds and, despite the efforts of the SPN, poaching is still a problem in Corcovado, as their (relative) abundance makes them easy prey. Around the Río Sirena estuary, especially, keep an eye out for the boat-billed heron, whose wide bill gives it a lopsided quality. The big black king vulture is present at Corcovado; a forager rather than a hunter, it still looks pretty ominous. There are many other smaller birds in Corcovado including, perhaps, the fluffy-headed harpy eagle. Though the harpy is thought to be extinct in Costa Rica, ornithologists reckon there is a chance that a few pairs still live in Corcovado, and in the Parque Internacional la Amistad on the Talamanca coast.

puesto. These provide an introduction to Corcovado without making you slog it out on the marathon trails, and can easily be covered in a morning or afternoon.

Paso Real to Panamá

Twenty kilometres north of Palmar on the Interamericana is the ferry at **Paso Real**. From here you can either continue on the Interamericana or take the tiny car ferry and drive a little-touristed route along a new paved road, which takes you through some spectacularly scenic country. The latter is little used by tourists except those few heading to the pretty mountain town of **San Vito**, the jumping-off point for the **Wilson Botanical Gardens** and **Parque Internacional la Amistad**.

Most people stick to the **Interamericana**, however, which switchbacks its way to the Panamá border following the wide and fast-running **Río Grande de Térraba**, which cuts a giant path through the almost unbearably hot lowland landscape, its banks coloured red with tropical soils. Rainstorms seem to steamroller in with the express purpose of washing everything away, and you can almost see the river rise with each fresh torrent. The area is prone to landslides in the rainy season, when you can find yourself stranded by a sea of mud. The last section of the trip down to **Panamá** is through an empty border region in which the highway itself is the major feature.

Boruca and Reserva Indígena Boruca

About 12km past the turn-off for Buenos Aires on the Interamericana, and then 18km up a bad road, is the village of **BORUCA**. This is officially within an **indigenous reserve** and, technically, foreign tourists need a better reason to come than simply to look around. However, because of its proximity to the highway, tourists do occasionally turn up, usually looking to buy local **crafts**. The women of Boruca make small tablecoths and purses on home-made looms; the men make balsa-wood masks, some of which are expressly intended for the *diablitos* (little devils) ceremony and procession that takes place on New Year's Eve. You can buy either from the artisans themselves or from the local co-operative, the Boruca Artesanías Group, for both of which you'll need a working knowledge of Spanish. Local people have little other outlet for their

---

The Borucas and the Fiesta de los Diablitos

Many indigenous peoples throughout the isthmus, and all the way north to Mexico, enact the fiesta de los diablitos – a resonant spectacle that is both disturbing and humorous. In Costa Rica the Borucas use it to celebrate New Year and to re-enact the Spanish invasion, with Columbus, Cortez and his men reborn every year. The fiesta takes place over three days and is a village affair: foreigners and tourists are not encouraged to come as spectators. On the first day a village man is appointed to play the bull; others disguise themselves as little devils (*diablitos*), with burlap sacks and masks carved from balsa wood. The *diablitos* taunt the bull, teasing him with sticks, while the bull responds in kind. At midnight on December 30 the *diablitos* congregate on the top of a hill, joined by musicians playing simple flutes and horns fashioned from conch shells. During the whole night and over the next three days, the group proceeds from house to house, visiting everyone in the village and enjoying a drink or two of home brew (*chicha*). On the third day, the "bull" is ritually killed. The symbolism is indirect, but the bull, of course, represents the Spaniard(s), and the *diablitos* the indigenous people. The bull is always vanquished and the *diablitos* always win – which of course is not quite how it turned out, in the end.

crafts (you won't find them in the San José shops), so a visit can be a good way of contributing to the local economy – though you'll need a 4WD to get there.

San Vito

The recently paved road from **Paso Real** to San Vito is steep and winding, with beautiful views. Just beyond Paso Real a tiny ferry (two cars only) crosses the Río Térraba on request. Even though the roads around here have improved, you'll have more peace of mind if you have a 4WD to deal with occasional washouts and landslides, from May to November especially.

Settled largely by post-World War II immigrants from Italy, **SAN VITO** is a clean, prosperous agricultural town with a lovely setting in the Talamancas. At nearly 1000m above sea level it has a wonderfully refreshing climate, as well as great views over the Valle de Coto Brus below. The town is growing as Costa Ricans discover its qualities, and will soon be an important regional hub, though for now there's nothing to do around here but visit the nearby **Wilson Botanical Gardens** (daily 7am–5pm; $8), 6km to the south. The gardens are the best in the country, and on the itineraries of many specialist bird-watching and natural-history tours. They make an excellent day-trip if you happen to be in the area, but unless you have a keen interest it's probably not worth making a special trip from San José. The huge tract of land is home to orchids, interesting tropical trees, and exotic flowers such as heliconias. There's good **birding** too, on the paths and in the surrounding lands, with more than 300 species in total. You can **stay** at the gardens in bunkhouses (②) or cabinas with private bath (⑥). Students and researchers with ID get reduced rates. Contact the OTS (☎240-6696, ⑩www.ots.ac.cr) for details; you must reserve in advance.

Parque Internacional La Amistad

Created in 1982 as a biosphere reserve, the **PARQUE INTERNACIONAL LA AMISTAD** (daily 8am–3.45pm; $6) is a joint venture by the governments of Panamá and Costa Rica to protect the Talamancan mountain areas on both sides of their shared border. Amistad also encompasses several **indigenous reserves**, the most geographically isolated in the country, where Bribrí and Cabecar peoples are able to live with minimal interference from the Valle Central. It is the largest park in the country, covering 2070 square kilometres of Costa Rican territory.

In 1983 Amistad was designated a World Heritage site, thanks to its immense scientific wealth. The Central American isthmus is often described as being a crossroads or filter for the meeting of the North and South American eco-communities; the Amistad area is itself a "biological bridge" within the isthmus, where an extraordinary number of habitats, life zones, topographical features, soils, terrains, and types of animal and plant life can be found. Its **terrain**, while mainly mountainous, is extremely varied on account of shifting altitudes, and ranges from wet tropical forest to high peaks where the temperature can drop below freezing at night. According to the classification system devised by L.R. Holdridge (see Contexts), Amistad has at least seven (some say eight or nine) **life zones**, along with six transition zones. Even more important is Amistad's function as the last bastion of some of the species most in danger of **extinction** in both Costa Rica and the isthmus. Within its boundaries roam the jaguar and the puma, the ocelot, and the tapir. Along with Corcovado on the

Osa Peninsula, Amistad may also be the last holdout of the harpy eagle, feared extinct in Costa Rica.

Too bad for keen natural historians and animal spotters, then, that the terrain is so rugged, for there is only limited access to Amistad. Indeed, only serious and experienced walkers and hikers should consider it a destination. There are few rangers in relation to the size of the area, and getting lost and/or running out of water and food is potentially fatal. Drinking from the many streams and rivers is not recommended, due to the presence of the giardia bacterium.

Practicalities

If you are really serious about exploring La Amistad's limited (and often unmarked and uncleared) trails, contact the Fundación de Parques Nacionales office in San José in advance. They may be able to hook you up with a local guide who knows the area. The small hamlet of **Altamira**, 50km northwest of San Vito, functions as the park headquarters, with a puesto maintained by a full-time ranger who can provide information. You'll need 4WD even to get here, whatever the season. From Altamira you can walk a demanding ten-kilometre-long trail, most of it uphill, to a flat ridge called **Las Tablas**, where it's possible to **camp**. Take water, tent and a three-season sleeping bag.

Near Las Tablas, bordering the park, *La Amistad Lodge*, 3km from the hamlet of Las Mellizas on the way to Sabalito (℡290-2251, ⓕ232-1913, ⓦwww.laamistad.com; ⓞ) has comfortable rustic rooms. It's on the Montero family farm, which also grows organic coffee and has a few kilometres of trails in its surrounding woods – the Monteros can provide transport if you ask in advance.

Paso Canoas and the Panamanian border

Duty-free shops and stalls lining the Interamericana announce the approach to **PASO CANOAS**. As you come into town, either driving or on the TRA-COPA or international Ticabus service, you'll pass the Costa Rican customs checkpoint, where everybody gets a going-over. Foreigners don't attract much interest, however; customs officials are far more concerned with nabbing Ticos coming back over the border with unauthorized amounts of bargain consumer goods.

To cross from Costa Rica into Panamá, most nationalities need a **tourist card**: though UK citizens need only bring their passport. Tourist cards should be collected in advance from the **Panamanian consulate**, or from the office of Copa, Panamá's national airline, in San José. Many people should also have a **visa** – Canadians, Australians and New Zealanders among them. You may also need a return ticket back to Costa Rica (or an onward ticket out of Panamá to another country), but bear in mind that immigration requirements frequently change, seemingly at whim, so always check with the Panamanian consulate before setting off.

The **migración** is on the Costa Rican side, next to the TRACOPA bus terminal. You'll have to wait in line, maybe for several hours, especially if a San José–David–Panamá City Ticabus comes through, as all international bus passengers are processed together. Arrive early to get through fastest. There's no problem **changing money**: there's a Banco Nacional on the Costa Rican side of the border and, beyond that, plenty of moneychangers. Note that Panamá has no paper currency of its own, and US dollars – called *balboas* – are used. It does have its own coins, equivalent to US coins, which are also in wide circulation. Note that you cannot take any **fruit or vegetables** across the border – even if they're for your lunch. They will be confiscated.

If you absolutely have to bed down in Paso Canoas, there are about a dozen rock-bottom budget **cabinas** and *hospedajes*. These are all extremely basic, with cell-like rooms, private bath and cold water. They can also be full on weekends. One place a cut above the pack is *Cabinas Interamericano* (no phone; ❶), on a side road to the right after the TRACOPA bus terminal, heading towards the border. Rooms are not bad, and there's a restaurant.

DAVID, the first city of any size in Panamá, is about ninety minutes beyond the border. Buses run from the Panamanian border bus terminal every hour or so until 5pm. From David it's easy to pick up local services, including the Ticabus to Panamá City, which you can't pick up at the border.

Parque Nacional Isla del Coco

Five hundred kilometres southwest off Costa Rica's Pacific coast, the remote **PARQUE NACIONAL ISLA DEL COCO**, integrated into the national park system in 1978, is these days most famous as "Dinosaur Island" in Steven Spielberg's blockbuster *Jurassic Park*. In the opening frames of the film, a helicopter swoops over azure seas to a remote, emerald-green isle: that's Coco. At 12km long and 5km wide, Coco is the only island in this part of the Pacific that receives enough rain to support the growth of **rainforest**. It also has an extraordinary wealth of **endemic species**: seventy plant species, sixty-four insect species, three spiders and four types of bird, all of which are found nowhere else in the world. Besides researchers and rangers, Coco has no human inhabitants.

Though evidence suggests that the island was known by pre-Columbian sea-going peoples from Ecuador and Colombia, in the modern age it was "discovered" by the navigator and sea captain Joan Cabezas in 1526. Attempts were made to establish a colony here in the early twentieth century, and nowadays wild descendants of the would-be settlers' pigs and coffee plants have upset the island's Galapagos-like ecosystem. Other threats include illegal fishing in its waters; the SPN has extremely limited resources for policing the island, as simply getting there by sea is so expensive. Besides biologists and divers, Coco attracts treasure hunters. It is said that over the centuries nefarious pirates buried bullion here, but in more than five hundred expeditions by tenacious treasure hunters, no one has yet found it. If you're interested in the island, now a UNESCO World Heritage Site, contact the Fundación Amigos de La Isla del Coco (☎256-7476, ⓦwww.cocosisland.org) which was founded in 1994 to help preserve the unique terrestial and marine biodiversity of Coco.

Getting to Coco entails major expense. In the North American winter months the ship *Okeanos Aggressor* leaves from Puntarenas (☎385-2628, ⓦwww.aggressor.com) for specialist ten-day **diving tours**. The price is about $3000 per person, excluding transport to Costa Rica and equipment rental, which is available once you arrive.

Travel details

Buses

Dominical to: Quepos (2 daily; 2hr); San Isidro (4 daily; 40min–1hr).

Golfito to: Playas Pavones and Zancudo (dry season only, 1 daily; 2hr 30min); San José (2 daily; 8hr).

Palmar to: San José (7 daily; 5hr 30min); Sierpe (5 daily; 30min).

Paso Canoas to: San Isidro (2 daily; 6hr); San José (6 daily; 9hr).

Playas Pavones and Zancudo to: Golfito (dry season only, 1 daily; 2hr 30min).

Puerto Jiménez to: San Isidro (2 daily; 5hr); San José (2 daily; 8–9hr).

San Gerardo de Rivas to: San Isidro (2 daily; 40min).

San Isidro to: Dominical (4 daily; 40min–1hr); Paso Canoas (2 daily; 6hr); Puerto Jiménez (2 daily; 5hr); Quepos (4 daily; 3hr 30min); San Gerardo de Rivas (2 daily; 1hr 40min); San José (12 daily; 3hr); Uvita (2 daily; 1hr 30min).

San José to: Golfito (2 daily; 8hr); Palmar (7 daily; 5hr 30min); Paso Canoas (6 daily; 9hr); Puerto Jiménez (2 daily; 8–9hr); San Isidro (12 daily; 3hr).

Sierpe to: Palmar (5 daily; 30min).

Uvita to: San Isidro (2 daily; 1hr 30min).

Lancha

Golfito to: Puerto Jiménez (daily at 11.30am; 1hr 30min), returning from Jiménez at 6am.

Flights

Golfito to: Puerto Jiménez (1 daily); San José (4 daily).

Puerto Jiménez to: Golfito (1 daily); San José (2–5 daily).

San José to: Golfito (4 daily); Palmar (1 daily); Puerto Jiménez (2–5 daily).

contexts

contexts

A brief history of Costa Rica

The peopling of Costa Rica probably took place sometime around 10,000 BC, about 25,000 years after the first *Homo sapiens* had crossed the Bering Strait into what is now the Americas (though the only thing to support this tentative date is a single flint arrowhead excavated in the 1890s in Guanacaste). Archeologists know almost nothing of the various people who inhabited modern-day Costa Rica until about 1000 BC. Certainly no written records were left.

Costa Rica before the Spanish

Pre-Columbian Costa Rica was a contact zone – a corridor for merchants and trading expeditions – between the Mesoamerican empires to the north and the Andean empire to the south. Excavations of pottery, jade and trade goods, and accounts of cultural traditions, have shown that the pre-Columbian peoples of Costa Rica adopted liberally from both areas.

When the Spaniards arrived in Costa Rica in the early sixteenth century, it was inhabited by as many as 27 different groups or clans. Most clans were assigned names by the invaders, which they took from the **cacique** (chief) with whom they dealt. The modern-day Zona Norte was home to the **Catapas**, the **Votos** and the **Suerres**; the extreme south of the Talamancas held the **Cabécars** and the **Guaymís**, whose influence spread to the modern-day Zona Sur and the Osa Peninsula. In the nearby Valle de Diquis and Valle de el General were the **Térrabas** and their sub-group the **Borucas**. The Valle Central contained the **Huetars**. Modern-day Guanacaste was the most heavily populated and farmed area in pre-Columbian Costa Rica, home to the **Chorotegas** and the older Nicoyan peoples.

Many of these groups had affinities with their neighbours in Nicaragua to the north and Panamá to the south. The Chorotegas in particular showed signs of cultural inheritance from the Olmec peoples of southern Mexico, while those of the extreme south and Osa Peninsula had affinities with peoples in Panamá and Colombia.

About 1000 BC, most of these groups would have been involved in **subsistence farming**. They also existed in a state of almost constant warfare. However, unlike in the Mesoamerican states and in the Inca empire, where war and domination had led to the establishment of complex, far-reaching empires, in Costa Rica no one group gained ascendancy, and the political position of the clans seemed to remain more or less constant throughout the ages, with no group imposing its language or customs on the rest. One reason could be that although these groups were only too willing to go to **war**, they did not do so in order to increase their territory. Perennially low population density in ancient Costa Rica meant that there was plenty of land, and plenty of space into which persecuted or vanquished groups could escape. Like the forest-dwelling tribes in Amazonia to the south, these pre-Columbian peoples waged war to capture slaves, victims for potential sacrifice, marriage partners, or simply for revenge.

As for **religion**, the clans were highly complex and specialized. Shamans were respected members of society, officiating at funerals, which were the most important rites of passage, especially in the Talamancan groups. Some clans had animal taboos that prevented them from hunting and killing certain beasts. The taboos neatly complemented each other: one group might not be able to hunt the tapir, for example, while the neighbouring clan in turn would be prohibited from hunting the main prey of another group. This delicate balance played itself out on various levels, promoting harmony between man and nature. Like everywhere from southern Mexico to Brazil, the jaguar was much revered among all the groups, and only hunted to provide shamans with pelts, teeth and other ritualistic articles.

Gender divisions were, to an extent, along familiar lines: men made war and performed religious duties, while women were confined to domestic roles. However, women of the Boruca group in the southwest went to war alongside men, and the Votos of the Zona Norte regularly had women chiefs. In many clans the inheritance of names and objects was matrilineal.

People lived **communally** in stockaded villages – especially in the Talamancan groups – called **palenques** by the Spaniards. Whole groups, not necessarily related by kin, would live kibbutz-like in a village big house. They organized work "gangs" who would tackle labour projects, usually agricultural. In most cases land was held communally and harvests shared to ensure the survival of all. **Social hierarchy** was complex, with an ascending scale of **caciques** and shamans occupying the elite positions.

The Chorotegas in Guanacaste in particular developed a high level of **cultural expression**, possessing a written, symbol-based language, and harvesting and trading such diverse products as honey, natural dyes, and cotton.

Costa Rica "discovered"

On September 18, 1502, on his fourth and last voyage to the Americas, **Columbus** sighted Costa Rica. Battered by a storm, he ordered his ships to drop anchor just off Isla Uvita, 1km offshore from present-day Puerto Limón. The group stayed seventeen days, making minor forays into the heavily forested coast and its few villages. The indigenous peoples that Columbus met – as he could not fail to notice – were liberally attired in gold headbands, mirrored breastplates, bracelets and the like, convincing him of potential riches. In fact, the **gold** worn by those first welcoming envoys would have been traded or come to the peoples of the Caribbean coast through inter-tribal warfare. There was very little gold in the area known as the Atlantic watershed – the eastern slopes of the Cordilleras Central and Talamanca. Rather it came from the southwest of the country near the Valle de Diquis, over the near-impenetrable hump of the Cordillera de Talamanca. With dreams of wealth, Columbus sailed on, charting the entire coastal area from Honduras to Panamá, including Costa Rica, and naming it **Veragua**.

In 1506 King Ferdinand of Spain despatched **Diego de Nicuesa** to govern what would become Costa Rica. From the start his mission was beset by hardship, beginning when their ship ran aground on the coast of Panamá, forcing the party to walk up the Caribbean shore. There they met native people who, unlike those who had welcomed Columbus tentatively but politely with their shows of gold, burned their crops rather than submit to the authority of the Spanish. This, together with the impenetrable jungles, the creatures that lived there and tropical diseases, meant that the expedition had to be abandoned.

Next came **Gil González**, in 1521–22, who concentrated on Costa Rica's Pacific coast, which offered safer anchorages. González and his men covered practically the entire length of Pacific Costa Rica on foot, baptizing as they went: the expedition priest later claimed that some 32,000 souls had been saved in the name of the King of Spain.

Gold, land and souls

The first Spanish accounts of Costa Rican indigenous peoples were made in the sixteenth century by "chroniclers", the official scribes who accompanied mapping and evangelical expeditions. In general these were either soldiers or missionaries who showed almost no talent for ethnography. Rather, they approached the pre-Columbian world as inventory-takers or suspicious accountants, writing terse and unimaginative reports liberally spiced with numbers and accounts of gold (although they found almost none). It was they who started the trend of portraying the cultures of the indigenous peoples of Costa Rica as "low" and underdeveloped; what they in fact meant was that there was little that could be expropriated for the Crown. Of the narratives which stand out is one by Columbus himself, who described the small welcoming party he received in 1502 in vivid and rather romanticized prose in his lettera rarissima, meant for the eyes of his sovereign.

Another, more important, account is by Gonzalo Fernández de Oviedo, whose comprehensive, nineteen-volume Historía General de las Indias, Islas y Tierra Firme del Mar Oceano was first published in 1535. Oviedo spent only ten or twelve days with the Chorotega peoples but he had a fine eye for detail, and recorded many aspects of the Chorotega diet, dress, and social customs. He also noticed that they spoke a form of Nahua, the language of the Aztecs and the lingua franca of Mesoamerica, an observation which has since convinced most historians of a direct cultural link between the empires to the north and the peoples of pre-Columbian Costa Rica and Nicaragua.

One of the first things the Spanish chroniclers noticed was that the indigenous peoples in the Talamancas in the southeast and the Greater Chiriquí in the southwest practised ritual sacrifice. Every full moon, prisoners captured in the most recent raid would be ritually beheaded. The Spanish, of course, were repelled, and so began the systematic baptism campaigns, and the destruction of indigenous "idolatry".

The indigenous peoples, meanwhile, began a campaign of **resistance** that was to last nearly thirty years, employing guerrilla tactics, full-scale flight, infanticide, attacks on colonist settlements and burning their own villages. There were massacres, defeats and submissions on both sides, but by 1540 Costa Rica was officially a Royal Province of Spain, and a decade later, the Conquest was more or less complete. Most of the key areas of the country had been charted or settled, with the exception of the Talamanca region, which remained largely unexplored for centuries.

Indigenous people in the colonial period

During the first years of the Spanish invasion those indigenous Costa Ricans who grouped themselves in large settlements, like the Chorotegas, proved more easily subjected, and were carted off by the Spanish to work in the mines, build the first Costa Rican towns, or co-opted to general slavery in the guise of farmwork. The more scattered groups fared better, in the main exiling themselves to the rugged Talamancas. By then, however, the real conquerors of the New World had arrived: smallpox, influenza, and measles. In the seventeenth and eighteenth centuries huge pandemics swept the country, among them the so-called **Great Pandemic** of 1611–60, in which whole towns and villages disappeared virtually overnight. **Caciques** as well as commoners died, leaving groups without leadership. Although colonial censuses are notoriously inaccurate, in 1563 it is reckoned that an estimated 80,000 indigenous peoples lived in Costa Rica; by 1714 the official count was 999. Today there are only about 5000 indigenous people in the country out of a population of nearly 3.5 million. For more on the current status of indigenous people in Costa Rica, see p.403.

In 1560 **Juan de Cavallon** and **Juan Vásquez de Coronado** – the first true conquistadors of Costa Rica – succeeded in penetrating the Valle Central, the area that would become most significant in the development of the nation. As Cortés had done in Mexico, the Spaniards of Costa Rica took advantage of existing rivalries among the native groups and played them off against each other. In this way they managed to dominate the groups of the Pacific coast with the help of tribes from the Valle Central.

In the early years of the colony, the Spaniards quickly established the **encomienda**, a system widespread in the Spanish crown's Central American possessions which gave the conquistadors and their descendants the right to demand tribute or labour from the indigenous population. The **encomienda** applied to all indigenous males in Costa Rica between the ages of 18 and 50, and to a lesser extent to women. Quotas were set for the donation of foods such as cacao fruit, corn, chicken, honey and chilli peppers. Although these are all foodstuffs the settlers could have grown and harvested themselves, the capacity for the **encomienda** to enrich the colonies was immense. From the Spanish point of view, this was compensation for the risks and hazards involved in coming to the New World. As many people have said, no man came to America to be poorer than he was in Europe.

Costa Rica's indigenous peoples resisted servitude to the colonials quite fiercely, although (in the words of one **cacique**) they did get tired of "running around in the jungle and hiding all the time". Nor was there total acceptance of the way the native population was treated during this period. High-ranking clergymen protested to their Spanish overlords, and as early as 1542 the **New Laws**, influenced by the passionate appeals of Fray Bartolomé de las Casas, decreed that colonizers had a duty to "protect" the indigenous peoples, and in 1711 the Bishop of Nicaragua, Fray Benito Garret y Arlovi, informed on the governor of Costa Rica for his brutal policies. These decrees assuaged the conscience of the Spanish crown, but what happened on the ground in the colonies, of course, was quite a different matter.

The early settlers

It seems more appropriate to discuss Costa Rica's lack of colonial experience, rather than a bona fide colonization. In 1562, **Juan Vásquez de Coronado** became the second governor of Costa Rica. Coronado has always been portrayed as the good guy, renowned for his favourable treatment of the indigenous peoples. It was under his administration that the first settlement of any size or importance was established, and **Cartago**, in the heart of the Valle Central, was made capital of the colony. During the next century settlers confined themselves more or less to the centre of the country. The Caribbean coast was the haunt of buccaneers – mainly English – who put ashore and wintered here after plundering the lucrative Spanish Main; the Pacific coast saw its share of pirate activity too, most famously when Sir Francis Drake put ashore briefly in Bahía Drake in 1579.

This first epoch of the colony is remembered as one of unremitting **poverty**. Within a decade of its invasion Costa Rica was notorious throughout the Spanish empire for its lack of gold. The settlers and their descendants, unlike those to the north and the south, who became wealthy on the gold of the Aztecs and Inca, never achieved their dreams of instant aristocracy. Instead, they were confronted with almost insuperable obstacles, including tropical fever, hunger, and belligerent natives. The Valle Central was fertile, but there was uncertainty as to what crops to grow. Coffee had not yet been imported to Costa Rica, nor had tobacco, so it was to subsistence agriculture that most settlers turned, growing just enough to live on. There were no export crops and no national markets for foodstuffs. Spanish fabrics, manufactured goods and currency became so scarce that by 1709 Valle Central settlers were forced to adopt cacao beans as currency. Goat's hair and bark were used as clothing fabrics, making your average eighteenth-century Costa Rican farmer look as wild and uncivilized as Romulus and Remus before the founding of Rome. In 1719, the governor of Costa Rica famously complained that he had to till his own land. To make matters worse, Volcán Irazú blew its top in 1723, nearly destroying the capital. With the emphasis on agriculture, and with little industry or trade, Costa Rica was unsurprisingly slow in founding urban settlements. 1706 saw the establishment of the second city (after Cartago) of Cubujuquí (present-day Heredia); in 1737 Villa Nueva de la Boca del Monte (later shortened, thankfully, to San José) was founded; in 1782 it was the turn of Villa Hermosa (present-day Alajuela).

The tough yeoman **settler farmers** who survived in these conditions are the most distinct figures in Costa Rica's early colonial history, and their independent, though impoverished, state is widely believed to be the root of the country's modern-day egalitarianism. Recent historical works, however, concede that while everybody in the early days of the colony may have been equally poor, social distinctions still counted, and where they did not exist, were manufactured, albeit in a much less virulent form than in other Central American possessions of the Spanish crown.

The history of banana-growing in Costa Rica is inextricably linked to the establishment of the railroads. Initially the brainchild of Costa Rican president Tomas Guardia, the San José–Puerto Limón railway – the "Jungle Train" – was built by American capitalist Minor Keith. From the outset in 1871, the idea behind the proposed railway was to establish an easy route for Valle Central coffee to reach the Caribbean coast, thus circumventing both the fluvial method of transporting the beans via the Río Sarapiquí, and the Puntarenas route, by which the crop had to travel around Cape Horn.

Almost immediately after construction began, however, the contractors faced a labour shortage. The lowlands of Limón province have a particularly brutal climate: continuously hot, muggy, and lashed by heavy rain. Yellow fever, venomous serpents, raids by bands of indigenous peoples and general exhaustion conspired to fell much of the workforce, initially made up of Highlanders, imported Chinese "coolie" labour, and Italians. Due to economic conditions in Jamaica at the time, there was a ready pool of black labour. Between 1874 and 1891 some 11,000 Jamaicans arrived in Costa Rica. The Highland majority did not respond well to this immigration, largely on grounds of race. Costa Ricans thought of themselves as white and often compared themselves favourably with the darker-skinned inhabitants of neighbouring countries. It is generally held that for the first half of this century a law existed prohibiting the migration of Afro-Caribbeans to the Valle Central.

In 1890 the train finally sparked and puffed its way out of the capital. Minor Keith's involvement in the history of Costa Rica did not stop here, as he had ingeniously planted bananas along the tracks in order to help pay for the train's construction. The fruit flourished and, as new markets opened up in Europe and the US, it became an exportable commodity: Costa Rica was the first Central American republic to grow bananas in bulk. In 1899 Keith and a colleague founded the United Fruit Company. The company, or Yunai, as it was called locally, came to transform the social, political and cultural face of Central America – and of all the countries in which it operated, it had the biggest dealings in Costa Rica.

Opinions of the Yunai oscillate between the belief that it was a capitalist scourge that gave Costa Rica its Banana Republic burden, and that it was the saving grace of the nation. Almost from the beginning, United Brands – as it came to call itself – gained a reputation for anti-union practices, deserting entire areas once labour showed any signs of being organized. That said, the banana companies have always generally offered high salaries, and many Highlanders would spend a year or two working on the banana plantations with the express purpose of getting together enough money to start a small farm, although workers would more often spend their salaries – for many years given in redeemable scrip instead of cash – on drink and dissipation. To a degree this was a deliberate plan by the company to have their labour force continuously in hock and therefore pliable.

As long as the United Fruit Company provided a steady flow of jobs, there was no real temptation for the Jamaicans and their descendants to leave the Caribbean coast, where they had effectively transported their own culture intact. In isolated Limón they could retain their traditional food, Protestantism, and play West Indian games like cricket, preserving their culture in the face of a much larger Highland majority. They could also use their ability to speak English to advantage – often Afro-Caribbeans attained high-ranking positions in the *bananeros* because they could communicate with the American foremen in their own language.

When the plantations began to close down in Limón in 1925 as a result of the dreaded banana maladies *Sigatoka* and Panamá disease, the fortunes of the Jamaicans changed. In the face of a pestilence so virulent that plantations could only run for about two or three years, the United Fruit company had to look elsewhere in the country for possible locations for their operations. While keeping their Limón plantations open, in 1934 they began acquiring land and planting bananas in the area around modern-day Quepos in the Central Pacific, and Golfito in the Zona Sur. This spelled bad news for the Afro-Caribbean workers as, unbeknown to them, United Fruit had signed a contract with the Costa Rican government stipulating that employment preference be given to native Costa Ricans. When the contract became public in September 1930, racial tensions rose to boiling point in Limón. Afro-Caribbeans were caught, unable to afford the passage home to Jamaica on the one hand and prohibited from taking work elsewhere in the country on the other. It seems that United Fruit itself did not have any qualms about employing Afro-Caribbeans; quite the opposite. Rather it was the government, along with the white plantation workers and the Highland elite who felt most threatened, and who in 1933 petitioned Congress to prohibit the entry of blacks into the country "because they are of a race inferior to ours".

In 1934 the most virulent strike yet seen in the Costa Rican *bananeros* began. It was organized by Carlos Luis Fallas, labour activist and novelist, who had been exiled to Limón as a result of his militancy on behalf of labour organizations in the Valle Central. As historian Michael Seligson puts it, sending Fallas to the *bananeros* "was like throwing Brer Rabbit into the briar patch. For the judges Limón was the Siberia of Costa Rica; for Fallas, it was the Nirvana of union organizers." Fallas proved a brilliant organizer, though initially the proposals he put forward to the Company were quite mild, requesting things like malaria drugs, snakebite serum, and payment in cash rather than scrip, which could easily be squandered. Nonetheless, the Company refused to recognize these proposals, and in August 1934 the strike began in earnest, tenaciously holding on in the face of physical harassment by the Company and police forces. For the next four years strikes and worker opposition raged on. In 1938 the Company finally pulled out of Limón province for good, deserting it for the Pacific coast.

Left behind in the economic devastation and unable to migrate within the country in search of work, the Afro-Caribbean population either took up cacao cultivation, hacked out their own smallholdings, or took to fishing or other subsistence activities. Overnight the schools, bunkhouses, American dollars, scrip economy, liquor and cigarettes disappeared, as did the US foremen and the ample plantation-style homes they had occupied. From about 1934 to 1970 the region was virtually destitute, without much of a cash economy or any large-scale employers. It is only now beginning to recover in terms of banana production – under the aegis of the national banana-franchise operators Standard Fruit Company – and only at considerable cost to the environment as more tropical forests are felled and more rivers polluted with the pesticides used on the fruit.

It is hard to appreciate the overwhelming presence that the Yunai wielded in communities until you have seen the schools and hospitals that it established, the plantation house-style accommodation it built for its managers, and the rows upon rows of barrack-like houses it provided for its workers. You can get a flavour of this in the banana towns of Limón's Estrella Valley and on the road from Jacó to Quepos, where you pass through a long corridor of African palm oil farms, United Brands' only major remaining investment in Costa Rica. The Company also left its mark on the collective consciousness of the region. Carlos Luis Fallas' novels *Mamita Yunai* and *Gentes y gentecillas*, Garcia Marquez's *One Hundred Years of Solitude*, and Guatemalan Asturias's masterly *El Papa Verde* all document the power of the Company in the everyday life of the *pueblitos* of Central America

Two other crucial factors went into the making of the modern nation. One was **coffee**, eventually to become Costa Rica's main export, a crop that requires many smallholders rather than large hacienda systems. Another factor in the unique development of the colony was **ethnic**: quite simply, the vast majority of peasants in Costa Rica were descendants of the Spanish colonists, rather than **indigenos** or **mestizos**, and as such were treated as equals by the ruling elite, who saw them as **hermaniticos**, or "little brothers".

Independence and prosperity

The nineteenth century was the most significant era in the development of Costa Rica. Initially, after 1821, when Central America declared **independence** from Spain, freedom made little difference to Costa Ricans. Although granted on September 15, 1823, the news did not reach Costa Rica until a month later, when a mule messenger arrived from Nicaragua to tell the astonished citizens of Cartago the good news. Rather than rejoicing in being freed from the Spanish – Spain had not paid much attention to the poor and isolated province anyway – a **civil war** promptly broke out among the inhabitants of the Valle Central, dividing the citizens of Alajuela and San José from those of Heredia and Cartago. This struggle for power was won by the Alajuela–San José faction, and **San José** became the capital city in 1823.

Costa Rica made remarkable progress in the latter half of the nineteenth century, building roads, bridges and railways and filling San José with neo-Baroque, European-style edifices. Virtually all this activity was fuelled by the **coffee** trade, bringing wealth that the settlers just a century earlier could hardly have dreamed of. The coffee story begins as early as 1808, when beans from Cuba or Jamaica – depending on which sources you believe – were first planted in the Valle Central. The plants thrived in the highland climate and by 1820 citizens of Cartago were being encouraged – ordered, even – to plant coffee in their backyards. But most significant in the early history of the coffee trade was the arrival in 1844 of English merchant **William Le Lacheur**. His ship, the **Monarch**, had emptied her hold of its cargo, and Le Lacheur arrived in the Pacific port of Puntarenas looking for ballast to take back to Liverpool. He travelled to the Valle Central where he secured a cargo of coffee beans, which he bought on credit, promising to return and pay in two years' time.

Until that point, most of Costa Rica's coffee had made its way to Chile, where it was mixed with a lower-grade South American bean, packaged for export under the brand of **Café de Valparíso** and sent to England, taking the long way around Cape Horn. With Le Lacheur's shipment, however, British tastebuds were won round to the mellow, high-quality bean. A trading partnership began that saw the Costa Rican upper classes using Sheffield steel cutlery and Manchester linens for most of the 1800s.

The **coffee bourgeoisie** played a vital role in the cultural and political development of the country, and in 1848 the newly influential **cafetaleros** elected to the presidency their chosen candidate, Juan Rafael Mora. Extremely conservative and pro-trade, Mora came to distinguish himself in the battle against the American-backed filibusterer William Walker in 1856, only to fall from grace and be executed in 1860 (see p.256).

The early twentieth century

The first years of the **twentieth century** witnessed a difficult transition towards democracy in Costa Rica. Universal male suffrage had come into effect during the last years of the nineteenth century, but class and power conflicts still dogged the country, with several **caudillo** (authoritarian) leaders, familiar figures in other Latin American countries, hijacking power. In general, however, these figures ended up in exile, and neither the army nor the church gained much of a foothold in politics. A number of radical labour initiatives were created during the 1920s, inspired by the Russian revolution, though for most of the twentieth century Costa Rica's successive administrations, whatever their political colour, have proved no friend of labour relations, beginning in 1924 when most **strikes** were outlawed. In 1931 the Communist party was formed, followed quickly by the National Republican party in 1932. The latter dominated the political scene for most of the 1940s, with the election in 1940 of the Republican (PRN) candidate **Rafael Calderón Guardia**, a doctor educated in part in Belgium and a devout Catholic.

It was Calderón who instigated the social reforms and state support for which Costa Rica is still almost unique in the region. In 1941 he established a new **Labour Code** which reinstated the right of workers to organize and strike, and a social security system providing free schooling for all. Calderón also paved the way for the establishment of the University of Costa Rica, health insurance, income security and assistance schemes, and thus won the support of the impoverished and the lower classes and the suspicion of the governing élites. One of those less than convinced by Calderón's policies was the man who would come to be known as **"Don Pepe"**, the coffee farmer José Figueres Ferrer, who denounced Calderón and his expensive reforms in a radio broadcast in 1941 and was then abuptly forced into exile in Mexico, from where he plotted his return.

The "revolution" of 1948 and after

The **elections of 1948** heralded the most eventful year of this century for Costa Rica. Constitutionally, Costa Rican presidents could not serve consecutive terms, so the election battle that year was between **Teodorico Picado**, widely considered to be a Calderón puppet, and **Ulate**, an ally of Figueres, who during two years in exile had become a heroic figure in some circles, returning to Costa Rica to play a key part in the **Acción Democratica**, a loose group of anti-Calderónistas. Ulate won the presidency, but the PRN won the majority in Congress – a fact that effectively annulled the election results.

For his part, **Figueres** was back on the scene and intent upon overthrowing Picado, who had stepped in and declared himself president in the face of the annulment. Figueres soon formed an opposition party, ideologically opposed to the PRN, calling them, somewhat ironically in view of the "republican" in their name, "communists". In March, **fighting** around Cartago began, culminating in an attack by the Figueres rebels on San José. To a degree, the battles were fought to safeguard the system of democratic election in the face of corruption, and in order to stem the clannishness and personality cults that dogged all Costa Rican political parties and presidential campaigns.

While Figueres' rebel forces were well equipped with arms, some supplied through CIA contacts, the militia defending president Picado was not: the national army consisted of only about 300 men at the time, and had to be supplemented by machete-wielding banana workers. Two thousand were dead by mid-April, when hostilities ceased. May saw the formation of the **Junta of the Second Republic**, with Figueres as acting president, despite an after-the-fact attack from Nicaraguan Picado supporters in December.

Figueres wanted above all to engineer a complete break with the country's past, and especially the policies and legacies of the Calderónistas. Seeing himself as fighting both communism and corruption, he not only outlawed the PVP, the Popular Vanguard Party – formerly known as the Communist Party – but also nationalized the banks and devised a tax to hit the rich particularly hard, thus alienating the establishment. The new **constitution** drawn up in 1949 gave full citizenship to Afro-Caribbeans, full suffrage to women and abolished Costa Rica's army. In a way, the **abolition of the army** fitted with political precedents in Costa Rica. Nearly thirty years before, in 1922, former president Ricardo Jiménez Oreamuno had given a famous speech in which he said: "the school shall kill militarism, or militarism shall kill the Republic . . . we are a country with more teachers than soldiers . . . and a country that turns military headquarters into schools." Although the warming sentiment behind Jiménez's words is oft-repeated in Costa Rica, the truth is somewhat darker. Figueres' motives were not utopian but rather a pragmatic bid to limit the political instability that had been the scourge of so many Latin American countries, and an attempt to save valuable resources. Today, while the country still has no army, the police forces are powerful, highly specialized and, in some cases, heavily armed. **Paramilitary** organizations do exist. Chief among them is the Free Costa Rica Movement (MCRL), formed in 1961 and still active, which has allegedly been involved in a number of deeds more reminiscent of the Guatemalan army's death squads than the spirit of a harmonious and army-free Costa Rica.

In 1951 Figueres formed the **National Liberation Party**, or PLN, in order to be legitimately elected. He was a genius in drawing together disparate strands of society: when the elections came around the following year he got the agricultural smallholder vote, while winning the support of the urban working classes with his retention of the welfare state. At the same time he appeased the right-of-centrists with his essentially free-marketeering and staunch anti-communist stance.

The **1960s** and **1970s** were a period of prosperity and stability in Costa Rica, when the welfare state was developed to reach nearly all sectors of society. In 1977 the **indigenous bill** established the right of aboriginal peoples to their own land reserves – a progressive measure at the time, although indigenous peoples today are not convinced the system has served them well (see p.403). At the end of the 1970s, regional conflicts deflected attention from the domestic agenda, with the Carazo (1978–82) administration announcing its support for the FSLN revolutionary movement in Nicaragua, who had finally managed to despatch the Somoza family into exile.

Storm in the isthmus: the 1980s

Against all odds, Costa Rica in the 1980s and 1990s not only saw its way through the serious political conflicts of its neighbours, but also successfully managed predatory US interventionism, economic crisis and staggering debt. Like many Latin American countries, Costa Rica had taken out bank and government **loans** in the 1960s and 1970s to finance vital development. But in the early 1980s the slump in international coffee and banana prices put the country's finances into the red. In September 1981, Costa Rica defaulted on its interest payment on these loans, becoming the first third-world country to do so, and sparking off a chain of similar defaults in Latin America that threw the international banking community into crisis. Despite its defaults, Costa Rica's debt continued to accumulate, and by 1989 had reached a staggering $5 billion, one of the highest per capita debt loads in the world.

To compound the economic crisis came the simultaneous escalation of the **Nicaraguan civil war**. During the entire decade Costa Rica's foreign policy – and to an extent its domestic agenda – would be overshadowed by tensions with Nicaragua and the US. Initially, the Monge PLN administration (1982–86) more or less capitulated to US demands that Costa Rica be used as a supply line for the Contras, and Costa Rica also accepted military training for its police force from the US. Simultaneously, the country's first agreement for a structural adjustment loan with the IMF was signed. It seemed increasingly clear that Costa Rica was on the path to both violating its declared neutrality in the conflicts of its neighbours and condemning its population to wage freezes, price increases and other side effects associated with the IMF restructuring.

In May 1984 the situation escalated with the events at the **La Penca** press conference, given by the US-backed Contra leader Edén Pastora. Held in a simple hut on the banks of the Río San Juan, the conference had minimal security. A bomb was apparently carried in to the hut by a "Danish" cameraman and concealed within an equipment case, and was intended to kill all. Miraculously, an aide of Pastora's accidentally kicked the case over, so that when it was detonated the force of the blast went up and down instead of sideways, thus saving the lives of most of those within, including Pastora himself. Although nobody is quite sure who was behind the bombing, it seems that the point of the carnage was to implicate Managua, thus cutting off international support and destabilizing the Sandinista government further. Both the CIA and freelance Argentine terrorists have been implicated. The immediate effect was to shock the Costa Rican government and the international community into paying more attention to the deadly conflicts of Nicaragua and, by association, El Salvador and Guatemala.

The Arias peace plan

In 1986 PLN candidate **Oscar Arias Sánchez** was elected to the presidency, and Costa Rica's relations with the US and Nicaragua took a different tack. The former political scientist began to play the role of peace broker in the conflicts of Nicaragua, El Salvador and, to a lesser extent, Honduras and Guatemala, mediating between these countries and also between domestic factions within them. In October 1987, just eighteen months after taking office, Arias was awarded the Nobel Prize for Peace, attracting worldwide attention.

Arias's **peace plan** focused on regional objectives, tying individual and domestic conflicts into the larger picture: the stability of the isthmus. It officially called for a ceasefire, the discontinuation of military aid to the Contra insurrectionists, amnesties for political prisoners and for guerrillas who voluntarily relinquished the fight, and, lastly and perhaps most importantly, intergovernmental negotiations leading to free and fair elections. The peace plan began, rather than ended, with the awarding of the Nobel Prize, dragging on throughout 1987 and 1988 and running into obstacles as, almost immediately, all nations involved charged one another with non-compliance or other violations. The situation deteriorated when the US stationed troops in southern Honduras, ready to attack Nicaragua. Meanwhile, Washington continued to undermine Costa Rica's declared neutrality, requesting in April 1988 that Arias approve Costa Rican territory as a corridor for "humanitarian aid" to the Contras. The same month, Arias met with US president George Bush in Washington. Arias's diplomatic credibility enabled him to secure millions of dollars worth of US aid for Costa Rica request without compromising the country politically. For its part, the last thing the US wanted was internal unrest in Costa Rica, its natural (if not entirely compliant) ally in the region.

However, while Arias had obviously stalled on the US using Costa Rica's northern border as a base from which to attack Nicaragua, he seemed to have fewer quibbles about what was happening in the south, in Panamá. In July 1989, CIA-supported anti-Noriega guerrilla forces (many of them ex-Contras) amassed along the Costa Rica–Panamá border in preparation for the US invasion of Panamá that would take place in December. Though Arias had gained the admiration of statesmen around the world, he proved to be less-than-popular at home. Many Costa Ricans saw him as neglecting domestic affairs, while increasing prices caused by the IMF's economic demands meant that conditions had not improved much in Costa Rica.

The 1990s

In 1990 the mantle of power shifted to **Rafael Calderón Fournier** (son of Calderón Guardia) who in the 1980s had been instrumental in consolidating the opposition that became the free-marketeering Partido Unidad Social Cristiana, or PUSC. A year later, Costa Rica was rocked by its most powerful **earthquake** since the one that laid waste to most of Cartago in 1910. Centred in Limón province, the quake killed 62 people and caused expensive structural damage. At the same time, nationals of El Salvador, Honduras, Guatemala and especially Nicaragua were looking to Costa Rica – the only stable country in the region – for asylum, and tension rose as the **refugees** poured in. In 1992 Costa Rica faced more trouble as it was brought to law in US courts for its failure to abide by international labour laws, a continuing black mark on the country's copybook for most of the twentieth century.

Until 1994, elections in Costa Rica had been relatively genteel affairs, involving lots of flag-waving and displays of national pride in democratic traditions. The elections of that year, however, were probably the dirtiest to date. The campaign opened and closed with an unprecedented bout of mudslinging and attempts to smear the reputations of both candidates, tactics which shocked many Costa Ricans. The PLN candidate – the choice of the left, for his promises to maintain the role of the state in the economy – was none other than **José María Figueres**, the son of Don Pepe, who had died four years previously. During the campaign Figueres was accused of shady investment rackets and influence-peddling. His free-market PUSC opposition candidate, Miguel Angel Rodriguez, fared no better, having admitted to being involved in a tainted-beef scandal in the 1980s. Figueres won, narrowly, though his term in office was plagued by a series of scandals. On a more positive note, in January 1995 a Free Trade agreement was signed with Mexico in order to try to redress the

Today you won't see much evidence of native traditions in Costa Rica. Only about one percent of the country's population is of aboriginal extraction, and the dispersion of the various groups ensures that they frequently do not share the same concerns and agendas. Contact between them, apart from through bodies such as CONAI – the national indigenous affairs organization – is minimal.

Although a system of indigenous reserves was set up by the Costa Rican administration in 1977, giving aboriginal peoples the right to remain in self-governing communities, titles to the reserve lands were withheld, so that while the communities may live on the land, they do not actually own it. This has led to government contracts being handed out to, for example, mining operations in the Talamanca area, leading to infringements on the communities themselves, which are further hampered by the presence of missionaries in settlements like Amubrí and San José Cabécar. The twelve "Indian reserves" scattered around the country are viewed by their inhabitants with some ambivalence. As in North America, establishing a reservation system has led in many cases to a banishing of indigenous peoples to poor quality land where enclaves of poverty soon develop.

Although the persecution of native peoples in Costa Rica is nothing like as bad as in Guatemala, in recent years there have been a number of disturbing indigenous rights violations, many of them documented by CODEHUCA (Comisión para la defensa de los derechos humanos en centroamérica). At the same time there is growing recognition of the importance of preserving indigenous culture and of providing reserves with increased services and self-sufficiency. In 1994 the first indigenous bank was set up in Suretka, Talamanca, by the Bribrí and Cabecar groups, to counter the fact that major banks have often refused indigenous business and initiatives credit. In addition, indigenous groups from around the country, realizing that they need a cohesive voice and common agenda, have banded together to rent a building in San José to be used as the headquarters for a united movement.

lack of preference given to Costa Rican goods in the US market by the signing of NAFTA. Costa Rica's economy received a further shot in the arm in 1996 when the communications giant INTEL chose the country for the site of their new factory in Latin America, creating thousands of jobs.

In February 1998 PUSC candidate **Dr Miguel Angel Rodriguez** was elected president, thus continuing the trend in Costa Rican politics for the past half-century, wherein power has been traded more or less evenly between the PLN and the PUSC. The new government committed itself to solving Costa Rica's most pressing problems, making improvements to the country's dreadful road system top priority, but financing this and other major public works by private investment. Increasingly, courting private money and catering to foreign interests are the order of the day. Still, problems dog the economy in the shape of increasing balance of payments difficulties, as well as pressures on the banana market from Ecuador's growing competition – banana plantation labour in Ecuador costs $3 a day, compared to $18 in Costa Rica.

The new millennium

Costa Rica's economic future rides on a wave created in the past, a constant see-sawing between the price of the country's bananas and coffee on world markets and the amount it pays for imports. Still, the economy continues to grow, in large part fuelled by **tourism**, and the government is beginning to claw back the massive public sector deficit through increased taxation, both on basic services like electricity and water and on restaurant meals and hotel bills.

As the Costa Rican economy grows, however, so do other indicators: inflation runs at around 17 percent, while the annual **population growth** is as high as 3.2 percent per annum – Costa Rica has the highest rural population density in Latin America, and there is tremendous pressure on land. The prognosis for the *campesino*, that now nearly forgotten former backbone of the country, is not good, as peasant agriculture becomes increasingly anachronistic in the face of the big banana, coffee, palmito and pineapple plantations. Furthermore, the burden of the welfare state in Costa Rica has become increasingly difficult for the state to carry. High external debts to service the country's respected system of social welfare mean that a staggering 30 percent of the government budget goes on keeping up interest payments to foreign banks.

Meanwhile, the prognosis for the **environment** could be bleak if the authorities continue their strategy of attracting large hotel and development groups. Even bleaker is the fact that in recent years the country has gained a reputation as a **sex tourism** destination, with increasing evidence that minors are involved in the business. Even so, the country's legal and judicial institutions are doing their best to combat the country's most pressing social problems, such as drug trafficking, domestic violence and increasing crime and disorder.

Landscape and wildlife

New World animals are believed to have crossed from Asia via the Bering Strait land bridge and migrated steadily southward through North America, evolving on the way. Because of Costa Rica's own celebrated position as a land bridge between the temperate Nearctic zone to the north and the Neotropics to the south, its varied animal life features tropical forms like the jaguar, temperate-zone animals like the deer, and some unusual, seemingly hybrid combinations such as the coati.

Habitats

Although roughly the size of West Virginia, Nova Scotia, or Wales, Costa Rica has nearly as many **habitats** as the whole of the US, including forests, riverside mangroves, seasonal wetlands and offshore marine forms such as coral reefs. Costa Rica has a remarkably varied **terrain** for its size, ranging from the plains of Guanacaste, where there is often no rain for five months of the year, to the Caribbean lowlands, thick-forested and deluged with a liberal 6000mm of precipitation annually. In terms of **elevation**, too, the country possesses great diversity: from the very hot and humid lowlands of Corcovado, the terrain rises within 150km to the chilly heights of Cerro Chirripó, at 3819m. For a detailed account of the lay of the land, and the effect that altitude has on temperature and rainfall, see Basics, p.48.

Life zones

Because Costa Rica's territory is almost bewilderingly varied, with similar geographical features found in many different places, it makes sense to speak of **life zones**, a detailed system of categorization referring primarily to forest habitats, developed in 1947 by biologist L.R. Holdridge to describe particular characteristics of terrain, climate and the life they support. Although he conceived the system in Haiti, with temperature and rainfall being the main determinants, this system has been used to create ecological maps of various countries, including Costa Rica. To read more about the cloudforest see p.304; for the dry forest, turn to p.243.

The most endangered of all the life zones in Costa Rica is the **tropical dry forest**, which needs about six dry months a year. Most trees in a tropical dry forest are deciduous or semi-deciduous; some lose their leaves near the end of the dry season, primarily to conserve water. They are less stratified than rainforests, with two layers rather than three or four, and appear far less dense. Orchids flower in the silver and brown branches, and bees, wasps and moths proliferate. Animal inhabitants include iguanas, white-tailed deer and some of the larger mammals, including the jaguar. The best examples are in the northwest, especially **Guanacaste** and **Santa Rosa** national parks.

The **tropical wet forest** is home, metre per metre, to the greatest number of species of flora and fauna, including the bushmaster snake and tapir, along with jaguar and other wild cats. Here the canopy trees can be very tall (up to 70 or even 80m) and, true to its name, it receives an enormous amount of rain – typically 5000–6000mm per year. Found in lowland areas, tropical wet forest is now confined to large protected blocks, chiefly the **Sarapiquí–Tortuguero** area and the large chunk protected by **Corcovado National Park** on the Osa Peninsula.

Premontane wet forests are found upon many of Costa Rica's mountains. Some trees are evergreen and most are covered with a thick carpet of moss. These forests typically exist at a high altitude and receive a lot of rain: the cover in **Tapantí National Park** in the southwest Valle Central is a good example, as is **Braulio Carrillo**, which has all five of the montane life zones within its boundaries. Many of the same animals that exist in the tropical wet forest exist here, along with brocket deer and peccaries.

Perhaps the most famous of Costa Rica's life zones are the tropical lower montane wet forests, or **cloudforests**, which occur in very isolated patches, mainly south of Cartago and on the Pacific slopes of the Cordillera de Tilarán. The cloudforest hosts many bromeliads, including orchids, and has an understorey thick with vines; its animal life includes tapirs, pumas and quetzals. Costa Rica's best known cloudforest is at **Monteverde**.

Tropical montane rainforest occurs at the highest altitudes; the tops of **Poás** and **Irazú** volcanos are good examples. Although large mosses and ferns can be seen, much of the vegetation has a shrunken, or dwarfed aspect, due to the biting wind and lofty altitude. Animals that live here include the Poás squirrel (endemic to that volcano) and some of the larger birds, including raptors and vultures.

At the very top of the country near **Cerro El Chirripó** is the only place you'll find **tropical subalpine rain páramo**, inhospitably cold, with almost no trees. Costa Rica is the northern frontier of this particular Andean type of *páramo*. Except for hardy hawks and vultures, birds tend to shun this cold milieu, although at lower elevations you may spot a quetzal.

Mangroves, wetlands and rivers

The **mangrove** is an increasingly fragile and endangered ecosystem that occurs along tropical coastlines and is particularly vulnerable to dredging: both the Papagayo Project in Guanacaste and the *Tambor Beach Hotel* in the Central Pacific have been accused of irresponsibly draining mangroves. With their extensive root system, mangrove trees are unique for their ability to adapt to the salinity of seaside or tidal waters, or to areas where freshwater rivers empty into the ocean. Because they absorb the thrust of waves and tides, they act as a buffer zone behind which species of aquatic and land-based life can flourish unmolested. Meanwhile, the beer-coloured mangrove swamp water is like a nutritious primordial soup where a range of species can grow, including crustaceans and shrimp as well as turtles, caimans and crocodiles, and their banks are home to a range of bird life.

Birds and reptiles are especially abundant in the country's remaining **wetlands**, which are typically seasonal, caused by the flooding of rivers with the rains, only to shrink back to pleated mud flats in the dry season. The **Caño Negro** seasonal wetlands in the Zona Norte and the Río Tempisque, within the bounds of **Palo Verde National Park** in Guanacaste, are the prime wetlands in Costa Rica.

Despite increasing silting and pollution caused largely by the banana plantations, Costa Rica's **rivers** support a variety of life, from fish, including the tarpon, to migratory birds, crocodiles, caimans and freshwater turtles. The waterways that yield the best wildlife-watching are the Tortuguero canals and the Ríos San Juan, Sarapiquí, Sierpe, and the Río Tárcoles in the Carara Biological Reserve on the central Pacific coast.

Marine habitats

Costa Rica's **coral reefs**, never as extensive as those in Belize, are under threat. Much of the **Caribbean coast** was seriously damaged by the 1991 earthquake, which heaved the reefs up above the water. The last remaining ones on this side of the country are at **Cahuita** and a smaller one further south at **Manzanillo** in the Gandoca–Manzanillo Wildlife Refuge. Though the Cahuita reef has been under siege for some time by silting caused by clearing of land for banana plantations, and pesticides used in banana cultivation, you can still see some fine – extremely localized – specimens of moose horn and deer horn coral. On the **Pacific coast** the most pristine reef is at **Bahía Ballena**, protected within Costa Rica's first marine national park, and also the reef that fringes Isla del Caño, about 20km offshore from the north coast of the Osa Peninsula.

Wildlife

It is a source of constant woe for guides in Costa Rica to have to deal with tourists who have paid their national park entrance fees and then expect to be reimbursed in kind by seeing a tapir, jaguar or ocelot. Many of the country's more exotic **mammals** are either nocturnal, endangered, or made shy through years of hunting and human encroachment. Although encounters do occur, they are usually brief, with the animal in question dipping quietly back into the shadows from which it first emerged. That said, however, it's very possible you will come into (usually fleeting) contact with some of the smaller and more abundant mammals.

Despite its reputation, Costa Rica does not have Central America's most diverse vertebrate fauna – that honour goes to Guatemala. However, Costa Rican **insects** and **birds** are particularly numerous, with 850 species of birds (including migratory ones) – more than the US and Canada combined. Costa Rica is also home to a quarter of the world's known **butterflies** – more than in all Africa – thousands of moths, and scores of bees and wasps.

Birds (*pájaros, aves*)

Bird life, both migratory and indigenous, is abundant in Costa Rica and includes some of the most colourful birds in the Americas: the **quetzal**, the **toucan** and the **scarlet macaw**. Many are best observed while feeding. Guides often point out quetzals, for instance, when they are feeding from their favoured **aguacatillo** tree, and you might catch a glimpse of the hummingbird hovering over a bright flower as it feeds on its nectar.

It's only fair that any discussion of birds in Costa Rica starts with the one that so many people come see: the brilliant green and red **quetzal**. With a range historically extending from southern Mexico to northern Panamá – more or less the deliniations of Mesoamerica – the dazzling quetzal was highly prized by the Aztecs and the Maya. In the language of the Aztecs, *quetzali* means, roughly, "beautiful", and along with jade, the shimmering, jewel-coloured feathers were used as currency in Maya cities. The feathers were also worn by Maya nobles to signify religious qualities and social superiority, and formed the headdress of the plumed serpent Quetzalcoatl, the supreme Aztec god.

Hunting quetzals is particularly cruel, as it is well known that the bird cannot (or will not) live in captivity, a poignant characteristic which has made it a symbol of freedom throughout Mesoamerica. The male in particular – who possesses the distinctive feather train of up to 1.5m long – is still pursued by poachers, and the quetzal is further endangered due to the destruction of its favoured cloudforest habitat. These days the remaining cloudforests (particularly Monteverde) are among the best places to try to see the birds (March–May is best), although they are always difficult to spot, in part due to shyness and in part because the vibrant green of their feathers, seemingly so eye-catchingly bright, actually means that they blend in well with the wet and shimmering cloudforest. Quetzals are officially protected in Costa Rica in Braulio Carrillo and Volcán Poás national parks in the Valle Central, in Chirripó in the Zona Sur, and in Monteverde.

The increasingly rare **scarlet macaw** (*lapa*), with its liberal splashes of red, yellow and blue, was once common on the Pacific coast of southern Mexico and Central America. The birds, which are monogamous, live in lowland forested areas, but these days your only chance of spotting them is in Corcovado National Park on the Osa Peninsula, and perhaps the Carara Biological Refuge in the Central Pacific, Palo Verde National Park or Lomas Barbudal Biological Refuge in Guanacaste. They are usually spotted in or near their nesting holes (they nest in tree trunks), in the upper branches, or while flying high and calling to one another with their distinctive raucous sqawk.

Parakeets are still fairly numerous and are most often seen in the lowland forested areas of the Pacific coast. You're also likely to see the **chestnut-mandibled** and **keel-billed toucans** (*tucánes*), with their ridiculous but beautiful banana-shaped beaks. The chestnut-mandibled is the largest; their bills are two-tone brown and yellow. Keel-billed toucans have the more rainbow-coloured beaks and are smaller, which is sometimes taken advantage of by their larger cousins, who may drive them away from a cache of food or hound them out of a particular tree. At other times, though, both types seem to commune quite happily. Other than humans, the toucan is thought to have few predators. They can be found in both higher and lower elevations, but in Costa Rica you are most likely to see them in the Caribbean lowlands, particularly the Sarapiquí area. They are most often spotted at dawn and in the afternoon as early as 4pm or 4.30pm – although dusk is best – sitting in the open upper branches of secondary forest. They also often fly low over the road from Guápiles to Las Horquetas.

In the **waterways** and **wetlands** of the country, most birds you see are **migratory** species from the north, including herons, gulls, sandpipers and plovers. Larger marine birds – pelicans and frigatebirds for example – come from much further afield, often making the journey from New Zealand or Cape Horn. Most migratory species are in residence between January and April, though a few arrive as early as November. The seasonal lagoons of the **Río Tempisque** basin in Guanacaste are home to the largest diversity and number of freshwater birds – both migratory and resident, in Central America. **Caño Negro** in the Zona Norte is another rewarding area for bird-watching.

Permanent residents of Costa Rican river areas include **cormorants**, and **anhingas** (sometimes called "snakebirds" in English, due to their sinuous necks). **Anhingas** are fishermen, impaling their prey on the knife-point of their beaks before swallowing. The elegant, long-limbed white **ibis** often stands motionless on river-level branches and banks; harder to spot and more endangered is the giant **jabirú stork**, most often seen in Caño Negro and on the Río Tempisque in Palo Verde National Park.

Travelling the Tortuguero canals or on the Río Sierpe down to Bahía Drake on the Osa Peninsula you are likely to see a **kingfisher** (*martín pescador*). The green kingfisher, with its deep forest-green back and distinctive crown is particularly lovely. The largest colony of the Nicaraguan **grackle** (*zanate*) makes regular appearances in Caño Negro; the only place in Costa Rica where these dark, crow-like birds nest. Other water birds include **brown pelicans** (*buchón*) and the pretty pink **roseate spoonbills**, found mainly in the Río Tempisque basin, where you can also see huge clumps of nesting **night-herons** (*cuacu*). The most common bird, and the one you're likely to come across hiking or riding in cattle country, is the unprepossessing grey-white **egret** (*garça*).

Of the raptors (hawks and eagles) the **laughing falcon** (*guaco*), found all over the country, probably has the most distinct call, which sounds exactly like it's Spanish name. The "laughing" bit comes from a much lower-pitched variation, which resembles muted human laughter. The laughing falcon preys on reptiles, including venomous snakes, biting off the head before bringing the body back to its eyrie, where it drapes it over a branch, sings a duet with its mate, and proceeds to dine. The sharp-eyed, mottled brown **osprey** eagle still has a reasonably good species count, despite the blows that deforestation have dealt to its rainforest habitat. You're most likely to see ospreys patrolling the skies of the canals between Barra del Colorado and Limón or in the Gandoca–Manzanillo Wildlife Refuge. The **harpy eagles** have not fared so well, and are thought to be locally extinct, due to widespread destruction of its favoured upper-canopy habitat. There is a chance that some may still live and hunt in the interior of Corcovado National Park on the Osa Peninsula, or within the rugged La Amistad International Park in the south of the country. Their bushy crowns give them a tousled look, rather than the usual fierce appearance of raptors, and they have a delicate, hooked beak.

You're unlikely to see much of owls, as they are nocturnal, but the **tropical screech owl** (*sorococa*) is commonly heard, even in the suburbs of San José, with its distinctive whirring call that builds to a screech or laugh as it takes flight. The unremarkable brown **oropéndola**, relative of the oriole, is best-known for its distinctive basketweave nest, which looks like a lacrosse net and droops conspicuously from tree limbs all over the country, especially in the Valle Central and Chirripó.

Hardly anyone gets through a day or two in Monteverde or Santa Elena without at least hearing the distinctive, metallic call of the **three-wattled bell-bird**. If you catch a glimpse of them you'll find that they look even stranger than their clunk-sounding clarion call, with three worm-like black sacks hanging off their beak. Monteverde is also a good place to watch the antics of the tiny thumb-sized **hummingbirds** (*colibrís*), who buzz about like particularly swift, engorged bees. Thanks to their wings' unusual round hinges, humming-birds can feed on flower nectar while actually hovering. They are numerous in Costa Rica, and some local types, like the purple-throated hummingbird, are particularly pretty.

The shrunken-shouldered **vulture** (*zópilote*) is not usually considered of interest to birders. That said, it is the one bird that almost everyone will see at some point, hanging out opportunistically on the side of major highways waiting for rabbits and iguanas to be thumped beneath the wheels of a passing vehicle.

Mammals (*fauna, animales*)

Costa Rica's **mammals** range from the fairly unexotic (at least for North Americans and Europeans) white-tailed deer (*venado cola blanca*) and brocket deer (*cabra de monte*), via the seemingly antediluvian, such as Baird's tapir or "mountain cow" (*danta*), to the preternatural or semi-sacred jaguar (*tigre*).

Now an endangered species, the **jaguar** is endemic to the New World tropics and has a range from southern Mexico to northern Argentina. Although it was once common throughout Central America, especially in the lowland forests and mangroves of coastal areas, the jaguar's main foe has long been man, who has hunted it for its valuable pelt and because of its reputation among farmers as a predator of calves and pigs. It is easily tracked, due to its distinctive footprint. Incredibly, the hunting of jaguars for sport was allowed right up until the 1980s, although the trade was hampered by the fact that it is illegal to import the pelts into most countries, including the US. Though you won't see a jaguar in the wild, one of the sorriest sights in Costa Rica is the captive jaguar – in a hotel's private zoo, for example – typically kept in small cramped cages where it can do little but pace back and forth. Considered sacred by the Maya, jaguars are a very beautiful mid-sized cat; nearly always golden with black spots, and much more rarely a sleek, beautiful black. They feed on smaller mammals such as agoutis, monkeys and peccaries, and may also eat fish and birds. Not to be confused with the jaguar, the **jaguarundi** is a small cat, very rarely seen, ranging in colour from reddish to black. Little studied, the jaguarundi has short legs and a low-slung body, and is sometimes confused for the tayra, or tropical mink. They are swift and shy, and although they live in many lowland areas and forests, are very rarely encountered by walkers.

Along with the jaguar, the tapir is perhaps the most fantastical form inhabiting the Neotropical rainforest, where it is called **Baird's tapir**. A distant relative of the rhinoceros, the tapir also occurs in the tropics of southeast Asia. Rather homely, with eyes set back on either side of its head, the tapir looks something between a horse and an overgrown pig, with a stout grey-skinned body and a head that suggests an elephant with a truncated trunk. Their antediluvian look comes from their prehensile snout, small ears, and delicate cloven feet. Weighing as much as 300 kilograms and vegetarian, they are extremely shy in the wild, largely nocturnal, and stick to densely forested or rugged land: consequently they are very rarely spotted by casual rainforest walkers. The tapir has proved to be very amiable in captivity, and is certain to be unaggressive should you be lucky enough to come upon one. Like the jaguar, its main foe is man, who hunts it for its succulent meat. Nowadays the tapir is protected to a degree in the national parks and preserves.

All Costa Rica's cats have been made extremely shy through centuries of hunting. The one exception, since its pelt isn't big enough to make it a worthwhile target, is the small, sinuous-necked **margay** (*tigrillo*), with its complex black-spotted markings and large, inquisitive eyes. It has been known to peek out of the shadows and even sun itself on the rocks. The **ocelot** (*manigordo*) is similar, somewhere between the margay and jaguar in size, but is another animal you are very unlikely to see. Of all the cats, the sandstone-coloured **mountain lion** (*puma*) is said to be the most forthcoming. It's a big animal, and although not usually aggressive towards humans, should be treated with respect.

Some of the animals you are more likely to see – because of their abundance and diurnal activity – look like outsize versions or variations on temperate-zone mammals: the **agouti** or **paca** (*tepezcuintle*), a large water-rodent, for example, or the mink-like **tayra** (*tolumuco*), who may flash by you on its way up a tree. Notable for its lustrous coat and snake-like sinuosity, the tayra can be fierce if cornered. The Neotropical **river otter** (*nutria*) is an altogether friendlier creature, although extremely shy. The **coati** (often mistakenly called *coatimundi*; *pizote* in Spanish) looks like a confused combination of a racoon, domestic cat and an anteater. There is also a tropical **racoon** (*mapache*) that looks like its northern neighbour, complete with eye mask. Nearly all of these are foragers and forest-floor dwellers.

The **peccary** (*saíno*), usually described as a wild pig or boar, comes in two little-differentiated species in Costa Rica: collared or white-lipped. They can be menacing when encountered in packs, when, if they get a whiff of you – their sight is poor so they'll smell you before they see you – they may clack their teeth and growl a bit. The usual advice, especially in Corcovado National Park where they travel in groups as large as thirty, is to climb a tree. However, peccaries are not on the whole dangerous and in captivity have proved to be very affectionate, rubbing themselves against you delightedly at the least opportunity.

You may well see an **anteater** (*hormiguero*) vacuuming an anthill at some point. Of the two species that inhabit Costa Rica, you're much more likely to see the **northern tamandua**, although it is largely nocturnal. It hunts ants, occasionally bees, and termites, digging into nests using its sharp claws and inserting its proboscis-like snout into the mound to lick up its prey. Far rarer, the **silky anteater** is arboreal, a lovely golden in colour, and hardly ever seen.

Costa Rica is home to four species of monkey. Most people can expect to at least hear, if not see, the **howler monkey** (*mono congo*), especially in the lowland forests: the male has a mechanism in its thick throat by which it can make sounds which sound like those from a gorilla. Their whoops are most often heard at dawn or dusk. The **white-faced or capuchin** (*carablanca*) **monkey** is slighter than the howler, with a distinctly humanoid expression on its delicate face. This, combined with its intelligence, often consigns it to being a pet in a hotel or private zoo. The **spider monkey** (*araña*) takes its name from its spider-like ability to move through the trees employing its three limbs – the third one is its prehensile tail, which it uses to grip branches. The **squirrel monkey** (*mono tití*) is presently only found in and south of Manuel Antonio National Park. Their delicate grey and white faces have long made them attractive to pet owners and zoos, and consequently they have been hunted to near extinction in Costa Rica. However, they are extremely gregarious – though they can be easily put off by too many people tramping through Manuel Antonio – and you may well catch sight of one.

Two types of **sloths** (*perezsosos*) live in Costa Rica: the **three-toed** sloth, active by day, and the nocturnal **two-toed** sloth. True to their name, sloths move very little during the day and have an extremely slow metabolism. They are excellently camouflaged from their main predators, eagles, by the algae that often covers their brown hair. In the first instance at least they are very difficult to spot on your own; a guide will usually point one out. Scan the V-intersections in trees, particularly the middle and upper elevations: from a distance they resemble a ball of fur or a hornet's nest. Sloths present something of a mystery in their defecating habits, risking life and limb to descend to the forest floor, once a week, to defecate. Their sharp taloned claws are best suited to the arboreal universe, and outside the tree limbs they are a bit lost, exposing themselves to predation by jaguars and other animals. No one has yet come up with a solid hypothesis as to this irrational behaviour.

Costa Rica has many species of **bats** (*murciélagos*) which literally hang out sleeping on the underside of branches, where they look like rows of small grey triangles. In Tortuguero, you may see a **fishing bat** skimming the water, casting its aural net in front in search of food: being blind, it fishes by sonar. For the best bat-viewing opportunities, head to Barra Honda caves on the Nicoya Peninsula, where they roost in huge numbers.

Amphibians and reptiles
(*anfíbios, reptiles*)

There are many, many **frogs** (*ranas*) and **toads** (*sapos*) in Costa Rica. Though they seem vulnerable – small, and with few defences – many tropical frogs look after themselves by secreting poison through their skin. Using some of the most powerful natural toxins known, the frog can directly target the heart muscle of the predator, paralysing it and causing immediate death. As these poisons are transmittable through skin contact, you should never touch a Costa Rican frog. Probably the best-known, and most toxic, of the frogs, is the colourful **poison dart frog**, usually quite small, and found in various combinations of bright red and blue or green and black. Even the innocuous-looking **shore** or **beach frog** can shoot out a jet of toxins; while it may not be fatal to humans, it can kill heedless cats and dogs who try to pick it up in their mouths.

Rainforest fauna and flora have an elaborate repertoire of ruses, poisons and camouflages which they put to a variety of uses, from self-protection to pollination. Many tropical animals are well known for their gaudy colour, which can mean one of two things: warning potential predators to keep away, or flaunting an invulnerable position at the top of the food chain. Particularly notable are the birds that inhabit the rainforest canopy: toucans, parakeets and scarlet macaws, not to mention the resplendent quetzal. Unfortunately, while flaunting the fact that they have hardly any predators, these beautiful birds make themselves vulnerable to perhaps the most threatening adversary of them all: humans. Advertising toxicity is another ingenious evolutionary development. The amazingly colourful poison dart frogs are a case in point, as is the venomous coral snake. These reptiles give the "keep away" signal loud and clear to potential predators, some of whom, after successive bad experiences, build up a species memory and cease preying upon them.

Some animals are camouflage experts. Again, camouflage serves one of two purposes: to be able to hide in order to ensnare prey, or to hide in order to avoid predators. The predatorial jaguar looks exactly like the mottled light of the ground floor of the rainforest, making it easier to both hide and hunt, while the clear-winged butterfly literally disappears into the air. Sloths, too, hide from their attackers, with a greasy green alga growing on their fur, making them look even more like the clump of leaves that they already resemble.

Then there are the mimics, usually insects, which have an evolutionary ability to look like something which they are not. The *asilidae* family in particular features many mimics: flies impersonate wasps and wasps disguise themselves as bees, all in the pursuit of safety or predation.

The more common ways in which tropical frogs defend themselves are through camouflage (usually mottled brown, green or variations thereon – they blend perfectly into the tropical cover) or by jumping, a good method of escape in thick ground cover. Jumping also throws snakes – who hunt by scent, and are probably their most prevalent predator – off track. You will most likely see frogs around dusk or at night; some of them make a regular and dignified procession down paths and trails, sitting motionless for long periods before hopping off again. The chief thing you'll notice about the more common frogs is their size: they're much stouter than temperate zone frogs. Look out for the gaudy **leaf frog** (*rana calzonudo*), star of many a frog calendar. Relatively large, it is an alarming bright green, with orange hands and feet and dark blue thighs. Its sides are purple, and its eyes are pure red, to scare off potential predators.

Travelling along or past Costa Rica's waterways, you may well see **caimans** and **crocodiles**. Crocs hang out on the muddy banks, basking in the sun, while the smaller, shyer caimans will sometimes perch on submerged tree branches, scuttling away at your approach. Both are under constant threat from hunters, who sell their skin to make shoes and handbags. Pot-bellied **iguanas** are the most ubiquitous of Costa Rica's lizards, as common here as chickens are in Europe or the US. Masters of camouflage, they can occasionally be spotted on the middle and lower branches of trees and on the ground. Despite their dragon-like appearance, they are very shy, and if you do spot them, it's likely that they'll be scurrying away in an ungainly fashion. In wetlands and on rivers, watch out for a tiny form skittering across the water: this is the **"Jesus Christ" lizard** (*basilisk*), so-called for its web-like foot and speed, which allows it to "walk" on water.

Costa Rica is home to a vast array of **snakes** (*serpientes, culebras*). Many of them, both venomous and non-venomous, are amazingly beautiful: this can be appreciated more if you see them in captivity than if you come across one in the wild. That said, the chances of the latter happening – let alone getting bitten – are very slim. Snakes are largely nocturnal, and for the most part far more wary of you than you are of them.

Out of 162 species found in the country, only 22 are venomous. These are usually well camouflaged, but some advertise their danger with a flamboyance of colour. One such is the highly venomous **coral** (same in Spanish) snake which, although retiring, is easily spotted – and avoided – with its bright rings of carmine red, yellow and black. The **false coral** snake, which is not venomous, looks very similar; a guide or a ranger will be able to point out the subtle differences. Of all the Costa Rican snakes the **bushmaster** (*matabuey*) is the one of which even guardaparques are afraid. The bushmaster, whose range extends from southern Mexico to Brazil, is the largest venomous snake in the Americas – in Costa Rica it can reach a size of nearly 2m. The most aggressive of snakes, it will actually chase people, if it is so inclined. The good news is that you are extremely unlikely to encounter one, as it prefers dense and mountainous territory – Braulio Carrillo, the Sarapiquí region and Corcovado, for example – and rarely emerges during the day.

Once the inhabitant of the rainforests, the fer-de-lance or **terciopelo** has adapted quite well to cleared areas, grassy uplands, and even some inhabited stretches, although you are far more likely to see them in places which have heavy rainfall (like the Limón coast) and near streams or rivers at night. Though it can reach more than 2m in length, the terciopelo ("velvet") is well camouflaged and very difficult to spot, resembling a big pile of leaves with its grey-black skin with a light crisscross pattern. Along with the bushmaster, the terciopelo is one of the few snakes who may attack without provocation. They are usually killed when encountered, due to their venom and fairly healthy species count. These are the ones you'll see coiled in jars of formaldehyde at rainforest lodges, often on display beside the supper table.

The very pretty **eyelash viper** (*bocaracá*) is usually tan or green, but sometimes brilliant yellow when inhabiting golden palm fruit groves. Largely arboreal and generally well camouflaged, it takes its name from the raised scales around its eyes. They are quite venomous to humans and should be given a wide berth if seen hanging from a branch or negotiating a path through the groves.

Considering the competition, it's not hard to see why the **boa constrictor** (*boa*) wins the title of most congenial snake. Often with beautiful semi-triangular markings, largely retiring and shy of people, the boa is one of the few snakes you may see in the daytime. Although they are largely torpid, it is not a good idea to bother them. They have big teeth and can bite, though they are not venomous and are unlikely to stir unless startled. If you encounter one, either on the move or lying still, the best thing is to walk around it slowly, giving it a good 5m berth.

For more details on precautions when dealing with snakes, see p.22 in Basics.

Insects (*insectos, bichos*)

Costa Rica supports an enormous diversity of insects, of which the **butterflies** (*mariposas*) are the most flamboyant and sought after. Active during the day, they can be seen, especially from about 8am to noon, almost anywhere in the country. Most adult butterflies take their typical food of nectar – usually from red flowers – through a proboscis. Others feed on fungi, dung and rotting fruit. Best-known, and quite often spotted, especially along forest trails, is the fast-flying **blue morpho**, whose titanium-bright wings seem to shimmer electrically. Like other garish butterflies, the morpho uses its colour to startle or shock potential predators. Far more difficult to spot, for obvious reasons, is the **clear-winged butterfly**.

Of the annoying insects, you'll surely get acquainted with **mosquitos** (zancudos), a few of which carry malaria and dengue fever (see p.21). In hot, slightly swampy lowland areas such as the coastal Osa or the southern Nicoya peninsulas, you may also come across **purrujas**, similar to blackflies or midges. They can inflict itchy bites, as can the **chiggers** (*colorados*) that inhabit scrub and secondary growth areas, attaching themselves to the skin, leech-like, in order to feed. Though not really bothersome, the **lantern fly** (*machaca*) emits an amazingly strong mint-blue light, like a mini lightning streak – if you have one in your hotel room you'll know it as soon as you turn out the light.

The ant kingdom is well represented in Costa Rica. Chief among the rainforest salarymen are the **leaf-cutter ants**, who work in businesslike cadres, carrying bits of leaf to and fro to build their distinctive nests. The ones to watch out for are the big **bullet ants** that resemble moving blackberries (their colloquial name is **veintecuatro** – "24" – meaning that if you get bitten by one it will hurt for 24 hours). Endemic to the Neotropics, carnivorous **army ants** are often encountered in the forest, typically living in large colonies, some of more than a million individuals. They are most famous for their "dawn raids", when they pour out of a hideaway, typically a log, and divide into several columns to create a swarm. In this columnar formation they go off in search of prey – other ants and insects – which they carry back to the nest to consume.

Among the many **bees and wasps** (*abejas*, *avispas*) are aggressive **Africanized bees**, which migrated from Africa to Brazil and then north to Costa Rica, where they have colonized certain localities. Although you have to disturb their nests before they'll bother you, people sensitive or allergic to bee-stings should avoid Palo Verde National Park.

Marine life

Among Costa Rica's **marine mammals** is the sea cow or **manatee** (*manati*), elephantine in size, lumbering, good-natured and well-intentioned, not to mention endangered. Manatees all over the Caribbean are declining in number, due to the disappearance and pollution of the fresh- and saltwater riverways in which they live. In Costa Rica your only reasonable chance of seeing one is in the Tortuguero canals in Limón province, where they sometimes break the surface. At first you might mistake it for a tarpon, but the manatee's overlapping snout and long whiskers are quite distinctive.

Five species of **marine turtle** nest on Costa Rica's shores. Nesting takes place mostly at night and mostly in the context of *arribadas*; giant invasions of turtles who come ashore in their thousands on the same beach (or spot of beach) at a certain time of year, laying hundreds of thousands of eggs. Greens, hawksbills and leatherbacks come ashore on both coasts, while the Olive Ridley comes ashore only on the Pacific. The strange blunt-nosed

loggerhead, which seems not to nest in Costa Rica, can sometimes be seen in Caribbean coastal waters.

The **green turtle**, long-prized for the delicacy of its flesh, has become nearly synonymous with its favoured nesting grounds in Tortuguero. In the 1950s it was classified as endangered, and, thanks in part to the protection offered by areas like Tortuguero, is making a comeback. Some greens make herculean journeys of as much as 2000km to their breeding beaches at Tortuguero, returning to the same stretch year after year. *Arribadas* are most concentrated in June and October. Green turtles are careful nesters: if a female is disturbed by human presence she will go back to the ocean and return only when all is clear.

The **hawksbill** (*carey*), so-named for its distinctive down-curving "beak", is found all over the tropics, often preferring rocky shores and coral reefs. it used to be hunted extensively on the Caribbean coast for its meat and shell, but this is now banned. Poaching does still occur, however, and you should avoid buying any tortoiseshell that you see for sale. Hawksbills do not come ashore in *arribadas* to the extent that green turtles do, preferring to nest alone.

Capable of growing to a length of 5m, the **leatherback** (*baula*) is the largest reptile in the world. Its "shell" is actually a network of bones overlaid with a very tough leathery skin. Though it nests most concentratedly at the Parque Nacional Las Baulas on the western Nicoya Peninsula, it also comes ashore elsewhere, including Tortuguero on the Caribbean coast. The **Olive Ridley** (*lora, carpintera* – also called Pacific Ridley) turtle nests on just a few beaches, among them Playa Nancite in Santa Rosa National Park and Ostional near Nosara on the Nicoya Peninsula. They come ashore in massive *arribadas*, and, unusually, often nest during the day. Olive Ridley eggs are as prized as any, but its species count seems to be fairly healthy. Among the freshwater **turtles** (*tortugas*) in Costa Rica is the **yellow turtle** (*tortuga amarilla*), most often seen in Caño Negro. The **black river turtle** and the **snapping turtle**, about whom little is known (except that it snaps), also inhabit rivers and mangrove swamps, and may occasionally be spotted on the riverbanks.

Though **dolphins** (*delfines*) and **whales** thread themselves through the waters of the Pacific coast, it is rare to see them. Dolphins are sighted in the Manuel Antonio and Dominical areas: for the best chance of a glimpse, take a boat trip at the Ballena Marine National Park. Getting to see a **whale** (*ballena*) is even harder. Though around Dominical, Bahía Drake and Isla del Caño, both sperm and humpback whales may be around in April and May, they are not dependable in their arrivals.

Fish (*pezes*)

Costa Rica is one of the richest sports-fishing grounds in the Neotropics. The best-known big-game fish in Costa Rica is the startlingly huge white **tarpon**. Other big fish prized for their fighting spirit are **snook**, **marlin**, and **wahoo** – all of which ply the waters of Barra del Colorado, Quepos and Golfito on the Pacific coast, and Playa Flamingo in Guanacaste. More laid-back are the **trout** (*trucha*) and **rainbow bass** (*guapote*) that live in the freshwater rivers and in Laguna de Arenal. Costa Rica also features a few oddities and evolutionary throwbacks, including the undeniably homely **garfish**, which inhabits the Caño Negro wetlands and the canals of Limón province. Snorkellers will see a number of exotic fish, including enormous, plate-flat **manta rays** and the

parrotfish, so-called less for its rich colouring than for its distinctive "beak" (actually a number of tiny teeth, welded together) which is used to munch coral. There's another set of teeth at the back of the mouth that then grinds the coral down in order to digest it. Many of the white-sand beaches throughout the Caribbean, including the one just south of Cahuita, are the result of eons of coral excreted by these fish. Other sea creatures include stingrays, oysters, sponges, ugly moray eels, sea urchins, starfish, spiny lobsters, and fat, slug-like **sea cucumbers** that lie half submerged in the sea bed, digesting and excreting sand and mud.

Sharks are generally found on beaches where turtles nest, especially along the northern Caribbean coast, on Playa Ostional in the Nicoya Peninsula – although not further south in Playas Nosara – and in the waters surrounding Corcovado.

The tropical rainforest

Many myths are perpetuated about the rainforest: that it is a representation of disorder (a natural chaos); that it is full of loud and startling sounds; that it is thick and impenetrable as well as mysterious. Along with these ideas, conveyed through fiction, poetry and the more colourful representations of the first European explorers of the tropics, go the colonial notions that it is a world unfinished, awaiting the seed of civilization, and it is in itself valueless and unprofitable.

Meanwhile, it's likely that in just forty years time the world's rainforests may not exist at all outside officially protected areas. Throughout the 1980s Costa Rica had one of the highest rates of deforestation in the world. So much of Costa Rica's forest is being logged, cleared or otherwise destroyed that it is estimated that by the year 2000 Costa Rica will not only have no forests left outside the protected areas, but will actually be importing timber: until twenty years ago, bringing wood to Costa Rica would have been the equivalent of taking coals to Newcastle.

The horizontal universe

Tropical forests exist only in a thin band roughly ten degrees on either side of the equator. Their main characteristic is the diversity of life they support, being home to around 40 to 50 percent of all living things on earth (barring marine ecosystems). But in biological terms, the tropical rainforest is still the Great Unknown. Scientists have catalogued fewer than one in six of their two million species, and it is often said that we know less about the workings of the rainforest than we know about the surface of the moon.

Though "rainforest" describes the typically diverse, typically wet tropical forests you encounter in most areas of Costa Rica, there are minute differences in altitude and climate. The unifying factor is, of course, rain. To qualify, a true rainforest must receive more than 2000mm annually, dispersed relatively equitably throughout the year – many receive as much as 5000mm or 6000mm. Most of what is discussed below pertains to **primary rainforest** (bosque primario) which has not been disturbed for several hundreds, or even thousands, of years. **Secondary growth** is the vegetation that springs up in the wake of some disturbance, like cutting, cultivation or habitation.

A tropical rainforest is characterized by the presence of several layers. At its most complex it will have four layers: the **canopy**, about 40–70m high, at the very top of which are **emergent** trees, often flat-topped; the **subcanopy** beneath the emergent trees; followed by the **understorey** trees, typically 10–20m in height; and finally the **shrub**, or ground, layer. Each strata is interconnected by a mesh of horizontal lianas and climbers.

The canopy often looks like a moth-eaten umbrella opened over the lower layers. The chief function of these very tall trees is to **protect** the layers below and to filter light. In very harsh downpours or tropical storms, it is the canopy that takes the brunt of the driving wind and rain, sometimes lightning, often being lashed about like a cat-of-nine-tails in the process. Sometimes they may be felled in particularly virulent storms, falling with a great crash and creating a hole in the upper layer through which light filters to feed the understorey below.

Up to 50 percent of the rainforests' mammalian population may at some point live in the trees, compared to about 15 percent of mammals in temperate-zone forests. The majority of the animals, especially insects, remain most of the time in a specific layer of the forest; some never leave their particular "floor". Species loss – in some cases leading to local extinction, as with the canopy-dwelling harpy eagle – takes place when the rainforest is felled, in part because many animals are not able to adapt to the new topography: they need their floor in order to survive.

Rainforest vegetation has a muffled quality. Mosses beard trees, vines and lianas seemingly strangle their host trees, and huge clumps of plants sprout from the armpits formed by tree branches. This results from **co-** or **interdependency** (sometimes called "mutuality"), another distinct feature of the tropical rainforest. Over millennia, birds and plants have had the entire year in which to engage in ecological interactions, unlike in the temperate zones, where winter shuts both plants and animals down for part of the year.

Rainforest **epiphytes**, plants which grow on other plants, present an example of **commensualism**, a form of symbiosis in which one species profits from its association with another without harming or benefiting the host. Sometimes the relationship is more parasitic, with the epiphyte taking nutrients from its hosts, as is the case with **bromeliads**, which resemble the leafy top of a pineapple turned upside down and stuck on a tree. **Orchids** are the flowering parts of these pineapple-like "weeds", as are pineapples. Bromeliads' leaves trap moisture; otherwise they take their nutrients from their host.

Co-evolution is where two species evolve more or less together due to mutual influence. Flowering plants and their insect pollinators are the best example you'll see in the rainforest. Birds, too, are important in this game of mutual survival. Hummingbirds, for example, pollinate flowers by picking up small quantities of pollen when they insert their long beaks into the flower to drink nectar, then transporting it to another flower. Some plants and birds build tight-knit relationships; deep flowers are pollinated only by long-beaked hummingbirds, more shallow ones by shorter-billed birds.

Experiencing the rainforest

Among the celebrated but false characteristics attributed to rainforests are **giganticism** and **density**. In reality, most rainforest tree trunks are thin, with the taller trees seeming to rise emaciated into the sun, sprouting like mushrooms atop the other layers in their search for light. Neither is primary rainforest as impenetrable as many visitors expect. It's actually roomy on the ground. Most growth goes on above your head – what the German explorer Alexander von Humbolt called "a forest above a forest". It's the **secondary forest**, which grows up after the destruction of primary growth, that is bushy and hard to penetrate.

During the day the primary forest cover can be quite **light**, except in perennially misty cloudforests or when it is raining. It's true that aside from secondary growth or where a tree has crashed, leaving a hole in the canopy, about 90 percent of the sunlight is captured by the upper layers before it reaches the ground. But when the sun is out, the rainforest light is almost bright in its translucence, a "light darkness", that is neither day nor night; rather as if a mesh of cheesecloth has been thrown over your head.

The true tropical rainforest is also not that **colourful**, unless you take into account incrementally differing shades of green and bark. Most orchids, for instance, grow in the upper canopy, as much as 40m above the ground, although you may see flashes of red in the form of heliconias, smiling-lip-shaped red flowers that grow in symmetrical bunches at eye level or lower.

Rather than hearing frightening screeches and feeling yourself being watched from all corners by the unseen eyes of tapirs and jaguars, you are likely to feel unexpectedly lonely in the largely **silent** tropical rainforest. Most walkers, unless they are trained or with a guide, do not see very much at all of other living creatures. Almost every living thing inside a tropical rainforest is shy of humans and/or well camouflaged, and many spend their days in semi-torpor or completely hidden. During the day it can be very quiet, except for birds and howler monkeys, two of the more voluble rainforest-dwellers. Once twilight begins to fall, though, the buzz and hum of the tropical forest crescendoes noticeably, with the intertwined croaks of frogs, the mating calls of toads, the whirr of crickets and the night cries of birds.

Among the most fantastic of the rainforest trees is the **walking palm**, whose finger-like roots are prehensile; in fact, they can actually move. If it is so inclined, the palm can "walk" more than 1m in its lifetime in search of water, stepping over inconvenient obstacles like logs. **Strangler vines** initially look disturbing; a sort of arboreal version of the boa constrictor that doesn't strangle, but rather out-competes host trees for light, eventually dehydrating them to death. Everywhere in the rainforest you will see dried-up, hollowed-out dead trees surrounded by the healthy stranglers they once supported. The loops of **lianas and vines** – stranglers and otherwise – are amazingly intricate, spiralling endlessly into complex **pas-de-deux**.

One of the most startling characteristics of some rainforest trees is their **buttresses**, which help anchor the tree in thin soil where runoff is considerable. These sometimes massive above-ground roots have bark that ranges from cement-hard to long peeling strips, called **exfoliating bark**. Some trunks also have huge **spines** that look as though they could have defended a medieval garrison. These are a protective mechanism, making it difficult for animals or humans to climb the tree.

Rainforest destruction

What the large-scale **destruction** of the rainforest will mean in terms of climatic change and the chemical composition of the air is not known. We do know, however, that the tropical rainforest performs vital photosynthesizing processes, affects **weather** patterns, and mitigates the greenhouse effect and a range of other changes occuring as a result of humankind's misuse of its environment. Tropical forests, particularly those at higher altitudes, do the usually richer lowland soils a big favour by acting as **watersheds** and absorbing most of the tremendous rainfall of the tropical climate. Without them, lowland agricultural soils would be washed away by torrents of water. Each year in Costa Rica about 725 million tons of **topsoil** are lost to wind erosion and water runoff – 83 percent of this happens in areas cleared and put under pasture. When it's bucketing down in the Valle Central in October, visitors will have a hard time believing that Costa Rica has a problem with water supply, or even desertification, as is the case in Guanacaste, but the watershed deterioration caused by deforestation has put the country at risk from both.

Many of the lower orders of living things that inhabit rainforests, like fungi and bacteria, have provided **medicine** with some of its most effective treatments against serious illnesses – good arguments, in human terms, for preserving the rainforest and the medical secrets it may divulge. Also lost when rainforests are felled are forest-dwelling indigenous **peoples** and their cultures. **Animals** and birds, including jaguars, tapirs, macaws, toucans and quetzals, lose their habitats or are hounded out into the open where they are easily killed by hunters.

The reason that such destruction takes place is, quite simply, that there is serious **money** to be made from the felling of tropical forests. **Loggers** fell the forest for the hardwoods it yields, using them to make expensive furniture prized for its durability and beauty. The most famous endangered hardwoods are mahogany and purpleheart, whose names evoke their lovely deep-blooded colour. Meanwhile, the big old oak trees of the cloudforests are used for timber and charcoal. Although the major deforesters often have the implicit support of the national government because they are earners of much needed foreign currency or foreign investment, they do not have total *carte blanche*. Loggers need a government permit, and the export of many rare tropical hardwood species is prohibited. But between a certain level of corruption and illegality, logging still takes place: the Costa Rican Forestry Office reckons that illegal cutting of rainforest trees accounted for 80 percent of forest losses between 1989 and 1991, and travellers who spend any amount of time on the nation's highways can expect at some point to find themselves stuck behind a slow-moving truck loaded with massive tree trunks swathed in chains – these are tropical hardwoods, trees hundreds or even thousands of years old, that are being lost for good.

Other perpetrators fell the trees for the land the forest stands on. **Bananas**, another large foreign-currency earner, only grow well in the hot, wet tropical lowlands. Other major agro-exports include coffee, tea and macadamia nut plantations, all grown for the foreign market. **Cattle-ranchers** have been clearing areas of rainforest for years. The first horses and cows were brought to Costa Rica by the Spanish as early as 1561. By 1950, approximately an eighth of the country was under pasture. The cattle industry in Costa Rica grew rapidly from the 1960s to the 1980s, largely funded by loans from the US to encourage lower-grade beef production and by rising beef prices on the international market. During much of the 1980s Costa Rica was the world's biggest exporter of beef to the US.

Cattle ranching takes up more land and yields less than any other type of farming and ranches create little local employment in comparison to banana or coffee plantations. The tropical soils of the pasture the cattle feed on are exhausted quickly, usually within three to ten years. By 1983 about 30 percent of the country was pastureland, much of it abandoned. Of all the forests cut during the 1960s and 1970s to make way for the growth of the cattle industry, about 90 percent are not regenerable. Meanwhile, since the late 1980s, tastes, both domestic and foreign, have changed, and the consumption and price of beef has dropped to such an extent that the future of large-scale cattle ranching seems in doubt.

Despite this, cattle continue to feature heavily in Costa Rica – especially in Guanacaste, where the cowboy and hacienda culture reigns supreme. Many haciendas have turned to non-traditional activities like tourism and have scaled down their herds in order to concentrate on the new trade, although in aspect and essence they remain working cattle farms. At the other end of the scale, the smallholder keeps cattle as a way of safeguarding against the risks of subsistence-level agriculture. Cows can be milked, slaughtered or sold, and in hard times – or in an inflationary economy such as Costa Rica's – they are a good investment for the *campesino*.

Another big threat to the survival of the tropical forest is **agriculture**. The very act of felling the rainforest renders the soil useless after a couple of years. Rainforest soils are, in fact, very poor in nutrients. The complex, dense appearance of the trees represents an attempt to compensate for this, as they have to build a store of crucial chemicals above ground, in their leaves and bark. When a rainforest tree is felled by a storm or by wind and comes crashing down, the nutrients are recycled by the ground vegetation within a matter of weeks (rather than months, as in the temperate zone). In this way essential chemicals are kept in constant exchange. These chemicals are located in the thin uppermost layer of soil – the humus – which is easily washed away, turned over for cultivation, or tramped into nonexistence by cows' hooves. The main exponent of slash-and-burn techniques in Costa Rica is usually the *precarista*, or squatter *campesino*, victim of unequal land distribution and poverty.

Costa Rica has the highest rural population density in Latin America, so there is tremendous pressure on **land**. Until the second half of this century, deforestation came under the legal definition of "improvement of the land", and the state still encourages deforestation by allowing the *campesino* to establish title to isolated patches of "unwanted" land, usually in remote areas, if he clears or otherwise "improves" it. (This is not just a Costa Rican phenomenon: in the eighteenth century, pioneer settlers to Canada and the United States were granted title to land according to the same criteria.) The effects of this colonization are most conspicuous along the roadsides and in the smaller communities of the Zona Norte, where you see smallholders' shacks built on poor, stump-studded land, dotted with the odd banana tree, vegetable patches, and a few cattle and pigs.

Archeologists and biologists speculate that the pre-Columbian isthmus peoples used the slash-and-burn method to plant crops of maize and *pejiballe*, and that this did not do long-term damage to the regenerative capacities of complex forest systems (for more on this, see p.238). Rather it is large-scale colonization, followed by burning, that ensure the rainforest will never recover. Burning renders long-term cultivation of anything from grasses to carrots impossible, as it definitively destroys the humus at the topmost layer of the former rainforest soil.

Forests of the future

Any real solutions to the problem of deforestation – rather than the preservation of existing forests – appear complex or unattainable. Historically, the blame for the near-total deforestation of the Central American isthmus lies with the conquistadors, who, in the search for domestic wealth, disrupted indigenous forms of sustainable cultivation to grow export crops, effectively turning the country into a coffee-and-banana republic. The concerns of the domestic elites and the consumer demands of the countries that import Costa Rican goods make it difficult to break the pattern. In what is essentially a third-world country, with little economic room for manoeuvre, it seems Costa Rica's rainforest can no longer just exist; instead, it must pay its own way in order to survive. In short, it must become **sustainable**.

A recent development in the sustainable use of rainforests is the entry of large **pharmaceutical** companies into the conservation effort. INbio (National Institute of Biodiversity) was founded in San José in 1989 as the first institute of its kind in the world, and is devoted to taking an entire inventory of Costa Rica's species, and training locals in species collection procedures. Many lower-order rainforest flora like fungi and bacteria are thought to possess potential anti-cancer, rheumatoid, and hypertension agents. INbio has recently signed a lucrative contract with Merck, one of the world's largest pharmeceutical companies, who have guaranteed that INbio (and the state) will receive "royalties" on any drugs successfully developed from samples INbio sends for investigation.

Debt payments and ecological concerns can even be successfully intertwined in **"debt-for-nature"** swaps. A complex arrangement still in the pioneering stage, this scheme allows organizations like the World Wide Fund for Nature to purchase a piece of Costa Rica's foreign debt, usually at a discount. Costa Rica's government in return issues short-term government bonds. The funds raised by selling these bonds to investors are funnelled into conservation. For the first world foreign banks and organizations who participate, debt-for-nature is seen in purely economic terms: an investment in the environment. Philosophically speaking, though, some justify it as the Third World being "paid back" for the First World's ravages, including carbon monoxide emissions and the deforestation that has long been encouraged by the markets and tastes of the developed world.

Conservation and tourism

Costa Rica is widely seen as being at the cutting edge of worldwide conservation strategy, an impressive feat for a tiny Central American nation. At the centre of Costa Rica's internationally applauded conservation effort is a complex system of national parks and wildlife refuges, which protect a full 25 percent of its territory, one of the largest percentages of protected land among Western-hemisphere nations. These statistics are used with great effect to attract tourists and, along with Belize, Costa Rica has become virtually synonymous with ecotourism in Central America.

On the other hand, the National Parks Service does not possess the funds to protect adequately more than half the boundaries of these areas, which are under constant pressure from logging and squatters (*precaristas*), and to a lesser extent from mining interests. In addition, the question uppermost in the minds of conservationists and biologists is what, if any, damage is being caused by so many feet walking through the rainforests.

Conservation in the New World tropics

The **traditional view** of conservation is a European one of preserving, museum-like, pretty animals and flowers; an idea that was conceived and upheld by relatively wealthy Old World countries in which the majority of the forests have long-since disappeared. In the contemporary world, this definition of conservation no longer works, and certainly not in the New World tropics, besieged as they are by lack of resources, huge income inequities, legislation that lacks bite, and the continual appetite of the world market for tropical hardwoods, not to mention the Old World zeal for coffee and picture-perfect supermarket fruits.

There's a leftist perspective on conservation that sees an imperialistic, bourgeois and anti-*campesino* agenda among the large conservation organizations of the North. By this reckoning, saving the environment is all very well but does little for the day-to-day realities of the 38 percent or so of Costa Rica's population who live below the poverty line. These people have, in many cases, been made landless and impoverished by, for instance, absentee landowners speculating on land (in the Zona Norte and in Guanacaste) or by the pulling-out of major employers like the United Fruit Company (in the Zona Sur near Golfito and on the Osa Peninsula). Many are left with simply no choice but to engage in the kind of activity – be it gold-panning or slash-and-burn agriculture – which is universally condemned by conservationists in the North.

Conservation in Costa Rica

Costa Rica has a long history of conservation-consciousness, although it has taken different forms and guises. As early as 1775, laws were passed to limit the destructive impact of *quemas*, or brush-burning. Meanwhile, a vogue developed in Europe for **botanical gardens**. The period from 1635 to 1812 saw the birth of some of Europe's most splendid gardens – including London's Kew Gardens, founded in 1730. Scientists-cum-adventurers in search of knowledge and botanists in search of flora descended upon the Neotropics.

The bulk of **preservation laws** were passed after 1845, concurrent with Costa Rica's period of greatest economic and cultural growth. That said, most of this legislation was directed at protecting resource extraction rather than the areas themselves – to guard fishing and hunting grounds and to conserve what were already seen as valuable timber supplies. In 1895 laws were passed protecting water supplies and the establishment of *guardabosques* (forest rangers) to fight the *quemas* caused by the regular burning of deforested land and pasture by cattle-ranchers. The forerunners of several institutions later to be important to the development of conservation in Costa Rica were founded by the end of the nineteenth century, including the Museo Nacional and the Instituto Físico Geográfico.

Much of the credit for helping establish Costa Rica's system of national parks has to go to **Olof Wessberg** and **Karen Morgenson**, longtime foreign residents who in 1963, largely through their own efforts, founded the Reserva Natura Absoluta Cabo Blanco near their home on the southwest tip of the Nicoya Peninsula. Wessberg and Morgenson helped raise national consciousness through an extensive campaign in the mid-1960s, so that by the end of the decade there was broad support for the founding of a national parks service. In 1969 Santa Rosa National Monument and Park was declared, and in 1970 the SPN (Servicio de Parques Nacionales) was officially inaugurated. Spearheaded by a recently graduated forester, Mario Boza, the system developed slowly at first, as the law which established Santa Rosa really existed only on paper: neighbouring farmers and ranchers continued to encroach on the land for pasture and brush-burning as before.

Although it remains a mystery, the murder of Olof Wessberg in 1975 on the Osa Peninsula is an illustration of the powerful interests that are thwarted by conservation. Wessberg was conducting a preliminary survey in Osa to assess the possibility of a national park there (the site of modern-day Corcovado). Although his assailant – the man who had offered to guide him – was caught, a motive was never discovered and the crime has not been satisfactorily solved.

The case of Tortuguero

National parks are now such an entrenched part of Costa Rica's landcape that they might be taken to have always been there. In fact most have been established in the last 25 years and the process of creating them is not always smooth. Tortuguero National Park on the Caribbean coast is a case in point.

Turtle Bogue (the old Miskito name for Tortuguero) had always been isolated. Even today access is by fluvial transport or air only, and before the dredging of the main canal in the 1960s it was even more cut off from the rest of the country. Most of the local people were of Miskito or Afro-Caribbean extraction, hunting and fishing and living almost completely without consumer goods. There was virtually no cash economy in the village, with local trade and barter being sufficient for most people's needs.

In the 1940s, lumbering began in earnest in the area. A sawmill was built in the village, and during the next two decades the area experienced a boom. The local lumber exhausted itself by the 1960s, but in the twenty-year interim it brought outsiders and a dependence on cash-obtainable consumer goods. Simultaneously, the number of green sea turtles began to decline rapidly, due to overfishing and egg harvesting, and by the 1950s the once-numerous turtle was officially endangered. The alarm raised by biologists over the green turtle's preciptous decline paved the way for the establishment, in 1970, of Tortuguero National Park, protecting 30 of the 35 kilometres of turtle-nesting beach and extending to more than 200 square kilometres of surrounding forests, canals and waterways. The establishment of this protective area put former sources of income off-limits to local populations, and villagers who had benefited from the wood-and-turtle economy either reverted to the subsistence and agricultural life they had known before or left the area in search of a better one. Nowadays, thirty years after the park was officially established, many locals make a good living off the increasing amount of tourism it brings, especially those with their own independent businesses, although others are relegated to low-paid positions in hotels and other services.

The establishment of the Tortuguero National Park effectively broke the boom-and-bust cycle so prevalent in the tropics, whereby local resources are used to extinction, leaving no viable alternatives after the storm has passed. In Tortuguero the hardwoods have made a bit of a comeback, and the green turtle's numbers are up dramatically from their low point in the 1950s and 1960s. Considering the popularity of the national park and its lagoons and turtle tours, there's no doubt that conservation and protection of Tortuguero's wildlands will have lasting benefits to locals, although there is some question as to how a tiny community like Tortuguero can absorb such high levels of tourism and retain its cultural integrity.

Under the Arias government a national conservation strategy was drafted in 1988, and soon after his election victory in 1994, president José Maria Figueres proclaimed, "We will build a constructive alliance with nature." The money to back these plans has come chiefly from increased taxation, something the country's middle and lower classes resent. His government has recently introduced a comprehensive range of tax hikes, including an electricity tax to encourage energy conservation and a carbon tax whose revenue will be directed to replanting tropical forests on exhausted cattle pastures. Figueres has also pledged to double the area of the country covered by national parks and wildlife refuges.

In autumn 1994 the government and the SPN raised entrance fees to most of the country's parks overnight by a thousand percent to $15. Uproar ensued, and even Costa Ricans (who continue to pay $1.50) could be heard to comment that the prices foreigners were being asked to pay were simply too high (following the outcry, the entrance charge was reduced to $6). Now the dust has settled, it is hoped that the fees will result in improved management, higher salaries and better training for rangers, and the purchase of more lands for preservation.

Eco-paradise lost: pesticides and pollution

There are, however, flaws in this Garden of Eden. Chief among them is the importance of the **agro-export** economy. The growth of the large-scale agro-industries depends on a continual supply of cheap labour and land, and the **pollution** wreaked by the pesticides used in banana plantations – the country's major agro-export – is becoming an increasing threat. Foreign consumers attach an amazing level of importance to the appearance of supermarket bananas and pineapples, and about 20 percent of potentially dangerous pesticides used in the cultivation of bananas serve only to improve the look of the fruit and not, as it is often thought, to control pestilence. Travellers who pass through banana plantations in Costa Rica or who take river trips, especially along the Río Sarapiquí, can't fail to notice the ubiquitous blue plastic bags. The pristine appearance of Costa Rican bananas are due largely to the fact that they grow inside these pesticide-lined bags, which make their way into waterways where they are fatally consumed by fish, mammals (such as the manatee) or iguanas. In the Río Tempisque basin armadillos and crocodiles are thought to have been virtually exterminated by agricultural pesticides.

Animals are not alone in being at risk from pesticides. In 1987 a hundred Costa Rican plantation workers sued Standard Fruit, Dow Chemical and Shell Oil for producing a pesticide that is a known cause of sterility in banana-plantation workers. Although the workers' claims were upheld in US courts, the companies have appealed. Since then several harmful pesticides have been banned, although every year six percent of all Costa Rican banana workers present claims for incidents involving exposure to pesticides – the highest such rate in the world.

Conservation initiatives

In recent years Mario Boza, a prominent conservationist, has been advocating a strategy of **macro-conservation**. By uniting concerns and "joining up" chunks of protected land, he argued, the macro-areas will allow larger protected areas for animals who need room to hunt, like jaguars and pumas. Most of all, they will allow countries to make more effective joint conservation policies and decisions. Macro-conservation projects currently include the Proyeto Paseo Pantera (all of Mesoamerica), El Mundo Maya (Belize, El Salvador, Guatemala, Honduras and Mexico), Si-a-Paz (Nicaragua and Costa Rica) and La Amistad International Park and Biosphere Reserve (Costa Rica and Panamá).

Arguably, however, the most revolutionary change in conservation management, and the one most likely to have the biggest pay-off in the long term, is the shift toward **local initiatives**. Some projects are truly local, such as the tiny grassroots organization TUVA and its selective logging of naturally felled

Conservation organizations in Costa Rica

The following list represents just a sample of the large number of conservation organizations working in Costa Rica, and there are many more local operations in addition. For details of voluntary conservation opportunities in Costa Rica, see p.63.

Fundación Neotropica, Aptdo 236-1002, Paseo de los Estudiantes, San José (☎253-2130, fax 253-4210). Well-established organization that works with several small-scale and (typically) local conservation initiatives in Costa Rica. Their Curridabat office sells posters, books and T-shirts in aid of funds. Accepts donations.

Rainforest Action Costa Rica, PO Box 99, Saxmundham, Suffolk, IP17 2LB, UK (☎01728/668501, fax 668680). A new programme run by the UK-based World Wide Land Conservation Trust. All donations go towards purchasing a piece of Costa Rican rainforest (£50 per acre is the current going price). Working closely with the Massachusetts Audobon society, they are particularly active on the Osa Peninsula, where they have been instrumental in blocking a planned woodchip mill and dock.

World Wide Fund for Nature, 1250 24th St NW, Washington DC, 20037 USA (☎202/293-4800); 90 Eglington Ave E, Suite 504, Toronto, Ontario M4P 2Z7 (☎416/489-8800); Panda House, Weyside Park, Godalming, Surrey GU7 1XR (☎01483/26444). Long a donor to projects in the Monteverde area, the WWF has recently expanded their funding to CATIE, a tropical agriculture research centre which acts as their Costa Rica office. They also support negotiations for debt-for-nature swaps.

rainforest trees on the Osa Peninsula, or the ecotourism co-operative of Las Delicias in Barra Honda on the Nicoya Peninsula.

Another initiative, even more promising in terms of how it affects the lives of many rural-based Costa Ricans, is the creation of **"buffer zones"** around some national parks. In these zones *campesinos* and other smallholders can do part-time farming, are allowed restricted hunting rights and receive education about the ecological and economic value of the forest. Locals may be trained as nature guides, and *campesinos* may be given incentives to enter into non-traditional forms of agriculture and ways of making a living which are less environmentally destructive.

In recent years Costa Rica's **waste disposal problems** have given the country a garbage nightmare, culminating in a scandal in 1995 over the overflowing of the Río Azul site, San José's main dump. The government fully recognizes the irony of this – rubbish lining the streets of a country with such a high conservation profile – and in an admirable, typically Tico grass-roots initiative, legions of schoolkids are now sent on rubbish-collecting after-school projects and weekend brigades. Even more ingenious is the national movement which sends Costa Rican schoolchildren to national parks and other preserves as **volunteers** to work on conservation projects during school holidays, thus planting the seeds for a future generation of dedicated – or at least aware – conservationists.

Tourism

Around 700,000 tourists a year come to Costa Rica – mostly from the US, Canada and Europe – an incredible number, considering that the population of the country itself is only a little over three million. In 1994, revenue to Costa

Rica from tourism was $700 million or more, surpassing earnings by banana exports for the first time in the country's history. In the North American winter months of December to March, it is estimated that the country's hotel rooms are at near-100 percent occupancy. Ten years ago it seemed unlikely that this small Central American country, peaceful but off the beaten track, would attract so many visitors. Along with the considerable charms of the country itself, its popularity today is linked with the growing trend toward eco-tourism.

If managed properly, low-impact **eco-tourism** is one of the best ways in which forests, beaches, rivers, mangroves, volcanos and other natural formations can pay their way – in *dólares* – while remaining pristine and intact. However, eco-tourism is a difficult term to define. It was often seen in relation to what it was not: package tourism, wherein visitors have limited contact with nature and with the day-to-day lives of local people. But as more and more organizations and businesses hijack the "eco" prefix for dubious uses, the authentic eco-tourism experience has become increasingly difficult to pin down. One of the best attempts has been put forward by ATEC, the Talamancan Eco-tourism and Conservation Association, which seeks to promote, as it says, "socially responsible tourism" by integrating local Bribrí and Afro-Caribbean culture into tourists' experience of the area, as well as giving residents pride in their unique cultural heritage and natural environment. Their definition is:

> Eco-tourism means more than bird books and binoculars. Eco-tourism means more than native art hanging on hotel walls or ethnic dishes on the restaurant menu. Eco-tourism is not mass tourism behind a green mask.
>
> Eco-tourism means a constant struggle to defend the earth and to protect and sustain traditional communities. Eco-tourism is a cooperative relationship between the non-wealthy local community and those sincere, open-minded tourists who want to enjoy themselves in a Third World setting and, at the same time, enrich their consciousness by means of significant educational and cultural experience.

There are more cynical views. For some, eco-tourism is a PR concept with a nice ring, but all in all no less destructive or voyeuristic than regular (package-holiday) tourism. Most, though, argue that if people are going to travel, they may as well do so in a low-impact manner that reduces destruction of the visited environment, and promotes cultural exchange.

Several pioneering projects in Costa Rica have set out to combine tourism with sustainable methods of farming, rainforest preservation, and scientific research. Some of these, like the Rainforest Aerial Tram and the Monteverde Cloudforest Reserve, are the most advanced of their kind in the Americas, if not the world. Not only does the Aerial Tram provide a fascinating glimpse of the tropical canopy – normally completely inaccessible to human eyes – but also offers a rare safe and stable method for biologists to investigate this little-known habitat. Income from visitors is funnelled into maintaining and augmenting the surrounding reserve. Monteverde, meanwhile, merely in preserving a large piece of complex tropical forest, gives scientists a valuable and stomping ground for taxonomic study. Tourism is just one of the main activities in the reserve, which has been a research ground for tropical biologists from all over the world, and provides revenue for maintenance and, hopefully, future expansion.

Rara Avis, a private rainforest preserve in the Sarapiquí area northeast of San José, is one of the larger and better established of such projects. The result of years of work by Amos Bien, a former administrator at nearby La Selva Biological Station, Rara Avis seeks not only to provide a memorable experience for those interested in tropical rainforests, but also to find ways of profitably harvesting rainforest products and at the same time give something back to the local community, offering small farmers living on the edges of deforested land a chance to make a profit from the forest without clearing it for cattle.

The huge growth of tourism in the country worries many Costa Ricans, even those who make their living from it. Is it just a fad that will fade away, only to be replaced by another unprepared country-of-the-moment? What – if any – are the advantages of having an economy led by tourism instead of the traditional exports of bananas and coffee?

More alarming is what many Costa Ricans see as the virtual purchase of their country by foreigners. Though many hotels and businesses are still Costa Rican-owned and managed, entire areas on the Pacific coast may as well be plastered with "Se Vende" signs as the government gears itself up to sell off yet more national resources and industries in its quest for foreign investment. It remains to be seen what effect this might have on small communities and local cultures.

At times the government seems bent on turning the country into a high-income tourist enclave. North Americans and Europeans will still consider many things quite cheap, but Costa Rica is already the most expensive country to visit in the region, and recently the tourism minister was quoted in the national press as saying that he had no qualms about discouraging "backpackers" (meaning budget tourists) from coming to Costa Rica. Better-heeled tourists, the thinking goes, not only make a more significant investment in the country dollar for dollar, but are more easily controlled, choosing in the main to travel in tour groups or to stay in big holiday resorts such as the Papagayo Project in Guanacaste and the *Hotel Playa Tambor* on the Nicoya Peninsula.

However, tourists with a genuine concern and interest in the country's flora, fauna and cultural life can choose from a variety of places to spend their money constructively, including top-notch rainforest lodges that have worked hard to integrate themselves with their surroundings. And those who want to rough it can still do so heroically in places like Corcovado and Chirripó. For now, at least, Costa Rica is one of the few countries in the world where eco-tourism can viably outlast and out-compete other, potentially more damaging, types of tourism.

Ecotourism codes of conduct

Though well-meaning, ecotourism codes of conduct can seem preachy and presumptuous. Still, in any attempt to define the term, or to go any way towards understanding its aims, it's useful to know what the locally accepted guidelines are. The Associación Tsuli, the Costa Rican branch of the Audubon Society, has developed its own short code of conduct for "Environmental Ethics for Nature Travel":

1 Wildlife and natural habitats must not be needlessly disturbed.

2 Waste should be disposed of properly.

3 Tourism should be a positive influence on local communities.

4 Tourism should be managed and sustainable.

5 Tourism should be culturally sensitive.

6 There must be no commerce in wildlife, wildlife products, or native plants.

7 Tourists should leave with a greater understanding and appreciation of nature, conservation and the environment.

8 Tourism should strengthen the conservation effort and enhance the natural integrity of places visited.

Books

The most comprehensive volumes written on Costa Rica tend to be about **natural history** – many make better introductions to what you'll see in the country than the glossy literature pumped out by the government tourist board and most guidebooks. Frustratingly, many of the most informative works on both natural and cultural history are out of date or out of print (designated "o/p" in the list below). You'll find a number of the titles listed below in San José bookshops, but don't expect to see them elsewhere in the country.

Those interested in **Costa Rican fiction** (which is alive and well, although not extensively translated or known abroad) will have much richer and varied reading with some knowledge of Spanish. Costa Rica has no single internationally recognized towering figure in its national literature, and in sharp contrast to other countries in the region the most sophisticated and best-known writers in the country are women. Carmen Naranjo is the most widely translated, with six novels and two short-story collections (plus some of the country's most prestigious literary awards) to her name, but there are a number of lesser-read writers, including the brilliant Yolanda Oreomuno, and an upsurge of younger women, tackling contemporary social issues like domestic violence and alcoholism in their fiction and poetry. The publication in the 1930s of Carlos Luis Fallas' seminal novel *Mamita Yunai*, about labour conditions in the United Fruit Company banana fields of Limón province sparked a wave of "proletarian" novels, which became the dominant form in Costa Rican fiction until well into the 1970s. Until recently Costa Rican fiction also leant heavily on picturesque stories of rural life with some writers – usually men – drawing on the country's wealth of fauna. There are a number of *cuentos* (stories), fable-like in their simplicity and not a little ponderous in their symbolism, featuring turtles, fish and rabbits as characters.

Travel narratives

Peter Ford, *Tekkin a Waalk* (UK, Flamingo, o/p). Journalist Ford was based in Managua for most of the terrible 1980s. After that his idea of a holiday seems to have been to "tek a waalk" (as it's called in the local patois) along the eastern coast of the isthmus. In the very short part of the book that deals with Costa Rica, Ford's boatmen overshoot the river entrance to Greytown, Nicaragua, and end up in the northeastern Costa Rican village of Barra del Colorado, much to the chagrin of the *migración* – Ford must be one of the few people ever to be deported from Costa Rica.

Paul Theroux, *The Old Patagonian Express: By Train through the Americas* (US, Houghton Mifflin/UK, Penguin). Somewhat out of date (Theroux went through about twenty years ago), but a great read nonetheless. Laced with the author's usual tetchy black humour and general misanthropy, the descriptions of his two Costa Rican train journeys (neither of which still run) to Limón and to Puntarenas remain apt – as is the account of passing through San José, where he meets American men on sex-and-booze vacations.

Culture and folk traditions

Roberto Cabrera, *Santa Cruz Guanacaste: una approximación a la historia y la cultura popular* (San José, Ediciones Guayacán). The best cultural history of Guanacaste, written by a respected Guanacastecan sociologist. Verbal snapshots of nineteenth- and twentieth-century hacienda life, accounts of bull riding, and details of micro-regional dances such as the *punto guanacasteco* (adopted as the national dance), *El torito* and the veiled dance.

★ **Paula Palmer**, *What Happen: A Folk History of the Talamanca Coast* (San José, Ecodesarrolos). The definitive – although now dated – folk history of the Afro-Caribbean community on Limón province's Talamancan coast. Palmer first went to Cahuita in the early 1970s as a Peace Corps vol-

unteer, later to return as a sociologist, collecting oral histories from older members of the local communities. Great stories and atmospheric testimonies of pirate treasure, ghosts and the like; complemented by photos and accounts of local agriculture, foods and traditional remedies.

Paula Palmer, Juanita Sánchez and Gloria Mayorga, *Taking Care of Sibö's Gifts* (San José, Editorarama). Manifesto for the future of Bribrí culture, ecological survival of the *talamanqueña* ecosystems and a concise explication of differing views of the land and people's relationship to it held by the *ladinos* and Bribrí on the KéköLdi indigenous reserve.

Conservation

★ **Catherine Caulfield**, *In the Rainforest* (US, University of Chicago Press). One of the best introductions to the rainforest, dealing in an accessible fashion with many of the issues covered in the more specialized titles. Her chapter on Costa Rica is a wary elucidation of the destruction that cattle ranching in particular wreaks, as well as an interesting profile of the farming methods used by the Monteverde community.

Marcus Colcheser and Larry Lohmann (eds), *The Struggle for Land and the Fate of the Forests* (US & UK, Zed Books). A volume of essays that divides rainforest issues into general theoretical discussions, followed by case studies. Although Costa Rica is covered only in passing, the chapter on Guatemala introduces relevant points, while the brief and accessible history of agrarian reform in Latin America puts the *campesino* and landlessness issues of Costa Rica in context.

Luis Fournier, *Desarrollo y perspectivas del movimiento conservacionista costarricense* (San José, EDUCA).

Seminal, if dry, survey of conservation policy from the dawn of the nation until present, by one of Costa Rica's most eminent scientists and conservationists.

Susanna Hecht and Alexander Cockburn, *The Fate of the Forest: Developers, Destroyers and Defenders of the Amazon* (US, Schocken, o/p/UK, Penguin). The best single book readily available on rainforest destruction, this exhaustive volume is written with a sound knowledge of Amazonian history. The beautiful prose dissects some of the more pervasive myths about rainforest destruction, and it's comprehensive enough to be applicable to any forested areas under threat in the New World tropics.

William Weinberg, *War on the Land: Ecology and Politics in Central America* (US & UK, Zed Books). Just one chapter, but a good one, devoted to Costa Rica. While not failing to congratulate the country for its conservation achievements, the author also reveals the internal wranglings of conservationist policy.

History and current affairs

Tony Avirgan and Martha Honey, *La Penca: On Trial in Costa Rica, the CIA vs. the Press* (San José, Editorial Porvenir). Avirgan, a journalist and longtime resident of San José, was wounded at the La Penca news conference bombing in 1984. After this, he and Honey sunk their teeth into the dark underbelly of US/CIA politics and operations in the area during the years of the Nicaraguan Civil War. In contrast to her more recent and more definitive book (see below), Honey concludes here that the attack was carried out by the CIA.

Mavis Hiltunen Biesanz, Richard Biesanz, Karen Zubris Biesanz, *The Ticos: Culture and Social Change in Costa Rica* (US, Lynne Reiner). An intriguing blend of quantitative and qualitative research, supported by personal interviews with many Costa Ricans, this book seeks to get under the skin of Costa Rican society, examining (amongst other things) government, class and ethnic relations, the family, health and sport, and managing to be rigorous and anecdotal at the same time.

Richard Biesanz, Karen Zubris Biesanz and Mavis Hiltunen Biesanz, *The Costa Ricans* (US, Prentice Hall, o/p). Rather outdated generalizations and idealizations about the Costa Rican "character". However, though descriptive rather than analytical, many of the authors' observations and conclusions, especially about sexual conduct, inequality and marriage, ring true.

★ Tjabel Daling, *Costa Rica In Focus: A Guide to the People, Politics and Culture* (US, Interlink/UK, Latin America Bureau). The most authoritative and up-to-date country guide, entertainingly illustrated with bits of Costa Rican current life, such as billboards and labels. The text offers an especially clear-eyed cultural and social analysis.

Marc Edelman and Joanne Kenen (eds), *The Costa Rica Reader* (US, Grove Atlantic, o/p). The best single introduction to the country for the general reader. The chronologically arranged essays are mainly by respected Costa Rican historians, academic in tone but not inaccessible. See especially Chilean sociologist Diego Palma's essay on current Costa Rican politics and class conflict, which exposes the myth of Costa Rica as a haven of middle-class democracy.

Omar Hernandez, Eugenia Ibarra and Juan Rafael Quesada (eds), *Discriminación y racismo en la historia costarricense* (San José, Editorial de la Universidad de Costa Rica). Most of these essays are written in the language and form of legal case studies, but nonetheless provide a history of the racial bias of legal discrimination in Costa Rica, and that of ethnicity in human rights abuses. Interesting counterpoint to Costa Rica's reputation for harmonious social relations, although probably only of use to specialists and those with a particular interest in race issues.

Martha Honey, *Hostile Acts – US Policy in Costa Rica in the 1980s* (US & UK, University of Florida Press). Those sceptical of elaborate conspiracy theories may have their minds changed by this exhaustively researched, weighty volume detailing the US's "dual diplomacy" against Costa Rica in the 1980s. In this heroic volume Honey concludes that the La Penca bomber was a leftist Argentine terrorist with connections to Nicaragua's Sandinista government.

Silvia Lara and Tom Barry, *Inside Costa Rica* (US, Inter-Hemispheric Resource Center/UK, Latin America Bureau). One title that will bring you up to date with most aspects of the country, although it has little to say about tourism, conservation, and culture. Left-leaning, argumentative, and analytical, the authors refuse to toe the party line on Costa Rica, and though the style is factual and somewhat dry, it is enlivened by flashes of humour and apt, well-supported conclusions.

Michael A. Seligson, *Peasants of Costa Rica and the Development of Agrarian Capitalism* (US & UK, University of Wisconsin). The best single history available in English, although only a university or specialist library will have it. Much wider in scope than the title suggests, this is an excellent intermeshing of ethnic and racial issues, economics and sociology along with hard-core analysis of the rise and fall of the Costa Rican peasant.

Various, *Between Continents, Between Seas: Precolumbian Art of Costa Rica* (US, Harry Abrams, o/p). Produced as a catalogue to accompany the exhibition that toured the US in

1982, this is the best single volume on pre-Conquest history and craftsmanship, with illuminating accounts of the lives, beliefs and customs of Costa Rica's pre-Columbian peoples as interpreted through artefacts and excavations. The photographs, whether of jade pendants, Chorotega pottery or the more diabolical of the Diquis' gold pieces, are uniformly wonderful.

Elías Zamora, *Acosta ethnografía histórica de Costa Rica, 1561 y 1615* (Spain, Universidad de Sevilla). Hugely impressive archival research that reconstructs the economic, political and social life in the province in the years immediately following the Spanish invasion. A masterwork, distressingly difficult to get hold of.

Wildlife, natural history and field guides

Paul H. Allen, *The Rainforests of the Golfo Dulce* (US, Stanford University Press). Obviously a labour of love, this is the best descriptive account of the lush rainforest cover found in the southwest of the country. It's a scientific book, with complete taxonomic accounts, although still very readable and with interesting photographs.

★ **Les Beletsky**, *Costa Rica: Ecotraveller's Wildlife Guide* (Academic Press). This readable wildlife and natural history handbook, written by a professional wildlife biologist, is a good compromise between a guidebook and a heavy field guide. The text is accompanied by photos and drawings; the plates showing species with photos of their typical habitats are particularly useful. Includes detailed information on about 220 bird, 50 mammal and 80 amphibian and reptile species.

Mario A. Boza, *Costa Rica's National Parks* (available in San José from Editorial Heliconia). Essentially a coffee-table book, this informed volume is a great taster for what you will find in the national parks. The text is in Spanish and English, and there are uniformly stunning photographs.

A.S. and P.P. Calvert, *A Year of Costa Rican Natural History* (US, Macmillan). Although now very old

– the year in question is 1910 – this is a brilliant, insightful and charmingly enthusiastic travelogue/natural history/autobiography by American biologist and zoologist husband and wife team. It features much, much more than natural history, with sections such as "Blood Sucking Flies", "Fiestas in Santa Cruz" and "Earthquakes". The best single title ever written on Costa Rica – the only problem is finding it. Try good libraries and specialist bookstores.

Stephen E. Cornelius, *The Sea Turtles of Santa Rosa National Park* (San José, Fundación de Parques Nacionales, o/p). Field guide to the four species of marine turtles who nest in Santa Rosa, and elsewhere. Full of detail about marine turtles' habits, but difficult to find.

Philip J. De Vries, *The Butterflies of Costa Rica and their Natural History* (US & UK, Princeton University Press). Much-admired volume, really for serious butterfly enthusiasts or scientists only, but illustrated with beautiful colour plates so you can marvel at the incremental differences between various butterflies.

Louise H. Emmons and François Feer, *Neotropical Rainforest Mammals – a Field Guide* (US, University of Chicago Press). Not written specifically for Costa Rica, but most mammals found in the country are covered here. Huge but portable, with more than 300 illustrations, and useful for identifying the flash of colour and fur that speeds past you as you make yet another fleeting contact with a rainforest mammal.

Joseph Franke, *Costa Rica's National Parks* (Mountaineers Books). A park-by-park discussion of the system of national parks and wildlife refuges, with detailed information on hiking and trails, as well as a topographical and environmental profile of each park. Useful if you're intending to spend any time hiking in more than one or two parks.

Daniel H. Janzen, *Costa Rican Natural History* (US, University of Chicago Press). The definitive reference source, with accessible, continuously fascinating species-by-species accounts, written by a highly influential figure, involved on a policy level in the governing of the national parks system. The introduction is especially worth reading, dealing in a cursory but lively fashion with tectonics, meteorology, history and archeology. Illustrated throughout with gripping photographs. Available in paperback, but still doorstep-thick.

Michael W. Mayfield and **Raphael E. Gallow**, *The Rivers of Costa Rica: A Canoeing, Kayaking and Rafting Guide* (US, Menasha Ridge Press). An essential book for serious white-water rafters and river or sea kayakers. Stretch-by-stretch and rapid-by-rapid accounts of the best rafting rivers south of the Colorado, including the Reventazon and Pacuaré.

Sam Mitchell, *Pura Vida: The Waterfalls and Hot Springs of Costa Rica* (US, Menasha Ridge). Jolly, personably written guide to the many little-known waterholes, cascades, and waterfalls of Costa Rica. Complete with detailed directions and accounts of surrounding trails. Available in English in San José.

Donald Perry, *Life Above the Jungle Floor* (Simon & Schuster, o/p). Nicely poised, lyrical account of biologist Perry's trials and tribulations in conceiving and mounting his Rainforest Aerial Tram (see p.138). Most of the book deals with his time at Rara Avis, where he conceived and tested his tram prototype, the Automated Web for Canopy Exploration.

F. Gary Stiles and Alexander F. Skutch, *A Guide to the Birds of Costa Rica* (US, Cornell University Press/UK, Black Press). All over Costa Rica you'll see guides clutching well-thumbed copies of this seminal tome, illustrated with colour plates to aid identification. Hefty, even in paperback, and too pricey for the amateur, but you may be able to pick up good secondhand copies in Costa Rica.

Allen M. Young, *Sarapiquí Chronicle: A Naturalist in Costa Rica* (Smithsonian Institute Press, o/p). Lavishly produced book based on entomologist Allen M. Young's twenty years' work in the Sarapiquí area and featuring a well-written combination of autobiography, travelogue and natural science, centring on the insect life he encounters.

Fiction

Miguel Benavides, *The Children of Mariplata* (UK, Forest Books). A short collection of even shorter stories, most of which are good examples of fable-like or allegorical Costa Rican tales. Many are written in the anthropomorphized voice of an animal; others, like "The Twilight Which Lost its Colour" describe searing slices of poverty-stricken life.

Carlos Cortés, *Cruz de Olvido* (México, Alfaguara). Told in the macho, exhausted and regretful tone of a disillusioned revolutionary, this novel charts the return of a Costa Rican Sandinista supporter from Nicaragua to his home country, where "nothing has happened since the big bang". The narrative marries the narrator's humourous disaffection with boring old Costa Rica and his investigation into the bizarre, excessively symbolic death of his son.

Fabián Dobles, *Ese Que Llaman Pueblo* (San José, Editorial Costa Rica). Born in 1918, Dobles is Costa Rica's elder statesman of letters. Set in the countryside among campesinos, this is a typical "proletarian" novel.

Fabián Dobles, *Years Like Brief Days* (UK, Peter Owen/UNESCO). The first novel by Dobles to be translated into English, this epistolary story is told in the form of a letter written by an old man to his mother, describing the village he grew up in and his eventful life.

Carlos Luis Fallas, *Mamita Yunai: el infierno de las bananeras* (San José). Exuberant, full of local colour, culture and diction: this entertaining, leftist novel depicting life in the hell of the banana plantations is a great read. It's set in the La Estrella valley in Limón province, where Fallas, a pioneering labour organizer in the 1930s and 1940s, was instrumental in forcing the United Brands conglomerate to take workers' welfare into account.

Amanda Hopkinson (ed), *Lovers and Comrades: Women's Resistance Poetry in Central America* (US, Interlink/UK, Women's Press, o/p). Heartfelt contributions by Costa Rican poets Janina Fernandez, Eulalia Bernard and Lily Guardia. Poems such as Bernard's "We are the nation of threes" shows that Costa Rican poetry is no less political and no less felt than the more numerous contributions from the countries torn by war in the 1980s.

Enrique Jaramillo Levi (ed), *When New Flowers Bloomed: Short Stories by Women Writers from Costa Rica and Panamá* (US, Latin American Literary Review Press). Collection of the best-known Costa Rican women writers, including Rima de Vallbona, Carmen Naranjo, Carmen Lyra and Yolanda Oreamuno. Most of the stories are from the late 1980s, with shared themes of domestic violence – a persistent problem in Costa Rica – sexual and economic inequality, and the tyrannies of female anatomy and desire. Look out especially for Emilia Macaya, a younger writer.

Tatiana Lobo, *Assault on Paradise* (US, Curbstone Press). Costa Rica's first great historical novel tells the story of the arrival of the Spaniards in Costa Rica and, as the title indicates, their destruction of the land and life of the indigenous peoples they encountered.

Carmen Naranjo, *Los perros no ladraron* (1966), *Responso por el niño Juan Manuel* (1968), *Ondina* (1982) and *Sobrepunto* (1985). In keeping with a tradition in Latin American letters but unusually for a woman, Naranjo has occupied several public posts, including Secretary of Culture, director of the publishing house EDUCA and Ambassador to Israel. She is widely considered an experimentalist and her novels can be found in Costa Rica, and her collection of stories *There Never Was Once Upon a Time* (US, Latin American Literary Review Press) is available in English.

Yolanda Oreamuno, *La ruta de su evasión* (San José, EDUCA). Oreamuno had a short life, dying at the age of 40 in 1956. By the time she was 24, however, she had distinguished herself as the most promising writer of her generation with her novel *Por Tierra Firme*. Technically brilliant, she is a great *scénariste*, with a continually surprising lyrical style. *La ruta* concerns a child sent to look for his father, who has disappeared, possibly on a drinking binge. The search is both actual and spiritual; the novel a complex weave of themes.

Barbara Ras, *Costa Rica: A Traveller's Literary Companion* (US, Whereabouts Press). This is probably the most accessible starting point for readers interested in Costa Rican literature, with flowing and well-translated stories arranged by geographical zone. The best stories are also the most heartrending – read "The Girl Who Came from the Moon" and "The Carbonero" for a glimpse of real life beyond the tourist-brochure images.

Yasmin Ross, *La flota negra* (México, Alfaguara). Originally a journalist from Mexico, Ross has made Costa Rica her home and in *La flota negra* has written one of the best-received novels set in Costa Rican in recent years. It takes as its starting point the story of the Black

Star Line, the shipping company that brought so many of the Caribbean immigrants whose descendants now make up the population of Limón, along with Marcus Garvey's visit to the province.

Anachristina Rossi, *La loca de Gandoca* (San José, EDUCA). One of the most popular novels to be published in Costa Rica in recent years, Rossi's book is really "faction", documenting in businesslike prose and with tongue firmly in cheek the bizarre and byzantine wranglings over the Gandoca-Manzanillo refuge, including the surveying of the indigenous Bribrí KéköLdi reserve.

Rosario Santos (ed), *And We Sold the Rain: Contemporary Fiction from Central America* (US, 7 Stories Press/UK, Ryan Publishing). Put together in the late 1980s, this collection attempts to show the faces of real people behind the newspaper headlines about guerrillas and militaries during the political conflicts of that decade. There are Costa Rican stories by Samuel Rovinski, Carmen Naranjo and Fabian Dobles.

Rogelio Sotela (ed), *Escritores de Costa Rica* (San José, Lehmann, o/p). Outdated, out-of-print and inaccessible in all but the best libraries, nevertheless this is still the definitive volume of Costa Rican literature up until the 1940s. Several fascinating sections, including one devoted to folklore. Much dreadful poetry, though.

Rima de Vallbona, *Flowering Inferno: Tales of Sinking Hearts* (US, Latin American Literary Review Press). Slim volume of affecting short stories by one of Costa Rica's most respected (and widely translated) writers on social life, customs, and the position of women.

Language

Although it is commonly said that everyone speaks English in Costa Rica, it is not really the case. Certainly many who work in the tourist trade speak some English, and there are a number of expats who speak anything from English to German to Dutch, but the people you'll meet day to day speak only Spanish. The one area where you will hear English widely spoken is on the Caribbean coast, where many of the Afro-Caribbean inhabitants are of Jamaican descent, and speak a distinctive regional creole.

If you want to get to know Costa Ricans, then, it makes sense to acquire some Spanish before you arrive. Ticos are polite, patient and forgiving interlocutors, and will not only tolerate but appreciate any attempts you make to speak their language. The rules of pronunciation are pretty straightforward. Unless there's an accent, all words ending in l, r and z are stressed on the last syllable, all others on the second last. Unlike in the rest of Latin America, in Costa Rica the final "d" in many words sometimes gets dropped; thus you'll hear "usté" for "usted" or "¿verdá?" for "¿verdad?" Other Costa Rican peculiarities are the ll and r sounds. All vowels are pure and short.

A somewhere between the A sound in "back" and that in "father".
E as in "get".
I as in "police".
O as in "hot".

A Costa Rican dictionary

Mario Quesada Pacheco *Nuevo diccionario de Costarriqueñismos* (San José, Editorial de la Universidad Technologica de Costa Rica). An entertaining, illustrated dictionary of slang and *dichos* (sayings) for Spanish-speakers interested in understanding heavily argot-spiced spoken Costa Rican Spanish. It's a fascinating compendium, giving the regional location of word usage and sayings, what age group uses them, and some etymology. It also reveals a wealth of localisms developed to describe local phenomena – witness, for example the number of different words for "wasp".

Basics

Yes, No	*Sí, No*
Please,	*Por favor,*
Thank you	*Gracias*
Where, When	*Dónde, Cuando*
What, How much	*Qué, Cuanto*
Here, There	*Aquí, Allí*
This, That	*Este, Eso*
Now, Later	*Ahora,*
	Mas tarde
Open, Closed	*Abierto/a,*
	Cerrado/a
With, Without	*Con, Sin*
Good, Bad	*Buen(o)/a,*
	Mal(o)/a
Big, Small	*Gran(de),*
	Pequeño/a
More, Less	*Mas, Menos*
Today, Tomorrow	*Hoy, Mañana*
Yesterday	*Ayer*

Greetings and responses

Hello, Goodbye	*Hola, Adiós*
Good morning	*Buenos días*
Good afternoon/	*Buenas tardes/*
night	*noches*
See you later	*Hasta luego*
Sorry	*Lo siento/*
	disculpeme
Excuse me	*Con permiso/*
	perdón
How are you?	*¿Cómo está*
	(usted)?
I (don't) understand	*(No) Entiendo*
What did you say?	*¿Cómo?*
Not at all/	*De nada*
You're welcome	

Do you speak	*¿Habla (usted)*
English?	*Inglés?*
I don't speak	*(No) Hablo*
Spanish	*Español*
My name is...	*Me llamo...*
What's your name?	*¿Como se llama*
	usted?
I am English/	*Soy Ingles(a)/*
Australian	*Australiano(a)*

Needs: hotels and transport

I want	*Quiero*
I'd like	*Quisiera*
Do you know...?	*¿Sabe...?*
I don't know	*No sé*
There is (is there)?	*(¿)Hay(?)*
Give me...	*Deme...*
(one like that)	*(uno asi)*
Do you have...?	*¿Tiene...?*
... the time	*... la hora*
... a room	*... un cuarto*
... with two beds/	*... con dos*
	camas/
... double bed	*... cama*
	matrimonial
It's for one person	*Es para*
	una persona
(two people)	*(dos personas)*
... for one night	*... para una*
	noche
(one week)	*(una semana)*
It's fine, how	*¿Está bien,*
much is it?	*cuanto es?*
It's too expensive	*Es demasiado*
	caro
Don't you have	*¿No tiene algo*
anything cheaper?	*más barato?*

U as in "rule".

C is soft before E and I, hard otherwise: *cerca* is pronounced "serka".

G works the same way: a guttural H sound (like the ch in "loch") before E or I, a hard G elsewhere: *gigante* becomes "higante".

H is always silent.

J the same sound as a guttural G: *jamon* is pronounced "hamon".

LL may be pronouned as a soft J (as in parts of Chile and Argentina) instead of Y: *ballena* (whale) becomes "bajzhena" instead of "bayena".

N is as in English, unless it has a tilde (accent) over it, when it becomes NY: *mañana* sounds like "manyana".

QU is pronounced like the English K.

R is not rolled Scottish burr-like as much as in other Spanish-speaking coun-

Can one...?	¿Se puede...?	7	siete
... camp (near) here?	¿... acampar aquí (cerca)?	8	ocho
		9	nueve
Is there a hotel nearby?	¿Hay un hotel aquí cerca?	10	diez
		11	once
How do I get to...?	¿Por donde se va a...?	12	doce
		13	trece
Left, right, straight on	Izquierda, derecha, derecho	14	catorce
		15	quince
Where is...?	¿Dónde está...?	16	diez y seis
... the bus station	... el estación autobuses	20	veinte
		21	veintiuno
... the nearest bank	... el banco mas cercano	30	treinta
		40	cuarenta
... the post office	... el correo	50	cincuenta
... the toilet	... el baño/servicio	60	sesenta
Where does the bus to... leave from?	¿De donde sale el autobus para...?	70	setenta
		80	ochenta
		90	noventa
I'd like a (return) ticket to...	Quisiera un tiquete (de ida y vuelta) para...	100	cien(to)
		101	ciento uno
		200	doscientos
		201	doscientos uno
What time does it leave (arrive in...)?	¿A qué hora sale (llega en...)?	500	quinientos
		1000	mil
What is there to eat?	¿Qué hay para comer?	2000	dos mil
		1990	mil novocientos noventa
What's that?	¿Qué es eso?		
What's this called in Spanish?	¿Como se llama este en Español?	1991	...y uno
		first	primero/a
		second	segundo/a
Numbers and days		third	tercero/a
1	un/uno/una	Monday	lunes
2	dos	Tuesday	martes
3	tres	Wednesday	miércoles
4	cuatro	Thursday	jueves
5	cinco	Friday	viernes
6	seis	Saturday	sabado
		Sunday	domingo

tries: *carro* is said "cahro", with a soft rather than a rolled R.

V sounds more like B: *vino* becomes "beano".

Z is the same as a soft C: *cerveza* is thus "servesa".

El idioma and tiquismos

Costa Rican Spanish is a living language full of flux and argot. Local slang and usage are often referred to as **Tiquismos** (from *Costarriqueñismos*, or Costa Ricanisms) or, as Costa Ricans will say when enlightening the foreigner as to their meaning, "*palabras muy ticas*". Some of the expressions and terms discussed below may be heard in other countries in the region, especially in Nicaragua and El Salvador, but still they are highly regional. Others are purely endemic, including barbarismos (*bastardizations*) and provincialismos (words particular to specific regions of Costa Rica).

The noun "Tico" used as a short form for Costa Rican comes less from a desire to shorten "Costarricense" than from the traditional trend toward **diminution** which is supposed to signal classlessness, eagerness to band together and desire not to cause offence. In Costa Rica the common Spanish diminution of "ito" – applied as a suffix at the end of the word, as in "herman*ito*"; "little brother" – often becomes "itico" ("herman*itico*"). That said, you hear the -ito or -itico endings less and less nowadays.

Costa Rican Spanish often displays an astounding **formality** that borders on servility. Instead of "*de nada*" ("you're welcome") many Costa Ricans will say, "*para servirle*", which means, literally, "I'm here to serve you". When they meet you, Costa Ricans will say "*con mucho gusto*"; "it's a pleasure", and you should do the same. Even when you leave people you do not know well, you will be told "*que le vaya bien*" ("may all go well with you").

Nicknames and a delight in the informal mix with a quite proper formal tone in spoken Costa Rican Spanish. Nicknames centre on your most obvious physical characteristic: popular ones include *flaco/a* (thin); *gordo/a* (fat), and *macho/a* (light-skinned). Terms of endearment are also very current in popular speech; along with the ubiquitous *mí amor*, you may also get called *joven*, young one.

Intimate address

It's difficult to get your head round forms of **second-person address** in Costa Rica. Children are often spoken to in the "usted" form, which is technically formal and reserved for showing respect (in other Spanish-speaking countries children are generally addressed as "tú"). Even friends who have known each other for years in Costa Rica will address each other as "usted". But the single most confounding irregularity of Costa Rican speech for those who already speak Spanish is the use of **"vos"** as personal intimate address – generally between friends of the same age. Many people on a short trip to the country never quite get to grips with it.

Now archaic, "vos" is only used widely in the New World in Argentina and Costa Rica. It has an interesting rhythm and sound, with verbs ending on a kind of diphthong-ized stress: vos sabés, vos queres (you know, you want), as opposed to *tu sabes/usted sabe* or *tu quieres/usted quiere*. If you are addressed in the "vos" form it is a sign of friendship, and you should try to use it back if you can. It is an affront to use "vos" improperly, with someone you don't know well, when it can be seen as being patronizing. Again, Costa Ricans are good-hearted in this respect, however, and put errors down to the fact that you are a foreigner.

Everyday expressions

Here are some everyday **peculiarities** that most visitors to Costa Rica will become familiar with pretty quickly:

¡acharã! expression of regret: "what a pity", like "*¡qué lástima!*"

adiós "hi", used primarily in the *campo* (country) when greeting someone on the road or street. Confusingly, as in the rest of Latin America, *adiós* is also "goodbye", but only if you are going away for a long time.

¿diay? slightly melancholic interjection in the vein of "ah, but what can you expect?"

fatal reserved for the absolutely worst possible eventuality: "*esta carretera para Golfito es fatal*" means "the road to Golfito is the very worst".

feo literally "ugly", but can also mean rotten or lousy, as in "*Todos los caminos en Costa Rica estan muy feos*" ("All the roads in Costa Rica are in really bad shape").

maje literally "dummy", used between young men as an affirmation of their friendship/maleness: it's used like "buddy, pal" (US) or "mate" (UK). There is no equivalent for women, unfortunately.

pura vida perhaps the best-known *tiquismo*, meaning "great" "OK", or "cool".

que mala/buena nota expression of disapproval/approval – "how uncool/great".

Luck and God

Both **luck** and **God** come into conversation often in Costa Rica. Thus you get the pattern:

"¿Cómo amaneció?"	"How did you sleep?"
	(Literally, "how did you wake up?")
"Muy bien, por dicha, ¿y usted?"	"Very well, fortunately, and you?"
"Muy bien, gracias a Dios."	"Very well, thank God."

Also, you will hear *dicha* and *Dios* used in situations that seem to have not much to do with luck or divine intervention: "*¡Qué dicha que usted llegó!*" ("What luck that you arrived!"), along with such phrases as "*Vamos a la playa esta fin de semana, sí Dios quiere*" ("We'll go to the beach this weekend, God willing"). Even a shrug of the shoulders elicits a "*¡Dios sabe!*" "God only knows." And the usual forms "*hasta luego*" or "*hasta la vista*" become in Costa Rica the much more God-fearing "*Que Dios le acompañe*" ("may God go with you").

"Where is your boyfriend?"

"*¿Dónde está su novio?/padres?*" ("Where is your boyfriend/family?") is a query women, especially those travelling alone, will hear often. **Family** is very important in explaining to many Costa Ricans who you are and where you come from, and people will place you by asking how many brothers and sisters you have, where your family (*padres*) live, whether your *abuela* (grandmother) is still alive . . . It's a good idea to get to grips with the following:

madre/padre	mother/father
abuelo/abuela	grandfather/grandmother
hija/hijo	daughter/son
hermano/hermana	brother/sister
tía/tío	aunt/uncle
prima/primo	cousin

Glossary

abastecedor a general store, usually in a rural area or *barrio* (neighbourhood) that keeps a stock of groceries and basic toiletries.

agringarse (verb) to adopt the ways of the gringos.

aguacero downpour.

ahorita "right now" (any time within the coming hour).

bárbaro fantastic, cool (literally "barbaric").

barrio neighbourhood (usually urban).

bomba gas station.

burro can refer to the animal (donkey), but is usually an adjective denoting "really big", as in "*vea este bicho sí burro*": "come see this *really* big insect".

campesino peasant farmer, smallholder.

campo literally countryside, but more often in Costa Rica "space", as in "seat" when travelling. Thus "*¿Hay un campo en este autobus?*": "is there a (free) seat on this bus?"

cantina bar, usually patronized by the working class or rural labouring class.

capa rain gear, poncho.

carro car (not *coche*, as in Spain).

cazadora literally, huntress; a beaten up old schoolbus that serves as public transport in rural areas.

chance widely used anglicism to denote chance, or opportunity; like *opportunidad*.

chiquillos kids; also *chiquititos*, *chiquiticos*.

chivo cute.

chorreador sack-and-metal coffee-filter contraption, still widely used.

choteo quick-witted sarcasm, something Costa Ricans admire, provided it's not too sharp-tongued.

conchos yokels, hicks from the sticks.

cordillera mountain range.

dando cuerda colloquial expression meaning, roughly, to "make eyes at", in an approximation of sexual interest (men to women, hardly ever the other way around).

evangélico usually refers to anyone who is of a religion other than Catholic, but particularly Protestant even if they are not evangelical. Such religions are also called *cultos*, belying a general wariness and disapproval for anything other than Catholicism.

finca farm or plantation.

finquero coffee grower.

foco flashlight/torch.

gambas buttresses, the giant above-ground roots that some rainforest trees put out.

gaseosa fizzy drink.

gasolinera gas station.

gringo not-at-all pejorative term for a North American. A European is usually *el Europeo*.

guaca pre-Columbian burial ground or tomb.

güisqui whisky (usually bad unless imported, and astronomically expensive).

hacienda big farm, usually a ranch.

hospedaje very basic *pensión*.

humilde humble, simple; an appearance and quality that is widely respected.

ICT Instituto Costarricense de Turismo, the national tourist board.

indígena an indigenous person; preferred term among indigenous groups in Costa Rica, rather than the less polite *índio* (Indian).

invierno winter (May–Nov).

jornaleros day labourers, usually landless peasants who are paid by the day, for instance to pick coffee in season.

mal educado literally, badly educated; a gentle if effective insult, especially useful for women harassed by hissing, leering men.

malecón seaside promenade.

marimba type of large xylophone played mainly in Guanacaste. Also refers to the style of music.

mestizo person of mixed race indigenous/Spanish; not usually pejorative.

metate pre-Columbian stone table used for grinding corn, especially by the Chorotega people of Guanacaste. Many of the archeological finds in Costa Rica are metates.

mirador lookout.

morenos offensive term for Afro-Caribbeans. The best term to use is *negros* or *Limónenses*.

muelle dock.

Neotrópicos Neotropics: tropics of the New World.

Nica Nicaraguan, from *Nicaragüense*.

palenque a thatched-roofed longhouse inhabited by indigenous people; more or less equivalent to the Native North American longhouse.

pasear to be on vacation/holiday; literally, to be passing through.

peón farm labourer, usually landless.

personaje someone of importance, a VIP, although usually used pejoratively to indicate someone who is putting on airs.

PLA National Liberation Party, the dominant political party.

pulpería general store or corner store. Also sometimes serves cooked food and drinks.

purrujas spectacularly annoying, tiny biting insect encountered in lowland areas.

PUSC Social Christian Unity Party, the opposition party-of-the-moment.

rancho palm-thatched roof, also smallholding.

redondel de toros bullring, not used for bullfighting but for local rodeos.

refresco drink, usually made with fresh fruit or water, sometimes fizzy drink, although this is most often called *gaseosa*.

regalar (verb) usually to give, as in to give a present, but in Costa Rica the usual command or request of "*deme uno de estos*" ("give me one of those"), becomes "*regaleme*". Thus "*regaleme un cafecito, por favor*": "could you give me a coffee?".

rejas security grille, popularly known in English as The Cage: the iron grille you see around all but the most humble dwellings in an effort to discourage burglary.

sabanero Costa Rican cowboy.

soda cafeteria or diner; in the rest of Central America it's usually called a *comedor*.

temporada season: *la temporada de lluvia* is the rainy season.

temporales early morning rains in the wet season (mainly in the Valle Central).

terreno land, small farm.

UCR Universidad de Costa Rica (in San Pedro, San José).

UNA Universidad Nacional (in Heredia).

verano summer (Dec–April).

index

and small print

Index

Map entries are in colour

INDEX Ⓘ

Twenty Years of Rough Guides

In the summer of 1981, Mark Ellingham, Rough Guides' founder, knocked out the first guide on a typewriter, with a group of friends. Mark had been travelling in Greece after university, and couldn't find a guidebook that really answered his needs.There were heavyweight cultural guides on the one hand – good on museums and classical sites but not on beaches and tavernas – and on the other hand student manuals that were so caught up with how to save money that they lost sight of the country's significance beyond its role as a place for a cool vacation. None of the guides began to address Greece as a country, with its natural and human environment, its politics and its contemporary life.

Having no urgent reason to return home, Mark decided to write his own guide. It was a guide to Greece that tried to combine some erudition and insight with a thoroughly practical approach to travellers' needs. Scrupulously researched listings of places to stay, eat and drink were matched by careful attention to detail on everything from Homer to Greek music, from classical sites to national parks and from nude beaches to monasteries. Back in London, Mark and his friends got their Rough Guide accepted by a farsighted commissioning editor at the publisher Routledge and it came out in 1982.

The Rough Guide to Greece was a student scheme that became a publishing phenomenon. The immediate success of the book – shortlisted for the Thomas Cook award – spawned a series that rapidly covered dozens of countries. The Rough Guides found a ready market among backpackers and budget travellers, but soon acquired a much broader readership that included older and less impecunious visitors. Readers relished the guides' wit and inquisitiveness as much as the enthusiastic, critical approach that acknowledges everyone wants value for money – but not at any price.

Rough Guides soon began supplementing the "rougher" information – the hostel and low-budget listings – with the kind of detail that independent-minded travellers on any budget might expect. These days, the guides – distributed worldwide by the Penguin group – include recommendations spanning the range from shoestring to luxury, and cover more than 200 destinations around the globe. Our growing team of authors, many of whom come to Rough Guides initially as outstandingly good letter-writers telling us about their travels, are spread all over the world, particularly in Europe, the USA and Australia. As well as the travel guides, Rough Guides publishes a series of dictionary phrasebooks covering two dozen major languages, an acclaimed series of music guides running the gamut from Classical to World Music, a series of music CDs in association with World Music Network, and a range of reference books on topics as diverse as the Internet, Pregnancy and Unexplained Phenomena. Visit www.roughguides.com to see what's cooking.

Rough Guide Credits

Text editor: Gavin Thomas
Series editor: Mark Ellingham
Editorial: Martin Dunford, Jonathan Buckley,
Jo Mead, Kate Berens, Ann-Marie Shaw,
Paul Gray, Helena Smith, Judith Bamber, Orla
Duane, Olivia Eccleshall, Ruth Blackmore,
Geoff Howard, Claire Saunders, Alexander
Mark Rogers, Polly Thomas, Joe Staines,
Richard Lim, Duncan Clark, Peter Buckley,
Lucy Ratcliffe, Clifton Wilkinson, Alison
Murchie, Matthew Teller (UK); Andrew
Rosenberg, Stephen Timblin, Yuki Takagaki,
Richard Koss (US)
Production: Susanne Hillen, Andy Hilliard,
Link Hall, Helen Prior, Julia Bovis, Michelle
Draycott, Katie Pringle, Mike Hancock, Zoë
Nobes, Rachel Holmes, Andy Turner
Cartography: Melissa Baker, Maxine Repath,

Ed Wright, Katie Lloyd-Jones
Picture research: Louise Boulton, Sharon
Martins
Online: Kelly Cross, Anja Mutig-Blessing,
Jennifer Gold, Audra Epstein, Suzanne
Welles (US)
Finance: John Fisher, Gary Singh, Edward
Downey, Mark Hall, Tim Bill
Marketing & Publicity: Richard Trillo, Niki
Smith, David Wearn, Chloë Roberts, Claire
Southern, Demelza Dallow, (UK); Simon
Carloss, David Wechsler, Kathleen Rushforth
(US)
Administration: Tania Hummel, Julie
Sanderson

Publishing Information

This third edition published October 2001 by
Rough Guides Ltd,
80 Strand, London WC2R ORL.
Penguin Putnam, Inc. 375 Hudson Street,
NY 10014, USA. Reprinted December 2002.
Distributed by the Penguin Group
Penguin Books Ltd,
80 Strand, London WC2R ORL
Penguin Putnam, Inc.
375 Hudson Street, NY 10014, USA
Penguin Books Australia Ltd,
487 Maroondah Highway, PO Box 257,
Ringwood, Victoria 3134, Australia
Penguin Books Canada Ltd,
10 Alcorn Avenue, Toronto, Ontario,
Canada M4V 1E4
Penguin Books (NZ) Ltd,
182–190 Wairau Road, Auckland 10,
New Zealand
Typeset in Bembo and Helvetica to an
original design by Henry Iles.

Printed in Italy by LegoPrint S.p.A

© Jean McNeil

480pp includes index
A catalogue record for this book is available
from the British Library

ISBN 1-85828-337-X

Help us update

We've gone to a lot of effort to ensure that
the third edition of The Rough Guide to
Costa Rica is accurate and up-to-date.
However, things change – places get
"discovered", opening hours are notoriously
fickle, restaurants and rooms raise prices or
lower standards. If you feel we've got it
wrong or left something out, we'd like to
know, and if you can remember the address,
the price, the time, the phone number, so
much the better.

We'll credit all contributions, and send a
copy of the next edition (or any other Rough
Guide if you prefer) for the best letters.
Everyone who writes to us and isn't already a
subscriber will receive a copy of our full-
colour twice-yearly newsletter. Please mark
letters: "Rough Guide Costa Rica Update"
and send to: Rough Guides, 80 Strand,
London WC2R ORL, or Rough Guides, 4th
Floor, 345 Hudson St, New York, NY 10014.
Or send an email to:
mail@roughguides.co.uk or
mail@roughguides.com

SMALL PRINT

Acknowledgements

From **Jean McNeil**: Thanks go first and foremost to Helena Chaverría and Mauricio Hernandez for their kind hospitality in San José and Puerto Viejo de Talamanca, as well as for the advice and support of their outstanding travel agency Camino Travel, especially Maricruz Quirós and Silvia in the San José office. Ramon Chaverría was hugely informative about Costa Rican history, politics and economics, as well as an enthusiastic sometime guide. Diego Ferrari was the perfect travelling companion because of his remarkable ability to strike up conversation and even friendships with total strangers. Polly Rodger Brown took on the task of updating four chapters for this edition and did it wonderfully. I would like to thank the many readers and travellers who wrote to me with updates and information for this edition. Thanks are also due to the following people for their friendship, help, hospitality – or mere willingness to chat – all or any of which contributed to the writing of this edition: Susanna and Birgit at the Arco Iris in Santa Elena; the Fonda Vela in Monteverde; Desafío tours in La Fortuna and Santa Elena; Flor Ugalde at Casa Rigeway in San José; Anita Muktyk at the Buena Nota in Manuel Antonio; Victor at the Mar de Luz in Jacó; Patricia and Lenny at the Sano Banano in Montezuma; Chuck at Casa Cook in Tamarindo; the Lagarta Lodge in Nosara; Don Gerardo and Doña Amalia at the Buena Vista Lodge in Rincón de la Vieja; Minor at the Borinquen Mountain Resort; the tourist information office in Liberia; Doña Emilia of Liberia; the Selva Verde Lodge in Sarapiquí; Prego/Europcar; and Richard and Marianne Morgan for their information and help with birdwatching.

From **Polly Rodger Brown**: Special thanks to all at Costa Rica Expeditions, particularly Richard Edwards, Priscilla Jimenez and Rodolfo Vargas; to Alex Quesada and Europcar; and Jean McNeil for her valuable advice and support. Thanks to all the following for their generous help and hospitality: Rodolfo Cornick; Jack E. Ewing; all at La Paloma Lodge; Shawn Larkin; Karen and John Lewis; Daryl Loth; Leonel Mata and all his brothers; Sara and Toine at Montana Linda; and Sofia Stein. Thanks also to the following people for great company and much-valued laughter on an often gruelling trip: George and Susan Atkinson; Gloria and Toby Cleaver and their friends Alanis Morrisette and Andy Pruter for one of the funniest nights of my life; Sue and Henry "Don Kiki" Neale; John and Anne McCall; Rick, Loni and the regulars at Sol y Mar; and Paulo "Treehouse" and Erick Palmer in Puerto Viejo. Finally I am hugely grateful to the men who pulled, pushed and dug me out of various rivers and muddy tracks, above all the fabulous Byron at Selva Bananito Lodge.

At **Rough Guides**, thanks to Narrell Leffman and Sean Hickey for additional Basics research; Susannah Wight for proofreading; Katie Lloyd-Jones for immaculate maps and superhuman patience; Sharon Martins for the many marvellous photos; and Helen Prior for all her pioneering efforts in bringing this first-ever new-look Rough Guide to completion.

Readers' letters

Thanks to all the readers who took the trouble to write in with their comments and suggestions (and apologies to anyone whose name we've misspelt or omitted):

Tiiu A. Adamek, K. Behr, Christina Beni, Laura Bidner, Rebecca Bohling, Les Bonwell, Roy and Audrey Bradford, Chip Braman, John Browning, Simon Calder, Carl Coates, Sonia and Kevin Connors, Kate Easthope, Peter & Gaby Eirew, Frank A. Fasick, Abigail Flack, Elliott Gotkine, Stephen Green, Tom Groot Irwin Halpern, Steven Hemsley, Kean Johal, John B. Kachuba, Felix Keller, Marianna Kepka, Boris Kester, Theresa M. Macintyre, Maddy Marr Jason Miller, Kathryn Mooney, Nikos Moreuos Clive and Gamze Newell, Smitty & Shawn Parratt, Dominique Ponzio, Carole Reed, Dave Ross, Bonnie Rubin Anne Schierenberg, Jessica Sinha, Josh Smallu, Erika Marin-Spiotta, Dr Carlos Guindon Standing, Val Taylor, John R. Wilkins, Justin Zaman.

Photo Credits

SMALL PRINT

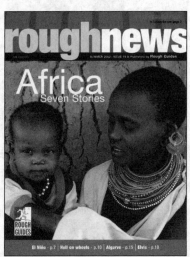

Rough Guides travel

Europe

Algarve
Amsterdam
Andalucia
Austria
Barcelona
Belgium
 & Luxembourg
Berlin
Britain
Brittany
 & Normandy
Bruges & Ghent
Brussels
Budapest
Bulgaria
Copenhagen
Corsica
Costa Brava
Crete
Croatia
Cyprus
Czech & Slovak
 Republics
Devon & Cornwall
Dodecanese
 & East Aegean
Dordogne
 & The Lot
Dublin
Edinburgh
England
Europe
First-Time Europe
Florence
France
French Hotels
 & Restaurants
Germany
Greece
Greek Islands
Holland
Hungary
Ibiza
 & Formentera
Iceland
Ionian Islands
Ireland
Italy
Lake District

Languedoc
 & Roussillon
Lisbon
London
London Mini Guide
London
 Restaurants
Madeira
Madrid
Mallorca
Malta & Gozo
Menorca
Moscow
Norway
Paris
Paris Mini Guide
Poland
Portugal
Prague
Provence & the
 Côte d'Azur
Pyrenees
Romania
Rome
Sardinia
Scandinavia
Scotland
Scottish Highlands
 & Islands
Sicily
Spain
St Petersburg
Sweden
Switzerland
Tenerife & La
 Gomera
Turkey
Tuscany & Umbria
Venice
 & The Veneto
Vienna
Wales

Asia

Bali & Lombok
Bangkok
Beijing
Cambodia
China

First-Time Asia
Goa
Hong Kong
 & Macau
India
Indonesia
Japan
Laos
Malaysia,
 Singapore
 & Brunei
Nepal
Singapore
South India
Southeast Asia
Thailand
Thailand Beaches
 & Islands
Tokyo
Vietnam

Australasia

Australia
Gay & Lesbian
 Australia
Melbourne
New Zealand
Sydney

North
America

Alaska
Big Island of
 Hawaii
Boston
California
Canada
Florida
Hawaii
Honolulu
Las Vegas
Los Angeles
Maui
Miami & the
 Florida Keys
Montréal
New England
New Orleans
New York City

New York City
 Mini Guide
New York
 Restaurants
Pacific Northwest
Rocky Mountains
San Francisco
San Francisco
 Restaurants
Seattle
Southwest USA
Toronto
USA
Vancouver
Washington DC
Yosemite

Caribbean
& Latin
America

Antigua & Barbuda
Argentina
Bahamas
Barbados
Belize
Bolivia
Brazil
Caribbean
Central America
Chile
Costa Rica
Cuba
Dominican
 Republic
Ecuador
Guatemala
Jamaica
Maya World
Mexico
Peru
St Lucia
Trinidad & Tobago

Africa &
Middle East

Cape Town
Egypt
Israel & Palestinian
 Territories

Jerusalem
Jordan
Kenya
Morocco
South Africa,
 Lesotho
 & Swaziland
Syria
Tanzania
Tunisia
West Africa
Zanzibar
Zimbabwe

Dictionary
Phrase-
books

Czech
Dutch
European
 Languages
French
German
Greek
Hungarian
Italian
Polish
Portuguese
Russian
Spanish
Turkish
Hindi & Urdu
Indonesian
Japanese
Mandarin Chinese
Thai
Vietnamese
Mexican Spanish
Egyptian Arabic
Swahili

Maps

Amsterdam
Dublin
London
Paris
San Francisco
Venice

Music

Acoustic Guitar
Blues: 100 Essential CDs
Cello
Clarinet
Classical Music
Classical Music: 100 Essential CDs
Country Music
Country: 100 Essential CDs
Cuban Music
Drum'n'bass
Drums
Electric Guitar & Bass Guitar
Flute
Hip-Hop
House
Irish Music
Jazz
Jazz: 100 Essential CDs
Keyboards & Digital Piano
Latin: 100 Essential CDs
Music USA: a Coast-To-Coast Tour
Opera
Opera: 100 Essential CDs
Piano
Reading Music
Reggae
Reggae: 100 Essential CDs
Rock
Rock: 100 Essential CDs
Saxophone
Soul: 100 Essential CDs
Techno
Trumpet & Trombone
Violin & Viola
World Music: 100 Essential CDs
World Music Vol1
World Music Vol2

Reference

Children's Books, 0–5
Children's Books, 5–11
China Chronicle
Cult Movies
Cult TV
Elvis
England Chronicle
France Chronicle
India Chronicle
The Internet
Internet Radio
James Bond
Liverpool FC
Man Utd
Money Online
Personal Computers
Pregnancy & Birth
Shopping Online
Travel Health
Travel Online
Unexplained Phenomena
Videogaming
Weather
Website Directory
Women Travel
World Cup

Music CDs

Africa
Afrocuba
Afro-Peru
Ali Hussan Kuban
The Alps
Americana
The Andes
The Appalachians
Arabesque
Asian Underground
Australian Aboriginal Music
Bellydance
Bhangra
Bluegrass
Bollywood
Boogaloo
Brazil
Cajun
Cajun and Zydeco
Calypso and Soca
Cape Verde
Central America
Classic Jazz
Congolese Soukous
Cuba
Cuban Music Story
Cuban Son
Cumbia
Delta Blues
Eastern Europe
English Roots Music
Flamenco
Franco
Gospel
Global Dance
Greece
The Gypsies
Haiti
Hawaii
The Himalayas
Hip Hop
Hungary
India
India and Pakistan
Indian Ocean
Indonesia
Irish Folk
Irish Music
Italy
Jamaica
Japan
Kenya and Tanzania
Klezmer
Louisiana
Lucky Dube
Mali and Guinea
Marrabenta Mozambique
Merengue & Bachata
Mexico
Native American Music
Nigeria and Ghana
North Africa
Nusrat Fateh Ali Khan
Okinawa
Paris Café Music
Portugal
Rai
Reggae
Salsa
Salsa Dance
Samba
Scandinavia
Scottish Folk
Scottish Music
Senegal & The Gambia
Ska
Soul Brothers
South Africa
South African Gospel
South African Jazz
Spain
Sufi Music
Tango
Thailand
Tex-Mex
Wales
West African Music
World Music Vol 1: Africa, Europe and the Middle East
World Music Vol 2: Latin & North America, Caribbean, India, Asia and Pacific
World Roots
Youssou N'Dour & Etoile de Dakar
Zimbabwe

Rough Guides music, reference & CDs

check www.roughguides.com for the latest news

NOTES

San Jose

Ricón de la vieja → grassy volcanic uplands
national park

Puerto Jimenez

la Leona

la sirena

los Patos

la Palma

San Gerardo de Rivas

Pacuaré Reserve
↑
Río

NOTES

TRAVEL
COSTA RICA

*ur one stop travel shop offers you
everything you need for a great time
in Costa Rica!*

We offer individual and group travel arrangements and
advice. Our services include:
- Domestic flight arrangements
- Car rentals
-Tours (volcanoes, rafting, jungle and much more!)
- Bus-schedules (locations and departure times)
- Reservations for hotels and lodges
- Transfers (from and to the airport, hotel and travel
destinations)
- Round trips (private tours or in small groups) and
important information

*ontact us now or upon arrival in our downtown
office!*

Camino Travel, calle 1, between 1 & Central Avenues
San José, Costa Rica
Tel. (506) 257-0107 or (506) 234-2530
Fax (506) 257-0243 or (506) 225-6143
e-mail: caminotr@racsa.co.cr
web site: www.caminotravel.com

The ideas expressed in this code were developed by and for independent travellers.

Learn About The Country You're Visiting

Start enjoying your travels before you leave by tapping into as many sources of information as you can.

The Cost Of Your Holiday

Think about where your money goes - be fair and realistic about how cheaply you travel. Try and put money into local peoples' hands; drink local beer or fruit juice rather than imported brands and stay in locally owned accommodation. Haggle with humour and not aggressively. Pay what something is worth to you and remember how wealthy you are compared to local people.

Embrace The Local Culture

Open your mind to new cultures and traditions - it will transform your experience. Think carefully about what's appropriate in terms of your clothes and the way you behave. You'll earn respect and be more readily welcomed by local people. Respect local laws and attitudes towards drugs and alcohol that vary in different countries and communities. Think about the impact you could have on them.

Exploring The World – The Travellers' Code

Being sensitive to these ideas means getting more out of your travels - and giving more back to the people you meet and the places you visit.

Minimise Your Environmental Impact

Think about what happens to your rubbish - take biodegradable products and a water filter bottle. Be sensitive to limited resources like water, fuel and electricity. Help preserve local wildlife and habitats by respecting local rules and regulations, such as sticking to footpaths and not standing on coral.

Don't Rely On Guidebooks

Use your guidebook as a starting point, not the only source of information. Talk to local people, then discover your own adventure!

Be Discreet With Photography

Don't treat people as part of the landscape, they may not want their picture taken. Ask first and respect their wishes.

We work with people the world over to promote tourism that benefits their communities, but we can only carry on our work with the support of people like you. For membership details or to find out how to make your travels work for local people and the environment, visit our website.

www.tourismconcern.org.uk

TourismConcern
Campaigning for Ethical and Fairly Traded Tourism

Will you have enough stories to tell your grandchildren?

©2000 Yahoo! Inc.

<u>Yahoo! Travel</u>

DO YOU
YAHOO!
?

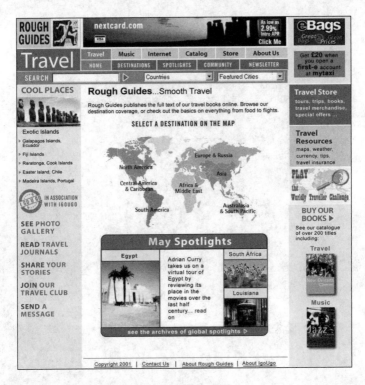